YO-CKN-595

ESSAYS IN MONGOLIAN STUDIES

Sechin Jagchid

Volume 3 in Monograph Series of the
David M. Kennedy Center for International Studies
Brigham Young University
Provo, Utah

Library of Congress Cataloging–in–Publication Data:

Jagchid, Sechin, 1914–
    Essays in Mongolian studies / Sechin Jagchid.
    332 p. cm.
    ISBN 0-912575-06-9 (pbk.)
    1. Mongolia — History. 2. Inner Mongolia (China) — History.
3. Mongols — History. I. Title.
DS798.5.J34 1988
951'.7 — dc19   87-26220
                                                        CIP

©1988 Sechin Jagchid
All Rights Reserved.
Printed in the United States of America.

This publication is available from:
Brigham Young University
David M. Kennedy Center for International Studies
Publication Services
280 Herald R. Clark Building
Provo, Utah 84602
801-378-6528

Contents

Foreword	v
Acknowledgements	vii
Introduction	ix

Maps

The Hsiung-nu and the Han (ca. 200 B.C.–100 A.D.)	xv
The Kitan, Tangut, and Sung of the Eleventh Century	xvi
The Mongol Empire of the Thirteenth Century	xvii
Mongolia During the Manchu-Ch'ing Period (1644–1912)	xviii
Twentieth Century Mongolia	xx

Part I: Prelude to the Mongolian Empire Period

1. Patterns of Trade and Conflict Between China and the Nomadic People of Mongolia	3
2. The Kitans and Their Cities	21
3. Kitan Struggles Against Jurchen Oppression — Nomadism versus Sinicization	34

Part II: The Mongolian Empire Period

4. Traditional Mongolian Attitudes and Values as Seen in the *Secret History of the Mongols* and the *Altan tobchi*	51
5. Some Notes on the Horse Policy of the Yüan Dynasty	67
6. Why the Mongolian Khans Adopted Tibetan Buddhism as Their Faith	83
7. Chinese Buddhism and Taoism During the Mongolian Rule of China	94
8. Buddhism in Mongolia After the Collapse of the Yüan Dynasty	121

Part III: The Manchu-Ch'ing Period

9. The Rise and Fall of Buddhism in Inner Mongolia (Part I)	131
10. The Manchu-Ch'ing Policy Toward Mongolian Religion	141
11. Mongolian Lamaist Quasi-Feudalism During the Period of Manchu Domination	155
12. Reasons for the Nondevelopment of Nomadic Power in North Asia Since the Eighteenth Century	173
13. Agricultural Development and Chinese Colonization in Mongolia	178
14. An Interpretation of "Mongol Bandits" (*Meng-Fei*)	186
15. The Sinicization of the Mongolian Ruling Class in the Late Manchu-Ch'ing Period	194

Part IV: The Modern Period

16. Prince Gungsangnorbu and Inner Mongolian Modernization	207
17. The Rise and Fall of Buddhism in Inner Mongolia (Part II)	234
18. Mongolian Nationalism in Response to Great Power Rivalry, 1900–1950	240
19. Discrimination Against Minorities in China	252
20. The Inner Mongolian Kuomintang of the 1920s	262
21. The Inner Mongolian Autonomous Movement of the 1930s	281

Part V: Folklore and Shamanism

22. Chinggis Khan in Mongolian Folklore	299
23. Shamanism Among the Dakhur Mongols	322
Index	333

Foreword

Historical studies of Mongolia have characteristically suffered from a Sinocentric view. Even Owen Lattimore's landmark thesis of a vital interconnection between China and her Inner Asian frontiers simply falls short of recognizing Mongolia as a country and a culture that should itself be the point of reference. Mongolia should not be thought of as a Chinese frontier region. Mongolia has its own vital and unique features, its own important historical contributions.

With unsurpassed expertise and personal experience, with a profundity and a breadth of learning based upon knowledge of Mongolian and Chinese sources, as well as a fluency in English and Japanese, Professor Sechin Jagchid incisively advocates the above perspectives of Mongolian history. In the monographic essays which comprise this book, he persuasively posits a Mongol-centric view. He explains and elaborates upon elements of modern Mongolian history that have been heretofore neglected by scholars who have approached the subject from other vantage points. After thoughtful consideration of his insights, one can never again think of Mongolia as simply an adjunct or frontier of China.

In the wide variety and versatility of topics represented — trade patterns, nomadic groups, interpretations of the *Secret History of the Mongols* and the *Altan tobchi*, the importance of the horse in the Asian steppes, agricultural developments in modern Mongolia, to list only a few — I am especially impressed with Jagchid's contributions to our understanding of Buddhism in Mongolia. He recognizes that Buddhism did not begin in that country. It is an import. And yet in carefully documented ways, Jagchid shows that Buddhism in time becomes a powerful internal, or one might even conclude, indigenous Mongolian force. It influenced the Mongolian independence movement of 1911. It became so intertwined with Mongolian culture and thought that it has become a unique expression or symbol of native traditions. We learn that Buddhism in Mongolia has become a double-edged sword, with both its bright and dark aspects. At times it seems to have succeeded in identifying with positive national aspirations and at other times to have been an albatross or a target of nationalistic, democratic, and socialistic movements, whose ecclesiastical quasi-feudalistic institutions were in the way.

Sechin Jagchid is a seasoned, world-class scholar in the field of Mongolian studies. At least since 1933, during his first year as a college student at Peking University, when he was active in the Inner Mongolian Autonomous Movement, he has been identified as a freedom fighter for the Mongolian people — fighting against all alien oppressors of whatever political, social, or ethnic background. He left his native Mongolia in 1949, the very year he wrote the Declaration of Autonomy of the Inner Mongolian Autonomous Movement.

Professor Jagchid taught Mongolian and Chinese history at all the leading universities in Taiwan; taught Mongolian language and literature at the University of London; lived in Japan from 1937 to 1939, and was Visiting Senior Researcher at Tokyo University for Foreign Studies in 1983–84; has published more than ten books and one hundred scholarly articles on Inner Asian topics; and continues to participate as organizer or panelist in professional conferences throughout the world.

For more than a decade, Jagchid has gained distinction in the United States as a popular and productive scholar at Brigham Young University, where he has taught classes in Asian history, Chinese history, and Inner Asian history. In 1982, he was the first Asian to receive BYU's prestigious Karl G. Maeser Research Award. In 1985, he was appointed an Associate of the David M. Kennedy Center for International Studies, under whose auspices this volume of articles is published.

For colleagues at BYU, Sechin Jagchid is a remarkable scholar whose extensive knowledge and exacting methods are only surpassed by his personal warmth, and by the affection and respect we feel for him, his wife, and his family.

Spencer J. Palmer

Acknowledgements

This book could not have been published without the support of the David M. Kennedy Center for International Studies of Brigham Young University, Provo, Utah. The author wishes especially to express his thanks to his colleague, Spencer J. Palmer, who initiated and pushed through the whole plan for publication and who wrote the Foreword. Thanks is also due to Ray C. Hillam, the director of the center who gave his full support to this plan. Particular thanks is expressed to Paul V. Hyer, who helped in both the writing and correcting of these papers, and to Roger R. Keller, who edited the papers, gave them uniform style, suggested the addition of maps, and provided headings and divisions to guide the new student as well as the seasoned scholar.

The author wishes to express his appreciation to Martin B. Hickman, the former dean of the College of Family, Home, and Social Sciences, and to De Lamar Jensen, Ted J. Warner, and James B. Allen, successive chairmen of the Department of History, who gave the author much kind encouragement during his thirteen years of teaching at Brigham Young University. Thanks is also due to Marilyn Webb and her associates in the Faculty Support Center who typed many of the manuscripts for original presentation.

The author expresses his cordial thanks to Deborah L. Coon, who supervised the publication process, to Gregory Gritton, who typed the entire manuscript, to Grant Paul Skabelund, who prepared the final manuscript and produced the index, to Rebecca Wetzel, who designed the maps, and to Melba Damico, who gave her full support through the entire process. Finally, I am indebted to my wife, Oyongerel, for writing all the Chinese characters in this collection, and for her patience and help over the years.

Introduction

Anciently, Mongolia was the cradle of powerful nomadic peoples who for centuries struggled against neighboring agrarian peoples, particularly those of the Middle Kingdom of China. In the thirteenth century, however, Mongolia became the base of an empire that dominated most of the known world for a time.

Modern Mongolia's role has changed radically from that of its earlier days. Landlocked as it is, it is usually seen as a buffer or frontier zone between the Soviet Union and the People's Republic of China. Consequently, in spite of its important strategic location and its historical and cultural uniqueness, Mongolia's role is either neglected or misperceived. Most publications on Mongolia that are available to western readers depend mainly upon materials prepared by non-Mongol writers. Therefore, these writings inherently convey a biased view.

The aim of these essays is to introduce readers to the views of a Mongolian historian. Some themes are new, but most provide different perspectives on old problems. It is also the author's desire to draw the readers' attention to the land and people of Mongolia, i.e., to the events, the cultural patterns, and the historical developments which shaped this land. Mongolia is not merely a satellite living in the shadow of powerful, giant neighbors. Rather, Mongolia is a nation to be recognized in its own right.

This book is based upon twenty-two articles which the author presented at various academic conferences and which were published in several countries over the past two decades. Delivered as separate presentations, they can now offer a connected and useful analysis of the history and cultural changes of the people of Mongolia over a two thousand-year period. Please note that the divisions which separate the articles are only general and are provided to help orient the reader.

Part I: Prelude to the Mongolian Empire Period

The article "Patterns of Trade and Conflict Between China and the Nomadic People of Mongolia" introduces the author's perspectives on the age old historical phenomena of war, peace, and trade relationships between the North Asian nomadic peoples and the sedentary Chinese. It points out that the nomadic invasions were economically motivated, and even though Chinese policy had political and military bases, peace depended upon trade in some form. Without trade, war resulted.

"The Kitans and Their Cities" is a short study of the impact of cities on the nomadic peoples, using the Kitans as a case study. The cities they built greatly accelerated the growth of Kitan power, but, when they were challenged by the Jurchens, the cities became targets for enemy attacks and hastened the downfall of their builders.

The article "Kitan Struggles Against Jurchen Oppression — Nomadism versus Sinicization" shows the bitter relationship between the two peoples, as well as the impact of Kitan rebellion upon the national security of the Jurchen. It also analyzes the factors involved in the disappearance of the Kitans and notes that their assimilation, or lack thereof, by the Mongols or the Chinese was decided by their responses toward these two different cultures. Those who were able to resist Jurchen domination insisted on their original nomadic life style.

Part II: The Mongolian Empire Period

The article "Traditional Mongolian Attitudes and Values as Seen in the *Secret History of the Mongols* and the *Altan tobchi*" argues that one is able to gain clear insights into the traditional moral, ethical, and religious values of the Mongols through the *Secret History* (the earliest extant Mongolian written source) and the *Altan tobchi* (another early collection of old Mongolian sayings and proverbs). Later, when they were converted to Buddhism, the Mongols were influenced by nationalistic and socialistic movements. Nevertheless, they still maintained many traditional Mongolian values, albeit in new forms.

"Some Notes on the Horse Policy of the Yüan Dynasty" discusses the function of the horse in the formation of a nomadic empire and the maintenance of a dynasty of conquest. It also provides some observations on administrative functions related to maintaining horses during the Mongol occupation of China.

Religion played an important role in Mongolian history, and this collection of essays includes several items on this subject. The first article, "Why the Mongolian Khans Adopted Tibetan Buddhism as Their Faith," explains the cultural gap between the Mongols and the Chinese. Although their lands were adjoining, their cultural distance was great. The Mongols had contact with Chinese Buddhism much earlier than with the esoteric Buddhism of Tibet. Nevertheless, their khans and ruling class eventually converted to the latter because of culture similarities with the Tibetans. A subsequent article, "Chinese Buddhism and Taoism During the Mongolian Rule of China," illustrates and analyzes Mongolian attitudes toward all foreign religions, taking as its beginning point the original Mongolian belief in Shamanism. It also discusses the Mongolians' administrative handling of Buddhism and Taoism, two conflicting religious groups in China, and further treats the success and failure of the Mongols in relation to these religions as the Mongols dominated China. "Buddhism in Mongolia After the Collapse of the Yüan Dynasty" deals with the continuing but declining influence of Buddhism and other foreign religions, i.e., Christianity and Islam, in the so-called "dark age" of traditional Mongolian history before the Mongols' reconversion to Buddhism beginning in the 1570s.

Another article on religion, "The Rise and Fall of Buddhism in Inner Mongolia (Part I)," is a brief narrative of the history of Buddhism in Mongolia. It emphasizes especially the second Mongolian conversion to Buddhism after the 1570s, its development, its positive and negative impact on the nation, its decline with the rise of nationalism, and its cultural changes in the modern period. This article is divided into two parts with the second part appearing as chapter 17.

Part III: The Manchu-Ch'ing Period

"The Manchu-Ch'ing Policy Toward Mongolian Religion" stresses the Mongolian attitude and devotion toward religion and the Manchu manipulation of the faith as an instrument in ruling and pacifying the Mongols. It also discusses the impact of the policy on Mongolian thought, behavior, economy, and politics.

The article "Mongolian Lamaist Quasi-Feudalism During the Period of Manchu Domination" is an extension of the foregoing discussion. It provides some insight into the Manchu establishment of Mongolian religious leaders as a bulwark of Mongolian feudalistic institutions paralleling the lay feudal lords. By this approach, the Manchus reached their political goal of fragmentation and rule.

The article "Reasons for the Nondevelopment of Nomadic Power in North Asia Since the Eighteenth Century" is a survey of the factors that caused the North Asian steppeland to change from the cradle of nomadic empires as well as a pivotal area in world geopolitics to the status of a pawn in great struggles for power. The Manchu-Jeünghar war is considered to be the turning point at which the great steppe ceased to be a base of operations for nomadic incursions into the neighboring agricultural districts or a refuge from foreign invasion.

"Agricultural Development and Chinese Colonization in Mongolia" is a brief account of the conflict between the Mongolian nomadic-pastoral economy and the Chinese agricultural economy which led to the cultivation of the nomadic grazing areas. This conflict eventually resulted in economic instability and political turbulence all over Mongolia.

A particularly important article concerning nineteenth century Mongolia is "An Interpretation of 'Mongol Bandits' (*Meng Fei*)." It refutes the old idea that the brave herdsmen who opposed Chinese appropriation of their pasture lands were "bandits." This was a false accusation made by Chinese authorities around the turn of the century. The "bandits" were actually distressed herdsmen who angrily took direct action to protect their people from Manchu-Chinese officials, Chinese settlers, and even from covetous Mongolian officials who betrayed them for personal gain by allowing the Chinese to cultivate their grazing areas without the consent of the people. This essay also identifies the emotions and sentiments that motivated these uprisings which eventually gave rise to anti-feudalistic and nationalistic movements.

"The Sinicization of the Mongolian Ruling Class in the Late Manchu-Ch'ing Period" points out the acculturation of the Mongolian ruling class to Chinese ways as a by-product of Manchu domination. In addition to discussing the causes of these processes, it also notes their positive and negative impact on Mongolia's modernization movement, on the rise of nationalism, and on the resulting loss of some original and unique cultural characteristics of the Mongols.

Part IV: The Modern Period

Modernization has long been a topic of special concern in Asia. The article "Prince Gungsangnorbu and Inner Mongolian Modernization" is a brief account of the activities of Mongolia's most enlightened ruling noble at the turn of this century. It cites his efforts toward modernization, his reforms, and his contribution to Mongolian education. It also illustrates the confrontation between the conservatives and the liberals in their attitudes toward modernization, as well as the impact of Gungsangnorbu's work on later democratic and nationalistic movements. It was some of these movements which impacted religion in Mongolia. Part Two of "The Rise and Fall of Buddhism in Inner Mongolia (Part II)" gives insights into these religious dynamics.

"Mongolian Nationalism in Response to Great Power Rivalry, 1900–1950" is a brief narrative of the rise of Mongolian nationalism, of the independence movement of Outer Mongolia, of the autonomous movement of Inner Mongolia, and of the entanglements of these events in the power conflicts between China, Russia, and Japan.

One article illustrates the historical and traditional Chinese attitudes toward the Mongols and national minorities of the so-called non-Han group. It addresses further the impact of these attitudes on the rise of nationalism among the minorities which opposed Chinese domination and the chauvinistic "great Han nationalism," thus leading to movements for separation and self-rule. The article is titled "Discrimination Against Minorities in China."

The essay "The Inner Mongolian Kuomintang of the 1920s" is linked with "The Inner Mongolian Autonomous Movement of the 1930s." Together they illustrate the unsuccessful attempts of the Inner Mongolian people for self-determination and self-rule under early modern Chinese governments and under the present-day Communists.

Part V: Folklore and Shamanism

"Chinggis Khan in Mongolian Folklore" illustrates how the Mongols worship their great historical hero in accord with their original Shamanistic religion, as well as the Khan's impact on them in both the past and the present. A short account, "Shamanism Among the Dakhur Mongols," discusses the historic religion of the Dakhurs, a people in Mongolia who were never converted to Buddhism. They continued their traditional Shamanistic practices until the notorious *Cultural Revolution* of Chinese Communist Maoists in the latter half of the 1960s.

Maps

The Hsiung-nu and the Han (ca. 200 B.C.–100 A.D.)

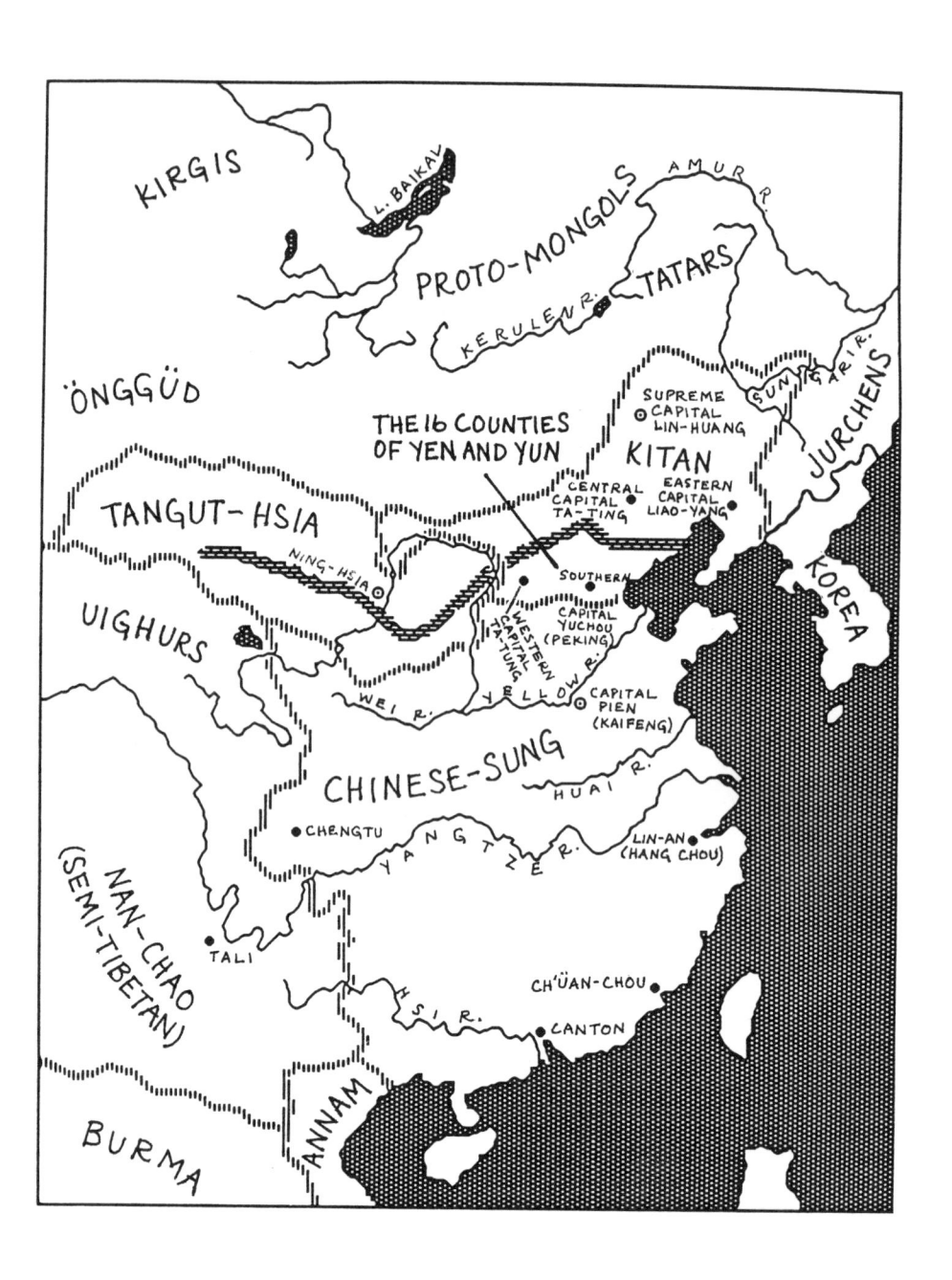

The Kitan, Tangut, and Sung of the Eleventh Century

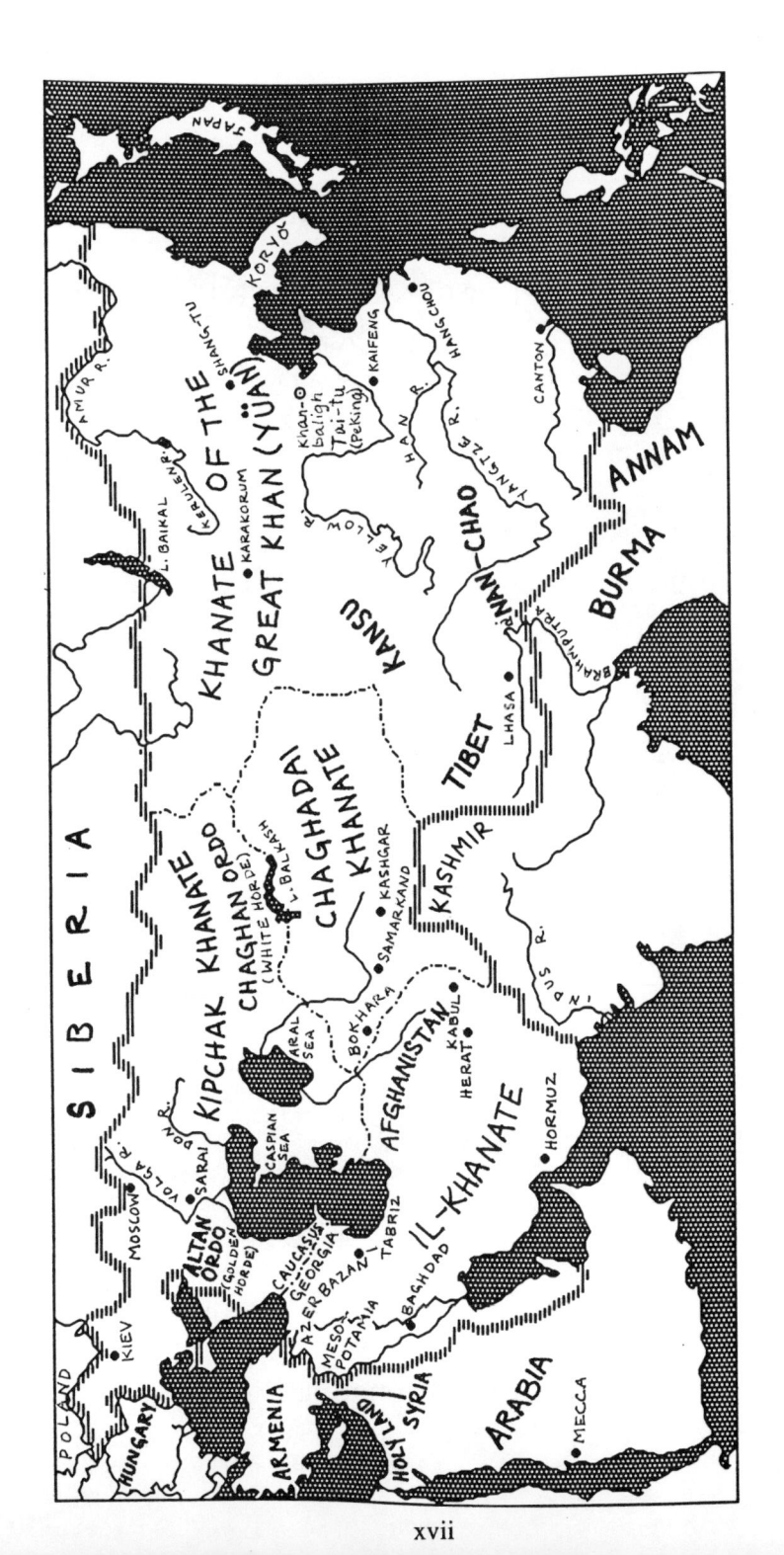

The Mongol Empire of the Thirteenth Century

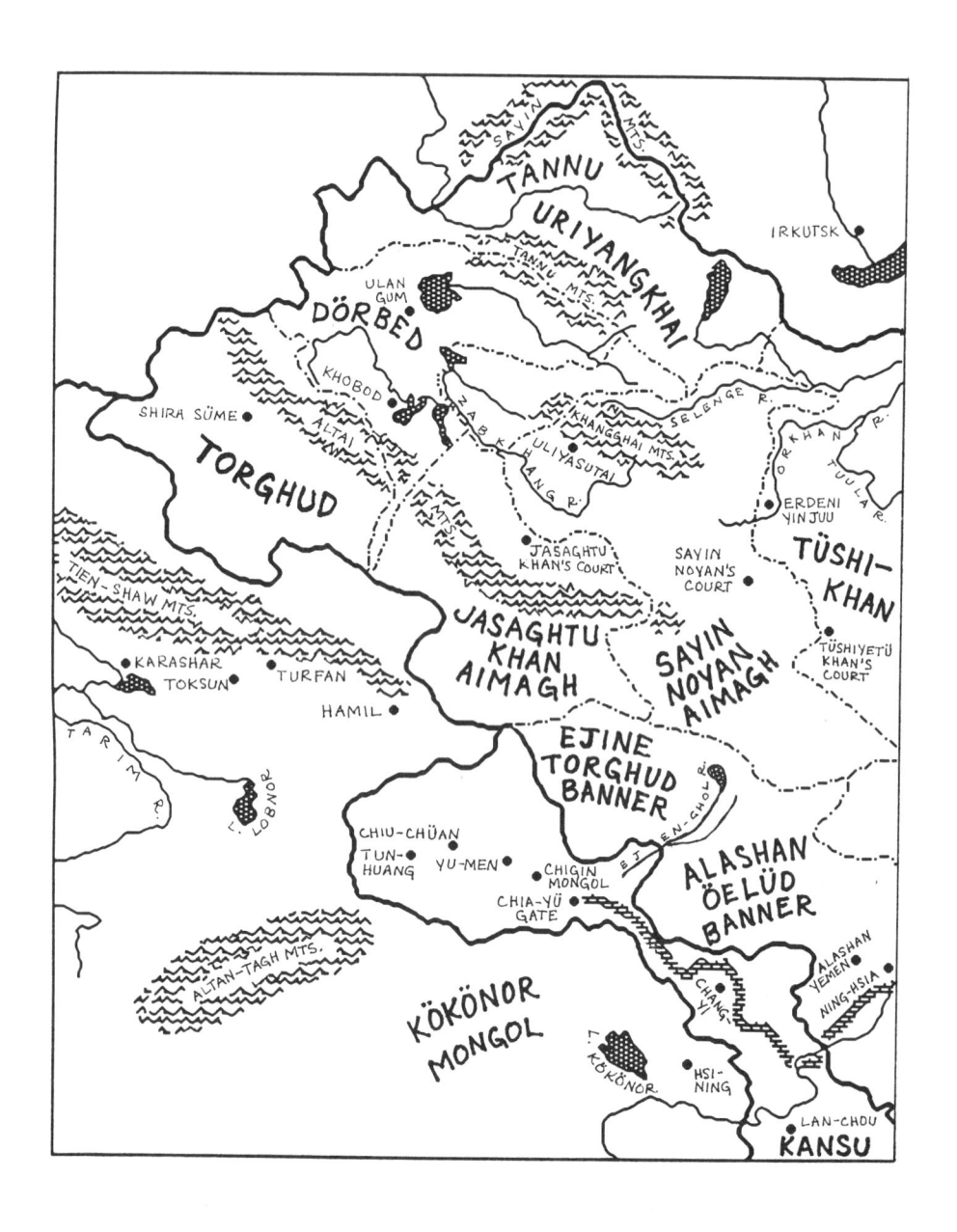

Mongolia During the Manchu-

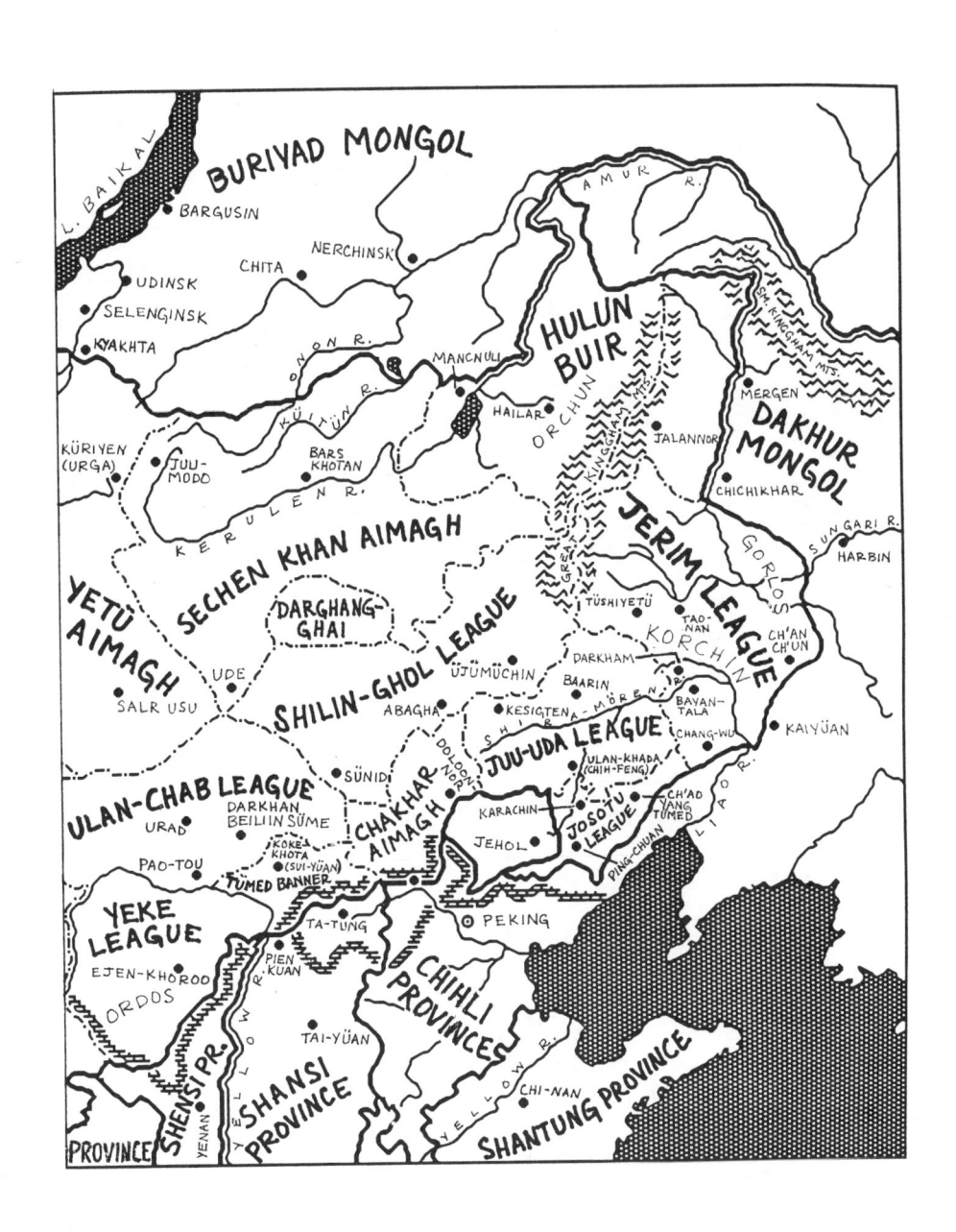

Ch'ing Period (1644–1912)

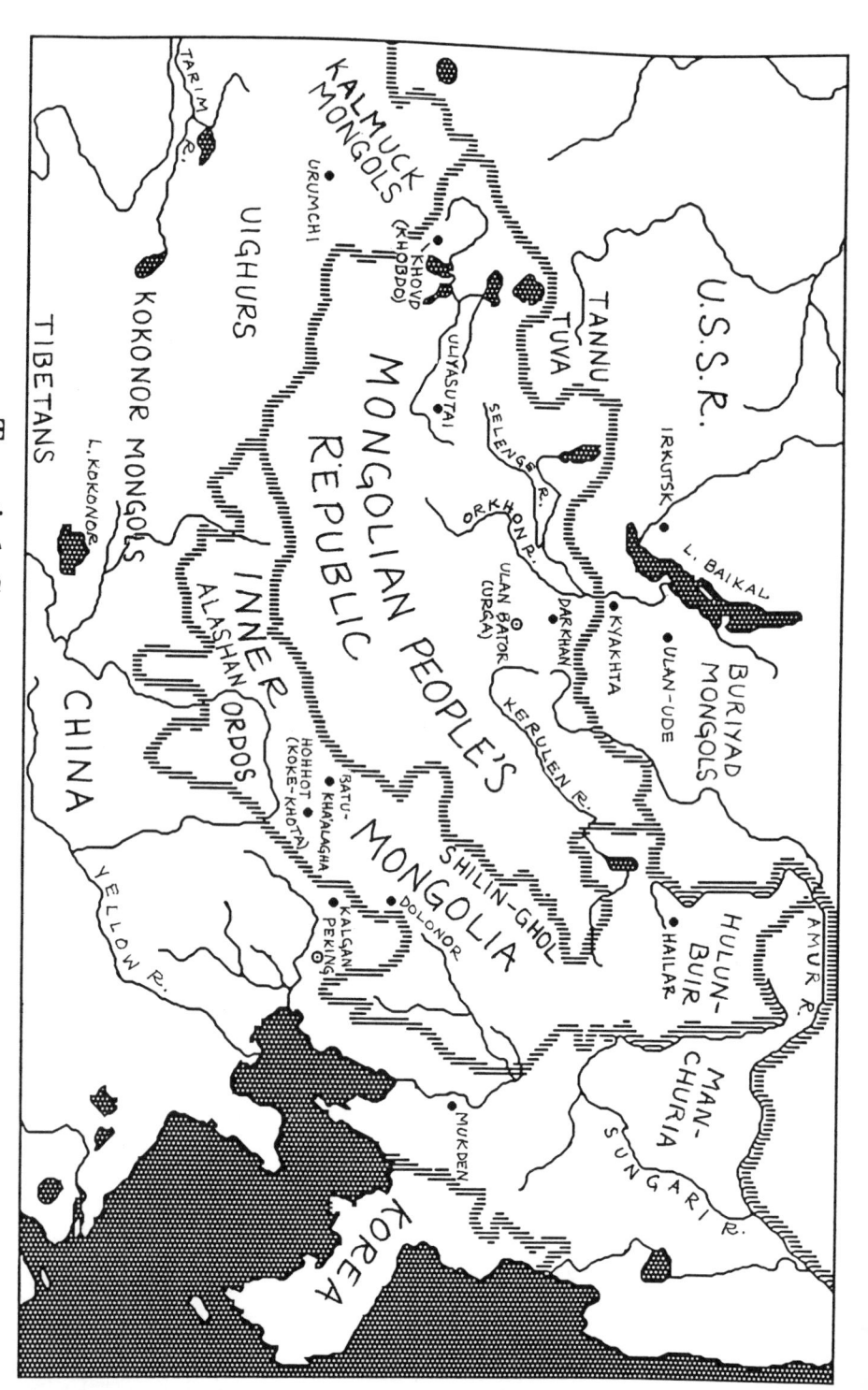

Twentieth Century Mongolia

Part I
Prelude to the Mongolian Empire Period

Chapter 1

Patterns of Trade and Conflict Between China and the Nomadic People of Mongolia

(Originally published in *Zentralasiatische Studien*, 1977, 11:177–204, Universität Bonn)

The struggle for survival and/or power between the northern nomadic peoples and the southern agricultural peoples is one of the main themes of traditional Asian history. Because of its unique geographical environment, the Eurasian steppe was a cradle for the development of many nomadic peoples and was also a base for their military operations against the southern agricultural territories. Sometimes the extension of nomadic power resulted in border encroachments, sometimes in intrusions into the heartlands of the neighboring peoples, and at other times in the creation of a new conquering dynasty. In the history of China, these conflicts occurred unceasingly from the beginning of history to the middle of the seventeenth century A.D. In considering these developments many questions arise. For example, what were the objectives of the nomadic people's military activity? Under what conditions were their military actions limited to border encroachments? Under what conditions did they occupy the agricultural territories and establish conquering dynasties? These are important historical problems and this paper contains some observations on these issues by a student of Mongolian history. A brief summary of pertinent historical factors are as follows.

1. Hindered by the environment — the cold and arid climate of the Gobi — limited by a primitive knowledge of technology, and constrained by the customs and traditions of their migratory life style, it was impossible for the North Asian nomadic peoples to produce crops and other products of an agricultural society. Therefore, economically they had to depend on supplies from their agricultural neighbors.

2. The differences of race and culture between the nomadic and agricultural peoples formed deep prejudices between the two, and historically the cultural distance between them was a more dominant factor than the geographical distance. Economically the agricultural Chinese were "affluent" when compared with their nomadic neighbors, and therefore had little interest in trade relations. Consequently, it was difficult to establish an ordinary system of trade or exchange. This caused the nomadic people, who were in want though militarily strong, to try to obtain their needs by force.

3. Between the nomadic and agricultural societies some types of exchange developed such as royal marriages, tribute, Chinese "bestowal," yearly payments, and frontier markets. When these did not exist, war, for the purpose of plundering agricultural products, took place immediately.

4. The actions of the nomadic peoples toward the agricultural societies were mainly based upon their economic need, and thus motivated by economic factors. However, the actions of the agricultural peoples toward their nomadic neighbors were primarily based on a desire for political gain or a military purpose.

5. The success or failure of the nomadic people in establishing trade relations with their agricultural neighbors generally depended upon their military abilities. The volume of exchange was usually in proportion to the size of the nomadic military power or perceived threat.

6. The wars launched by nomadic peoples against agricultural regions were a kind of economic production, a method of getting rich. The cost of war was only a burden to the enemy. Consequently, when a capable and ambitious leader emerged, traditionally he would initiate an invasion against the agricultural areas in order to increase the wealth of his people and his own prestige.

7. Since the nomadic people's objective in war was to gain agricultural products and manufactured goods which they badly needed, they ordinarily had no political or territorial ambitions. Unless they gained some cooperation or encouragement from the agricultural region, they were not interested in occupying the land or establishing a permanent administration to rule the area.

Having briefly listed seven factors which led to trade or conflict between the nomadic peoples of Mongolia and the peoples of China, each factor will now be examined in detail.

Geographic and Environmental Factors

The great master of Taoism and famous traveler of the thirteenth century, Ch'ang-ch'un Chen-jen, when he mounted the divide or watershed between the Middle Kingdom and the Northern Steppes on his way from Shantung to visit Chinggis Khan in Afghanistan during the latter's campaign against Khorezm, said:

> Gazing southward over the mountains of the T'ai-hang Range, I beheld scenery both beautiful and lovely; but looking toward the north, the only thing I could see was the cold desert and arid grass. The environment of the Middle Land ceased absolutely from here![1]

Thus, the first impression of the Taoist scholar was that the land of the Northern nomads was a cold, arid desert, a wilderness unsuitable for an agricultural way of life. Many Chinese writers and poets have described the natural environment and the landscape of the Mongolian steppes in their works. "The land of Hu [Northern barbarian] is covered with snow in the eighth month." "The cattle and sheep will be seen while the wind sweeps the grass." However, they paid almost no attention to the basic needs of the nomadic people and to their economic dependency on agricultural societies.

Among the Chinese emperors, only Wen-ti (r. 179–158 B.C.) of the Han Dynasty seems to have perceived the real economic situation of his nomadic neighbors. In a cordial letter to the *Shan-yü* (or Khan) Lo-shang (r. 175–161 B.C.) of the Hsiung-nu, he wrote:

> The Han and the Hsiung-nu are neighboring countries with a mutual rivalry. The Hsiung-nu are situated to the north where the land is cold and where winter comes early. Therefore [we] have ordered our officials to present [you] the *Shan-yü* a definite quantity of grain each year, also food stuffs, gold, embroidered cloth, silk, quilts, and other goods. As a result there is tranquility under heaven and happiness among the people.[2]

This communication shows a rather profound insight into nomadic life, and although he did not wish to have a more intimate contact with the Hsiung-nu,[3] neither did he wish to make his opponents suffer from a lack of agricultural products. No doubt Han Wen-ti knew that the alternative was endless war. Unfortunately, most other Chinese rulers neglected this decisive factor which often determined whether there would be peace or war. They usually tried to cut off trade relationships and to weaken their rivals. Consequently, the struggle for existence caused the nomadic peoples to carry out military operations and to attack the Chinese frontier for their needs.

Nomadic peoples were limited by the natural conditions of their environment and they lacked man-power due to their thin population base. The benefits of farming under such severe difficulties were not as great as the benefits of raising animals and hunting game. However, this does not mean that the nomadic people did not need agricultural products. On the contrary, since they themselves could not produce them, they were all the more dependent on neighboring agricultural societies.

According to historical records, some nomadic leaders utilized exiled captive Chinese to farm and labor for them.[4] Thus, the common nomadic people came to feel that farming was the labor of a subordinate people, and that for themselves the only proper way of life was pastoral. Hunting supplemented their basic livelihood and was also a form of amusement. Therefore, the nomadic peoples persisted in their old traditions and refused to adopt an agricultural way of life.[5] On the other hand, compelled by the basic needs of life, they still had to obtain agricultural products by force from their neighbors when peaceful trade relations were shut off.

Racial and Cultural Factors

The prejudice between different peoples is usually worsened by the shadow of cultural distance. Pan Ku, the second great Chinese historian, mentioned unreservedly the Chinese prejudice against their nomadic neighbors in his classical document, *Han Shu*.

> The barbarians are covetous for gain, human faced but animal hearted. . . . As for clothing, costume, food, and language, the barbarians are entirely different from the Middle Kingdom. They live in the cold wilderness of the far north. They follow the grazing fields herding their flocks and hunting game to maintain their lives. Mountains, valleys, and the great desert separate them from us. This barrier, which lies between the interior and the alien, was made by heaven and earth. Therefore, the sage rulers, considering them beasts, neither established contact with them nor subjugated them. It would cost a huge sum and we would be deceived if any agreement were established. It would involve our troops in vain and cause the enemy to fight back, if an invasion were carried out against them. Their land is impossible to cultivate and it is impossible to rule them as subjects. Therefore, they are always to be considered as outsiders, never as citizens. Our administration and teachings have never reached their people. Our Imperial calendar has never been bestowed upon them. Punish them when they come in and guard against them when they retreat. Receive them when they offer tribute as a sign of admiration for our righteousness. Restrain them continually and make it appear that all the blame is on their side. This is the proper policy of sage rulers toward the barbarians.[6]

Here the so-called "proper policy" clearly shows how prejudice was deepened by the cultural differences of the two peoples. This common misunderstanding hindered equal and mutually beneficial contacts between the two societies. Of course, there was also a strong prejudice among the nomads against the agriculturalists. This had its own negative influence on relations between the two peoples. However, dominated by their "proper policy," the court of China always tried to force all contacts and trade relationships into an unequal relationship. In other words, trade had to be carried out under the condition of "offering tribute as a sign of admiration of our righteousness," or else "all the blame is on their side." Consequently, any proposals for trade had to be submitted as a tribute. However, since the conditions and degree of the so-called "admiration of righteousness" had no established objective standard, the matter was always decided according to the subjective needs of the agricultural court. Therefore, often the "submissions for tribute" from the nomadic leaders were rejected and bloodshed and wars along the frontier ensued. The characteristic denunciation of the nomads as "covetous for gain" is further evidence of the economic dependence of the nomadic people on their agricultural neighbors.

Again, in the record of the *Hou-han Shu,* there is a policy statement by a minister regarding the Hsien-pei people. He said:

> Heaven created the mountains and rivers, the Ch'in dynasty built the Great Wall, and [we] the Han established fortresses and walls. These all aim to divide the interior from that which is alien and to distinguish [us] from those of different traditions. If there is no dangerous aggression against our country, we should not struggle for intercourse with such worm-like barbarians.[7]

This unwillingness to have any contact with aliens dominated the traditional policy of Chinese courts toward nomadic peoples for millennia. Also, from the idea "if there is no dangerous aggression against our country" it is not surprising to discover that if the power of the nomadic group were not yet a vital threat to the court of the agricultural society, then their hopes for trade would usually be frustrated. This was one of the main factors leading to war. The endless encroachments of the Mongols against Ming frontier areas were primarily for this reason.

Differences of nationality and culture between the nomadic and agricultural peoples deepened into traditional prejudices, one against the other. Historically the cultural distance between the two, each having different life styles, was more important than geographical distance. Economically, the farm production of peasants was comparatively more rich or brought a higher level of self-sufficiency than the herding activity of nomads. Agricultural peoples had practically no dependence on their nomadic neighbors, and, consequently, they had little incentive to establish systematic trade or exchanges. When the demands of the nomadic peoples were impossible to reject, the leaders of the agricultural society then tried to transform inevitable trade contacts into a subordinating relationship. Simply speaking, any trade had to be carried out under the conditions of "offering tribute as a sign of admiration of righteousness." Of course, such a high-handed policy toward nomadic people was based upon the independent strength or self-sufficient economic foundation of the agricultural society.

From ancient times to the middle of the seventeenth century, the "closed-door policy" of agricultural China against the nomadic people beyond the Great Wall was intended to annihilate these wanderers by choking off their economic lifeline. This policy greatly hindered the establishment of a regular, peaceful, and reciprocal trade system between the two peoples. As already noted, a major result was unilateral action out of economic necessity on the part of the nomads, i.e., military threats, looting, war, and bloodshed. A lack of trade was the main factor stimulating the northern nomadic peoples to continually invade the Chinese frontier. The traditional Chinese policy of "barbarians beyond the Wall" was directly related to the origin of the modern closed-door policy of the Ch'ing court against the "barbarians from beyond the ocean." Both led to war and unequal treaties.

Some Modes of Exchange

The nomadic people of Mongolia, hampered by their natural environment, restricted from agriculture by their way of life, economically dependent on the agricultural society of China, and confronted with the closed-door policy of the Chinese courts, had no choice but to adopt military force to meet their needs. In relationships between the two societies, without some system of exchange to meet the needs and desires of the nomadic society, it was impossible to restrain the nomads from military ventures. Unfortunately, most officials of the dynastic courts of China did not understand the nature of the economic dependence of their northern neighbors. They not only neglected to utilize this situation to develop a profitable relationship for themselves, but they also hindered the growth of regular trade for the benefit of others. Even so, they were sometimes compelled to alter the status quo and allow some type of trade in order to maintain peace. This trade was often generated by a nomadic military victory.

Royal marriages (和親) were ostensibly to establish peace between the leaders of both the agricultural and nomadic spheres. In fact, however, there were many daughters of Chinese emperors married to the "barbarian" leaders, but very few daughters of the nomadic rulers who were married to members of the Chinese royal households.[8] The institution of "royal marriage" was founded in the Han dynasty under the pressure or military threat of the Hsiung-nu.[9] From the perspective of a nomadic khan, a Chinese princess was taken as a wife as a trophy gained through military strength. However, on the Chinese side, the court constantly explained that bestowing a princess in marriage was a special royal favor to a nomadic ruler. Whatever the explanation, the main reason this arrangement was welcomed by nomadic rulers was the rich dowries and workmen that accompanied the royal princesses, plus the yearly gifts of agricultural products resulting from these marriages. However, the quantity of the gifts occasionally did not meet the nomads' needs, and intrusions along the border inevitably occurred. Nevertheless, large-scale war was usually prevented by such marriage relationships. The fact that royal marriage relationships were established under the shadow of the military influence of nomadic leaders was one unique phenomenon in the historical contact of the two peoples.

"Tribute" was also a type of trade exchange that was usually initiated by nomadic rulers and authorized by the Chinese courts. Except for a very small portion which was actually presented to the Chinese emperors, the main part of the so-called "tribute" was commonly domestic animals or hunting and pastoral products. These were the commodities for exchange, and items that were purchased officially by the court were usually converted into a definite price equivalent. On the basis of this standard, bestowals were granted to the tributaries. In other words, it was an exchange of "bestowal" for "tribute," unequal in form but not necessarily unequal in fact. Therefore, many powerful nomadic rulers demanded through threats or use of force that the courts of the agricultural society of China accept their "petition for tribute." If the "petition" was rejected, then war often broke out immediately. This was also a common phenomenon during the two centuries of the Mongol-Ming relationship.

The "bestowals" or "grants" were theoretically gifts to nomadic rulers from the Chinese court in the name of the Son of Heaven. However, except for a symbolic portion which was a real gift, the rest was often goods in return for "tributes." Sometimes a "bestowal" was not an exchange item but a unilateral present to the nomadic people. For instance, after the rebellion of Au Lu-shan and Shih Ssu-ming (755–58 A.D.) the great T'ang dynasty of China began to decline. After that, whether to pacify internal rebellions or as a counter against the power of a foreign enemy, the Tu-fan or Tibetans, the T'ang dynasty depended upon the military help of the Uighurs. In order to reward their "merit," the Son of Heaven granted them each year numerous items as a "bestowal"[10] and also allowed them to trade horses to the Chinese. These were the well known "Uighur horses" of the T'ang history.[11]

"Yearly payment" (歲幣) was the term used by the Sung dynasty for presenting silver and silk unilaterally to the rulers of the Kitan, Jurchen, and Tangut under the latter's military threat. Consequently, in the records of both Kitan and Jurchen these were recognized as "tribute."[12] This type of one-sided contribution usually appeared only when a nomadic people (or a half-farming/half-hunting people such as the Jurchen) had already occupied a great area of Chinese agricultural territory and had established a dual-system of government over both agricultural and nomadic peoples. However, they were still motivated by their long standing and traditional objectives of war in formalizing a system to extract agricultural and manufactured goods from an enemy they had subdued.

The four exchange relationships were measures that the court of the agricultural society used (based upon their abundant economic power) to purchase peace from the nomadic people. They were stimulated by military might and threatened aggression.

Besides these four institutionalized exchanges, the "frontier market" was the most regular form of trade and also the most effective measure for peace. The function of border markets became quite evident as early as the Han period, and reached a peak late in the Ming times, i.e., from 1570 to the end of the dynasty in 1644. Peace in the two military districts Hsüan-fu and Ta-tung was perfectly preserved because the Ming court established permanent "frontier markets" or "tributary markets" for Altan Khan, a powerful leader of Western Inner Mongolia. However, war continued in the military districts of Chi-chou and Liao-tung because the Ming court could not reach a similar settlement with the Great Khan of Mongolia. Unfortunately, this effective method for both peace and trade did not bear the beneficial fruit it should have, because it was misused by the Chinese. The court either rejected proposals to establish "markets" or used them as a military trap against the nomads. In this connection, Ssu-ma Ch'ien mentions a particular tragedy in his *Shih chi:*

> After ascending the throne, Emperor Wu-ti [r. 140–88 B.C.] clearly made it his policy to continue the establishment of royal marriages, to tighten his control over frontier market places, and to give more supplies to outsiders. Therefore the Hsiung-nu, from the Shan-yü [khan] down to the ordinary people, all became pro-Han [Chinese]. The authorities made the old man of the city of Ma-yi Nieh I, their spy in exchanging goods with the Hsiung-nu. Tempting the Shan-yü, he pretended to betray the city of Ma-yi. The Shan-yü believed him, and coveted the wealth and goods of Ma-yi, and violated the border of Wu-sai with a hundred thousand cavalry. The Han ambushing him with three hundred thousand soldiers . . . tried to capture the Shan-yü and kill him. After that, the Hsiung-nu cut off the practice of intermarriage . . . and began to invade the borders of Han increasingly. Even so, the Hsiung-nu still desired trading places and coveted Han goods. Also the Hans often trapped them by the trick of opening a marketing place.[13]

From such stories, it is not difficult to see to what degree the "frontier market" contributed to peace, and also what difficult circumstances the Hsiung-nu fell into because of the deception of the Han authorities. Of course, the establishment of frontier markets was an important goal and at times it was achieved militarily by the nomadic peoples.

The objective of most nomadic aggression was economic. However, the agriculturally based governments of China were generally motivated by political considerations or military security in dealing with nomadic neighbors. Ssu-ma Ch'ien interpreted the ancient relationship between the northern, non-Chinese people, and the Western Chou as follows.

> King Wu . . . expelled the barbarians to the north of the Ching and Lo rivers.[14] [He] referred to them as vassals of the wastelands [huang-fu 荒服] and required them to offer tribute at definite times. Two hundred years later, the rule of Chou declined, and [its] King Mu attacked the Ch'üan-jung ["dog-like barbarians"

犬戎], [990 B.C.]. . . . From that time the vassals of the wasteland refused to come to court.[15]

This ancient account serves as a key to understanding the relationship between the Chinese and the nomadic people. It makes clear that the objectives of the two peoples were different. From the Chinese records it is obvious that the nomads wanted to obtain "bestowals" in exchange for "tribute." The Chinese court demanded that this exchange be carried out as a form of tribute, and designated the "tributaries" as "vassals of the wasteland," in order to establish that the authority of the Son of Heaven had been established over the barbarians. The various cases recorded in Chinese records suggest that the actions of the agricultural state were politically motivated.

From this study of the long history of the tributary system of the Middle Kingdom, we may summarize as follows.

1. In "tributary" relationships between the nomadic peoples and the Middle Kingdom, the nomads were mainly the initiators. They pressed for opportunities to "offer tribute" and even used military power to pressure rulers in China to accept their "petitions." The frequency and the volume of the "tribute" activity increased with the growth of nomadic power. The "tributary" relationship between the Oirads and the Ming dynasty is a typical example. Nomadic leaders apparently did not consider the form of so-called "tribute" a serious problem. Also a "loss of face" was not a problem for them as it was for Chinese rulers. Nor did they worry about damaging their political prestige or status. The content of the exchange was their main concern, and economic satisfaction took precedence over the form of the contact. On the other hand, it was common for courts in China to reject "petitions for tribute," as occurred in the majority of cases. When rejection was impossible, trade missions were authorized, but only under the designation of "tribute mission" which exaggerated the power of the Son of Heaven to both the "barbarians" and their own peasants inside the Great Wall.

2. The pattern of tributary relationships between China and the petty agricultural states on the south was quite different from that noted above. It was almost always China which was the initiator of the relationships. Often the powerful courts of the Middle Kingdom, by military measures, forced the subjugation of weaker peoples to the Son of Heaven. Their presentation of tribute was a symbol of obedience. These tributary states, however, in offering tribute did not seek so-called "bestowals" in exchange. They were forced to accept the unequal terms of tributary status, and while recognizing their role as vassals they often petitioned for a suspension of their obligations or an extension of the time period between tributary missions required of them. These petitions suggest that they were compelled to offer tribute to China and are in marked contrast to the actions of the northern nomadic powers which pressed the Middle Kingdom to accept their "tribute." The political motivations of courts in China remained essentially the same whether directed toward the South or the North.

Ruler or Ruled?

It is difficult to determine in detail, due to a lack of material, whether the "politics" of tributary relationships really affected the nomadic peoples. To what degree were they truly influenced? Was there a consciousness of being under subjugation through the system? These problems still await analytic study to establish the historical facts. However, from the difference between the Chinese and Turkic texts in the well-known Orkhon inscriptions[16] it is not difficult to discover that there was no common understanding of the official relationship between the Turks and T'ang. Consequently, from the Chinese point of view, while noble ranks and official titles granted by the emperors to the nomadic leaders is evidence that they did put "barbarian rulers" under the favor and authority of the Son of Heaven, such "authority" did not really restrain the rebellious activities of a powerful nomadic ruler. For instance, the Emperor Yung-lo (r. 1402–24) invested with the rank of *wang* (prince) both of the leaders of the Oirad and the Ta-tan. However, it produced no real obedience, and Yung-lo himself finally died on what proved to be his last expedition against the Mongols.[17] All these facts indicate that from the Chinese standpoint, this pattern of diplomatic calculation based on their traditional political philosophy brought them the appearance of political status and achievement. From the standpoint of the nomadic people, however, the diplomatic arrangements did not result in that for which their designers hoped. The reason for the failure was that vain ranks and titles did not meet the material or economic needs of the nomadic peoples. This kind of policy, i.e., emphasizing the political design but neglecting the economic needs of China's neighbors, could never achieve positive or permanent results. In a memorial to the Ming Emperor (1571) expressing thanksgiving for the rank of "Shun-yi Wang" (順義王) for himself and for other official titles granted his relatives, Altan Khan said:

> We, your vassals who have grown up among the Northern Barbarians, do not really understand the rituals of vassalage. . . . Our people have increased but clothing is not sufficient. . . . Along the border there was no place allowed for trade. Since we could not obtain cloth to wear, and because wool or furs are too hot for summer . . . we therefore violated the frontier and committee evil deeds. . . . Consequently, our men and horses were often killed and wounded. . . . Now the Imperial Decree has shown mercy on us, has bestowed upon me the rank of Shun-yi Wang, and has allowed us to present tribute and to establish frontier market places. We, your vassals, are very grateful for your heavenly mercy. . . . This will make me, your vassal, and also my brother, nephews, sons, and grandsons grateful from generation to generation and we will never rebel again.[18]

Altan and his descendants eventually achieved a permanent peace with the Ming on the conditions of establishing frontier markets and making an oath to "never rebel again." Interestingly, the same story was recorded differently in the Mongolian materials. Sagang Sechen Taiji, in his notable work, *Erdeni-yin tobchi,* said:

> Altan Khan dispatched troops into China, invading and plundering. The Ming were greatly threatened and sent envoys to Altan Khan, gave him the title of Sun Ong, and presented to him a gold seal to carry out a great rule together with Emperor Lung-ch'ing of the Great Ming.[19]

This shows a different interpretation among the Mongols of a situation which was embarrassing to the Chinese.

Early in the reign of Wang Mang (r. 9–23 A.D.), his policy toward the Hsiung-nu and their response confirm the view that the activities of nomadic peoples were usually determined by economic considerations but the activities of the court of the Chinese agricultural society were usually dictated by political interests. After Wang Mang usurped the Han throne and established his new dynasty under the name of Hsin, he sent an envoy to the Hsiung-nu to present the Shan-yü gold and silk in large quantities. He also exchanged the old seal of the Hsiung-nu which was granted them by Han Hsüan-ti (r. 73–49 B.C). The old seal's inscription read "The Imperial Seal of the *Shan-yü* of the Hsiung-nu."[20] Wang Mang gave them a new seal with the inscription "The Stamp of the Hsiung-nu *Shan-yü* of the Hsin." The Hsiung-nu complained that the old seal was *"hsi,"* an imperial seal, but that the new one was *"chang,"* merely a stamp of an ordinary official, making the *Shan-yü* no different from a vassal. However, they were pleased with the rich gifts and sent horses and cattle to Wang Mang to express their thanks.[21]

This story indicates that the ruler of the Hsiung-nu, in order to achieve economic benefits, accepted political subordination. This does not mean that political concessions were conditional and limitless. Afterwards, encouraged by his achievement, Wang Mang again offered gold and other precious things to the Hsiung-nu to buy them off and divide them into several smaller groups. He tried to create fifteen *shan-yü* and finally inflamed the Hsiung-nu. They launched a terrible invasion and looted south of the Great Wall.[22] This war continued even after the fall of Wang Mang.

Royal marriage alliances, noted above as a unique aspect of the exchange or trade carried on due to the pressure of the Hsiung-nu, were paradoxically initiated by the Han court. Ssu-ma Ch'ien recorded the viewpoints of both the initiator of the policy, Liu Ching, and the Emperor, Kao-ti of Han, in his work, *Shih chi*.

> At that time, Mao-tun was the *Shan-yü* (r. 209–174 B.C.). His military strength was powerful as his archers numbered three hundred thousand and [he] invaded the frontier several times. The Emperor [Kao-ti], worried about this, consulted Liu Ching. Liu Ching counseled, "The realm has just been settled and the soldiers are tired of fighting. . . . it is impossible to overcome [them] by force. . . . Mao-tun demonstrates [his power] through military force. . . . It is impossible to convince him through good heartedness and righteousness. The only thing possible is to plan for the future and to make his son and grandson our vassals. However, Your Majesty may not be willing to do so." The Emperor replied, "If it works, why not. Let us try." Liu Ching then said, "If your Majesty really approves, then give him the Elder Princess to be his wife, also give him rich presents. When the barbarians realize that the Han Emperor has given his daughter in marriage with rich presents, they will admire [us] and will make her the *Yen-chih*.[23] If she gives birth to a son he will be established as the crown prince and will succeed [his father] as *Shan-yü*. Why is it thus? Because they need rich gifts from the Han. If Your Majesty gives the things which are abundant in the Han realm, but rare in their land, from time to time, and sends a person of eloquence to persuade [them] through propriety, then, while Mao-tun is alive he will be [your] son-in-law and when he dies [your] grandson will become the *Shan-yü*. Who has heard of a grandson who dares to disobey his grandfather? Therefore [we] gradually make them our vassals without using military force."[24]

As a matter of fact, the policy of a royal marriage alliance from beginning to end did not achieve the purpose Liu Ching designed. However, the food and manufactured goods which were offered to the nomadic rulers did have an economic influence and reduced the high tide of conflict. Later, in the Sui period (589–618 A.D.), Chinese princesses became a political bridge between the two opposing powers.[25] Some became centers of intelligence for the Chinese court,[26] and others eventually became the means of sowing dissension among the nomadic rulers.[27] All these activities reinforce the contention that the objectives of the agrarian rulers toward their nomadic neighbors were mainly political.

Nomadic Military Power

The possibility of establishing a trade agreement with the Chinese usually depended upon the level of the military strength of the nomadic state concerned. If it were not powerful enough to impress the agricultural state, then its demands were usually ignored or rejected. This was especially the case when the steppe nomads were not unified, or when the various nomadic groups were still struggling among themselves. A long journey for trade often had to be carried out under strong military protection. There is much historical evidence that most nomadic groups, after having established their power, first organized a powerful alliance and then began to seek permission to "offer tribute" to the court inside the Great Wall. The court's response to the "petition" was then based on the realization that a new nomadic coalition could develop as a challenge to old nomadic opponents, and such a development was naturally welcomed. A well-known pattern which was part of the diplomatic design to insure the security of China was a policy of "attacking those near-by and establishing friendly relations with those afar," that is, the policy of "checking barbarians with barbarians." There is a record in the *Account of the T'u-chüeh* found in the *Chou-shu* which notes:

> At the time of the Tu-men [Bumin Khan] his tribe became powerful. They began to come to [our] border to purchase silk and quilt, and hoped to have communication with the Middle Kingdom. In the eleventh year of Ta-t'ung (545), Tai Tsu[28] sent an envoy . . . to them. Their countrymen were happy and said: "Now the envoy of a great kingdom has arrived. Our country will rise."[29]

This story denotes that at the time of Bumin Khan the Turks had already established themselves as a power. This made it possible to direct a trade caravan from the area of the Altai Mountains, passing through the Gobi steppes (which were under the rule of Jou-jan), to the border of the Tabghach Wei. This is strong evidence of the power of the Turks, and is also the main reason why the Wei court agreed to establish trade ties with them. In other words, the objective was to make better contact with the new Turkic power in order to encircle and counter their old enemy, the Jou-jan.

According to the historical record, after the collapse of the Mongolian Yüan dynasty (1368) and the emergence of the Ming court, the size and frequency of "tribute" missions remained generally at a very low level. However, by the middle of the Ming dynasty, when the Mongols had regained much of their power, both their frequency and the volume of "tribute" exchange increased. The *Ming shih-lu* records the situation as follows.

> In times past the Oirad envoy missions usually numbered not more than five persons. Now [1442] the envoys from Toghtobukha[30] and Esen are numbered in the thousands. In addition, there are [many] traders.[31]

Implicit in this statement is the fact that the volume of trade under the guise of tribute between the nomadic peoples and the Chinese agricultural state depended mainly upon the comparative power of the nomadic state. Thus, a part of "tribute" exchange was carried out under the military threat of nomadic rulers who were supposedly "vassals."

The Effects of War

Periodic campaigns launched by the nomadic powers into agricultural areas usually transferred the bad effects of war onto the peasants, while the nomads enjoyed the benefits. War, for the nomadic people, was a sort of "production," i.e., a means of increasing wealth. For the warriors it usually meant success and riches. Therefore, when a powerful and talented leader appeared he was often inclined by tradition to launch a war, to loot agricultural areas south of the Great Wall in order to increase the wealth of his people. A secondary result was the consolidation of his personal power and prestige. As a result of the long term embargo policy of the rulers of the agricultural state of China, nomads and their leaders were conditioned to believe that there was almost no other way to obtain needed food and other agricultural products except by war or military threat. In the thirteenth century, Chinggis Khan and his generals shrewdly exploited this traditional economic motivation to stir up the desire for war among their people. They effectively maintained military law and distributed booty equitably to the men who followed them in battle. Sometimes, even the conquered lands and the people themselves were divided and given to Mongol nobles and generals as fief or reward. Therefore, through military victories the livelihood of the nomads greatly improved, the morale of the people was raised, and war rather than being a waste of wealth, increased it. In contrast, from the beginning to end, war was inevitably an economic loss to the enemies of the Mongols. General Peng T'a-ya of the Southern Sung (1127-1276) discussed the strategy of the Mongols in his *Hei-ta shih-lüëh* as follows.

> When they launched a campaign into the territory of others, they immediately loot the area. As Master Sun Wu maintains, this is the strategy of obtaining a food supply from the enemy.[32]

This situation already existed very early, before the Mongols appeared in world history. Regarding the Hsiung-nu's disposal of booty, Ssau-ma Ch'ien records:

> In their campaigns . . . they distribute booty and make slaves of the prisoners. Therefore in war everyone strives for personal gain. . . . Seeking loot they attack their enemy as a swarm of birds.[33]

In the "Wei-shu" section of the *San Kuo Chih* there is the following note regarding the personality of K'o-pi-neng, the leader of the Hsien-pei people who occupied Mongolia in the second and third centuries.

> K'o-pi-neng originally was the [leader] of a small group of Hsien-pei. Because of [his] boldness, fairness in the execution of law, and unselfishness in wealth, he was supported by all and became the *ta-jen* [leader of the tribal alliance]. . . . He commanded more than one hundred thousand horsemen. During campaigns, he divided the loot evenly among the warriors with no selfish consideration at all. Therefore, the people served [him] with all their might and the *ta-jen* of other tribes held him in high esteem.[34]

Since war was a method of increasing the wealth of the nation and people, their fighting spirit was high, and thus it was easy to win victories against their opponents.

The war between the Kitan and the Sung dynasties in 1004 was ended on the condition that *sui-pi* (歲幣), a definite amount of silver and silk, would be presented by the Sung court to the Kitan. This course was a result determined by the traditional military objectives of the nomadic peoples. In the year 1042 another crisis broke out between these two and this also was solved when the Sung agreed to increase the volume of *sui-pi*. In the negotiations it seems that the words of the Sung envoy greatly influenced the thinking of the Kitan emperor and persuaded him to agree to the Sung concession. In the "Biography of Fu Pi" in the *Sung-shih*, it is recorded that he counseled the Kitan ruler as follows.

> When the Court of the North established friendship with the Middle Kingdom, the profits will be monopolized by the monarch and nothing will be obtained by the vassals and underlings. In the case of war, then the profits will belong to the vassals and underlings. However, any disaster will be blamed on the monarch. Therefore, one who advocates war is planning for himself.[35]

According to this view, war was promoted for the benefit of the generals and the troops, but the nomadic ruler agreed to peace because of the possibility of gaining more goods and riches through peace. However, a decline of the morale of the nomadic people was also a result of the establishment of a peace which did not provide any economic satisfaction for the mass of the people.

Territorial Expansion

The writer has stressed the view that the objective of the military actions of the nomadic people was mainly to gain food and wealth and that they usually had no political designs or territorial ambitions. There were some exceptions when the nomadic people received cooperation or encouragement from within the agricultural society. In the ancient *Shih chi* there is the following interesting record of an admonition given to Mao-tun by his wife while he was besieging the Han Emperor within Chinese territory (202 B.C.).

> Then the *Yen-chih* [khatun or queen] said to Mao-tun, "Two lords should not make hardships for each other. Now [we] are in Han territory but when all is considered this is not the land in which [you], the *Shan-yü* should live. . . . I hope that [you], the *Shan-yü* will consider this matter." Mao-tun . . . accepted the *Yen-chih's* words and opened a path in the corner of the siege encirclement. Finally [Kao-ti] escaped and met his main forces, while Mao-tun left with his troops. The Han also withdrew their forces and sent Liu Ching as an envoy to establish an alliance through a royal marriage.[36]

This is a typical case making clear that the objective of the military campaigns of Mao-tun was neither to capture the Han Emperor nor to occupy the farming lands of China. The hope rather was economic gain as a result of victory in war. This explains why Mao-tun agreed to release Han Kao-ti and to accept a royal marriage alliance.

In the middle of the sixth century, the Turks established themselves as a strong power in Inner Asia. Meanwhile, south of the Great Wall there appeared two antagonistic regimes of Ch'i (550–77) and Chou (559–81). Both of these struggled to win military support from the Turks in order to increase pressure against the other. In the spring of 564 an allied force of Chou and Turkic warriors launched a war against Ch'i. However, the aims of these two allies were entirely different. The purpose of Chou was to crush their mortal enemy, Ch'i, but the objective of the Turks was only to loot agricultural products and to capture laborers to serve them. They were not interested in the extermination of Ch'i nor the occupation of Chinese territory. In the "Account of the T'ü-chüeh" in the *Chou-shu* there is a narrative reflecting the military maneuvers of the allied forces of Chou and the Turks against Ch'i as follows.

> In the war against Ch'i . . . [we] asked the [T'ü-chüeh] to dispatch their forces eastward to attack Ch'i. . . . In the third year of [Pao-ting 563] . . . the Imperial Decree instructed Yang Chung, the Duke of Sui[37] to move forward with ten thousand together with the T'ü-chüeh to attack the Ch'i. . . . Ssu-chin [Mughan Khan, r. 553–72] came to meet us with one hundred thousand cavalry. In the first month of the next year, [the allied forces] attacked the ruler of Ch'i at Chin-yang [present-day Tai-yüan in Shansi]. [The city] was impossible to take. . . . Then Ssu-chin sent out his troops to loot and returned.[38]

The "Biography of Yang Chung" in the *Chou-shu* adds that:

The T'ü-chüeh forces set out to loot. In the area . . . from Chin-yang down to Luan-ch'eng [present-day Luan-ch'eng in Hopei] almost the entire population and animals were captured or killed.[39]

Clearly, the aims of the Chou and the Turks were entirely different.

The Chinese T'ang dynasty also at its beginning sought military help from the Turks, saying, "We would like to have the Khan's forces enter the Capital [Ch'ang-an]. The people and the land should go to the Duke of T'ang, but the wealth — silk, gold, and other precious things — should be given to the T'ü-chüeh." Once again it is clear that the objective of Turkic military assistance to T'ang was not for territorial nor political gain, but to obtain "wealth, silk, gold, and other precious things."[40]

Later, in 756, the Uighur forces helped the T'ang to pacify an internal rebellion. Such cooperation indicates that the objectives of the Uighurs were the same as those of the earlier Turks, i.e., they sought neither territorial nor political influence, but rather the confiscation of the wealth and treasure of the rebels, the looting of cities, and obtaining of rich yearly grants from the T'ang court.

The following is recorded in the "Accounts of Hui-he" in the *Chiu T'ang-shu*.

After the West Capital [Ch'ang-an] was recovered, the Uighur troops wanted to enter the city and loot. This was eventually stopped by the Prince of Kuang-p'ing.[41] Later, when the East Capital [Lo-yang] was recovered, the Uighur entered the treasury and confiscated all the money and silk. Again, in the city and villages they looted for three entire days plundering immeasurable wealth and goods. The Prince of Kuang-p'ing also presented the Uighur with embroidery, silk and other precious things. . . . Later when Emperor Su-tsung (r. 756–62) returned to the West Capital . . . he again bestowed upon them embroidery, silks, fabrics, gold, and silver containers.[42]

The *Hsin T'ang-shu* adds, "each year twenty thousand pieces of silk were granted to them."[43]

In the middle of the fifteenth century the Oirad Mongols became very powerful. In a battle at T'u-mu (a fortress along the Great Wall west of Peking) in 1449, even the Emperor Ying-tsung (r. 1436–49, 1457–64) was captured by Esen, but this victory did not bear fruit for the Oirad. When the Ming Emperor Ching-tsung (r. 1449–57) came to power, it was no longer possible for the Oriad to force ransom from the abducted emperor, Ying-tsung. Finally Esen sent him back without any conditions. This again suggests that the motive of the Oirad was not political or territorial aggrandizement.

In the sixteenth century, the Mongols under Altan Khan's leadership regularly invaded Chinese areas for almost five decades and even threatened Yen-ching, the Ming capital, several times in order to force the Ming to open up frontier markets. In 1550, when the forces of Altan appeared before the gates of the capital, the Ming held a court conference to consider the crisis and among all the ministers only Yen Sung,[44] regarded by Chinese historians as "treacherous," recognized the situation as no great threat. He maintained that Altan and his troops were "merely a group of food-looting bandits, nothing to worry about."[45] Yen Sung alone recognized the economic motivations behind the military actions of China's northern nomadic neighbors. Another minister Hsü Chieh[46] took the danger very seriously, and worried that the enemy might propose some embarrassing political demands. He said, "If they only demand money, pearls, and jade, that is all right, but if they demand some things which we cannot accept, then what shall we do?"[47] Compared with Hsü Chieh, Yen Sung had greater insight — that the objective of Altan was economic, not political.

This discussion has suggested that the military objective of the Inner Asian nomadic peoples, whether it be through invasion or involvement in the civil wars of China, was to obtain agricultural products vital to their very livelihood. Even nomadic military aid to China was actually a kind of exchange of services for supplies. However, in the case of the relationship between the Tu-fan, or Tibetans, and the T'ang dynasty there is an exception. The campaigns launched by the Tibetans against the T'ang were mainly for territorial occupation. The reason for this may be explained by the fact that the Tibetans were a semi-farming, semi-nomadic people, and, therefore, their concept of land usage was quite different from that of the purely nomadic peoples north of the Great Wall. This may also explain why after 756 the T'ang court established an alliance with the Uighur against the Tu-fan. The Tibetans were a competing neighbor with territorial ambitions while the Uighur were merely a people "covetous for gain," but void of territorial and political ambition. Consequently, the T'ang court devised a rather brilliant policy of checking Tibetan expansion with Uighur power. A related problem — the long struggle for control of the Silk Road and Central Asia between the Han and Hsiung-nu — also suggests that the purpose of the Hsiung-nu was to obtain economic benefits, while the objective of the Han was to enlarge its military influence and to occupy territory.

The above analysis does not include all the objectives of every nomadic action, especially in cases where they gained support from or had close relations with the agricultural society south of the Great Wall or where the nomads became acculturated, adopted an agricultural life style, and became Sinicized. In such circumstances the nomadic rulers tried to occupy the land, to rule the people, and to establish some kind of Sinicized regime within Chinese territory. These cases are generally known as the "dynasties of conquest" or "dynasties of infiltration."

The first great dynasty established in China by a northern nomadic people was the Tabghach Wei (386–556).[48] This political state was a masterpiece established by the nomadic people who admired the Chinese way of life, and who became Sinicized deliberately. The second important case was the Liao dynasty (907–1125) established by the Kitan. From the beginning Kitan rulers were supported by their Chinese minister Han Yen-hui[49] and by other Chinese. Also Kitan rulers actively utilized Chinese who escaped north of the Great Wall to plant crops for them.[50] These factors increased the Kitan's interest in Chinese affairs. Consequently, they became involved in internal struggles, helped the Later Chin (936–46) to overthrow the Later T'ang (923–35), and took the "sixteen districts of Yen and Yün"[51] as a reward for their military assistance. The Kitan state was the first nomadic empire which sought land and people as a reward and which was not satisfied with only silk, gold, and precious things as were the Turks before them.

With the rise of the Mongolian empire, Chinggis Khan (r. 1206–27) invaded North China in 1211 and 1213. He withdrew his forces only after they reaped a great harvest in wealth and agricultural products. They did not occupy any land or make any political demands of the Sinicized Jurchen-Chin dynasty. Granted, this may have been because the Mongols lacked enough powerful weapons to attack Chinese walled cities, but an even more important reason may be that they did not get Chinese or Kitan support. The *Secret History of the Mongols* relates the withdrawal of the Mongol forces as follows.

> They [the Jurchen] presented a daughter with the title of Imperial Princess [to the Khaghan], and brought forth gold, silver, embroidered work, silk, and other wealth from the city of Jungdu [Peking], and pressed our soldiers to accept them as much as possible. Therefore, Chinggis Khaghan withdrew his forces from attacking the city. . . . As much as possible, our troops carried these

embroideries, silk, and other wealth on horseback and even used soft silk to tie the loot on the horses (section 248).

Thus, Chinggis Khan's objectives in these invasions still followed the traditional pattern of acquiring agricultural wealth and products to meet needs, but not to establish a permanent administration over the land and people. Doubtless, Chinggis's two invasions were a prelude to the later occupation of North China. However, it seems that a change of policy was the main factor leading to the Mongol occupation. This change of attitude toward agricultural areas might be due to the support or cooperation of such powerful Chinese families as those of Shih T'ien-ni, Yen Shih, Chang Juo, and Tung Tsun.[52]

Chinggis Khan's military action in Central Asia of Khorezm (Central Asia) and the destruction and looting of cities in Transoxiana was again motivated by the old traditional desire to seize wealth and craftsmen. In his decision to establish a system of protracted occupation over this area, he seems to have been encouraged by Yalavaj and his son Mas'ut, Western Asian officials. The *Secret History* notes:

> After Sarta'ul [Khorezm] was pacified, Chinggis Khaghan ordered the establishment of a *darughachi* in each city to rule over it. . . . From Urgenj there came . . . Yalavaj and Mas'ut, father and son, to visit Chinggis Khaghan and explain a system for the administration of cities. Because their words were reasonable, [the Khagan] appointed the son, Khurumushi Mas'ut together with the *darughachis* that were established to rule . . . the [Transoxianian] cities, and the father Yalavaj was appointed over the city of Jungdu [Peking] of Kitad [Cathay]. . . . Because Yalavaj and Mas'ut knew how to administer cities, they were appointed to rule the people of Kitad (section 263).

This account suggests that the establishment of a permanent nomadic administration in an occupied agricultural territory was a result of the encouragement by members of the gentry in the agricultural society. Why did the Mongol leader make Yalavaj, an alien, the governor of North China? The evidence reveals that although Chinggis Khan had already received the cooperation of some Chinese military men, he had not yet recruited learned Chinese administrators to serve in his civil service. Yeh-lü Ch'u-ts'ai, the Sinicized Kitan scholar, was then in the Mongol camp, but his career as a leading minister in the Mongolian court came in the reign of Ögödei Khan (r. 1229–41). Also because of cooperation between Ye-lü Ch'u-ts'ai and his Chinese colleagues, the Mongol rulers established a permanent system which bridged temporarily the gap between the clique of Yeh-lü Ch'u-ts'ai, which advocated ruling China according to a Chinese approach, and the clique of Yalavaj and Mongol conservatives. However, this internal tension finally resulted in a split in the Mongolian empire and the creation of the Yüan dynasty (1260).

The establishment of the Yüan court and especially the subjugation of Southern Sung (1227) by Khubilai Khan (r. 1260–94) resulted from the persuasion of Khubilai's Chinese ministers. This is a well known historical event which does not need further explanation. However, other Chinggisid princes opposed Khubilai, mainly because of their lack of concern for agricultural territory and their conservative nomadic attitudes. Their views, which opposed Sinicization, finally led to a split in the Mongolian empire. Evidence of this is seen in the *Yüan shih* as follows.

The princes in the northwest sent envoys to court and protested saying, "Our tradition is different from that of the Chinese. Now [you] are residing in Chinese territory, establishing a capital and cities, and adopting Chinese institutions, laws, and regulations. What is the purpose in all this?"[53]

Besides the foregoing, two other conquering dynasties, the Chin and the Ch'ing, should be mentioned. Both were established by the Jurchen and their descendants, and both were semi-hunting and semi-agricultural people. Since their life was different, it is expected that their conception of land and their objectives were also different from those of purely nomadic peoples as the Hsiung-nu, the Turks, the Uighurs, and the Mongols.

Notes

1. *Ch'ang-chun Chen-jen hsi-yu-chi* (長春真人西遊記 Wang Kuo-wei, *Meng-ku shih-liao ssu-chung* edition) 1:16b.
2. *Shih chi* 110, Accounts of Hsiung-nu, 19ab.
3. Ibid., 14a.
4. Before their occupation of Chinese territory, the Kitan had already established some cities for Chinese refugees, and captives farmed for the Kitans. Before the Mongols established the Yüan dynasty, they also built cities as settlements for captured laborers such as Chimkhai City (鎮海城) in Western Mongolia.
5. Even in the late 1940s, a majority of the Mongols were influenced by such traditions.
6. *Han-shu* 94 B, Account of the Hsiung-nu B, 32ab.
7. From the words of Ts'ai Yung (蔡邕), *Hou Han shu* 90, Account of the Wu-huan and Hsien-pei, 17b.
8. Yü-wen Yung (宇文邕), Kao-tsu of the Northern Chou Dynasty married the daughter of Mughan Khan of the Turks and made her his empress. See *Chou-shu* 50, "Biography of the Empresses," 3b–4b.
9. *Shih chi* 99, Biography of Liu Ching (劉敬) 4ab, and Ibid. 11o, "Account of the Hsiung-nu," 12ab.
10. The T'ang court, in order to "reward the merit" of the Uighur in the recovery of their two capitols, "granted twenty thousand pieces of silk each year" to them. See Hsin T'ang-shu 217a, Account of Uighurs, 4b.
11. See Sechin Jagchid, *"Tui Hui-ku-ma wen-t'i ti yi-ke kan-fa* (對回鶻馬問題的一個看法) On the Problem of 'Uighur Horses," *Shih-hou Monthly* (食貨月刊) vol. 1, no. 1, April 1971, Taipei.
12. An entry in the eleventh year of Ch'ung-hsi (重熙 1042) "Annals of Hsing-tsung" 2d, *Laio shih* 19, says "In the second ninth month, Yeh-lü Jen-hsien (耶律仁先) sent messengers to report that the Sung agreed to increase additional silver silk each ten thousand of taels and pieces, and in the official documents it would be entitled as *kung* (貢 tribute)."
13. *Shih chi* 110, Account of Hsiung-nu, 21ab.
14. The two rivers of Ching and Lo are in the north central part of Shensi province.
15. *Shih chi* 110, Account of Hsiung-nu, 2b.
16. The contents of the Chinese and the Turkic inscriptions of the same stone tablet of Kul Tekin in the Orkhon River valley do not coincide with one another.

17. Emperor Yung-lo died in the year 1424 (on his return from his last invasion against Mongolia) at Yü-mu-ch'uan (榆木川), a place which seeps to be in the Ba'arin Banner of Juu-uda League, Inner Mongolia.
18. *Hsüan-lan-t'ang ts'ung-shu* (玄覽堂叢書) vol. 1, "The Tributary Report of Shun-yi Wang, Altan and Other Vassals of the Northern Barbarians (*Pei-ti Shun-yi Wang An-ta teng chen kung-piao-wen*)."
19. *Meng-ku yüan-liu ch'ien-cheng* (蒙古源流箋証) 6:21b.
20. The name of the seal of Hsiung-nu that was given them by Han Hsüan-ti was "Hsiung-nu Shan-yü hsi,(匈奴單于璽)," in order to show it was a seal of a chief of state. Therefore it did not bear the words of "Han Hsiung-nu" or "the Hsiung-nu of the Han." In other words, the Han court did not exaggerate the status of the Hsiung-nu.
21. *Han-shu* 94b, Account of Hsiung-nu B, 20b–23b.
22. Ibid.
23. *Yen-chih* (閼氏) was the official title of the wife of the *Shan-yü* of the Hsiung-nu, and is similar to the Turkic-Mongol word *Khatun*.
24. *Shih chi* 99, Biography of Liu Ching (劉敬), 4ab.
25. The Princess Ch'ien-chin (千金公主) of Chou helped to establish a relationship between her husband Ishabara Khan of the Turks and Emperor Wen-ti of Sui, who had seized power from the Chou. Princess Ning-kuo (寧國公主), daughter of Emperor Su-tsung of T'ang, married Ke-le Khan of the Uighurs and consequently a friendly relationship was established between the two powers.
26. The Sui gave Princess Yi-an (義安公主), a daughter of the royal household, in marriage to Jan-kan, a prince of the Turks, and thereafter the actions of the Turks were usually reported to the Sui court through her and also Jan-kan.
27. Sui Wen-ti gave a daughter of his household to Tölis, younger brother of Tu-lan Khan, in order to sow dissension among the Turks.
28. Yü-wen T'ai (宇文泰), Tai-tsu of Chou by this time was the prime minister of Western Wei.
29. *Chou-shu* 50, *yi-yü* (foreign lands) B, Account of the T'u-chüeh, 3a.
30. Toghto-bukha is known as Daitsung Khaghan in the Mongolian materials.
31. See the entry for the wu-yin day of the first month in spring of the Cheng-t'ung seventh year (1442), Ying-tsung 88, *Ming shih-lu*.
32. *Hei-ta shih-lueh* (黑韃事略 Wang Kou-wei, *Meng-ku shih-liao-ssu-chung* edition), 20b.
33. *Shih chi* 110, "Account of the Hsiung-nu," 11a.
34. *Wei-shu* 30 of *San-kou chih*, "Account of Hsien-pei," 11a.
35. *Sung-shih* 313, "Biography of Fu Pi (富弼)," 2a–3a.
36. *Shih chi* 110, "Account of Hsiung-nu", 12ab.
37. Yang Chung (楊忠) was the father of Yang Chien (楊堅), Sui Wei-ti.
38. *Chou-shi* 50, *yi-yü* (foreign lands) B, "Account of T'u-chüeh," 6b.
39. *Chou-shu* 19, "Biography of Yang Chung," 21b.
40. *Chiu T'ang-shu* 57, "Biography of Liu Wen-ching (劉文靜)."
41. Prince Kuang-p'ing (廣平王) Li Yü (李豫) later became Emperor Tai-tsung (763–75) of T'ang.
42. *Chiu T'ang-shu* 195, "Account of Uighur," 3b–4a.
43. *Hsin T'ang-shu* 217 A, "Account of Uighur," 4a.

44. *Ming shih* 308, "Biography of Yen Sung (嚴嵩)."
45. The entry of the *jen-wu* day of the eighth month of the twenty-ninth year of Chia-ching (1550), Shih-tsung, *Ming shih-lu* 364.
46. *Ming shih* 213, "Biography of Hsü Ch'ieh."
47. See note 45.
48. Before the Tabgach (To-pa) Wei, several small or short-lived kingdoms were established by non-Chinese people, for instance, the Han, Chao, Yen, Ch'in, etc., in the Sixteen Kingdoms Period (308–97 A.D.). Some of them were dynasties of conquest and others were dynasties of infiltration, but because the latter did not establish a firm base or administration, they are not discussed in this paper.
49. *Liao shih*, "Biography of Han Yen-hui (韓延徽)."
50. At the time of the Five Dynasties (907–60), wars and riots continued in the Middle Kingdom and great numbers of Chinese farmers sought refuge in the territory of Kitan. They farmed and supplied agricultural products to the Kitan. This increased the Kitan's interest in farming land, and their confidence in ruling farming people.
51. The Sixteen Districts of Yen and Yün were: Yu, Chi, Ying, Mo, Cho, Tan, Shun, Hsin, Wei, Ju, Wu, Wei, Yü, Ying, Huan, and Shou. They are presently included in the Northern Hopei Province (including Peking) and Northern Shansi Province.
52. The biographies of Chang Juo (張柔), Shih T'ien-ni (史天倪), Tung Tsun (董俊), and Yen Shih (嚴實). See *Yüan shih* 148.
53. *Yüan shih* 125, Biography of Kao Chih-yao (高智耀).

Chapter 2

The Kitans and Their Cities

(Originally published in *Central Asiatic Journal*, 1981, 25:70–88)

Introduction: The Kitans' Purpose for Building Cities

The earliest contact between the nomadic Kitans and the Chinese town and city dwellers was during the T'o-pa Wei Dynasty (386–557). The T'o-pa rulers were Sinicized nomads, but the masses of their kingdom were mainly Chinese. Several centuries later, however, at the beginning of the tenth century, the Kitans began the construction of cities themselves. They built their cities with great commitment and energy and became the first nomadic group to construct cities on a large scale in the traditionally nomadic world of present-day Mongolia. However, several centuries before Kitan urban development, when a nomadic Turkic group was considering the same matter, a farsighted leader expressed a perceptive awareness of the implications of such an undertaking. This is noted in the "Account of the Turks" in the *Hsin T'ang shu* (History of the T'ang Dynasty).

[Bilge Khan] desired to construct cities and Buddhist and Taoist temples. But [the Chancellor] Tonyukhukh said, "The Turks are only one one-hundredth the size of the T'ang [Chinese masses]. Nevertheless [we] are able to resist [the T'ang pressure] because of our nomadic mobile life style and our talent in military arts that derived from our hunting customs. When powerful [we] can invade; when weak, [we] can retreat. Even the largest of T'ang armies is ineffective. If we adopt a sedentary urban life style, we will be captured after only one defeat. Moreover the teaching of the Buddhists and Taoists serve merely to make people benevolent and weak, but not vigorous and militant." His advise was accepted by [the Khan].[1]

This dialogue suggests that the Khan had an inclination to establish a city in order to transplant sedentary agrarian culture into the nomadic world. Opposition from Tonyukhukh was a worry to his fellow Turks, because it meant that the city and the resulting cultural change might well bring about Sinicization and destroy the Turks' national identity. In contrast, the Kitan hope was that city building might facilitate the nomadic rulers in utilizing Chinese manpower and talent to exert stronger control over their agricultural subjects and thus to transform their own "kingdom on horseback"[2] into a consolidated empire. Clearly, the danger was that once these cities were turned into Chinese centers they might actually work against the interests of their own nomadic people. The above dialogue foreshadows later developments among the Kitans.

Around the 840s the Kirgiz forced Uighur power from northern Mongolia. This newly victorious nomadic group had no intention of possessing the grazing fields south of the Gobi. Soon the Chinese T'ang power inside the Great Wall also declined. This released the Kitans from enemy oppression from two sides from which they had suffered for centuries. Thus, the above factors provided an opportunity for the Kitans to become the greatest nomadic power north of the Great Wall.

In the beginning of the 900s, Kitan forces were reorganized under a talented leader, Yeh-lü A-pao-chi, and transformed from a powerful clan or tribal alliance into a unified, well-established, orderly nomadic nation or *ulus* with its power base in the Shira-mören river valley, the "Land of Pine and Desert," as the Chinese called it. At that time the Chinese were suffering from the wars and turmoil of the period of the "Five Dynasties of the Ten Kingdoms" (907–60). Therefore, there was a constant flow of Chinese refugees into the Kitan realm who were seeking a peaceful life. In 907, Yeh-lü A-pao-chi was proclaimed Khan, and with their increasing power the Kitans began to cross the Chinese border. They looted the cities and towns and brought back artisans and peasants as booty to strengthen their nomadic economy. How to administer Chinese affairs and how to organize their manpower for further development became one of the most important problems of the Kitan nation builders.

The long historical Sino-nomadic relationship showed that without Chinese cooperation there would be no possibility for a nomadic power to consolidate its rule as a dynasty of conquest over the Middle Kingdom. In other words, the Kitan rulers needed the advice and support of their Chinese subjects. This may be the reason why the Kitan rulers enthusiastically built so many cities and settled so many Chinese in their native territories.

The Kitans were traditionally nomadic, so their cities were constructed without past experience or earlier precedence. The emergence of cities inside the Kitan domain was symbolic of a greater cooperation and cultural exchange between the Kitans, Chinese, Uighurs, Tungusic Parhaes, and other minor groups of peoples. They were also evidence of a collective endeavor to found a new Kitan empire and make the transition from a purely nomadic "kingdom on horseback" to a complex state. The contemporary Sung historian O-yang Hsiu in his *Wu-tai shih-chi* (Historical Record of the Five Dynasties) briefly recorded the Kitan policy.

> [Yeh-lü] A-pao-chi had the Chinese to cultivate crops and following the example of Yu *chou* [present-day Peking] [he] established cities, dwellings, shops, and markets. With these the Chinese were satisfied, settled down, and had no desire to return.[3]

Concerning early city construction the colophon of the "Annals of T'ai-tsu" in the *Liao shih* (History of Kitan-liao), records:

> Shu-lan[4] [uncle of Yeh-lü A-pao-chi] attacked Yü-chüeh and Shih-wei[5] on the north, and invaded Yi *[chou]*, Ting *[chou]*,[6] Hsi and Shi[7] in the south. [He] started to build cities, caused the people to farm, and organized them. [He] already had the desire to enlarge the realm and increase the population. Thus, when T'ai-tsu [Yeh-lü A-pao-chi] was later installed as the Khan, it was possible [for him] to establish the nation [swiftly].[8]

This record reveals that the Kitan course of establishing cities early, the settling of the agricultural people within their domain, and their cultivation of crops formed the original power base upon which Yeh-lü A-pao-chi launched his career for the subsequent establishment of the Kitan empire. In the same annals the following reference is found regarding city building of Yah-lü A-pao-chi before he was proclaimed Khan, in 907.

> In the seventh month of ... the [second] year of T'ien-fu of T'ang [902], [A-pao-chi] attacked the Ho-tung [present Shansi Province] ... and captured ninety-five thousand people. ... In the ninth month [he] built the city of Lung-hua *chou* [sub-prefecture] on the south of the Huang River [Shira-mören], and started the construction of [the Buddhist monastery] K'ai-chiao *ssu*. In the spring of the

next year [903], [A-pao-chi] attacked the Jurchens and took three hundred families into captivity.... In the ninth month [he] attacked Ho-tung, and in the tenth month invaded the northern [region] of Chi [present-day northeast Hopei Province] and returned with captives.... The next year [904], the eastern section of the city of Lung-hua *chou* was broadened.[9]

This account demonstrates that the Kitans had already started their city building project five years before Yeh-lü A-pao-chi's rise to the khanship. The purpose was to settle the Chinese and Jurchen captives in order to strengthen the power of the Yeh-lü family and to further the establishment of a great Kitan nation. The building of the above mentioned monastery suggests that the Kitan leaders not only desired to employ Chinese manpower for construction, but were also looking forward to cultural changes. The new cities that were built are referred to in Chinese sources as *Han ch'eng* "Chinese cities."[10] In addition to the Chinese captives, people from other areas such as Jurchen, Parhae, and Korea in the east, and Tang-hsiang (Tangut) and T'u-yü-hun in the west were also settled under the same conditions.

The "Monograph on Geography" in the *Liao shih* notes the various types of urban units established.

Five *ching* [capitals], six *fu* [prefectures], one hundred fifty-six *chou* [subprefectures], and *chün* [military administrative districts] type cities, two hundred and nine *hsien* [districts], fifty-two tribes, and sixty subordinate [petty] states.[11]

This brief note shows that the Kitans possessed more than one hundred fifty cities. However, a part of them were urban developments already established in occupied Chinese and Parhae territories before the Kitan takeover.

These Kitan cities which will be discussed below may roughly be categorized into the following four types: 1) the capitals; 2) the fief-like settlements of the nobles; 3) centers for trade and handicraft production; and 4) frontier towns or cities.

The Capitals

The Supreme Capital

The most significant cities of the Kitans were their five capitals. Among them Shang-ching, the Supreme Capital, was of greatest importance. The construction of this city is the first evidence in the history of Mongolia that a nomadic power created a large city in the steppe from nothing and made it a sedentary site for the headquarters of their entire nation. The "Monograph on Geography" in the *Liao shih* says:

Shang-ching [the Supreme Capital] [identical with] Lin-huang *fu* ... governed twenty-five cities of *chün, fu, chou* [level] and ten *hsiens*.... Shang-ching was where [Emperor] T'ai-tsu started [his] career.... In the first year of T'ien-hsien [926], returning from his subjugation of Po-hai [Parhae], [he] began to enlarge the wall of this city and to build a palace.... In the southeast corner there was the T'ien-hsiung *ssu* [monastery]. The circumference [of the city] was twenty-seven *li* [about nine miles].... In its north side was the Imperial City.... East of South Street were located the Garrison Office and the Salt and Iron Agency.... On the south of the Lung-ssu Street was the [office of] Lin-huang *fu* [prefecture], and next to it was the [Office of] Lin-huang *hsien* [district]. On the southwest was Chung-hsiao *ssu* [monastery].... South of the monastery was the [Office of] Ch'ang-t'ai District. On the west was the [Taoist temple] T'ien-ch'ang *kuan*. On the southwest was the Imperial Academy and on the north [of the academy] was the Temple of Confucius. . . . The southern [section of the city] was called the Chinese city . . . with shops and stores. . . . On the east of the South Gate was the Uighur quarter. All of the Uighur traders and merchants staying in Shang-ching gathered here. On the southwest [of the gate] was then T'ung-wen Quarter to accommodate the envoys from foreign countries. Southwest of this was the Lin-huang Quarter to accommodate the envoy from the Kingdom of [Tangut] Hsia.[12]

The contemporary Sung historian, O-yang Hsiu, recorded in his *Wu-tai shih-chi:*

[Yeh-lü A-pao-chi] made his residential area the Supreme Capital and built Hsi-lo [the West Building]. . . . The Kitans worship spirits and honor the sun. On the first day of each month [they] bow eastward toward the sun. [On the occasions of] their great congress *[khuraltai]* and other national gatherings they always treat the east as the honorable direction. . . . Therefore the doors of their dwellings [are] . . . all directed toward the east.[13]

The *Liao shih* also includes an excerpt from the *Hsien lu chi* (陷虜記 the Record of a Captive among the Barbarians) by Hu Chiao who was held hostage by the Kitan between 951 and 953.

In the Supreme Capital, the West Building, there are houses, markets, and shops. Cloth is used for exchange but not money. There are silk and satin craftsmen, eunuchs, Buddhist monks and nuns, and Taoist monks. The Chinese here are mainly from the regions of Ping, Fen, Yu and Chi [present-day central Shansi Province and northern Hopei Province].[14]

The *Liao shih* provides two biographies of the city's architects or engineers.

K'ang Mo-chi . . . in his young age was appointed an officer of Chi *Chou* [present-day Chi *hsien*, northeastern Hopei Province]. [Emperor] T'ai-tsu [Yeh-lü A-pao-chi] invaded Chi *chou* and took him. Appreciating his talent [the Emperor] ordered him to serve in the [Imperial] Headquarters. All Kitan-Chinese affairs that [were] assigned to Mo-chi were all settled reasonably through consultation and discussion, and the Emperor was pleased. . . . Later [he] was promoted to the post of Leftside Premier. In the third year of Shen-ts'e [918] the Imperial Capital was established. Mo-chi supervised the laborers and exhorted them. The task was accomplished within a hundred days.[15]

Han Yan-hui . . . was a man from Yu *chou* [present-day Peking]. . . . Later the Marshal [of Yu *chou*], Liu Shou-kuang[16] sent [him] as his envoy to [the Kitan]. T'ai-tsu was angry and took him hostage. Empress Shu-lü[17] admonished [the Emperor] and said, "He insists that he will not yield. He must be a man of integrity." Then T'ai-tsu called him and talked with him. He was appreciated and assigned to work on military affairs. . . . Later [he] advised [T'ai-tsu] to build cities and towns to settle the Chinese who had surrendered. He arranged marriages for them and had them cultivate and farm to maintain their livelihood. Since then the deserters have decreased.[18]

All of these records suggest that the pattern on construction of Kitan cities was essentially a duplication of Chinese cities. It is clear that Yu *chou* was the blueprint for Shang-ching, the Supreme Capital of Kitan. The designers were of the Chinese elite and included K'ang Mo-chi, Han Yen-hui, and others. The labor forces were mainly Chinese refugees, exiles, and captives. The purpose of this great undertaking was to settle the Chinese, Parhaes, and other captive peoples, and to mobilize them in the great task of Kitan empire building. The cities served as symbols of greater cooperation than before between the Kitans and the Chinese and other peoples they ruled they enhanced peace, prosperity, and a mutually beneficial coexistence. They also symbolized the Kitans' willingness to transplant an agricultural life style into their nomadic world. Instead of the former nomadizing headquarters, the new capital cities gradually developed into permanent centers of the Kitan nation.

In the midst of all this, the Kitans managed to maintain their nomadic tradition. They built permanent capitals on one hand, and on the other continued their migratory system of *nai-po* (捺鉢), the four seasonal camps of the Khan. Again the direction in which the front door of the main building and yurts faced showed the influence of the Kitans' nomadic tradition carried into their new agricultural, sedentary city life. This may also indicate that the Kitans' policy of dualism carried over into their state buildings. In the Northern Division *(Pei-yüan* 北院 *)* of their court the Kitans ruled according to their traditional nomadic institutions while in the Southern Division *(Nan-yüan* 南院 *)*, dominated by the Chinese and other agricultural people, affairs were conducted in conformity with the Chinese system.

Besides the ruling Kitan elite, there were the Chinese scholars, officials, monks, nuns, musicians, actors, shopkeepers and artisans, the Uighur trading and merchant group, the Parhaes, the Jurchens, and various emissaries from foreign countries. This all suggests that the Supreme Capital was the first great cosmopolitan city, hosting numerous different cultures that appeared in historical Mongolia.

The Central Capital

In addition to and resembling the Supreme Capital, a so-called Central Capital was built by the Kitans after they invaded Sung China in 1004. As the result of this military action the Chinese agreed to present tribute yearly to the Kitans, which was recorded in the Chinese sources as *sui-pi* (歲幣), yearly payment. Following this victory the Kitan Khan Yeh-lü Lung-hsü (Emperor Sheng-tsung, r. 983–1031) decreed that there be established a new capital in the territory of present-day Kharachin Banner[19] which was the old site of the headquarters of the King of Hsi. Regarding this urban center the "Monograph on Geography" of the *Liao shih* records:

> The city wall was built in the twenty-fifth year of T'ung-ho [1007], and in it were settled Chinese households. It was named *Chung-ching* [Central Capital] and the *fu* [prefecture] was named Ta-ting. In the Imperial City [within the capital] there was an Ancestral Temple [of the Imperial Family].... The Ta-t'ung Quarter [was built] for the Sung envoy, the Ch'ao-t'ien Hostel for the Silla envoy and the Lai-pin Hostel for the Hsia envoy. [It] governed ten *chou* [sub-prefectures] and nine *hsien* [districts].[20]

This shows that the establishment of the Central Capital, the second metropolitan city in historical Mongolia, came much later than the construction of the Supreme Capital and was a symbol of increased Kitan power and prosperity. This city was also filled with Chinese and its construction was no different from that of the first one.

The Eastern Capital

Tung-ching, the Eastern Capital, Liao-yang *fu* of ancient times, was actually a Chinese power base in present-day Manchuria that confronted the Korean states of Chosen and later Koguryo. From the early 700s to the early 900s, present-day southern Manchuria was occupied by Parhae (Po-hai in Chinese), a kingdom established under a ruling household of Tungusic-Korean origin. In 919, the Kitan Khan Yeh-lü A-pao-chi subdued this kingdom, and in 926 absorbed it into his own empire, renaming it Tung-tan (Eastern Kitan). He made his eldest son Yeh-lü T'u-yü the ruler and Liao-yang the capital of this newly occupied territory. The "Monograph on Geography" in the *Liao shih* records the establishment of the Eastern Capital as follows.

> In the forth year of Shen-ts'e [914], [Emperor T'ai-tsu] ordered the restoration of the old Liao-yang city, moving both Parhae and Chinese families here to settle. Also a *fang-wei chou* [sub-prefecture for defence] was established there. . . . In the third year of T'ien-hsien [928], [the Court again] moved the people of Tung-tan to settle in and promote [the status of this city] . . . to a capital. . . . The Imperial City [within it] was located in the northeast corner. . . . The outer city was called the Chinese city. . . . A morning bazaar gathered in the south marketplace and the evening one in the north marketplace. . . . On the west of the [main] street were the [monasteries] Chin-te *ssu*, Fu-ma *ssu*, and Chao tou-to *ssu*. . . . In Kuei-hua *ying* [the acculturation camp] were stationed more than one thousand men, and most of the exiles from north of the Yellow River gathered here. . . . In the thirteenth year of T'ien-hsien [938] the name . . . was changed to Tung-ching [Eastern Capital]. It governed eighty-nine prefectures, sub-prefectures, military administrative districts and cities, and nine districts.[21]

This excerpt demonstrates that the Kitan city known as the Eastern Capital was a political center and military stronghold which enabled the Kitans to rule over the territory they annexed from Parhae. However, its inhabitants were mainly Parhaes and Chinese. The reason for calling the city a capital was probably to emphasize the integral nature of the territory it ruled as an indivisible part of the kingdom. Of course in continued to play its traditional role as a strategic point in relationship to Korea in the east.

The Southern Capital

Nan-ching, the Southern Capital, also known as Hsi-chin *fu* or Yu *chou*, was anciently the site of the capital of the old State of Yen in the Warring States period (403–221 B.C.) and presently is Peking, capital of the People's Republic of China. The *Liao shih* records the situation of this city during the time of the Kitans.

Because the [Kitan-] Liao had contributed great help, [the Emperor] Kao-tsu [Shih Ching-t'ang, r. 936–42] of Chin presented sixteen *chou* [sub-prefectures] including Yu *chou* to [Liao]. [Emperor] T'ai-tsung [Yeh-lü Te-kuang, r. 927–47] promoted Yu Chou as Nan-ching [the South Capital] and was also named Yen-ching [the Capital of Yen]. . . . The Imperial City was located in the southwest corner. . . . The buildings, shops, markets, offices, hostels, and Buddhist and Taoist monasteries were numerous and impossible to describe. . . . This city governed six sub-prefectures and eleven districts.[22]

The Western Capital

This city was developed on the site of the earlier capital of the T'o-pa Wei (386–557), the first dynasty of conquest in Chinese history. Known as Ta-t'ung or Yün *chou* before the Kitans' takeover, it has been the most important city of Northern Shansi Province from ancient times until today. Regarding this urban center the *Liao shih* records:

> [Emperor] Kao-tsu of Chin took over the throne of the [Later] T'ang. Because of the Kitans' assistance [he] conceded to them the land on the south of the mountain and the north of Tai [present-day Tai *hsien*, Shansi Province].

Consequently, Ta-t'ung came under [Kitan] domination and was made Hsi-ching [Western Capital]. . . . After a capital was established there, it became an important district and only a first ranking prince was qualified to be its governor. In the eighth year of Ch'ing-ning [1062] the Hua-yen *ssu* [monastery] was built there to accommodate stone and bronze images of the [Kitan] Emperors. . . . It governed two sub-prefectures and seven districts.[23]

According to the above passage both the Southern Capital and the Western Capital (also known as Ta-t'ung *fu*) were obtained from the Chinese as the price of Kitan military support. These two cities were focal points of Kitan territory south of the Great Wall. Both cities were political and military centers of occupied Chinese land and strongholds in the Kitans' confrontation against Sung and Hsia. These major economic centers for supplying the needs of the Kitan homeland north of the Great Wall were chosen as capitals for the same reason Liao-yang City was promoted as the Eastern Capital. Again the three capitals outside the Kitan homeland were all centers of national defense.

The Fief-like Settlements of the Nobles

Approximately one century before Christ the great Chinese historian, Ssu-ma Ch'ien, stated that the nomadic Hsiung-nu warriors "in their campaigns . . . distributed their booty and made slaves of their prisoners."[24] Later, in the beginning of the T'ang Dynasty (618), the Chinese Emperor requested that the Turkic Khan assist him in his struggle for the throne under the following conditions. The *Hsin T'ang shu* states:

[The Emperor of T'ang] is willing to pacify the Capital city with the Turks and allow the gold, fabric, boys and girls all to go to [you] the Khan. [The Khan] was greatly pleased and immediately dispatched two thousand cavalry.[25]

These passages reveal that the nomads demanded Chinese manpower to support their economic development. The captives, whose fate was the same as that of other booties, were distributed among the heads of the clans or tribes as their underlings or slaves. Because of long contact with the agrarian people the Kitans were able to manipulate cleverly the manpower and talent of the Chinese and Parhaes. While maintaining their own traditional nomadic lifestyle on the steppes, the Kitan nobles built walled cities for their agrarian captives. These supplemental economic centers were located north of the Great Wall or elsewhere in the Kitans' own domain in Mongolia. Here the captives worked to supply some of the Kitans' agricultural needs as well as to maintain their own needs. By concentrating their captives in these cities under supervision, the Kitans were also able to prevent rebellion and escape. Chinese lived in the urban centers, while the Kitans inhabited the surrounding countryside.

In the Kitan-Liao period these cities were called *tou-hsia ch'eng* (投下城), meaning the cities or settlements in the fiefs under the nobles. The *Liao shih* states:

All subordinate sub-prefectures and military administrative districts were established by the princes, imperial relatives, ministers, and the chiefs of tribes for settling their captives or war prisoners. Princes, imperial relatives, and princesses were allowed to build cities but others [dignitaries] were forbidden to do so. The court named these regions and prefectures and appointed the governor-generals, but allowed the nobles to appoint magistrates for them from among their own underlings. . . . Taxes from the stores and markets were collected for the [nobles] who were entitled to them [as the lords of the cities].[26]

Most "Chinese cities" *(Han ch'eng 漢城)* and the cities of the Parhaes belonged to this category of *tou-hsia ch'eng*. Following are a few selected examples from the long record of the *Liao shih*.

1. Lin-huang *hsien* [district]. In the beginning of T'ien-tsan [922], [Emperor] T'ai-tsu [Yeh-lü A-pao-chi] campaigned southward into [the] areas of Yen and Chi [present-day north and northeast Hopei Province]. He dispersed and settled the captured people and families north of the Huang River [Shira-mören], an area good for agricultural purposes. This district was named Lin-huang [the vicinity of the Huang River]. The families living here numbered three thousand five hundred.[27]

2. Pao-ho *hsien*. The population of this city had originally inhabited Fu-li *hsien* of Parhae. After [Emperor] T'ai-tsu took over Lung *chou*, he moved the people of Fu-li and settled them on the south of the Supreme Capital. In the eighth year of T'ung-ho [990], because this population belonged to the Imperial household, a [district] was established and put under the rule of Chang-min Palace. The families here numbered four thousand.[28]

3. Yüeh-wang *ch'eng* [City of Prince Yüeh]. The uncle of T'ai-tsu, Shu-lu, the Prince of *yü-yüeh* [于越 Lord Chancellor], campaigned westward against the Tang-hsiang and T'u-yü-hun [peoples], capturing and settling them in this location for the purpose of grazing cattle. This city was built twenty *li* [about seven miles] on the southeast of [Tsu-] *chou*. The families numbered one thousand.[29]

4. Hui *chou*. [This city was established] by the Eldest Princess of the [States of] Ch'in [and] Chin, the daughter of [Emperor] Ching-tsung [Yeh-lü Hsien, r. 968–82], to settle ten thousand underlings assigned to accompany her in her marriage.[30]

5. Yüan *chou*. Chin-te, an Imperial maternal uncle, built this city [to settle Chinese people he had captured]. The families numbered five hundred.[31]

6. Feng *chou*. Yeh-lü A-mo-li joined conquering expeditions, gathered captives and established a city. [He] petitioned [the Court] to recognize it as Feng *chou*. [The Emperor Sheng-tsung] appointed Yen Kuei, a house slave of [Yeh-lü A-mo-li], to be its magistrate.[32]

Centers of Trading and Handicraft Production

In addition to these occupied cities south of the Great Wall and the five capitals mentioned, several newly established cities inside the Kitan domain served as centers for trading and handicraft production.
The *Liao shih* records:

1. I-k'un *chou*. Empress Ying-t'ien[33] . . . provided great assistance in [Emperor] T'ai-tsu's expansion of the realm and the pacification of Parhae. The captured talented artisans mainly came into her possession. . . . There [this] subprefecture was established.[34]

2. Ch'ang-lo *hsien*. [Emperor] T'ai-tsu invaded Parhae state, moved the people, and established this district in which to settle them. The families numbered four thousand, one thousand of which presented iron [to the Court] in tribute.[35]

3. Tsu *chou*. [Emperor] T'ai-tsu captured the people of Wei *chou* [present Wei *hsien*, west Hopei Province] and established a fortress in which to settle them. His purpose was to have then mine and refine the silver of Hsien River.[36]

4. Hung-ching *hsien* [Emperor] Shih-tsung [Yeh-lü Juan, r. 947–51] established [this district] as a place to settle the captive families from Ting *chou* [present Ting *hsien*, central Hopei Province]. These people were talented, professional textile workers.[37]

These four cities are examples of production centers. They were also border towns for the purpose of trade and commerce. The "Monograph on Economy" of the above book records:

[Emperor] T'ai-tsu established Yang-ch'eng on the north of Tan-shan to promote trade through various routes. [Emperor] T'ai-tsung took Yen and established it as the Southern Capital. . . . Markets and appropriate offices were established. The same thing occurred in the other four capitals and the [cities of] the sub-prefectures and districts. . . . In Southern Hsiung *chou* [present-day Hsiung *hsien*, Hopei Province], Kao-ch'ang [Uighur territory in present-day western Kansu Province], and Parhae markets were established for exchanging the commodities of the Sung in the south, the tribes in the northwest, and Korea [in the east].[38]

According to the institutions of the Kitan-Liao and later the Jurchen-Chin, these exchange centers were known in Chinese as *chiao-ch'ang* (榷場).

Military and Defence Centers

Outside their original domain the Kitans possessed three main military centers — the Eastern Capital, the Southern Capital, and the Western Capital. Inside their own homeland their military centers were the Supreme Capital and the Central Capital. A few frontier cities in remote areas also served the purpose of border defense. The *Liao shih* states:

Frontier defence cities in the northwest border of the Kingdom of Liao were established for the purpose of stationing troops in them.[39]

Troops were stationed along the eastern border for defense against Korea and the Jurchen. . . . There were one prefecture, two sub-prefectures, two cities, seventy castles, and eight camps.[40]

The *Liao shih* also lists nine frontier defence cities:

1. Ching *chou*.

2. Chen *chou*. This city was built in the twenty-second year of T'ung-ho [1004] on the site of the old K'o-tun *ch'eng* [Khatun City]. . . . Twenty thousand cavalry men selected from all the tribes were stationed here for a defense against countries such as Shih-wei (室韋), Yü-chüeh (羽厥), and so forth. . . . Also more than seven hundred exiled Parhae, Jurchen, and Chinese

families were sent to settle in the [three] sub-prefectures of Chen, Wei, and Fang. This city was more than three thousand *li* [one thousand miles] from the Supreme Capital in the Southeast.

3. Wei *chou*.

4. Fang *chou*.

5. Ho-tung *ch'eng*. The name of this city is a transliteration of the original name Khatun city.[41] ... The Liao people rebuilt it and made it a fortress to prevent border incursions. The Jurchens of the Kao *chou* usually robbed and disturbed travelers in this area, and therefore they were moved and resettled here. The city was one thousand seven hundred *li* [about six hundred miles] from the Supreme Capital in the southeast.

6. Ching-pien *ch'eng*. Originally this city was the grazing lands of twenty Kitan tribes. Because the Yü-chüeh on the north usually robbed them, this city was built for defense. It was one thousand five hundred *li* [five hundred miles] from the Supreme Capital in the southeast.

7. P'i-pei-ho [River] *ch'eng*. This city controlled the territory of the northern frontier. Five hundred soldiers were stationed here. . . . It was one thousand five hundred *li* from the Supreme Capital in the south.

8. Chao *chou*. This city was established in the third year of K'ai-tai [1014], by the settling of Jurchen families there.

9. Ta-lai wang *ch'eng* [City of Prince Dalai?]. This city was established in the ninth year of Ta-k'ang [1083] along the Lü-chü [Kerülen] River.[42]

The nine cities mentioned above were mainly established as a defense for the Kitan northern border against other proto-Mongolian nomadic tribes. The major forces stationed there were Kitan warriors, and the Parhaes, Jurchens, and Chinese were used as supplemental manpower.

The location of many of these cities is still difficult to identify. According to the Mongolian historian Kh. Perlee, Kitan cities found and excavated in the present-day Mongolian People's Republic include Emgentiin balgas, Taliin ulaan balgas, Khadaasangiin balgas, Chin-tolgoi, Dersen kerem, Öglöchiin kerem, Baruun kerem, identified as the city of Chen *chou*, and Züün kerem as the city of P'i-pei River.[43] According to the Chinese (PRC) historian, Ch'en Shu, the cities of Chen *chou*, Wei *chou*, Fang *chou*, Ho-tung *ch'eng*, and Chao *chou* were located in the vicinity of present-day Ulan-bator. Ching-pien *ch'eng* is identified as Bars *khot*, and Tal-lai wang *ch'eng* was located in the vicinity of Jalai-nor in Hulun-buir, eastern Inner Mongolia.[44]

Postscript: Cities in Mongolia after the Fall of the Kitans

For two centuries the cities discussed were power centers of the Kitans. However, after the Jurchens rose to power, and after 1115, the cities immediately became targets and were turned into Jurchen power bases for suppressing the Kitans. Unfortunately, this tragedy proved that the foresight of Tonyukhukh approximately three and one-half centuries earlier was truly perceptive.

Eventually the Kitan city dwellers and the Jurchens were assimilated by the Chinese and lost their identity. But the majority of the Kitans on the steppe maintained their nomadic traditions and continued their struggle against Jurchen rule. Two centuries later, however, they amalgamated with the nomadic Mongols.

The final revolt by the Kitans against the Jurchens took place in the 1160s. Kitan forces devastated almost the entire Jurchen territory north of the Great Wall, but failed to occupy the cities, many of which originally had been established by their own ancestors. They attacked Lin-huang (the old Supreme Capital of Kitan-Liao), Hui-ning (the old Jurchen capital, located in the vicinity of present Harbin), Tung-ching (Liao-yang, the old Kitan Eastern Capital), Pei-ching (the old Kitan Central Capital), Ning-ch'ang, Hsien-ping, Han *chou,* Chi *chou,* Hsin *chou,* Shang *chou,* Yi *chou,* T'ai *chou,* Ch'üan *chou,* and Li *chou.* Among these cities the Kitans managed to take over only Han *chou* and Hsien-ping, but did not occupy them for any considerable length of time. Because of their failure to occupy the cities, which were the power base of the Jurchens, the Kitans' attempt to restore their kingdom ended in vain.[45]

Later, in the early 1200s, with the emergence of Mongolian power many Kitan leaders joined the Mongol forces to attacked and occupied the Jurchen cities. These events suggest that unless a nomadic people gained significant military power or joined with a greater power, they had very little chance of taking over and occupying city centers. This was, of course, not only the experience of the Kitans but also of the Mongols when they were not able to reoccupy Chinese cities after the collapse of their Yüan Dynasty.

The building, settling, and holding of cities was basically contradictory to the life of the nomadic peoples, but it was an important historical phenomenon in Sino-nomadic relationships in Inner Asia. The development of the cities inevitably brought Chinese influences, which affected the politics, the economy, and even the lifestyle of the Kitans, but made no significant difference in the expansion of Chinese power into nomadic lands. Instead of the customary *ordo* or headquarters, cities became the power centers of the Kitan empire. In addition to the above-mentioned factors, the great difference in the ratio of the agricultural to nomadic population hastened the growth of the cities and the decline of the nomads. All of these factors viewed together suggest that the city building of the Kitans was not a long-term historical gain but rather a loss. Though perhaps a bitter experience for the early Kitans, the experience has set a precedent for Chinese urbanization among the Inner Mongols of the twentieth century.

Notes

1. *Hsing T'ang shu,* 215 B., *chuan* 140 B. "Account of the Turks" 2, 1a.
2. *Shih chi,* 123, *chuan* 63, "Account of Ta-wan," 4a.
3. *Wu-tai shih-chi,* 72, "*Ssu-yi fu-lu*" (Appendix for the Four Barbarians), 3a.
4. Shu-lan (述瀾) also known as Shih-lu (釋魯). See *Liao shih* 64, *piao* 2. "The Table of Imperial Sons," 3a.
5. Some historians identified the Shih-wei people as proto-Mongols.
6. Present-day central Hopei Province.
7. Both the Hsi (奚) and Shi (霫) ethnic groups were similar to the Kitan people. In Chinese they were recorded in different characters, but were pronounced the same. Later these two peoples were absorbed by the Kitans. See the reference in the *Wu-tai shih-chi,* 74, "Appendix for the Four Barbarians," 3, 1a–2a.
8. *Liao shih,* 2, *chi* 2, "Annals of T'ai-tsu," 2, 8b.
9. Ibid., 1, *chi* 1, "Annals of Tai-tsu" 1, 1b–2a.
10. See Yao Ts'ung-wu (姚從吾), "Shuo A-pao-chi shih-tai ti Han-ch'eng" (說阿保机時代的漢城) On the Chinese Cities of A-pao-chi's period), *Tung-pei-shih lun-ts'ung,* Taipei, 1959, 1:193–216. See also Karl A. Wittfogel and Feng

Chai-sheng, *History of Chinese Society Liao,* The American Philosophical Society Edition, Philadelphia, 1949, 142–43.
  11. *Liao shih,* 37, *chih* 7. "Monograph on Geography," 1, 2a.
  12. Ibid., 2a–5a.
  13. *Wu-tai shih-chi,* 72, "Appendix for the Four Barbarians," 5a.
  14. *Liao shih,* 37, *chih* 7, "Monograph on Geography," 1, 5ab.
  15. Ibid., 72, *chuan* 4, "Biography of K'ang Mo-chi (康默紀)," 1a.
  16. On Liu Shou-k'uang (劉守光) see his biography in *Chiu Wu-tai shih,* 135.
  17. Also known by her title as Empress Ying-tien (應天太后); see her biography in *Liao shih* 71, *chuan* 1, "Biographies of the Empresses," 2a–3b.
  18. Ibid., 74, *chuan* 4, "Biography of Han Yen-hui (韓延徽)," 2ab.
  19. Originally this location was in the Kharachin Central Banner. After the Communist takeover this banner was unified with the Kharachin Right Flank Banner and was renamed the Kharachin Banner, Juu-uda League, Inner Mongolia.
  20. *Liao shih,* 39, *chih* 9, "Monograph on Geography," 3, 1ab.
  21. Ibid., 38, *chih* 8, "Monograph on Geography," 2, 1a–3a.
  22. Ibid., 40, *chih* 10, "Monograph on Geography," 4, 1a–2a. For a more detailed record see Yeh Lung-li (葉隆禮), "*Chi-tan Kuo-chih*" (契丹國志 The Gazetteer of the Kingdom of Kitan), *chüan* 22.
  23. Ibid., 41, *chih* 11, "Monograph on Geography," 5, 2a.
  24. *Shih chi,* 110, *Chuan* 50, "Account of Hsiung-nu," 11a.
  25. *Hsin T'ang-shu,* 88, *chuan* 13, "Biography of Liu Wen-ching (劉文靜)," 2a.
  26. *Liao shih,* 37, *chih* 7, "Monograph on Geography," 1, 11b–12a.
  27. Ibid., 3a.
  28. Ibid., 3a.
  29. Ibid., 6b.
  30. Ibid., 12a. The Chinese term is *yün-ch'en* (媵臣), similar in meaning to the Mongolian term *injes.*
  31. Ibid., 12b.
  32. Ibid., 79, *chuan* 9, "Biography of Yeh-lü A-mo-li," 4ab.
  33. Also known by her family name as Empress Shu-lü; see note 17.
  34. Ibid., *chih* 7, "Monograph on Geography," 1, 10a.
  35. Ibid., 11b.
  36. Ibid., 39, *chih* 9, "Monograph on Geography," 3, 3b.
  37. Ibid., 6b.
  38. Ibid., 60, *chih* 29, "Monograph on Economy," 2, 1ab.
  39. Ibid., 37, *chih* 7, "Monograph on Geography," 1, 13b.
  40. Ibid., 36, *chih* 6, "Monograph on Military Affairs and Garrison System," 2, 13a–14a.
  41. According to the study of recent years there were more than two Khatun cities.
  42. Ibid., 37, *chih* 37, "Monograph on Geography," 1, 13b–14b.
  43. Kh. Perlee, *Khyatan nar tednii Mongolchuudtai kholbogdson ni* (Kitans' Involvement with the Mongols), Ulan-bator, 1959, 84–93, and *Mongol ard ulsiin ert dundad üeiin hot suurinii tobchoon* (An Outline of the Ancient and Medieval City Ruins in Mongolian People's Republic), Ulan-bator, 1961, 56–68.
  44. Ch'en Shu (陳述), *Chi-tan shê-hui ching-chi shih-kao* (契丹社會經濟史稿 A Manuscript of the History of Kitan's Society and Economy), Peking, 1978, 100–103. See also Wittfogel, 45.

45. See Sechin Jagchid, "Kitan Struggle against Jurchen Oppression, Nomadism versus Sinicization," a paper presented in the First Western U.S. Meeting on Central Asian Studies, Berkeley, 13–14 April 1980 (chapter 3 in this work).

Chapter 3

Kitan Struggles Against Jurchen Oppression — Nomadism versus Sinicization

(Originally published in *Zentralasiatischue Studien*, 1982, 16:165–85, Universität Bonn)

Introduction

Both the Kitans and the Jurchens were peoples of the Altaic language group in the southeastern end of Inner Asia. However, the cultural backgrounds of these two peoples were different. The Kitans were basically a nomadic people who used hunting as a means of supplementing their living. The Jurchens were a half-agricultural, half-hunting people. The interrelationship of these two neighboring peoples was always established on the basis of who conquered whom. In addition to this, both established a dynasty of conquest in the Chinese agricultural lands.

The Kitans' rule over the Jurchen people began in the early part of the tenth century and ended in the early part of the twelfth century. The Kitans required the Jurchens to join the royal hunting expeditions, to pay as tribute falcons and eagles, and to serve in the army. The Kitan rulers treated the Jurchens as a subordinate foreign satellite. Following the original tradition of the Jurchens, the Kitans divided them into several tribes, recognizing their tribal leaders as "great princes" *(ta-wang 大王)* who would rule over their own people. However, the real power over Jurchen lands (present-day Manchuria) was held by the Kitan authorities, *hsiang-wen* (詳穩), who were appointed by the Kitan Khans. The official history of the Kitans, the *Liao shih*, includes many biographies of the Chinese, P'o-hai (Parhae), and Uighur elites, along with eminent Kitans, but no biographies of Jurchen leaders. Apparently, under Kitan domination, the Jurchens were overlooked, and none of them were appointed to important positions in state affairs.

The Jurchens' revolt against the Kitan was essentially an external event or aggression from the outside, which eventually resulted in the downfall of the ruling Kitans. The specific reason for the Jurchen rebellion was the excessive Kitan demand for the famous greyfalcons. Clearly, the demands of a nomadic power were quite different from those of an agricultural kingdom.

The political experiences of the Kitan elite greatly aided the Jurchens in founding their new state. Therefore, the official history of the Jurchens, the *Chin shih*, contains many biographies of the elites of the Kitan and the Hsi, a related people of the same origins as the Kitans. This suggests that the Kitans aided in the founding of the Jurchen Chin empire, the third dynasty of conquest in Chinese history. The Jurchens viewed the Kitans as their internal subjects or citizens, which was different from the way the Kitans had treated the Jurchens. Consequently, the Kitan rebellion was an internal revolt of an oppressed people against alien rulers of a different race. However, many Kitan subjects loyally supported their Jurchen rulers, making important contributions because of their political experience. This important historical fact cannot be neglected.

Both rebellion and loyalty suggest that an ideological split among the Kitan people existed which originated because of differing attitudes towards adoption or rejection of

Chinese culture. During the period of Kitan domination of Chinese land, a group of Kitan elites had already been Sinicized. The Jurchens also occupied North China, and, following in the footsteps of the early Kitan elites, accepted Chinese culture as their own. Therefore, the Sinicized Kitans did not think of the Jurchens as cultural aliens. However, the Kitans who remained in their homeland, "the territory of pines and deserts" (*sung-mo* 松漠), continued their traditional nomadic way of life. These Kitans considered the Chinese aliens. They found it more difficult to reach a common understanding with their gradually Sinicizing and foreign Jurchen rulers. This was the basic reason for the different attitudes among the Kitan people towards their Jurchen overlords. By the end of the Jurchen Chin Dynasty, these differing attitudes had become even more pronounced. The following are two examples.

In 1215, Chinggis Khan occupied the city of Yen (Peking), summoned the Kitan scholar, Yeh-lü Ch'u-ts'ai, and said, "Liao and Chin were enemies of long generations, and now I have gained revenge for you." In his reply Yeh-lü Ch'u-ts'ai said, "My grandfather and my father served in the Chin Court. Since we were their vassals, how can I seek revenge against my lords?" The Mongol Khan was moved and pleased by his words.[1]

Shih-mo Ye-hsien was a descendant of the Kitan Liao. His grandfather swore not to serve in the Chin court, took his tribe, and migrated afar. His father, who also refused to serve the Chin, had five sons and Yeh-hsien (Esen) was the second. At the age of ten, hearing the story of the destruction of his country from his father, he became angry and said, "I, your son, will take revenge!" Later he was known as a powerful and capable person and the Chin court appointed him the headman of the His tribe. He transferred this post to his elder brother and said, "In order to protect our clan, you take it temporarily." Then he escaped and hid in the deep wilderness of the north. Upon hearing that Chinggis Khan had come to power, he immediately came alone with only one horse.[2]

Another interesting phenomenon was that most Kitans who remained loyal to the Jurchen rulers adopted Chinese personal names. Those who opposed the Jurchens continued to use their traditional Kitan names, except those who had adopted the Chinese word *Hsiao* as their family names.[3] This indicates that those Sinicized Kitans who migrated to China had settled there mainly following the changing of the dynasties recognized the legality of the new Jurchen Chin regime. However, those nomadic Kitans who were not Sinicized and remained in their homeland firmly rejected alien domination from outside. In addition, this also shows that the agricultural world to the south of the Great Wall was the cultural melting pot of Asian history. The Kitans, the Jurchens, and all other people who entered this region were reshaped into one cultural unit, losing their differences and prejudices against one another. In the steppe land of Inner Asia to the north of the Great Wall, separatism was a part of the nomadic way of life. Therefore, it was easy for tribalism or racism to grow. Likewise, it was difficult for prejudice and mutual rejection to die.

The Jurchens' Attitude and Policy toward the Kitans

Whether the Kitans showed good will or hatred toward the Jurchens partially depended on the attitude and policy of the Jurchen rulers. The following tactics played a prominent role in Jurchen policy from the beginning to the end.

Massacre as a method of intimidation

The Jurchens frequently massacred the Kitan inhabitants in an area where a rebellion occurred. In the autumn of 1132, the Jurchens executed Kao-li, a commander of the Kitan troops, and his entire household. Then the Office of the Marshal *(Yüan-shuai fu* 元帥府 *)* ordered the generals to search for the Kitan rebels of Yeh-lü Yü-tu's party and to execute the Kitans residing in all the circuits *(tao* 道 *)*. As a result, riots broke out which continued for more than a month. Many Kitan chieftains and other leaders escaped with their followers to the Kingdom of Hsia (Tangut) or to the north of the desert (Mongolia). After the riots were subdued, all the Kitans who had not escaped and who had surrendered to the Chin were "turned into ashes."[4]

In 1183, Yeh-lü Wo-han, a head of the grazing organization *(ch'ün-mu* 群牧*)*, gathered together one hundred thousand troops. Calling himself the Emperor of Later Liao, he formed an alliance with the Mongolian tribes in the north. The Jurchen Lord ordered the Marshal Ho-shih-lieh Sa-ho-nien to attack the rebels. The Marshal captured Yeh-lü Wo-han and brought back fifty carts of ears and noses of the enemy.[5]

This high-handed policy was apparently quite effective for the moment in putting down the Kitans' revolt. However, in the long run it caused the Kitans to hate the Jurchens even more, and helped to maintain a strong Kitan desire for rebellion.

The use of aliens to attack aliens

Using Kitans and foreigners to attack other foreigners was a common Jurchen strategy. In 1311, Prince Nien-han gave ten thousand Jurchen and Chinese troops to Yeh-lü Yü-tu (a Kitan general who had surrendered) and had him go north to attack the Kitan Prince Yeh-lü Ta-shih[6] at the city of Ho-tung on the north of the Desert. After the troops left, the family of Yeh-lü Yü-tu was taken hostage in a Jurchen city.[7]

Yü-wen Mao-chao, the contemporary author of *Ta-Chin-kuo chih,* criticized the Jurchen policy and said, "The strategy of the Great Chin is always to use talk of peace to complement their attack and to use traitors to trap the rebels."[8] He also pointed out that this type of deceitful policy eventually caused Yeh-lü Yü-tu to become greatly disappointed and to rebel.

The use of Kitan military resources for further expansion

"The Monograph of Military Affairs" of the *Chin shih* contains many entries which mention the use of Kitan forces. According to Yü-wen Mao-chao, in the year 1160, when the Jurchen Emperor Hai-ling (Wan-yen Ti-ku-nai, r. 1148–61) mobilized his forces to carry out an expedition against the Southern Sung, he ordered the conscription of all the able bodied men from the Jurchen, Kitan, and Hsi peoples.[9] This record shows the importance of the Kitan forces in Jurchen military actions. However, this forced conscription shook Kitan society and finally caused mass rebellions.

Conciliation for pacification

The real strength of the Kitan people caused the Jurchen rulers to show conciliatory "goodheartedness" toward their Kitan subjects. However, the Jurchens could not negate the fact that they practiced a policy of "whip and carrots."

In 1116, the Jurchen Emperor declared, "Since the destruction of Liao forces, there are multitudes of people coming to surrender from the four directions; therefore, special relief should be provided for them. From now on, the Kitan, Hsi, Chinese, Parhae officials and people, and the Jurchens under the Liao administration who have surrendered, been captured, or returned from exile should not be treated as criminals. Their chieftains should be reappointed as officials and [we should] allow them to live according to their ways."[10]

In the spring of 1125, relief supplies were distributed to the newly surrendered Kitan people, and in the autumn the captured Kitan Khan was given the title of *Hai-pin Wang*

(海濱王 the prince of the seashore).[11] Later in the spring of 1141 he was again promoted to the rank of the Prince of Yü (豫王).[12]

These examples show a magnanimous attitude on the part of the Jurchen rulers toward their Kitan subjects. They hoped thereby to gain the Kitans' appreciation and to secure Kitan aid in the founding of a new Jurchen empire. This policy was effective among the Sinicized Kitans. However, the cruel nature of the Jurchen ruling class caused this policy to come to a halt before it had become completely effective among other Kitans. For instance, in 1161 the Jurchens executed all the royal descendants of the imperial households of the Kitan Liao and Chinese Sung (who had been captured earlier in 1126). Such incidents made it difficult for the magnanimous acts to change the antagonistic attitudes of the non-Sinicized Kitans towards their alien conquerors.

Fragmentation for assimilation

Because Jurchen power was based upon the destruction of the Kitan nation, the Jurchen rulers had to be cautious in dealing with the remaining power of their former mortal enemy. Therefore, after the establishment of the Chin dynasty, an important task of the Jurchen rulers was dispersing the Kitan people and assimilating them into the Jurchen and Chinese societies. The court ordered that the Jurchen military-civilian units of *meng-an* (one thousand soldiers) and *mou-k'e* (one hundred soldiers) stationed in Chinese land be allowed to intermarry with the Kitans and Chinese.[13]

After the suppression of the 1162 rebellion of Yeh-lü Wo-wo (耶律窩斡), the Kitans were absorbed into the Jurchen *meng-an* and *mou-k'e*. In the fall of 1163, the Emperor ordered the dismissal of the Kitan *meng-an* and *mou-k'e*.[14] Later in 1177, because the Kitans remaining in areas of the southwestern and northwestern military zones (*chao-t'ao ssu* 招討司), were still antagonistic and untrustworthy in times of crisis, they were ordered to move into the Jurchen lands of Wu-ku-li-shih-lei Tribe and Shang-ching.[15]

This policy of fragmentation and assimilation did not work well among the nomadic Kitans. Also, the Jurchen rulers, recognizing the importance of horses for military use, reluctantly organized the nomadic Kitans into many pastures (*ch'ün-mu*) to maintain their traditional way of life in their old homeland.[16] Usually the rebellions broke out among these nomadic Kitans.

The Revolts and Rebellions

The Kitan revolts and rebellions apparently continued unceasingly from the beginning to the end of the Jurchen Chin dynasty. However, the main revolts occurred in three distinct periods: 1) at the beginning of Jurchen rule when its power was not yet fully established; 2) at the time of an internal power struggle; and 3) at the time when Mongolian power became a decisive threat. Thus, the revolts of the Kitan people were interlaced with the rise, the existence, and the fall of the Jurchen rule. The Kitans' military strength and political experience, as it was infused into the Jurchen empire, increased the strength of the latter. At the same time, this Kitan element was a subversive factor, and one of the principal elements which shook the foundation of Jurchen power. Consequently, each time a Kitan rebellion broke out, it caused considerable damage to the real strength of the Jurchens.

The uprisings of Yeh-lü Yü-tu

The courageous fighting spirit of the Jurchen people was the principal external reason for the destruction of the Kitan Liao empire. However, inability, mistrust, and misgivings of the last Khan, Yeh-lü Yen-hsi (r. 1101–25), and internal conflicts among the Kitan leaders were also important factors contributing to the end of Kitan rule. Given this situation, the Jurchens eliminated the Kitan leaders one by one. Some Kitan leaders were forced to defect to the enemy side. The story of Yeh-lü Yü-tü is one example. However, he was never trusted by his new lord.

In 1125, the Jurchens invaded the Chinese Sung. Yeh-lü Yü-tü was appointed the Marshal Supervisor of the Right Flank. Forty thousand Sung troops came to save Tai-yüan (present Sansi province). Yeh-lü Yü-tü defeated them on the north of the Fen River. So, Yeh-lü Yü-tü was appointed the Governor of Hsi-ching, the West Capital (present-day Ta-t'ung). But in 1132, Yeh-lü Yü-tü planned a revolt and was exposed by several Kitan leaders. Yeh-lü Yü-tü escaped, but his companion, Hsiao Kao-liu, the Military Commander of Yen-ching (Peking), was executed, and the Governor-General of Wei-chou (present-day Wei-hsien, Hopei Province) committed suicide. Soon Yeh-lü Yü-tü and his sons were killed and their heads were presented to the Chin court.[17]

According to the "Biography of Yeh-lü Yü-tü" in the *Chin shih,* from the beginning of his career to its end he was neither loyal to his Jurchen overlords nor was he trusted by them. When he first surrendered, the people who followed him were also forced to surrender. Consequently, they watched for a chance to escape from the Jurchens. The exposure of Yeh-lü Yü-tü shows the conflict and lack of harmony among the Kitans and the difficult situation of these surrendered Kitan leaders. Nevertheless, in war against the Chinese Sung, they fought courageously and faithfully. This suggests that cultural and racial considerations were still major determining influences in their attitude towards an alien people. It also indicated the importance of Kitan military strength in the expansion of the Jurchen Chin empire. Finally, the unsuccessful plan to rebel indicates the true feeling of Kitan military leaders towards the new Jurchen rule.

The mass rebellion headed by K'ua-li and Sa-pa

The dark period of the Jurchen Chin dynasty under the rule of its tyrant, Emperor Hai-ling, 1148–61, was also the zenith of Jurchen power. The Emperor tried to bring together the military forces of the entire country to invade the Chinese Sung and to unify the "universe" under his own rule. The utilization of Kitan military strength was an important part of his ambitious plan. However, the heavy conscription of Kitan soldiers eventually led the Kitan people to rebel. The records that are found in the *Chin shih* describe these events.

The Emperor Hai-ling carried out his southern campaign against the Sung and the whole country was disturbed. By that time all the able bodied men of the Kitan tribes were conscripted to serve in the army. The tribal people did not want to go and petitioned the envoy. Fearing the Emperor, the envoy did not dare to report this to the court. Consequently, the tribal people rebelled.[18]

In 1161, the southern expedition took place. The Kitans along the northern border area, fearing that their families, wives, and children might be looted by neighboring alien enemies, refused to conscript all males into the army. Therefore they rebelled.[19]

Hsio Huai-chung, a Hsi, was the Military Commander of the Northwest Circuit. Hsiao yü, the Vice-Prime Minister, and a group of Kitans plotted to reestablish their own empire using descendants of the Kitan Liao Emperor. They sent an envoy to contact Hsiao Huai-chung and Yeh-lü Lang, the Governor-General of the same circuit, for help. Hsiao Huai-chung reported the plot to the court. Hsiao Yü and his group were all executed. Then Hsiao Huai-chung was promoted to the post of Vice-Director of Military Affairs *(shu-mi fu-shih* 樞密副使*),* and was also given the rank of prince. When Sa-pa rebelled, Hsiao Huai-chung, Pu-san Ssu-kung, the General-Director of Military

Affairs, and other generals were ordered to attack the rebels. However, the war ended without success. The troops pursued Sa-pa but could not overtake him. Emperor Hai-ling assumed that since both Hsiao Huai-chung and Hsiao Yü were Kitans, they had plotted together. So when Sa-pa rebelled, fearing that all Kitans might join together, he sent an envoy to the army and executed Hsiao Huai-chung and his entire household.[20] The Emperor also put to death all the male members of the descendants of the Yeh-lü family of the imperial household of the Kitan Liao and the Chao family of the captured Chinese Sung. In all, more than 130 persons died.[21]

These events show that the Kitan revolt was sparked by the attempt to conscript so many Kitan men to fight against the Chinese Sung. The Jurchen Emperor Hai-ling first ordered the Kitan and Hsi generals to attack their rebellious countrymen in order to fragment the Kitan unity. But soon he executed all the generals because of his suspicions and their failures. This also shows that the rebellious Kitan forces were not as easy to put down as the Emperor had originally planned. The plot to restore the Kitan imperial family and their state infuriated the Jurchen tyrant. The resultant executions of the Yeh-lü family and the innocent Chinese Chao family increased the hatred of the Kitan people.

The exact date of the beginning of this revolt was not clearly recorded. One source says that in 1159, at the time of the great conscription of Tai-chou,[22] Ting-yuan-a-pu and his followers rebelled and fled. Wen-ti-han I-shih-man with the forces of seven commanders of a hundred men captured Tin-yüan-a-pu, stopped his followers, and brought them back to the army. Soon the Kitans rebelled again, and defeated the six *meng-an* troops of Hui-ning[23] at Ti-mu mountain. The rebels then occupied the territories of Hsin-chou[24] and Han-chou.[25]

Another source reported that in 1161, the invasion against the Sung occurred. All troops and the commanders of hundreds and of thousands were moved to the battlefront, and therefore none of the districts had defence forces. K'ua-li, a Kitan, occupied Han-chou and besieged Hsin-chou. All districts both near and far were frightened. Later, K'ua-li lifted the sieges and marched toward the East Capital (Tung-ching).[26]

At present, no available material identifies Ting-yüan-a-pu as either a Kitan or a Jurchen. But the fact that the Kitan rebellion headed by K'ua-li was inflamed by the Ting-yüan-a-pu incident indicates that he may have been a Kitan. Little is recorded about the life or activities of either K'ua-li or Sa-pa.

The *Chin shih* does tell us that Sa-pa originally was an interpreter for a frontier military director's office *(chao-t'ao-ssu)*. Taking advantage of Kitan opposition to conscription, he invited the Kitans to kill the Jurchen military director *(chao-tao shih* 招討使) to steal the armor of three thousand men, and to rebel. The rebel leaders tried to restore to power a descendant of the last Kitan Khan. The four Kitan pastures in front of the mountain (Hsing-an Range?) and all the pastures in back of the mountain immediately responded. The eight officers of the *mou-k'e* (hundreds) who were pasturing on the north of the mountain killed their officers, took their horses, and joined Sa-pa. The Jurchen Junior Governor *(shao-yin* 少尹*)* of Hsien-ping[27] wanted to capture the family members of K'ua-li. But K'oa-li and his party tempted the slaves of rich families to rebel. Within a few days they gathered together more than two thousand slaves. They took over Han-chou and the country of Liu-ho,[28] and then they moved towards Hsien-ping. The Junior Governor confronted them but was defeated, and the city of Hsien-ping fell into the hands of the Kitans. The Kitans plundered the treasury and used the money to recruit troops. K'oa-li attacked Chi-*chou*,[29] but here he was defeated. Collecting the remnants of his forces he then moved towards the East Capital, Tung-ching but failed to seize it. By that time Prince Wan-yen Wu-lu[30] was the Governor of the East Capital. He resisted the enemy with only four hundred soldiers. K'ua-li retreated and then united with Sa-pa.

Seeing the tense situation Emperor Hai-ling dispatched the General-Director of Military Affairs, Pu-san Ssu-kung, with other Kitan generals commanding ten thousand troops to attack the rebels. The battle took place in the vicinity of Lin-huang, the old capital of the Kitan Liao dynasty. There was no victory for either side. However, Sa-pa, feeling the pressure of the great Jurchen force, decided to escape to Kara Kitai in Central Asia. He began to move his forces west. Pu-san Ssu-king and his troops pursued them, but could not catch them. Because of their lack of success, Pan-san Ssu-kung and other Kitan generals were all put to death by the Jurchen ruler. After this setback Emperor Hai-ling ordered two Jurchen high commanders, Pai Yen-ching and Ho-shih-lieh Chih-ning,[31] to station their troops in the north for defence against the Kitans.

Meanwhile Sa-pa and his Kitans had moved west, but the Kitans who lived north of the Hsing-an mountains refused to follow him. Instead they supported another leader, Yi-la Wo-wo, who killed Sa-pa. Following this internal struggle, Wo-wo moved back to the east again.[32]

The record of these incidents again suggests that the direct cause of the Kitan rebellion was the forced conscription. The rebellion itself was not a well-organized movement but more of a mass revolt. Both K'ua-li and Sa-pa obtained reinforcements for the rebellious groups, but they failed to organize them into a solid body for a Kitan-Liao restoration.

Some shrewd Kitan or Hsi leaders decided to take advantage of this situation. They plotted to restore a member of the old Kitan imperial household as ruler. They probably intended to set him up as a puppet, using his prestige to establish a Kitan regime of their own. This plot could have caused K'ua-li and Sa-pa's rebellion to take on more of a political flavor. However, the Jurchens used this plot as a pretext for executing many Kitan leaders and descendants of earlier Kitan Khans. This caused the Kitan rebellion to lose its political strength so that it was no longer a threat to the Jurchens as an organized, politically motivated revolution.

Another significant event in this rebellion was the liberation of the slaves. This gave some social-revolutionary flavor to the original ethnic rebellion. However, the disorganized nature of those involved was a hindrance to further united action.

The desire of Sa-pa to join the Kara Kitai in the west suggests that the connection between the Kitans in Central Asia and their fellow countrymen in southeastern Inner Mongolia had never been fully severed. Moreover, the tie to Kara Kitai was deeply impressed on the hearts of many Kitan people. Even so, migration of this type could not solve the problem of the Kitans who still remained in their homeland under Jurchen oppression. It was for this reason that the people eventually killed Sa-pa and moved back to the east with a new leader, Yi-la Wo-wo, who would continue to fight the Jurchens in the "land of pine and desert."

Although the rebellion of the Kitan masses could not halt Emperor Hai-ling's invasion against the Sung, it did reduce the strength of the Jurchen southern expeditionary forces to a considerable extent. The execution of many high generals also hurt the morale of the whole army. This not only affected Hai-ling's southern invasion, but it also provided Prince Wan-yen Wu-lu, the Governor of the Eastern Capital, a good chance to usurp power and proclaim himself the Emperor of Chin. The resulting power struggle between Prince Wu-lu and Emperor Hai-ling ended shortly after the assassination of Hai-ling in his headquarters near the Yangtze River in southeastern China. Prince Wu-lu, who later became the Emperor Shih-tsung (r. 1161–89), was also in a difficult situation. When he confronted Kitan K'ua-li, as the Governor of the East Capital, he had only four hundred soldiers. Thus, the Kitans were a considerable threat to the new Jurchen regime. Only when Pai Yen-ching and Ho-shih-lieh Chih-ning, two high commanders of the northern forces of Hai-ling, the former Emperor, came to support the Emperor Shih-tsung did his position become a little more secure.

The new Emperor's first important task was to address the Jurchens' internal problems. He therefore went to Chung-tu (Peking) to look after the national matters. Before the assassination of Hai-ling, the Chinese Sung had won a minor victory at Ts'ai-shih[33] along the Yangtze River. However, they did not have enough strength to counter-attack the Jurchens in this crisis. Even so, a tense situation between the Chinese and the Jurchen still remained. Therefore, Emperor Shih-tsung tried his best to pacify the rebellious Kitans through persuasion, but the Kitans did not respond to his overtures. This indicates that the Kitan people wanted to take advantage of Jurchen difficulties in order to free themselves from alien domination. This may have caused the Emperor Shih-tsung, who was a well-known Confucian Jurchen ruler, to have strong prejudices against the Kitans in his later reign.

The rebellion headed by Yi-la Wo-wo and its aftermath

The internal struggles of the Kitans and their return to the east did not end their rebellion. The "Biography of Yi-la Wo-wo" states that when the Kitans arrived in the area southeast of Lin-huang, the old capital of Kitan-Liao, Emperor Shih-tsung sent a Kitan, Yi-la Cha-pa, to persuade Yi-la Wo-wo to surrender. However, this imperial envoy himself surrendered to Yi-la Wo-wo. Soon the Kitans attacked Lin-huang and killed the Jurchen Governor, but could not take the city. Near the end of 1161 or the beginning of 1162, Yi-la Wo-wo proclaimed himself the Khan. He called his reign in Chinese T'ien-cheng (天正 Heavenly Uprightness).[34]

Yi-la Wo-wo's proclamation shows the growing power of the Kitan rebels. It also indicates the changing character of the revolt from a mass rebellion into a comparatively organized politically motivated revolution. This increased the pressure upon the newly organized Jurchen government.

According to the "Biography of Yi-la Wo-wo," after Pai Yen-ching and Ho-shih-lieh Chih-ning came to support Emperor Shih-tsung, the new Jurchen court was able to send troops to fight against the Kitans. However, the first effort of the Jurchens again ended in failure. In early 1162, the Jurchen court appointed the Vice-Right-Marshal Wan-yen Mo-yen to take command of all the available troops and to go northward to attack Yi-la Wo-wo. In the early spring of that same year, the Emperor decreed that anyone who would leave the Kitan rebels and willingly surrender would be pardoned unconditionally. Both slaves and freemen would be pardoned equally. Those officials who had joined the rebels but who surrendered with their followers would be rewarded with official posts. Anyone who could capture or kill Yi-la Wo-wo would be rewarded with hereditary high rank, an official post, and salary.

This shows that even though the newly-reorganized Jurchen court was able to send troops to attack the Kitans, the attacks were unsuccessful. Therefore, the Jurchen ruler launched a political attack, tempting the rebels to surrender through heavy bribes. The offered liberation of slaves, in particular, was a direct counter-attack against the strategy of the Kitan leaders who created social conflict among their enemies. This political offensive was successful. It gradually brought about the dissolution of the weakly-organized Kitan unification. The high bounty for the capture of Yi-la Wo-wo indicated how much of a threat he was to the Jurchen regime.

The Kitans' military tactics apparently were not different from the traditional military tactics of nomadic people. The Kitans were quick to attack and to retreat, making it difficult for the agricultural, semi-hunting Jurchens to pursue them, especially since the Jurchens were already somewhat Sinicized. However, the Kitans were limited by their lack of effective weapons. They were not able to occupy the more politically-significant cities, such as Lin-huang and Tung-ching. Even so, they devastated a large part of the territory under Jurchen rule. This is especially true of the land north of the Great Wall, i.e., present-day Inner Mongolia and Manchuria which was the original territory of the Kitans and the Jurchens. This territory was covered with the dust of Kitan cavalry. But since the Kitans could not take over the cities, they were not able to occupy the land effectively. They did take temporary possession of several cities, but they were unable to maintain their rule for a longer period.

The Jurchen military leaders were also discontented. Earlier, at the time of Emperor Hai-ling, the Jurchen commanders were executed because of their failures. Even after the Emperor Shih-tsung came to the throne, the situation remained unchanged. Nor did the victories of the new military commander Wan-yen Mo-yen have much effect. Consequently, he was also demoted from the post to commander-in-chief. He was replaced by Pu-san Chung-yi, with Ho-shih-lieh Chih-ning and other generals as staff officers.

This change of personnel did not bring any immediate success. However, the resolution of internal problems made it possible for the Jurchen Emperor, his court, and his generals to concentrate their total energies on the Kitans. At the same time fragmentation had take place in the camp of the Kitans. Thus, the whole situation was gradually reversed.

The official record describes the final events. Jurchen military forces followed Yi-la Wo-wo closely and attacked him at a place named Hua-tao. The Kitans were badly defeated and more than ten thousand persons were killed. As a result, many minor leaders and their people surrendered. Those Kitans were all pardoned and given supplies. Then, even more Kitans came to surrender, and the rest lost their fighting spirit.[35]

But Yi-la Wo-wo did not surrender. He gathered more than ten thousand remaining troops and sought help among the Hsi tribes. From time to time he attacked the regions between Ku-pei-k'ou and Hsing-hua. The Emperor ordered Wan-yen Mo-yen and Wan-yen Ssu-ching to invade the land of Hsi with a heavy force. In the fall the Jurchens defeated the Hsi tribes. Those who refused to surrender were killed and their wives, girls, and children were distributed to the Jurchen soldiers.[36] These records show that the Jurchen rulers simultaneously carried out a harsh policy to threaten the Kitan and Hsi people and a moderate policy to soften and to fragment the rebels.

Yi-la Wo-wo then moved west. He tried to pass through the West Capital (Ta-t'ung) to the Kingdom of Hsia to seek refuge. However, a large force pursued him, and many of his followers deserted in the middle of the journey. Since it was impossible for him to continue west, he turned north and entered the desert.[37] Thus, the defeated Ya-la Wo-wo followed in the footsteps of Sa-pa. However, there is no evidence to suggest that Yi-la Wo-wo also desired to go to Kara Kitai.

Finally, Ya-la Wo-wo's followers betrayed him. He was brought to the camp of the Jurchen commander Wan-yan Ssu-ching along with his mother, his wife, and his children. Wan-yan Ssu-ching presented Yi-la Wo-wo and his party to the court for execution. His head was chopped off at the market place of the capital (Peking). His arms and legs were chopped off and sent to be hung in important cities.[38] Then the Crown Prince and the court officials conveyed their congratulations to the Emperor. They announced the end of Yi-la Wo-wo to the people of the realm and in foreign countries.[39]

In this manner the Jurchen court officially ended the Kitan rebellion inspired by the leadership of K'ua-li, Sa-pa, and Yi-la Wo-wo. The formal celebration in the court and the statement sent to their subjects and to foreign countries show the importance and seriousness of the Kitan rebellion in the history of Jurchen Chin.

Internal disintegration was the main cause of Yi-la Wo-wo's defeat, but this did not keep the hard-minded Kitan leaders from continuing to fight the Jurchens. In the spring of 1163, Cha-pa, K'ua-li and their party escaped to Sung. The Sung generals knew that the Kitans were good fighters. Therefore they used the military knowledge and tactics of the Kitan leaders in their struggle against the Jurchens along the border lands. They occupied several cities, and caused the Jurchens to suffer several setbacks.[40]

The Kitan rebellion led by K'ua-li, Sa-pa, and Yi-la Wo-wo ended tragically after lasting four years (1159–63). It devastated almost all the original territory of the Kitan Liao and the Jurchen Chin which is most of present-day Inner Mongolia and Manchuria. The official historical record of the Jurchen Chin, the *Chin shih*, records this rebellion in two annals of the emperors, and in twenty-three biographies of the elites, indicating the seriousness of the event. The rebellion severely damaged the economy of the Chin state and disrupted the life of the people.[41]

After occupying the throne (1161), the Emperor Shih-tsung found the resolution of the Kitan problem to be one of his most important concerns. Since he himself had experienced the Kitan threat, he tried hard to fragment the Kitans and to assimilate them into his own Jurchen people. After the pacification of Yi-li Wo-wo the Emperor commanded the abolishment of the Kitan *meng-an* and *mou-k'e*. Thus, those Kitans who had surrendered from the camp of Yi-li Wo-wo were to be put under the rule of Jurchen *meng-an* and *mou-k'e*. All their horses were requisitioned. Later the Emperor decided that it was unfair to treat the Kitans who had not joined the rebellion the same as the surrendered rebels. He therefore allowed those Kitans who had not joined the rebellion to remain as they were.[42]

The Jurchen Emperor and his court tried their best to appease and to pacify the Kitans, and endeavored to find a long-lasting solution to the conflict. But the results again were negative and uprisings continued. In the summer of 1164, Pu-su-yüeh, a follower of Yi-la Wo-wo, was captured and executed.[43] In the early spring of 1169, the Kitan Wai-Shih-la rebelled. He was captured and executed.[44] In the winter of 1183 when the Tsu-pu (a Mongolian tribe) rebelled again, Wan-yen Hsiang was stationed at Pei-ching. Just then Te-shou T'o-so, a head of a Kitan grazing organization, rebelled and occupied Hsin-chou. He called his reign *Shen-sheng* (神聖 Saintly-holiness). His troops were rumored to be about one hundred thousand. Both the people nearby and far away were frightened. Wan-yen Hsiang then mobilized the troops of the Shang-ching area and other districts to attack the Kitan rebels. He captured Te-shuo T'o-so and brought him to the Capital. It was at this time the court officials expressed a desire to halt the offering to heaven and to alter the calendar.[45]

These records make clear that thirty years after the death of Yi-la Wo-wo the Kitan rebellion still continued. The Kitan rebels even called their leaders Khan and fought for the establishment of an independent state. In addition, they formed alliances with the Tsu-pu or other Mongolian tribes for reinforcement. This was the precedent for a later Kitan-Mongolian alliance under Chinggis Khan. The fact that a head of a pasture acted as the leader of the rebellion demonstrates that the nomadic Kitans never changed their hostile attitudes toward their Jurchen overlords. The desire of the court officials to halt the offering to heaven and to alter the calendar indicates the seriousness of the Kitan problem and its unfavorable influence.

As has been mentioned, the direct cause of the Kitan rebellions was the conscription of Kitan forces for the invasion of the Chinese Sung. This suggests that the Jurchen overlords badly needed the Kitan military strength to support imperial expansion. Unless the Jurchens were aided by the Kitans, they would not be able to subdue the Chinese or to establish a larger empire. The Jurchens also depended heavily on the support of the Sinicized Kitans in civilian administration. The Kitans were necessary for the support of the Jurchen empire, but at the same time Kitan power created problems. It could also shake the foundations of the kingdom. The loyalty and the experience of the Sinicized Kitan elites gave the Jurchens many advantages, but the antagonistic feeling of the traditional nomadic Kitans toward their Jurchen overlords, became one of the main reasons for instability in the Chin empire.

In the summer of 1201, the Emperor Chang-tsung (Ma-ta-ke, r. 1190–1208) announced that the Kitans who had served in the army and achieved military merit should be rewarded equally with the Jurchens according to the regulation of bestowals. In addition they should be allowed to raise horses and to serve as officials.[46] This might have been a fruitful policy in winning the support of the Kitans. However, it came too late. It happened only five years before Chinggis Khan ascended the throne.

The Kitan rebellion at the time of the rise of the Mongols

Because of their nomadic culture, the Kitans were more similar to the Mongols than to the Jurchens. This is probably one of the main reasons why many Kitan leaders allied themselves with the "northern tribes" to fight against their alien overlords, the Jurchens. The rise of Chinggis Khan (Temüjin, r. 1206–27) and the unification of the Mongols apparently stimulated greatly the Kitans in their traditional antagonism toward the Jurchens. Seeing their own weakness, these rebellious Kitan leaders came to realize the necessity of joining with the Mongols. Consequently, following the expansion of the Mongolian power, the nomadic Kitans fought the Jurchens along with the Mongols. The Sinicized Kitans, following in the footsteps of their ancestors who served the Jurchens, served the Mongols as principal advisors in ruling China.

The Jurchen rulers apparently discovered this approaching danger and had tried to prevent it. However, their efforts again provoked the Kitans and stirred a new rebellion. The leader of this movement was Yeh-lü Liu-ko. According to his biography in the *Yüan shih*, Yeh-lü Liu-ko was head of a thousand men along the northern border under the Jurchen administration. When Chinggis Khan came to power in the north, the Jurchens became suspicious of the Kitans. They ordered each Kitan household to be closely watched by two Jurchen families. Yeh-lü Liu-ko felt insecure. In the year 1212 he escaped to Lung-an (present-day Nung-an Kirin) and Han-chou to gather men to loot the area. The local authorities sent armed forces to oppose him, but they were defeated. He then united with Yeh-ti to organize troops. In several months they gathered more than one hundred thousand men. They supported Yeh-lü Liu-ko as Marshal and Yeh-ti as deputy. The length of their camp area was more than thirty miles, and all the territory of Liao-tung (Southern Manchuria) was shaken.[47]

By this time Chinggis Khan had already begun his expedition against the Jurchens (1211), invading the territory south of the Great Wall. Before this invasion, Kitan leaders such as Shih-mo Yeh-hsien, Yi-la Nieh-erh, Yeh-lü A-hai and his younger brother Yeh-lü Tu-hua had joined Chinggis Khan's camp. Both the rise of Chinggis Khan and the cooperation of the Kitan leaders with him stirred up more Kitan rebellions during the Mongolian invasion. In the summer of 1213, the Jurchen court sent an envoy to appease the Kitans who had gathered and were making a disturbance in the territory of the Circuit of Hsien-p'ing.[48] In the summer of the same year, a Kitan officer transferred Ku-pei-k'ou, an important fortress along the Great Wall, to Chinggis Khan.[49] In the spring of 1215, the Jurchen court reluctantly pardoned the Kitans who had disturbed the area of Pei-ching (Lin-huang).[50] At the same time Yeh-lü Liu-ko had established his alliance with

Chinggis Khan, and the Capital of the Jurchen Chin (Peking) was under siege by the Mongolian forces. Therefore, the Jurchen could take no harsh measures against the Kitans. Even so, according to the Chin material, in the winter of 1215 the Jurchen Governor of Liao-tung reported his victory over Yeh-lü Liu-ko.[51]

In addition to these events, several Kitan or Hsi generals had joined the Mongolian forces in North China. Their activities indicate a strong desire to retaliate against the Jurchens. However, these merely represented individual reactions. They did not lead an organized revolt of the Kitan people. The only meaningful movement was the rebellion headed by Yeh-lü Lui-ko. However, this movement failed to establish a Kitan state because of disunity among the Kitan leaders.

According to the biography of Yeh-lü Liu-ko, the Jurchen court commanded a general in the area to attack the Kitan rebels with a large force, and announced that anyone who could bring one tael (one ounce) of bones of Yeh-lü Liu-ko would be rewarded with an equal weight of gold and one tael of his flesh with silver of the same weight. In addition the man would be given the post of a commander of a thousand as a hereditary privilege. Yeh-lü Liu-ko felt it impossible to resist alone, and sought reinforcements from Chinggis Khan. The Khan sent troops to support him and to defeat the Jurchens.

In the spring of 1213, the Kitans established Yeh-lü Liu-ko as King (*wang* 王) and his supporter, Yeh-ssu-pu as Prince *(chün wang)*. They named their kingdom the "Liao," and organized a governing body. The next year, 1215, the Jurchen Chin court sent an emissary to persuade Yeh-lü Liu-ko to surrender, offering him heavy bribes. However, this demand was rejected. The Chin Emperor was angered and ordered a force of four hundred thousand soldiers to attack, but they were defeated by Yeh-lü Liu-ko. Following this victory, many local Jurchen officials surrendered to the Kitans. Thereupon, Yeh-lü Liu-ko took possession of most of the cities in Liao-tung. They made Hsien-p'ing the capital and named it Chung-ching (Central Capital). The Jurchens attacked Yeh-lü Liu-ko with one hundred thousand troops, but again the Jurchens were defeated.

In 1215, Yeh-lü Liu-ko occupied Tung-ching, the Eastern Capital of the Jurchens, while Chung-tu, the Central Capital (Peking) was taken over by the Mongols. However, this victory bore bitter fruit for the Kitans, as dissension erupted among their leaders. Yeh-ssu-pu and others tried to persuade Yeh-lü Liu-ko to call himself emperor, but Yeh-lü Liu-ko refused. He said, "I have given my oath to be a vassal of the Great Mongolian State. How can I deny my own words and call myself the emperor of the east?" The multitude insisted on their proposal, but Yeh-lü Liu-ko refused and instead he secretly went to pay his respects to Chinggis Khan. The Khan was greatly pleased and conferred upon Yeh-lü Liu-ko the title of the King of Liao (Liao Wang).

While Yeh-lü Liu-ko was at the headquarters of the Khan, Yeh-ssu-pu falsely announced his death and killed all the Mongols in the Kitan camp. In 1216, some Kitan leaders supported Yeh-ssu-pu as emperor at Teng-chou (present-day Hai-cheng, Liao-ning province). They continued to use the word "Liao" as the name of their country. Soon afterwards Yeh-ssu-pu was killed by his own followers, and the Jurchens at Kai-chou (present-day Kai-p'ing, near Dairen) came to attack. Just then Yeh-lü Liu-ko arrived with Mongolian forces, and when the opposition group moved east Yeh-lü Liu-ko pursued them. He brought back his family and a part of the Kitan people to Lin-huang, the old capital of the former Kitan empire. A Kitan remnant retreated to Korea, disintegrated, and dispersed. Finally, in the year 1218, the remaining Kitan people were brought back to their homeland.

In the year 1220, Yeh-lü Liu-ko died. Chinggis Khan was then campaigning in western Inner Asia. In 1226, the Khan returned and Yeh-lü Liu-ko's widow petitioned the Khan to decide a successor to her deceased husband. The Khan accepted her petition and appointed Yeh-lü Liu-ko's eldest son, Hsüeh-ch'ê (Seche), to succeed to his father's rank. In 1229, Hsüeh-ch'ê followed Ögödei Khan (r. 1229–41) in invading the Jurchen Chin. In 1230, the Khan commanded him and the Mongol general Sartai to carry out an expedition toward the east to collect the remnants of his father's people. From 1230 to 1237 Hsüeh-ch'ê recovered more than six thousand Kitan households. Hsüeh-ch'ê died in the year 1238, and his son Shuo-kuo-nu succeeded to his rank and was appointed the governor of the Circuit of Kuang-ning.[52] He changed his name to Shira in Mongolian style. In 1251, Möngke Khan (r. 1251–59), recognizing Shira's merit in a Korean expedition and his family's service to the state, bestowed upon him a special golden tiger head seal and commanded him to assist the Mongolian princes in that area.[53]

The above records show both the Kitans' antagonism toward the Jurchens and their loyalty to the Mongols. Yeh-lü Liu-ko's cooperation with the Mongols was seemingly very natural. It was not brought about by outside pressure. Rather Jurchen oppression generated it. However, internal conflicts among the Kitan leaders brought about the failure of Yeh-lü Liu-ko's reunification movement, just as it had done with his forerunners. The Kitan rebellions from beginning to end lacked a great leader talented in the art of politics and organization. Even so, all the leaders were united in their desires to restore Kitan Liao. The Mongols were on the side of Yeh-lü Liu-ko, but this did not mean that they would support the restoration movement. In reality the rapid growth of Mongolian power left no place for an independent state of the Kitan people. Consequently, the policy that Yeh-lü Liu-ko tried to follow, i.e., the setting up of a vassal state, might have been quite practical and reasonable. However this policy was completely disrupted by power struggles among the Kitan leaders themselves. Chinggis Khan and his descendents trusted both the father and the sons of the Yeh-lü family. They allowed them to gather their own scattered people and to continue using the title Liao Wang. Hsüeh-ch'ê was appointed to be the commander of a thousand. As a result this Kitan leader became half-Mongol. In addition, the change of Shuo-kuo-nu's name into Shira indicates that this family had been thoroughly Mongolianized. This might be the reason why Möngke Khan ordered him to serve the Chinggisid princes in present-day Manchuria, and considered him a Mongol. At the time when Yeh-lü Liu-ko began to revolt against the Jurchens, the population of the Kitan under him was reportedly six hundred thousand. However, after the internal conflict and disruption this number sharply decreased. Many Kitans apparently left their main group, disappeared, and finally lost their racial identity.

Postscript

The existence of the Kitan problem during the Jurchen Chin dynasty is an important historical event. The Jurchens were aided in their rise to power by the political experience and the military strength of the subjugated Kitans. However, the riots and rebellions of the Kitans were a major factor in the disintegration of Jurchen power. Without the Kitans' military strength the Jurchen empire could not expand. Yet, the existence of Kitan power was also a serious problem which brought instability to the Jurchen nation. The Jurchen rulers had to take into consideration the Kitans' strength, but they were unable to give up their traditional prejudice toward their mortal enemy, the Kitans. Consequently, Jurchen policy toward the Kitans was two-faced and contradictory, and in the long run could not achieve a fruitful result. Moreover, it did not diminish the Kitans' desire for the restoration of their own country. Instead, the heavy oppression led to numerous Kitan rebellions which were a constant threat within the Jurchen Kingdom.

The Kara Kitai realm in Central Asia, established by Yeh-lü Ta-shih, had always been an attraction to the Kitans who remained in their homeland under Jurchen domination. It had some limited influence on the rebellions in the "land of pine and desert." This suggests that the existence of Kara Kitai had had political significance to all Kitan people. On the other hand, the recovery of their homelands in the "land of pine and desert" was the hope of the Kitans in Central Asia. Neither group realized its dream.

The rebellious Kitan leaders tried to obtain some foreign aid, but never succeeded. They desired to cooperate with the Hsia (Tangut), but the Hsia people had no need to support the Kitans and no desire to offend the powerful Jurchens. Though the Chinese hoped to stir up internal conflict in the Chin, they had insufficient strength to carry out a counter-attack against their enemy. Nevertheless, Jurchen expansion toward Sung was reduced by Kitan rebellions. At the same time, these rebellions were also hindered Jurchen rulers from managing their northern border effectively against the Mongols. Indeed, the "northern tribes" had always been supporters of these rebellious Kitans.

The Kitan leaders and peoples who fought Jurchen rule were primarily traditional nomads. The Sinicized Kitans, gradually following the Sinicization process of the Jurchens, blended together and lost their desire and need to resist the Jurchens. Similarly, the nomadic Kitans remaining in the "land of pine and desert" were gradually and naturally assimilated by the Mongols because of cultural similarities. Both the Sinicized Kitans and the Sinicized Jurchens were assimilated and disappeared into a human Chinese sea. From the perspective of the Kitans, their resistance against the Jurchen rule marked the end of their national history.[54] It was a glorious but tragic end.

Notes

1. "The Biography of Yeh-lü Ch'u-ts'ai (耶律楚材)," *Yüan shih* (Abbr.: YS) *Po-na* edition, 146:1a.
2. "The Biography of Shih-mo Yeh-hsien (石抹也先)," YS, 150:1a–2b.
3. Many leaders of Hsi (奚) tribe used the Chinese word "Hsiao" (蕭) as their family name. In addition the Shu-lü (述律) clan of the Kitans also used the same word instead of the word "Shu-lü."
4. Yu-wen Mao-chao (宇文懋昭), "*Ta-Chin-Kuo Chih*" (大金國志、The Records of the Great Chin State), reprinted in Taipei, 1967–68. The author was a Jurchen Chin living near the end of the dynasty.
5. Ibid., 132.
6. Yeh-lü Ta-shih (耶律大石), the founder of the Kara Kitai in Central Asia. See "The Annals of Emperor T'ien-tso", *Liao shih* (Abbr.: LS), 30:4a–7a.
7. Yü-wen Mao-chao, 63–64.
8. Ibid., 65.
9. Ibid., 111.
10. "The Annals of Tai-tsu," *Chin shih* (Abbr.: CS), 2:10b–11a.
11. "The Annals of Tai-tsung," CS, 3:5b–6a.
12. "The Annals of Hsi-tsung," CS, 4:7a.
13. "The Monograph of Military Affairs," CS, 44:1a.
14. "The Annals of Shih-tsung," CS, 6:12a.
15. Ibid., 3b–4b. Shang-ching (上京) was the old capital of the Jurchen Chin, in the vicinity of present-day Harbin City, Manchuria.
16. "The Monograph of Geography," CS, 24:17b–18a. See "The Monograph of Officials," CS, 57:22a.
17. Cf. "Biography of Yeh-lü Yu-tü (耶律餘睹)," LS, 102, and CS, 132.
18. "The Annals of Shih-tsung," CS, 6:1b.
19. "The Monograph of Military Affairs," CS, 44:3b.

20. "The Biography of Hsiao Huai-chung," CS, 91:12a.
21. "The Annals of Hai-ling," CS, 5:21ab.
22. Tai-chou, in the vicinity of present-day Ch'ang-ch'un, Kirin Province.
23. Hui-ning was the old capital of Chin and was also known as Shang-ching. See note 14.
24. Hsin-chou, in the vicinity of present-day Tieh-ling, Liaoning.
25. Han-chou, present-day Ch'ang-tu, Liaoning. See "The Biography of Wen-ti-han I-shih-man (溫迪罕移室懑)," CS, 91:3b.
26. Tung-ching, present-day Liao-yang, Liaoning. See "The Biography of Wu-yen Ch'a-la," CS, 86:9b.
27. Hsien-p'ing, present-day K'ai-yüan, Liaoning.
28. Liu-ho, in present-day Liaoning.
29. Chi-chou, present-day Nung-an Kirin.
30. Shih-tsung, Wang-yen Wu-lu ascended the throne in 1161. At that time his rank was still the Duke of the State of Ts'ao (曹國公).
31. See biographies of Pai Yen-ching and Ho-shih-lieh Chih-ning in CS, 84 and 87.
32. See "Biography of Yi-la Wo-wo (移剌窩斡)," CS, 133:6a–8b.
33. Ts'ai-shih, present-day Tan-tu, Anhui province.
34. Ibid., 8b–99a.
35. Ibid., 15a–16a.
36. Ibid., 16a–a. See "The Annals of Shih-tsung," CS, 6:8b.
37. Ibid., 16b.
38. Ibid., 16b–17a.
39. "The Annals of Shih-tsung," CS, 6:ab, n43, 17b.
40. "The Biography of Yi-la Wo-wo" CS, 133:17ab. Yü-wen Mao-chao, 121. "The Biography of Ho-shih-lieh Chih-ning," CS, 87:3b. "The Biography of Pu-san Chung-yi." CS, 87:9b. In "The Annals of Kao-tsung" of *Sung Shih*, this event is not recorded.
41. Of "The Annals of Shih-tsung," CS, 6:12b and 14b.
42. Of "The Biography of Wan-yen Wu-pu-ho," CS, 90:6ab.
43. "The Annals of Shih-tsung," CS, 6:14a.
44. Ibid., 22b.
45. Of "The Biography of Nei-tsu [Wan-yen] Hsiang," CS, 94:7ab. This rebellion was also recorded in "The Annals of Chang-tsung, II," CS, 10:13b. However, it put Te-shuo T'o-so as T'o-so Te-shou and the date as 1196. It was also recorded in Ta-chin Kuo Chih in a little different way. Cf Wan-yeh Mao-chao, 132.
46. "The Annals of Chang-tsung, III," CS, 11, 9a.
47. "The Biography of Yeh-lü Liu-ko," YS, 149:1a.
48. "The Annals of Wei-shao Wang," CS, 13:6a.
49. "The Annals of Tai-tsu," YS, 1:17a.
50. "The Annals of Hsüan-tsung," CS, 14:7a.
51. Ibid., 15a.
52. Kuan-ning Circuit, presently the land on the east of Yi-wu-lü Mountain Range, Liaoning.
53. See "The Biography of Yeh-lü Liu-ko," YS, 149.
54. By this time Kara Kitai had already been annexed by Güchülüg, the prince of Naiman, in the year 1211 or 1212.

Part II
The Mongolian Empire Period

Chapter 4

Traditional Mongolian Attitudes and Values as Seen in the *Secret History of the Mongols* and the *Altan tobchi*

(Originally published in Indiana University Uralic and Altaic Series,
Aspects of Altaic Civilization II, 1978,134:89-114)

The *Secret History of the Mongols*[1] still the earliest extant record in the Mongolian language. The *Altan tobchi*[2] contains about 80 percent of the original text of the *Secret History* plus many additional old traditions, dialogues, and proverbs. The *Altan tobchi*, though compiled by Lobsangdanjin in the late seventeenth century or the early eighteenth century, drew on the sources that were much older. Because of their antiquity, the author consulted these two sources for the observations stated here concerning early Mongolian norms of morality. These traditional values naturally changed with the flow of time and as Mongolian attitudes or emotions were transformed. However, in their inner essence there was an important continuity.

Heaven and Filial Love

Traditional Mongolian culture arising from unique geographical influences and a nomadic life style is clearly different from the culture of the agricultural areas of East Asia. However, it still belongs to the general category of Asian culture, and was never entirely cut off from other Asian moral traditions. Two important examples are seen in the veneration of heaven and the sentiment of filial love.

Möngke Tenggeri, or Everlasting Heaven, was the highest deity of Mongolian Shamanism. Veneration of heaven, of course, was the expression of a religious emotion, and the Mongols regarded heaven as the source of all power. The very first sentence of the *Secret History* claims that the ancestors of Chinggis Khan were born by the mandate of Heaven *(Tenggeri).*[3] Also, the record continually emphasizes that the success of the Khan stemmed from the power of Heaven and Earth.[4] This sentiment was reflected by a Chinese writer of the Sung dynasty when he spoke of "Chinggis Khan, the One Blessed of Heaven" (天賜成吉思汗 *tien-tz'u ch'eng-chi-ssu han).*[5] The *Secret History* not only claims that the victory of the Khan was based on help from Heaven,[6] but also that Jamukha, the mortal enemy of Chinggis Khan, actually recognized that Heaven assisted Chinggis in defeating him.[7] Similarly, when young Temüjin[8] was first attacked by the Taichi'ud tribe and later by the Mergid, he went in both cases to the Burkhan mountain and expressed thanksgiving for the mercy of the Mountain and of Heaven in allowing him to escape these dangers.[9] In his prayer he humbly acknowledged that Heaven and the holy mountain had protected his "insignificant flea or ant-like life" from danger.[10] In early Mongol records there are these and other expressions of humility toward Everlasting Heaven.

The worship of Heaven was religious in nature, but there was a transference to daily life such that fear and worship of Heaven influenced the development of self-restraint in such rulers as Chinggis who had absolute power. In their imperial decrees the Mongols customarily used the phrase "by the power of Everlasting Heaven."[11] Even in warnings to their enemies they would say "the results will only be known by Heaven."[12] It may seem to some that the Mongols were putting on airs and insulting others in these statements, but in analyzing the data from the *Secret History*, these statements actually appear as humble expressions revealing a desire to avoid being too proud before the blessings granted by Heaven.

The filial love of children for parents is another Mongolian moral value in the Asian tradition. However, the nature of Mongolian filial love has been somewhat different from that of the filial piety of Chinese Confucianism, which tended to be more ritualistic than emotional. Both were reflections of filial love, but their expressions differed. In the early clan system of Mongolian nomadic society, in order to strengthen blood relationships, the focus on a common ancestor was greatly emphasized. In addition to the *Secret History*, other Mongolian historical records, including the genealogy of the royal household of Chinggis Khan and the genealogy or lineages of other important households, were carefully kept. Ancestral veneration was an important religious and political ceremony for all classes. Many instructions in the *Secret History* emphasize the value of the words or teachings of the ancestors *(yekes)* and elders *(ötögüs)*.[13] Among the Mongols filial love is a spontaneous form of love, embodying both attachment and obedience. It was not a canonical or dogmatic matter as advocated by Chinese Confucian scholars.

According to the *Altan tobchi,* Chinggis Khan asked his second son Chaghadai on a certain occasion what sort of festival was the most meaningful. His son's answer was the Near Year's Day banquet. The Khan then said:

No! If you were not born and if no name were given you;
If you came not from your mother's womb to see the light;
What New Year could you enjoy,
And to whom could you give a name?
From this time you must remember the day of procreation by your father,
And the giving of birth by your mother.
Wine and dine happily together.
This is the best festival.[14]

Thus, a Mongolian tradition is the expression of great appreciation to one's parents from whom life came.

The *Secret History* records that a quarrel was about to break out between Chinggis Khan and his second younger brother Khasar, instigated by the politically ambitious shaman, Kököchü.[15] Their mother, Kö'elün, hearing of it, immediately rushed to the spot and severely rebuked Chinggis Khan. After this rebuke, Chinggis said, "I have caused my mother to be very angry. I am afraid. I feel very shameful!"[16] So saying, he left his younger brother's place quietly. His expression of filial love and obedience was emphasized by the author of the *Secret History,* and seems to be a reflection of the moral values or social norms of the Mongolian society at the time.

The *Secret History* further records that after being supported as the Great Khan, Chinggis, in order to strengthen the code of law he established, decided to get rid of his own paternal uncle, Da'aritai, who earlier transgressed the military regulations by plundering for booty, rebelling against Chinggis, and surrendering to his rival Ong Khan of the Kereyid. His decision, however, was countered by the admonition of his respected associates Bo'orchu, Mukhuali, and Shigikutughu. They emphasized that this man was the only existing younger brother of the Khan's father, and that therefore his household should not be exterminated. The record says Chinggis was moved to tears and even his nose was irritated like one who had inhaled smoke.[17] The incident also demonstrates the deep emotion associated with filial love and the high regard for blood ties.

The word *ëbügen*[18] frequently appears in the *Secret History* to show a veneration of old persons. On some special occasions unrelated elderly people are called *echige*, "father,"[19] and *eke*, "mother."[20] This custom shows a deep regard for elderly persons, and calls into question Chinese records which hold that North Asian nomadic peoples usually "honored the strong but despised the elderly." Certainly dynamic power was respected in the nomadic society, and both the terms *bökö*, "wrestlers," and *mergen*, "experts in archery," were used as honorable titles for outstanding men. Chinese views probably arose from the fact that veneration towards elderly people in a nomadic society was not as ritualistic as the honor paid to the aged in the agricultural society of China.

After the Yüan Dynasty (1260–1368) was established, many Confucian classics were translated into Mongolian but only the *Book of Filial Piety (Hsiao-ching* 孝經) remains today. This may suggest that many of the principles of the orthodox school of Confucian ethics were not compatible with the values of nomadic society, and that only the content of the *Hsiao-ching* was acceptable to Mongolian moral tradition and was therefore carefully preserved.

"Fire in the Eyes"

In Mongolian society from the time of the *Secret History* to the present day there has been a dislike for a pale face. Mongols usually praise those children and youth who have "fire in their eyes and a light on their face."[21] The marriage engagement between young Temüjin and Börte was decided in part because the parents of both sides recognized that the two children belonged to the special group having "fire in their eyes and a light on the face."[22] Even when Temüjin was captured by the Taichi'ud and released and saved by Sorkhan-shira, it was because he had these characteristics.[23] According to the *Yüan shih*, Chinggis Khan promoted a young Uighur, Meng-su-ssu, because he had "fire in his eyes."[24] The praising of active, earnest, and zealous youth is an old tradition which is still very much alive in present-day Mongolia.

Beauty and Bravery

The beauty of women and the prowess and bravery of men were highly valued by Mongolian society, and *Gho'a*, which means "beautiful," has long been a common name of women, while *bökö* ("wrestler") and *ba'atur* ("brave man" or "hero") appears in the titles and names of men. For instance, in the *Secret History*, Dei Sechen, father of Börte, said to Yesügei, the father of Temüjin:

From early days among us, the Onggirad,
The appearance of the sons of our daughters has been magnificent!
The countenance of our daughters is beautiful![25]

Beautiful women and heroic men are often the subjects of stories in Mongolian society. The natural expressions of love by a woman were not forbidden, as was customary in the restrained agricultural society of China. The *Secret History* notes that when Yesügei kidnapped Kö'elün from her husband, Chiledü, she was unrestrained in expressing her love, sympathy, and sorrow for her former husband.[26] Later, when Börte was captured by the Mergid and then eventually released in a war against the Mergid, on meeting her husband Temüjin on the battlefield, she rushed forward and embraced him.[27]

A similar story is recorded in the *Secret History* when discussing the war of Chinggis Khan against the Taichi'ud. Khada'an, the daughter of Sorkhan-shira, who had saved the life of Chinggis Khan, barely escaped death by the sword and came to Temüjin. When she met Chinggis they embraced each other[28] in a natural flow of love and emotion. This display of feeling again differs from the more restrained relationships between men and women in agricultural society south of the Great Wall.

Concerning bravery, the *Secret History* records that after the Taichi'ud were exterminated by Chinggis Khan, the warrior, Jebe, having surrendered boldly, told the Khan that it was he who shot the Khan's horse and almost took his life. The Khan admired his boldness and made him one of his personal companions.[29] Later this man became a distinguished general during the building of the Mongol Empire.

In the *Altan tobchi*, there is a long verse describing how Chinggis Khan praised the bravery of his generals who fought valiantly with no regard for their lives.[30] The *Secret History* makes a clear contrast between bravery and cowardice in the account of Chinggis Khan's expedition against the Naiman. Khor-sübechi, a general of the Naiman, criticized the cowardice of Tayang Khan, but praised the bravery of the father: "Your father, Inancha Bilge Khaghan, during his march against the enemy, never showed the backs of his men nor the hip of a horse to his foe,"[31] meaning that this Khan never retreated or turned aside. The *Secret History* also points out that Tayang Khan was despised even by his mother and son because of his cowardice. Although this trait may be exaggerated or idealized, it is traditional in Mongolian society to honor bravery and despise cowardice.

Chastity

In order to protect the purity of blood relations in a clan or lineage, the chastity of women was very strictly maintained. For instance, the chastity of Khulan, a Mergid girl who eventually became a *Khatun* of Chinggis Khan, is greatly praised. She was brought to the Khan from the battlefield by Naya'a, one of the Khan's generals. Both Khulan and Naya'a were greatly appreciated by the Khan because of the strictly chaste relationship observed by the two as they journeyed to the Khan's camp.[32]

The *Altan tobchi* mentions certain instructions of Chinggis Khan to his daughter, Alkha Begi, as follows:

The body is a temporary thing,
But one's reputation is everlasting.[33]

Again the Khan asked his companion, general Bo'-orchu, to instruct Checheyigen, another daughter of the Khan, when she was going to marry:

When you speak you must have wisdom;
In your conduct you must honor chastity.[34]

Although sexual standards began to decline from the end of the seventeenth century, chastity was still an ideal valued highly among the Mongols.

Extending Assistance

Helping people in danger, assuming nothing neutralized this intention, has been one of the traditional ideals of Mongolian nomadic society. The *Secret History* records an incident in which Temüchin escaped while being held as a hostage of the Taichi'ud and came to the home of Sorkhan-shira. Fearing the Taichi'ud, Sorkhan-shira hesitated to allow Temüjin to hide in his home. However, his two sons Chimbei and Chila'un argued with him, persuading him with an old proverb to assist one in danger.

When a bird is chased by a sparrow-hawk and flies into the bush, the bush will save it. How can you now put a person off this way who has come to us?

Thus saying, they risked their own lives to save Temüjin.[35] The *Yüan shih* mentions a similar altruistic incident.

I-na-ssu [great-grandfather of T'u-t'u-ha] had been a lord in the land of the Kimchak for generations. Huo-tu [Khodu], the lord of Mergid, escaped and arrived there and I-na-ssu received him. T'ai-tsu [Chinggis Khan] sent an envoy and instructed him saying: "Why do you hide a deer . . . bearing my arrow? . . ." I-na-ssu replied: "A bush still can help save the life of a bird that has escaped from the sparrow-hawk. Am I not better than grass and wood?" T'ai-tsu then commanded the generals and armies to attack him.[36]

The above incident reveals that this proverb, repeated over generations, is evidence of an altruistic pattern, a common element in the moral system of all the nomadic people on the Eurasian steppes.

Unity

Whether involving the dissolution or the formation of clan alliances, the internal unification of one's own clan is highly valued in nomadic society. In this connection the *Secret History* records that Alan-gho'a, a legendary female ancestor of Chinggis Khan, on seeing that her five sons were separating and going their individual ways, gathered them in and told each of them to take an arrow in his hands and break it. She then put five arrows together and told them to try to break them. After they failed to do so, she admonished them saying:

All of you are as these five arrows. If you separate you will be easily broken by anyone as separate arrows; but if you unite together like the five arrows as one heart and one body, then no matter who it be, they cannot go against you.[37]

The same lesson is stressed in the *"Biography of T'u-yü-hun"* (吐谷渾) found in the *Wei-shu*.

A-chai was established as a ruler. He had twenty sons. . . . When he was about to die, he gathered all his sons and younger brothers and told them, "Each of you take one of my arrows. Break it and throw it on the ground." He then ordered Mu-li-yen, younger brother of his mother to break one. Again he said, "You take nineteen arrows and break them." But Mu-li-yen could not do so. A-chai said, "Now do you understand? A single one is easily broken, but it is difficult to destroy a multitude. If you cooperate in the use of your power and unify with one heart, then the state will be very solid!" After saying this he died.[38]

This example of the arrows was commonly used to persuade people in steppe society to unify. It seems to have been a common tradition of all North Asian nomadic peoples.[39]

The *Secret History* records that Kö'elün rebuked her sons Temüjin and Khasar after they killed Begder, their brother by a different mother. She pointedly warned them using an old proverb: "Except for your shadow, you have no other companion; except for a tail, you have no other whip."[40] This was a common warning of that period which served to admonish people not to separate from blood relatives but to cooperate and unite together.

This high regard for clan or tribe was strengthened following the establishment of the Mongolian Empire by Chinggis Khan. However, after the collapse of this great empire and a long period of internal warfare, there was a reversion to tribalism and unified power was reduced. The *Altan tobchi* records that Toghon of the Oirad, criticizing his opponent Arughtai and the disunity of the Eastern Mongols, said:

They are like a camel herd without a male camel,
A cattle herd without a bull,
A horse herd without a stallion,
A sheep herd without a male sheep.[41]

The *Altan tobchi* records an incident when Abgirchin Jinong rebelled against his own Khaghan and was moving to surrender to the enemy Oirad. Kharghucha Taiji admonished him, saying: "One who is inclined toward outsiders will never prosper. Only one who protects his own blood relationships will increase and flourish."[42] After his surrender, the Jinong was eventually killed by the leaders of the Oirad. Their excuse was:

Is it possible for one who does not love his own relatives to love our relatives? Is it possible for one who does not love his own state to love our state? Is it possible for one who does not love his own reputation to be concerned about our reputation?[43]

All these sayings reveal that loyalty to one's own tribe was a high principle, but that rebellion against it was a great shame and an immoral act.

Following the decline of Mongol unity and the period of fragmentation and rule by Manchu-Ch'ing rulers, the consciousness of broad loyalties was lost in the rise of strong tribalism. Such tribalism became a real hindrance to the reunification of the Mongols and to the rise of a nationalistic movement at the beginning of this century. Gradually, however, nationalism did occur, along with a feeling of patriotism for the new Mongol nation.

Revenge

Tribal attachment strengthened natural inclinations to reward loyalty and to avenge treachery. Thus, there was a strong tendency towards vendetta in early Mongol society. The *Secret History* records that in order to avenge the capture of Ambaghai Khan by the Tatar and his subsequent execution by the Jurchen-Chin, the Borjigid and the Taichi'ud carried on a long feud with the Tatar in a vain attempt to gain revenge through a decisive victory.[44] Yesügei, father of Chinggis Khan, was one of the leaders in this feud.[45] The hatred between the Tatar and the Borjigid increased, and Yesügei was poisoned by the Tatar and died. This was the main reason why Chinggis Khan eventually attempted to exterminate the entire Tatar tribe.[46] Later, the Mergid attack on Temüjin and their capture of his wife Börte was to gain revenge against Yesügei who had kidnapped Kö'elün from her husband Chiledü, a man of the Mergid.[47] Later Chinggis Khan exterminated many Mergid for political and military reasons, but also to avenge himself against his old foe. In his first victory against the Mergid, Temüjin victoriously proclaimed that "the feud of man has been revenged."[48] Later, in the year of the ox, 1205, as Chinggis Khan dispatched his famous general Sübe'etei on an expedition against the Mergid who had migrated to Central Asia, he recalled the earlier feud.

When I was young the three Mergid [groups] . . . encircled the Burkhan mountain three times to threaten me. Toward this rival people, I now again swear that we will attack them unto the end of lengths and unto the bottom of the depths.[49]

This statement highlights his desire for vengeance.

When Temüjin was formally proclaimed the Great Khan of the Mongols (1206), he praised the merit of General Boroghul with the words: "to avenge our hatred and to satisfy our grudge against the enemy."[50] Thus, vendetta, blood feuds, and mandatory revenge strongly colored the attitudes and morality of Mongol society. All members of a clan had the obligation to take revenge against the foes of their clan.

Gratitude

On the positive side, rewarding the grace of a benefactor was also an honored virtue. Thus, Temüjin commanded his descendants to worship the Burkhan mountain to show gratitude that his life had once been saved by the holy mountain.[51] The *Secret History* also mentions many times that Chinggis Khan showed gratitude to the family of Sorkhan-shira, who saved his life and helped him escape from the Taichi'ud.[52] Again, the Khan always showed his special concern for the family of Menglig, who helped his widowed mother Kö'elün, himself, and his young brothers when they had been abandoned by the Tai-ci'ud leaders in the wilderness. Chinggis remembered that Menglig was a trusted follower of his father, Yesügei. Moreover, he did not punish Menglig or other members of his family as he could have done after Kököchü, son of Menglig, was found to be plotting against the Khan. Chinggis's revenge was limited to the son, who was executed.[53] Concerning the case of Menglig, he said:

When we were born, we were born together; as we grew, we grew together. Your blessings and good fortune have been a satisfaction and boon to me.[54]

The *Secret History* also shows that gratitude for earlier help from Yesügei was the reason why the Kereyid Ong Khan joined forces with Yesügei's son, Temüjin, to attack the Mergid.[55]

The above incidents are but a few examples illustrating the bonds of affection, personal loyalty, and the importance of expressing gratitude towards one's benefactors. In the *Secret History* a set term for kindness or mercy is *tusa*, the motivation for voluntary assistance. *Ghabiya*, a term used for assistance which is obligatory, was not ordinarily used in such cases as the above. Therefore, it is clear that the actions of which we speak were in appreciation for the kindness of a benefactor. They were not merely an obligatory reward *(ghabiya)*.

Customary patterns of vengeance and reward assisted Chinggis Khan in his accomplishments. For instance, the invasion against the Jurchen Chin was to avenge an old hatred of Ambaghai Khan.[56] In time, the traditional attitudes discussed opened the way for the Mongols to accept more easily the Buddhist law of cause and effect and to be thoroughly converted to Buddhism.

Balancing Gratitude and Revenge

In balancing gratitude and revenge, the question would arise whether one should be strict or tolerant. Both attitudes were present when Chinggis Khan unified Mongolia and established order. He established the *Jasagh,* a law code, and applied it consistently. Many people receive the impression that Chinggis Khan, in establishing his great empire through military means, must have been an inflexible man. There is much truth in this notion. But on the other hand, he was a rare ruler in East Asia, for he did not kill even one of his former followers — evidence that he was a man of great tolerance. In the *Secret History* are found some examples. When the Idughud (king of the Uighurs) decided to join the Mongols, he sent an envoy to Chinggis Khan bearing the message:

> When I heard of the great fame of Chinggis Khan, I felt as happy as when the clouds disappear permitting the sunshine to appear or when the melting of the ice permits the river quietly to flow.[57]

The surrender of the Uighur king to Chinggis seems to have been prompted by the benevolence of the Khan, not merely by his military power.

As mentioned, the *Secret History* records that after Kököchü was executed the Khan severely rebuked Menglig and afterwards said:

> It is shameful and ridiculous that words spoken in the morning are changed in the evening, or that statements of the evening are reversed the next morning. Therefore, what I have said earlier let us not forget.

After Chinggis's anger was appeased, he said graciously: "If they were only able to restrain their sinful tendencies, then who could compete with the descendants of Menglig *ecige* [old father]?"[58]

The *Altan tobchi* presents cases in which it seems the Khan had difficulty in making a decision because of conflict between law and emotions. There is, for example, the question of punishing a man named Shilimen.

> Shilimen of Ughurtai quit his duty in the royal guard without authority to do so. Before the Khaghan father spoke to the people, Chaghadai Akha [elder brother] said, "Punish Shilimen to establish a precedent of warning to the masses! If we do not punish Shilimen, how can we rule the people?" . . . But Shilimen defended himself and . . . Chinggis Khan then decreed — "Who destroys things established by whom? Who tortures those gathered by whom? Torture them after I leave but not while I still live!" After Chaghadai walked out, Chinggis Khan made his pronouncement: "Chaghadai is correct and you Shilimen are wrong, but because you made great efforts many times I now forgive you once. However, this should not be imitated by others as a pattern."[59]

This story also indicates that Mongol society honored affection more than law and valued tolerance above punishment. The *Shih-huo chih* of the *Yüan shih* records that:

> At the beginning of Yüan there was no definite institution to collect taxes from the people. When Shih-tsu [Khubilai] established the [tax] law, it was based on the principles of generosity.[60]

Also, in the *Hsing-fa-chih* of the *Yüan shih* we read:

> The positive aspect of the law and the punishment system of the Yüan was merciful and tolerant, but its negative side was that it was too loose. They did not know how to strengthen it.[61]

Generosity, mercy, and tolerance arose from the original ethics of nomadic society in Mongolia, and they were not developed further after the Mongols occupied China. There is evidence, however, that Mongolian traditions did affect the institutions of the Yüan

Dynasty established in China. According to the Chinese interpretation, "There were originally no definite institutions"[62] in Mongol society before the conquest. They occurred only after Chinese tradition was adopted. In reality, the institutions in steppe society were merely different and went unrecognized by Chinese writers.

The Military Man

The ideal military man as recorded in the *Altan tobchi* is of interest and is portrayed in the following quotation.

> Chinggis Khan praised his generals and of his great companion, Bo'orchu, he said: "The son of Nakhu Bayan is my hero, the good Bo'orchu!
> In contacts with neighbors his character is [as friendly] as a spotted calf;
> At the time of melee he never pays attention to his own life and body;
> That is my hero Bo'orchu!
> As a friend of others, his character is [as friendly] as a black calf;
> But in meeting the enemy he rushes into battle like a flying eagle;
> That is my hero Bo'orchu!
> Laughing and talking [with friends] his personality is [as friendly] as a pure black calf;
> But in confrontation with a mortal enemy, he rushes in and out like an attacking hawk;
> That is my hero Bo'orchu!
> Playing and smiling [with people] his personality is [as friendly] as a new born calf;
> But in attacking he rushed downward just like a gerfalcon;
> That is my hero Bo'orchu![63]

These verses were written in the old spirit of nomadic society, according to which one should treat one's fellow tribesmen with tolerance and friendliness but the enemy with mercilessness and cruelty. According to the observations of the author, present-day Mongols still possess these two tendencies in peace and war.

Self-Control

In traditional Mongolian society a troublemaker was not welcome, and in this regard the *Altan tobchi* records Chinggis Khan as having said: "Do not grab the beard of a sitting man. Do not touch the legs of a resting person!"[64] In order to reduce trouble, persons were encouraged to be reasonable, not emotional. A person able to control his anger was honored in Mongolian society as a model of good behavior. The *Secret History* records an important occasion when Temüjin and Jamukha were about to separate under strained circumstances. Temüjin kept quiet and said nothing against Jamukha,[65] even though some expression of doubt as to their friendship would have been justified. Also, it records an incident in which the ambitious shaman, Kököchü, made trouble between the brothers of Chinggis Khan, an incident which almost erupted into open conflict. Before making the final decision to get rid of this shaman, the Khan made a conscious attempt to control his emotions and to keep silent.[66] On another occasion, when his two sons Jochi and Chaghadai, competing to be the successor to the throne, quarreled in front of their father, the Khan again kept silent and made no immediate judgment. Finally, the silence of the father caused the two sons to make a compromise, and both supported their younger brother Ögödei as successor to the throne. This, in fact, was quite acceptable to the Khan.[67]

Great self-discipline and the ability to control his anger also made Chinggis Khan able to accept criticism and admonishments from his vassals. According to the *Secret History*, Chinggis said: "You Bo'orchu and Mukhali, persuade me to do those things which I should do until I accomplish them, and you stop me from doing those things which I should not do until I stop doing them. Thereby, I am able to be seated on this great throne."[68] These stories also indicate that in Mongolian society a quick response was not necessarily praiseworthy. Rather, a slow and comparatively careful decision was preferred.

When it speaks of the bad tempered and obstinate Chaghadai, the *Secret History* records: "Chinggis Khan said: 'Chaghadai is tough-minded and easily angered. Kököchüs [you] should be there in the morning and the evening to admonish him.'"[69] Thus, a hot temper and violent behavior were not welcome in nomadic society.

Before Temüjin ascended the throne as the Great Khan, two important incidents occurred because women could not control their emotions. The first was a quarrel between the widow of Ambaghai Khan and Kö'elün, the mother of Temüjin. Eventually the trouble caused young Temüjin and his mother to be abandoned in the wilderness by the Taichi'ud leaders.[70] The result was that the Borjigid and the Taichi'ud became mortal enemies and feuded between themselves. The second incident was caused by quarreling women of the Jürkin clan, which led to a conflict between Chinggis Khan and the Jürkin leaders.[71] It appears that the *Secret History* assumes that women were less able to control their emotions than men.

In the *Altan tobchi* a saying of Chinggis Khan is recorded in which he declares:

Do not spoil the state,
Merely because you were struck by the horn of a male antelope;
Do not forsake your own people,
Merely because you were struck by the horn of a ram;
Do not mix with evil persons,
Merely because you were struck by the horn of a bull![72]

The meaning is that one should not be confused and commit some great violence because of a small matter that one should endure. The same record gives the Khan's admonition to his daughter Alkha Begi: "No friend is better than your own brilliant and wise heart. No enemy is worse than your own angry and crooked heart."[73] He also instructed his sons: "If one is able to control anger that has already reached his mouth, then whom can violence and indignation ever overcome?"[74] Maxims like these are common in Mongolian historical literature.

Many other Mongolian records show the value placed on self-control in nomadic society. When Khubilai became the "Son of Heaven" as ruler of China, he followed the admonitions of his ancestors and tried to control his anger. According to the *Yüan shih*, Shih-tsu (Khubilai) commanded his ministers:

If We are angry against one who is judged guilty and command you to execute him, you should not kill him but wait for one or two days. Then, report to Us again [and await Our final decision].[75]

Decisiveness

A nomadic and hunting life required the people of the steppe to struggle against the natural environment and to have decisive wills during clan wars and the establishment of their great empires. In this regard the *Altan tobchi* records the instructions of Chinggis Khan to his sons as follows.

Climb to the top of high mountains!
Go to the ports of the great oceans!
Do not hesitate only because the way is too long.
If you try you will reach there!
Do not fear because the burden is heavy.
If you try you can bear it!
Meat-eating teeth hide in the heart.
If the body is strong, it can only overcome a single man.
If the will is strong, it will overcome a multitude![76]

When his daughter Alkha Begi was going to marry, Chinggis Khan instructed her similarly on proper attitudes.

Decide in your mind to be one of my feet!
During expeditions be my supporter;
When galloping be my good horse! . . .
Be careful and steadfast;
Be afraid of nothing![77]

The *Altan tobchi* also records that when his eldest son, Jochi, was going to occupy the land of Kipchak, Chinggis Khan asked his faithful companion Bo'orchu to advise the son.

If you feel there is a mountain that you cannot cross,
Do not wonder, "How can I pass it?"
If you decide there is nothing that you cannot pass through,
Then you will be able to pass through it!
When you can climb boldly,
Then the beautiful colors and fine music on the other side of the mountain will
   all appear before you.
If you feel there is a river that you cannot cross,
Do not wonder, "How can I cross it?"
When you cross it in an orderly way,
Then the carts and horses on the far bank of the river will all appear before
   you![78]

This same commitment is recorded in the *Chinggis Boghda-yin durasghal-un tegübüri*. The words of Chinggis Khan are as follows.

If you climb the mountain which is impossible to climb,
You will reach the top.
If you cross the river which is impossible to cross,
You will reach the other bank![79]

A decisive heart and an unshakeable will are always praised by the Mongolian people. Even in the 1940s, in the pastoral zone of Inner Mongolia, when a traveller met a wolf he would not harm it. The wolf was regarded as a symbol of decisive will, and, it was believed, might be good luck for the traveller in reaching his destination.

Loyalty

Loyalty was another prime value of traditional Mongolian feudalistic society. At the time he established his great empire, Chinggis Khan emphasized loyalty. There are many stories about this virtue recorded in the *Secret History*. For instance, after Chinggis crushed his mortal enemies, the Taichi'ud, a man named Naya'a and his father, who had been with them, came to Chinggis. On their way they captured Targhutai-kiriltugh, the chief of the Taichi'ud. The father decided to kill him, but Naya'a stopped his father and released the man because he was once their *tus*, or original lord. After they came to the Khan and reported the story to him, along with Naya'a's loyalty to his original lord, Naya'a was honored by the Khan.[80]

Loyalty was admired, even when exemplified among the enemy. Chinggis Khan attacked the Kereyid, among whom Ong Khan and his son Senggüm were hiding. One of their vassals, Khadagh Ba'atur, fought valiantly and made it possible for Ong Khan and his son to escape. After the warfare had ended, Khadagh surrendered to Chinggis Khan, readily acknowledged his role in the battle, and asked for execution. But instead, Chinggis praised his loyalty and bravery by saying:

He risked his own life in fighting in order not to forsake his lord *[tus]* but to aid his escape and protect his life. What a great man! Is he not a worthwhile companion?[81]

After Chinggis Khan defeated the Naiman (1204), his enemy, Jamukha, was captured by his own companions and brought to the Khan. Disapproving of their action, Chinggis said, "These people betrayed their own lord. How can I trust them?" With this he had them executed in the presence of Jamukha.[82] Such stories as these suggest that Chinggis Khan utilized special occasions to emphasize loyalty. Because of his efforts to develop this moral trait, he had outstanding success in ruling his underlings. There is no case of a general or vassal rebelling against him, nor was he ever forced to execute any of his close officers or men because of treachery.

Both the *Altan tobchi* and the *Chinggis Boghda-yin durasghal-un tegübüri*[83] record a thought of the Khan regarding loyalty.

A man of two hearts is not a man, but should be considered as a woman;
A man of one heart is more than a man, and should be honored as a precious thing;
A woman of one heart is no more a woman but should be valued as a man;
A woman of two hearts is not a woman, but merely a dog!
How can one make a companion of such a person?[84]

These words might be regarded as a general proverb of Chinggis Khan's times. It clearly emphasizes that in Mongolian society whole-heartedness or single-mindedness was greatly honored, while a person with a changeable heart was greatly despised. Loyalty is a vital standard of feudalistic morality. During the long period of quasi-feudalistic institutions in Mongolia, person-to-person relationships were extremely important and loyalty to one's own lord was praised.

At the same time, the Mongolian people had a strong, immovable loyalty to their beliefs. This is why the Mongols were such devoted followers of Buddhism for almost four hundred years. Now times have changed, but the tradition of loyalty is still there.

This trait did not decrease because of the decline of Buddhism, but rather changed to a commitment to new principles.

At times the Mongols have been seen by others as a stubborn people who are very difficult to convince of the value of new ideas. More accurately, this "stubbornness" is really steadfastness and loyalty, whether to men, ideas, or institutions. They also joke about themselves, saying "Do not tell the Mongols of a particular way. After they are aware of it, they will always go that way!"

Faithfulness

The word *batu,* which means faithfulness, honesty, and solidness, is a traditional Mongolian name for both males and females. The *Secret History* mentions that when young Temüjin established a close relationship with young Bo'orchu, the father of Bo'orchu, Nakhu-Bayan, instructed them on how to be good companions. He said that they should never separate from each other, and indeed they followed this instruction all their lives.[85]

Needless to say, unfaithfulness was despised by the Mongols. For instance, there is the case of Seche Begi and Taichu, who swore to support Temüjin as Khan, but eventually rebelled against him. When they were finally captured, Chinggis Khan asked them, "What did we pledge together?" Seche Begi and Taichu answered, "Since we did not fulfil our pledge, let us now be dealt with according to our own words."[86] The Khan disposed of them according to their vows.

The only political propaganda or psychological warfare that Chinggis Khan carried out against Ong Khan of the Kereyid was a rebuke for his unfaithfulness. Also, after Jamukha was captured, Chinggis showed a desire to have him become his companion. But this proposal was rejected by Jamukha who said:

> When we were young . . . I made a mutual vow with Khaghan *Anda,* I spoke words that I should not have forgotten. . . . Later, instigated by others . . . we spoke hard words to each other. Therefore, unless the black skin of my face be peeled off, I can have no face to see the warm color of [you, my] Khaghan *Anda.* I spoke words that I should never have forgotten and therefore unless the red skin of my face be peeled off, I really have no face to see the real appearance of my ambitious *Anda!*[87]

The Mongolian people honored a solemn vow and one could not lightly break one's word. Even in recent times, a proverb common in pastoral areas says: "Once you have said yes, you should not later complain of pain." The implication is that after a matter is agreed upon, there should be no regret at the outcome. In the modern period there is ample evidence that Mongolian leaders, assuming that other people behaved on the same principles as themselves, were cheated by hollow promises made by those with whom they dealt in foreign affairs.

Words and Deeds

Mongolian society also focuses on a person's behavior rather than on vain words. The *Altan tobchi* illustrates this in the words of Khuyildar.

> To speak hundreds of words is no better than only to keep a good nature;
> To speak hundreds of words is no better than to properly accomplish a matter.

In ten thousand words there may be one correct item;
In hundreds of words there may be one good intent.[88]

These verses hold that a ruler should not only speak properly, but should develop a good nature and accomplish good deeds. The *Altan tobchi* records the Khan's instruction to his judges as follows.

The state under the Khaghan cannot be developed in darkness . . . You must work single-mindedly. Avoid taking sides against anyone. Your word should not show discrimination! . . . You should not hang bells on the fringe of your coat nor should you hang a sled on the seat of your trousers![89]

This means that a man should be open and unselfish. He should not do things which would be a stumbling block to himself or others.

The *Secret History* records that the Grand Judge, Shigi-khutughu, at the time of the surrender of Jungdu (present-day Peking), the capital of the Jurchen Chin, refused to take bribes from top officials of the enemy. He said, "Formerly Jungdu belonged to the Jurchen Emperor. But now it belongs to Chinggis Khan. How can one take the treasure of Chinggis Khan and give it to others secretly?"[90] This proper behavior was greatly appreciated by the Khan. These and many other examples show that Mongolian society honors the fruits of work but not vain words.

Conclusion

The above incidents and items from the *Secret History* and the *Altan tobchi* give clear insight into the traditional moral and ethical values of the Mongolian people. Later, following the development of Buddhism, the collapse of the quasi-feudalistic system, the development of nationalism, and the socialistic revolution, new attitudes and values brought great cultural change among the Mongolians. The people are, however, still Mongols and though they face new circumstances, many traditional values continue under new forms.

Notes

1. In this paper all quotations from the *Secret History of the Mongols (S.H.)* are free translations of the author himself based upon the *Ssu-pu ts'ung-k'an* edition of the *Yüan-ch'ao pi-shih*.

2. The quotations from the *Altan tobchi (A.T.)* are also free translations from the *Altan tobchi (nova) (Scripta Mongolica* I, Harvard-Yenching edition). The author also has partially translated this text into Chinese and published it in *Bulletin*, no. 2, of the China Council for East Asian Studies, 1963, Taipei.

3. *S.H.* 1.

4. Ibid., 2.

5. Chao Hung (趙珙), *Meng-ta pei-lu* (蒙韃備錄) *Kuan-chih* (官制) section, *Meng-ku shih-liao ssu-chung* (蒙古史料四種) edition, 10b.

6. *S.H.* 119.

7. Ibid., 201.

8. The name *Temüjin* is used in this paper to denote events which took place before the title Chinggis Khan was assumed.

9. *S.H.* 80.

10. Ibid.,103.
11. P'eng Ta-ya (彭大雅), Hei-ta shih-lüeh (黑韃事畧), Meng-ku shih-liao ssu-chung edition, 12b.
12. The last words in the reply of the Great Khan Güyüg to Pope Innocent IV, Bertold Spuler, History of the Mongols, 9. See also the letter sent to the Pope by the Mongol general Baiju and handed over to the Dominican Ascelinus. Cf. Eric Voegelin, "Mongol orders of submission to European Powers," Byzantine 15, (1940–41), 289. See Denis Sinor, "The Mongols and Western Europe," A History of the Crusades, vol. III (ed. by Kenneth M. Setton and Harry W. Hazard, Wisconsin, 1975), 519–20.
13. S.H. 70, 78.
14. A.T., 2:2.
15. Also known as Teb-Tenggeri, son of Menglig of the Khongkhutan. See Francis W. Cleavers, "Teb Tenggeri," UAJ. 39 (1967)
16. S.H. 244.
17. Ibid., 242.
18. Ibid., 72, 73.
19. Ibid., 69, 246.
20. Ibid., 103.
21. Ibid., 62.
22. Ibid., 66.
23. Ibid., 82.
24. Biography of Meng-su-ssu (孟速思), Yüan shih, 142:16b.
25. S.H. 64.
26. Ibid., 55, 56.
27. Ibid., 110.
28. Ibid., 146. According to Yüan shih, 106, Khada'an seems to be Ha-ta huang-hou (哈荅皇后) of the Fourth Ordo of T'ai-tsu (Chinggis Khan).
29. S.H. 147.
30. A.T., 1:96–106.
31. S.H. 194.
32. Ibid., 197.
33. A.T., 2:19.
34. Ibid., 20.
35. S.H. 85. This proverb has been a puzzle to many scholars. A. Mostaert has presented a discussion on this matter in his Sur quelques passages de l'Histoire Secréte des Mongols (HJAS 13, December 1950), 311–13.
36. The Biography of T'u-t'u-ha, Yüan shih, 128:14a.
37. S.H. 19, 22.
38. "The Biography of T'u-yü-hun," Wei shu, 101:12a.
39. Yao Ts'ung-wu, (姚從吾) "Ts'ung A-lan niang-niang che-chien hsün-tzu shou-tao K'e-e-lun t'ai-hou ti hsün-chieh Ch'eng-chi-ssu-han (從阿闌娘娘折箭訓子說到訶額侖太后訓戒成吉思汗)," Ta-lu tsa-chih (大陸雜誌) vol. 22, no. 1 (1961).
40. S.H. 77,78.
41. A.T., 2:134–35.
42. Ibid., 137.
43. Ibid., 140.
44. S.H. 53, 58.
45. Ibid., 59.
46. Ibid., 133, 154.

47. Ibid., 102.
48. Ibid., 113.
49. Ibid., 199.
50. Ibid., 214.
51. Ibid., 103.
52. Ibid., 82–87, 146, 219.
53. Ibid., 68, 69, 72, 73, 168, 204, 245, 246.
54. Ibid., 204.
55. Ibid., 117.
56. D'Ohsson (according to Rashid al-Din) Chinese tr.,1:69.
57. *S.H.* 238.
58. Ibid., 246.
59. *A.T.*, 2:62–64.
60. *Shih-huo-chih* (Monograph on Economy), *Yüan shih*, 93:2b.
61. *Hsing-fa-chih* (Monograph on Law), *Yüan shih*, 102:2b.
62. Ibid., 1ab.
63. *A.T.*, 1:104–5.
64. Ibid., 2:67.
65. *S.H.* 118.
66. Ibid., 244–45.
67. Ibid., 254–55.
68. Ibid., 205.
69. Ibid., 243.
70. Ibid., 70–72.
71. Ibid., 130–33.
72. *A.T.*, 2:67.
73. Ibid., 2:19–20.
74. Ibid., 2:30.
75. *Hsing-fa-chih* of the *Yüan shih*, 102:3a.
76. *A.T.*, 1:104–5.
77. Ibid., 2:19–20.
78. Ibid., 2:87–88.
79. *Chinggis Boghda-yin durasghal-un tegübüri* (Peking, 1926), 41–42.
80. *S.H.* 149.
81. Ibid., 185.
82. Ibid., 200.
83. *Chinggis Boghda-yin durasghal-un tegübüri*, 42.
84. *A.T.*, 2:57–58. See *Chinggis khaghan-u chidagh* (Peking 1927) 75a.
85. *S.H.* 93.
86. Ibid., 136.
87. Ibid., 201.
88. *A.T.*, 2:59.
89. Ibid., 2:65.
90. *S.H.* 252.

Chapter 5

Some Notes on the Horse Policy of the Yüan Dynasty

(This article was originally coauthored with Charles R. Bawden and published in *Central Asiatic Journal*, December 1965, 10:246–68)

The importance of the horse to the peoples of the north-central Asian steppes can hardly be overestimated. Its economic and military value is well-known. It provided the nomadic people with transport and food for daily life, and in time of war gave them the mobility to concentrate their forces against the settled peoples of the agricultural areas, to attack and to withdraw at will, and to reorganize and to reinforce themselves if defeated. Further, autumn, the time when the farmer is occupied with the harvest, was also the best time for the military exploitation of the horse which is then in its peak condition. The nomadic people were enabled to campaign at a time most profitable to them and most inconvenient to the enemy. The value of the horse to the nomadic people is expressed very succinctly by *Yüan shih:*

> Yüan arose in the northern areas. By nature they are good at riding and archery. Therefore, they took possession of the world through this advantage of bow and horse.[1]

Though the account goes on to say that such phenomenon can hardly have occurred in former times, it must be evident that this statement is not true merely of the Mongols. It is also true of other nomadic peoples who attacked China previously with greater or lesser success. However, in this paper we will limit ourselves to Mongol imperial times basing our remarks on evidence from the *Secret History of the Mongols* and later writings.

Numerous passages of the *Secret History* and other texts bear witness to the basic importance of the Mongol's horse. It was needed for moving, herding, hunting, fighting, and as a source of drink. In early times it was even a source of meat. The horse was traditionally considered the first of the five categories of domestic animal, the *tabun khoshighun mal*. We mention as examples of the horse's importance the following.

1. *Secret History* 3, in enumerating the ancestors of the Mongols, lists Torkholjin Bayan with the name of his wife, the name of his servant, and the colors of his two horses. His epithet *bayan,* rich, appears to rest upon his possession of the two good horses singled out for mention.

2. *Secret History* 90. When Temüjin and his brothers were nearing manhood and were improving their lot, they owned eight horses and a ninth which was used for marmot-hunting. When the eight were stolen by enemies, Temüjin and his future companion Bo'orchu risked their lives to recover the horses. This memorable episode is recorded not only here and in other chronicles such as *Altan tobchi,* but also in Chinese sources.[2]

3. *Secret History* 99. For lack of a horse Temüjin's wife had to be transported by an ox-cart at the time of an attack by the Mergid and she was subsequently captured.

4. *Secret History* 168. Weakness in the horses could serve as a pretext for avoiding unwelcome meetings. Chinggis was able to stay away from a treacherous meeting planned by Ong Khan on the grounds that it was spring and his horses were too thin and must first be fattened. Juvaini records a similar excuse made by Batu to avoid meeting Oghul Ghaimish to elect a new Khan after Güyüg's death.[3]

5. *Secret History* 131. The man chosen to hold the horse for Chinggis at a potentially dangerous meeting was a specially trustworthy companion — his brother Belgütei.

6. *Secret History* 124. When Temüjin became Khan, his first concern was to appoint his trustworthy companions, Belgütei and Kharaldai, to look after the geldings, while three other trusted men were appointed to oversee the horse herds. This action, together with the control of sheep and carts instituted at the same time, appears to mark the beginning of the mobilization of resources which ultimately allowed the Mongol expansions to take place. Moreover, indicating how seriously the care of the animals was taken, the *Keshig* or bodyguard of the Yüan emperors, while of high rank and responsible for acting as government officials, remained hereditarily responsible for looking after the imperial horses as *ulaghachi, morinchi,* and *kötöchi.*[4]

The above examples point to the practical importance of the horse. We should mention also two ceremonial uses of the horse among the Mongols.

1. According to *Secret History* 141 the swearing of an oath was confirmed by cutting a stallion and a mare through the middle. Centuries later the treaty of alliance between the Kharachin Mongols and the Manchus was similarly confirmed by the killing of a white horse and a black ox.[5]

2. When a Mongol emperor died, the body was prepared in an especially elaborate manner. Then a shamaness would ride a horse before the coffin, wearing new clothes, and leading another horse with a gold-ornamented saddle and bridle and covered with *na-shih-shih,*[6] and called the *Chin-ling-ma,* "Golden spirit horse."[7]

Mongolia's richness in horses is well testified. *Yüan shih* says:

> Because in the ten thousand *li* of the steppes they pasture and breed horses, the imperial horses can hardly be numbered.[8]

Meng-ta pei-lu (蒙韃備錄),[9] a report by Chao Hung who came to Mukhali's army and met him in 1221, is more explicit. In its section on horse policy, *Ma-cheng,* it states:

> The land of the Tatars is rich in water and grass and suitable for sheep and horses. In the first year or two after birth their horses are ridden hard and trained in the grasslands. Then they nourish them for three years and afterwards ride them again. Because they were trained early on they do not kick or bite. Herds are formed of thousands or hundreds, yet they are quiet, with no neighing. When they dismount, they do not need to tie up the horses. They will not stray. Their nature is extremely good. In the daytime they never feed them with fodder. Only when night comes do they let them out to pasture. They pasture them on the steppe according to where the grass is green or withered. When morning comes they saddle and mount them. They never give them beans or grain at all. When they go on campaign every man has several horses, and they alternate horses daily. For this reason the horses never get exhausted.[10]

A text of a slightly later date, *Hei-ta shih-lüeh,*[11] refers to the reign of Ögödei Khan (r. 1229–41). Of the Mongols' horses, it records:

Their horses graze on the steppes and without fodder. In the sixth month they eat green grass and become fat. When the strong ones get four teeth they geld them, and so they become broad and strong and powerful. They are tame and do not have a bad character. They can put up with wind and cold. If they are left a long time without being gelded, then it is just the opposite. Moreover, they are [then] easily startled and cannot be managed. The horseshoes are thin, and for fear of stones they plate [the hooves] with iron or board, and call this "foot-rough," *chiao-se* (脚涩).[12] When they run quickly they do not let them eat their fill. When they take off the saddles they tie them with the head looking upwards to wait for their breathing to calm down and for the hooves to get cold. Then they let them go to water and grass. The herdsmen are called *wu la ch'ih,* [*ulaghachi*].

To this account the commentator Hsü T'ing adds:

I examined the horse-raising methods of the Tatars. From the beginning of spring they stop fighting. All the good horses used in the war they let go free to water and grass, and do not allow them to be ridden or moved. Only when the west wind is about to blow do they take them and tie them up. They tether them around the tents and feed them with a very little water and grass. After a month the fat drops away and they ride them. They will not sweat over several hundred *li*. For this reason they can bear long distances and campaigns. Ordinarily while they are moving they do not allow them to eat water and grass. If in their exertions they do eat water and grass, this does not go to fat but causes sickness. This is a good method of raising horses. The Southerners [i.e., Chinese] do the opposite and therefore there is much sickness amongst their horses. Of the male horses they keep the really good and strong ones as stallions[13] for breeding, and the rest of them are gelded. Therefore there are none which are not strong. The ungelded ones are put to look after the groups of mares, and never join the groups of geldings. The geldings and the mares form groups apart. Mostly a herd of horses consists of four to five hundred head. Each herd has only two *ulaghachi* to look after it. They hold a "cock-heart iron"[14] in their hands to beat them with instead of a whip. When the horses catch sight of this they are afraid. Every morning and evening each *ulaghachi,* leading the horses in his charge, stands before the owner's tent for a while, and then they disperse. When they water the horses, their wells are sufficient only to water four to five horses, and there is an order of precedence. They come slowly, drink their fill, and go away. Then the next ones come. If one jumps his turn, the *ulaghachi* will flourish the iron and beat it. They will bow their heads and stop. As for the mares, each stallion will kick and bite her and make her come back. If the stallion of some other herd comes and trespasses, then the stallion of the herd will kick and bite him and make him go away. They each distinguish and control their own. This is very interesting.

Later on the text reports:

Their armies consist of the men from fifteen upwards. They have cavalry but no infantry. Every man has two to three mounts or six to seven mounts. Each fifty riders form a unit.

To this Hsü comments:

When I travelled in the steppes, I never saw anyone walking. As for the army heads, each man rides one horse and has five or six, or three or four, horses following him as a rule, to be ready for an emergency. Even the poor have to have one or two.[15]

We have gone into some detail in quoting these early records to illustrate the ideal state in a war-like nomadic society and to contrast it with the situation in China later in the dynasty. A greater abundance of horses existed in the steppes than under the Yüan dynasty when Mongol soldiers are reported to have no horses at times, and a requisition could produce as few as forty-seven horses from a whole province.

When we turn our attention to official records, we find that the "Military Monograph" of the *Yüan shih* provides only the most general information about horse-management policies.[16] It begins by noting the various offices established for horse management.[17] Then it limits itself to an enumeration of horse-grazing areas,[18] to information about the branding of horses and about the use made of horses for food, enjoyment,[19] and religious sacrifice.[20] What it records clearly demonstrates the continuing "Mongolianness" of the ruling family in China, at least as far as their attitudes toward the horse were concerned. We mention this only briefly, and intend to concentrate rather on another facet of Yüan horse policy, namely the extraordinary procurement of horses for military purposes. This, strangely enough, is not dealt with in the military monograph's section on horse policy, but much interesting information can be obtained from an independent text entitled *Ta-yüan ma-cheng-chi* (大元馬政記) "Records of the Horse Policy of the Great Yüan Dynasty"). This is a collection of official documents put together during the Yüan dynasty, but apparently unknown to the compilers of *Yüan shih*, though *Hsin Yüan-shih* makes some use of it in its "Military Monograph." Its colophon informs us that the text was examined in 1887 by Wen T'ing-shih, who wrote:

> This copy is copied from that of Miao Hsiao-shan [also Miao Ch'üan-sun 1844–1919], apparently a copy by Hsü Hsing-po [also Hsü Sung 1781–1848]. Now the copy [of what, is not clear] is kept in the *Han-lin Yüan* (翰林院). These two volumes have been lost.

K'o Shao-wen, compiler of *Hsin Yüan-shih*, adds: "The *Ma-cheng* of *Yüan-tien-chang* (元典章) is too short, so how fortunate it is that we have these two volumes."

Further information about the book was kindly supplied by Professor Yao Ts'ung-wu (姚從吾) who wrote that it was preserved in *Yung-lo ta-tien* (永樂大典), whence Hsü copied it in 1809. The edition from which the present manuscript copy was made comes from the *Kuang-ts'ang-hsüeh-ch'ün ts'ung-shu*, edited by Chi Fo-t'o (also Chi Chüeh-mi), and printed in Shanghai in 1916. It was reprinted in 1937 by the Wen-tien-ko (文殿閣), Peiping, in the series *Kuo-hsüeh wen-k'u* (國學叢書).

The manuscript consists of 28 unnumbered folios, each of 121 columns of a maximum of 32 characters.

The Military Horse Policy of the Yüan Dynasty

Two horse management problems seem to have faced the Mongols during and after their occupation of China, and two facets of imperial policy can be distinguished. On the one hand, while a large part of Southern Sung, China remained unsubdued, it was necessary to deny horses to the Chinese as far as possible to prevent illicit trade and smuggling. On the other hand, the Mongol emperors once established in China found themselves having to deal with rebellions from within their own ranks and in outlying areas. To try to cope with rebellions such as those of Arigh-bukha, Khaidu, and Nayan and to restore unity to the empire in areas where horses were still plentiful and military mobility superior, they demanded periodic and extraordinary levies of horses from the population of China itself.

Operations southward

The earliest record in *Ma-cheng-chi* concerning operations against China dates from the reign of Ögödei. His main objectives were to maintain the horses (partly realized by ordering the manufacture of standard troughs), to establish a firm boundary between Mongol-held territory and China, and to establish an intermediate zone between the two territories in which horses were not to be used except by certain classes of people.

The relevant texts are as follows.

First, from the section *Ma-cheng tsa-li* "(馬政雜例), Various Regulations Concerning Horse Policy:"

An Imperial Decree of the 24th day of the 6th month of the 4th year of T'ai-tsung huang-ti [1232], commanding the collector T'o Tuan and others:

Now at present there is a deficiency of horse troughs, except in Tung-sheng, Yün-nei, and Feng-chou.[21] There are, according to an examination of the families under the control of this *lu* [i.e., Hsi-ching lu] altogether 1627 families. Each family shall make one trough, 5 feet long, 1 foot 4 inches wide, Mongol style. Everywhere they shall prepare carts and oxen and before the 10th day of the 7th month shall send them in and hand them over to the Camp. There must be no delay or disobedience. If anyone offends he shall be punished by *aldashi*. Approved.

Second, from the same section, "Criminal regulations:"

An Imperial Decree of the 6th month of the 2nd year of Chih-yüan (1265). To the *Chung-shu-sheng*:[22]

Referring back: previously, Khaghan Huang-ti [i.e., Ögödei] and Meng-ke huang-ti [Möngke Khan] frequently issued Imperial Decrees to forbid anyone to take horses and smuggle them across the frontier. In recent years, too, this has been forbidden, but it has never ceased. Now along the frontier zone persons both good and bad are riding horses irregularly, and the military officials supervising the border and the civil officials controlling the people have not been paying attention to forbidding or preventing this, and so men who do not fear the law are smuggling [horses] over the southern frontier and thereby assisting the enemy. So unless the entry-points along the frontier are blocked, we fear that many officials and people will be executed.

We command all the army staffs[23] and the commanders of the ten thousands controlling the fighting to prohibit this firmly, and further we determine that in the area south of the Yellow River, eastwards from T'ung-kuan[24] up to Ch'i-hsien,[25] the people, — i.e., Buddhists, Taoists, scholars, Christians, Mohammedan teachers, Uighurs, Jurched, Kitans, Chinese of Ho-hsi [i.e., Tangut], Koreans, and all manner of workmen, hunters, merchants, prostitutes, innkeepers, and men without duties in offices — are not to ride horses, and, no matter what manner of person they are, they are not to use horses either for pulling carts, turning millstones, or ploughing the land. And in addition, at all the big and small ferries along the Yellow River, officials are to be dispatched to patrol and prevent this. Mongols, Chinese soldiers and messengers, and persons working in the offices may ride horses, but even so they must produce evidence to be examined, with the seal of their superior officers, and only then may they go, but apart from this, no one without a document to serve as evidence may take horses and pass the Yellow River and ride or sell them.

From Ch'i-hsien to Yi-chou[26] all is put under *Shu-mi-yüan*[27] and we order more military posts to be set up and constant patrols made. Except for the Mongols and the Chinese soldiers and those who are allowed to ride horses along the frontier, those not permitted to ride horses are, within three days from the day when this Imperial Decree arrives, to take the horses they have now and sell them in the market or to the offices of their own *lu* according to the regulations, at a suitable regulated price for the times.

If anyone rides a horse contrary to these regulations, or conceals horses, or passes off [others'] as his own, or uses them irregularly, all must report this, and those people must be arrested and taken into custody and examined, the truth got, and the guilty are to be executed. The horses are to be examined and valued, and the price given to the informer. A list is to be drawn up of those permitted to ride. We command that this be done.

[There follow details of the officials permitted to use horses and the number of horses allowed them.]

Regular horse procurement

In its introductory paragraphs, *Ma-cheng-chi* speaks of the regular exactions of horses and sheep made from the people in ordinary times.

As for the people's horses, there is a percentage system. When the number reaches 100, one is taken. If it reaches 30, one is taken likewise. If less than this they are exempt. It is the same with cattle and sheep. The places where this percentage applies are 15 in all. Should there be military operations and horses be lacking at the frontiers, then they shall be commandeered at an official price to supply the emergency. This is not the ordinary system.

It is not absolutely clear from this text how the regular exactions were calculated, since thirty horses seem to have attracted the same tax as one hundred. Moreover, some modifications of the system seem to have taken place at different times according to certain decrees found in the section *Ch'ou-fen yang-ma* (抽分羊馬), "Taxation of sheep and horses."

Thus, a decree of Ögödei's, dated in the fiftieth year of T'ai-tsung (1223) states:

From those families which have horses, cattle, and sheep up to 100 head, there shall be taken by the state one mare, one cow, and one ewe. Where the mares, cows, and ewes reach ten, one mare, cow, and ewe shall likewise be taken.

This decree may be compared with the exactions of one sheep per hundred mentioned in the *Secret History* in a context where Ögödei is expressing his intention to treat the people kindly and to spare them want.[28] The rate of exaction is sharply increased in an imperial decree of 1250, dated by the reign of Ting-tsung, Güyüg Khan.

Imperial Decree received, directing one horse, sheep, or cow to be taken from ten in the herds of people of every sort.

Though this decree is dated from Güyüg's reign, it actually refers to the regency of his widow Oghul-Ghaimish, during which the affairs of the state fell into disorder and taxes were notoriously misapplied.[29] Though the numbers in these two decrees are not too easy to interpret, they may point to confusion in the tax system, while in the following decree, dated 1252, the second year of Hsien-tsung, Möngke Khan ordered exactions at the rate of one animal per hundred and may reflect Möngke's policy of sparing the people as much taxation as possible.[30]

Special requisitions of horses for military purposes

The compulsory buying or commandeering of horses at official prices for special purposes is dealt with in two sections of *Ma-cheng-chi*, i.e., in *mai-ma* (買馬) and *Shua-ma* (刷馬). Compulsory purchases are mentioned as early as Ögödei's reign in a decree dated 1238 (tenth year of T'ai-tsung), but on this occasion the horses were needed not for campaigning but for reinforcing the post-stations to transport official goods and silks granted to the nobles. Oxen were priced at twenty *liang*. The price for a horse was fixed at thirty *liang*,[31] since horses were difficult to acquire in the southern *lu's*. Extraordinary purchases for military purposes appear to date from the beginning of Khubilai's reign. Though chronologically out of place here we quote from the *Shua-ma* section, a decree of Khubilai's reign dated 1293 (thirtieth year of Chih-yüan) which clearly and briefly characterizes the abnormal exactions.

Imperial Decree received. Apparently said: Because the rebellious princes [i.e. Khaidu and others] have not submitted, the time has now come for military operations. Collect 100,000 horses from all the provinces and give the price accordingly. Imperial agreement.

Later in 1310 (third year of Wu-tsung Chih-ta), a report from the *Ch'eng-hsiang* Beg-bukha stated that after discussion with officials of the *Shang-shu-sheng*[32] and *Shu-mi-yüan*, Chabar and the other princes and imperial sons-in-law of the western regions, who had not attended court for many years, were beginning to come to submit.[33] To strengthen their troops, stations, and material, it was suggested that a horse requisition be made, and Imperial agreement was obtained.

These two decrees, taken together, illustrate, firstly, the difficulties of the Yüan emperors when faced with rebellion from the north. They were deprived of access to Mongol horses and breeding grounds which were available to the enemy and aided his mobility. Secondly, they show that when the rebellious princes submitted without their territories, they too lacked horses and were unable to keep up opposition to the dynasty or to recover their lost lands.

The first decree of Khabilai's reign was issued in his first year, 1260 (first year of Chung-t'ung), to the *Hsüan-fu-ssu*.[34] The decree (text approximate) in *Ho-mai-ma* (和買馬) said:

On the day this decree arrives 10,000 riding horses are to be bought compulsorily in the *lu's* concerned. Excepting riding horses for officials on military duty, the regular soldiers on military duty, and persons going to court, all riding horses are to be registered and collected. According to the usual prices, one *ting* of silver should buy five horses, but at the actual time the price may be varied up or down. We need only fit horses.[35] Families with riding horses may retain one horse from five for the original owner to ride. Officials on active duty may also retain one horse. After compulsory purchase, registration, and branding are completed, the *durughachi* of the civil administration is to look after them and forward them to K'ai-p'ing-fu [i.e., the area around Shang-tu] and hand them over. Do not allow any to get lost or exhausted on the way. As for the price for the compulsory purchase, the officials of the *lu* concerned are to hand it over immediately without causing the people difficulties, regardless of what category [of account] it is in. Agreed.

[There follow detailed numbers of horses to be obtained from various *lu's*].

More direct mention is made of the military use for which the collected horses were destined in a further decree issued the following year. Again the text survives approximately in *Ho-mai-ma*.

To the Branch *Chung-shu-sheng*. Just now Arigh-bukha has been defeated at Hsi-mu-tu nao-erh [Shimültü na'ur] and has retreated in disorder. Now we hear that in the north the snow is heavy, and they are coming back here again. Though it is not certain they will come, we must take precautions. If there are horses fit for riding, they are to be bought up at one *ting* per five head.

There follows the following document.

The same day, a further Decree was received. To the *lu's* of Hsi-ching, Hsüan-te, and Pei-ching.[36] Make compulsory purchases of horses. Fit horses are to be bought at one *ting* of silver for five head. Horses thin and unfit for riding are also to be registered. Let the original owners keep these and look after them. If they are to be used later, they shall be bought according to the regulations, too. Get them when needed. Do not delay. If favor is shown or bribes taken, or horses concealed or omitted, then those who hide them or show favor or take bribes shall be punished according to military law. The fit horses received are to be handed over to the dispatched officials and distributed to the Mongol foot-soldiers to ride. If there are surplus horses for riding, report this to the throne.

Comparing the decrees of these two years we may note a growing desperation, for unfit horses also are included in the registrations. Moreover, the existence of Mongol foot soldiers who need horses contrasts sharply with the reports mentioned earlier of the richness in mounts of the Mongol armies in the early part of the thirteenth century. We may mention here also the first document in the section *Shua-ma*, a report of *Shu-mi-yüan* dated 1275 (Chih-yüan 12), requesting permission, which was granted to collect twenty-five hundred horses to give to the infantry troops commanded by Yesüder and others.

To illustrate the purchasing process implied in the documents in the *Ho-mai-ma* section, we quote rather fully from an imperial decree of 1289 issued by Khubilai (twenty-sixth year of Chih-yüan). This decree was an answer to a report by the *Shang-shu-sheng* and was received by the *Ping-pu*.[37]

The money for the compulsorily purchased horses has already been checked, dispatched, and officials sent to bring it to each place to be handed over. We have drawn up a list of what is to be done, and We command the *Hsüan-wei-ssu*[38] of each *tao* and the *Tsung-kuan-fu* of each *lu*[39] to appoint their main officials to do

the purchasing jointly [with these officials] and further, the documents are to be forwarded to their subordinates. Do as above.
1. [Places and amounts of paper money listed].
2. Appoint the *Hsüan-wei-ssu* of each *tao* and the *Tsung-kuan-fu* of each *lu* to make the compulsory purchase jointly [with the dispatched officials] and all the fit horses belonging to all the officials of the *Hsüan-wei-ssu, An-ch'a-ssu*,[40] *Chuan-yün-ssu*,[41] *Tsung-kuan-fu*, and all *yamens*, to the Buddhists, Taoists, Mohammedan teachers, Christians and *O t'o*,[42] regardless of whether they are military or civilians or whatever sort of people they are, are all to be compulsorily bought and immediately branded, and the proper price determined and immediately given to the owner.
3. Each *jamchi* [post-rider] may have one main horse and keep two supplementary horses. The remaining horses are to be bought as above.
4. When the dispatched officials bringing the money arrive, it is to be received and checked against the amount and reported to the *sheng*. The responsibility as to whether the affair is carried out quickly or slowly, and whether the horses are good or weak, will rest upon the officials of the *Hsüan-wei-ssu* and of each *lu*.
5. Buy fit horses of four years and above. Even if they are older, if they are fat and strong and fit for work, they are likewise to be bought.
6. If powerful and influential families conceal horses or shelter [others'] horses, punish them with 107 blows. The horses are to be confiscated.
7. If short value is given instead of the proper purchase price, or official monies are misapplied, and someone informs, or it comes through officially, this must be reported and punished severely.
8. If the officials of the various offices carry out the matter expeditiously and the horses are fat and good, this must be specially considered and reported to the Throne. If there is any negligence and the horses or the numbers are unsatisfactory, they are to be punished.
9. The numbers of horses bought [except in certain localities mentioned] are to be made up into transports of one or two hundred. Appoint and dispatch capable main officials to manage the forwarding to the capital and the handing over in succession. The offices through which they pass during the transport must supply men to lead the horses according to the regulations. The transporting officers are to feed and water them at the proper times. Do not let them get weak or thin. In cases of sickness, the official on the spot is to send immediately for a vet to treat them. If, when compared with the degree of fatness when first acquired, they get thin and weak, or die on the way, the transport officer must provide compensation and be punished.
10. When the horses have been bought, open registers and list the [owners'] names, color and age, degree of fatness, and price, and report to the *sheng*.
11. The original horses of the families of *Tanmachi*[43] and *Tangut Turkhugh*[44] are not included in this requisition. But they are not to buy the horses of others. If there is any offence, the seller and the buyer are each to be given 107 blows and the horse and the price are to be confiscated.
12. If the purchase money now dispatched is not enough, report at once to the *sheng*. If the money dispatched is not all used up, the appropriate amount is to be returned.
13. The price of horses is to be established according to *Chung-t'ung* paper money:

Each gelding	Best quality	5 *ting*
	Middle "	4 "
	Low "	3 "
Each stallion	Best "	4 "
	Middle "	3 "
	Low "	2 *ting* 20 *liang*
Each small horse	Best "	3 "
	Middle "	2 *ting* 25 *liang*
	Low "	2 "

Four days later a further order was received by the *Ping-pu* which included mention of a notice to be displayed in Ta-tu (Peking) and elsewhere to inform the public of the purchases. It was evidently necessary not only to remind the officials of the penalties for evasions, but also to encourage them by admitting past abuses and promising reform.

In previous requisitions of horses the price to be paid was not all paid exactly. In the present requisition the *Ping-pu* is to draw up clear prices and send officials to pay money over to the owners face to face. We fear that some horse-owning families may not come and hand over their horses to the office and will conceal them, or that influential and powerful people may conceal horses and shelter [others'] horses on this pretext.

The penalties enumerated in this order seem to have increased in severity for they provide equal punishment for neighbors on each side of an offender. One paragraph of the public notice defines those officials allowed to keep their horses.

Officials of 2d rank and above may keep	5 horses.
" " 3d " " "	4 "
" " 4th and 5th ranks " "	3 "
" " 6th and 7th ranks " "	2 "
" " 8th rank and below " "	1 horse.

Four years later, in 1293, in an order by *Chung-shu-sheng* (thirtieth year of Chih-yüan), the numbers of horses which officials actually on duty might retain was reduced, while even fewer horses were allowed to officials not actually on duty.

1st rank	5
2d "	4
3d "	3
4th and 5th	2
6th and below	1

Until 1293 horses seem to have been bought by public money set aside for this purpose. However, in a report of that year by the *P'ing-chang cheng-shih*[45] Tege and Nachin a suggestion was made. After discussion with the *Shu-mi-yüan* and *Yü-shih-t'' ai*[46] it was determined that officials in receipt of salary should contribute money for the purchase of ten thousand horses.

The horse requisitions must have caused personal dislocations and difficulty for the people of China, but adverse economic side-effects are also suggested in various documents. A report in the *Ho-mai-ma* section from the *Ch'eng-hsiang* Sang-ke[47] and others, dated 1289 (twelfth month of the twenty-sixth year of Chih-yüan), i.e., the same year as the decree mentioned in detail above — proposed moderation in the collection of horses from the Chinese cities in the Fu-li area.[48] If all horses were purchased, the result would have been to remove horses from that part of North China. He asked that only the geldings and stallions be bought, not mares, and this was agreed.

The requisitions appear to have caused other economic difficulties. In 1293 a report was made (thirtieth year of Chih-yüan) by the *Chung-shu p'ing-chang cheng-shih* Tege and Nachin.

In previous horse collections, all were sent to the capital by the same way, and all the horses were crowded together and made a nuisance for the people, and trod down the rice-fields. Further, many died. Now, wherever the horses are collected, let them be driven by the shortest route.

An order in 1295 (first year of Ch'eng-tsung Yüan-chen), recorded in the section *Ma-cheng tsa-li*, was issued by the *Chung-shu-sheng* at the request of the *Ta-ssu-nung-ssu*[49] and was also directed to the welfare of the people. It forbade those in control of military horses to let horses go about by themselves or to eat up or tread down and ruin mulberry trees, fruits, lands, and crops. Offenders were to be punished.

Finally, as recorded in the section *Ch'ou-fen yang-ma,* in 1303 (seventh year of Ch'eng-tsung Ta-te), at the request of the *Lien-fang-sze*[50] of the *Yü-shih-t'ai*, the *Chung-shu-sheng* commanded the *Ping-pu* to forbid the sheep and horse collectors from disturbing the *chou* and *hsien* administrations and upsetting the people every year. It was requested that the *Hsüan-hui-yüan*[51] make strict regulations for this purpose.

It appears from a report of the *Ch'eng-hsiang* Wan tse (Öljei)[52] and the *P'ing-chang* Sai tien chih[53] and others, dated 1298 (second year of Ta-te), that five special requisitions of horses were made during Khubilai's reign under the category of *shua*-collections. However, these can hardly have been carried out with complete success, for the final requisition produced only seventy thousand horses instead of the one hundred thousand required. The reason may be that the number of horse raising families had declined due to the requisition policy.

In fact it may be deduced from a selection of documents that the situation regarding horse procurement worsened in the latter part of Khubilai's reign. The first of these is an Imperial Decree of 1287 (twenty-fourth year of Chih-yüan) recorded in the section *Shua-ma*.

> According to a submission by Yang Tsung-t'ung.[54] Horses have already been requisitioned from those Buddhist monks, Christians, Taoists, and Mohammedan teachers of North China who had them. Those south of the Yangtse have not yet been requisitioned. Now, what need have the monks and Taoists, sitting in their temples, for horses? Command Yang Tsung-t'ung to go with the dispatched officials and make the requisition jointly, and hand over [the horses] to the province of Chiang-Huai (江淮) and send them to Chen-nan-wang (鎮南王).[55] Report the number. Those who conceal them shall be punished and the informers rewarded.

and:

> On the 9th day of the 8th month of that year the *P'ing-chang* Sang-ke and others submitted: The Chiang-Huai Province reports: The monks, Christians, and Taoists south of the Yangtse always ride in sedan chairs when they go out, and there are few horsebreeders. In Hangchou city 100 horses were requisitioned, and in the rest of the territory south of the Yangtse the requisition has been completed. Altogether 1,503 horses [have been requisitioned]. Hindu, the Tsung-

kuan of Huai-an lu,[56] was dispatched to convey them to Chen-nan-wang, and the hand-over has been completed.

Chiang-huai Province	1206 horses
Chiang-hsi "	140 "
Fu-chien "	47 "
Hu-kuang "	290 "

The second document was a report to the throne in 1288 (twenty-fifth year of Chih-yüan) by the *Hu-pu* (Final Ministry)[57] of the *Shang-shu-sheng*. It recommended that in the area of Lung-hsing-fu horses must be requisitioned by the feudal lords and immediately given to the army moving north. Those who concealed horses should be punished much more severely than before, i.e., they should be beheaded and the head displayed on the city gates. This was agreed. Yet from this requisition, with its stern penalties, only 143 horses were obtained and handed over to the army.

Third, in a document from *Chung-shu-sheng* to *Yü-shih-t'ai* dated 1293 (thirtieth year of Chih-yüan), recorded in the *Shua-ma* section, the buying and selling of horses was specifically prohibited.

At the beginning of the fourteenth century the great rebellions subsided, and the material, as recorded in the section of *Ho-mai-ma*, ends with the reign of Ch'eng-tsung. However, later documentation is still available in the section *Shua-ma*, showing that requisitions continued. In 1317 (fourth year of Jen-tsung Yen-yu) a report by the *T'ai-shih-yu-ch'eng-hsiang* Temüder[58] was accepted by the emperor. The largest horse collection recorded is an order of 250 thousand. No reason is given for this large requisition. It may have been for purposes of reinforcement. After this, only relatively minor requisitions were made. The last records are from 1329 or 1330 (first year of T'ien-li). However, by the end of the period with which we are concerned, the character of the collections appears to have changed. Horses were collected not so much for their military use as for their fine appearances. A report in the introductory part of our text, contemporary with its composition, states that horses of various colors and of fine appearance, of which details are given, had to be sent in, and that the emperor would sit in his palace and watch them.

Conclusion

Our material permits us to consider only briefly the horse management policy of the Yüan dynasty inside China, as exercised in the areas centering on Ta-tu. Even after the collapse of the rebellions and the reestablishment of imperial control over the grass lands of Mongolia up to Karakorum, no material concerning the horses of Mongolia is to be found amongst the decrees recorded in *Ta-yüan ma-cheng-chi*. Hence, our account of the horse policy of the Yüan dynasty is necessarily limited in this respect. The only direct mention of Mongolia itself occurs in the earlier, introductory part of the text. It is recorded that in 1323 (third year of Ying-tsung Chih-chih) an Imperial Decree demanded the collection of one thousand horses every third year from the *aimaghs*, to be given to the *Shang-ch'eng-ssu* (上乘寺) for use in imperial processions and for persons working in the palace. Thus, it appears that horses for imperial use were still brought from Mongolia. The next year (first year of T'ai-ting) a report by Hun Tan stated that there were great losses of horses in the *aimaghs* and asked for the purchase of ten thousand to replace them.

What we have shown by this brief survey of selected documents is the significance of the horse from the Mongols' military, economic, and religious points of view. The

Mongols were able to establish their empire because of the abundance of their horses, as is illustrated by our early texts. Having established the empire they were unable, from the imperial center in China, to acquire enough horses to support a regular and realistic horse policy which would have given them the constant mobility necessary to act successfully against rebels and to retain the unity of the empire. Without horses, Mongol armies, whether imperial armies or those belonging to weary rebellious princes, were unable to assert their powers fully. The Mongols, having conquered China with the horse, soon lost their superior mobility which could have given them control over the whole empire.

Notes

1. *Yüan shih* (Po-na edition) 100, *Ping-chih* (Military Monograph) 3, 1a.
2. *Yüan shih* 119, *Chuan* (Biographies) 6, and *Yüan-wen-lei* (元文類) 23, *T'ai-shih kuang-p'ing chen-hsien-wang pei* (太師廣平真憲王碑).
3. J. A. Boyle, *The History of the World-Conqueror* (Manchester University Press, 1958), 263.
4. *Yüan shih* 99, *Ping-chih* 2, *Ssu ch'üeh hsüeh* (四却薛) "The four keshig", fol. 2b.
5. *Altan tobchi nova*, 2:192.
6. *Na-shih-shih* or *nachid*. See *Secret History*, *chin-tuan-tzu* "gold brocade" and Boyle, 218 with a footnote referring to Pelliot, *Une ville musulmane dans la Chine du nord sous les Mongols*.
7. *Yüan shih* 77, *Chi-ssu-chih* (The Monograph on Religious Ceremonies) 6, 17b.
8. *Ping-chih* 3, 1a.
9. Edited, with *Hei-ta shih-lüeh* (黑韃事略), by Wang Kuo-wei (王國維), reprinted in Taipei, 1962, in *Meng-ku shih-liao ssu-chung* (蒙古史料四種).
10. *Meng-ta pei-lu*, 8b.
11. By P'eng Ta-ya (彭大雅) commented at about the same time by Hsü T'ing (徐霆).
12. *Hei-ta shih-lueh*, 18b–19a. The use of boards for horseshoes, unusual among the Mongols, is confirmed in a note by Wang Kuo-wei: "In the *Wu-tai shih-chi ssu-i fu-lu*, Kan Chü-hui was sent to Yü-t'ien [Khotan] and reported: From Kan-chou westwards one begins to cross the desert-wastes. The Kan-chou people told the ambassadors of Chin to make 'wooden-rough' *(mu-ssu)* shoes for the horses' hooves. The shoes have four holes, and in the horses' hooves they also bore four holes and tie them together. The camels' hooves they wrap in yak-skin, and then they can go. Tu Fu (杜甫) says in a poem: 'The good horses have newly bored hooves.' Hence by T'ang times people must have done this."
13. *Yi-la ma* (移剌馬), glossed as *kung ma* (公馬).
14. *Chi hsin t'ieh* (鷄心鉄).
15. Ibid., 19ab.
16. *Ping-chih* 3, *Ma-cheng* (馬政).
17. Fol. 1r-1v. In 1263 Khubilai established the *Ch'ün-mu-so* under the *T'ai-fu-chien* (太府監). This was raised to *Shang-mu-chien* (尚牧監), then to *T'ai-p'u-yüan* (太僕院) and then the name was changed to *Wei-yü-yüan* (衛尉院). This *yüan* was abolished and the *T'ai-p'u-ssu* (太僕寺) established under the *Hsüan-hui-yüan* (宣徽院) and later put under *Chung-shu-sheng* (中書省). These offices administered the horses of the great imperial *ordo*

or inheritance. [The term *ordo* is discussed in a long article entitled *Ordo-kao* by Yanai Watari in his *Mokoshikenkyū* (蒙古史研究), 663-768.]

18. "East beyond Tan-lo [part of Korea], north past Huo-li-t'u-ma [uncertain location], west to Kan-su, south including Yünnan, fourteen places in all." These places are enumerated later under the heading Tung-lu "Eastern Route," leaving open the possibility of the existence of further areas.

19. "When the court went to Shang-tu, the head of the *T'ai-p'u-ssu* and his subordinates all accompanied it and drove the horses outside the Chien-te gate. They took the fat ones which could be milked with them, got rid of the weak and thin ones and sent them back to the herd. From the Emperor to the royal princes and officials, all set up tents of *t'o lo* (脫羅) felt to act as milking halls. When the court returned to the capital, the head of *T'ai-p'u-ssu* sent messengers in advance to collect horses for fifty *yün-tu* (醞都) to come to the capital. *Yün-tu* is the name for a cart holding milk. When the horses came, the *Ha-ch'ih* (哈赤) and *Ha-la-ch'ih* (哈剌赤), acting as court officials had to feed them personally and brew black [i.e., pure] mares' milk to offer as the imperial food. This was called 'fine milk.' Every *yün-tu* had forty mares. For each mare the officials gave one bundle of fodder and eight *sheng* of pulse, and for each colt one bundle of fodder and five *sheng* of pulse. If the pulse was expensive it was to be made up with half of millet [hsiao-tao 小稻]. The royal princes and officials and below also had a ration of mares' milk. The number of *yün-tu* was as before, but the horses were cut down by one fourth. This was called 'course milk.' The fodder and grain were taken each ten days from the *Tu-chih-ssu* (度支寺) and the officials checked every ten days also to examine whether the horses were fat or thin." N.B. For *Ha-la-ch'ih* as the name of the man who looked after the royal mares prepared good koumis see *Yüan shih* 128, "Biography of T'u-t'u-ha (土土哈)." An explanation for *ha-ch'ih* is lacking. For *T'ai-p'u-ssu*, see, as well as *Ping-chih* 3, *Yüan shih* 90, *Pai-kuan-chih* 6. It was placed under an official of the second rank and has charge of the imperial geldings. There was a further office called *Shang-ch'eng-ssu* (上乘寺), under an official of the third rank, which also controlled the imperial saddles and bridles, carts, geldings, mules, and so on. *Tu-chih-ssu* seems to be the same as *Tu-chih-chien* (度支監), *Yüan shih* 90, *Pai-kuan-chih* (百官志 Official's Monograph) 6. This office looked after the horses' fodder supplies.

20. From Khubilai onwards the imperial tombs had their own *yün-tu* and got mares' milk to provide for the sacrifices. This was called "The Mare-milking of the Golden Tombs" *(Chin-ling chi-ma* 金陵撒馬*)*. After five years all was given to the guards of the tombs.

21. Tung-sheng (東勝) is in present-day Muu-mingghan and Tümed, Yün-nei (雲內) in Sarachi (Tümed), and Feng-chou (豐州) in Tümed near Feng-chen.

22. *Chung-shu-sheng* (中書省). See *Yüan shih* 85, *Pai-kuan-chih* 1, fol. 2v. foll.

23. *T'ung-chün-ssu* (統軍司). See *Yüan shih* 86, *Pai-kuan-chih* 2, fol. 3r, which mentions the replacement of the *T'ung-chün-ssu* in Honan Province by a *Hsing-shu-mi-yüan* (行樞密院). Both bodies seem to have existed only in war-time.

24. T'ung-kuan is at the great eastward turn of the Yellow River in Shensi province.

25. Ch'i was established by Yüan as Ch'i-chou-lu under Honan Province. Now it is Ch'i-ch'un hsien.

26. Yi-chou in present-day southern Shantung province.

27. *Shu-mi-yüan* (樞密院). *Yüan shih* 85, *Pai-kuan-chih* 2.

28. Paragraph 279. From each herd, one two-year-old sheep was to be given for the imperial food, and from each one hundred sheep, one was to be given to the poor and needy of the same clan.
29. Cf. d'Ohsson, *Histoire des Mongols*, 2:251, and Boyle, 265 for her poor administration.
30. *Yüan shih* 2, *Pen-chi* (Annals) 2, *Ting-tsung pen-chi*, fol. 9b, mentions the extraordinary taxations carried out after Güyüg's death, though not directly referring to his widow, and says that Ögödei's system was thereby brought into confusion. The following chapter, 3b, describes the reform of abuses of the tax-system put into effect by Möngke Khan immediately.
31. Prices were later expressed in terms of paper currency and suffered from the general inflation. We see later that a good quality stallion was priced at five *ting* while a low quality stallion, in itself less valuable than a corresponding gelding, was priced at two *ting* twenty *lang*. Inflation of the paper currency is dealt with in *Yüan shih* 93, *Shih-huo-chih* 1 (食貨志 Economy Monograph) *Ch'ao-fa* (鈔法 Monetary System).
32. *Shang-shu-sheng:* (尚書省) *Yüan shih* 85, *Pai-kuan-chih* 1.
33. For Chabar's submission to the Emperor, see d'Ohsson, 3:520.
34. *Hsüan-fu-ssu:* (宣撫司) *Yüan shih* 91, *Pai-kuan-chih* 7. Apparently a temporary occupation administrative unit.
35. But in 1277 (fourteenth year of Chih-yüan) a command from the *Chung-shu-sheng*, recorded in the section *Ho-mai-ma*, ordered that horses of all sorts be registered and branded and then returned to their owners, whether blind, ulcered, glandered, or pregnant. Moreover, even the horses for pulling boats belonging to the *Ts'ao-yün-ssu* (漕運司 see *Yüan shih* 85, *Pai-kuan-chih* 1, 14a under *Ching-chi-tu ts'ao-yün shih-ssu* and 15b under *Tu ts'ao-yün shih-ssu*), that is, horses essential for the transport of rice in North China, were to be branded but returned for use as tug-horses for the time being.
36. Hsi-ching, in present-day N. Shansi, centering on Ta-t'ung, Hsüan-te in NW Hopei, centering on Hsüan-hua, and Pei-ching, the area of Juu-uda League, Inner Mongolia.
37. *Ping-pu:* (兵部) *Yüan shih* 85, 26b.
38. *Hsüan-wei-ssu:* (宣慰司) *Yüan shih* 91, *Pai-kuan-chih* 7, 4b.
39. *Chu-lu tsung-kuan-fu:* (諸路總管府) *Yüan shih* 91, 13b.
40. *An-ch'a-ssu:* (按察司) *Yüan shih* 86, *Pai-kuan-chih* 2, 30a-31a. See under *Su-cheng lien-fang-ssu* (肅政廉訪司).
41. *Chuan-yün-ssu:* (轉運司)*Yüan shih* 91, 9b-12a.
42. For *o t'o* (斡脫), *ortakh*, see Boyle, 209, n. 18, "a merchant who formed a commercial association with a ruler or great man." The word seems to refer to non-Chinese, Mohammedan merchants and moneylenders.
43. For *Tanmachi* see *Yüan shih* 98, *Ping-chih* 1, 2a.
44. For *turkhagh* see *Yüan shih* 98, *Ping-chih* 1, 2b. "The sons and younger brothers of the nobles and generals and commanders are taken to join the army and are called *chih-tzu-chün* (質子軍), also *t'u-lu-hua-chün*." In the *Secret History turkhagh* is a guard or body-guard of trustworthy companions. Hence, the *turckagh* seems to have enjoyed a traditionally respected position, even though composed at a later date of Tanguts as well as Mongols.
45. *P'ing-chang cheng-shih:* (平章政事) *Yüan shih* 85, 3a-3b.
46. *Yü-shih-t'ai:* (御史台) *Yüan shih* 86, 27bv.
47. Biography in *Yüan shih* 205, *Lieh-chuan* 92.

48. The area of North China under the direct administration of *Chung-shu-sheng*.
49. *Ta-ssu-nung-ssu:* (大司農司) *Yüan shih* 87, *Pai-kuan-chih* 3, fol. 2r.
50. *(Su-cheng) lien-fang-ssu:* (肅政廉訪司) *Yüan shih* 86, fol. 30r.
51. *Hsüan-hui-yüan:* (宣徽院) *Yüan shih* 87, 14a.
52. Biography in *Yüan shih* 130, *Lieh-chuan* 17.
53. Biography in *Yüan shih* 125, *Lieh-chuan* 12.
54. Biography in *Yüan shih* 202, *Lieh-chuan* 89, 3v. He was perhaps a Tibetan monk, named Yang-lien-chen-chia, and was appointed by Khubilai as *Tsung-t'ung* (Director General) of Buddhism south of the Yangtse. He is notorious for having dug up the tombs of the Sung emperors. See *Cho-keng-lu* (輟耕錄) 4, *Fa Sung Ling-ch'in* (伐宋陵寢 Digging of the Sung Tombs).
55. See *Yüan shih* 107, *Tsung-shih shih-hsi-piao* (宗室世系表) 12a. He was Toghon, the ninth son of Khubilai.
56. Now the northern part of Chiang-su province.
57. *Hu-pu:* (戶部) *Yüan shih* 85, *Pai-kuan-chih* 1, fol. 9r.
58. Biography in *Yüan shih* 205.

Chapter 6

Why the Mongolian Khans Adopted Tibetan Buddhism as Their Faith

(Originally published in *Proceedings of the 3d East Asian Altaistic Conference,* Taipei, 1969, 108–28)

In recent years the author has collected material on Mongolian-Tibetan relations. This work began with the relationship between the early Mongolian empire and the Tibetan Sa-skya-pa theocratic regime. If this relationship had not existed, the history of these two people would have developed differently. Of all the problems inherent in this relationship, the problem concerning why the Mongolian khans selected Tibetan Buddhism as their faith seems to be the most interesting one.

Before the Mongols made any contacts with peoples of other cultures, their religion was pantheistic Shamanism, a faith common to the nomadic North Asian peoples. It was easy and natural for the people of the steppes of North or Inner Asia to humble themselves before the blue sky hanging above their heads and the boundless open earth lying under their feet. Their lives and welfare depended on the mercy of Heaven and Earth. Consequently, Heaven *(Tenggeri)* and Earth *(Etügen)* became the first objects of worship. Of course, this followed a pattern of religious thought common in Eastern Asia. In particular, it is similar to the Chinese idea of *Huang-t'ien Hou-t'u* (皇天后土), the kingly Heaven and queenly Earth. The personified or deified heaven, *Möngke Tenggeri* or Everlasting Heaven, was the highest of all gods. All heavenly spirits were deities, but they could not share the glory of *Möngke Tenggeri,* the supreme god. Men and women who could be in contact with or communicate with *Möngke Tenggeri, tenggeris,* and other spirits were known as *bö'es* and *idügens* in Mongolian. The men of god who could communicate with *Möngke Tenggeri* were usually honored with the title of *Teb Tenggeri,* or *Kao-t'en-jen* (告天人) in Chinese, which means "the Heavenly reporter." Kököchü, the ambitions *bö'e* who was finally liquidated by Chinggis Khan, is an example of an honored *bö'e* who had the title of *Teb Tenggeri.*[1] The duty or the power of a "Heavenly reporter" was to tell or explain *ji'arin,* the "will of Heaven," to the people and pray for the khan.[2]

Following the expansion of their empire, the Mongols began to make contact with many foreign religions. However, from the Mongols' traditional point of view, different religions were nothing but branches of their traditional pantheistic teachings. Different objects of worship were merely additional deities among the shaministic gods. If foreign priests, monks, or *khojas* were willing, like the Mongolian *bö'es,* to communicate with Heaven and pray for the khan, they would be honored as *bö'es.* The more priests or *bö'es* that prayed for the long life of the khan and the tranquility of the people the better. Therefore, the Mongols had no hostility toward foreign religions but treated them all equally and with honor. Because of their pantheistic beliefs, the Mongols felt no necessity to sustain one religion and oppress another. Moreover, in the doctrines of the outside religions there was, more or less, the call to honor Heaven. Therefore, their masters, leaders, or elders were recognized by the Mongols as *kao-t'ien-jen's* and were treated as mediators between Heaven and men. This may explain why Ch'iu Ch'u-chi, Ch'ang ch'un Chen-jen (邱處机長春真人), the great leader of the Taoist Ch'üan-chen sect (全真教), was warmly welcomed and greatly honored by Chinggis Khan in his camp at Snow Mountain.[3]

The Mongols made it clear to the leaders of every foreign religion that unless they could win support from the Mongolian rulers, they would meet a terrible fate which might be the end of their religion. As a result, religious leaders not only accepted the Mongols' demand that they pray for the khan and the state, but also tried hard to win the Mongolian rulers' sympathy and support. Even though very old, the Chinese Taoist leader, Ch'iu Ch'u-chi, had to travel thousands of miles from home to pay homage to Chinggis Khan in the "Western Region," and the Tibetan lama, Sa-skya Pandita, the fourth great master of the Sa-skya-pa, also had to come personally to the camp of Kötön,[4] the commanding prince of the Mongolian forces in the area of Ch'in (Shensi), Lung (Kansu), and Tibet.

The Mongols, who started from a small, unknown nomadic tribe, but who in a very short time established themselves as conquerors of the world, could not avoid mingling with foreign cultures and different ways of life. Therefore, they had to select those new things which would be useful. This attitude applied to foreign religions. As contact with such religions increased, the Mongolian rulers began to feel that their originally simple and primitive religion could not match the foreign religions which had profound philosophical teachings and magnificent rituals. They felt that their religion was not adequate to the spiritual needs of world conquerors. This may be one of the reasons why different members of the Mongolian ruling class at one time or another adopted Buddhism, Christianity, or Islam. But why, among so many religions, did the Mongolian khans of the Yüan dynasty in China choose Tibetan Buddhism as the royal religion and honor the lamas of the Sa-skya-pa as imperial instructors — *ti-shih* (帝師)? Besides the reasons usually given by monks and clergymen, such as "by affinity" (*irügel* in Mongolian and *yüan* 緣 in Chinese), "the will of God," or "the destiny decided by Heaven," there should be a historical and cultural rationale.

In his later days Chinggis Khan divided his land and people among his sons and brothers. He bestowed the native land of Mongolia on his youngest son, Tolui, and the lands of Central and Northwest Asia on his other three sons, Jochi, Chaghadai, and Ögödei. The princes of Tolui's family, therefore, had a hereditary economic tie with North China. As a consequence they were more or less influenced by Chinese culture.

Shigi-khutukh, the *yeke jurghuchi* of the Mongolian empire of Chinggis Khan's time and the lord governor of North China during Ögödei's reign, was the only important person among all the Mongolian ministers and generals who had any deep concern for China's agricultural land.[5] Also in Ögödei's time, the *yeke bichigchi* or "prime minister,"[6] Yeh-lü Ch'u-ts'ai (耶律楚材), was a great protector of Chinese culture during the Mongolian occupation of North China. This man was known as a leading Confucianist and devoted Buddhist. Both Prince Möngke and Prince Khubilai of Tolui's line, who were soon to become emperors of China, may have been influenced by these two ministers.

Among Chinese religious leaders, the Taoist Ch'ang-ch'un furthered his Ch'üan-chen sect in China through the personal honors that Chinggis Khan bestowed on him, but he did nothing to influence the religious development of the Mongols. Another great leader was the Buddhist monk Yin Chien (印簡) known by the honorific title Hai-yün Fa-shih (海雲法師).[7] According to his biography in *Fo-tsu li-tai t'ung-tsai* (佛祖歷代通載) volume 21, he received the title *kao-t'ien-jen*, "Heavenly reporter," from Chinggis Khan through the recommendation of Mukhali,[8] the commander-in-chief of Mongolian forces in North China. Later, in the year *hsin-mao* (1231), he had further gifts bestowed upon him by the *Khaghan* Ögödei. Again, in the year *ting-yu* (1237), he received the honorific title *Kuang-t'ien chen-kuo ta-shih* (光天鎮國大師), "Great Master of Glorifying Heaven and Pacifying the State," from the second Empress of the Emperor T'ai tsu (Chinggis Khan). However, the most meaningful thing that he did and the most important to later history was his preaching of Buddhism to Khubilai at the latter's princely residence in the year of *jen-yin* (1242). Through this preaching the monk not only won Khubilai's sympathy and support for Chinese Buddhism, but also succeeded in planting the basic truths of Buddhism in the heart of the future khan which finally made him receptive to Buddhist teachings and led him to favor Buddhism over other religions. In Yin Chien's biography it states:

> In the year *jen-yin* (1242) the Great Prince Khubilai invited the Master to his pavilion and asked him about the general ideas of the Law of the Buddha. At first the Master explained the teaching of men and Heaven, and the relation between cause and effect. Next he explained several key words of the Law to open the Prince's heart. Then faith grew in the heart of the Prince, so he asked for the disciplined heart of a bodhisattva.
>
> At the time Secretary Liu Ping-chung[9] was in the service of attendance [to the Prince]. [The Prince] again queried, "Does the Law of the Buddha provide the way for the world to enjoy tranquility?" The Master said, "In the realm of the Law it provides life to the four kinds of living beings.[10] These facts are all included in the realm of the Law of the Buddha. In this realm the four universes[11] are merely as small as a bit of dust in the great earth. Then, how small would the four seas[12] be? However, as for the tranquility or unrest of a state, everything depends upon the joy or suffering of the people. The making of joy or suffering or peace or danger has to depend upon politics. Of course, it also depends upon the will of Heaven. . . . In the teaching of the Law of our Buddha, the function of the Court has already been pointed out clearly. It is neither easy nor difficult, but it might be impossible for Your Highness, the Prince, to practice. It would be better to invite wise men and learned scholars from all parts of the realm to query them about the history of tranquility and the decline of states, now and then. Your Highness may learn something by listening to them."
>
> The Prince asked again, "Among the three religions [Buddhism, Taoism, and Confucianism] which one is the most honorable, which law is the best, and which is the outermost?" The Master answered, "Among all sages only Buddhist monks are not tricky. Therefore from ancient times, Buddhism has always been held above the others. Consequently, according to the Royal Decree of the

Imperial Ancestor, the Empress Mother[13] proclaimed that Buddhist monks should stand at the head and that no Taoist priest should be allowed to be placed before a monk."

The Prince bestowed upon him a pearl coat, golden silk, and a seamless garment, and honored him as his instructor. The Prince asked him to stay, but the Master insisted on leaving. Before his departure the Prince asked, "After you leave, how shall I keep the Law of Buddha?" The Master said, "Faith is difficult to grow. Good will is not easy to develop. Since it has emerged, it is important to hold it fast with all your heart. Please do not forget the heart discipline of a bodhisattva. Do not find fault with the Three Jewels [Buddha, Law, and Community of Monks], and always be mindful of the sufferings of the people. Rule them and pacify them kindly. Promotion and punishment should be just and fair. Administration should be carried out without prejudice. Use good men and take correct advice. Every task should be useful and practical in its time. Always do beneficial works for others. These are the Laws of the Buddha."[14]

From the above it is evident that the Chinese monk Yin Chien had explained to Khubilai why Buddhism was necessary for a ruler. During the political unrest after the death of Ögödei Khan, the monk's suggestions seemed to have been accepted by the ambitious young prince who was earnestly trying to find some way to re-establish good order and effective administration in the empire. From the above passage words such as "Faith is difficult to grow. Good will is not easy to develop. Since it has emerged, it is important to hold it fast with all your heart," and "faith grew in the heart of the Prince; so he asked for the disciplined heart of a bodhisattva," show that Khubilai already had some faith or strong interest in Buddhism well before Yin Chien's departure. Also, the biography mentions the presence of Liu Ping-chung who was then a Buddhist monk and later became one of the important establishers of the state in the Yüan dynasty. Since his job was to attend the young prince, he had ample opportunity to influence the prince toward the teachings of the Buddha. All these things could happen to Khubilai because the territory of Tolui's family was situated in the eastern part of the Mongolian empire. In Hsing-chou,[15] especially, a well known city of high civilization in North China in the personal territory of Sorkhaghtani Beki Khatun,[16] the mother of Möngke Khan and Khubilai Khan, there was a good chance for the princes of this family to become acquainted with famous Chinese scholars and monks.

Struggles between the Taoists and the Buddhists are legendary in Chinese history. Chinggis Khan bestowed special honors on Ch'ang-ch'un Chen-jen and accorded special privileges to Taoist priests and temples. This was because the Khan himself had very little understanding of or concern for Chinese culture and had no prejudice for or against any Chinese religion. Therefore, this learned and talkative Taoist "immortal," who dared to discuss philosophical problems with him, won his trust and rich gifts. Had he not done so, the khan would not have been more favorable to the Taoists than to the others, and he would have not allowed the temples of the Ch'üan-chen sect to be a refuge for North China scholars in wartime. However, this action of the great khan did not win applause from all Confucian scholars. For instance, the Sinicized Kitan Confucianist and "prime minister" of Ögödei, Yeh-lü Ch'u-ts'ai, was the one who complained against the "unrighteous activities" of Ch'ang-ch'un. This Kitan scholar endeavored to administer state affairs with Confucius's teachings and to govern the inner man with the Law of the Buddha. Under his administration Chinese culture and Confucian traditions were protected. However, in his famous work *Hsi-yu lu* (西遊錄), he expressed his dissatisfaction with Ch'ang-ch'un and even accused him of being a fraud. Thus, following the expansion of Taoist influence, the anti-Taoist feeling of Buddhists and Confucianists alike became more and more intense. From the records of *Chih-yüan pien-wei lu* (至元辨偽錄) it is easy to discover that the Chinese scholars who persuaded Khubilai to accept the teachings of Confucius, such as Yao Shu, Tou Mo, and Chang Wen-ch'ien,[17] were all important attendants or witnesses at the official debate between representatives of the two opposing religions. They were also united against the Taoists. In such an environment it was easy for Khubilai to favor Chinese Buddhism over Taoism.

Why the Mongols failed to adopt Nestorianism is another interesting question. Nestorianism was the first foreign religion known to the Mongols. Before Chinggis Khan came to power this "rebellious" sect of Christianity had already entered western and middle Mongolia through Syria, Western and Central Asia, and the land of the Uighurs. The Nestorian missionaries did win some converts from the Naiman and Kereyid tribes, but they failed to develop it into a common faith for the people. Sorkhaghtani Beki Khatun, daughter of a Kereyid noble and mother of Möngke Khan and Khubilai Khan, was a devoted Nestorian. The *Yüan shih* refers to her belief in Nestorianism as follows.

> On the *wu-yin* day of the ninth month, the first year of T'ien-li [1328] ... the Emperor commanded the Kao-ch'ang [Uighur] monks to perform the Buddhist ritual (fo-shih 佛事) at the Yen-ch'un Ko, and the *Yeh-li-k'o-wen* (也里可溫) to perform the Buddhist ritual at the Shrine Palace of Hsien-yi Chuang-sheng Huang-hou (莊聖皇后) [Sorkhaghtani]."[18]

> On the *ping-shen* day of the third month, the first year of Chih-yüan [1335], the ministers of *Chung-shu-sheng* (中書省) reported, "Now the mother of Emperor Shih Tsu [Khubilai], Pieh-chi [Beki] T'ai-hou (別吉太后), is worshipped in the *shih-tze ssu* (十字寺) of Kan-chou Lu, Kansu province.[19] The form of the ritual has to be decided." This was accepted [by the Emperor].[20]

In the above-mentioned passages the term "Buddhist ritual" is not used in its strict sense but refers to religious ritual in general, including the Christian ritual. *Yeh-li-k'o-wen* was the term used for Nestorian Christians,[21] and *shih-tzu ssu*, which meant "temple of the cross" in Chinese, was the term for Christian churches in Yüan times. These facts indicate that even in the latter Yüan, the Mongolian court was still treating the Christian faith of the Khatun with respect. However, the faith of Sorkhaghtani Beki Khatun did not determine the religious beliefs of her sons, Möngke and Khubilai. This suggests that pantheistic Shamanism was still the dominant religion of Mongolian society. The Mongolian royal family was, therefore, not bothered by the contradictory doctrines of the different religions. Besides, it is also easy to see that neither Western Christianity nor Nestorianism was suited to the cultural and social conditions — either nomadic or agricultural — of East Asia. The Christians gained some converts at the beginning, but Christianity was not finally accepted by the mass of the people. For instance, Nestorian Christianity, after being nomadized in Central Asia, once flourished among a part of the

Uighurs, Naimans, Kerityeds, and Ongguds. The pantheistic Mongols, however, were not bothered by the doctrines and worship practices of the Nestorians. Yet, the Nestorians' monotheistic teaching was too hostile to the pantheistic or shaministic tradition of the ordinary Mongol. Consequently, the Nestorians isolated themselves from the masses, and did not take root in the shaministic and polytheistic Mongolian society, as did polytheistic Buddhism. Nestorianism finally withered up without bearing any fruit. On the other hand, Christianity's failure may also suggest that the Christian priests in Mongolia, in personal ability, wisdom, learning, and virtue, could not match the famous Taoist Ch'ang-ch'un, the Chinese monk Yin Chien, the Kashmiri monk Na-mo, or the Tibetan lama Phags-pa. Thus, they were unable to win the confidence and support of the khans.

However, some Catholic scholars, basing their arguments on early missionary accounts, suggest that Möngke Khan did accept Christianity. No evidence for this can be found in either Chinese or Mongolian materials. On the contrary, the khan was a Mongolian traditionalist with little inclination toward Buddhism. This misunderstanding may have come from the fact that the khan, in accordance with his pantheistic traditions, allowed Christian priests to pray for him and to perform their religious ceremonies in his royal courtyard.

In the *Yüan shih,* volume 202, the "Biography of Monks and Taoists" *(Shih lao chuan),* it is recorded, "While the Yüan were rising in the north, they were already favorable to Buddhism."[22] This is documentary evidence of a growing attraction to Buddhism. The Biography of Yin Chien (Hai-yün) of the *Fo-tsu li-tai t'ung-tsai* volume 21, and volumes 4 and 6 of the *Chih-yüan pien-wei lu* mention that before the Yüan was established (1260) there were already many Buddhist monks working actively in the khan's court. It stands to reason that all these activities were not entirely in vain.

Among the Buddhist monks active at the pre-Yüan Mongolian court, Na-mo of Kashmir is especially noteworthy. In the "Biography of T'ieh-ke [Tege]," in the *Yüan shih,* it says:

> T'ieh-ke [Tege] . . . was a man from Kashmir. . . . Both his father O-t'o-chi [Otochi] and his uncle Na-mo [Namu] were disciples of the Buddha. One day the O-t'o-chi brothers said to each other: "The world is full of unrest, and our country is declining, but in the northeast there is the sign of the Son of Heaven. Why should we not go and follow him?" So they came together and were received by T'ai-tsung [Ögödei Khan]. Ting-tsung [Güyüg Khan] made Na-mo his instructor. . . . Hsien-tsung [Möngke Khan] honored Na-mo with the title of *kuo-shih* [國師 state instructor], bestowed upon him a jade seal, and appointed him to administer the Buddhist affairs of the empire."[23]

The great founder of the Buddhist faith in Tibet, Master Padmasambhava, also came to this Land of Snow from a country between Kashmir and Afghanistan where Tantra was popular. Padmasambhava was the founder of the old Red Sect, Snying-ma-pa, and later the Sa-skya-pa developed as a new focus for Tibetan Buddhism just before the Mongolian invasion. These two sects had some differences in their teachings and ceremonies, but they did not differ from each other as drastically as the later Yellow Sect differed from the old Red. Thus, the original doctrine of the Kashmiri lama Namu may from the very beginning have been relatively similar to Tibetan Buddhism. Namu's activities at the courts of Ögödei, Güyüg, and Möngke accomplished a great deal of pioneering work toward the later development of the Sa-skya-pa among the members of the Mongolian royal host. When Möngke put Namu in charge of Buddhist affairs, Namu found himself in an especially good position to enhance the development of Buddhism throughout the empire.

At the very time that this Kashmiri master was active in Karakorum, the Mongolian invasion and occupation of Tibet reached its climax. At the same time, the Sa-skya Pandita was preaching the Law of the Buddha at the camp of Prince Kötön, the supreme commander of the Mongolian forces in the Tibetan area. Khubilai was then on his way to campaign against Ta-li (Yünnan) and Tibet, and the young Phags-pa Lama, nephew of the Sa-skya Pandita, was acting as a kind of royal priest at Khubilai's palace. All these factors combined to further the progress of Tibetan Buddhism among the Mongolian nobles.

The Sa-skya Pandita's visit to Prince Kötön's camp was a highly important event in Mongolian-Tibetan history. It may even have had more historical significance than the talk between Chinggis Khan and Ch'ang-ch'un. During his stay at the camp the lama not only converted Kötön, but also provided Phags-pa with a chance to become acquainted with Khubilai, who eventually became the great benefactor of Tibetan Buddhism.

There is a story about Khubilai himself which may explain why he was so benevolently disposed toward Buddhism and came to trust the lamas. The biography of Tege in the *Yüan shih* says:

> Formerly, Shih-tsu [Khubilai] served Hsien-tsung [Möngke] and was very intimate. However, they became somewhat estranged because of some misrepresentations. The State Instructor [Namu] advised Shih-tsu to humble himself and be careful. Then they became harmonious as before. Afterwards, when the Emperor [Khubilai] was appointing Tege, he said, "I do this in order to reward the State Instructor."[24]

The background to this story is essentially as follows. While Khubilai was governing North China he trusted Chinese scholars to rule China according to traditional Chinese ways. This made the conservative Mongolian ministers of Möngke Khan's court very angry. They misrepresented the situation to the khan and caused him to suspect his brother's intentions. This unhappy story was also recorded in the biography of Yao Shu in the *Yüan shih*.[25] Under these difficult and embarrassing circumstances, Khubilai asked the Kashmiri lama to act as his intermediary and help him rebuild his brotherly ties with the khan, so that he could regain the political and military power that he would need if he were to have a chance for the throne. From this account we see why Khubilai was so well disposed personally toward the Buddhists.

As mentioned before, from the time of Ögödei Khan the Mongolian royal house had had contact with Buddhism, yet, why, from all the sects of Buddhism, did Khubilai select Tibetan Buddhism as his personal faith[26] and honor the master of Sa-skya-pa, Phags-pa Lama, as his instructor? Political reasons aside, cultural similarity between the Mongols and Tibetans and their common distance from the Chinese may have been the main factors which caused Khubilai to make this historic decision.

Mongolia and Tibet are high plateaus of Inner Asia. Their open arid steppes and their cold weather make them well suited for nomadism. Because of their similar geography,

Tibet and Mongolia have developed similar ways of life, forms of economy, and types of culture. There were cultural interactions between the Mongols and other Altaic peoples such as the Turkic Uighurs and Tungusic Manchus. Yet, the Mongols and Tibetans shared the same type of nomadic pastoralism. Therefore, from the perspective of cultural distance, it was still easier for the Mongols to mingle culturally with semi-nomadic Tibetans than with the agricultural Chinese. Similarly, other neighboring agricultural peoples around China, such as Koreans, Japanese, and Vietnamese, accepted more Chinese cultural influences than nomadic neighbors like Turks, Uighurs, Tibetans, and Mongols. This reflects a basic cultural differentiation between nomadism and agricultural life. Similarly, the religion which was acceptable to Tibetans, who had the same shaministic background, was also easier for the Mongols to accept.

It is true that Tibetan Buddhism has developed several great monastic centers, such as the monastery of Sa-skya-pa, the seat of Phags-pa Lama, etc. However, the abbots and monks in the monasteries and the people settled around them were still members of the old Tibetan pastoral society that held firmly to their nomadic traditions. This pattern occurred not only in Tibet. It was also evident in Inner and Outer Mongolia and in the Kansu and Kohonor Tibetan areas until the Communist occupation. This may suggest that on the one hand, Phags-pa and his disciples were great lamas or famous monasteries, and on the other hand, that they were also to some extent representing the traditional nomadic elements of Tibetan society. It is also true in Khubilai's case that he and his descendant were Sons of Heaven in the great city of Khanbaligh (Peking), while, at the same time, they were nomadic rulers from the other side of the Great Wall. Thus, the words of Tibetan lamas would be understandable and acceptable to members of the Mongolian ruling class.

From the time of the Mongolian empire to the day of the establishment of the Yüan dynasty, there were always two groups among the Mongolian leadership. One was inclined to expand the empire toward the west, and the other toward the south. The leaders predisposed toward the south were mostly interested in the Chinese way of life and culture. Khubilai was the leader of this group. They were always in opposition to the conservative Mongolian traditionalists who had more concern for the "Western Region." However, like other Mongolian rulers, Khubilai himself still held traditional Mongolian attitudes toward foreign cultures, despite his personal contact with Chinese monks and scholars and his interest in Chinese culture. This helps us understand why a pro-Chinese Mongolian ruler like Khubilai finally adopted Tibetan Buddhism as his religion and as the religion of his household and court. Moreover, from a Buddhist point of view, all the sects in Tibet and China were disciples of the same Buddha. The branch in Tibet, however, had deeper knowledge of Tantric teachings.

Originally, the primitive religious faith of Tibet, which was known as *Bon* or the "Black Faith," was a branch of Shamanism. Its priests, *bon-pos,* were similar to the Mongolian shamans, *bö'e.* Later, Sron-btsan sagam-po, the founder of the Tibetan empire, married Bal-mo khri-btsun, a Nepalese Princess, and Wen-ch'eng Kung-chu (文成公主), a Princess of the Chinese T'ang dynasty. With these marriages, Buddhist monks from Nepal and China arrived in Tibet to preach their Buddhism. However, the real development of Tibetan Buddhism came at the time of Khri-sron Ide-btsan. This ruler invited great teachers from India and Kashmir to his kingdom, and among them was the great master Padmasambhava. In the meantime, Chinese monks, following the way that had been opened to them by the royal marriage, also came to the Land of Snow. Unfortunately, the doctrines of the Indian masters and the teachings of the Chinese monks sometimes seemed to contradict each other, and this made it difficult for the Tibetans to decide which group was preaching the truth. Finally, according to some reports the Tibetan court ordered the two opposing groups to hold an open debate. The Tibetan authorities chose the Indian-Kashmiri group as the winner, and then sent the Chinese monks back to their homes and closed the door to Chinese Buddhism in Tibet. The victorious sect transcended the strong shaministic *bon-po* faith by its overwhelming "supernatural power," overcame the *bon-po's*, and molded them in its own fashion. In other words, the Tibetan Buddhists reconciled themselves to a degree to the original shaministic faith and accommodated the nomadic religious traditions of the Tibetans. Thus, we see how Tibetanized Buddhism fit into the nomadic culture of the "Land of Snow" much more naturally than the Sinicized Buddhism which had already accommodated itself to an agricultural civilization.[27]

In the "Annals of Shun-ti [Toghontemür]" in the *Yüan shih*, there is a story as follows.

In the twenty-second year of Ch'ih-cheng [1362], the Crown Prince [Ayurshiridara] was sitting in the Ch'ing-ning Palace, [and] many Tibetans and Korean monks were also seated in a long row. The crown prince said, "Mister Li Hao-wen[28] has taught me the Confucian scriptures for many years, but their meaning is still not too clear to me. Now I am hearing the Law of the Buddha, and I can understand it after only a night." Afterwards, the Crown Prince became more and more interested in Buddhist studies.[29]

This story took place at a time when the Yüan dynasty was almost a century old. Nevertheless, the Mongolian Crown Prince was still finding the philosophical traditions of Chinese scholars difficult to comprehend, whereas Tibetan Buddhism he found easier. This would indicate that Mongol acceptance or rejection of outside cultural elements largely depended upon the similarity of a given culture to the nomadic culture of the Mongols themselves. Also, it suggests that geographical proximity was no match for cultural distance.[30]

Notes

1. See *Secret History of the Mongols (S.H.)* 224–26. See F.W. Cleaves "Teb Tenggeri," *Ural-Altaishe Jahrbücher*, 1967, 39:248–60.
2. Ibid., § 121 and 244.
3. See Yao Ts'ung-wu's (姚從吾) paper, "Chinggis Khan's Trusting Chiu Chu-chi and Its Contribution to Preserving Chinese Heritage in the Early Stage of Yüan (1215–58)," *Bulletin of College of Arts*, National Taiwan Univ., no. 15 (August 1966).
4. Kötön, son of Ögödei. See *Yüan shih*, 107:7r. T'u Chi (屠寄) in his *Meng-wu-erh shih-chi* (蒙兀兒史記), 37, wrote a brief biography of him. The actual name of this Mongolian prince (Kötön) is a problem for the Mongolist. However, I believe this name was taken from the place name Khotan or Khotana which is now known as Ho-t'ien (和闐), Udan (兀丹) in the *S.H.*, and Yü-tien (于闐) in early times. In *Yüan shih*, 62:32r, it was written as Hu-t'an

(忽炭), which is another transcription of Khotan [See Feng Ch'eng-chün (馮承鈞), *Hsi-yü ti-ming* (西域地名), 44.] The Mongols customarily used place names as the names of their children. For instance, the name of the brother of Ködön, Khashi, or Ho-shih (合失) is evidently taken from the place name Ho-hsi (河西), "on the west of the Yellow River," which eventually was the Chinese name for the Tangut area. Therefore, that brothers might bear the names Khashi and Ködön, which geographically and economically are closely related to each other, is not difficult to understand.

5. *S.H.* 103. *Yeke jarghuchi* means "great judge," who in reality he was both chief justice and prime minister.

6. Yeh-lü Ch'u-ts'ai's officials Chinese title was *Chung-shu-ling* (中書令) which means prime minister. However, this term was only a loose translation of the Mongolian title *yeke bichigchi*, which means "grand secretary."

7. In Yüan times, the Chinese scholar Ch'eng Chü-fu (程鉅夫) wrote a biography of this monk entitled "The Inscription for the Pagoda of Hai-yün, Abbot Chien (海雲印簡和尚碑)," and this is included in his collection, *Hsüeh-lou chi* (雪樓集), 6.

8. "Biography of Mukhali," *Yüan shih*, 119.

9. "Biography of Liu Ping-chung (劉秉忠)," *Yüan shih*, 157.

10. Namely, living beings that are born from the womb, like men and animals; from eggs, like birds and fish; from moisture, like worms; and from change, like lives in heaven and hell.

11. In Buddhist teachings, there are four universes or four continents, and our world is only a part of one "continent," Jambudvipa.

12. "Four seas" is a Chinese term for China, its neighboring people, and lands in four directions. It is similar to the term *t'ien-hsia*.

13. For example, the wife of Ögödei Khan and the mother of Güyüg Khan, Törgene Naimanjin Khatun.

14. *Taisho Daizokyo*, vol. 49.

15. Hsing-chou (邢州), now Shun-te (順德) of Hopei Province.

16. There is a biography for this Khatun in *Yüan shih*, 116, although it is brief. T'u Chi in his *Meng-wu-erh shih-chi*, 19, has written a biography of her, which is a little better than the one in the *Yüan shih*. Lately, Liu Yi-kuang (劉義光) has published "Some Notes on the Mongol Chuang-sheng Huang-hou Sorkhaghtani (記蒙古莊聖皇后莎兒哈黑塔尼事)" in *Ch'u-pan yüeh-k'an* (出版月刊), no. 13 (June 1966).

17. Biographies of Yao Shu (姚樞), Tou Mo (竇默), and Chang Wen-ch'ien (張文謙) of *Yüan shih*, 157 and 158.

18. *Yüan shih*, 32, "Annals of Wen-tsung," 10b.

19. Now Chang Yeh (張掖) of Kansu province.

20. *Yüan shih*, 38, "Annals of Shun Ti," 14r.

21. See Ch'en Yüan (陳垣), "On *Yeh-li-k'e-wen* (也里可溫考)."

22. *Yüan shih*, 202, *Shih-lao-chuan* (釋老傳), 1a.

23. Ibid., 123, "Biography of Tieh-ko (鐵哥)," 13b.

24. Ibid., 14v.

25. This story is clearly recorded by Yao Sui (姚燧) the nephew of Yao Shu, in his work "The Inscription of the Tomb of Yao Wen-shien-kung, Deputy Minister of the Chung-shu-sheng (中書左丞姚文獻公神道碑)." See *Mu-an chi* (牧庵集), 15.

26. Some scholars doubt that Khubilai accepted Buddhism as his personal faith, and believe the assertion to be an exaggeration made by Tibetans lamaist historians. However, from the *Biography of the Imperial Instructor Phags-pa (Ti-shih Pa-ssu-pa hsing-chuang)* (帝師八思巴行狀), by Yüan Chinese scholar Wang P'an (王磐), in 1280, it is clear that Khubilai and his household accepted Buddhism. See *Taisho Daizokyo*, 49:707. For the personal relationship between the khan and the lama, see S. Jagchid's paper, "Khubilai Khan and Phags-pa Lama (忽必烈可汗與八思巴喇嘛)" in *Shih-hsüeh hui-k'an* (史學彙刊), vol. 2, August 1969.

27. At the time when the Mongols made their second conversion to Tibetan Buddhism, the Third Dalai Lama declared that he had overcome the gods and spirits of Mongolia and turned them into the protecting angels of Buddhism. See *Erdeni-yin Tobcih* (Ulan Bator edition, 1958, 1961), 242–43.

28. In the "Biography of Li Hao-wen (李好文)," *Yüan shih*, 183, his post is recorded as instructor to the crown prince, but there is nothing to this.

29. *Yüan shih*, 46:8b.

30. I offer my sincere thanks to Joseph Fletcher of Harvard University and to Hedehiro Okada of Washington University, both of whom kindly helped me with the manuscript and provided advice and criticism during their short stays in Taipei.

Chapter 7

Chinese Buddhism and Taoism During the Mongolian Rule of China

(Originally published in *Mongolian Studies, Journal of the Mongolia Society,* 1980, 6:61–97)

Chinggis Khan and the Buddhists

The purpose of this paper is not to discuss the religious faith of the Mongols themselves but to concentrate on the *relationship* of the Mongols to Chinese Buddhism and Taoism in the thirteenth century.

A difficult question to answer accurately is whether it was the Chinese Buddhists or the Taoists that contacted the Mongols first. According to available sources it seems that the Buddhists made the earliest contacts. When the Mongols invaded North China during the Jurchen-Chin dynasty, the famous monk, Yin-chien (also known as Master Hai-yün), had already made personal contact with the *Kuo-wang ("king of a state") Mukhali*,[1] Commander-in-chief of the Mongolian forces and the top Mongolian administrator in North China. Through this powerful leader's recommendation, Yin-chien received the honorable religious title *Kao-t'ien-jen* from Chinggis Khan. According to the Yüan monk Nien-ch'ang's account, *Fo-tsu li-tai t'ung-tsai,*[2] Master Hai-yün, sixteenth abbot of the Lin-chi Sect,[3] was born in the year *jen-hsu* (1202) and died in the year *ting-ssu* (1257). In his youth he was a disciple of Master Chung-kuan and was later received in audience by Chinggis Khan. The *Fo-tsu li-tai t'ung-tsai* records:

> When the Master was thirteen years old[4] [1214] Emperor Chinggis was campaigning in the realm under Heaven. Just then the Master was in Ning-yüan when the city fell. [The Master], among all the people, personally approached the presence of the Saintly [Emperor]. [The Emperor] advised him [to allow his hair to grow and] to wear a coil. The Master answered, "If [I] follow the style of the Nation [Mongols], I can not keep the style of a monk." Whereupon [The Emperor] made a decree allowing [him] to continue his original practice.

The *T'ung-tsai* continues:

> When the Master was eighteen [1219], the Heavenly troops approached again. *Tai-shih kuo-wang* [Mukhali][5] directed the troops to attack Lan-ch'eng.[6] All the people escaped and dispersed [but] the Master remained to serve Chung-kuan as usual. ... The next day, the city surrendered, and the honorable Shih Tien-tse[7] Marshal of Ching-lo and the honorable Li Ch'i-ko,[8] the Marshal of Yi-chow, discovered that the appearance of the Master was extraordinary ... [his] response and the answers were uncommon. So [they] honored Chung-kuan as a teacher, and firmly engaged in a gold and rock-like friendship with the Master. The *Kuo-*

wang put Chung-kuan and the Master under the direct rule of the Emperor Chinggis. . . . Chung-kuan rode in a light cart pulled by a yellow calf which the Master drove personally . . . and arriving in Ch'ih-ch'en[9] after one year . . . Emperor Chinggis issued an Imperial Decree to *Kuo-wang* Mukhali saying: "The old elder and the young elder, whom you reported to me through an envoy, are truly *kao-t'ien-jen*. Furnish them nicely with clothing and food, make them the head men, and take good care of them. Their purpose is to report to Heaven and nobody is allowed to disturb them. This has to be carried out [carefully] by the *darkhan*."[10] Upon receiving this Decree, the *Kuo-wang* bestowed upon them great mercy and invited them to stay [in the monastery of] Hsin-an hsiang-ch'üan-yüan. The *Kuo-wang* offered the title of *Tzu-yün cheng-chüeh ta-ch'an-shih* [慈雲正覺大禪師 The great guru of merciful cloud and real awakening to truth] to Chung-kuan, and [the title of] *Chi-chao yin-wu ta-shih* [寂照英悟大師 The master of the light of tranquility and brilliant understanding] to the Master. All their needs were supplied by the office. Thus, the name of the Young Elder began to be known. [When the master was] nineteen [1220], Chung-kuan . . . passed away. . . . [Later] the Master entered Yen [Peking] and stayed at [the monastery of] Great Ch'ing-shou-ssu . . . [Afterwards] the master moved from [one monastery] to [another, such as] Hsing-kuo, Hsing-an, and Yung-ch'ing of the Lai-yan[11] [area] and the Great Ch'ing-shou monastery [of Yen]. These were all instructed by the orders of *Tai-shih Kuo-wang* and other important ministers.[12]

By the time Hai-yün was thirteen, in 1214, Chinggis had been campaigning against the Chin for three years, and the Mongolian forces were besieging Yen (Peking). Consequently, Chung-kuan and Hai-yün had the opportunity to meet Chinggis Khan. The khan's tolerance towards the young acolyte and his master was probably due to traditional Mongolian Shamanistic practices. On the other hand, Hai-yün's bold refusal to obey the Khan's order might have actually pleased the Khan because of his disposition to honor a straight-forward person. However, the short visit had no further significance for Chinese Buddhism.

The Mongols occupied Yen (Peking) in 1215. In 1216 Chinggis, "conferring [the rank of] *Tai-shih kuo-wang* [on Makhali], allowed [him] to manage the lord-chancellor's affairs as though they already had imperial authorization, and decreed: 'On the north of the T'ai-hang [Mountains] We alone will rule; south of the T'ai-hang you [rule] your best.'"[13] In Hai-yüns eighteenth year, 1219, Mukhali sent Hsiao Temür from Yün (present-day Ta-t'ung) and Shou (present-day Shuo-hsien) to attack K'o (present-day K'o-lan) and Lan (present-day Lan-hsien).[14] Amid this great turmoil Hai-yün was discovered by Shih T'ien-tse and Li Shou-chung, Chinese military leaders under the Mongols, and they recommended him to their Commander-in-chief, Mukhali. Apparently, Mukhali had a good impression of both Chung-kuan and Hai-yün, for Mukhali recommended them to the Imperial camp and had them pray for the Khan. This recommendation was important both for obtaining Heaven's blessings for the Khan and to indicate the Mongols' concern for the religious activities of the Chinese subjects. Chinggis returned to Mongolia in the spring of 1215, too early for Hai-yün and his master to pay their respects personally to the Great Khan. Yet, Chinggis Khan decreed: "The old elder and young elder . . . are truly *kao-t'ien-jen*. . . . Make them the headmen, and take good care of them." From this statement one may infer that both master and disciple had already been recognized by the Khan as chief shamans and appointed headmen over Chinese Buddhist affairs. Consequently, they were given honorary Chinese-style religious titles of distinction.

Thus, it appears that Chinese Buddhist leaders had the earliest contacts with the Mongolian authorities. The words, "take good care of them [the Chinese Buddhists] . . . nobody is allowed to disturb them" together with the honor given them is sufficient evidence to confirm this. Judging from the style and wording, it appears that this decree was made orally, either by the Khan or by other high Mongolian authorities, and was translated into Chinese word by word. The decree is entirely different from the Khan's decree made later for the famous Taoist Ch'iu Ch'u-chi (印處机)

Chinggis Khan and Taoism

Chinese Taoism by this period had developed into two main streams, mainly because the political confrontation between the Jurchen-Chin and the Chinese Sung. To the north in the realm of Chin, was the Chüan-chen Sect (全真教) headed by Ch'iu Ch'u-chi, (also entitled, Ch'ang-ch'un Chen-jen, "the perfect man of everlasting spring"). To the south of the Yangtze River was the Cheng-yi Sect (正一教) led by Chang T'ien-shih (張天師), "The heavenly instructor," and his household.[15] In the early thirteenth century, there was still no need for the Cheng-yi Sect and its leaders to establish contact with the Mongols. However, due to the military threat of the Mongols, the Chüan-chen Sect was pressed to sue for the favor of the invaders. Ch'ui Ch'u-chi, head of the sect, was brought to the attention of Chinggis Khan by a Chinese courtier, Liu Chung-lu. In 1219, the Khan dispatched Liu to Shangtung to invite this famous Taoist to his court. The meeting took place during Chinggis's western expedition against Khorezm. It is unclear whether he wanted to meet the "Perfect Man" or whether it was due to a consistent Mongolian policy of summoning religious leaders whom they could reach.

Upon his arrival in Afghanistan Ch'iu Ch'u-chi immediately established friendship with Yeh-lü ch'u-ts'ai, an important Kitan scholar and statesman at the court of Chinggis Khan, who was emotionally attracted to Buddhism but intellectually espoused Confucianism for its political philosophy. This relationship soon deteriorated and Yeh-lü Ch'u-ts'ai later censured Ch'iu as a liar who misled the Khan. In his *Hsi-yu-lu* (西遊錄 *A Western Travelog*), Yeh-lü Chu-ts'ai used a purported dialogue with a visitor to express his negative attitude towards the Taoist leader.

> The guest asked, "Is it possible to hear how it was that Master Ch'iu came to an audience [with the Khan]?" The recluse[16] said: "Formerly, a person named Wen from the Liu family[17] came to the court [of the Khan] as a physician. He said, 'Master Ch'iu, who is now three hundred years old, has a secret way of nourishment for longevity,' and recommended him to the Throne."[18]

Yeh-lü Ch'u-t'sai evidently was skeptical of Ch'iu's claim to be three hundred years old. But, it is understandable that the "world conqueror" would anxiously desire an endless life. This desire of Chinggis was the same as that of the Emperor Ch'in Shih-huang-ti (r. 246–210 B.C.) and Emperor Han Wu-ti (r. 140–88 B.C.).

According to the late Yüan scholar, T'ao Tsung-yi's *Ch'o-ching-lu*, Chinggis Khan's decree to the Taoist Ch'iu Ch'u-chi was as follows.

As soon as [We] humbly discovered [you] *hsien-sheng* [teacher],[19] in [your] retreat in the old territory of Shantung, We limitlessly admired and were sincerely concerned about [you]. There are stories that [King Wen] invited [T'ai-kung Wang] to ride on his own cart at the Wei River,[20] and that [Liu Pei] visited the grass hut [of Chu-Ko Liang] three times.[21] However, with many mountains and rivers between [us], it is impossible for Us to fulfill the ceremony of welcoming you in person. But We will devoutly cleanse Our body with baths and eat vegetarian food. . . . [We] invite [you], the teacher, to condescend in your immortal steps and come to Us, notwithstanding the deserts and the remoteness. [You] may faithfully instruct Us for the sake of the people and the state, and sympathetically provide the nourishing method for Our body. We will serve you in person beside [your] immortal seat. We earnestly hope that even one phrase from the remnant of your spit may sustain [Us].[22]

Here, for the Chinese courtier, Liu Ch'ung-lu, the so-called "nourishing way for the body" was perhaps the only method to gain a promotion. To accomplish the purposes of the Khan and himself, Liu, as a special emissary, went in 1219 to summon the immortal Taoist from Shantung. The elegant Chinese decree that Liu delivered to the Taoist Master was very different from the one written in a pure Mongolian tone that the Khan sent to Mukhali regarding the Buddhist leader, Hai-yün. The Mongolian leaders had not yet been Sinicized and were yet unable to phrase their ideas in the style of the above decree. Therefore, the latter decree is somewhat suspect. It might have been altered by the envoy or by the Taoist recipients. The decree was very different in style from others found in the *Secret History of the Mongols* and from the Yüan colloquial decrees to both Buddhist and Taoist temples collected in the *Ta-Yüan sheng-cheng kuo-ch'ao tien-chang*.[23] Chinggis Khan did not have an appreciation of Chinese culture (as did his grandson, Khubilai), and certainly was unacquainted with Chinese historical anecdotes about Tai-kung Wang and Chu-ko Liang. Moreover, the expression of "devotedly cleansing Our body with baths and eat vegetarian food" is entirely out of character for a warrior hero of the nomadic world. The same is true of the notion that "even one phrase from the remnant of your spit may sustain Us."

Chinggis Khan's historic conversation with Ch'iu Ch'u-chi took place in the snowy mountains of Afghanistan. It was a novel chat between the world conqueror, who had spent his life at war and on horseback, and a religious leader, who lived a quiet life in retreat and mediation. Though the talk did not really satisfy the Khan, it did result in mutual understanding and respect and greatly influenced later historical events.

Taoist records assess the meeting as very successful. During the audience, Ch'iu Ch'u-chi was excused from the ceremony of bowing and was given the title *shen-hsien* (神仙), "the Immortal," by the Khan. In the *Ch'ang-ch'un chen-jen hsi-yu-chi* (長春真人西遊記), an account by Li Chih-ch'ang, a disciple who accompanied Ch'iu on his long journey, it is recorded that, "The Emperor . . . remarked to his followers, 'The Immortal explained the nourishing way of life three times and greatly impressed my heart.'"[24] However, in an account in the *Ta-Yüan Chih-yüan pien-wie-lu* (大元至元辯偽錄), written by the Yüan monk Hsiang-mai (祥邁), the story is somewhat different: "In the later part of the eighth month of the year *jen-wu* [122], Master Ch'iu arrived at the Imperial camp. All his answers to [the Throne] were quite common."[25]

The conversation in Afghanistan was summarized in the *Yüan shih*, as follows.

[Ch'iu] Ch'u-chi said that one who desires to unify the great realm under Heaven must not kill people. When [Ch'iu] was asked about a policy of rule, [he] answered that to honor Heaven and to love the people is basic. As for longevity and long reign, [he] stressed the purification of the heart and reduction of lust; and [Emperor] T'ai-tsu [Chinggis Khan] was deeply impressed by his words. . . . One day when it was thundering T'ai-tsu asked about this phenomena and Ch'u-chi answered, "Thunder is a warning of Heaven. Of the sins of man nothing is worse than being unfilial. Being unfilial [to parents] is disobedience against Heaven. Therefore, Heaven gives a thunderous warning. It is said that there are quite a few unfilial persons in the territory. Your Majesty should clarify the warnings of Heaven to guide the multitudes." This was accepted by T'ai-tsu. In the year *kuei-wei* [1223], T'ai-tzu commanded a grand-scale hunt in the east mountains and his horse stumbled. Ch'u-chi admonishingly said, "The way of Heaven is to have pity on living beings. The venerable age of Your Majesty is high, and is not suitable for hunting." Because of this T'ai-tsu stopped hunting for quite a long period.[26]

Ch'iu Ch'u-chi's comments seem reasonable considering Mongolian life and activity at the time. First, the injunction to stop killing was the general attitude of all religious persons, not merely the doctrine of the Taoist Chüan-chen Sect. Though a high moral standard, it was an impossible precept for Chinggis Khan who was then waging his Western Campaign. The Taoist's negative injunction was not supportive, and his comments were much different from the services and prayers of the later Imperial Instructors, Phags-pa Lama[27] and Master Chan-pa,[28] which advocated conquering the Southern Sung to shorten a bloody war. Consequently, the psychological influences on Mongolian leaders were also different. Second, Ch'iu's warning to honor Heaven was already the center of original Mongolian religious beliefs. Li Chih-ch'ang's record confirms this: "The Khan gathered the heir-apparent, the princes, and the ministers and said, 'The Chinese honor the Immortal just as you worship Heaven.'"[29] Therefore, advice to honor Heaven was acceptable and nothing new. Third, love for the people was the topic stressed. In fact, Ch'iu Ch'u-chi was pleading the cause of the people under Mongolian occupation. This may have been one of his purposes in traveling so far to visit the Khan. It was also the reason that he became so famous.[30] Fourth, Ch'iu spoke of thunder. To fear thunder was customary in Mongolian Shamanism and Ch'iu linked this with the problem of unfilial behavior, or disobedience to parents, an offence of which he considered the Mongols to be guilty. As a Chinese, misunderstanding nomadic culture, Li Chih-ch'ang wrote, "Now it is heard that according to the native [Mongolian] custom there is much unfilial behavior."[31] But it seems clear from the *Secret History* that the Mongols ordinarily emphasized obedience and honor toward their ancestors, parents, and elders. Chinese Confucian filial-piety was a matter of ritualistic obedience. Mongolian obedience and love toward one's parents were more emotional then ceremonial. Consequently, Mongolian filial piety was usually misunderstood by Chinese intellectuals. Ch'iu Ch'u-chi and his disciple Li Chih-ch'ang are a case in point. Fifth, Ch'iu's injunction to stop hunting was consistent with his own agrarian background, but such admonitions were lost on steppe nomads for whom hunting was a way of life. For instance, even the most

Sinicized Confucian ruler, the Jurchen Emperor Shih-tsung (Wan-yen Wu-lu, r. 1161–89), did not accept this view. He said, "This matter [hunting] is not understandable to scholarly [Chinese] vassals."[32] Finally, some Chinese historians suggest that Chinggis Khan's return from his western campaign was the result of Ch'iu Ch'u-chi's persuasion.[33] This seems improbable. In fact, Chinggis Khan's expedition against Khorezm was already successful and his return was the natural result.

Chinggis Khan's chief reason for meeting with Ch'iu Ch'u-chi was to learn the secret of longevity. Li Chih-ch'ang records:

> After settling in the hostel, [the Master] immediately went for an audience. The Emperor comforting [him] said, "[You] did not respond to the invitations from other countries, but traveled tens of thousands of miles to arrive [here]. We are greatly pleased. [The Master] replied, "The reason that [I], a person of the countryside, accepted the Decree to come was [the will] of Heaven." The Emperor was pleased and allowed [the Master] to be seated. After a meal [the Emperor] asked, "As a *chen-jen* ["the perfect person"] from afar, what kind of medicine of perpetual life do you have to help Us?" The Master replied, "There is a way to prolong life but no medicine for perpetual life as such." The Emperor appreciated his honesty and [ordered] two tents to be erected east of the Imperial Pavilion to accommodate the Master. [Later] the interpreter asked; "You are addressed as *Tenggeri möngke kümün*. Is that what you call yourself or do other people so address you?" The Master said, "It is not [I], a person of the countryside, who calls myself that. I am called that by others." The interpreter again asked, "What were you called in the old days?" [The Master] replied [to the Emperor], ". . . people of the world call [me] *hsien-sheng* [teacher]." The Emperor asked Chimkhai, "What should the perfect person be called?"[34] Chimkhai replied, "Some persons call [him] respectfully the teacher, the perfect person, or the immortal." The Emperor said, "From now on let [him] be called the immortal."[35]

It is not difficult to see that the Chinggis Khan's hope was to obtain the "medicine of perpetual life." His quest failed, but he was not distressed. He calmly approved of Ch'iu's honesty, thus, exercising self-control. Yet, because this famous Taoist had "not responded to the invitation from other countries but had traveled tens of thousands of miles" to meet Chinggis Khan, the Khan expressed his pleasure. It appears that he wanted to impress the Chinese, with whom he was actually waging a psychological war. In order to emphasize this fact, the Khan had his interpreter ask the Taoist whether the high title, *Tenggeri möngke kümün*, "the Heavenly everlasting person" was self assumed or whether it had been conferred on him by others. Apparently, the Khan was trying to find out whether the Taoist was an imposter.

In conferring a title on the Chinese visitor, the Mongolian monarch made a very careful choice among the three alternatives of "teacher," "perfect person," and "immortal" *(shen-hsien)*. From this one may infer that the conversation did not convert the Khan to the teachings of the Taoist, although he remained a supporter. This differed from the later conversion of his grandsons. Prince Kötön accepted the Sa-skaya Pandita as his teacher and Kubilai Khan made the Phags-pa Lama the Imperial Instructor of his realm. It is difficult to determine the original translation of the Chinese word *shen-hsien* into

Mongolian at this period. Nevertheless, it may have had a meaning similar to the Mongolian term *sakighulsun*, i.e., "godly spirit," "protecting spirit," "immortal," "fairy," or "deity." If so, it was compatible with Shamanistic beliefs.

The late Professor Yao Ts'ung-wu has discussed in detail the above "conversation on a snowy mountain" in his article *"Yüan Ch'iu Ch'u-chi nien-p'u"* (元邱處機年譜 The Chronological Biography of Ch'iu Ch'u-chi of the Yüan Dynasty).[36] However, this writer would like to point out several important accomplishments by both sides. For Ch'iu Ch'u-chi his leadership in the religious world was firmly guaranteed by the Khan. The Taoist priests and temples of North China were protected and exempted from tax and corvée duties. Through these special privileges Ch'iu was able to provide safe refuge for many intellectuals and others in the Taoist temples during troubled periods of the Mongolian conquest. Consequently, Ch'iu Ch'u-chi has been highly praised up to the present day. Chinggis Khan also achieved results from the meeting which supported his Mongolian strategy. The Jurchen Chin Emperor and officials of the Chinese Sung dynasty had invited the Taoist several times, but were all politely refused. Later, when he decided to visit Chinggis Khan, he explained to his followers, "Whether I go or stay is up to Heaven. It is not a matter understood by men. There will come a time when it will be impossible to remain uninvolved."[37] Then in his audience with the Khan he said, "The reason [I] . . . accepted the decree to come was because it was [the will] of Heaven."[38] Implicit in Ch'iu's reply was the notion that of those who invited him only Chinggis Khan was the true Son of Heaven with a Mandate to unify the universe, and the only sovereign to whom Ch'iu should pay his respects. In this manner Chinggis had achieved a psychological coup in his political propaganda.

The Taoist's traveling companion, Li Chih-ch'ang, recorded the events of Ch'iu's return trip to Yün-chung (present-day Ta-t'ung in Shansi).

> The Imperial envoy A-li-hsien desired to go to Shantung to appease the people through a proclamation [of pardon] and requested that the [Master's] disciple Yin Chih-ping accompany him. The Master said, "It is not yet agreeable to the will of Heaven. Even if you went, what would be the benefit?" A-li-hsien bowed and said, "If the *Kuo-wang*[39] approaches with heavy troops [many] lives will be destroyed. [I] wish the Master to say a word of mercy." After a long time the Master said, "Even if this cannot save them, it is still better than to sit and watch the people die." [He] then ordered Ch'ing-ho[40] to accompany the envoy, and gave them two statements for pacification.[41]

This is a good example of the cooperation of Ch'iu and his sect with the Mongols. By such activity both the Master and his sect established special prestige in North China. They did not oppose the Khan, and, moreover, publicized the Khan favorably. Further, the noted Confucian scholar, Yüan Hao-wen,[42] estimates that by the end of the Chin dynasty and the beginning of the Yüan, 20 percent of the population of North China was under the influence of the Chüan-chen Sect.[43] Thus, a good relationship between Chinggis Khan and the leader of this powerful group was a great victory in his campaign against the Chin.

Chinggis Khan's contact with Ch'iu Ch'u-chi was probably the Khan's first encounter with the cultivated, philosophical, religious leader, and he was obviously greatly impressed. Earlier the Khan had had brief contact with the Buddhist monk Hai-yün, but the Khan was no more favorably inclined to Chinese Buddhism as a result. Chinggis Khan could not have known of the long struggle between Taoism and Buddhism in Chinese history. Eventually, however, the Khan granted special privileges to the Taoist leader which enabled him to provide refuge for Chinese intellectuals in his Taoist temples. This action disappointed both Buddhist monks and Confucian scholars. The situation was clearly recorded by Yeh-lü Ch'u-ts'ai in his *Hsi-yu lu*. The expansion of Taoist influence stimulated the Buddhists to launch a counterattack during the reign of Möngke Khan (r. 1251–59). On New Year's day 1229, Yeh-lü Ch'u-ts'ai wrote the following.

I was summoned by Imperial Decree and proceeded west for tens of thousands of *li*. The only thing effective in calming my heart against temptation was meditation on the boundless Sea of Law [of the Buddha]. Therefore, to recompense the compassion of the Buddha, [I] record my views against falseness and the rejection of [Taoist] trash. In the *wu-tzu* year [1228], [I] arrived in the Capital. . . . The local people asked [me] about affairs in foreign lands. Worrying how to answer [these questions], [I] wrote [this] *Hsi-yu-lu* as witness of my concern. It contains many [records] concerning the debate on the true and false teachings of the three saints. Someone ridiculed me as a person fond of arguing. In response I said, "In the *Lun-yü* of Lu[44] it says, 'Names should be rectified,' [and] again it says, 'Thoughts should have no falsehood.' These make a distinction between truth and falsehood, and should not be neglected. As for the way of Yang Chu, Mo Ti, Tien P'ien, and Hsü Hsing, all bear falsehoods against Confucius.[45] The followers of the Ninety-six categories of the Western Region, Tz'u-fan, Pi-lu, K'ang-p'iao, Pai-ching, and Hsiang-hui, are all false [groups] against the Buddha.[46] The doctrine of Ch'üan-chen, Ta-t'ao, Hun-yüan (混元), T'ai-yi, and the three [persons of] the Chang [family], are all heresies against Lao Tzu.[47] As for the transmutation of gold and silver, immortality pills, transubstantiation [of bones], and tonics all are a necromancy of heterodox teachings and not the proper way of Po-yang [Lao Tzu]. All these were forbidden in earlier days as is clearly recorded in the established laws. Now the state has been established and both tolerance and mercy are emphasized. Consequently, falsehoods and recklessness grow, and it is not yet possible to distinguish truth [from heresy]. In ancient time, the Ch'in [Dynasty] of the Ying [family] burned the classics and buried scholars [alive]. Han [Yu][48] of the T'ang Dynasty condemned the Buddha and Lao Tzu. All are distortions [against the truth]. Mencius denounced [the theories] of Yang [Chu and] Mo [Ti] and condemned them as trash. This is the correct argument for Confucius. I would like to publish them. Even were the three saints [Confucius, the Buddha, and Lao Tzu] alive again, they would not change this theory."[49]

In this preface, Yeh-lü Ch'u-ts'ai openly condemned Ch'iu Ch'u-chi's Ch'üan-chen Sect as a false faction distorting the proper teachings of Lao Tzu's Taoism. He maintained that it should be forbidden by law. He also suggested that the tolerant, broadminded policy of the Chinggis Khan allowed the spreading of many false teachings which should be prohibited in the future. Chinggis Khan passed away in 1227 and his son Ögödei ascended the throne in 1229, the year Yeh-lü Ch'u-ts'ai wrote the above views. This same year

Yeh-lü Ch'u-ts'ai was promoted to the position of premier *(Chung-shu-ling)*. All these events were unfavorable for the Taoist Ch'üan-chen Sect. However, Ögödei Khan did not alter the traditional Mongolian policy of religious tolerance, so the Buddhist counterattack against the Taoists was postponed for two decades. During this changing political situation, the great Taoist Master Ch'ui Ch'u-chi also died. From that time the Taoist movement was not active as were the Buddhists under the leadership of the outstanding monk Hai-yün.

Buddhism Among the Mongols

Concerning the Buddhist movement among the Mongols, the *Yüan shih* records: "When the Yüan arose in the north they already honored Buddhism."[50] The record must have some historical basis, but the account is unclear about the time, the persons involved, and other details. As for the monk Hai-yün, the Yüan literati Ch'eng Chu-fu[51] composed the following Inscription for him entitled *Hai-yün Chien-ho-shang ta-pei* (The Inscription of the Pagoda of Hai-yün, the Abbot Chien). This was recorded in Ch'eng's collection *Hsüeh-lo chi* (vol. VI). A more complete biography is found in the *Fo-tsu li-tai t'ung-tsai* by the Yüan monk Nien-ch'ang, and is quoted here.

In the eleventh month of the *hsien-mou* year [1231], the Master received bestowals from Khaghan Emperor [Tai-tsung, Ögödei]. . . . In the *chi-wei* year [1235], the Court . . . decided to examine the monks and the Taoists and [their] scriptures. The Elder Wan-sung[52] sighed and said, "From the beginning of the [Mongolian] National Dynasty, the monks stopped their lecturing classes for a long, long time, and only a few of them learned the scriptures. He then asked the Master to manage the matter together with other elderly monks. The Master responded calmly, "[You] should encourage the multitude of monks to learn the scriptures through this [incident]. The Lord Emperor must have some deeper intentions. According to my observation monks nowadays have little concern about the commandments, do not study profoundly, and stay far away from the truth. Therefore, the Heavenly Dragon moved the Court to issue the examination . . . order to save [the Law] from its destruction. Under the protection of the Three Jewels [the purpose] of the Saintly Decree will not fail. [The Master] then met with the imperial emissary, and all measures and regulations were resolved according to the admonitions of the Master. [Wan-sung], the Premier Hsia-li,[53] told the Master, in the word of the Great *Noyan* [Shigi-] Khutugh,[54] "Following the Saintly Decree [we] dispatched officials to examine the scriptures. Those who are able to read should be allowed to remain as monks. Those who are unable to read should be sent back to lay life." The Master said, "[I], a rustic monk, have not learned the scriptures, and am not able to read even one character." The Premier said, "If [you] can not read, how can [you] be an elder?" The Master said, "Can the Great *Noyan* read the characters?" Upon hearing these words the lords of the territories who were present were all astonished. The Premier again said, "What can we do then?" The Master said, "A person who understands this business and is brilliant in the Law of Buddha should know that the law of the world is the Law of Buddha. The passions of the Way will not differ from the emotions of human beings. In ancient times people arose from being small tradesmen establishing great merits in the world, and were recorded in history. A thousand years later [they] are still [honored] as if they were alive. Moreover, at present the saintly brilliant Son of Heaven is [ruling] above, [whose] light is just like the sun and the moon shining upon [us]. Can an examination of the monks and the Taoist priests be handled like that of the scripture-learning youngsters, testing them by the same method as the traditional examinations for officials? The State should cultivate tens of thousands of good deeds and honor the Three Jewels, in order to serve Heaven and to prolong the blessed reign of the State for ever and ever. This is the only use of us monks. Besides this there is nothing to be said." The Premier reported these words to the Great *Noyan*, and they were accepted. A memorial was sent [to the Emperor] and since then, though there were tests, no monk was defrocked. [Later, the Emperor] decreed that all problems should be settled according to the regulations of T'ai-tsu [Chinggis Khan] and he allowed them to remain as monks.[55]

This record illustrates the efforts of such Buddhist elders such as Wan-sung and Hai-yün to maintain the position of the monks. It is also obvious that there were many unqualified persons in the ecclesiastical bodies of both Buddhism and Taoism, and the great majority of them were unable to read their own scriptures. The last part of this record says, "all should be settled according to the regulations of T'ai-tsu and [the Emperor] allowed them to remain as monks." Apparently, Chinggis Khan had already established special arrangements for the Buddhists that are unclear from the records.

The relationship between the prominent Buddhist Hai-yün and the Confucianists was recorded by a monk of the period.

When the Duke of Yen-sheng [K'ung] Yüan-t'suo,[56] crossed the [Yellow] River and proceeded to the temple and tomb [of Confucius] at Ch'ü-fu, the Duke brought a letter from Yen [Shih][57] of Tung-ping[58] allowing him to visit the Master and [asking him] to speak to the Great *Noyan* for him so that he might assume his rank. The Master spoke for him saying, "Confucius has a good knowledge of the ancient records. [He] attained the way of ultimate uprightness, the ritual of the three basic principles, and the five constant virtues. [He clarified] the cause of life, of blessings and disasters, the way of king and vassal, father and son, husband and wife. [He clarified] the principle of governing a kingdom, of ruling a household, and of pacifying the realm under heaven. [He] straightened the [human] heart and the sincerity of thought. From Confucius until the present, succession to the rank of the Duke of Yen-sheng has reached fifty-one generations. All those who obtain the kingdom allow them to succeed and to continue offering services [to Confucius] uninterrupted." Hearing these words, the Great *Noyan* accepted the idea of the Master and ordered [K'ung Yüan-ts'uo] to attain to the rank and to continue the services. The Master again petitioned for Yen [Tzu][59] and Mencius who had preached the truth of Confucius and had had their descendants continue [their rank and service] unceasingly. Besides, [the Master] also spoke for those who learned the teachings of [Duke of] Chou and Confucius, and they were all exempt from their corvée duties, and made diligently to practice their teachings and to be useful to the state.[60]

Although this might be one-sided it still has a core of truth. In 1233, when the Chin capital, Pien, was under Mongolian siege, K'ung Yuan-t'suo had taken refuge in the city. If Yeh-lü Ch'u-ts'ai had not admonished Ögödei Khan, the city of Pien might have been destroyed. The Khan proclaimed that except for the Jurchen ruling family of the Wan-yen clan, all people in the city were pardoned. Thus, Yeh-lü Ch'u-ts'ai saved the life of K'ung Yuan-ts'uo. Also, it can be imagined that through the influence of both Yeh-lü Ch'u-ts'ai and Hai-yün, Shigi-khutugh agreed to provide favorable treatment for the descendents of Confucius and Confucian scholars. Consequently, the credit for protecting Chinese intellectuals was not due solely to the Taoist Ch'üan-chen Sect.

Nien-ch'ang also recorded Hai-yün's activities in the Mongolian Court.

In the first month of the *tin-yu* [1237] the Second Empress of Emperor T'ai-tsu offered the Master the title of *Kuang-t'ien chen-kuo ta-shih* [灌頂鎮國大師The Great Master of Glorifying Heaven and Pacifying the State]. In the winter of the year chi-hai [1239], the Master was again appointed Abbot of the Great Ch'ing-shou Monastery (慶寿寺).[61]

Here the so-called "Second Empress of Emperor T'ai-tsu" was probably Khulan Khatun of the second *ordo* of Chinggis Khan.[62] The title of *Kuang-t'ien chen-kuo ta-shih*, which is non-Mongolian, may have originated with some Chinese scholars. The Great Ch'ing-shuo Monastery was the main temple of Yen (Peking). As mentioned, in the year 1220 Hai-yün entered Yen and settled in this monastery. The record says, "The Master was again appointed Abbot of the Great Ch'ing-shou Monastery," which infers that Hai-yün had ceased to be the Abbot of the monastery, the center of North China Buddhism, for a period of time, and then was reappointed because of his growing reputation and prestige in the Buddhist world. As noted in the previous chapter, the most meaningful thing Hai-Yüan did, and the most important for later history, was his teaching of Buddhism to Khubilai, making him receptive to the Buddhist teachings and causing him to favor Buddhism over other religions.

Undoubtedly, the influence of the great Phags-pa Lama on Khubilai Khan was also a critical factor. Nevertheless, the Chinese Buddhist scholar Liu Ping-chung, influenced the Mongolian rulers to appreciate Chinese Buddhism. Liu, who later became one of the important founders of the Yüan state, was originally a monk attached to the princely residence of Khubilai. In attending the young prince, he had ample opportunity to influence him with the teachings of the Buddha. All these things could happen to Khubilai because the territory of Tolui's family was situated in the eastern part of the Mongolian empire. In Hsing-chou[63] especially, a city of high civilization in North China in the territory of Sorkhaghtani Beki Khatun,[64] the mother of Möngke Khan and Khubilai Khan, there was a good chance for the princes to become acquainted with famous Chinese scholars and monks. In addition, Hai-yün and Liu Ping-chung had an intimate personal relationship as master and disciple. Consequently, in the struggle of Taoists against the Buddhists, Liu was naturally on the side of the latter. Nien-ch'ang recorded Liu Ping-chung's first visit to Mongolia.

> Master Hsü-ching ... [conducted the ceremony] of shaving the hair and turned him into a monk. Because he knew the [Confucian] classics and was talented in literature, [his master] ordered [him] to do the secretarial work. Later [he] traveled to Yün-chung [present-day T'a-tung, Shansi Province] and stayed at the

Nan-t'ang Monastery. Then Master Hai-yün was summoned to the north for an audience and arrived at Yün-chung. Hearing of his talent in art [the Master] asked him to go with him. He refused this request [but] Hai-yün insisted, and Liu Ping-chung was forced to go.[65]

Thus, Liu's acquaintance with Khubilai came through the recommendation of Hai-yün. This was recorded also in "The Biography of Liu Ping-chung" in the *Yüan shih* (157). Liu, half-monk, half-Confucian, scholar later became one of the main planners for the Yüan Dynasty and recommended many important Chinese scholars to Khubilai. The position of the Mongolian court in the Buddhist-Taoist struggle was obviously influenced through such contacts.

Concerning Hai-yün's activities in the Mongolian Court, Nien-ch'ang in his *T'ung-tsai* recorded:

In the *i-ssu* year [1245, the Master] received instructions from the Sixth Empress[66] to conduct a prayer service at Wu-tai [Mountain][67] for the blessings of the State. . . . In the year *ting-wei* [1247] Emperor Güyüg ascended the throne,[68] ordered the Master to administer to the monks, and bestowed upon him ten thousand tales of white gold [silver]. The Master conducted a great prayer service at Hao-t'ien Monastery for the blessings of the State. The heir-apparent, Ha-la-chi,[69] invited the Master to come to [Khara-] khorum, settled [him] at T'ai-p'ing hsing-kuo Monastery, and honored him extraordinarily. In the year *hsin-hai* [1251], Emperor Möngke ascended the throne, conferred a merciful decree, provided favorable treatment, and again appointed the Master to administer the affairs of all monks in the realm under heaven. All exemptions of duties were [set] according to the old regulations. In the first month of *ping-ch'en* [1256], receiving a Sacred Decree, the Master conducted a service at hao-t'ien Monastery.[70]

This record confirms that Hai-yün was trusted by the Mongolian Court and allowed to conduct official state prayers quite early. Invited to settle in Kharakhorum, he had many chances to influence the Mongolian ruling class to favor Buddhism. Hai-yün was continually ordered to administer Buddhist affairs during the reigns of Güyüg Khan (1246–48) and Möngke Khan (1251–59). This was not only a personal success for Hai-yün, but also influenced Mongolian policy toward religious affairs in China. "The Annals of Hsien-tsung [Möngke Khan]" in the *Yüan shih* records, "The monk Hai-yün was in charge of Buddhist affairs and the Taoist Li Chen-ch'ang[71] was in charge of Taoist affairs."[72]

The exemption of duties "was [decided] according to the old regulations," but it is difficult to judge when and how the "old regulations" were established. Since there was a record from the time of T'ai-tsung (Ögödei Khan) which says, "According to the regulation of Tai-tsu [Chinggis Khan] he allowed them to remain as monks," the original regulation must have been made by Chinggis Khan. The *Ta-Yüan sheng-ch'eng kuo-ch'ao tien-chang* records:

On the sixteenth day of the fifth month of the thirty-first year of Chih-yüan [1294] the *Chung-shu-sheng* [the premier's office] received a Sacred Decree which said, "In the Sacred Decrees of the Former Emperors, Chinggis and

Ögödei, it has been said, 'Release the [Buddhist] monks, the Christian priests, and the Taoist priests from all their corvée duties and taxes. Have them report to Heaven and pray for [Our] long life. Now according to this precedent of the Former [Emperors'] Sacred Decrees, exempt [them] from their corvée duties and taxes and have them report to Heaven and pray for [Our] long life. This is by His Majesty.[73]

Thus, both Chinggis and Ögödei Khan exempted the Buddhist, Taoist, and Christian priesthoods from corvée duties and taxes according to traditional Mongolian broadmindedness toward all religions.

The aforementioned "Biography of Tege" mentions the arrival of the Kashmir lama, Na-mo, in the Mongolian Court and says, "Hsien-tsung [Möngke Khan] honored Na-mo with the title of *kuo-shih* [State Instructor], bestowed upon him a jade seal, and appointed him to administer the Buddhist affairs in all the realm under heaven."[74] However, it is difficult to decide whether this event happened before or after Hai-yün's appointment. Nevertheless, this set the first precedent for appointing a non-Chinese monk to administer Buddhist affairs in the empire, including in China. In other words, this was a forerunner of the institutionalized function of *Ti-shih,* the Imperial Instructor, a post always occupied by the great lamas of the Tibetan Sa-skya sect.

Buddhist/Taoist Conflicts and Debates

Through the meeting of the famous Taoist master Ch'iu Ch'u-chi with Chinggis Khan, the Ch'üan-chen sect obtained special and favorable support from the Mongols and consequently "flourished like the sun in the middle of the sky."[75] This Taoist sect was then able to save many people, but also inevitably attracted the hostility of Buddhism. The evil deeds of the Taoists listed by Hsiang-mai in the *Ta-Yüan Chih-yüan pien-wei-lu* are likely exaggerated and prejudiced. Nevertheless, they are not all false accusations.

The author has always felt that there were devious undercurrents in this relationship. As noted, the style of Chinggis Khan's so-called decrees to Ch'iu Ch'u-chi is purely Chinese and has no Mongolian flavor at all. Certainly these were not the words of the world conqueror, Chinggis Khan. Moreover, in later days, "Cultivation of the Hu (化胡經)," was the main factor in the fall of the Chüan-chen sect.

Attached to the *Hsi-yu chi,* and collected by Wang-Kuo-wei in his *Meng-ku shih-liao ssu-chung,* were five decrees from Chinggis Khan to Ch'iu Ch'u-chi. Two are in excellent Chinese literary style. Three were in the Yüan colloquial style. In other words, these were direct translations from Mongolian oral or written texts and are more trustworthy than the two elegant Chinese texts; all texts being related to the matter of the exemption of the Taoists from tax and duties. In one dated from the twenty-fourth day of the ninth month of the *kuo-wei* year (1223), the Khan said, "Earlier I gave you a decree telling you to administer to all good people who left their homes to become devotees. Rule over the good ones, and the bad ones are up to you, the Immortal Ch'iu. Only you will make decisions."[76] Here the phrase, "good people who left their homes to become devotees" had a broader meaning than the word *hsien-shen* which meant "teacher" in Chinese but "Taoist" to the Mongolians. It may mean that both the Taoists and the Buddhist monks were put under the rule of the Immortal Ch'iu. If so, it no doubt caused great dissatisfaction among the Buddhists, and eventually incited them to launch a counterattack against the oppressive power of Taoism.

According to Li Chih-ch'ang's *Hsi-yu-chi*, the will of Ch'iu Ch'u-chi was, "to have the disciple Sung Tao-an to administer religious affairs, Yin Chih-p'ing to assist, Ch'ang Chih-sung to serve as deputy, and Wang Chih-ming to continue in his former positions, with Sung Te-fang and Li Chih-ch'ang to give counsel."[77] The *"Shih-lao chuan"* in the *Yüan shih* says, "His disciple, Yin Chih-ch'ang, and others received the document with the Imperial Seal to administer the affairs of their religion. . . . [At the time of Emperor Shih-tsu [Khubilai], in the fourth generation [after Ch'iu Ch'u-chi] Chi Chih-ch'eng . . . had a high reputation in the Taoist religion."[78] In general, after the death of Ch'iu Ch'u-chi the Taoists were not as active as Buddhists. This was probably due to the rise to power of Ögödei Khan and his appointment of Yeh-lü Ch'u-ts'ai, a devote Buddhist, as his premier for Chinese affairs. Even so, the Taoists were not neglected by the Mongolian court, and Taoist leaders "received documents with the Imperial Seal to administer the affairs of their religion." When Möngke Khan ascended the throne (1251) he appointed Li Chen-ch'ang to oversee Taoist affairs.[79] (This "Li Chen-ch'ang" is a mispronunciation of the name Li Chih-ch'ang, the author of *Hsi-yu-chi* and Ch'iu Ch'u-chi's counselor in the Ch'üan-chen Sect.)

The long historical conflict between Taoism and Buddhism was not merely a cultural struggle between two different religions, one of Chinese origin and the other of Indian background. It was also a political and economic conflict. The destruction of the Law of Buddha, historically, complicated the historical backdrop and was unknown to the Mongolian rulers during their early occupation of China. However, when the Buddhist monks discovered that their opponents had gained support from Chinggis Khan, they immediately recalled these painful historical experiences suffered in the past, and tried to find some way to influence the Mongolian court in order to prevent a recurrence of "the disaster against the Proper Law."

The efforts of Na-mo and Hai-yün influenced the Mongolian rulers to review their policy toward Chinese religions. Moreover, the conversion of Prince Kötön to Tibetan Buddhism and the personal relationship between Prince Khubilai and Phags-pa Lama greatly aided the Chinese Buddhists to expand their influence in the Mongolian court. First of all, they discredited Ch'iu Ch'u-chi, accusing him of dishonesty in dealing with Chinggis Khan. To gain the support of the new Khan Möngke in retaliating against the Taoists, they asserted that they were the victims of evil Taoist activities. The Yüan *Hanlin* scholar Chang Po-ch'un,[80] in his preface to the *Ta-yüan Chih-yüan pein-wei-lu*, the work of the monk Hsiang-mai, said:

> The Taoist Ch'iu Ch'u-chi, Li Chih-ch'ang, and others destroyed the T'en-cheng Confucian Temple of Hsi-ching [presently Ta-t'ung, Shansi] and turned it into [the Taoist temple] Wen-ch'eng Kuan. [They] destroyed the image of Buddha Sakyamuni, the white jade [image] of Kuan-yin [Avalokitésvara], and the sacred pagoda of Buddhist relics. [They] plotted against and occupied four hundred eighty-two Buddhist monasteries, and spread false words of Wang Fu,[81] the *Lao Tzu pa-shih-i hua-t'u* [老子八十一化圖] The eighty-one conversion figures of Lao Tzu] to mislead the people. Then the Elder [Fu-] yü of the Shao-lin [Monastery] led the honorable instructors to the Court and petitioned [the case] to the former Emperor Möngke.[82]

First debate

Upon receiving this Buddhist petition, Möngke Khan decreed a debate in the year 1258 between the Buddhist monks and the Taoists. Hsiang-mai continued:

Then His Majesty, the Emperor [Khubilai], established the city at Shangtu and was ordered by the Former Emperor [Möngke], as the heir-apparent of the kingdom entrusted with the future [of the State] through the Sacred Decree, to assemble the elite of the nine schools[83] again to discuss and to distinguish between the truth and falseness of the two ways of the monks and the Taoists. Accepting the Sacred Decree of the Former Emperor, His Majesty, the Emperor, decided to summon the two sides of Buddhism and Taoism with the Elder of the Shao-lin [Monastery] as the head of the monks and Chang *Chen-jen* as the head of the Taoist priests to come to the palace at Shangtu to debate face to face in the presence of [His Majesty] in the Grand Hall. Also present were the State Instructor Na-mo, the State Instructor Phags-pa,[84] and State Instructor of Tibet, the monks from the state of Ho-hsi [the region of the former Tangut Hsia], the monks from the five outer *lu* [routes],[85] the monks from the State of Ta-li.[86] Also present were those from China: Yüan-fu the Elder Ch'ao, and Feng-fu the Elder Heng of Chung-tu [Peking]; K'ai-chüeh the Elder Mai of P'ing-luan *lu* [presently eastern Hopei Province]; Elder Ch'in of Ta-ming [presently southern Hopei]; the Young Master Ta-pi, the Director Su-mo-shih-kua, the Interpreter Mönggüdei of Chen-ting [presently Pao-ting, Hopei]; the Head Lecturer Hsün of Pei-ching [presently Ba'arin Banner, Inner Mongolia]; Head Lecturer Kuei of Ta-ming; Shou, the Record Keeper of Monks' Affairs of Chung-tu [Peking]; the T'zu-fu Head Lecturer Lang, Lung-men Head Lecturer Yü and His Excellency the Senior Guardian of the Heir-Apparent Ts'ung [Liu Ping-chung],[87] and other monks totaling more than three hundred; Confucian scholars Tou Han-ch'ing,[88] Yao Kung-mao[89] and others; Premier Meng-su-su,[90] Vice-Premier Lien,[91] Premier Molkhachi, Chang Chung-ch'ien[92] and two hundred others [officials and scholars] to witness; and the Taoist priests Chang *chen-jen* Wang *hsien-sheng* from Mantzu [South China]; the Record Keeper of the Taoist Affairs; Fan Chih-yin; the Judge of the Taoist Affairs, Wei Chih-yang; Lecturer Chou Li-chih and more than two hundred others to debate with the [Buddhist] monks.[93]

The presence of so many dignitaries and luminaries illustrated how great and significant the meeting was. It also shows the deep concern of both Möngke Khan and Prince Khubilai. Besides the Buddhist and Taoist opponents, many Confucian scholars attended including Yao Shu, Tao Mo, Chang Wen-ch'ien, and Lien Hsi-hsien. The crux of this great debate was recorded in "The inscription for the destruction of the false scriptures of the Taoist collections in all districts as commanded by the Sacred Decree" *(Shen-chih fen-hui chu-lu wei-Tao-tsang-ching chih pei)*. The inscription was composed by the *Han-lin* Scholars T'ang Fang, Yang Wen-yü, Wang Kou,[94] Li Ch'ien,[95] Yen Fu,[96] Li T'ao and Wang P'an[97] in the year 1284.

[Your] vassals, [Wang] Pan and others, carefully referred to the record by Khataisari, the General Director of Buddhism. In the time of the reign of Emperor Hsien-tsung [Möngke], the Taoists produced a book called *Lao-chün hua-hu ch'eng-fo ching* [老君化胡成佛經] The Scripture of Lao

Tzu's Transformation to Buddha through the Conversion of Barbarians] and *Pa-shih-i-hua tu* [八十一化figure The Eighty-one Conversion Figures]. It was engraved on wooden blocks, [printed] and distributed to the [lands of] four directions. The words are vile, shallow, and extravagant. [Their] purpose is to despise Buddhism and to elevate their own teachings. The Great Master of Kashmir, General Director Lan-ma [No-mo] and [Elder of] Sho-lin [Monastery] Fu-yü, memorialized the matter [to the throne]. At that time, His Majesty was at [his] princely residence. [Former] Emperor Hsien-tsung ordered the two parties — Buddhists and Taoists — to proceed to His Majesty's palace to debate. Both of the parties agreed that if the Taoists won then the monks would wear hats and become Taoist; if the monks won then the Taoists would shave [their] hair and become monks. The monks asked the Taoists, "Your book is named the *Scripture of Transformation to Buddha through the Conversion of the Barbarians.* What does the [word] Buddha mean?" The Taoist answered, "The Buddha is the [great] awakening. It means the awakening of heaven and earth, the awakening of *yin* and *yang,* the awakening of benevolence and uprightness." The monk said, "It is not so. The awakening means self-awakening, to awaken others, the fulfillment of the deed of awakening and the clear completion of the [above] three awakenings. Therefore, this is said to be the Buddha. It is not limited only to the awakening of heaven and earth, *yin* and *yang,* and benevolence and uprightness." His Majesty said, "I also understand by heart that benevolence and uprightness are the words of Confucius. [They] said that Buddha is the awakening of benevolence and uprightness. Their theory is wrong." The Taoist again proceeded and presented the *Shih chi* and other books and tried to talk more and win by chance. The Imperial Instructor Pandita Phags-pa said, "What book is it?" [The Taoist] said, "It is the book about the emperors and kings of earlier dynasties." His Majesty said, "Now it is purposed to discuss religion. Why should all hang on these emperors and kings of earlier dynasties?" The Imperial Instructor said, "In our India, there is also a *Shih chi* [record of history]. Have you heard of it?" [The Taoists answered, "Not yet." The Imperial Instructor said, "Let me explain it to you. In India the King Bimbasara praised the merit of Buddha and said, 'Above heaven and under heaven there is nothing equivalent to Buddha. In the ten directions of the world there is also nothing able to compare with the Buddha. Of all that I have seen in the world none is able to match the Buddha. When he was speaking these words, where was Lao Tzu?" The Taoist could not answer. The Imperial Instructor again asked, "Is the theory of the conversion of the barbarians [recorded] in your *Shih chi?"* [The Taoist] said, "No." The Imperial Instructor said, "Since it is not in the *Shih chi,* and again is not recorded in the *Tao-te ching,* it is clear that this is a falsehood!" The words of the Taoists were submitted and Minister Yao Shu said: "The Taoists are defeated." His Majesty commanded that the punishment be performed as it has been agreed upon and dispatched the envoy Toghon to proceed to the Lung-kuang Monastery to shave the hair of the Taoist Fan Chih-ying and seventeen other persons to make them monks, and burnt forty-five books of false scriptures. In the realm under heaven the two-hundred thirty-seven Buddhist Monasteries that had been occupied by the Taoists were all ordered to be returned [to the Buddhists].[98]

From these records it is clear that this great debate was a struggle between the Taoists and an alliance of Buddhists and Confucian scholars. The background for this debate involved not only religious contradictions but also political and cultural conflicts. The most decisive argument against the Taoists was that of Phags-pa. This not only increased his personal prestige and brought him reverence from Khubilai, but also greatly influenced Chinese society with its traditional culture and thought. Of course, the influence of Na-mo should not be neglected.

The great debate was also recorded in the Tibetan *Hor Chos'byung* (a history of Mongolian Buddhism) by Jigmed-namkha.

> Then in China there were many people of wrong views. They were the followers of the ancient Tai-shang Lao-chün (太上老君) and were called *shing-shing* (先生). Considering this matter as a harmful thing to both themselves and others, the Khan commanded [Phags-pa] to extinguish these evil persons and to cause them to follow the Proper Law [of Buddha]. There upon through the principle of proper reason he subdued this heresy, swiftly extinguished the leading figures of the *shing-shing*, turned their wrong views into proper views, and ordered them to become monks to develop the Law of Buddha Shakyamuni.[99]

The Tibetan record indicates that the event was a significant victory in Buddhist history and was highly praised by Tibetan Buddhists. In fact, however, the event did not overcome Taoist activities effectively, and therefore, after Khubilai became Khan (r. 1260–94) the Buddhists again petitioned the court to destroy the Taoist scriptures. This was again authorized by Khubilai Khan and in the winter of 1281 he ordered the Buddhists and Taoists once again to debate their doctrines. The decree says:

> Formerly, according to the Decree of Emperor Möngke, in the year of *wu-wu* [1258], the monks and the *hsien-sheng* [Taoists] carried out a debate on the Law of Buddha. The Taoists lost. . . . Upon this, the *Hua-hu-ching* (化胡經) and other scriptures, which were falsely made from the lies of the Taoists, together with their wooden blocks, were ordered to be burnt and destroyed. At present, because it was reported that the Taoists did not destroy those scriptures and wooden blocks, which should be destroyed, but hid them, [the Court] sent the Vice-Premier Chang, the Deputy-Premier Chang, Minister Chiao, together [with the monks], the General-Director [of Buddhist Affairs] Chüan, the Record Keeper of Buddhist Affairs Chen-tsang, and other Judges of Buddhist Affairs, head lecturers, and elders, and the Taoists Chang *t'ien-shih*,[100] Chi-*chen-jen*, Li chen-jen, Tu *chen-jen* and others to go to the inner part of Ch'ang-ch'un Kung to collect them. Now Vice-Premier Chang and the others returned and reported: "The Scriptures of the [*Tao*]-tsang [the cannon of Taoism], except *Tao-te-ching* which is the real scripture of Lao Tzu, are all creations of later persons. Most of them calumniate the teaching of Buddha [and] steal the words of Buddhism. Moreover, some of them were copied from the books of the *yin-yang* [school], medical, and other words of many scholars but with their names changed. The annotations are distorted and erroneous, and have lost their original truth. [The Taoists] have falsely made charms and amulets, and absurdly told people that those who wear them . . . would not be drowned in water, burnt

in fire, or wounded by swords and knives. When Chang *t'ien-shih*, Chi *chen-jen* and Li *chen-jen* were ordered to test them in fire, they all implored for mercy and said, 'These are all false. [We] dare not try.' . . . Again the report of Chi *chen-jen*, Li *Chen-jen*, and Tu *chen-jen* say: 'The [collection] of scriptures of *Tao-tsang*, with the exception of the *Tao-te-ching* of Lao Tzu, are groundless words fabricated by later people. [We] are willing to have all of them burnt. It will also make us feel cleaner.'" This was authorized by the Throne [by saying], "From now on the Taoists should follow the *Tao-te-ching* of Lao Tzu for their practices. If there are those who prefer the scriptures of Buddha they may become monks. If they are not willing to become monks they should marry and go back to their lay life. Except for the *Tao-te-ching* these groundless scriptures in the *Tao-tsang* that were created from falsehood, together with their wooden blocks, should all be burnt and destroyed."[101]

Second debate

In the earlier debate convened by Möngke Khan, both No-mo and Phags-pa were leading figures and influenced the Mongolian court's final decision. This second debate was the result of a proposal by another Tibetan lama, the State Instructor Chan-pa (Damba?). His biography (in the *Fu-tsu li-tai t'ung-tsai*) says:

In the year *hsin-ssu* [1281], the Master [Chan-pa] read the *Hua-ha ching* [The Scripture of the Conversion of the Barbarians] and the *Pa-shih-i-hua tu* [The Eighty-one Conversion Figures] which were groundless and false. The Master sighed and said, "This really deludes the proper [ones] through falsehood!" Consequently, [the Master] reported it [to the throne]. [The Emperor] decreed that the great and virtuous one of Buddhism and the *Han-lin* scholars were to proceed to the Ch'ang-ch'un kung to debate and prove [the true and false doctrine].[102]

According to the Taoist record *Hua-hu ching*, Lao Tzu went west to convert the barbarians. Even T'ien-chu (India), the holy land of Buddhism, it was claimed, came under the influence of the teachings of Lao Tzu. According to this Taoist notion the Buddha was not only transformed into Tai-shan Lao-chün (Lao Tzu) but was even made Lao Tzu's disciple. This greatly offended the Buddhists, and consequently, all debates were concentrated on this crucial topic.

Hsiang-mai summarized the philosophical contradictions in this theory. He stressed that: 1) The establishment of T'ien-tsun [天尊 the honorable god of heaven] is false and without credible basis; 2) The creation of the chronicle regarding inescapable destruction is false; 3) The Taoist idea of three worlds is false; 4) The Taoist claim of being instructors of the emperors of all earlier dynasties is false; 5) Lao Tzu's claim of having emerged from the *Ling-pao san-tung* [three spiritually precious caves] is false; 6) The claim of traveling to and converting the nine heavens is false; 7) Taoists stealing from the Buddhists scriptures and teachings should be condemned; and 8) The myth of Lao-chün's crystallization from the breath to form the universe is false.[103] All these criticisms were based upon both Buddhist religious philosophy and historical facts and should not merely be taken as one-sided, groundless accusations against Taoism.

The Results of the Buddhist Victory

The victorious Buddhists continued to undermine Taoist influence and to extend the Buddhist movement from North China to the south. Along with these events, the excavation of the imperial Sung tombs fanned the hatred of the elite on the south of the Yangtze River. This event was recorded in detail by T'ao Tsung-yi in his *Ch'o-ching-lu* (vol. IV). Many transgressions were attributed to the monk Yang-lien-chen-chia, who used the money gained from raiding the Sung tombs for Buddhist enterprises. This was in retaliation for the pro-Taoist attitude of the former imperial household of Southern Sung (1127–1278).

The Buddhist-Taoist conflict undoubtedly existed before the Mongolian occupation. After the collapse of the Southern Sung, Yang-lien-chen-chia came to the Chiang-che area (present-day Kiangsu and Chekiang) as the General Director of Buddhism South of the Yangtze River. It appears that he was used by the Buddhists to retaliate against the Taoists. This act resulted in the excavation of the Sung tombs and was one of the great mistakes of the Mongolian rulers in China. In his *Ch'o-ching lu* (vol. XII) T'ao Tsung-yi wrote: "In the Chih-yüan period [1264–94], the Buddhist monks became overbearing. [They] turned Taoist temples into Buddhist monasteries and shaved Taoist priests. Also, many great tombs were excavated."[104] However, in Chang Po-ch'un's preface for the *Ta-yüan Chih-yüan pein-wei-lu* it reports quite differently.

At that time, the General Director of Buddhist Affairs on the South of the Yangtze River, Master [Yang-] lien-jen-chai, greatly cultivated saintliness and in three years, from the spring of the twenty-second year of Chih-yüan [1285] to the spring of the twenty-fourth year [1288], rehabilitated more than thirty Buddhist monasteries. For instance, the [Taoist temple] Ssu-sheng kuan was [originally the Buddhist monastery] Ku-shan ssu. The Taoist Hu *ti-t'ien* [manager] and others forsook falsehood and came to the truth. Those who abandoned Taoism, and became monks were some seven or eight hundred persons.[105]

Concerning Yang-lien-chen-chia, there is no information about his origins or the sect to which he belonged. The *Ta-yüan chih-yüan Pein-wei-lu* records his name as "Yang, the Master, Lien-chen-chia." The *Yüan shih* calls him Lien-chen-chia and Lien-chen-chia-wa, which may be Chinese transliterations of the Tibetan word Rin-chen dgah-ba. The Chinese word "Yang," it seems, is not related to the Tibetan word Rin-chen dgah-ba. The Mongolian transliteration of the name would be read as either "Rinchin" or "Erinchin," recorded in the *Yüan shih* as I-lien-chen. This case is similar to that of Chia Ta-la-hun,[106] whose name is a combination of the Chinese family name Chia and the Mongolian word *targhun* ["the fat"]. If the speculation is correct this questionable monk must have been a person from the Chinese Yang family who adopted the Tibetan Buddhist name Rin-chen dgah-ba. However, in the Chinese tradition a monk rarely put his family name with his religious name. This problem still needs further study.

The Mongolian mistake related to the tombs resulted from religious conflict but also from a lack of understanding of Chinese history. As a result, from the beginning to the end of the Mongolian occupation of China, balanced policies toward both Chinese Buddhism and Taoism were never forthcoming.

In the Buddhist-Taoist struggle all sects of Buddhism, even those of Kashmir and Tibet, joined in an alliance against the Taoists. Consequently, the Taoist Chüan-chen sect, once firmly supported by the Mongolian court, collapsed after the two great debates. With the establishment of the Yüan Dyasty in China, the Cheng-yi sect, headed by the *t'ien-shih* ("heavenly instructor") Chang Tsung-yen, assumed the leadership of Taoism instead of Ch'iu Ch'u-chi's Chüan-chen sect. Other sects, such as the Chen-ta and Tai-yi sects, gained visibility at court, but they were not as influential as the Cheng-yi sect. The relationship between the court and the sect, the contract between the Khan and the *t'ien-shih*, and the honor these Taoists received from the Mongols have been ably discussed by Sun K'o-kuan in his paper, *"Yüan-tai Cheng-i-chiao k'ao"* (元代正一教考 A Study of the Ching-yi Sect of the Yüan Dynasty),[107] and there is no need for any additional discussion here. The way Khubilai Khan treated the *t'ien-shih* Chang Tsung-yen, entitling him *shen-hsien* ("immortality"), was quite similar to his grandfather Chinggis Khan's handling of Ch'iu Ch'u-chi. The *"Shih-lao chuan"* in the *Yüan shih* says:

> After the pacification south of the [Yangtze] River [Emperor] Shih-tsu dispatched an envoy to summon [the *t'ien-shih*]. When he arrived, [the Emperor] sent court officials to meet him outside the capitol. At the audience, [the Emperor] said to him, "Formerly in the year *chi-wei* [1259], We came to O-tu [presently west of Wu-chang] and sent Wang I-ch'ing to visit your father, [the former *t'ien-shih*]. Your father reported to Us, saying, 'Twenty years from now, the realm should be unified.' The words of the immortal have already come to pass." Consequently, [the Emperor] allowed [him] to be seated and dine.[108]

This was the same manner in which Chinggis Khan waged psychological warfare through the Immortal Ch'iu Ch'u-chi. Whether or not the honored treatment of the Taoist Cheng-yi sect by the Mongolian court removed the hatred in the heart of the Chinese people created by misguided Mongolian religious policies should be carefully studied in the future. In general the Yüan Emperors adopted a comparatively evenhanded policy toward all religions under their control. Of course, this approach was based on the traditional polytheistic beliefs in Shamanism. The Mongols probably thought that the term *t'ien-shih*, "the instructor of heaven," had a similar meaning to *Teb-Tenggeri* in Mongolian. This might have been one of the factors that interested the Mongolian court in the Cheng-yi sect.

Government Supervision of Religion

According to available materials, such as the decrees collected in the *Ta-yüan sheng-cheng kuo-ch'ao tien-chang*, Buddhist monks and Taoist priests were treated equally. At least officially there is no unequal treatment apparent from an examination of the laws. The "Monograph of Officials" in the *Yüan shih* records: "The Ministry of Rituals . . . administers the affairs of . . . worship, . . . confers titles on godly persons . . . and administers matters pertaining to the literati, monks and Taoists."[109] It continues: "The Hsüan-cheng Yüan (宣政院) . . . has jurisdiction over . . . Buddhist monks and [their] disciples, and rules the land of Tibet."[110] This office was "headed by the State Instructor."[111] Thus the handling of Buddhist affairs was separated from the ordinary civil administration and the monks were put under the protection of a special and powerful office headed by a Tibetan religious leader. Locally, especially south of the Yangtze River, the *Kuang chiao tsung-kuan-fu* (廣教總管府 the General Director's Office for Propagating Religion) was established as a Buddhist administration. Later this office came under the Branch Office of the *Hsüan-chen Yüan* in Hangchou. In addition to these organizations, a special office, *Kung-te-shih ssu* (功德使司) The Office of the Emissary for Meritorious Affairs) was abolished and reestablished from time to time. All these facts indicate that the Mongolian-Yüan court's concern for Buddhism was much deeper than that for Taoism.

Carrying out religious services and building religious centers were major activities for the faithful of Buddhism and Taoism. The activities were seen not only as blessings for the welfare of their deceased ancestors but also as beneficial to themselves and to society. The Mongolian authorities often required the religious organizations to pray for the long life of the khan and for blessings for the state to express their loyalty. On the other hand, at court the Buddhist monks, Taoists, and other religious groups were active in order to win the confidence and support of the khan, and to gain such privileges as exemptions from taxes and duties. In this atmosphere both Buddhism and Taoism carried on the construction of Buddhist monasteries or Taoist temples. This eventually created a great financial deficit for the Yüan administration.

The dynastic history records:

In the first year of *Tai-ting* [1324] . . . [Chang] Kuei . . . proceeded to Shangtu to petition [the Emperor] saying: . . . "From ancient times the Saintly Kings sincerely concentrated their attention on politics to move Heaven and Earth and to affect the gods and the spirits; but they never tried to obtain blessings through the Buddhist monks and Taoists to disturb the people and damage the state. For example, in the thirtieth year of *Chih-yüan* [1295] there were only one hundred and two Taoist and Buddhist services, but in the seventh year of *Ta-te* [1303] when the [office of] *Kung-te shih ssu* was reestablished the number of services reached more than five hundred. This year the number has already increased more than four times its original [numbers]. The monks again bribe the courtiers to practice Buddhist services, taking divination as [their] pretext to cheat the Court by increasing offerings and donations. They pretend to carry a special decree, and the officials dare not check, but promptly supply their wants. In addition, the Buddhists should be clear and pure, without desire and without want. However, the monks are greedy for interest and gain. They go contrary to their own teachings. The expense is vast in gold, silver, money and cash. Each year much money is spent; many times more than in the period of *Chih-yüan* [1264–94]. All the offerings are taken by them and the money contributed is again monopolized. The fat and flesh of the people are squeezed to satisfy their personal desire and to support their wives and children. Since they have not practiced the way of holy mediation and here blasphemed Heaven and the Gods, how can they provide blessings? In recent years, although there were more Buddhist services, the age of the former Emperors did not last long and there were disasters one after another. It is absolutely clear that these services do not bring forth good results. [We, your] vassals have discussed [and now petition that Your Majesty] abolish the [office of] *Kung-te-shih ssu* and the services that existed before the thirtieth year of *Chih-yüan* [1295]. Taoist and Buddhist services for the anniversary and deaths of the former Emperors should only be carried out under the supervision of the [Office of] *Hsüan-ch'eng-yüan,* and the rest should be reduced or abolished. The courtiers should not be allowed to memorialize [the Emperor] and falsely increase the items. If there is any special decree, it should be rememorialized by *Chung-shu sheng* [the office of the premier] and then carried out." All of these proposals were eventually rejected by the Emperor.[112]

This citation is a brief description of the political and economic problems created by an uncritical belief in Buddhism and by the honors given to Taoism. However, to the Mongol Khans, the above remonstrance was less persuasive than the words of a *kao-t'ien-jen,* "a Heavenly reporter."

Conclusion

The Khans of the Yüan dynasty accepted Tantryana Tibetan Buddhism as their religious belief and honored the masters of the Sa-skya-pa sect as their Imperial Instructors, and thus promoted the development of Tantric Buddhism in China. Tibetan Buddhism was accepted by the Mongolian nobility because of the cultural similarities between the Mongols and the Tibetans. But it was rejected by the Chinese, especially by the intellectuals, because of basic cultural difference between the Chinese and the Tibetans. Consequently, most Chinese materials on this subject are one-sided and based upon their prejudices against an alien culture. In fact, most Imperial Instructors remained silent on state affairs, and were ordered not to be involved in politics. The case of Tibet was an exception. As a result of the excessive belief in Buddhism and the exorbitant honor given to monks, many illegal activities took place among the clergy. Although this was not entirely neglected by the Yüan court, Chinese historians still commonly claimed that "half of the Yüan realm was destroyed by the monks." Of course this is an exaggerated, subjective interpretation of the Mongolian rule.

In short, the Mongolian Khans' selection of their own religious faith was based upon their traditional nomadic culture. Nevertheless, their attitudes and policies toward Buddhism and Taoism in China gave rise to many deviations in their administration. This may have been a result of basic differences and misunderstandings between nomadic culture and that of the agricultural world of China.

Notes

1. "Biography of Mu-hua-li," *Yüan shih,* 119.
2. The Yüan monk, Nien-ch'ang's (念常) *Fo-tsu li-tai tung-tsai* (佛祖歷代通載 22 volumes) is collected in the Japanese Taisho edition *Daizokyo* (大正大藏經). It is also collected in the *Ssu-ku ch'üan-shu* (四庫全書), but the Mongolian and Tibetan personal names are all distorted. The latter was printed by the Commercial Press in Taipei.
3. The Lin-chi (臨濟) sect, a branch of the Chan (禪 zen), was founded by Lin-chi yi-hsüan chan-shih (臨濟義玄禪師) of the T'ang Dynasty. See Yüan scholar, Chao Meng-fu (趙孟頫), "Lin-chi cheng-tsung chih pei

(臨濟正宗之碑)" (the inscription of the Lin-chi proper sect), *Sung-hsüeh-chai wen-chi* (松雪齋文集), vol. 9, *Ssu-pu t'sung-kan* (四部叢刊) edition, 99.

4. According to Western counting, Hai-yün's age was only twelve.

5. According to the "Biography of Mu-hua-li," in the *Yüan shih*, the title of *t'ai-shih kuo-wang* (太師國王) was conferred on him by Chinggis Khan in the year *t'ing ch'uo*, 1217.

6. Lan-ch'eng, present-day Lan-hsien, Shansi Province.

7. See "Biography of Shih Tien-tse (史天澤)," *Yüan shih*, 155. However, the biography does not mention this event.

8. In "Biography of Li Shou-hsien (李守賢)," *Yüan shih*, 150, it says that the commander of the Yi-chou army, Li Ting-chih, had his younger brother, Li Shou-chung (李守忠), temporarily direct the southern army. This Li Shou-chung was identical to this Li Chi-ko which meant the seventh brother of the Li family.

9. Ch'ih-ch'eng, present-day Ch'ih-ch'eng *hsien*, Chahar Province, during the Yüan dynasty belonged to Yün-chou.

10. *Darkhan* is a Mongolian high rank, and it is difficult to identify who this *darkhan* was.

11. Lia-yang, probably present-day Lia-shui *hsien*, Hopei Province.

12. See Nien-ch'ang, 21:9a–11a, 12ab.

13. "The Biography of Mu-hua-li" 4b.

14. Ibid.

15. In North China the Taoist religion was divided into three sects, Chüan-chen (全真), Tai-yi (太一), and Cheng-ta (正大); on the south of the Yangtze River there were two sects, Cheng-yi (正一), and Mao-shan (茅山). Later from the Cheng-yi sect there developed a branch known as Hsüan-chiao (玄教). See note 110.

16. The translation of the Chinese Buddhist term *chü-shih* (居士) identifies Yeh-lü Chu-ts'ai who usually called himself Chan-jan chü-shih, i.e., "a tranquil recluse."

17. Liu Wen was another name of Liu Chung-lu.

18. Wang Kuo-wai (王國維, *Meng-ku shih-liao ssu-chung* (蒙古史料四種), Taipei, 1961, 230.

19. *Hsien-sheng* (先生) is a general term for a learned person, such as sir, teacher, or mister, but in the period of the Mongolian Empire it was the term that the Mongols applied to the Taoists. This word was even mispronounced as *shing-shing* in many Mongolian and Tibetan materials.

20. For King Wen (d. 1135 B.C.) of Chou, see Ssu-ma Ch'ien, "The Annals of Chou," and "Biography of the Household of T'ai-kung Wang," *Shih chi*, vols. 4 and 32.

21. "Biography of Chu-ko Liang," *San kuo-chih*, 35:2a.

22. Wang-kuo-wei, 231-233, and T'ao Tsung-yi (陶宗儀) *Ch'o-ching-lu* (輟耕錄), Taipei, 1962, 10:150–51.

23. See the decrees of the Yüan emperors to the Buddhists and the Taoists that were collected in the *Ta-Yüan sheng-cheng kuo-ch'ao tien-chang* (大元聖政國朝典章), reprinted by the Palace Museum, Taipei, 1976.

24. Wang Kuo-wei, 356.

25. Ibid.

26. "Shih-lao chuan" (Biography of the Buddhists and the Taoists), *Yüan shih* 202:9b–10a.
27. S. Jagchid, *"Hu-pi-lieh k'o-han yü Pa-ssu-pa la-ma"* (Khubilai Khan and Phags-pa lama), *Shih-hsüeh hui-k'an* (史學彙刊), no. 2, Taipei, 1969, and *"Ta-Yüan ti-shih Pa-ssu-pa la-ma shih tsen-yang-ti i-ko-jen?"* (What Kind of Person Was the Imperial Tutor of the Great Yüan, Phas-pa Lama?), *Chung-hua wen-hua fu-hsing yüeh-ken* (中華文化復興月刊), vol. 4, no. 4, Taipei, April 1971.
28. Chan-pa, see "Shih-lao chuan" of the *Yüan shih*, 202:3ab, and see Nien-ch'ang, 21:29b.
29. Wang Kuo-wei, 359. See also Peng Ta-ya's words in his *Hei-ta shih-lüeh* (黑韃事略): "All the matters are all up to the heavens, and this is no different than the Tatar lord to his subjects." Ibid., 488.
30. Yao Ts'ung-wu (姚從吾) *"Chin Yüan Ch'üan-chen-ch'aio ti min-tsu ssu-hiang yü chiu-shih ssu-hsiang"* (全真教的民族思想與救世思想 The Nationalistic Thought and World Salvation Thought of the Ch'üan-chen sect at the Period of Chin and Yüan). *Tung-pei-shih Lung-ts'ung* (東北史論叢), Taipei, 1959, 2:175–204.
31. Wang Kuo-wei, 358.
32. During the Jurchen Chin Dynasty only one Chinese vassal who approved of hunting activity is to be found. See the "Biography of Liang Hsiang," *Chin shih*, 96:13ab. See also Yao Ts'ung-wu, *Tung-pei-shih lun-ts'ung*, 2:118–73.
33. Ibid., 194–95.
34. The "Biography of Chen-hai" in the *Yüan shih* makes no mention of this matter.
35. Wang Kuo-wei, 340.
36. Yao Ts'ung-wu, 194–95.
37. Wang Kuo-wei, 229–30, 340.
38. Ibid., 267.
39. Here the *kuo-wang* was Boro, the son of Mokhali, who died in the year 1223.
40. Ching-ho. See Wang Kuo-wei, 402–3.
41. Ibid., 372–73.
42. See the attached "Biography of the Son Hao-wen" to the "Biography of Yüan Te-ming in the *Chin shih*, 126.
43. Yao Ts'ung-wu, 262.
44. *Lun-yü (Analects)* of the State of Lu is the collection of the wisdom of the sage Confucius.
45. Yang Chu, Mo Ti, T'ien P'ien and Hsü Hsing were the leaders of the different schools other than Confucianism in the pre-Ch'in period.
46. The Ninety-six Categories were seemingly the Chinese non-orthodox schools of India at the time of Buddha and the rest were seemingly the Chinese non-orthodox Buddhist sect.
47. See note 15. The Ch'üan-chen, Ta-tao (大道), Hung-yüan and T'ai-yi were the sects in Taoism. The three persons of the Chang family were the founders of the Taoist religion, Chang Ling (張陵) or Chang Tao-ling (張道陵), Chang Heng and Chang Lu (張魯) of the Eastern Han Period (25–220 A.D.).
48. See the "Biography of Han Yü (768–824) in the *Hsin T'ang-shu*, 101.

49. Yeh-lü Ch'u-ts'ai, *Chan-jan-chü-shih wen-chi* (湛然居士文集), *Ssu-pu-ts'ung-k'an*, Taipei edition, 8:84.
50. "Shih-lao-chuang," *Yüan shih*, 202:4b.
51. "Biography of Ch'eng Chü-fu (程鉅夫)," *Yüan shih*, 172.
52. At the West Chang-an Street, Peking, there is the pagoda of Wan-sung lao-jen (elder). In *Chan-jan-chü-shih wen-chi* there are several poems written by Yeh-lü ch'u-ts'ai for the elder Wan-sung (萬松).
53. A mispronunciation of Yeh-lü, the original is Hsia-li, and in the *Ssu-pu ts'ung-k'an* edition, was changed to She-li.
54. The Mongolian term *noyan* means noble or official. Shighi-Khutugh was the *Yeke-jarghuchi* (Grand Judge or Premier) of the Mongolian Empire. See "Biography of Hu-tu-hu" in K'o Shao-wen's (柯紹忞) *Hsin Yüan shih*, 126.
55. Nien-ch'ang, 21:13a–14b.
56. K'ung Yüan-ts'uo (孔元措) was the fifty-first generation descendant of Confucius. Duk of Yen-sheng (衍聖公) was the hereditary rank title of the K'ung family.
57. See "Biography of Yen Shih," *Yüan shih*, 148.
58. Tung-ping, present Tung-pin, Shantung province.
59. Yen Hui, the leading student of Confucius.
60. Nien-ch'ang, 21:4ab.
61. Ibid., 14b–15a.
62. See the "Biography of Kulan Khatun," *Men-wu-erh shih-chi* (蒙兀兒史記), the work of T'u Chi (屠寄), 19:2a–3a.
63. Hsing-chou, present-day Shun-te, Hopei Province.
64. There is a biography for this Khatun in *Yüan shih*, 116, although it is too brief. T'u Chi in his *Meng-wu-erh shih-chi*, 19, has written a biography of her, which is a little better than the one in *Yüan shih*. Lately, Liu I-kuang has published his *"Chi Meng-ku Chuang-sheng huang-huo Sorkhaghtani shih,"* in *Ch'u-pan yüeh-k'an*, no. 13, 1966.
65. Nien-ch'ang, 21:17ab.
66. Niamanjin (or Naimaljin) Khatun, the widow of Ögödei Khan. Mother of Güyüg Khan (r. 1246–48), Törgene Naimanjin Khatun. There is a brief account of this Khatun in T'u Chi'a's work, 19:5b.
67. Wu-t'ai Mountain is one of the Buddhist holylands in China with both Chinese Buddhist monasteries and Tibetan Buddhist lamaseries. It is located in eastern Shansi Province.
68. This is a mistake. The correct date is 1246.
69. This prince, Ha-la-chi, seems to be Kharachar, a son of Ögödei Khan. See *Yüan shih*, 107, the entry of the sons of Tai-tsung in the "Tables of the Imperial Household."
70. Nien-ch'ang, 21:17a.
71. Li Chen-ch'ang (李真常) is an erroneous record of Li chih-ch'ang (李志常).
72. "Annals of Hsien-tsung," *Yüan shih*, 3:3a.
73. The entry of *shih-lao* (monks and Taoists) of volume 6 of the Li-pu (礼部), *Ta-Yüan sheng-cheng kuo-ch'ao tien-chang*, 33. The Palace Museum editon, Taipei 1976.
74. "Biography of Tieh-ko (Tege), *Yüan shih*,125:13b.

75. Yao Tsung-wu, "Ch'iu Ch'u-chi nien-pu (邱處機年譜)," *Tung-pei-shih lun-tsung*, 245.
76. Wang Kuo-wei, 399.
77. Ibid., 393.
78. "Shih-lao chuan" in the *Yüan shih*, 202:10b.
79. See note 73.
80. "Biography of Chang Po-ch'ung (張伯淳)," *Yüan shih*, 178.
81. Wang Fu (王浮) was a Taoist leader of Eastern Chin period (316–419) who had failed in his debate against the Buddhists.
82. Nien-ch'ang, 21:39ab.
83. The "nine schools" were the Confucian, Taoist, Naturalist *(yin-yang)*, Legalist, Dialectician *(ming)*, Moist (the followers of Mo Tzu), and *tsung-heng* (a school of political alliances and strategies), Agriculturalist and others.
84. Phags-pa was given the title of *Ti-shih*, or the Imperial Instructor, in the sixteenth year of Chih-yüan (1279), after the nirvana of this great lama.
85. *Lu* in Yüan times was a unit under the *hsing-sheng* (province) and above the *hsien* (district).
86. Ta-li, also known as Nanacho, present-day Yünnan Province, was a kingdom of semi-Tibetan people, ended by the Mongols in 1253.
87. See "Biography of Liu Ping-chung," *Yüan shih*, 157. The title of *Tai-pao*, or the Senior Guardian of the Heir-Apparent, was given to him much later after this event.
88. See "Biography of Tou Mo," *Yüan shih*, 158.
89. See "Biography of Yao Shu," *Yüan shih*, 158.
90. He was the Uighur minister Meng-su-ssu. See "Biography of Meng-su-ssu," *Yüan shih*, 124. He had been the *jarghuchi* and therefore he was called by the Chinese as *cheng-hsiang*, the Premier.
91. He was another Uighur Confucian scholarly minister Lien Hsi-hsien who was well-known as Lien the Mencius (Lien Meng Tzu). See "Biography of Lien Hsi-hsien," *Yüan shih*, 126.
92. See "Biography of Chang Wen-ch'ien," *Yüan shih*, 157.
93. Hsiang-mai (祥邁), *Chih-yüan pien-wei-lu* (至元辨偽錄), Yangchou Ts'ang-ching-yüan, 1907 edition, 4:20b–21a.
94. "Biography of Wang Kou," *Yüan shih*, 164.
95. "Biography of Li Ch'ien," *Yüan shih*, 160.
96. "Biography of Yen Fu," *Yüan shih*, 160.
97. "Biography of Wang Pang," *Yüan shih*, 160.
98. Hsiang-mai, 6:1a–2b.
99. Hjigs-men mam-mkha, *Chen-po hor-gyi-yul-du dam-paihi-chos ji-ltar-byun-bahi-tshul-bsad-pa rgyal-bahi-bstan-pa-rin-po-che gsal-bar-byed pahi-sgron-me*, 1819. The Japanese edition was translated by Koho Hashimoto and was published in Tokyo, 1940, under the title of *Moko ramakyo shi* (The History of Mongolian Lamaism).
100. This Chang *T'ien-shih*, the Heavenly Instructor Chang, was Chang Tsung-yen, the thirty-sixth *tien-shih* after Chang Tao-ling the founder of Chang-yi t'ien-shih sect of Taoism.
101. Nien-ch'ang, 21:30a–31b. Also in this entry there is another record of an imperial decree on the twelfth day of the twelfth month of the same year.

102. Ibid., 21:45b.
103. Ibid., 21:29a–31b.
104. T'ao Tsung-yi, 202. See note 22.
105. Nien-ch'ang, 3:40ab.
106. "Biography of Chia Ta-la-hun," *Yüan shih*, 151.
107. Sun K'o-k'uan (孫克寬), *Sung Yüan Tao-chiao chi fa-chan* (宋元道教之發展 The Development of Taoism at the Time of Sung and Yüan), vol. II, Taiwan 1968.
108. "Shih-lao Chüan," *Yüan shih*, 202:11a.
109. The entry of *Li-pu* (ministry of ritual), in the "Monograph of Officials, I," *Yüan shih*, 85:21ab.
110. The entry of *Hsüan-cheng yüan*, in the "Monograph of Officials, I," *Yüan shih*, 87:8a.
111. Ibid.
112. "Biography of Chang Kuei (張珪)," *Yüan shih*, 175:10b–11b.

Chapter 8

Buddhism in Mongolia After the Collapse of the Yüan Dynasty

(Originally published as *Traditions Religieuses et Para-Religieuses des Peuples, Altaïques*, Paris, 1972, 49–58)

The state of Buddhism in Mongolia from the year 1368 (when Toghontemür Khan was driven out from his capital city Tai-tu or Khanbaligh by the Chinese Ming forces and retreated to Mongolia) until the year 1578 (when Altan Khan of Tümed met the Third Dalai Lama, Bsod-nams rgya-mtso, and accepted Buddhism as his faith and that of his people) is an interesting period. Most historians indicate that after the collapse of the Yüan dynasty, the Mongols were cut off from their contacts with the outside world. Consequently, all the religions in Mongolia such as Buddhism, Christianity, and Islam began to decline and eventually disappeared, while Shamanism, the original belief of the Altaic peoples, regained the prestige which had been captured by Tibetan Buddhism for almost a century.

During the Yüan dynasty the high priests of the Mongolian royal house were mostly the lamas of Sa-skya-pa, an important sect of Tibetan Buddhism. This sect declined before the collapse of the Yüan dynasty. Its theocratic regime, which was established by the early Mongol khans, was transferred to another powerful sect, the Phag-mo-grub-pa. However, at the end of the Yüan dynasty, the post of *ti-shih* (帝師), the imperial instructor, was still occupied by the head lama of Sa-skya-pa. Yet, the abbots of an opposing group, the Karma-pa, were also highly honored by the Mongol court. Notwithstanding their religious differences or their political struggles in Tibet, they were all cut off from Mongolia after the retreat of Toghontemür Khan from China. Thus, none of these denominations could continue to work actively or send teachers to Mongolia. Consequently, they all changed their aim and took Yen-ching, the Capital of the newly established Ming dynasty, as their preaching center to gain support from the Chinese emperors. Naturally their activities in Mongolia diminished. Moreover, the Mongols were facing the threat of Ming forces from outside and civil war from inside, which was a great hindrance to the lamaistic sects mentioned above. Even so, it is impossible to say that there was no Buddhist movement in Mongolia after 1368.

Shen Tseng-chih (沈增植) and Chang Erh-t'ien (張爾田) were the first Chinese scholars who paid attention to this problem and discussed it in their work, *Meng-ku yüan-liu ch'ien-cheng* (蒙古源流箋証 *Some Notes on the Erdeni-yin tobchi*). They noted:

> According to the *Hsi-yü Chüan* (西域傳) of the *Ming shih*, in the seventh year of Hung-wu [1374] the State Instructor of Kharakorum.To-erh-chi chüeh-lieh-ssu-shih pa-tsang-pu sent his Main Lecturer (講主), Ju-nu wang-pu, to the Court to present a bronze image of Buddha and relics. The *Shih Kai* (史概) also stated: "In the 11th year of Cheng-t'ung [1466], Yeh-hsien

[Esen] asked for title, silver seal, and ritual instruments, and this was rejected [by the Emperor]." Evidently, the instructors of the Red sect did not disappear on the north of the desert. (vol. VII, 1b.)

Also, at the same place, Chang Erh-t'ien spoke as follows:

According to the book of *Hua-yi Yi-yü* (華夷譯語), there was a decree to recognize the monk Yi-lin-chen tsang-pu as the abbot of Wan-shou Temple of T'ai-ning.[1]

Consequently in the beginning of the Ming dynasty, the lamas were honored among the people of Three Garrisons [三 衛 Uriyangkha]. Those lamas seem to belong to the Red sect.[2]

These accounts indicate activity among the Tibetan lamas in Mongolia after the collapse of the Yüan dynasty. Since it is difficult to find any record of these activities in the Mongolian materials, the author has had to depend upon the Chinese records.

In the entry for Wu-hsü day of the second month of the seventh year of Hung-wu (1374), *T'ai-tsu*, volume 87 in the *Ming shih-lu* (明實錄), it says:

To-erh-chi chüeh-lieh-shih-ssu pa-tsang-pu, the State Instructor of Ho-lin [Karakorum] of the old Yüan, sent his instructor Ju-nu wang-shu to the Court to present a petition and a bronze image of Buddha, a relic, a piece of white *khadagh* cloth,[3] and one jade seal, one jade stamp, four silver seals, five bronze seals, and three tablets with golden writings which were bestowed on him by the Yüan [emperors].

Accordingly, the [Emperor] proclaimed in [his] decree to the Ministry of Rites, that the image of Buddha and the relics should be presented to a Buddhist temple, and Ju-no wang-shu should be accorded the embroidered monk gown, boots, and other necessities.

Also the entry for Keng-ch'en day of the fifth month of the seventh year of Hung-wu (1374) of the above mentioned book, volume 89, states:

To-erh-chi chüeh-lieh-shih-ssu pa-tsang-pu, the State Instructor of Ho-lin [Karakorum] and Wang Wen-shu-nu, the *ping-chang* (平章 governor) of Kansu Province arrived in the Capital [Nanking]. The State Instructor presented an image of Buddha, relics, and two horses. In the Royal Decree [the Emperor] commanded that the image of Buddha and the relics be sent to Chung-shan Temple, that an embroidered monk gown should be bestowed on the State Instructor and a silk gown on Wang Wen-shu-nu, and that both should be accorded housing, furniture, other necessities, and clothing for their followers.

These accounts agree with the record of the *Hsi-yü chuan* of *Ming shih* which was quoted by Shen Tseng-chih and Chang Erh-t'ien. The materials show that there was still a Tibetan State Instructor in Karakorum seven years after the collapse of the Yüan dynasty. It is difficult to discover whether or not the surrender of the State Instructor, To-erh-chi chüeh-lieh-shih-ssu-pang-tsang-pu or Rdo-rje bka-sis dpal-bzan-po, to the Ming court affected the Buddhist faith of the Mongolian ruling class. However, it would be easy to understand how this treacherous action would limit the Mongols' trust in the Tibetan lamas whom they had honored while in power south of the Great Wall.

The entry for Chia-tzu of the twelfth month of the second year of Cheng-tung (1437 or 1438), *Ying Tsung,* volume 37 of *Ming shih-lu* says:

> [The Emperor] bestowed the title of *Tze-shan hung-hua Ko-shih* [善喜弘化國師 the State Instructor of Mercy, Benevolence, and Broad Teaching] on Ha-ma-la shih-li [Kamala-sila or Kamali-sri], the title of *Yu chüe-yi* [右覺義 Right Explainer of Righteousness] of *Seng-lu ssu* [僧錄司 Bureau of Religion and Monks] on Ta-tsang, and the titles of *Chih-hui* [指揮 Director], *Ch'ien-hu* [千戶 Head of a Thousand], and *Chen-fu* [鎮撫 Governor] on Ta-lan t'ieh-mu-erh [Dalan-temür] and others. Ha-ma-la-shih-li noted that as the envoy of tributary missions, he had come to the Court and received bestowals on several occasions. However, in order to facilitate visits to the Royal Residence, he asked [the Emperor] to bestow a title on him. The Ministry of Rites reported the matter to the Emperor and received the above decree. Also, [the Emperor] bestowed one suit of monk gown to Ha-ma-la shih-li and a hat and a belt to Ta-lan tieh-mu-erh.

The event recorded here occurred seventy years after the collapse of the Yüan dynasty. It suggests that not only were there Buddhist monks or lamas living among the Oirads, but they were also working actively for the Oirad rulers and involving themselves in diplomatic affairs between the Chinese and the Mongols. This Kamala-sila, who received the title of "State Instructor" from the Ming Emperor, probably was not a Tibetan monk but a Mongolian lama with a Buddhist name. If this were not so, he would have had difficulty coming to the Ming court as an envoy of the Oirads. The fact that he was given the honorable title of State Instructor by the Ming Emperor shows that he was held in relatively high esteem by the Oirads. However, the Oirads who appeared in the *Secret History of the Mongols* almost disappeared in the *Yüan shih*. This suggests that during the Yüan period their relation with the imperial court in Khanbaligh was not particularly intimate. Even so their leaders were still influenced by Buddhism, the imperial faith of the Mongol khans. Therefore, even seventy years after the downfall of the Yüan dynasty there were still high lamas working actively among the Oirads. This may also suggest that among opposing groups, known as Ta-Tan (Eastern Mongols) in the Ming materials, there were active Buddhist monks.

The entry for *Yi-yu* day of the fourth month of the summer of the eighth year of Cheng-t'ung (1443) *Ying Tsung,* volume 103, *Ming shih-lu,* reports:

> Formerly, Ch'ieh-wang shih-chia [Tsha-dban Sakya], the Deputy Commander of the Ch'ih-chin [Chingin] Mongol Garrison[4] sent the Director, Pa-tu-ma [Badma] to present a letter to Jen Li,[5] the Count of Ning-Yüan (寧遠伯) and the Commander, to ask permission for [him and his people] to move to Yeh-k'e pu-la [Yeke Bulagh] to escape the threat of the Oirad. Because the land was in the vicinity of Su-Chou [now Chiü-ch'üan of Kansu Province], it was rejected by [Jen] Li. Afterwards, Ch'ieh-wang chia-shih reported that he was going to build a temple in the mountains of that area and asked for a donation of colored paint and help of craftsmen. [The Emperor] sent this report to the Ministry of Rites, and it was discussed by the officials. The [Ministry] decided: The barbarians are people

of a different race. If the request to build a temple is granted, then they will move in and live there, and it will become a problem for future days. Therefore, their request should be rejected. The Emperor approved this decision.

This record suggests that the Chingin Mongols, who were to the south of the Oirads, still believed in Buddhism and that their chiefs were trying to establish a temple in the 1440s to worship Buddha.

The entry for Keng-ch'en day of the first month of the eleventh year of Cheng-t'ung (1446), *Ying Tsung,* volume 137, *Ming shih-lu,* says:

> Yeh-hsien [Esen], the Wa-la [Oirad] Tai-shih (太師) reported that the head of his tributary mission, *Kuan-ting Kuo-shih* (灌頂國師) Ch'an-ch'üan [禪全 Byams-chen] Lama, had mastered the teaching of Buddhism, and thus asked [the Emperor] to bestow on him a [high] title, silver seal, and monk gown of golden embroidery. Also [he] asked for a painting scroll of five categories of Buddhas, rings, thunder-bolt (杵), drums, lined jewelry covers, sea shells, and other ceremonial instruments. This was sent to the Ministry of Rites for discussion. The Minister, Hu Ying[6] and other officials reported concerning this matter that there was no precedent, so they would have to ask [the Emperor] to decide. The Emperor said, "We have always followed the regulations laid down by Our forefathers to appease the foreign barbarians. Since there is no precedent for the incorrect request of Yeh-hsien [Esen] why should We be forced to comply? Do not give them to him."

This record suggests that at the time when the Oirads were at their peak, their most powerful leader, Esen, was still worshipping Buddha and honoring monks. Also this record provides the fact that the lama, who was honored by Esen, had the Chinese style religious title of *Kou-shih* or *Kuan-ting Kou-shih.* Esen asked the Emperor of the Ming dynasty to bestow on the monk not only a high Chinese title but also everything he needed in the performance of his rituals and meditation. Regardless of the fact that Esen's request was rejected, it still proves that this emissary, Byams-chen lama, was an important man and honored by the Oirad leader. Also, this record shows us that the missions which were sent to Ming court by Toghon and his son, Esen, were usually headed by a lama. These facts lead us to conjecture that besides these high lamas who usually acted as emissaries there might have been other lamas who did not involve themselves with politics but only practiced their holy work as priests and preachers of the Law of Buddha.

Again in the entry for *Hsin-yu* day of the eleventh month of the third year of Ching-t'ai (1452), *Ying-tsung,* volume 223 (*The Appendix of the Abandoned Emperor, Chen-li Wang* 郕戾王, vol. 41), *Ming shih-lu,* it was recorded that:

> Yeh-hsien [Esen] again sent in a request for monk's hats and gowns, images of Buddhas, tents, golden seals, silver bottles, and other ritual instruments for his State Instructor, San-ta shih-li [Gsang-bdag-Sri] and the barbarian monk, Sa-hui t'ieh-mu-erh [Sakhuitemür], and others. These were all rejected [by the Emperor].

This account substantiates the suggestion that has just been made. It also indicates that just one year before the death of Esen (1452) there was not only *Kou-shih,* a State

Instructor, but there were also some others honored "barbarian" lamas — either Tibetan or Mongol — among the Oirad people.

All these above mentioned materials are related to the Oirads. The only record that was found in the Chinese materials concerning the religious beliefs of the Ta-tan or Eastern Mongols has already been quoted by Shen Tseng-chih and Chang Erh-t'ien in their book. The origin of this record was noted in the *Hua-yi Yi-yü*. It says: "The monk, Yi-lin-chen tsang-pu [Rin-chen bzan-po], is still in the post of abbot at Wang-shu Temple of the T'ai-ning Garrison." This is the only evidence which shows that at the beginning of the Ming dynasty there were still Buddhist monks living among the Uriyangkha people in southeastern Mongolia. However, we still lack other materials dealing with the Buddhist activities in that area after this period. Although we cannot suggest that the Buddhist movement in eastern Mongolia had entirely stopped, it is possible to surmise that Buddhist activities were not as widespread as in Oirad territory. This might have been the result of their geographical relation with Tibet or of the political gaps between eastern and western Mongolia during this period. Later, Esen was overthrown by his opponent, Alagh, and the power of Oirad declined. They began to retreat westward to the land between Altai and T'ienshan mountains. Afterwards, almost no record of them is to be found in the Ming Chinese materials. Consequently, it is impossible to study Oirad religious activities.

From the time of Esen's death in 1453 to the year of Altan Khan's conversion to Buddhism in 1578, there is almost no detailed record of the religious activities of the Mongol people.[7] Consequently, it seems that Buddhism became very weak in this 125-year period. Therefore, Sagang Sechen, the author of *Erdeni-yin tobchi* recorded the will of Altan Khan before his death and said:

> Formerly there was no Law of Buddha, and my ancestors had no scriptures and teachings [to follow] but worshipped the *ongghuns* and *cheligs*[8] only. (E. Haenisch's Ulan Batar edition, 79v–80r.)

From these records it may be possible to conclude that after the retreat of the Yüan imperial household from Khanbaligh, the devotion of the Mongol khans and leaders of Eastern Mongolia, Ta-tan, to Buddhism decreased. They were not as zealous as the Oirad leaders. This also suggests that among the Eastern Mongols Buddhism gradually disappeared and that Shamanism, the original faith of Altaic people, still survived. Even so, there is evidence to show that Buddhism, however feeble, exerted an influence on the hearts of the Mongols.

First, the *Erdeni-yin tobchi* and the *Altan tobchi* recorded that at the great ceremonial gathering, the Third Dalai Lama preached the Law of Buddha to Altan Khan and other Mongol leaders. He emphasized the story of Phags-pa Lama and Khubilai Khan and depicted himself as the reincarnation of Phags-pa Lama and Altan Khan as the reincarnation of Khubilai Khan.[9] This is strong evidence that even as late as the 1570s the Mongols were still honoring the story of Phags-pa Lama, the Imperial Instructor of the great Yüan Dynasty. This may also suggest that the Law of Buddha which was taught by the lamas of Sa-skya-pa still existed in Mongolia. Second, the *Erdeni-yin Erike* also recorded the story of Abadai Khan, who developed the teaching of Buddha among the Khalkha people of Northern Mongolia. It says:

Abadai Khan sent envoys to Lighdan Khan of Chakhar to bring back the manuscripts [of the holy scriptures] which were formerly written in Mongolian [language] by Sa-skya Pandita. (Ulan Bater edition 89v.)

The arrival of Sa-skya Pandita at the camp of Prince Kötön[10] (1246–47) was during the reign of Güyüg Khan (1246–48). Thus, from then until Lighdan Khan (r. 1604–34) the Mongolian translations of the Buddhist scriptures, made during the Mongolian empire and the Yüan dynasty, were still preserved. Since the translations were the work of the Sa-skya-pa lamas, their Buddhism, however it may have declined, continued up to Lighdan Khan's day.

Summary

In general, after the collapse of the Yüan dynasty, Tibetan Buddhism existed in Mongolia, and it was honored and believed, especially by the Oirad leaders. However, from the year 1453 to the year 1566 or 1578, its activities became very weak. It is also a fact that in this period the Dge-lug-pa, or the Yellow Sect established by Tsun-ka-pa, had not yet spread among the Mongols. Therefore, the continuation of Buddhism in Mongolia seems to have been perpetuated by the Sa-skya-pas, Karma-pas, and the members of other sects of Tibetan Buddhism. The survival of the old Shamanistic faith is beyond dispute.

Turning to Christianity, the Roman Catholic Church had been very active in Khanbaligh, Hangchow, and other places south of the Great Wall, but had made no progress in Mongolia. It was impossible for the Catholics to compete with Nestorianism which had a long historical presence in Central and North Asia. Nestorianism did not continue into modern times. However, having a number of believers among the *khatuns*, generals, ministers, and other important members of the Önggüd, Kereyid, and Naiman tribes, it was possible for Nestorianism to continue to exert a small influence even after the end of the Yüan dynasty. Consequently, some scholars believe the name of a young Mongol khan, Magha-Gürgis in Mongolian,[11] and Ma-ku-k'e-erh-chi-ssu (馬古可兒吉思) in Chinese,[12] to be a Christian name, i.e., Marco Gorgis or Mar Gorgis. Recently, Prof. Hidehiro Okada wrote an interesting paper on this problem entitled *Virgin Mary in 15th Century Mongolia*.[13]

There was also an Islamic presence. Most Chinese materials called Batula of the Oirad (or Wa-la) Mahmud. The name of the head of the Oirad envoys to the Ming court in 1447 was Pir Mohammed.[14] These facts demonstrate that some Oirads were followers of Mohammed. Even later, just before Dayan Khan's re-unification of Mongolia, one of the powerful leaders of Western Mongolia was named Ismail.[15] These records support the idea that Islamic activities existed together with Christian Nestorianism and Buddhism within the Shamanistic Mongolian society. This branch of Islam may be the origin of the Islamic *sumun* of the Alashan Banner of Western Inner Mongolia.

Notes

1. Tái-ning (泰寧 or 大寧) was one of the three Ugiyangkha garrisons that was established by the Ming emperor, Hung-wu, in the year 1389. The late Sei Wada did very detailed research on the Three Uigyangkha Garrisons. See *Studies on the History of Far East (Mongolia)*, 107–424.

2. Here the so-called "Red Sect" is a loose term for all sects besides the Dge-lug-pa, and does not really mean the Snying-ma-pa.

3. *Khadagh* is a piece of silk with Buddhist designs. It is used as a present to honor and to bring the recipient peace and blessings from Buddha or heaven.

4. Chingin Mongol (赤斤蒙古) occupied the land — as it is now called — of "Yü-men (玉門) *hsien* and An-hsi (安西) *hsien* of Kansu province. It is said the Chih-chin (赤斤 Chigin) Lake of Yü-men *hsien* was the place where the garrison was stationed.

5. "Biography of Jen Li (任礼)," *Ming shih*, 155.

6. "Biography of Hu Ying (胡濙)," *Ming shih*, 169.

7. Only the *Erdeni-yin tobchi* recorded that in the year 1566 Khutughtu Sechen Khung Taiji of the Ordos tribe invaded Tibet, and on his way home he brought back three preachers of the Law of Buddha and promoted their activities among the Mongol people.

8. The Chinese translation of *ongghon* and *chelig* is *tu-shen* (土神), the "lords of earth," which really means local deities.

9. See *Meng-gu yüan-liu ch'ien-cheng*, 7:9a and *Altan tobchi* (Nova), *Scripta Mongolica*, I, Harvard-Yenching Institute, 2d sect., 180–85.

10. Kötön was son of Ögödei Khan and was dispatched as the commander-in-chief to West China and Tibet by his father. See *Yüan shih*, 107:7r. T'u Chi (屠寄) in his *Meng-wu-erh Shih-shi* (蒙兀兒史記), 37, wrote a brief biography of him.

11. Makha or Magha Gürgis, see *Altan tobchi* (Nova), 2d Sect., 151, and *Chinggis-khaghan-u Chidagh*, 45.

12. This young khan was known in *"Ta-tan Chuan," Ming shih*, 327:9b, 10b, by different names, i.e., Ma-erh-k'e-erh (麻兒可兒) and Ma-ku-k'e-erh-chi-ssu (馬苦可兒吉思).

13. *Bulletin of the Institute of China Border Area Studies*, no. 1, Chengchi University, Taipei, 1970.

14. Entry for *chia-chen* of the eleventh month of the twelfth year of Cheng-t'ung (1447) *Ying-tsung* 160, *Ming shih-lu*.

15. See *Chinggis Khaghan-u Chidagh* 49b, and *Ta-tan Chuan* of the *Ming shih* 327, 13b–14a.

Part III
The Manchu-Ch'ing Period

Chapter 9

The Rise and Fall of Buddhism in Inner Mongolia (Part I)

(Originally published in *Studies in History of Buddhism,*
A. K. Narain, ed., New Delhi, 1980, 93–109)

A National Conversion to Buddhism

As we consider the continuing role of Buddhism in Inner Mongolia, it seems appropriate to reiterate some points made in the previous three chapters. As previously noted, before their great empire was established, the Mongolians' religion was the traditional polytheistic or animistic Shamanism common to all North Asian and Altaic nomads. The Mongols began as a small, unknown nomadic tribe, but in a very short time they established themselves as world conquerors. In doing so, they could not avoid mingling with foreign cultures and religious beliefs. As these contacts increased, Mongolian rulers began to feel that their religion was inadequate for meeting the spiritual needs of a world empire. This may account, in part, for the tendency of some members of Mongolia's ruling class to adopt, at one time or another, Buddhism, Christianity, or Islam.

The Mongolian Khans' choice of religion was probably based on cultural similarities between Mongols and Tibetans and their mutual distance, geographically and culturally, from the Chinese. Tibetan Buddhism was the official religion of the court of Khubilai Khan (r. 1260–94), the founder of the Yüan dynasty. While he and his descendants were "Sons of Heaven" in the Middle Kingdom, they were also nomadic rulers from the other side of the Great Wall, the watershed between the nomadic and agricultural worlds. In general, the teachings of the Tibetan lamas were more easily understood and accepted by the members of the Mongolian ruling class than the teachings of the Chinese monks.

The Buddhism developed by Khubilai Khan and Phags-pa, the Great Master of Tibetan Saskya-pa,[1] flourished only among the Mongolian ruling class. Consequently, following the collapse of the Yüan (1368) and the isolation of Mongolian lands, Buddhism faded away along with other foreign religions, making possible the revival of the old Shamanistic faith. This period came to be known as the "dark ages" in most Mongolian records, but because Buddhism had flourished during the Yüan period, it subtly influenced Mongolia's traditional faith and culture and consequently sowed the seeds for a future revival.

The decline of Mongolian power and the Buddhist religion did not last long. The Mongols soon were able to reestablish their position as a powerful nation against the Chinese Ming Dynasty (1368–1644). In the mid-sixteenth century, Altan Khan[2] of the Tümed[3] tribe on the south of the Gobi carried out a military campaign into Tibetan territory and reestablished intimate ties between Mongolia and Tibet, thus creating conditions conducive to the extensive development of Buddhism in Mongolia. This military victory unexpectedly resulted in the conversion to Buddhism of both Altan Khan and his nephew, Khutughtu Sechen-Khong-Taiji, of the Ordos tribe.[4]

In 1577 Altan Khan sent an emissary to Tibet to pay respects to the Great Master of the Dgelugs-pa, Bsod-nam rgya-mtsho. The following year, the Mongolian patrons and the Tibetan master met at the bank of the Lake of Kökönor (Chinghai) to enact a ceremony to promulgate the Law of the Buddha. Altan Khan presented to the master the title of "Vachir-dara Dalai Lama" and the master rewarded Altan Khan with the title "Tsakrawar Sechen Khan." Consequently, with the support of a powerful Mongolian patron, the Dgelugs-pa, the sect of the Dalai Lama, achieved eminence above all others in Tibet. In addition, Altan Khan's prestige in Mongolia increased due to the blessings of the exalted religious leader of the "Land of Snow."

The Dgelugs-pa, the Yellow Sect, had been founded by the Great Master Tsongkha-pa and was led after his *nirvana* by his two great disciples. Bsod-nam rgya-mtsho, who received the title of "Dalai Lama" from Altan Khan, was viewed as the third reincarnation of one of the two disciples of Tsongkha-pa and called himself "the Third Dalai Lama." The person eventually designated as Panchen Lama[5] was considered the reincarnation of the other great disciple.

Altan Khan's conversion, of course, hastened the spread of Buddhism in Mongolia, and the Great Khan Tümen,[6] whose headquarters were then in the eastern part of Inner Mongolia, also accepted Buddhism as his faith. Both of these conversions had far-reaching influence, even bringing about the conversion of the leader of the Central Asian Oriad Mongols, who were enemies of both the Great Khan and Altan.

After Altan Khan and other Mongolian nobles received Buddhism, the Third Dalai Lama appointed Dongkhar-Manjushiri Khutughtu as his representative, and stationed him at Köke-Khota (Chs. Kuei-hua Ch'eng), the capital city of Altan Khan, there to expound the Law of the Buddha among the Mongols.

Altan Khan died in 1583, and in 1585 the Third Dalai Lama came to Köke-Khota to pray for him and to broadcast the Law of Buddha in the Ordos and other parts of Western Inner Mongolia. This made Köke-Khota the first center of Buddhism in Mongolia. Abadai Taiji, the leader of the Khalkha Mongols to the north of the Gobi, also proceeded to the city to accept the Law from the Great Master.[7]

The Third Dalai Lama "showed the light" of *nirvana* (i.e., died), in Inner Mongolia in 1588, and the Fourth Dalai Lama was born in the household of Altan Khan.[8] Thus, the "Golden descendants" *(Altan uragh)* of Chinggis Khan were joined with the orthodox line of Tibetan Buddhism.

During this period, those who went to Mongolia to preach Buddhism came not only from the Yellow Sect but from others, usually mistakenly known as the "Red Sect."[9] Tibetan Buddhism soon spread all over Mongolia, even reaching Manchuria, where the Manchu imperial household was converted.[10]

Buddhism developed among the Khalkha Mongols on the north of the Gobi mainly because of the knowledge of Buddhism and political prestige among the households of the First Jebtsundamba Khutughtu,[11] who were members of the "Golden descendents" of Chinggis Khan. As a result, a unified system of leadership was established in the ecclesiastical world of Outer Mongolia. These unified religious institutions, together with practical politics, gradually brought together under the leadership of the First Jebtsundamba Khutughtu the fragmented Mongolian tribes on the north of the Gobi.

Because of the Manchu-Jeüngharian war, the Khalkha nobles under the leadership of this high lama surrendered to the suzerainty of the Manchu-Ch'ing.
The dynamics of religious and political unification and separation were most important to the history of Mongolia. The Imperial Tutors (Chs. *ti-shih*) of the Yüan Court had carefully avoided political involvement in other than Tibetan affairs, but after the revival of Buddhism in Mongolia, politics and religion became entangled from time to time. For example, Lighdan, the last Great Khan of Mongolia, was a patron of the Yellow sect. He built many monasteries, sponsored the translation of the Tibetan Buddhist Cannon, the Kanjur, into Mongolian, and because of his zealous efforts for the development of Buddhism, was given the religious title of "Khutughtu Khan."[12] Later, influenced by political struggles, Lighdan shifted his support, which had been directed to the Yellow Sect, to the "Red Sect." As a result, he lost his prestige among the Mongolian majority which mainly supported the Yellow Sect. Finally, after his defeat by Manchus, Lighdan fled to Kökönor and died there in 1634. After his death, the influence of the "Red Sect" in Mongolia began to decline.

The Influence of Buddhism on Mongolian Life and Culture

As already mentioned, the acceptance of honorable titles from Tibetan religious leaders by Mongolian nobles had a negative effect upon politics, for it forced the nobles to recognize that Tibetan ecclesiastical power was greater than their own lay authority. Following a precedent set by Altan Khan, Abadai Taiji of the Khalkha received the honorable title of "Khan" from the Third Dalai Lama. Afterwards, Törölbaikhu,[13] a noble of the Khoshod Mongols, who provided full military support to the Yellow Religion received the title of "Güüshi Khan" from the Fifth Dalai Lama. The same Master, immediately thereafter gave the title of "Boshoghtu Khan" to Galdan,[14] ambitious lord of the Jeünghar (Dzungar) Mongols. All this suggests that the political position of the Dalai Lama *vis-à-vis* Mongolian lay nobles was essentially the same as that of the Roman Catholic Pope *vis-à-vis* the medieval lay rulers of Europe. Without the support of the Dalai Lama, a Mongolian lay ruler could not assume leadership even among his own people. This situation not only hindered the unification of the Mongolian tribes, but also increased foreign involvement in Mongolia's internal politics.

Following Chinggis Khan's unification of Mongolia in 1206, a quasi-feudalistic nomadic system began to develop. During this period, all feudal lords and all nobility were lay men, none were monks or ecclesiastics.[15] However, after the conversion of Altan Khan, there was a new development in Mongolian society: the emergence of the ecclesiastical nobility. Among these were the members of the "Golden descendents," who left their homes and became devotees of the noble class and the high lamas who were beloved and honored as prophets. This new class of ecclesiastical nobles, together with the lay nobility, eventually formed the two pillars of modern Mongolian quasi-feudalism. It was a significant change in the socio-political history of Mongolia.[16]

The ecclesiastical nobility was strengthened by the policies and statutes of the court at the time of the Manchu domination of Mongolia (1636–1911).[17] The high lamas, with such religious titles as *khutughtu, nom-un khan, pandita, chorji, shabrang,* and *khubilghan,* made up the ecclesiastical nobility. The lamas were called by the Mongols "gege'en," which literally means "enlightened one." This word was introduced to the West as "living Buddha" through the Chinese mistranslation, *Huo-fuo*. Most high lamas were the abbots of monasteries, some of them even possessing land and underlings, or *shabinar*. According to Manchu-Ch'ing Law, the number of high lamas officially recognized by the Court as ecclesiastical nobles were as follows:

> Twelve persons in Köke-Khota Tümed, nine in Chakhar, two in Shire'etü-Küriye, three in Korchin, one in Ghorlos, six in Eastern Tümed, six in Üjümüchin, one in Kha'uchid, one in Abagha, five in Abakhanar, two in Sünid, one in Dörben-ke'üd, five in Urad, and one in the Ordos; all together, fifty-five persons.[18]

Most of the above-named lamas were Mongols or others reincarnated in Mongolia, and were officially recognized by the Manchu-Ch'ing Court as lamaist nobles. In addition, many abbots or owners of smaller temples were recognized as reincarnations *(khubilghan)* by the local people, but were not listed in the official file of the Manchu-Ch'ing Court. According to tradition, after their deaths, their new incarnation, the *khubilghan,* inherited the former incarnation's rank, titles, property, and even *shabinar* (lay disciples).[19]

Still more honorable than those mentioned above, were the lamas of the highest religious rank, *khutughtu,* born or reincarnated in Tibet or other Tibetan-speaking areas, such as Kham or Amdo. This group included the four great Mongolian *khutughtu:* 1) Jangjia Khutughtu, 2) Galdan-Shiréetü Khutughtu, 3) Mingyur Khutughtu, and 4) Jilung Khutughtu.

"The Eight *Khutughtu* of Peking" included the Dongkhar Khutughtu, Goman Khutughtu, Namkha Khutughtu, Asar Khutughtu, Ragua Khutughtu, Ajia Khutughtu, Gungtang Khutughtu, and Togon Khutughtu. In Dolon-nor there was Shikür-Shire'etü-Noyan-Choriji Khutughtu. These nobles were similar to Mongolian lamaist nobles and, especially in Inner Mongolia, enjoyed the same feudalistic privileges as the lay nobility.

During the Manchu-Ch'ing period, those Mongolian lay nobles who held administrative power were called *jasagh,* which means "ruler," and those who had no such power were called "the nobles in leisure." For the ecclesiastical nobles — those who possessed people (*shabinar,* the lay disciples) but no land, the Court established a special administrative system outside the jurisdiction of the ordinary league and banner system. Such offices as *lama tamagha* and *jasagh lama* were created to deal with the administration of the monasteries, lamas, and lay disciples. This measure, introduced to bring about the fragmentation and subjection of the Mongols, caused a further split in the already divided society. At that time, the Ch'ing Court policy was ostensibly that the lamas were not to be involved with lay politics.

Religion sometimes has a more powerful influence on human life than does law. The conversion of a nation to a certain religion means that its people will accept that religion's principles as their basic pattern for life. When the Mongolian-Yüan Khans were converted to Buddhism, the religion was accepted only by the upper class, whose influence was much weaker than in the late sixteenth century when the whole Mongolian nation received Buddhism as its faith. After the collapse of the Yüan Dynasty, the Mongols had suffered extensively from both foreign invasion and internal tribal wars. As a result, the people felt that life was vain and sorrowful. Following the second conversion of the Mongolian nobles, they began to regain hope for peace and gained a deep faith that provided them comfort. The desire of both nobles and the common people was to follow the Law that would lead them to the realm of the Buddha. They repented of their sins and worked for blessings. This psychological change brought peace and stability to Mongolia, but it also resulted in weakness and decline. The traditional martial spirit was replaced by an unrealistic hope for the next life.

When Altan Khan was converted to Buddhism, the nobles promised to honor and support the four kinds of ecclesiastics, freeing them from serving in campaigns, from the hunt, from performing other labors, and exempting them from all tax obligations. At this time, the insulting, scolding, or beating of a monk began to be treated as a transgression against the nobles themselves. As a result, a new class of ecclesiastical nobles, with a status higher than that of the common people, arose in Mongolian society. A monk's duty was to read scripture and carry out religious work. He had no corvée obligations or taxes. In other words, he had no obligation to the lay administration. In the early days this sort of honor had been given only to persons of highest merit. Now, however, anyone who became a monk received this special treatment, which obviously encouraged parents to send their male children to the monastery. Unfortunately, the rapid growth of ecclesiastics greatly damaged the military forces, the nation's productive power, and the rate of population growth in Mongolia.

While the initial conversion to Buddhism of the Mongolian Khans and nobles of the Yüan Dynasty had not interfered with Shamanistic beliefs, the second conversion, in the latter part of the sixteenth century, was a complete surrender to the Tibetan Yellow-sect. The Tibetan religion strictly forbade its believers from following heathen practices. This, in turn, implied the complete suppression of Shamanism. Though the lamas absorbed Shamanistic, pantheistic Mongolian deities such as *Tenggeri, Luus,* and others into the fold as protectors of the Buddhist Law, they used the political power of the converted nobles to destroy Shamanistic idols and to forbid Shamanistic practices.[20] In addition, Buddhist rituals replaced those of Shamanism, and lamas replaced the shamans in the worship of the deities of the mountains and rivers, in divination, in cleansing, and even in mystic or magical practices. Buddhism also prohibited the burying of horses with the dead and the offering of animal sacrifices. Basically, it closed the door opened earlier by Mongol Khans to the dissemination of all religions. These new religious measures forced any remaining Shamanistic practices underground, branded them as dishonorable, and radically altered the Mongols traditional religious life. From a cultural, historical perspective, this change was a major step forward from a primitive, animistic belief to a religion of profound philosophy and discipline.

Translation of Buddhist scriptures into Mongolian also had a profound effect on Mongolian culture. The translation of the *Kanjur,* promoted by Lighdan, the last great Khan of Mongolia, was a significant contribution. The spread of these Buddhist scriptures enhanced the development and uniformity of the Mongolian writing system, and Buddhist names (mainly in the Tibetan language) eventually comprised more than 60 percent of all Mongol names. The construction of temples, the sculpting and painting of images, and the making of religious instruments and decorations brought progress to Mongolian architecture, painting, sculpting, and handicrafts. Tibetan art, strongly influenced by Indian art, had a major influence on Mongol art.

Among the influences of Buddhism, however, the economic factor was the most affected. From ancient times, the Mongols had been limited by geographical conditions and a nomadic way of life. Consequently their economy was one of scarcity. Their relationship with the southern agricultural people of China always was determined by economic factors.[21] In peaceful trade, the Mongols exchanged their livestock and pastoral by-products for those items necessary for their livelihood, such as foodstuffs, silk, cloth, and agricultural or manufactured goods. Their reliance on the increase of their flocks and herds was the most critical economic factor for the Mongols. After their thorough conversion to Buddhism, the practices of Buddhist ceremonies, establishment of monasteries and temples, and donation to and support of monasteries and lamas accounted for the greatest part of the peoples' expenditures. When Mongolian feudal lords donated to the monasteries in Tibet, they often ordered their people to contribute likewise from their herds.[22] Thus, a great portion of Mongolian wealth and surplus productions was sent out of the country, precluding any possible accumulation of wealth. It led to poverty among the people and limited the Mongolian economy. In addition, the exodus of males from their homes to the monastery separated a tremendous portion of the labor force from production. The enlargement and the excessive number of monasteries contributed to a further decline in the country's economy.

The number of celibate monks increased rapidly, and in later generations it became common for families to keep only one lay son, in order to continue the patriarchal line, and to send all other sons to the monastery. As a result, in the last three centuries the Mongolian population has decreased rather than increased.[23]

Despite these problems, the monasteries were the center of faith, culture, economy, education, and traditional medicine in the nomadic Mongolian society. Their great and long-lasting contribution should not be neglected.

When the Manchus began their rise to power, the Inner Mongols on the south of the Gobi Desert were already converted to Buddhism and they surrendered to the Manchus. For a period they were allies of the Manchus, but gradually became their vassals. In 1691, the Khalkhas, on the north of the Gobi, were persuaded by the First Jebtsundama Khutughtu to also surrender to the Manchus. The Manchu rulers, experts in the art of politics, did not neglect the potential power of Buddhism, and used it to manipulate the Mongols. Of this, Emperor Ch'ien-lung (r. 1736–95) wrote in *La-ma-Shuo* (喇嘛說 On the Lamas):

> The Yellow Religion both outside and [inside the empire] is ruled by both [the Dalai Lama and the Panchen Erdeni] and all Mongols follow them wholeheartedly. Therefore, to develop the Yellow Religion is a measure to win over the Mongols. The consequence [of this policy] should be patronized. This is not to honor vainly or to flatter the Tibetan monks as happened in the Yuan dynasty.[24]

The measures taken toward Tibetan Buddhism by the Manchu Court were, as we see, aimed at strengthening their control over the Mongols. Even at the end of the Ch'ing Dynasty, there still were those who openly praised the success of this Manchu policy to weaken Mongolia. One such analyst said, "The rule of our dynasty over the Mongols is to establish more feudal units, to divide their power, to honor Buddhism, to control their birth rate, and thus to half the disaster of the Hsiungnu and Uighur. The art is really marvelous."[25]

Manchu-Ch'ing's religious policy and Buddhist influence in Mongolia fed on one other, placing the Mongols in a desperate situation. The unifying influence of the First

Jebtsundamba Khutughtu had threatened the Manchu policy of fragmentation and rule. Therefore, after the passing of the Second Jebtsundamba Khutughtu, the Emperor Ch'ien-lung cleverly established the policy that future reincarnations be born in Tibet, hoping to prevent the union of Mongolian lay-political and ecclesiastical religious power.[26] At the same time, however, the Manchu emperors endeavored to establish the Jangjia Khutughtu[27] as the Holy One of Inner Mongolia, and, therefore, as an imperial instrument to halt the influence of the Jebtsundamba Khutughtu from expanding south of the Gobi. During the previous three centuries the construction of monasteries had been uninterrupted in Inner Mongolia. At the earliest Buddhist center of Köke-Khota there were more than ten large monasteries. Later, at the time of Emperor K'ang-hsi (r. 1662–1722) and Emperor Yung-cheng (r. 1723–35) the Köke Süme (Hui-tsung ssu) was built in 1691 and the Shira Süme (Shan-yin ssu) at Doloön-nor in 1731. Emperor Ch'ien-lung (r. 1736–95), imitating the architectural style of Tibet, established in 1770 the Potala (Pu-to-tsung-ch'eng ssu) and the Tashilumbu (Hsü-mi-fu-shuo ssu) in Jehol. Consequently, Köke-Khota, Doloön-nor, and Jehol became the centers of religious administration in Inner Mongolia. There, the offices of the *Lama Tamagha* were established to carry out religious administration.

In Peking, Emperor Yung-cheng donated his own princely residence as the Imperial Lamaist Monastery, Yung-ho-kung (雍和宮). There were also in the Capital many other great lamasaries, such as the Yellow Temple (Huang ssu), where the relic of the Sixth Panchen Erdeni[28] was placed, and Sung-chu ssu, the residence of the Jangjia Khutughtu. Most important was the Tsandan Juu Temple (Chan-tan ssu),[29] originally built by Khubilai Khan at the time of the Mongolian Empire. Wu-tai mountain monastic center in Shansi Province also provided a strong attraction for Mongolian pilgrims.

The great monasteries of Inner Mongolia were famous for various reasons. The Monastery of Badghar (commonly known as Wu-tan-chao or Kuang-chüeh ssu in Chinese) in the Mongnai Mountains (Chs. Ta-ching-shan) of Ulanchab League, was famous for its strict discipline and profound studies in Buddhology. The Chaghan-dayanchi-yin Süme (Chs. Jui-ying ssu) of Josotu League, was the most populous monastery, once reaching ten thousand. The Shire'etü-Küriye Süme, of the same League, was unique in that it had administrative power over a banner and its people. The Janglung Pandits Gege'en Keid[30] (Chs. Pei-tzu miao) of Shilinghol League, although not large numerically, was also important.

Because Buddhism was so influential, the great hope of Mongolian monks was to study in Tibet. There, the three great monasteries, especially Jebon (Hbas-spuñs), maintained special dormitories for students from Inner Mongolia. Lamas who could not go to Tibet sought to travel to the famous monasteries of Kumbum and Labrang in the Tibetan districts of Kökönor and Kansu. At the very least they would go to Urga and Badghar in Outer and western Inner Mongolia for further study.[31]

Notes

1. Sechin Jagchid, "Ta-Yuan ti-shih Pa-ssu-pa la-ma shih tsen-yang-ti yi-ko-jen" (大元帝師八思巴喇嘛是怎樣的一个人 Phags-pa Lama, Imperial Tutor of the Yüan Dynasty), *Chung-hua Wen-hua fu-hsing yüeh-k'an* (中華文化復興月刊), April 1971, 4:12–19.

2. Altan is known as An-ta (俺答) in the *Ming shih* and other Chinese materials. He was not the Great Khan, but received a *khan* title from the Great Khan. Because of his contribution to the development of Buddhism in Mongolia, he also was titled Sayin Gege'en Altan Khan (the word *gege'en* means "enlightened"). See also Sei Wada (和田清), *Tōshi kenkyo Moko-hen* (東亜史研究蒙古篇) Studies on the History of the East — Mongolia), Tokyo, 1959, 753–812.

3. Ibid., 690–716.

4. Ibid., 716–38.

5. Panchen Erdeni or the Tashi Lama was known as the reincarnation of the second great disciple of Tsongkha-pa, the founder of the Yellow Sect.

6. Tümen Khan (r. 1558–92) is also known as Jasaghtu Tümen Khan in Mongolian materials and as T'u-man (土蠻) in the *Ming-hih* and other Chinese materials. During his time the Khan only had control over the Left Flank forces, while the Right Flank forces were under the domination of Altan.

7. The Records on the meeting date and place of Abadai Taiji and the Third Dalai Lama are not all identical. Some suggest it took place in Tibet; others suggest it was at Köke-Khota. The latter seems more dependable.

8. The father of the Fourth Dalai Lama, Sümer-mergen-khong-taiji, was a grandson of Altan Khan.

9. Strictly speaking, the "Red Sect" is identified only with the Nyingma-pa sect, though a general view, somewhat misleading, is that the so-called "Red Sect" includes all sects except the Gelug-pa, the Yellow Sect.

10. In 1631 (the fourth year of Tien-ts'ung) the Monument of the Great Chin (Manchu) Lama, *"Ta-Chih la-ma fa-shih pao-ta-chi pei"* was established in memory of Tibetan Lama Ülüg-darkhan-nangsu.

11. The First Jebtsundamba Khutughtu, Tsanabatsar (1635–1732) was a son of Gombodorji, Tüshiyetü Khan of the Khalkha Mongols. See C. R. Badwen, *The Jebtsundamba Khutukhtus of Urga*, 1961, Wiesbaden, 8–20, 46–67.

12. The Mongolian translation of the Kanjur was done during the rule of Lighdan Khan (r. 1604–34), but it was not possible to publish it because of the defeat of the Khan by the Manchus. Later, it was published in Peking at the time of K'ang-shi (1662–1722). The Mongolian translation of the Tanjur was accomplished at the time of Yung-cheng (1723–35).

13. Lighdan Khan, after his defeat by the Manchus, retreated to western Inner Mongolia, where he allied himself with Choghtu Taiji of Khalkha to carry out an invasion of Tibet. Their purpose was to assist the so-called "Red Sect" to restore its power over the Yellow Sect of the Dalai Lama. Törölbaikhu, the leader of the Khoshod tribe of the Oriad Mongols, led his forces to help the Yellow Religion. By this time Lighdan Khan had died and Choghtu's forces were entirely destroyed by Törölbaikhu and the "Red Sect" was also subdued by him. Therefore, in fact, Törölbaikhu was the one who assisted the Fifth Dalai Lama to establish his theocratic rule over Tibet.

14. Galdan accepted from the Fifth Dalai Lama the title "Boshoghtu Khan," which means "the Khan of the mandate of heaven." This greatly encouraged the ambition of Galdan to unify all Mongolia, and eventually caused the Manchu-Jeün-gharian War which lasted seven decades.

15. In the very early period of Mongolian history, there were some clan leaders or *noyan* who had the title of *begi* or *beki*. They were shamans. However, none of them were real ecclesiastical monks.

16. See Sechin Jagchid, "Mongolian Lamaist Quasi-Feudalism During the Period of Manchu Domination," *Mongolian Studies,* 1974, Bloomington,1:27–54 (chapter 11 in this work).

17. In 1624, the Khorchin tribe of Inner Mongolia allied itself with the Manchus. Later in 1636, all Mongolian nobles on the south of the Gobi presented the title of *Boghda Sechen Khan* to the Emperor T'ai-tsung of the Manchus, and officially recognized him as the sovereign of Mongolia. The surrender of the Khalkha Mongols took place in 1691 and the Manchu military occupation of the Jeün-ghar realm began in 1757.

18. See *Ta-Ching hui tien* (大清會典), 974:8b. Both the Chakhar and the Hulunbuir areas are not listed in this section.

19. These lay disciples *(shabinar)*, were originally the underlings or *khariyatu* of the nobles who offered them to high lamas whom they honored. These *shabinars* were only obliged to serve their religious overlords and their temples, but were released from their old obligations toward their feudal lords.

20. Radnabadara, *"Zaya Pandita-yin Namtar"* (The Biography of Zaya Pandita), Damdinsürüng, ed., *Mongghol uran jokiyalun degeji joghun bilig orushibai*, 1959, Ulan-Bator, 320–26, and Sagang Sechen, 252.

21. Sechin Jagchid, "Trade, Peace and War Between the Nomadic Altaics and the Agricultural Chinese," *Bulletin of the Institute of China Border Area Studies,* no. 1, 1970, Taipei, 35–80.

22. Radnabadara.

23. According to the author's personal experience, the pure pastoral area of Shilinghol League, at the beginning of the Ch'ing dynasty was divided into ten banners which contained 180 *sumun*. Each *sumun* was a unit of 150 men in an army reserve and at the same time it was also a civilian administrative unit of about 150 families. If each family contained five persons, the total number of the families would be about 16,200 and the whole population would be at least 81,000. However, the 1942 statistic of this league records 11,872 families and 52,706 persons.

24. Ho-ling (和琳), *Wei-Tsang t'ung-chih* (衛藏通誌), 1965, reprinted in Taipei, 27b–28a.

25. See the preface by Chen Chan-jan (陳澹然) for *Ch'ou-Meng chü-i* (籌蒙芻議 A Rustic Opinion on Mongolian Policy) by Yao Hsi-kuang (姚錫光), Peking, 1908, reprinted in Taipei, 1966.

26. The Second Jebtsundamba Khutughtu was also born in the family of Tüshiyetü Khan. He was unhappy because of the long involvement of the Khalkha Mongols in the Manchu-Jeün-gharian War. Therefore, after his death (1757), the Ch'ing Court influenced the Mongolian ecclesiastical and lay authorities to restrict the finding of the reincarnation of this high lama to the "Holy Land" of Tibet. However, at the present time, the documentary material on this top secret policy is not yet available for study.

27. The First Jangjia Khutughtu was a follower of the emissary of the Fifth Dalai Lama to the Ch'ing Court. The second reincarnation was a great master of profound knowledge in Buddhism and received the title of *Ta-kuo-shih* (大國師 the Great

Tutor of the State). Also, from the second to the late eighth incarnation the same title was perpetuated by the Court as an instrument to solve Mongolian problems.

28. The Sixth Panchen Lama (1738–80) came to Jehol to visit the Emperor Chien-lung. He was received with great honor. The great Monastery of Tashilumbo or Hsü-mi-fu-shuo-ssu at Jehol was established in his honor. In 1780 he died in Peking. The Emperor established a pagoda for him at the Yellow Temple (Huang-ssu) outside the wall of Peking.

29. This monastery was destroyed by the Allied forces after the defeat of the Boxer's resistance in 1900.

30. The Pandita Gege'en Keid originally contained only a few more than fifty officially authorized lamas, but in the late nineteenth and early twentieth centuries the number of the lamas reached more than one thousand.

31. This article is continued as chapter 17.

Chapter 10

The Manchu-Ch'ing Policy Toward Mongolian Religion

(Originally published in *Tractata Altaica, Denis Sinor, Sexagenario optime de rebus altaicis, Merito dedicuta*, Otto Harrassowitz, Wiesbaden, 1976, 301-19)

The political talent of the Manchu rulers is clearly demonstrated by the fact that they successfully ruled over the Middle Kingdom for 260 years and did so as a small minority among the Chinese masses. They brought their homeland of Manchuria, plus Mongolia, Turkistan, and Tibet, into the Middle Kingdom — a geopolitical unit comparable to present-day China. They shrewdly welded into one group many different peoples with divergent territories and traditions who then cooperated in spite of their many contradictions. They achieved amazing balance and tight control. They maintained general acquiescence in spite of undercurrents of dissatisfaction and rebellion. This stability was a great compliment to the Manchu art of administration.

Manchu rulers devised a set of policies suitable to each subjugated population and caused the peoples to respond, as it were, to the "benevolence and mercy" of the Manchu emperors. In reality the people were already locked in their cages. The Manchu-Ch'ing dynasty was interrupted by Western powers and forced to change its policies toward subjugated peoples, thereby stimulating nationalistic consciousness. This eventually caused separatist movements to rise against Manchu rule quite apart from the Han-Chinese revolution (1911). Had this not occurred, the great enterprise established by the Manchus in China and East Asia might not have been shaken and ended quite so quickly.

From the standpoint of control, the Han (Chinese) were, of course, the Manchus' principal subjects and main problem. Before entering China proper in 1644, the Manchus had already established a strong alliance with the Mongols south of the Gobi through intermarriage and other shrewd policies. They planned to utilize the joint forces of the Manchus and the Mongols against the Chinese. Later they manipulated religious institutions to link the Manchus, Mongols, and Tibetans together[1] and to isolate them from the Islamic Turkic peoples, as well as from the Chinese. Through the adoption of Chinese institutions and the traditional examination system, the Manchu rulers made the Chinese accept them as Sons of Heaven, while considering the peoples of Mongolia, Tibet, and Turkistan as foreign subordinates. At the same time, the Manchus created the positive assumption among the Mongols, Tibetans, and Turkic-Uighurs that they were the Khans and thus their protectors. Of the various Manchu policies, that toward the Mongols was possibly the most effective. The Manchus early adopted a quasi-feudal system and a special religious policy to rule over the whole of Mongolia. This system is not to be discussed in this paper. However, an attempt will be made to analyze the Manchu-Ch'ing policy toward Mongolian Lamaistic Buddhism.

Cultural Significance

Both the Manchus and Mongols are Altaic speaking peoples. However, their premodern ways of life were basically different. The Manchus were originally a half-hunting, half-agricultural people while the Mongols were mainly nomadic. Both belonged to the same language family and a cultural belt of similar North Asian people. In matters of religion they followed Shamanism, a common belief-system of North Asian peoples. Toward the latter part of the sixteenth century, the Mongols were converted to Tibetan Buddhism, commonly or mistakenly known as Lamaism. Later the Manchus, influenced by Mongol tribes which settled near them, began to accept Buddhism, but they were never as devout as the Mongols. While Lamaist missionaries came to Mongolia from the holy land of Tibet, a few went as far as Manchuria and even converted some Manchu leaders. Nurhachi's personal faith was recorded on the "Inscription of the Precious Pagoda of the Great Lama Master of the Great Chin."[2]

> Master Ulug Darkhan Nangsu [d. 1621] was a man from Tibet [dbUs gTsang]. He was born in the land of the Buddha, and achieved a great understanding of the truth. After passing through the great law, he became very anxious for the salvation of all mankind. He did not hesitate to undertake the long, difficult journey to the Mongol tribes in the east to promote the holy religion and broadly expand the mercy of Buddha. . . . After his arrival in our country, Emperor Tai-tsu [Nurhachi, r. 1616–27] honored him with reverential respect as a teacher, and richly provided for him.[3]

This inscription was created in 1631 by Emperor Tai-tsung (r. 1627–43). Although it suggests that early Manchu emperors believed in Buddhism, its influence among the Manchus was not as profound as it was among the Mongols. Buddhism never entirely displaced Shamanism in Manchu religious activities. The situation was quite similar to the first Mongol conversion to Buddhism during the reign of Khubilai Khan (r. 1260–94).

In the Imperial record, Emperor Yung-cheng (r. 1723–35) states:

> When I was young, I liked to read theological books and to marvel at the possibility of being able to become a Buddha. . . . In my whole life I deeply contemplated the chain of cause and effect. The Jangjia Kjutughtu was really my mentor and the teacher who gave me proof. Other Buddhist monks also came to my princely residence . . . such as [the teacher] Chia-ling-hsing . . . the Po-lin Abbot[4] . . . also Master Chien-fo-yin and others. After I met them and conferred with them for a long, long time, I realized their ability was limited and I was unable to find even one answer to my questions.[5]

A similar story is that of Ayorshiridara, the Crown Prince of Toghontemür Khan (1333–68) of the Mongol-Yüan dynasty. The *Yüan shih* records this story.

> In the twenty-second year of Chih-cheng [1362] the Crown Prince was sitting in the Ching-ning Palace. Many Tibetan and Korean monks were also seated there in a long row. The Crown Prince remarked, "The [Chinese] Master Li Hao-wen[6] taught me Confucian scriptures for many years but their meaning was still not too clear to me. Now I am hearing the Law of the Buddha [from monks] and can

understand it after only one night." After this the Crown Prince became more and more interested in Buddhist studies.[7]

These two stories indicate that the Mongols and Manchus, because of similar religious backgrounds, were inclined toward Tibetan Buddhism.[8]

Later, after ascending the throne, Emperor Yung-cheng dedicated his personal, princely residence to the Buddha, and it became Yung-ho kung (雍和宫), still well-known as the great Lamaist Temple of Peking.[9] This event originated in his personal religious interests and should not be interpreted solely as a political measure aimed at the Mongols. In the imperial palace in Peking there is a hall filled with Lamaist images where lamas formerly performed religious rituals for the well-being of the emperor and his imperial household. Also, on Jade Island (Ch'ün-tao) in the imperial garden of Pei-hai Lake there is a Lamaistic pagoda, another monument to Manchu religious interest. To celebrate his mother's birthday, Emperor Ch'ien-lung established many Lamaist temples and religious ceremonies. Offerings at the Imperial Tombs were carried out by Manchu lamas.[10] All these facts suggest that the faith of the Manchu imperial household was primarily Lamaist Buddhism, a fact which greatly helped the Manchu rulers win the confidence and support of the Mongols who held the same religious beliefs.

Political Motivation

Emperor Ch'ien-lung (r. 1736–95) frankly stated the Manchu policy towards Mongolian Lamaism, or the "Yellow Religion," in his inscription "On the Lamas" *(Lama shuo)*.

The Yellow Religion both outside and [inside the empire] is ruled by both [the Dalai Lama and the Panchen Erdeni] and all Mongols follow them wholeheartedly. Therefore, to develop the Yellow Religion is a measure to win over the Mongols. The consequence [of this policy] is no small matter because [the religion] should be patronized. This is not to honor vainly or to flatter the Tibetan monks as happened in the Yuan dynasty.[11]

When the Manchus were establishing their empire, Mongolian society, through a nomadic quasi-feudal system, had already become more fragmented than unified. However, the rise of the great religious leader, the First Jebtsundamba Khutughtu (1635–1723) from the noble house of the Khalkha Tüshiyetü Khan, had begun to reunify the Mongols. The move of the Khalkha to surrender themselves to the Manchu-Ch'ing was led by this great Lama (1691). The Buddhist faith of the Manchu court was one of the important reasons which led the Lama to persuade these nobles to take this action.

As the historical record notes, Galdan's first encroachment against the Khalkha (1688) was encouraged by the theocratic power of Lhasa. Near the end of the Manchu-Jeüngharian War (1688–1757), a Khalkha rebellion, led by Prince Chinggunjab, took place against Manchu domination. It was ended through the influence of the Second Jebtsumdamba Khutughtu (1724–75).[12] Such events as these eventually led Emperor Ch'ien-lung to give special attention to all policies toward Mongolian Lamaism.

Politically, Manchu measures affecting Mongolian religion may be divided into three main approaches.

1. To regulate church systems as part of an overall state system under the rule of the government. All religious ranks or titles, such as *khutughtu, nomun khan, chorji, ghabchu,* and *khubilghan*,[13] had to be authorized by the government and bestowed by the emperor.

2. To give special honor to high lamas, elevate their social position, and show imperial devotion and favor towards Buddhism, in order to utilize their religious influence to increase Mongol loyalty toward the Manchu court. For instance, when the First Jebtsundamba Khutughtu died in Peking (1723), Emperor Yung-cheng unprecedentedly came personally to express his condolences and issued an imperial decree.

> The Khutughtu was greatly revered by My Imperial Father, and was treated with great honor. Our Imperial Father ascended to the remote regions on the *chia-wu* day, and now it is evident that the Khutughtu's nirvana is also on the *chia-wu* day. The fate of both the Buddha [Khutughtu] and the Sacred One [the Emperor] proved unmistakably that the Khutughtu should not be compared with other ordinary monks. Our Royal Self has presented *khadagh*[14] and offered tea [to the Khutughtu] in order to express Our deep concern. Let this decree be noted by all Khalkha khans, Royal son-in-laws, various *khutughtu* and their underlings.[15]

3. To build great imperial temples in Peking, Mukden, Jehol, Dolonor, and Urga as concrete evidence of the Buddhist faith of the Manchu imperial household and as a measure to strengthen the influence of Buddhism as an instrument of control in Mongolia.

Reading between the lines and judging from actual results, the true purpose of the Manchu religious policy toward Mongolia aimed at the following.

1. To establish Lamaist institutions as a counterbalance to the secular power of Mongolian princes.

2. To limit the power of the great Mongolian religious leaders and to forestall the unification of theocratic power and political power.

3. To reduce political ties and relations between Mongolia and Tibet and to strengthen the ties between Mongolian monasteries and Peking institutions.

4. To create a high governmental religious leader as a political instrument to check the influence of local Mongolian leaders.

Main Aspects of Manchu Policy Toward Mongolia

What has been termed Mongolian, nomadic, quasi-feudalism stemmed from the relationship between the feudal princes and their people. At the time of the Mongolian Yuan dynasty, Khubilai Khan granted the great master, Phags-pa, the rank of *ti-shih* (Imperial Instructor) and made his monastery of Sa-skya the center of Tibetan government. However, in Mongolian society there were neither "noble lamas" nor "lama nobles" among the *noyad* class of princely lords. The rise of lama nobles occurred after the second conversion of the Mongols to Buddhism in the late sixteenth century. This basic orientation was reaffirmed and reinforced by the Manchu emperors. They granted lama nobles the same feudalistic privileges that the lay nobility enjoyed, and confirmed them as overlords in their own domain. Consequently, these lama nobles, together with their counterparts the lay nobles, became the two main pillars of a Mongolian quasi-feudal socio-political system. This policy generated no unity among the fragmented Mongols either under the lay nobility or under a theocratic authority. Rather, their loyalty was directed to the Manchu Emperor.[16] As a result, the Mongolian people eventually split into two groups: the common *arad* under lay lords and the *shabinar*[17] under the theocratic lords. There was the rise of the factions — a *khara* ("black") or lay segment, and *shira* ("yellow"), the lamas. The struggle for power between these two groups has also been a main current in modern Mongolian history.[18]

Through the leadership of the First and Second Jebtsundambas, fragmented northern Mongolia began to reunite. Their inclination toward religious unification also began to influence the Mongols south of the Gobi. Moreover, these two great religious leaders were from the family of Tüshiyetü Khan of Khalkha. In other words they were descendants of Chinggis Khan. This wedding of lay power, theocratic power, politics, and religion was viewed as a threat which could lead to the reunion of Mongolia under a theocratic leader of the old imperial household of Chinggis Khan. This would not benefit the Manchu court, and consequently the Manchus sought to limit the power of the Jebtsundamba Khutughtu, while still showing great reverence. After the outbreak of Chinggunjab's incident[19] already mentioned, Emperor Ch'ien-lung decided not to allow further developments of this type in Mongolia, and, therefore, after the unexpected "nirvana" of the Second Jebtsundamba, the Emperor determined that the reincarnation of this high lama should henceforth be found in Tibet, not in Mongolia. Thus, the Manchus removed the possibility that Mongolia's highest religious leader could ever emerge from among the descendants of Chinggis Khan. In the inscription of *La-mo-Shuo*, "On the Lamas" (喇嘛說), which was written by Emperor Ch'ien-Lung himself and was erected in the Yung-ho-kung (雍和宮), the Royal Lama Temple in Peking, he said as follows.

> Now the *khubilghans* of the Dalai Lama, the Panchen Erdeni, and the Jebtsun [danba] Khutughtu who were worshipped by the four tribes of Khalkha, are usually transferred through the [relationship of] brothers, uncles, nephews, and relatives. It seems that the *khubiglhans*, who handle religious affairs, all come from one family. Thus, it is no different from the succession of the [lay] titles. For instance, the great *khubilghans* that are worshipped in the Inner and Outer *Jasaghs* of Mongolia and were reincarnated in the families of the princes are as follows: The Shire'etü Khutughtu is the uncle of the Prince of Khalkha, Güren Efu[20] Lhawang-dorji. The Daghba Khutughtu is the son of the Prince of Alashan, Lobsang-doriji. . . . The Khutughtu of Jambalorji, the Khambu Nomun Khan, is the son of the Tüshiyetü Khan Tsedendorji. There are [so many] cases like this, it is impossible to mention them individually. . . . If this defect can not be remedied, it would be transferred to each other only through their personal selfishness and cause the decline of the Yellow religion. Then it would be neglected and distrusted by both the Mongols and Tibetans and might even cause riots.[21]

Because of this measure all reincarnations of the Jebtsundamba Khutughtu from the third forward were found in Tibet without any exceptions. Consequently, the Emperor's policy blocked the developing union of Mongolian theocratic and lay power. This regulation led to the separation of the reincarnations of high lamas in Mongolian leagues and banners from the blood relations of the lay nobles, thereby establishing a breach between these two groups. However, the Manchus could not foresee that in the twentieth century, the powerful figure who would lead the Mongols against them to independence would be the Eighth Jebtsundamba Khutughtu, a Tibetan lama by birth but a Mongolian by spirit.

By these policies the Emperor Ch'ien-lung on the one hand recognized the Yellow Religion headed by the Dalai Lama and the Panchen Erdeni. He promoted the belief in the reincarnation of Mongolia's highest religious leader while stipulating that he be found in Tibet. Simultaneously, he tried to curtail the intimate religious tie between Mongolia and Tibet by ending the influence of Tibet's religious leaders in Mongolia and Lhasa's role in the recognition of Mongolian reincarnations.

According to earlier traditions all new incarnations of Mongolian theocratic nobles had to be formally confirmed by the Dalai Lama or the Panchen Erdeni. This usually took the form of confirmation through an oracle from the spirits of the Protectors of the Law. Of course, the real authority in such decisions was exercised by the theocratic court of the Dalai Lama or the Panchen Erdeni. Thus, it was quite easy to bring Mongolian and Tibetan theocratic power or politics under one Vatican-like monastic influence. As the Son of Heaven, Emperor of the Middle Kingdom, Emperor Ch'ien-lung shrewdly adopted the ancient Chinese strategy of disallowing the unification of non-Chinese peoples. Therefore, in the fifty-seventh year of his rule (1792) he established the "Golden *Bomba* [bottle]" system. One *bomba* was placed in Lhasa and administered by the Manchus *amban* ("minister") stationed in Lhasa. Another *bomba* was located in the great lamasery of Yung-ho-kung in Peking where the drawing of lots determined which of the candidates would be installed as a new reincarnation. This was supervised by the Minister of the Li-fan-yuan.[22] Emperor Ch'ien lung said in his inscription "On the Lamas":

> The fact that all the *khubilghans* are reincarnated in one family is nothing but selfishness. How could Buddha be selfish! Consequently, this has to be prohibited. Here, I made a golden bottle, and sent it to Tibet. The names of the candidates of the reincarnated *khutughtu* should be written and placed in the bottle, after they have been suggested by the masses, and should be decided by drawing sticks [from the bottle]. Although it cannot remedy all the defects, it will certainly be fairer than previously when it was decided by one man's will.[23]

In the passage in the *Tien-shu Ch'ing li-ssu* of the *Li-fan Yüan* of the *Ta-Ch'ing hui-tien*, there is an explanation of the resolution. It says:

> The lamas of high virtue, who are capable of reincarnation in this world by miracle, are *khubilghans*. The names of the candidates should be placed in the Golden Bomba Bottle, and the decision made according to the lot that has beet drawn [from the bottle]. This evidence should be reported [to the Emperor] to await Imperial decision.

The original note on the passage gives a more detailed explanation. It says:

> Formerly, the reincarnation of a *khutughtu* usually depended upon the Dalai Lama's Lhamu *choijung*[24] who invited the spirit [of Lhamu] to possess his body to point out the [birth] place of the [new] *khubilghan,* and then [his disciples] went out to search [for his new reincarnation] to worship it. In the

57th year of Ch'ien-Lung [1792], after the pacification of Kurka [Nepal] the Emperor Kao tsung Ch'un-huang-ti ruled Tibet well, attacking the falsity of Lhamu *choijung*, and especially granting one Golden Bomba Bottle which was placed in the great hall of Potala. After the *nirvana* [death] of the Dalai Lama, the Panchen-Erdeni, the Jebtsundamba Khutughtu, the reincarnated *khutughtus*, or great lamas of both Tibet and Mongolia, the name, date, and hour of birth of the candidates should be put into the Golden Bomba Bottle. Then invite the lamas to recite scripture, and under the supervision of the *Amban* of Tibet (駐藏大臣), draw one lot [from the bottle] to decide the [new] *khubilghan*. Another Golden Bomba Bottle is to be placed in the Yung-ho-kung. If the *khutughtus* of both Inner and Outer *Jasaghs* are prevented from going to Tibet for recognition, they should ask the chief of their league *(chighulghan)* to make a tentative decision, and report it to the [Li-fan] Yüan.[25] Then [the name of the candidates] should be written carefully on the lots, the lots put into the Golden Bomba Bottle of Yung-ho-kung, and the *Jasagh da-lama*[26] invited to recite the scripture, while the lots are drawn under the supervision of the Minister of *Li-fan Y″an*. (vol. 64:7b–8a)

In this way the Lamaist administration was put at least in part under the jurisdiction of *Li-fan-yuan*. All such matters as the recognition of a new reincarnation of a *khubilghan*, his formal installation, his rank, his title, the number of monks in a temple, and the administration of all great lamasaries had to be authorized by the *Li-fan-yuan*. The Ch'ing court established four leading *khutughtus:* the Jangjia Khutughtu, the Minjur Khutughtu, the Galdan-shire'etü Khutughtu, and the Jilung Khutughtu. Another eight high level khutughtus were stationed in Peking from time to time including: the Dungkor Khutughtu, the Gomon Khutughtu, the Namkha Khutughtu, the Osar Khutughtu, the Ajiya Khutughtu, the Ragua Khutughtu, the Gungtang Khutughtu, and the Tugon Khutughtu. Besides the Jebtsundamba Khutughtu of Urga (present-day Ulanbator), all prominent incarnate high lamas were ordered to personally come to Peking every six years and pay homage to the Emperor by a system of rotation. A *Lama Tamagha*, or Lama Office, was established in Peking to supervise Lamaist affairs under the guidance of the *Li-fan-yuan*. Also, similar Lamaist agencies were established at Jehol, Dolonor,[27] and Wu-tai-shan.[28] The Manchu rulers thus sought to elevate the religious status of Peking. Nevertheless, it could never match Tibet and the holy city of Lhasa. Still, administratively, Peking became more closely related to the Mongolian lamasaries than were the theocratic courts of Lhasa or Tashilumpo.

The measures of the Manchu court to control the theocratic power in Mongolia were rather negative measures. The Manchu approach was not as effective as it would have been had they established a religious leader of their own who could have been utilized politically. This idea was, however, a factor in the rise of the Jangjia Khutughtu to a high position.

According to his own confession recorded in the *La-ma shuo*, Emperor Ch'ien-lung recognized the leading position of the Dalai Lama and the Panchen Erdeni in the realm of Yellow Religion. However, he was reluctant to recognize the Jebtsundamba Khutughtu's position as the third highest ecclesiastic of the Lamaistic world and the preeminent leader of the Church in Mongolia. Moreover, he ignored the Jebtsundamba Khutughtu's claim to leadership over all Mongolia, and only acknowledged him as the religious leader of the

Khalkha. On this point the Emperor Ch'ien-lung quite agreed with Galdan, leader of the Jeünghar Mongols and the opponent of Ch'ien-lung's grandfather, Emperor K'ang-hsi, in their struggle for rule over Khalkha.[29] At its highest point the status of the Jebtsundamba Khutughtu never rivaled the supreme position of the Dalai Lama and the Panchen Erdeni of Tibet, but his position in Mongolia had no parallel. Consequently, the Manchu court felt the necessity of creating a religious figure in Mongolia to counterbalance the power of the Jebtsundamba Khutughtu.

The First Jangjia Khutughtu, Aghwanglobsangchoildan, was originally one of the delegates from the Fifth Dalai Lama,[30] and came to Peking in the year 1683. At a ceremony held to pay their respects to the Emperor K'ang-hsi, Aghwanglobsangchoildan's attitude greatly pleased the Emperor. Other members of the Dalai Lama's delegation returned to Tibet without Aghwanglobsangchoildan, who, by command of the Emperor, remained in Peking to pray for the well-being of the royal household. Later, when a disturbance broke out in Tibet after the death of the Fifth Dalai Lama (1682), Aghwanglobsangchoildan was sent to Lhasa as an envoy of the Emperor to settle the problem of selecting a new reincarnation of the Sixth Dalai Lama (1697).[31] Because of his merit he was appointed abbot of the imperial temple at Dolonor and given the responsibility of developing the Yellow Religion in both Inner and Outer Mongolia. In the year 1705, the emperor gave him the title Ta-kuo-shih (大國師), "Great Teacher of the State." The next year the Emperor built the great temple, Sung-chu Ssu, for this lama and appointed him to the highest religious post which supervised the temples in Peking, Jehol, and Dolonor. He was revered by the Emperor Yung-cheng before the latter ascended the throne, and consequently, Aghwanglobsangchoildan was reincarnated as the Second Jangjia Khutughtu, Rolpaidorji, and was further honored in the court of Emperor Yung-cheng. In 1731, the Emperor built for him the great lamasery Shira Süme (Shan-yin Ssu) in Dolonor. Later the Emperor Ch'ien-lung bestowed upon him the title of *Chen-hsing huang-chiao ta-tse ta-kuo-shih* (振興黃教大國師), "Great Developer of the Yellow Religion and Great Merciful Teacher of the State." When the Khalkha Prince Chinggunjab headed a rebellion against Manchu rule, the Jangjia was appointed as a special envoy to Urga to confer with the Second Jebtsundamba in an effort to appease the people of Khalkha. From this time on, all successive reincarnations of the Jangjia Khutughtu carried the political function of appeasing the Mongolian masses for the sake of Manchu domination.

Honored by the Manchu court, the position of the Jangjia Khutughtu was elevated politically to the fourth position in Lamaist Buddhism. His influence forestalled the development of the Jebtsundamba's power in Inner Mongolia. Clearly, the policy of the Ch'ing court was to isolate Mongolian theocratic power, so that it could not interfere in lay matters. Thus, although the Jangjia Khutughtu was a useful counter-balance to the influence of the Jebtsundamba Khutughtu, it was still not intended that he be openly involved in lay politics. Moreover, from the third reincarnation, Jebtsundamba Khutughtus were all Tibetans and had decreasing concern for Mongolian politics. With this changed situation Jangjia Khutughtus gradually lost their important political role. However, when the Eighth Jebtsundamba Khutughtu[32] headed the Independence Movement of Outer Mongolia, the young Sixth Jangjia Khutughtu[33] immediately became an important figure in the manipulations of the Peking Government in the newly established Republic of China. He was used to check the influence of the great Khutughtu of Urga, and also to pacify a disturbed situation in Inner Mongolia. In order to make him more influential, Yüan Shih-kai, the first President of the Republic, formally recognized his old title of *Ta-kou-shih*, "Great Teacher of the Republic."

The above facts suggest the importance of religious factors in the Manchu policy toward Mongolia and Tibet. This policy was cunningly planned and skillfully carried out. Consequently, general criticisms of the Manchu policy toward Mongolian Buddhism note that the thoughts and actions of the Mongols were restricted by Lamaistic Buddhism which retarded the development and contributed to the downfall of the nation. Moreover, the power of the lamas and the negative influences of Buddhism increased day after day until eventually the Mongols lost their militant spirit and turned to vain desires for the next world. Seeking great blessings from the Buddha, exemption from taxes and corvée duties granted to lamas, and the high reverence bestowed by society, parents kept one son at home to continue the family line while all the rest of their sons entered temples to become monks. This caused a decrease in population, kept men from productive activity, and turned them into pure consumers. The surplus production and economic power of the Mongolian society was invested in monasteries and religious works, rather than being invested in production. This vicious cycle caused a sharp decline in the Mongolian economy, and was one of the things the Mongols suffered under the foreign domination of the Manchus from 1624 to 1911.[34] The overall effects of Manchu policy were the decline of the Mongol nation, but this was not solely the result of Manchu manipulation of Mongolian religion.

The basic purpose of Manchu policy toward Mongolia was to curtail the power of the Mongols as a people who would otherwise be difficult to rule. Still the Mongols could not be so weak that they could not support the Manchu imperial court. During the crises of the Tai-p'ing Rebellion (1850–60), the Sino-Anglo-French War (1857–60), and the Nein-fei rebellion (1853–68), Mongolian volunteers under the leadership of Prince Sengerinchin[35] assisted the Manchus in fighting their enemies both inside and outside the Middle Kingdom. These actions prove the success of Manchu policy toward the Mongols. In contrast, the Independence Movement of Outer Mongolia (1911) is evidence of failings in Manchu rule. These failings were a direct result of the changing situation in Asia and the modification of policies toward Mongolia in the latter part of the Ch'ing Dynasty when the Manchus had become fully Sinicized.

While Manchu rulers carried out their religious policies toward the Mongols, they concurrently implemented a policy of militarism. All Mongolian males from fifteen to sixty were listed in the military files. Of course, this was not designed to strengthen or preserve the military might of the Mongols, but rather to utilize the Mongolian forces to maintain Manchu rule. Consequently, according to Ch'ing law, it was difficult for a Mongol male to get permission to become a lama, and this control was originally quite tight. The Lamas of every temple were registered and unless a lama received a *tu-tieh* (度 諜), or official diploma of recognition, he was not qualified as a monk and was subject to severe punishment.

The Emperor Shun-chih in 1658 directed that, "The lamas and their disciples, unless their names [and numbers] are registered in the *[Li-fan] Yüan* shall not be allowed to increase."[36] Later, in the first year of his reign K'ang-hsi (1662) ordered:

> People of the dependencies [Inner and Outer Mongolia], the Mongolian Eight Banners,[37] and the Chakhar[38] who wish to send family members to [temples] as

disciples of lamas, and those who wish to retain *gelun* or *bandi*[39] that came from outside, must report their names to the *[Li-fan] Yüan* and register in the file. Transgressors will be punished for the crime of hiding a man in service.[40]

Again in the tenth year of K'ang-hsi (1671) the Emperor mandated:

In the land of . . . Mongolia, except for lamas registered in the files, all other lamas and *bandis* in the pasture shall be expelled from the temples. Anyone refusing to be expelled, or hiding such a person, or one who secretly makes his underling a *bandi* — or if any such case is discovered — then the transgressing prince . . . duke, *jasagh*, or *taiji* will be fined one entire year's salary. If the *taiji* has no salary then the fine will be fifty horses and dismissal from his post. If a transgressor be [a person without official post] then he shall be punished with one hundred strokes. His ruling prince . . . duke or *taiji* shall be fined nine months' salary. The fine for . . . [other officials] is eighteen animals. The . . . head of a ten household unit [shall be punished] with one hundred strokes. One-third of the animals fined shall be given to an informer. When the informer is a slave, he shall then be released from slavery. Persons who became *bandi* secretly, and lamas and *bandi* who are detained, shall be made laymen and sent back to their original banner.[41]

In Mongolia all the ranking horsemen and the men on the military roles were forbidden to be *ubashi*[42] without authorization. Anyone transgressing this rule shall be punished as in cases of becoming a *gelun* or *bandi* secretly. The aged, disabled, or persons whose names are eliminated from the military rolls are allowed to move according to their own will.[43]

The Mongolian women are not to be allowed to become *chibghancha* [nun]. Transgressors shall be punished as in cases of unauthorized *bandi*.[44]

In 1775 Emperor Ch'ien-lung decreed: "Originally *taiji* were not allowed to become lamas without authorization. However, because the Mongols are so devoted to Buddhism, if someone among the *taiji* now wishes to become a lama, he should not be prevented."[45]

In 1817 the Manchu court decided that: "Lamas who petition for *tu-tieh* [registration and recognition], should have it granted by the *[Li-fan] Yüan*. At the end of the year all cases shall be collectively reported to the Throne."[46]

From the regulations given (1658–1817), it is clear that the main Manchu principles were: 1) to maintain Mongolian army resources, and 2) to prohibit the sons of lay nobles from becoming lamas. The Ch'ing court exercised strict controls to prevent an increase in monks, and did not actively encourage Mongol males to leave home and become devotees as is commonly thought. Clearly this would have been counterproductive, for according to Ch'ing policy, local Mongolian administration was a combined military-civilian system. In every *sumu*,[47] there were to be fifty soldiers and one-hundred able-bodied men. Every three years a review or inspection was carried out by the chief of the league, and all numbers, results, and so forth were reported to the emperor. Veteran elders in a banner office informed the author in the early 1930s that the inspection occurred in Inner Mongolia in the latter part of the Ch'ing period just before the "Boxer Rebellion" (1899–1900). However, it had become a mere formality. Due to the increase of lamas and lack of able-bodied men, banner officials usually falsified both the list of lamas, many of whom had no *tu-tieh,* and also the list of able-bodied men.

These last observations suggest that the Mongolian ruling class, being influenced by their devotion to Buddhism, ignored the orders of the imperial court in order to achieve blessings in the next life. They did not wish to sin by prohibiting a person from becoming a lama. Instead, they preferred to transgress imperial orders. Manchu officials, on their part, although aware of the situation, did not restrain the increase in the number of lamas. They discovered a tendency which they could not stop. Whether they intentionally contributed to the tendency is still a difficult question and impossible to answer due to a lack of reliable materials. As the 1775 decree shows, the court gave up its prohibition against Mongolian nobles becoming lamas and is good evidence suggesting that even Emperor Ch'ien-lung experienced difficulty in stopping the Mongols from leaving the lay life to become monastic devotees. By studying the Lamaist regulations established in Ch'ing times it is easy to discover that controls eventually became quite loose. This may have been due to two things. First, it was difficult to control persons wishing to become lamas,and second, with the Sinicization of the Manchu rulers, Mongolia was not as important as it had been.

The Pandita Gene'en Keid of Abakhanar Banner, Shilinghol League, was one the great monasteries of Inner Mongolia. In early 1943 there were still more than eight hundred lamas there, and twenty years earlier the number had been more than one thousand. However, the authorized *tu-tieh* for this temple by the Ch'ing court was only about fifty.[48] In a matter such as this, it would not be fair to place the blame for the increase in lamas and the decline of the Mongolian population entirely on the Manchu rulers. The Mongolian ruling class also cannot escape its responsibilities.

Notes

1. Religious ties were extremely important in the political relations between the Manchus, Mongols, and Tibetans. They believed that the Dalai Lama himself was Avalokitesvara, that the Manchu Emperor was the reincarnation of Manjusiri, and that the Mongolian Khan was the reincarnation of Vajra-bani.

2. After Nurhachi ascended the Khan's throne (1616), he adopted "Chin" or "Hou Chin" (the Later Chin) as the official title of his kingdom.

3. This text is recorded in Inaba's (稻葉君山) *Shin-cho zen-shi* (清朝全史 Early History of the Ch'ing Dynasty).

4. Pai-lin Ssu (柏林寺), a famous Buddhist Monastery in Peking.

5. *Wei-Tsang t'ung-chih* (衛藏通志) top volume 11–12b (*Ch'ien-hsi-ts'un-she* 漸西村舍 edition).

6. In the "Biography of Li Hao-wen (李好文)," *Yüan shih* 183, his position is recorded as an instructor to the crown prince, but there are no details given.

7. *Yüan shih* 46, "The Annals of Shun-ti," 8b.

8. In the thirteenth century, the Mongols first made contact with the Chinese Buddhists but were finally converted to Tibetan Buddhism. See Sechin Jagchid, "Why the Mongolian Khans Adopted Tibetan Buddhism As their Faith," *Proceedings of the Third East Asian Altaistic Conference,* 1969, Taipei (chapter 6 in this work).

9. See Ferdinand D. Lessing's work, *Yung-ho kung.*

10. In the fifty-first year of Ch'ien-lung (1786), it was decided by the Emperor that: "There should be twenty lamas in both the Lung-fu ssu (隆福寺) temple at the East Royal Tombs, and Yung-fu ssu (永福寺) temple at the West Royal Tombs, also a da-lama should be appointed." See *Ch'ing tai pien-cheng t'ung-k'ao* (清代邊政通考), 193, the chapter "The Titles of Lamas."

11. The inscription La-ma shuo (喇嘛說) was composed by the Emperor Ch'ien-lung himself in the fifty-seventh year of his reign (1792), and the monument was erected in the great lamasery, Yung-ho kung, in Peking. This inscription was originally written in Chinese and was translated into the Manchurian, Mongolian, and Tibetan languages, all carved on the same monument. This inscription is also recorded in the first volume of the *Wei-tsang t'ung-chih,* 27a–30.

12. See Charles R. Bawden, *The Modern History of Mongolia,* 118–33; N. Isjamts, *Mongol ard tumnii 1755-1758 onii tusggar togtnoliin zebsegt temtsel,* 1962, Ulaabaator. Li Yü-shu (李毓澍), *Wai-meng cheng-chiao chih-tu k'ao* (外蒙政教制度考), Taipei, 1962, 389–92.

13. *Khutughtu,* a Mongolian word, means "the great blessed one." *Nom-un Khan,* means "the king of scriptures." *Chorji,* a Tibetan word, has the same meaning as *Nom-un Khan. Ghabchu* or *Kabhchu,* another Tibetan word, means great teacher with profound knowledge of scriptures. *Khubilghan,* a Mongolian word, means "the reincarnated one."

14. A *khadagh* is a piece of white or light blue silk scarf with Buddhist designs. According to Mongolian and Tibetan custom, the presentation of a *khadagh* expresses highest honors and greatest blessings to the receiver.

15. See Chang Mu (張穆), *Meng-ku yu-mu-chi* (蒙古游牧記), vol. VII, "General Instruction on the Khalkha," a note from the "Ping-ting Chun-ke-erh fan-lueh" (平定準噶爾方略).

16. See Sechin Jagchid, "Mongolian Lamaistic Quasi-Feudalism During the Period of Manchu Domination," *Mongolian Studies* (Bloomington, Indiana, 1974), 1:27–54 (chapter 11 in this work).

17. *Shabinar,* or "disciples," had feudal-like characteristics as underlings of a lamasery or a theocratic noble. The ordinary people are known as *arad.* They were all *albatu,* i.e., they had corvée duty to serve and had to pay taxes to their overlords.

18. *Khara,* "black," really means a layman of the married segment of society. *Shira* means "yellow." The yellow color is symbolic of Tibetan Buddhism, hence the "Yellow Religion." The term *shira* came to be applied to theocratic authorities, lamas, and the people under their jurisdiction.

19. See note 12.

20. Gurun-Efu is "royal son-in-law" in Manchu. The word *gurun* means state, and *efu* means son-in-law.

21. See *Wei-tsang t'ung-chih,* 1:28b–29b.

22. *Li-fan Yüan* (理藩院), or the Ministry of Dependencies, was the Ch'ing office to administer Mongolian, Tibetan, Chinese, Turkistan, and certain other foreign affairs. Later in 1861, the *Tsung-li ke-kuo shih-wu ya-men* (總理各國事務衙門) or a "foreign ministry" was established and the administration of foreign affairs began to move from the *Li-fan yüan* to this new ministry.

23. See note 11.

24. Lhamu *choijung* means Lhamu the Protector of Law or angel. Lhamu is a very ferocious Lamaistic goddess, and she is one of the main protectors of the Law of the Dalai Lama.

25. The *Ta-Ch'ing hui-tien* says: "In the second year of Tao-kuang [1822, the Emperor] directed that 'When a [new] *Khubilghan* is going to be recognized, the banner to which he belongs must report the matter to the Li-fan Yüan in a formal sealed document, and then the [names] should be allowed to be put into the [Golden] Bottle and the lots drawn.'" 975:13ab)

26. These *jasagh da-lamas* of the *tamagha* are the leading lamas of the headquarters of the lama administration.

27. Dolonor (Dolo'on-naur) is also known in Chinese as Tuo-lun or Tuo-lun-no-erh. It is situated in the northeastern part of Chakhar Aimagh and is not too far from the ruins of Shandu, summer capital of Khubilai Khan. It was also the place where the Khalkha nobles surrendered to Emperor K'ang-hsi in 1691.

28. Wu-tai-shan (五台山) is a mountain in the area of Wu-tai Hsien, in Eastern Sansi Province. It was traditionally a holy land for both Lamaist Buddhism and Chinese Buddhism.

29. The pretext for Galdan's invasion of Khalkha in 1688 was to punish the First Jebtsundamba Khutughtu for presumptuous behavior, i.e., he sat together on a seat of equal rank with a formal delegate of the Fifth Dalai Lama to discuss a peace settlement among the Khalkha leaders.

30. This delegate was the same one mentioned in note 29. His rank was the Shire'etü Khutughtu of the Gandan Monastery in Lhasa and his personal name was Aghwanglodijamso.

31. The Fifth Dalai Lama died in 1682, but the Tibetan authorities kept this secret and utilized the deceased lama's name, to carry out a policy contradictory to that of the Ch'ing court. Later this covert tactic was revealed to the Emperor K'ang-hsi. In the succession to the Holy Seat, the Tibetans installed a young reincarnation who was rejected by the Emperor. A disturbance then broke out, and the Emperor took advantage of the situation to interfere in Tibetan affairs. He finally sent the Jangjia Khutughtu to Lhasa to install his Sixth Dalai Lama on his Holy Seat (1697).

32. The Eighth Jebtsundamba Khutughtu, Aghwangchoijinimadanjin-wangchugh was born in Tibet in 1870 and installed in Urga in 1874. He headed the independence movement and was supported as Khan by the Khalkha nobles. In 1919 he was forced by the Chinese warlord Hsu Shu-cheng to give up all political activities. He was supported by White Russian forces and in 1920 again proclaimed independence from China. In 1921, the Mongolian People's Revolutionary Party sustained by a Soviet Red Army destroyed the White Russian forces in Mongolia and established a socialistic government under Soviet influence. This high lama was recognized as the symbolic head of state. He died in 1924.

33. The Sixth Jangjia Khutughtu, Sangjiejab, was born in Kokonor, a Tibetan area, in 1891 and proceeded to Peking in 1899. After the new Republic of China was established he was utilized as an important instrument to appease or otherwise manipulate the Mongols. Later he became associated with the Shansi warlord, Yen Hsi-shan, in efforts to carry out pacification work in Inner Mongolia. In 1933, during the Inner Mongolian Autonomous Movement, he was persuaded by Yen Hsi-shan to try to stop the

movement. Subsequently, the National Government in Nanking granted him the title *Meng-chi hsuan-hua-shih* (蒙旗宣化使), Special Envoy to Appease the Mongolian Banners. This anti-Mongol posture provoked young Mongolian activists and intellectuals and consequently stirred up an anti-religious movement among them. He died in Taiwan in the late 1950s.

34. In 1624 the Khorchin tribe of Eastern Mongolia surrendered to the Manchus, and from this time on many tribes on the south of the Gobi desert followed. In 1911 Outer Mongolia declared their independence from the Manchu-Ch'ing, and the dynasty ended that same year.

35. On Senggerinchin, see his biography in the *Ch'ing shih* (Taipei, 1961), vol. 405, *lieh-chuan* 191.

36. *Ch'ing-tai pein-chen t'ung-k'ao* (Taipei, 1959), "Lamaist prohibitions," 385.

37. After the Mongols south of Gobi surrendered to the Ch'ing, the Manchus reorganized a group of Mongols into supplementary forces in the Manchu Eight Banner system. These Mongols were soon Manchurianized or Sinicized and became a group of "Banner Men," separated from the Mongols. San-tuo, the last *amban* of Urga, who was very high-handed in his dealings with the Mongols, was a man from the Mongolian Eight Banners stationed at Hangchou.

38. The Chakhar rebelled against Manchu rule in 1675. Therefore, their quasi-feudal autonomous privileges were abolished by the Ch'ing court and the administration of their region was separated from other ordinary leagues and banners. However, this event happened much later than the circulation of this decree.

39. A *gelün* is a ranking lama who has already taken the second vow and has become a senior lama, a *bhikshu* in Sanskrit. *Bandi* or *gesel* are junior lamas or lesser disciples of a lama.

40. *Ch'ing-tai pien-cheng t'ung-k'ao*, 386.

41. Ibid.

42. *Ubashi* is a lay male Buddhist meditator at home. A female meditator is known as *ubasanja*.

43. *Ch'ing-tai pien-cheng t'ung-k'ao*, 386.

44. Ibid.

45. Ibid., 387.

46. Ibid.

47. *Sumu* was the basic local administrative unit and also a military unit under the *khushu'un* (banner). Today, in the Mongolian People's Republic, a *sumu* is still the local administrative unit under the regional *aimagh* (province), but the structure is different from the old days.

48. According to the author's personal investigation.

Chapter 11

Mongolian Lamaist Quasi-Feudalism During the Period of Manchu Domination

(Originally published in *Mongolian Studies, Journal of the Mongolia Society*, vol. I, 1974)

Introduction

It is disputed among scholars of Altaic studies whether "feudalism" really existed in Mongolian history. However, Chinese historical works, especially the official or semiofficial records of the Ch'ing Dynasty, always use the term *feng-chien* (封建) to describe Mongolian society and its political system from the establishment of the empire until recently. The term *feng-chien* in its strict meaning may not exactly correspond to the word feudalism in the West. Yet, it is difficult to find a suitable substitute in English. Therefore, the term "quasi-feudalism" is tentatively used in this paper.

The unification of the Mongol people under Chinggis Khan and the establishment of the great empires transformed Mongolian social structure from a clan-centered system into a quasi-feudalistic one. These quasi-feudalistic characteristics became more and more pronounced after the decline of the khans' power and the collapse of the empire. The Mongolian khans had accepted Tibetan Buddhism as their personal faith, but in the nomadic quasi-feudalistic society, which was mainly based upon the relationship between the feudal lords and their people, there were neither noble lamas nor lama nobles among the class of feudal lords, the *noyans*. During the second conversion of Mongols to Buddhism in the late sixteenth century, under the persuasion of Altan Khan, a change occurred in Mongolian quasi-feudalistic society. Later, during the Manchu period, because policies toward the Mongols were designed to appease and to weaken them through feudalistic controls, through fragmentation,[1] and through their religious beliefs, the original quasi-feudalistic system was strengthened and formalized by Manchu laws. In order to diminish the strength of the nomadic people when mobilized, the Manchu rulers planned to lock fragments of the nomadic Mongol units into small pieces of land, the *notughs*[2] or fiefs. Also, in order to counterbalance the power and influence of the lay nobility, many high lamas were placed among the feudal lords who ruled over lands and people. This was the reason why the high lamas and the lay nobles became the *two* pillars of modern Mongolian quasi-feudalistic society. However, the Manchu Emperor, Ch'ien-lung (r. 1736–95) realized that the Mongols might reunite under their spiritual leader, the Jebtsundamba Khutughtu, and become a great hindrance to Manchu domination. Thus, he transferred this highest religious seat of Mongolia to the Tibetan lamas. He could not, however, foresee that the Tibetan lama who sat on the throne would eventually become a leader of both the lay and religious worlds, and become the theocratic monarch of Mongolia at the beginning of this century.

The Noble Lamas and the Lama Nobles

In Yüan times, the Mongolian emperors were devout supporters of Buddhism, and many abbots of the great Tibetan lamaseries were granted special privileges. Some of the abbots were made feudal lords in various Tibetan territories. However, it is difficult to find any descendants of the Mongolian royal house who became monks and were then established as noble lamas. In 1578, Altan Khan, the leader of the Tümed tribe of the Mongols to the south of the Gobi, accepted Tibetan Buddhism as his own personal faith. Through his personal influence he made Buddhism the belief of all Mongols, whether nobles or ordinary people. From then on a new class of noble lamas and lama nobles began to appear in Mongol history. Noble lamas were those who had been born into the families of the *Altan Uragh,* the Golden Descendants of Chinggis Khan, but left their homes and became lamas. Lama nobles were the great and virtuous lamas who were trusted and believed by the *khans* or *noyans* (nobles). During the lifetime of these lamas, there were *noyans* who would offer some of their own people or vassals to serve as *shabinar*[3] (underlings) to the lamas. After their death, because of the belief in reincarnation, "spiritual boys" (靈童) would succeed to their seats, would enjoy the property of their temples, and would rule over the lama disciples and lay *shabinar*. This kind of reincarnated lama gradually became the theocratic or lama noble.

According to *Jigmid-namkha,*[4] the first time that the descendants of *Altan uragh* left their homes and became monks was when the Third Dalai Lama, Sodnam-jamtso, proclaimed the Law of Buddha to Altan Khan at the beach of Kokonor Lake in 1578. The book says: "Three members from the Khan's household, and one hundred persons from the family of *noyans* were ordered to leave their homes to become monks."[5] However, it is impossible to know now who the three members were.

The next important person was the Fourth Dalai Lama, Yondan-jamtso, the great grandson of Altan Khan. He was recognized as the reincarnation of the former Third Dalai Lama and was seated on the throne. Since he lived in Tibet and took the role of a Tibetan leader, he was no longer a Mongolian noble. However, the Maidari Khutughtu, who was dispatched by him to Mongolia to preach the Law of Buddha, finally became one of the great lama nobles of Mongolia.

As for Western Mongolia, the *Biography of Zayaa Pandita*[6] mentions that in 1616 all the *noyans* of the four Oirad *aimaghs* decided that each of them should make one of their sons a monk. The Chinese material *Huang-ch'ao fan-pu yao-lüeh*[7] records twenty-one important *noyans* of approximately the same period as the four Oirad *aimaghs*. Among them were three lamas. In other words, one seventh of the nobility were lamas. It shows that among the Oirads the power or influence of the lamas was not negligible.

Concerning Northern Mongolia, the *Huang-ch'ao fan-pu yao-lüeh* (vol. 3, Khalkha) tells the story of Tümenken, the founder of the Sayin Noyan Aimagh, who helped the Yellow sect defeat the "Red" in the religious struggle. Then it mentions his second son's (Danjin Lama) connection with the Ch'ing Court. This Danjin Lama received the honorable title of *Nom-un Khan,* "the King of Law," from the Dalai Lama of Tibet, while also being recognized by the Manchu emperor as "one of the eight *jasaghs* of Khalkha." After his death, there was no reincarnation to succeed to his religious post, but his son took over his lay position as *noyan*. As a lama, Danjin was quite different from the rest of the Yellow sect. He had a homelife, wives, and children. He was also a typical example of the later high lama nobles who enjoyed land as their fief and *shabinar* as their subjects.

The highest noble lama or greatest lama noble of Khalkha or Mongolia was the well-known Jebtsundamba Khutughtu.[8] The first incarnation was born in the house of Tüshiyetü Khan, and led the Khalkhas to accept the protection of the Manchu Emperor against the invasion from Jeünghar (Dzungar). The second reincarnation was also born in the same house of the Tüshiyetü Khan.[9] They became the spiritual leaders of Mongolia with high prestige in Mongolian politics. Consequently, the Manchu Emperor, Ch'ien-lung, plotted to hinder Mongolian reunification under their "Living Buddha" who by birth was also a member of the Mongolian nobility. He took advantage of the death of the Second Jebtsundamba Khutughtu to establish an unwritten regulation to prevent new reincarnations being found in Mongolia, saying they could only be found in Tibet. However, he did not foresee that a "spiritual boy," after he was enthroned on the seat of Law of Mongolia, could be naturally and completely integrated as a Mongol and a Mongolian lama noble, or that he would be honored, trusted, and believed as his former Mongolian reincarnations. Therefore, the Eight Jebtsundamba Khutughtu was able to lead the Mongols to resist, and even to dare to declare independence from, the Manchus.

Because of the nomadic life of the Mongol people and their devotion to Buddhism, not only did the lamaseries become the centers of economic and cultural life with learned and virtuous lamas becoming honored by the masses, but it also enabled these lamas to become involved in politics and to establish a position of equality over against the lay nobility.[10] At least some of them became the abbots of temples which to some degree enjoyed certain prerogatives and the obedience of lay *shabinar*.

Some of the virtuous Tibetan lamas who came to Mongolia to preach the Law of Buddha returned to Tibet after their task had ended. Some, however, stayed and died in Mongolia, and were later even reincarnated in Mongolia. Many of the latter ones received some sort of honorable title and gradually became the theocratic nobility in the Mongolian quasi-feudalistic societies (for example, the Maidari Khutughtu, etc.). Some among them were originally Tibetans. Their reincarnations were always born in the Tibetan area, but they enjoyed temples, properties, and even fief land or grazing fields of their *shabinar* in Mongolia. The size of this group of lama nobles was not small. The well-known Jangjia Khutughtu, the Shire'etü Khutughtu, the Kanjurwa Nom-un Khan, should be included in this category.

The Titles and Seals of the Lama Nobles

Because of the lack of material, it is difficult to go back to the time before the Ch'ing. The system was seemingly established or legalized during the first part of the Ch'ing Dynasty. In Ch'ing times the lamas who were qualified as lama nobles had to have one of the following titles: the *khutughtu*, the *nom-un khan*, the *chorji*, the *pandita*, the *shaburong*, the *khubilghan*, and the *gege'en*. Among them the great ones would enjoy lands, temples, and people in vassalage, and the small ones would at least be the abbot of a temple. They were all *khubilghans*, or in other words, they had to be reincarnated lamas. From generation to generation they were succeeded by their reincarnations who occupied their seats and enjoyed their prerogatives. Their social position was far higher than the ordinary monks. No matter what kind of knowledge of the Law of Buddha they had, they were always more highly honored than monks, whether from noble houses or common families, who were not reincarnated lamas. It was then firmly believed by the people that the more generations of reincarnations they had, the more spiritual or miraculous powers they possessed. Consequently, they had to create a legend which traced their first incarnation back even to the time of Buddha, thereby elevating themselves to a higher position.

The highest of these titles was *khutughtu*. The lowest was *shaburong*, and most of the *shaburongs* were not abbots of a temple. According to *Ta-Ch'ing hui-tien* they were not listed as lama nobles,[11] and in reality they were little honored outside their own banners. The meaning of the Tibetan word *chorji* is "the king of the holy scritpure," and therefore its Mongolian translation is *nom-un khan*. Both words were used as honorable titles, but did not necessarily indicate any special degree of knowledge of the Law of Buddha.

With reference to important lama nobles, the note in the *Lamas in the Capital* section of the *Tien-shu ch'ing-li-ssu* of the *Li-fan-Yüan shih-li* (理藩院事例) of *Ta-Ch'ing hui-tien* says:

> The *lamas* who are stationed in the Capital and who, from generation to generation have developed the Yellow Religion, are as follows: The Jangjia Khutughtu, The Galdan Shire'etü Khutughtu, Minjur Khutughtu, and the Jilung Khutughtu, . . . the rest of the *khutughtus* in the Capital are: the Dongkor Khutughtu, the Ghomon Khutughtu, the Namkha Khutughtu, the Osar Khutughtu, the Ajia Khutughtu, the Ragua Khutughtu, the Gungtang Khutughtu, and the Tugon Khutughtu. In Dolonor is the Shirkür Shire'etü Noyan Chorji Khutughtu. (67:6ab)

In this list, the Jangjia, the Galdan Shire'etü, the Minjur, and the Jilung *khutughtus* were the so-called "Four Great *Khutughtus*." According to the Ch'ing laws the Dalai Lama and the Panchen Erdeni of Tibet, and the Jebtsundamba Khutughtu of Mongolia, were the highest ranking lamas. The rest of the *khutughtus*, the Dongkor, the Gomong, the Namkha, the Osar, the Ajia, the Ragua, the Gungtang, and the Tugon were the well-known "Eight Great Khutughtus in the Capital." The Shikür Shire'etü Noyan Chorji Khutughtu was the *khutughtu* that was specially stationed at Dolonor, the religious and economic center of Inner Mongolia.

The above mentioned *khutughtus* came mostly from and were incarnated in Tibet or the Tibetan areas. Yet, many of them had temples, properties, lands, and even lama and lay disciples, *shabinar*, in Mongolia. For instance, the Jangjia Khutughtu, the Ajia Khutughtu, and some other *khutughtus* all enjoyed lands and people in the vicinity of Dolonor. Even so, it was not they who formed one of the two pillars of the ecclesiastical and lay feudalism of Mongolia. Rather, it was they who from generation to generation were incarnated in Mongolia. According to the evidence of *Lamas of the Mongolian and Tibetan Tribes* in the section *Lama Titles* of the *Li-fan-Yüan shih-li* of the *Ta-Ch'ing hui-tien* the following were lama nobles.

> These are [high] lamas in the areas of Küke-Khota Tümed, Chakhar, the forty nine banners of the Inner *Jasagh*[12] Khalkha, and Alashan-Ö'elüd. Among those who are registered as *khubilghans* in the file of the *[Li-fan] Yüan*, there are the following: There are sixteen in Küke-Khota [Tümed], nine in Chakhar, two in

Shire'etü Küriye, three in Khorchin, one in Ghorlos, six in [the East] Tümed, six in Abkhanar, two in Sünid, one in Dörben Ke'üd, five in Urad, one in Ordos, nineteen in Khalkha, and two in Alashan. (974:8b)

This official document apparently does not refer to Western Mongolia or to the Oirad territories. Most of the high lamas in this list possessed temples, property, and *shabinar*. However, only a few held lands as fief. Those who possessed land will be discussed in the fifth part of this paper.

These lama nobles, despite the fact that they already possessed high religious ranks and titles, either had to be officially recognized again by the Manchu Court, or they had to receive a new title from the emperor. Some of them even had to wait for the bestowal of an official seal. The following are the principal measures that the Ch'ing Court took to settle this sort of problem.

1. The first condition for a lama noble was that he had to be a *khubilghan* and already registered in the file of *Li-fan Yüan*. In other words, they had to have the proper qualifications as a "reincarnation," be formally recognized by the Ch'ing government, and their names had to be carefully recorded in the file of *Li-fan Yüan*. After passing through these procedures, they then became lama nobles recognized by law. Their official positions were quite different from those *gege'ens* or *shaburongs* whose names were not officially listed in the file of *Li-fan Yüan*.

2. The first time that the Manchu Court gave a seal to a lama was in the tenth year of Shun-Chih (1653) when the Emperor presented a golden seal to the God King of Tibet, the Fifth Dalai Lama, Agwanglobsangjamso.[13] The first time the court gave a seal to a Mongolian lama was eight years later (1661). The Emperor Shun-chih bestowed an official seal on Danjin Lama of Khalkha. This lama had the high religious rank of *Nom-un Khan*, as well as being one of the important lay nobles of Khalkha. This was the beginning of the Ch'ing Court's recognition of a high lama as a feudal lord over people and land. However, Khalkha had not as yet come under the jurisdiction of the Manchus. Moreover, the religious position of Danjin Lama did not last long. His descendants continued his lay line and succeeded him as lay *noyan* of his people and lands.[14]

3. In the eighteenth year of K'ang-hsi (1679) the Emperor approved "the giving of seals to those *jasagh da-lamas*,[15] and regulations (禁條) and charters (度牒) to the *gelüngs* and the *bandis*. But no seals should be given to them."[16] This is the beginning of the Ch'ing's official lama system of administration and the establishment of the *lama jasagh*. The word *jasagh* means "the man who rules or administers" in Mongolian. In the lay system he is the *noyan*, the feudal lord, who took responsibility for the administration of a banner. All nobles who could not possess the title of *jasagh* by imperial appointment or by succession were called the *sulu noyad*, the "leisured nobles," who had no right or responsibility to deal with the administration of the banner to which they belonged. The *jasagh lama* was the high lama official who administered the various affairs of the lamas. There was no reincarnation system for a *jasagh lama*, and neither was it a lifelong position. He was only a lama official who might be removed at any time. He was a subordinate to a reincarnated *khubilghan* and was responsible to him for looking after the lay business of the temples, disciples, and *shabinar*. The *jasagh lama* was not a feudal lord, but he increased the power and influence of the high lama nobles, such as the Jangjia Khutughtu and others. The word *gelung* is *bhikshu* in Sanskrit. Before the Manchu subjugation of Mongolia, there were many *gelungs* who carried out the

regulations of the Law, and some of them were involved in political affairs.[17] The word "regulation" here meant both governmental regulations and religious restrictions. The charter was the diploma of a monk. This was an old Chinese system. The monk, who got such a charter, would be officially relieved of the obligations of a lay man, such as military service, taxes, etc. On the other hand, it was also a measure to limit the lama nobles to a definite number, and, of course, a restriction prohibiting the lama from lay activities, especially in politics. As for the *bandis,* these denoted the ordinary or common lamas, and they will not be discussed in this paper.

4. The Manchu emperor's canonization of the chief Mongolian noble lama, the First Jebtsundamba Khutughtu, was in the thirty-second year of K'ang-hsi (1693), two years after the Khalkha's surrender to the Manchus. Even so, it was nothing but a formal recognition of the status quo.

5. In the third year of Ch'ien-lung (1738), concerning the matter of the Second Jebtsundamba Khutughtu, the Emperor said in an imperial decree: "The same title should be bestowed on the new reincarnation of the Jebtsundamba as was held by his former reincarnation. The title of Ch'i-fa [啟法 The Enlightener of the Law of Buddha] Jebtsundamba Lama should be left [to him] as it was, but a new title should be given."[18] From this fact it is easy to see that the procedures for the establishment of a new reincarnation of the theocratic nobility and the succession of the lay nobility were nearly the same. They were all authorized by the Emperor.

6. In the fourth year of Ch'ien lung (1739), the Emperor bestowed a seal upon the Dongkor Manjushiri Khutughtu, the tutor of the Jebtsundamba Khutughtu. This is further evidence that some high lamas were made important theocratic nobles through the power of the Ch'ing emperors.

7. Besides those lama titles mentioned above, there were also many Chinese-style titles, such as: *Kuan-ting* (灌頂 the perfect), *Pu-shan* (普善 universally virtuous), *Kuang-tz'u* (廣慈 broad and merciful), *Ch'i-fa, lung-chiao* (隆教 the developer of Buddhism), *An-sheng* (安生 the tranquilizer of all living beings) and *Hui-wu* (慧悟 apprehension of wisdom), *ta kuo-shih* (大國師 the great teacher of the state), *kuo-shih* (國師 the teacher of the state), *ch'an-shih* (禪師 the teacher of meditation), etc. All these titles were a symbol of the Sinicization of original Tibetan and Mongolian titles. However, because of the difficulty of translation and the differentiation in culture, it was not generally accepted by the ordinary Mongols. Consequently, this plan did not bear fruit.

The Recognition of a "Khubilghan"

As has been mentioned above, a qualified lama noble had to be a *khubilghan* regardless of whether he was in a high religious position or a low one. *Khubilghan* is a Mongolian word which originally meant "transformation" or "the transformed one." However, in Buddhism it means "incarnation" or "the reincarnated one." A lama noble had to be the reincarnation of a virtuous man who had been recognized and honored by the emperor, the nobles, and the masses. The *khubilghans* in the Ch'ing documents were all authorized by the emperors and were recognized through formal and legal processes. However, in both Mongolia and Tibet there were still many minor *khubilghans* whose names were not listed in the Ch'ing documents.[19] All the *khubilghans* who were recognized through a definite religious process and were formally installed in their seat, were generally addressed with the honorable title *gege'en*, which means the "light." Its loose Chinese translation is *huo-fu* (活佛), the living Buddha.

Before the *nirvana* or the death of a virtuous lama, his disciples would present him with a request begging him, for the sake of the salvation of all living things, to return to the human world again. After the *nirvana*, they would invite a virtuous monk to recite the scripture and to divine for him. Then they would go out to search for a "spiritual boy" according to the instructions of their former *gege'en* and of the diviner. This "spiritual" boy had to show some special characteristics to prove himself the real reincarnation of the former one. Of course, such miracles were usually exaggerated into legendary tales, but this was the original way of finding a new reincarnation. Later, after the Mongols surrendered to the Manchus, the Manchu emperor, in order to manifest his authority over Mongolia, proclaimed that all the *khubilghans* should be recognized according to the law of his court. However, this regulation was only a restriction on important *khubilghans* whose names were listed in the file of *Li-fan Yüan*.

Before the latter part of the reign of Emperor Ch'ien-lung, this regulation seems to have merely required a report and registration after the reincarnation was installed. Later the Emperor Ch'ien-lung became aware that most of the Mongolian theocratic nobles were born into the families of the lay *noyans*, and, as noted in the prior chapter, he became especially alert to possible reincarnations of Jebtsundamba Khutughtu. He worried about the re-unification of lay and theocratic powers which might lead the Mongols to reorganize into a unit which could challenge the domination of the Manchu court.

It is not difficult to see that the Mongolian lay nobles had ambitions to make their own sons *khubilghans*, and so to keep the spiritual influence of the theocratic leaders in the hands of their households. At the same time, it seems that the lamas and the leaders of large temples also tried to establish close ties with the powerful lay *noyans* by accepting their sons as *gege'en* to increase their authority and influence in the lay world. Of course, this was not what the Manchu ruler wanted to see happen. Consequently, he had to find some means to "remedy" the "defects." The "remedy," as previously noted, was the use of the "Golden Bomba Bottle," and the prohibiting of the *khubilghans*, or the reincarnations, from being born in the houses of the Mongolian lay nobility.

The aims and results of these policies were as follows.

1. They emphasized that the Emperor and his court would not tolerate the unification of the Mongolian lay and theocratic nobilities through blood relationships. Therefore, the court had to take decisive measures to crush political ambitions of Mongolian laity and lamas.

2. Instead of the spiritual instruction of the Dalai Lama's protector of Law, Lhamu *choijung*, the regulations concerning the Golden *Bomba* Bottle were established to identify a new *khubilghan*. Thus, theoretically and religiously it was still managed by the Dalai Lama. In reality, it was orchestrated by the *Amban* of Tibet or a Minister of *Li-fan Yüan* and finally decided by the emperor himself. It not only prohibited the powerful Mongolian or Tibetan nobles from influencing the Lhamu *choijung* by suggesting their sons or brothers to be the *khubilghans*, but also put the authority of the Ch'ing court above religion. It made the *khubilghan* and his disciples grateful and obedient to their Manchu rulers.

3. Because the installation of *khubilghans* or *khutughtus* had to go through the same procedure of imperial decision, it supported their political position as equals to the lay feudal lords. Thus, politically, it emphasized the counterbalancing of the *shira* (yellow) or theocratic element over against the *khara* (black) or lay element in Mongolian society, and split the Mongol people into two large and opposed groups.

4. Emperor Ch'ien-lung prohibited Mongolian theocratic leaders from being reincarnated in the families of powerful lay nobles. Again utilizing the death of the Second Jebtsundamba Khutughtu, the emperor arranged affairs so that no reincarnation of this line could be sought in Mongolia. Thereafter he was to be found in Tibet, and was to proceed to Mongolia to sit on his throne by the "imperial order" of the emperor. Thus, the emperor hoped to decrease the Jebtsundamba Khutughtu's political influence among the Mongol people.

5. Except for the new reincarnation of the Jebtsundamba Khutughtu, who was still tentatively recognized by the Dalai Lama or the Panchen-Erdeni and then approved by the emperor himself, the rest of the Mongolian *khutughtus* were encouraged to complete procedures in Peking through the *Li-fan Yüan*. This enabled the emperor to make all decisions, increasing the influence of the court in Peking and separating the intimate and mutually dependent relationship between Mongolia and Lhasa.

There was one exception to these regulations. In a decree of the fifty-ninth year of Ch'ien-lung (1794) it records:

> The Chaghan Nom-un Khan of Kokonor is a *jasagh* and has the responsibility of ruling over [his people and] the fief. Therefore, for greater convenience in this matter his *khubilghan* has to be honored and trusted by his underlings. Henceforth, after the *nirvana* of the Changhan Nom-un Khan, if the candidate for his *khubilghanate* is honored by his underlings, then no matter whether it is a relative of his or not, the name should be put into the Golden *Bomba* Bottle and the lot drawn. Do not apply the new regulations inflexibly.[20]

This decree shows that the Chaghan Nom-un Khan was one of the Mongolian feudal lords who enjoyed land, people, and the power of administration, and did not differ from other lay nobles. In this case even the Emperor had to accept the situation and he made no attempt to apply his new regulations by force.

The Administrative Powers and Fiefs of the Lama Nobles

Mongolian nomadic quasi-feudalism was founded upon the relationship between the *noyan* (feudal lord) and the *arad* (people). The land or the *notugh* (fief) was of secondary importance. Therefore, from the feudalistic point of view, there was little difference between the lay *noyans* and the lama nobles who also enjoyed rights over both people and lands.

At the very beginning of the *Li-fan Yüan shih-li* of the *Ta-Ch'ing hui-tien*, it says:

> To the South of the Great Desert is Inner Mongolia, . . . divided into forty-nine banners. . . . [Northward] across the Great Desert is Outer Mongolia, . . . [which] is divided into eighty six banners.[21] . . . One head officer, the *jasagh*, is established for each banner to have charge of public affairs. If there is no *jasagh* [the administration of that banner] should be in the hands of the *Chiang-*

chün (general) the *tu-t'ung* (military governor), or the *amban* (minister).... The lamas who rule the masses administer public affairs in the same manner as the *jasaghs*. (63:1a–12b)

The meaning here of the word *jasagh* is a "ruler" or an "administrator." Among the Mongolian nobles, regardless of whether their title were *khan, wang, beile, beise, gung, taiji*, or *tabunang*,[22] if they were not a *jasagh* by appointment or by succession, they remained merely a *sula noyan* or a "noble at leisure." These "nobles at leisure" also had some personal *khariyatus* (underlings), but enjoyed neither *notugh* (fief) nor administrative power.

The forty-nine banners of Inner Mongolia and eighty-six banners of Outer Mongolia were all typical quasi-feudalistic units and were ruled by the *jasaghs* or by succession. Only if the Mongolian nobles rebelled against the Manchu court were they divested of the feudal privileges with their fiefs then administered by generals, military governors, or *ambans*, such as the Chakhar, the Tümed, etc.

"The lamas who rule the masses and administer public affairs in the same manner as the *jasaghs*," is one of the main themes of this paper. This rule evidently enabled those lamas who had a large number of *shabinar* (lay underlings) to enjoy the privilege of administrative power in public affairs in the same way as the lay *jasaghs*. This was a legal recognition and guaranteed the coexistence of a lay and theocratic quasi-feudaldist system in Mongolia.

The history of the *shabinar* (vassals of a high lama) began almost at the same time as the second conversion of the Mongols to Buddhism in the late sixteenth century. A *shabinar* was created when a young male member of a noble family left his home to become a lama and his father or the household gave him some of his *arad* (people) to be his *shabinar* to serve him forever. Or it began when the lay nobles, to express their deep reverence for a lama of great virtue, offered him some of their people as his *shabinar*. The duties of *shabinar* were usually lighter than those of the *arad* under the control of a lay noble. At least, if it were not war time, there would be no military service. Therefore, some ordinary *arad* voluntarily (or selfishly) asked permission from their lay feudal lords to become *shabinar* of a temple or of a high lama. Consequently, the number of *shabinar* was always increasing, resulting in the expansion of the administrative power and prestige of the theocratic nobility. Those high lamas who had *shabinar* in large numbers would naturally be equivalent to a lay *jasagh*, even enjoying a piece of land as their fief. Those who had fewer in number would usually be equivalent to the "nobles at leisure." Of course, there were many who possessed only a few families of *shabinar* and were as powerless as the ordinary lay *taiji* or *tabunang*.

After the death of the First Jebtsundamba Khutughtu (1723, the first year of Yung-cheng), it was decided that the Khutughtu should not administer both religious and lay affairs. Therefore, the Emperor Yung-cheng established two lama officials in Urga. The first, the *Erdeni Shangsadba*, was to settle the civil affairs of the *shabinar*, and the second, the *Khambu Nom-un Khan*, was to take care of religious matters.[23] However, in reality the system merely recognized an established fact. *Khambu Nom-un Khan* is a mixture of Tibetan and Mongolian words, which means the "teacher of Law and king of scripture." His responsibilities were purely religious, a discussion of which is not included in this paper. The *Erdeni Shangsadba* is a similar linguistic mix meaning the "precious manager of the temple." In Mongolian custom the *shangsadba* was always the highest lama official of a temple under the abbot, *gege'en*. The one established in Urga, however, was different from the rest. He was not only a lama official of the temple, but also the high official over the civil affairs of the *shabinar*. The legalization of the status quo established the foundation of the theocratic quasi-feudalism of Mongolia. Later, following the increase in numbers of the *shabinar* of the Jebtsundamba Khutughtu, the political position of the Erdeni Shangsadba was elevated to the same level as the chiefs of the four leagues of Khalkha. Consequently, at the beginning of this century, the lamas who were in this post played important roles in the independence movement.

There were a few among the theocratic nobility who were not installed through reincarnation but by succession from father to son, such as the abbot of the Shire'etü Küriye in Josotu League, Eastern Inner Mongolia, and the abbot of the Shire'etü Juu in Köke Khota, Western Inner Monoglia. Both of these great temples possessed land and *shabinar* in large number. All the lamas were legally allowed to marry wives and father children. Therefore, these theocratic nobles were succeeded by their descendants and were no different from the lay nobles. But their titles were not *wang* or *taiji* but titles with religious characteristics such as *jasagh da-lama*. In a decree of the second year of Ch'ien-lung (1737), the Emperor said:

> Both the Erdeni Pandita Khutughtu and the Jaya'a Pandita Khutughtu of Khalkha enjoy large numbers of *shabinar* independently. They carry out official and military services alongside the people who are under the *jasaghs* and *sumun janggis*. Bestow official seals on them so that they may govern their *shabinar*.[24]

This shows that in Khalkha, along side and sometimes under the Jebtsundamba Khutughtu, there were still other great theocratic nobles. The Erdeni Pandita Khutughtu and the Jaya's Pandita Khutughtu had large numbers of underlings who performed military service in the war against the Jeünghar (Dzungar) together with the people under the lay nobles. Therefore, the Emperor bestowed official seals on them and made them quasi-feudalistic units as a reward.

Again, in the twentieth year of Ch'ien-lung (1755), imitating the establishment of the *Erdeni Shangsadba* for the Jebtsundamba Khutughtu, the Ch'ing Court established the *Jasagh lama Shangsadba* for the Jangjia Khutughtu and bestowed an official seal on him. All the reincarnations of the line of Jangjia Khutughtu were Tibetans, however, and they normally carried out various political missions among the Mongols for the Manchu emperors. Yet, because of support from the Manchu emperors, they were honored by the Mongols and received large numbers of *shabinar* from the Mongolian princes and nobles. Consequently, they became the premier theocratic feudal lords in Inner Mongolia, and most of their *shabinar* were centered in the vicinity of Dolonor where the fief was located.[25]

Again in the Ta-Ch'ing hui-tien, it says:

> In the 24th year of Ch'ien-lung (1759), the Emperor approved the report that the *shabinar* of Noyan Khutughtu, Lobsang-jamyang-danjin of Khalkha, should be organized into one *sumu*[26] and ruled by himself. Let them carry out their service in the original *aimagh*, and bestow [on him] the seal of "Director (總管) of [the *Shabinar*] of the Noyan Khutughtu." (947:16a)

The above records sketch the theocratic quasi-feudalist system of that period. The largest unit was that of the Jebtsundamba Khutughtu. His *shabinar* were far more numerous than the population of several banners, and, therfore, his unit was as large as one of the four leagues of Khalkha. The second largest were the Shire'etü Küriye of Josotu and the Changhan Nom-un Khan of Kokonor. Their *shabinar* were organized into two separate banners. The third class was merely organized into one *sumu*, though of course there were many minor theocratic nobles or abbots of small temples whose names cannot be found in the records of *Li-fan Yüan*. These also possessed some *shabinar* and were under the administration of the various banners to which they belonged, and are not a subject of discussion in this paper.

The fiefs of the Mongolian nobles were known as *notugh*, which originally meant "the native land" or "the permanent living place." It was also recorded in the *Secret History of the Mongols* and *Yüan shih* as *nontugh*.[27] In the official documents of the Ch'ing Dynasty it was called *yu-mu* (游牧), the pasturage. Consequently, the *yu-mu*, or the *notugh* was the foundation of nomadic livelihood for both the feudal lord and the people. It was their common grazing field and was not private property belonging to any lord. The *jasagh* was the ruler or governor of the *yu-mu*, but he could not take it as his own. He had, of course, no right to transfer it to any one else.[28] The same applied to high theocratic nobles who held the *yu-mu* or fief. According to the evidence of *The Mongolian Pasturage Lama Tribes* (蒙古游牧喇嘛部落) in the section on *Territory* (疆理) of the *Li-fan Yüan* of the *Ta-Ch'ing hui-ten*, the territories that were distributed to the high lamas as fiefs were as follows.

In Inner Mongolia, the pasturage of the *Jasagh lama* of the Shire'etü Küriye is located outside the Wall of Fa-k'u (法庫邊) of Mukden (盛京), having a common border with Naiman Banner on the north and Tümed Left Banner on the southwest.

In Khalkha, the pasturage of the Jebtsundamba Khutughtu is attached to the Tüshiyetü Khan *Aimagh*, and is located on the southwest of Kentei Mountain and the north of the Khan Ula (mountain). [The settling place of] his followers is *Küriyen*, and is located in the Middle Banner of the Tüshiyetü Khan Aimagh.

The pasturage of the Erdeni Pandita Khutughtu is attached to the Sayin Noyan Aimagh, and is located in the area of Orogh Nor, having a common border with the Sayin Noyan Banner to the east, and the Middle Banner to the west, at the waterhead of the Tuin-ghol (river).

The pasturage of the Ch'ing Süj"gtü Nom-un Khan is attached to the Sayin Noyan Aimagh, and is located in the valley of Chaghan Chichirlig River, having a common border with the Last Banner of the Right Flank to the east at Baidarigh River, and the Right Rear Banner of the Right Flank to the west.

The pasturage of the Naru Panchen Khutughtu is attached to the Jasaghtu Khan Aimagh, and is located in the valley of Jabkhang (Tzabkhan) River, having a common border with the Middle Banner of the Left Flank and the Rear Banner of the Right Flank to the west and the Middle Rear Banner of the Sayin Noyan Aimagh to the northeast.

The pasturage of the Changhan Nom-un Khan is attached to the Kokonor Mongols, and is located on the east bank of the Yellow River, joining the border of the Khoshod Middle Banner of the South Left Flank to the south, and the Tibetan (番子) area of the *Kui-te T'ing* (貴德廳 *t'ing* means district) to the north. (966:11a–12a)

Besides these, in the vicinity of Dolonor there were the pasturages of the *shabinar* of the thirteen great *gege'ens* of Mongolian and Tibetan origin, who had their seats in the imperial temples of Hui-tsung (彙宗) and Shan-yin (善因).[29] There were: 1) the Jangjia Khutughtu; 2) the Ajia-Khutughtu; 3) the Shire'etü Khutughtu; 4) the Kanjurwa Nom-un Khan; 5) the Shikür Shire'etü Noyan Chorji Khutughtu; 6) the Arkha Gege'en; 7) the Jiran Gege'en; 8) the Nomun-Khan Gege'en; 9) the Dalai Khambu Gege'en; 10) the Gül Küke-yin Lama; 11) the Donkor Khutughtu; 12) the Samsa Gege'en; and 13) the Emchi Lama.

The *jisas*, the managers of the two imperial temples, also had their own *shabinar*. Of course, there were still other similar temples that were not listed in the record of the *Ta-Ch'ing hui-ten*, e.g., the Shire'etü Juu at Köke-Khota, etc.

The above materials suggest that the relationship between the feudal lords and their underlings was quite similar to that between the Mongolian theocratic nobles and their lay partners. The only difference was that the population of the *shabinar* was much smaller than that of the ordinary *arad* under the lay *noyans* or *jasaghs*. Similarly, the land controlled by theocratic nobles was not comparable to the great territories of the laity.

Privileges and Duties

As mentioned in "Titles and Seals" above, the Mongolian theocratic nobility enjoyed many titles and ranks. They had their own underlings, the *shabinar*, who had the duties of paying taxes and serving them. These privileges in essence provided equality with the lay nobility. Consequently, their duties toward the Manchu emperors were also similar to those of their lay partners, i.e., attending the emperor at court and paying tribute to him. The section of the *Wang-hui ch'ing-li-ssu* (王會清吏司) of *Li-fan Yüan* in th Ta-Ch'ing hui-tien states:

> On every New Year's day, the princes of the Inner *Jasagh* have to proceed to the Capital for audience, according to their rotations. (65:3a)

> The Yearly Audience of the Khalkha [nobles] are divided into six rotations. (68:2a)

> The rotations of the great lamas, who are stationed both to the south and north of the [Gobi] Desert in Mongolia are divided into six, and the audiences take place once a year. (68:3b)

Clearly, the Manchu emperor made equal demands for yearly audiences on both the Mongolian theocratic and lay nobles.

The entry under *The Lamas Yearly Rotation* in the section on the *Royal Audience* *Li-fan Yüan* of *Ta-Ch'ing hui-tien* (vol. 984) states:

The Yearly Rotation of Lamas: With the exception of Jebtsundamba Khutughtu, all the great lamas of the forty-nine banners of Inner *Jasagh*, Kuei-hua City (Köke Khota) Chakhar, Alashan, Khalkha, Küriyen (Urga), Sire'etü Küriyen, etc., are organized into six rotations, and each year one of the rotations has to come to the Capital.

The names were as follows:

The first rotation includes eleven members:
    The Naru'a Panchan Khutughtu of Khalkha
    The Noyan Khutughtu of Khorchin
    The Daghbu Khutughtu of Alashan
    The Maidari Khutughtu of Tümed
    The Biligtu Nom-un Khan of Kha'uchid
    The Pandita Lama of Abkhanar
    Aghwang Dundub Khutughtu of Ordos
    The Erdeni Dayanchi Khutughtu of Kuei-hua City
    Yanchachin Lama of Kuei-hua City
    Lobsang-damba-rabjai Lama of Ordos
    The Mergen Pandita Khutughtu of Khalkha

The second rotation includes ten members:
    The Erdeni Nomchi Lobun Chorji Lama of Chakhar
    The Erdeni Ilaghughsan Lama of Khalkha
    Raghba-ochir Da-Lama of Tümed
    Lhama-jamba-shirab-jamso Lama of Abkhanar
    Bars-dorji Lama of Urad
    The Chois Khabutu Dayanchi Khutughtu of Kuei-hua City
    The Choiji Toyin Khutughtu of Kuei-hua City
    Tobsang Lama of Alashan
    Lobsang-dobdan Lama of Üjumüchin
    The Yughojur Khutughtu of Chakhar

The third rotation includes ten members:
    The Daiching Chorji, Lobsang-dandar Lama of Chakhar
    The Shiwa Shire'etü Khutughtu of Khalkha
    Jangchub-dorji Lama of Küriyen
    The Shaburong, Yondan-jamso Lama of Ordos
    The Güseri (?) Chorji, Aghwang-sodba Lama of Üjümüchin
    The Güüshi, Lobsang-choijur Lama of Abkhanar
    The Donkor Pandita Lama of Urad
    The Niyang-niyang Khtughtu of Kuei-hua City
    The Güüshi Minjur Chorji Lama of Chakhar

The fourth rotation includes ten members:
    The Ching Sujugtu Nom-un Khan of Khalkha
    Lobsang-jamchan Nom-un Khan of Khalkha
    The Ayushi Mergen Chorji Lama of Tümed

Lobsang-rashi Da-Lama of Sunid
Agwang-lobsang-pongchugh Lama of Üjümüchin
Lobsang-nima Lama of the Mani-yin Süme of Abkhanar
Lhamu-jamba-getü-pongchugh Lama of Urad
The Shire'etü Khutughtu of Kuei-hua City
The Dayanchi Khutughtu of Kuei-hya City
Lhamu-jamba-lobsang-danba Lama of Chakhar

The fifth rotation includes ten members:
The Erdeni Pandita Khutughtu of Khalkha
The Jaya'a Pandita Khutughtu of Khalkha
The Süsügtü Chorji, Aghwang-shirab Lama of Tümed
Molum-lhamu-jamba-lobsang-diwa Lama of Üjümüchin
Baija-sabdung (?) Lama of Abkhanar
Saghru-aghwang-jamyang Lama of Shire'etü-Küriyen
The Güüshi, Lobsang-dampil Lama of Urad
The Darkhan Chorji Khutughtu of Kuei-hua City
The Chaghan Dayanchi Khutughtu of Kuei-hua City
The Dalai Khutughtu of Chakhar

The sixth rotation includes nine members:
The Chaghan Dayanchi of Tümed (Monggholjin)
The Kanjurwa Erdeni Khambu Lama of Sundid
Molon-lhamu-jamba-ghonchugh-rashi Lama of Üjümüchin
The Erdeni Mergen Lama of Abkhanar
The Mergen Dayanchi of Urad
The Jaya'an Pandita Khutughtu of Kuei-hua City
The Ombu Jamsan Lama of Kuei-hua City
The Emchi Darkhan Chorji Lama of Chakhar
The Güüshi Jamchan-yungrui Lama of Chakhar.

The above are the important theocratic nobles[30] who enjoyed a position of importance similar to that of the lay princes in the Mongolian quasi-feudalistic society during the Manchu Ch'ing period. In the Ch'ing laws there were many regulations which show that the so-called "Rotation for New Year Audience" had to be carried out under all circumstances. The aim of this policy was apparently: 1) to be sure that the personal relationship between the Manchu court and the Mongolian feudal lords remained close and intimate; 2) to keep the Mongolian leaders busy in preparation for a long journey and thus, to prevent them from having time to plan something else; and 3) to create an economic burden and decrease the strength of the Mongolian leaders.[31]

Concerning the tribute system, the section of *Ju-yüan ch'ing-li-ssu* (柔遠清吏司) on the cases of *Li-fan-yüan* of the *Ta-Ch'ing hui-tien* states:

> The tribute from the Outer *Jasagh* should be presented at the time of the New Year Audience. There is no definite quantity for the sheep, horses, incense, woolen cloth, swords, and other equipment [that they present]. The lama's tribute is also the same. Only the Jebtsundamba Khutughtu, Sechen Khan, and

Tüshiyetü Khan present the "tribute of nine white" each year. Then the Emperor bestows them richly [with gifts] and sends [their envoys home]. (68:4a)

Concerning the definition of the "nine white" the original note says:

Each year the Jebtsundamba Khutughtu sends envoys to present one white camel and eight white horses, and this is acknowledged as the [tribute of] nine white. The Sechen Khan and Tüshiyetü Khan also sent envoys to present the nine white. (68:4a)

Again the section on contributions (貢獻) of the Outer *Jasagh* of the same book states:

In the thirtieth year of K'ang-hsi (1691),[32] [the Emperor] approved: Since Tüshiyetü Khan and Sechen Khan were allowed to retain their titles of *khan*, they were authorized to present tribute of one white camel and eight white horses as in former times. The rest were not allowed to present the "tribute of nine white." (986:3ab)

The above mentioned regulations show that according to the law, both lama and lay nobles were requested to present tributes, the quality and the quantity of the presents depending upon their ranks, titles, and positions. The fact that only Jebtsundamba Khutughtu and the nobles who enjoyed the title of khan were allowed to present the "tribute of nine white" was the important symbol of vassalage to the Manchu emperor of the top class of Mongolian nobles. In other words, it was also an acknowledgment from the Manchu emperor that the Jebtsundamba had a rank and position equal to that of a vassal khan. With this political standing and his long established prestige, it is easy to understand why, at the end of the Ch'ing Dynasty, the Eighth Jebtsundamba Khutughtu was qualified to be the leader of the independence movement of Khalkha and was supported as a *Khaghan* by both lama and lay feudal lords.

Notes

1. There is a well-known historical story, that Chia Yi (賈誼) tried to persuade the Emperor Wen-ti of the Han to diminish the power of the feudal lords and to strengthen his control over them. See the Biography of Chia Yi in the *Han Shu* 48.

2. See the Biography of Tei Sechen (特薛禪) in the *Yüan shih*. The original note says: "*Nontugh* (農土) similarly means territory (in Chinese)," 118:5b. Also see section 219 of the *Secret History of the Mongols*.

3. *Shabi* means disciple and *nar* is the suffix of plural number. The whole word, *Shabinar*, means the "disciples." However, according to its quasi-feudalistic characteristics, the term *shabinar* or disciples should be explained as the vassal or the underlings of a lamasery or a theocratic noble. The ordinary people were known as *arad*. The people who belonged to the lay and lama nobles were called *khariyatu*, which means underling or vassal. Moreover, all the people under the rule of the feudal lord were known as *albatu*. The meaning of this word is "the people who have a duty to pay taxes and serve their *noyan* (lord)."

4. The original name of this book in Tibetan is *Chen-po hor-gyi-yul-du dam-paihi-chos ji-ltar-byun-bahi-tshul-bsad-pa rgyal-bahi-bstan-pa-rin-po-che gsal-bar-byed pahi-*

sgron-me, which means "The Light of the Jewel Lamp of the Victorious Religion; It Records the Development of the Righteous Law in the Land of Great Mongolia." The name of the author was Hjigs-med nam-mkhah. In Mongolia his work is generally known under the name of *Hor choi jung*. It has been translated into German by G. Huth and into Japanese by K. Hashimoto, and was published under the name *Moko ramakyoshi (The History of Mongolian Lamaism*蒙古喇嘛教史), 1940.

5. See Hashimoto, *Moko ramakyoshi*, 235.

6. Zayaa Pandita (or Jiyagha Pandita 1599–1662) was a very famous lama learned in both Buddhism and literature. He reformed the Mongolian writing system. See his abbreviated biography in Dandingsurung's *Jaghun Bilig*.

7. The *Huang-Ch'ao Fan-pu Yao-lüeh* (皇朝藩部要略) was written by Chi Yüen-shih (祁韻士) and read by Chang Mu (張穆). The preface was written by Li Chao-lo (李兆洛), in the nineteenth year of Tao Kuang (1839).

8. The First Jebtsundamba Khutughtu had many names, but his best-known name was Tsanabatsar (1635–1723). He was the son of Gombodorji, the Tüshiyetü Khan of Khalkha.

9. The Second Jebtsundamba, Lobsang-dambi-dungmi (1724–57) was the son of Dondobdorji, who was then Tüshiyetu Khan, and the great grandson of Gombodorji.

10. Before the Manchu occupation of China Proper the envoys between Manchuria and Khalkha were usually lamas.

11. However, there were some exceptions, such as the Shaburong Lama of Gorlos whose name appeared in the list of the third Rotation of the New Year Audience. In Tibetan areas the Shaburongs' positions were recognized by the Ch'ing Court. See the note on the Tibetan lamas in the *Tien-shu ch'ing-li-ssu* (典屬清吏司) section of *Li-fan Yüan* (理藩院) in *Ta-Ch'ing hui-ten* (大清會典).

12. The so-called "forty nine banners of the Inner *Jasagh*" meant the forty nine banners and the six leagues of Inner Mongolia. Among them the Mongols of Chakhar, Kulun-buir, and Küke-Khota Tümed were not included.

13. The honorific title that the Manchu Emperor had given to the Fifth Dalai Lama (1616–80) was The Great Self-existent Buddha of the Western Heaven, Leader of Buddhism of the Universe, the Universal Ochir Dhara Dalai Lama (西天大自在佛領天下釋教普通瓦齊爾達喇達賴喇嘛).

14. Danjin Lama was the son of Tümenken, the founder of the Sayin Khan *Aimagh* of Khalkha. Chang Mu's *Meng-ku yu-mu chi* (蒙古游牧記), vol. 8, says: "In the 12th year of Shun-chih [1655], his sons and younger brothers came to the Court. [The Emperor] granted a decree to Danjin Lama, appointing him one of the *Jasagh* of the Left Flank [of Khalkha] and commanding him to present the tribute of nine white as did the three Khans [of Khalkha]."

15. The word for "seal" is *tamagha* in Mongolian. The place to put the seal was named *tamagha-yin ghajar* in Mongolian and *yin wu ch'u* (印務處) in Chinese, and it was the headquarters or the center of administration. The *yamen* (衙門) of a *jasagh* was usually known as *jasagh-yin tamagh-un ghajar*. In order to deal with the administration of the lamas, a *Lama Tamagh-yin ghajar* was established under the direct control of the *Li-fan Yüan*. However, the power and function of this headquarters was very limited, and was not comparable to the *Hsüan-cheng Yüan* (宣政院) of the Mongolian Yüan Dynasty. In *Ta-Ch'ing hui-tien* there is a record of giving a seal to the

Ching Süjügtü Nom-un Khan, in the twentieth year of Ch'ien-Lung (1755). It says: "The three kinds of writings of Manchu, Mongolian, and Tibetan should be carved separately." This shows the style of the seals of the high lamas.

16. See *Ta-Ch'ing hui-tien*, 974:9a.

17. See note 10. For instance, the Ilaghughsan Khutughtu, who was the envoy of both the Fifth Dalai Lama and Güüshi Khan of the Kokonor Mongols, and brought their goodwill to Emperor T'ai-tsung in the year 1642.

18. See *Ta-Ch'ing hui-tien* (the Li-fan Yüan part), 974:12b–13a.

19. It seems that only a small number of these minor *khubilghans* had the qualifications of a "reincarnation" at the beginning of the Ch'ing Dynasty, and had not been officially recognized by the Ch'ing Court. However, most of them were those who did not report themselves to the *Li-fan Yüan* after the law had been promulgated. Therefore, in his decree of the fifty-seventh year of Ch'ien-lung (1792) the Emperor said: "Those abbots of the unknown small temples, and those ordinary lamas who were not the reincarnations of former *khubilghans* should not be recognized as *khubilghans*." See *Ta-Ch'ing hui-tien* (*Li-fan Yüan* part), 975:11b.

20. See *Ta-Ch'ing hui-tien*, 95:12b.

21. This denotes the eighty-six banners of the four Khalkha *aimaghs* only and does not include the two Dörbet *aimaghs*.

22. In these high ranking titles, the *khan, taiji,* and *tabunang* are Mongolian terms. However, the word *taiji* is a mispronunciation of the Chinese "crown prince," *Tai-tzu* (太子). *Tabunang* means royal son-in-law. The leaders of Uriyangkha, that were known as Kharachin in Ch'ing times, were the sons-in-law of *Altan uragh*, the Golden descendants of Chinggis Khan, and therefore they took the title of *tabunang*. *Beile* and *beitse* were Manchu terms which originally meant prince. After the Manchus established their Ch'ing Dynasty, they adopted the Chinese title *wang* for prince, *kung* for duke, and listed *beise* and *beitze* between them. The *wangs* were divided into two degrees as *ch'in-wang* (親王) and *chüen-wang* (郡王), and the *kung* into *Chen-kuo-kung* (鎮國公) and *fu-kuo-kung* (輔國公).

23. See *Ta-Ch'ing hui-tien*, 974:10b.

24. Ibid., 974:12b.

25. The First Jangjia Khutughtu was a Kokonor Tibetan lama. In the twenty-second year of K'ang-hsi (1683), he came to the Ch'ing Court as one of the followers of the famous Tibetan teacher, Aghwang-lodui-jamtso. His talent strongly impressed the Emperor and he received the title of Khutughtu. The second reincarnation, Rolpai-dorji, was well-known as a profound scholar of Buddhism and was especially trusted by Emperor Yung-Cheng, both politically and religiously. From his time on all his reincarnations played an important role in appeasing the Mongols on behalf of the Ch'ing Court, and consequently their position was much higher then the rest of the *khutughtus*. The last reincarnation, Sangjiejab, who died in Taipei, was appointed as the Appeasing Emissary For Mongolian Banners (蒙旗宣化使), but his efforts ended in failure and could not stop the Autonomous Movement of Inner Mongolia in 1933.

26. The Mongolian term for *tso-ling* (佐領) is *sumu*, which was the administrative and military unit under the banner. In Inner Mongolia it was organized on the basis of 150 families or 150 men prepared for military service.

27. See note 2.

28. From the end of the Ch'ing Dynasty some of the covetous Mongolian princes associated themselves with the illegal Chinese merchants and local warlords in selling the grazing land for cultivation. Thus, the Mongolian "cowboys" lost their livelihood. This provoked them into taking up weapons for revenge. These rioters were known as the "Mongol bandits." This was a principal force affecting the independence movement of Outer Mongolian and the instability of Inner Mongolia.

29. The Hui-tsung Temple is generally known by the Mongols as Küke Süme (the Bule Temple). It was built by Emperor K'ang-hsi at the place where the Khalkha leaders came for the audience and surrendered to him in the year 1691 (the thirtieth year of K'ang-hsi). The Shan-yin Temple was built by Emperor Yung-Cheng, and it was known by the Mongols as Shira Süme (the Yellow Temple).

30. Some of the names in this list were the personal names of the lamas and some were their official titles.

31. In other words, it was a system similar to the Japanese *sankin kodai* which the *shogun* used against the *daimios* under him in the period of Tokugawa.

32. This was the year that Khalkha surrendered to the Manchus.

Chapter 12

Reasons for the Nondevelopment of Nomadic Power in North Asia Since the Eighteenth Century

(Originally published in *Proceedings of the Second East Asian Altaistic Conference*, Seoul, September 1986, 2–12)

Although the geography of Asia may be divided into three zones — the oceanic, agricultural, and nomadic — continental Asian history is dominated by the competition or the cooperation, the fighting or the intermingling, between the nomadic peoples of the northern steppes and the agricultural peoples of the "Middle Kingdom."

The agricultural Chinese had a much different attitude toward the oceanic regions and the small states to the south of China than they did toward the nomadic states to the north, which continually posed the threat of invasion. The southern states were compelled to recognize Chinese suzerainty when China was strong and were able to ignore it when China was weak. The ocean was important only as a boundary to China. The territory which comprised China was usually termed *ssu hai chih nei* (四海之内), "the land surrounded by the four seas," and little concern was shown regarding matters abroad or *hai wai* (海外), "outside the sea." To the agricultural Chinese, the sea was little more than a mysterious expanse of water which stimulated the imagination and harbored dangerous pirates. The Chinese did not realize that powerful nations might one day attack them from beyond the sea.

On the other hand, the nomadic peoples of the steppes were always wary of the danger to their security which might come from south of the Great Wall. When there was no pressure from the south, the nomads herded their flocks, hunted game, and moved about the steppes in relative contentment and peace. The great expanse of land on the north and northwest of Mongolia was to the nomads a "sea of grass." Whatever hunting and gathering peoples lived within this nearly empty area were subordinate to the herding nomads, and when these nomadic peoples were oppressed by the agricultural Chinese in the south, this area provided an excellent refuge. Just as the Chinese had not conceived of being threatened from across the ocean, it was inconceivable to the nomadic peoples that a foreign power might attack them from the north or the west.

With the beginning of the eighteenth century, the age-old situation outlined above changed radically. For the agricultural Chinese, the ocean changed from a bulwark against invasion to a broad and easy road by which Western powers were able to reach Asia for trade, missionary work, and exploitation. This new oceanic role took the attention of China away from the north and caused it to be focused on the seacoast in an attempt to withstand the new and terrible foreign threat.

At the same time, the vast steppe areas, which had previously furnished a ready refuge for the nomadic Mongols when they were forced to migrate or flee, fell into the hands of the newly developing power of Tsarist Russia. Parts of Central Asia and Siberia became the base for this new alien power confronting the Mongols, and this change restructured the whole picture of Asian history. The new actors on the stage of Asian history increased, and some of the prominent actors of the past were deprived of their traditional roles.

Due to the natural limitations of the steppes, the Altaic nomadic peoples were unable to adopt an agricultural life, and their pastoral ways of life only supplied their needs in relation to animal products. As they were unable to produce agricultural goods themselves or to manufacture goods which they needed, the nomads had to depend on their southern neighbors for many products. When it was impossible to satisfy their needs peacefully, the nomads, as we have seen before, would try to gain these products by plunder. Therefore, their leaders always fixed their gaze upon the south, and when they were able to organize a strong force, they would invariably carry out an expedition to the south. If they met defeat, they could always retreat to the Gobi, "the dry sea," where they could rest, regroup their forces, and plan another campaign. Even if the armies of the southern agricultural states entered the Gobi, the nomads could still move farther north or northwestward to regroup and await another opportunity.

The military power of the southern agricultural states did intrude into Mongolian and penetrate the Gobi during the reign of Emperor Wu-ti (r. 140–87 B.C.) and Emperor Ho-ti (r. 89–105 A.D.), both of the Han Dynasty, and again during the reign of Emperor Yung-lo (r. 1403–24 A.D.) of the Ming Dynasty. The Chinese armies defeated the nomadic armies and crushed the threatening regimes. However, the Chinese still could not effectively control or permanently occupy the steppes. They could not administer the region or the "Barbarians" because of the great mobility of the people and the difficulties presented by the great "dry sea," the Gobi. The armies from the south were only able to drive off the nomads who threatened their borders, forcing them to withdraw for a short time. Before long the nomads reinforced themselves and returned to herd their horses under the shadow of the Great Wall. This military game of hide-and-seek brought no permanent solution to the subjugation of the northern nomadic peoples. On the contrary, the Chinese campaigns sometimes brought economic crises and disaster to the agricultural people themselves.

As has been mentioned, one reason the northern nomadic peoples could advance and retreat so freely was that they were all expert horsemen and the great territories to the north or the northwest of the Gobi were devoid of any alien powers. But beginning with the eighteenth century the expansion of Russia toward the east caused this nomadic refuge to disappear.

Beginning in the late seventeenth century the nomadic peoples of North and Central Asia began to be pushed back by the overwhelming power of the southern Manchu-Ch'ing Empire, and at the same time they began to feel the heavy pressure of Tsarist Russia from the north. Consequently, they were wedged between two great powers and lost their freedom to migrate. In time, they were forced to submit themselves to one or the other of the great powers. With direct contact between the Manchu-Ch'ing Empire and Tsarist Russia and with the subsequent settlement of the national border, came an irrevocable limit which bound the nomadic peoples and stopped their free movement and traditional tactics. This was the greatest threat that the nomadic peoples had ever faced. It was far greater than any natural catastrophe on the steppes.

After the collapse of the Yüan Dynasty, the Mongols had retreated to Mongolia where they maintained the Northern Yüan State for some time. They then divided into two groups, the Mongols (Ta-tan) in the east and the Oirads (Wa-la) in the west. When powerful enough, they both moved south again, drew near the Great Wall, and paid little attention to Russia in the north. In time the Oirads were defeated by the eastern Mongols. Following the traditional route, the Oirads moved northwest to the vicinity of the Altai Mountain Range where they consolidated their strength and formed a new powerful regime, the famous Jeünghar (Dzungar) empire of the Oirad Mongols.

Later, in the fifteenth century, Mongolia was reunited under the reign of Dayan Khan and became a significant threat to the Ming Dynasty. Dayan Khan himself, as well as his descendants, followed the traditional patterns without alteration. They concentrated their attention on the south, camped in their royal headquarters, and stationed their troops not too far from the Great Wall. Even when Dayan Khan distributed people and territories to his sons as their fiefs, he placed most of them in southern Mongolia. Only his youngest son received the great land to the north which was known as Khalkha. Consequently, most of Dayan Khan's people and forces were concentrated south of the Gobi, and the northern areas of Mongolia were comparatively empty. When the Manchu tribe arose in the early seventeenth century on the east of Mongolia, they gradually subjugated by alliance or by pressure Mongol tribes on the south of the Gobi. The Khalkha Mongols were powerless and weak by comparison. Therefore, when the Khalkhas came under the threat of the Jeünghars (Dzungars), they wavered between the alternatives of surrendering to the Tsar on the north or seeking protection from the Manchu Emperor to the south. Eventually, because of religious and cultural ties, they chose vassalage to the Manchu Emperor.

The Jeünghar empire, which struggled against Russian expansion in Central Asia, almost conquered the territories of Koko-nor and Tibet and occupied about half the territory of what is now the Mongolian People's Republic. It was to be the last nomadic state which followed the development patterns of the old nomadic empires. However, from the beginning of its growth, it encountered difficulties which other nomadic states had never experienced. The Jeünghars tried the old policy of expanding their power toward the southeast where they met strong resistance from the Manchu Empire, then at its peak. To the rear of the Jeünghars, Tsarist Russia had just reached a new level of prosperity and power under Peter the Great. As a result, the Jeünghars had to fight for their lives against both the Manchus and the Russians, a crisis which no other nomadic power had ever faced. Furthermore, they were engaged in a war against an enemy within their own homeland.

The struggle finally absorbed all their strength in a series of decisive battles. They could no longer use the old military tactics of fleeing into the land of the far northwest to escape from mortal defeat and to recover their strength in the boundless stretches of the steppes. In the end, when their leader, Amurtsana, was defeated, he did escape into Russian territory (1757), but he went alone. Without a following of warriors, he had no opportunity to restore his tribe or to return to the stage for another scene in the drama of Central Asian history. Thus, the change in the basic dynamics of power in Inner Asia prevented the emergence of a really powerful nomadic empire in Central Asia.

When Galdan Khan of the Jeünghar empire was defeated by the Manchu Emperor Kang-hsi at Juu-Modo near the Tula River of Outer Mongolia (1696), it was the first time in history that Mongol horsemen were routed by the fire of the "Red Coated Big Guns" *(Hung-yi ta-p'ao* 紅衣大炮*)*. The cannons had been cast by the Manchus with the assistance of Jesuit missionaries. It was also the first recorded occasion when nomadic tactics bowed to modern weapons. While the Mongols in defeat felt the inevitable tide of modern civilization, they were still landlocked in Inner Asia by the wilderness of Siberia and the isolationism of the Ch'ing Empire. Therefore, they had no opportunity to reap the benefits of modern civilization or to modernize as other peoples.

From earliest times, the emergence of a nomadic power was usually preceded by struggles among the nomadic tribes. One tribe might absorb another, and thus its power would increase. At other periods, because of certain political, military, or economic aims, tribes joined voluntarily to form powerful confederations. It must also be remembered that the main strength of the nomadic peoples was their capacity to move rapidly. As they moved, they usually absorbed whatever groups lay in their path. Thus, nomadic groups grew like a snowball rolling down a mountain, i.e., in the beginning it seems very small, but as it continues to roll, the ball grows larger and larger, and finally strikes the earth like a mighty clap of thunder.

Originally, the concept of land among the nomadic peoples was similar to the concept of the sea among oceanic peoples. They did not share the idea, common among agricultural people, that man and land are inseparable. A nomadic chief could lead his people in a great sweep from the east to the far west. They were not tied to particular grazing fields, and this mobility allowed tactics which no agricultural people could duplicate. The advantage, however, disappeared with the Manchu policies which controlled the Mongols. The shrewd Manchu rulers adopted the policy of the Han Dynasty, i.e., that of "establishing feudal lords but reducing their strength" (*Han shu*, 48, chuan 18, "Biography of Chia Yi," Po-na edition 11a). The Manchus divided the original Mongol tribes into many small "banners." They also made a sweeping change in the Mongolian feudalistic system by specifying *land* relationships as well as the nomadic man-to-man feudal relationship. They located the Mongol feudal lord with his vassals and peoples in a definite territory as part of a new Mongol "banner" system, each banner possessing its own grazing fields and land. The feudal lords and their people could only move within the bounds of their common pastures while herding and hunting, and they were never allowed to go beyond the set borders. If anyone did so without official permission, not only the person but also his overlord, the Mongol prince, was punished. Since this policy was strictly enforced, the Ch'ing rulers effectively limited the previously nomadic groups to small territorial areas. Thus, the possibility of the sudden emergence of a nomadic power on the steppes was absolutely destroyed.

In early years, disturbances or wars sometimes drove nomadic tribes into alliances through negotiation or force, thus forming powerful political or military bodies. However, the Manchu rulers of the Ch'ing court successfully appeased Mongol aristocrats under their control by a shrewd policy of marriage alliances. They conditioned the Mongol aristocrats to be restrained and satisfied in the separate, small "kingdoms." If the Mongols did not become personally involved in rebellions or treasonous activities against the emperor, they enjoyed considerable autonomous power. On the other hand, the emperor assumed the responsibility for protecting the Mongol princes from aggression and made them feel content and prosperous. The Ch'ing emperors promoted the princes to high status, gave them honored titles and ranks, bestowed rich gifts upon them, and, as noted, bound them in marriage with Manchu daughters of the royal household. The Mongols saw that their princes were favored by the emperors, and thus lost their incentive to rebel against the Manchus. In this way the Manchus stopped any disturbances among the Mongols themselves, disturbances which had previously led to the emergence of a great leader with organizing genius. His genius usually led to the creation of a new nomadic power. However, Manchu policies shut off forever any opportunity for the Mongols to establish their own state.

Religious prejudices were also a significant hindrance in forming a new nomadic power. Because Altan Khan adopted the "Yellow Sect" of Tibetan Buddhism and supported it as the common faith of the Mongol people in the late sixteenth century, the teaching and discipline of Buddhism greatly influenced and limited the customs, society, and activities of the nomadic Mongols. It changed the traditionally powerful militant spirit of the Mongols into concerns for the next life, and thus the Mongols dared not commit any "sin." Among all possible sins, war was considered one of the greatest.

In Central Asia the Mongols were converted to Buddhism, and the Turkish people had earlier become the followers of Islam. Because of the prejudices between these two religions, the Mongols and Turks always viewed each other with enmity. This is another reason why there was no unified regime in the vastness of Central Asia after the Jeünghar empire.

As noted previously, the prime reason northern nomadic peoples invaded southern agricultural lands was due to the nomads' desire for grain and manufactured goods which they could not produce in their pastoral culture. Chinese dynasties always thought that if the nomads fell into dire poverty, they might perish and disappear. They never seemed to discover that poverty caused the nomadic power to invade the Chinese lands to supply their needs. When wars broke out due to these economic factors, they usually ended with the agricultural states allowing the nomads to trade along the Great Wall or with the Chinese giving the nomads grain, cloth, and other goods which they had required. Thus, the nomadic peoples came to feel that if they wanted supplies to maintain their existence, they had to organize themselves into powerful units capable of threatening their southern neighbors. However, when the Russians and the Manchus occupied Central and Northeast Asia, both abandoned the negative policies of economic blockade and encouraged their merchants to trade among the nomads. This policy brought great benefits to the merchants and made it convenient for the nomadic peoples. They could exchange in a peaceful manner animals for needed goods in the vicinity of their tents. Although extortion by the merchants was notorious, when compared with trade through war and bloodshed it was still worthwhile for the Mongols. Thus, the historical reasons for the nomadic peoples to unite and to struggle for the basics of life passed away forever.

Chapter 13

Agricultural Development and Chinese Colonization in Mongolia

(Originally published in *Proceedings of the Montana Academy of Sciences*, 1968, 28:134–43)

In April 1960, Mr. Tsendanbal, the Prime Minister of the Mongolian People's Republic, declared in the National Assembly (Khural) that Mongolia had successfully made the transition from a pastoral-nomadic country to an agricultural state. However, agriculture did not develop naturally in Mongolia. In the northern regions, especially in the Buriyad areas, it has been carried out under heavy political pressure. To the south in Inner Mongolia it was developed in combination with the Chinese colonization of Mongol pasture land which was one of the most important factors leading to the Outer Mongolian struggle for independence in 1911 and the Inner Mongolian movement for autonomy from China, especially between 1933 and 1945.

Today Inner Mongolia is under Chinese Communist control, and the continued existence of the Mongols as a nation is threatened by the long standing Chinese pressure upon Mongolian lands. There is also much evidence that Chinese chauvinism against minority people is being stepped up under the Communists in order to assimilate minorities into the dominant Chinese population. For example, the main reason why Ulanfu was demoted[1] after being Inner Mongolia's leader was because he was sowing the seeds of "Mongolia for the Mongols." In other words, his error was advocating that "the nationalistic character of the [Mongolian Autonomous Region] must be elevated," a slogan which opposed Chinese chauvinism.

In 1945, just after the Communist occupation of Inner Mongolia, the population of the west Üjümüchin Right Banner of Shilinghol League was around ten thousand, of which only three hundred were non-Mongols. Several years later the population of the same Banner increased to fifteen thousand and then to thirty thousand. Obviously, there is no possibility that the original Mongols tripled in population in these few years. Without doubt several years after the Communist occupation, the Chinese farmers who were forcibly settled on Üjümüchin land had doubled the original Mongolian population of the same area. Today Red China is a political threat to many countries and brings demographic pressures to bear on her neighboring states because of her more than seven hundred million people.[2] However, this pressure can not be compared to that which she has imposed upon the minorities within her borders. The following discussion reflects the historical background to this problem as it developed on the Mongolian frontier of China.

It is difficult to say whether the North Asian steppe peoples had adopted any form of agriculture before the third century B.C., while still occupying parts of North China, now known as northern Hopei and Shansi provinces. However, it is evident that as they retreated into the "Dry Sea" or Gobi area they became completely nomadic. Thus, the first famous Chinese historian, Ssu-ma Ch'ien, writing before the first century B.C., described the life of the Hsiung-nu and explained that "they are forever moving about following the watering places and grazing fields, and they have no cities, houses, or farming lands."[3]

The first written record of Chinese colonization of Mongol lands was in the year 214 B.C. when the Ch'in general Meng T'ien defeated the northern nomadic peoples and occupied land on the south of the big bend of the Yellow River, now known as the Ordos Area of Inner Mongolia. The purpose of settling Chinese farmers in this newly occupied land was undoubtedly to make this territory an integral part of the Ch'in Empire. However, two decades later, following the collapse of the Ch'in Dynasty and the emergence of the powerful Hsiung-nu empire, the Chinese settlers who had been forced onto this land all retreated to their native areas.

Many accounts can be found in the history of the Han Dynasty (206 B.C.–220 A.D.) showing that numerous Chinese thought life among the Hsiung-nu people was easier than life in China. Thus, they migrated and took refuge to the north of the Great Wall. Although there are no records which indicate whether these Chinese fugitives were used by the Hsiung-nu nobles as artisans or farmers, judging from what is known about later nomadic peoples, it is possible that these Chinese helped the Hsiung-nu cultivate agricultural lands. During the long struggle between the Hsiung-nu and the Han Chinese, the Ordos area once again fell into the hands of the Chinese. This area was not only an important strategic point against the Hsiung-nu on the north, but it was also a key point in the control of the Silk Road on the west. The Han court followed the pattern of the Ch'in and moved Chinese farmers into the area to colonize it.

In the third and fourth centuries, both the Hsien-pei and the Wu-huan, probably proto-Mongol peoples, occupied Mongolia following the decline of the Hsiung-nu empire. It seems that they practiced a little farming in eastern Inner Mongolian territory. However, there is insufficient material available either to prove or disprove this.

After establishing the Wei Dynasty (387–556) in north China the Tabgatch (or To-pa) people began to be Sinicized, and Mongolia proper was occupied by the Jou-jan (or Juan-juan, ?–550) who were much more nomadic than the Tabgatch. The *Wei shu*, the dynastic history of the Tabgatch Wei, notes that on one occasion the nomadic Jou-jan people asked the Wei to supply them with seeds (521). However, this appears to have been a compiler's mistake, and the reference probably refers to grain rather than to seed, since the same account notes that this group of nomadic people moved near the Great Wall in the winter and migrated north of the Gobi in the summer.[4] Such movements would make settled agricultural activity extremely difficult if not impossible.

During the era of the Turk (T'u-chüeh) empire (550–745) numerous Chinese people lived in Mongolia both as refugees and as prisoners of war. Once again, there is no record which establishes that these Chinese developed agriculture in Mongolia. To the contrary, it is stated in the *Hsin T'ang Shu* that the famous minister Tonyukhukh admonished Bilge Khan (r. 716–34) that the Turks, in striving for existence, should not adopt the lifestyle of the sedentary agricultural Chinese.[5]

Following the end of the T'u-chüeh Turks, a related people, the Uighurs, established their empire in Mongolia (745–847). In 762, as a result of a petition from the T'ang emperor, the Uighur suppressed a Chinese rebellion in the city of Lo-yang, the eastern capital of the T'ang Dynasty, and occupied it for a year. At this time the Uighur Khan converted to the Manichean religion. This old Persian religion espoused vegetarianism, and consequently the Uighur had to develop some sort of agriculture in Mongolia before their migration to the area of the Tien-shan mountains after 847. There is no indication that Mongolia had any type of agriculture during the Kirghis occupation (847–924).

In Eastern Inner Mongolia during the time of the Kitan Empire (907–1125) some agriculture developed. However, the Kitans do not seem to have farmed themselves, but it was done by Chinese who had fled into Mongolia or had been captured in war by the Kitan. The Kitan ruler treated those Chinese liberally and utilized them in a systematic plan for agricultural production. The Chinese were settled in several cities to farm under the supervision of the Kitans. Thus, the Kitans were the only northern nomadic power which could supply all their food from within their own territory before occupying Chinese lands. The ruins of Kitan cities have been found in Outer Mongolia and have become the object of intensive studies. However, it is not possible to determine as yet whether agriculture was carried on in connection with these particular cities far to the north in the interior of Mongolia.

During the twelfth century the Jurchen Chin Dynasty (1115–1234) built a secondary wall to the north and outside the Great Wall in order to protect their northern border against the Mongols. The dynastic history of this period, the *Chin shih*, makes note of the *t'un-t'ien* (屯田), rather unique establishments in which troops stationed there carried on agricultural activity. This agriculture, of course, was accomplished not by Mongols but by the Jurchen and probably some Chinese.

Later, according to Chinese records, at the beginning of the Mongol Empire the Mongolian diet was composed of meat and milk with very little or no grain. It seems safe to assume that agriculture was not practiced. After the establishment of the empire Chimhai (Chinese = Chen-hai) a city was set up in Outer Mongolia with the object of supplying agricultural products for people north of the Gobi. The city appears to have been in the region of the Orhon River. Chamhai was the name of an important minister who supervised the city. The agriculture was carried on by captives, not by the Mongols themselves. There is mention in the records of a group called *Chung-t'ien jen* (屯田人), i.e., farmers who cultivated to the north of the Gobi. There is also evidence of agricultural activity a little later in the vicinity of the old Mongol capital, Kharakhorum. One stone inscription found in the vicinity has some mention of an agricultural problem of grain production and of transportation, but again it is difficult to believe that this involved Mongol farmers. All of these agricultural settlements or cities seemed to have totally disappeared with the collapse of the Yüan Dynasty (1368).

It was a full two centuries before any further agricultural activity in Mongolia is mentioned in the Chinese records. There was nothing until the time of Altan Khan and the Tümed Tribe who collected Chinese farmers escaping from the Ming due to heavy taxes, etc. These Chinese agricultural settlements under Mongol rule were located mostly in southwestern Inner Mongolia around present-day Hohhot (Köke-Khota). The Mongols called them *baishing*, no doubt taken from the term used by the Chinese in referring to the common people. This was the first incident of free Chinese settling and cultivating lands in Mongolia under Mongol protection.

It is very difficult to determine from historical records exactly when the Mongols themselves began to develop agriculture. One of the first accounts is found in the *Ming shih-lu*, which says the Uiryangkha Mongols beyond the Great Wall to the northeast of Peking came to the Chinese for plows and seed. These people were what later came to be known as the Kharachin Banners of eastern Inner Mongolia. It appears that from Ming times to the present, some Mongols in these regions carried on agricultural activity. Yet at the same time, there is a long series of records according to which the Mongols came into Chinese areas to trade horses and pelts for grain and other products. There is a possibility that the Mongols made weapons out of the plows they purchased and did not actually use them for agricultural purposes, since there was a perpetual embargo on weapons sales to Mongolia. However, it was seldom possible to enforce it fully.

The earliest reference in the Ch'ing records concerning Mongolian agriculture is in a decree by the Emperor T'ai-tsung (r. 1626–43), which substantiates the fact that there were Mongolian farmers near the Manchu settlement regions who were carrying on some sort of agriculture. The next reference is in the *Ta-Ch'ing hui-tien* (大清會典 Collection of Ch'ing Laws and Regulations), in 1650, according to which "for every fifteen men among the subordinate Mongols there shall be granted a piece of land twenty *li* in length and one *li* in width."[6] This is further proof of Mongolian agricultural activity in very early Ch'ing times. However, it should be noted that this condition concerned only a limited area of eastern Inner Mongolia and was not widespread among the Mongol people as a whole. The general policy of the Manchus was not to encourage the Mongols to become too involved in agriculture.

By the latter part of the seventeenth century, a new trend developed. There was a continuing dribble of Chinese into Mongol territories escaping from China proper. This marks the real beginning of Mongolian agriculture which was copied or learned by the Mongols from the Chinese settlers. In the beginning there was no concern among the Mongols for the protection of their pastures. However, this changed later as pressures grew upon the Mongol pastoralists and finally led to the emergence of political problems between the Mongols and the Chinese.

In the year 1748, the Manchu-Ch'ing court made three decisions on the colonization problem in eastern Inner Mongolia.

> The Mongol lands which have been mortgaged to Chinese should be returned to the original [Mongol] landowners according to the year limitations of the mortgages. Those lands, 1643.30 *ching*[7] in the Tümed Beise Banner, 400.80 *ching* in the Kharachin Beise Banner, and 431.80 *ching* in the Kharachin Jasagh Banner are the farming lands of the Mongol people. In other banners there is no such land situation, consequently the Chinese are not allowed to occupy or cultivate such lands as mentioned above. The *jasaghs* [Mongol ruling princes] of these banners must clearly determine the land ownership, the mortgagers, the rental payments, the time limitations, list them in detail, and send it to the *t'ung-chih* (同知) and the *t'ung-pan* (通判) [Manchu officials in Mongol border areas]. This should follow the pattern of the Kuei-hua-cheng area where the Mongols have withdrawn their lands [from the Chinese settlers].

> The Chinese who have rented lands or houses must pay their rent according to their contract. If anyone refuses or postpones and prolongs the payments and charges are brought by the owner, then . . . [the Manchu officials] must take charge of the case and collect the rent for the owner. In any case in which a tenant does not pay his rent for three years, then the land or house must be returned to the owner.

The Mongol nobility, officials, and lamas are mostly rich, but those under them and the soldiers are mostly poor. However, sometimes those who are rich through their privileges allow Chinese to cultivate public land [pastures]. Consequently, poor Mongols are more handicapped by this. From now on according to their circumstances, one-third of the land of the rich princes, nobility, officials, and lamas should be turned over to the poor Mongols to farm.[8]

In the above record we can see that around the middle of the eighteenth century there were a few banners, both in eastern and western Inner Mongolia, where the Mongols themselves did some farming. However, some of the lands had been mortgaged to Chinese settlers. This situation caused the Manchu Court to worry about what consequences and problems might arise for their Mongolian administration. Consequently, they tried to force the Chinese to return the lands to the Mongol owners. Also, because of such problems Manchu officials were dispatched and stationed in Mongolian border areas. Later, they became regular officials over those Chinese settlements.

It is also clear that even in quite early times there were already some Chinese tenants who refused to pay rent to the Mongol landowners. Further, some selfish Mongol nobility and officials turned the public pastures over to Chinese settlers for personal gain. This caused the common people to suffer from the loss of the common grazing fields.

In 1749 another decision was made by the Ch'ing Court announcing that: "Except for those Chinese who have already settled in the banners of Kharachin, Tümed, Aukhan, and Ongni'ud, no more Chinese are to be allowed to settle or cultivate [in Mongolia]. . . . *Jasaghs* and Mongol officials who dare for personal gain to allow Chinese to settle and cultivate or mortgage land from them shall receive the same punishment as those who commit the crime of hiding fugitives. . . . Cultivated land must be distributed among the poor Mongols of that same banner. Chinese who mortgage land shall be heavily punished and be sent back to their home province by the local [Manchu] authorities. As for cases of Chinese settlers in Chakhar areas, these should be handled by Manchu officials and in Kharachin . . . the Chinese must be sent back to their original home lands."[9]

Later, in the year 1772 the Ch'ing Court declared, "Manchu and Chinese inside the Great Wall must not enter Mongol areas outside the Great Wall to cultivate land there. Those who transgress this regulation shall be punished according to the law."[10]

By the time of Chien-lung (1736–95) of the Ch'ing Dynasty, Mongol land problems were limited to the areas of the southeastern border areas of Josotu and Juu-uda leagues, the Chakhar area, and the Tümed Banner of the Hohhot area. Later in the reign of Chia-ch'ing (1795–1820) the same kind of problem arose in the area of Jerim league in eastern Inner Mongolia. By this period the total size of the land farmed by Chinese had become enlarged. It was no longer even calculated in Ch'ing (15.13 acres) but *li* (1.890 English feet). For instance, a document in 1812 mentions that:

Chinese cultivation is allowed in . . . Khorchin Left Flank Rear Banner . . . which is bordered by the Liao River on the west and the Surbakhan River on the east, 120 *li* in length. It extends from the Taip'ing Mountains on the north to Liu-tiao-pien [a border wall] on the south, 52 *li* in width.[11]

This document shows the rapid development of the Chinese settlements in eastern Inner Mongolia. It seems that the Ch'ing court had already relaxed the restraints against Chinese settlers and was trying to encourage the Mongols to make concessions to Chinese agriculture in Mongolia by increasing the income to Mongol nobility. Another document of 1811 records that:

> Half of the income from the rent of the cultivated land of Changtu-erg [in the above mentioned Khorchin Banner] shall be given to the *jasagh*, and the other half . . . shall be distributed fairly among the nobles, officials, troops, and common people.[12]

This is good evidence that permission for Chinese agriculture profited the prince and the nobles greatly. Therefore, through such temptations some of the covetous nobility, in order to increase their personal wealth, allowed more Chinese to settle in their banners.

Later, following the Sinicization of the Manchu Court and the expansion of Russian power toward China, the Manchu rulers, in order to protect their northern border area, changed their former policy protecting Mongol pastures from Chinese cultivation and adopted a policy encouraging Chinese settlement to the north of the Great Wall. With such encouragement a great stream of Chinese peasants flowed into Mongolia. Because of the increase of Chinese settlers, Manchu officials stationed in the border area of Inner Mongolia were formally appointed as local magistrates and the new Chinese settlements became Chinese districts or *Chou* and *hsien*. In addition, because of the declining power of the Mongol banners, these Manchu magistrates began to interfere with the administration of the Mongols and tried to gain more pasture lands for cultivation by Chinese immigrants. Also, Chinese merchants and money lenders, backed by the Manchu officials, began to take lands as security for monies which they had lent to the Mongol princes at a high interest rate.

By the beginning of this century the above mentioned policy of the Ch'ing Court was fostered by Manchu officials both in eastern and western Mongolia. In the east, the Bureau of Mongol Affairs *(Meng-shih-chu蒙事處)* was established under the Office of the Governor General of Sheng-Ching (Mukden) which dealt with the business of Chinese colonization in the banners of Jerim league. In the west, the Governor General of Suiyuan, I-ku,[13] was appointed as the Minister of Colonization. Thus, he laid a heavy hand on the Mongol people of both the Ordos and Ulanchab areas. In 1905, General I-ku executed seven Mongol officials who were leaders opposed to Chinese cultivation. This caused rebellions to break out all across these two areas. Finally, the Ch'ing Court was forced to make a concession, dismissed I-ku from his post, and temporarily ceased further cultivation.

Since the Mongol lands settled by the Chinese were the public pastures, there was a direct affect on the livelihood of the common herdsmen who were forced to give up their best grazing fields without any compensation. The league and banner organization, under the domination of Manchu and Chinese magistrates, could not simultaneously protect the Mongols, collect the rent from the Chinese, and maintain jurisdiction in their own territories. Because of this, some herdsmen eventually took up their weapons and began attacking the newly established Chinese political centers for revenge. Such men are known as "Mongol bandits" in modern Chinese history. The increase of so-called "Mongol bandits" indicates a growth in Chinese settlements in Mongolia. However, the killing of Manchu and Chinese magistrates and settlers did not make the Ch'ing Court change its policy, especially in eastern Mongolia. This situation did not change even after the establishment of the Chinese Republic. In 1911, Outer Mongolia declared independence and a group of so-called "Mongol bandits" marched north and joined the movement. One of their leaders, Toghtogh *Taiji*, was appointed Vice-Minister of Military Affairs in the newly established government in Urga (Ulan-bator).

In Outer Mongolia, in the 1720s, during the period of Manchu-Jeüngharian War, farming was carried out by the troops of the Manchu General Fu-erh-tan who was stationed in the vicinity of the temple Erdeni-yin Juu in the Orkhon River valley in order to supply food for his army. This was the first time that land in Khalkha was farmed by a non-Mongol people under non-Mongol supervision. However, there is no record to show that this farming activity was continued after the war ended. The location, it seems, was not far from the modern Arbai-keer collective farm of the Mongolian People's Republic.

By the end of the Ch'ing Dynasty it seems that there was no Chinese cultivation in Outer Mongolia. Nevertheless, rumors of the abolishment of the traditional league and banner system, of the establishment of a Chinese style administration, and of Chinese colonization increasingly reached Urga. These rumors made the people of Outer Mongolia anxious about their future. This was one of the main factors in their desire to gain independence.

During the early years of the Republic of China, and in order to win the support of the Mongols, the Peking Government proclaimed that the traditional administrative rights of the Mongol princes would remain as before. However, the warlords of North China, especially Chang Tso-lin in Manchuria, continued their aggressive policy toward the Inner Mongolian banners and occupied the best pastures. More migrant Chinese settlers caused the establishment of Chinese administrations in Mongol territory.

Just before the Manchurian incident of 1931, eastern Inner Mongolia was under the domination of the warlord Chang Hsüeh-liang. Under him more lands were taken by force without compensating the Mongol herders. This policy of settlement by military force was carried out by Tsou Tso-hua, who was the General Director of Colonization for the Northeastern Mongolian Banners *(tung-pei meng-chi tun-ken tu-pan* 東北蒙旗 屯墾督辦).

In western Inner Mongolia, Fu Tso-yi was the main figure in the colonization of Mongol land. By the end of the Ch'ing Dynasty all of the fertile soil along the great bend of the Yellow River was settled by Chinese. Later, in the 1930s, Shih Hua-yen was appointed by the well-known Shansi warlord Yen Hsi-shan to be the Director of Military Cultivation in Mongol area. They planned to settle their retired soldiers on Mongol pastures. This became one of the main reasons for the Inner Mongolian Autonomous Movement of 1933.

In eastern Inner Mongolia during Japanese occupation the land problem was temporarily solved through the arbitration of Japanese officials. The Mongols reestablished their rights of land ownership in many places, but the Chinese rights of perpetual lease were also recognized together with a set schedule of rental fees. The revenues from the land rent were used as the main funds to establish a modern school system and to develop education.

From 1945 on Inner Monglia began to come under the influence of the Chinese Communists. In order to win the support of the Mongols, the Communists proclaimed that there would be no further cultivation of Mongol pastures. However, this was merely empty propaganda. After they strengthened their control, they forgot this promise and brought Chinese migrants from all over China and settled them in all places "suitable for agricultural production." Consequently, remaining Mongolian areas such as Shilinghol, Hulunbuir, Ulanchap, and the northern parts of Joo-uda, Jerim, and Chakhar were all changed into new settlements for these forced settlers. This was not a special treatment by the Chinese Communists reserved for Mongolia, for it was also a common practice toward all minority peoples under Chinese power, e.g., the Tibetans and the Uighurs. Because of the chauvinistic expansionism of the Chinese Communists, many Inner Mongolians sought asylum in the land of their brothers — Outer Mongolia. This also has become one of the main reasons for conflict between Red China and the Mongolian People's Republic which is keenly aware of the heavy pressure of the Chinese population.

Notes

1. The demotion of Ulanfu occurred during the Cultural Revolution, after the death of Mao Tse-tung. At the "victorious end of the Cultural Revolution," he was rehabilitated and promoted to the position of Vice-Chairman of the People's Congress of the PRC.
2. At present the Chinese population is a little more than one billion.
3. *Shih chi*, 110, "Account of Hsiung-nu," 1b.
4. *Wei shui*, 103 "Account of Juan-juan," 1b, 20ab.
5. *Hsin-T'ang-shu*, 140B, "Account of T'u-chüeh," 1a.
6. *Ch'ing-tai pien-cheng t'ung-k'ao* (清代边政通考), edited by Mongolian and Tibetan Affairs Commission, Taipei, 1959, 248.
7. One *ch'ing* (頃) contains one hundred *mu* (畝). One *mu* is about 733 square yards.
8. *Ch'ing-tai pien-cheng t'ung-k'ao*, 248.
9. Ibid., 248–49.
10. Ibid., 249.
11. Ibid., 251.
12. Ibid., 250.
13. For I-ku (貽穀), see biography in *Ch'ing-shih*, 1961, 454.

Chapter 14

An Interpretation of "Mongol Bandits" (*Meng-Fei*)

(Originally published in *Altaica, Proceedings of the 19th Annual Meeting of the Permanent International Altaistic Conference*, June 1976, Helsinki 113-21).

Interaction between two peoples of different cultures inevitably results in misunderstandings and conflict. This is particularly true when there is little basis for mutual understanding, no means to resolve conflict, and when the power of one side is superior to that of the other. Although interaction between the Chinese and the peoples of Mongolia has had a long history extending over several thousand years, a relationship of mutual respect and peaceful coexistence never developed. Instead, the relationship was almost always one of mutual antagonism, of invasion or counter-invasion, of oppression and reaction. Before the middle of the seventeenth century, the Mongols were invariably the intruders, but thereafter it was Mongolia that was invaded by the Chinese.

The word "aggression" is difficult to define and is politically sensitive. Naturally, neither side wants to be branded as an aggressor in the complex relationship between two peoples in a disputed border area. Nevertheless, there are few people who have perceived the complex differences between nomadic peoples invading China and Chinese agriculturalists entering Mongolia.

The invasion of nomads into agricultural areas was usually motivated by economic need and followed a pattern of raiding and plundering. Even in cases where nomadic peoples occupied agricultural regions and established a conquering dynasty, their basic goal rarely exceeded economic exploitation. Their rule did not cause a basic change in the lifestyle or agricultural production, nor did it destroy the economic basis of the agricultural people. Thus, after a nomadic invasion and occupation had run its course, the situation usually returned to the social and economic norms which had existed before the nomadic people came. The results of nomadic invasions south of the Great Wall were violent but had only a temporary impact. They were not a mortal blow to the future viability of sedentary Chinese society.

In contrast, the expansion of Chinese agricultural peoples into nomadic areas, made possible by their stronger nation-state and military power, resulted in more permanent political control and economic development. The land was often occupied and cultivated permanently. The result was a thorough and basic change in the society and culture of the Mongolian region colonized. In changing the basic economy and the related lifestyle, the viability of the nomadic society was destroyed as the people were forced from the land and thus removed from their economic base.

While the migration of the present farmers was not usually violent, it was generally permanent — a mortal blow to nomadic life. Beyond the Great Wall the irresistible pressure of the enormous Chinese population was the main factor bringing the nomads to a point of assimilation or of violent reaction to avoid extermination. This militant phase in the relationship between the Mongols and the Chinese reached its peak in the latter part of the last century and the early decades of this century. Those Mongols who adopted militant action to avoid assimilation continually appear in the Chinese records as "Mongol Bandits" (蒙匪 Meng-fei). A brief analysis of this phenomenon will be attempted here, but first some background should be traced.

Anciently, during the confrontation between the nomadic Hsiung-nu and the Han-dynasty, a Chinese official, Chung-hang Yüeh, who had surrendered to the nomadic side, took special pains to warn the Shan-yü (Khan of the Hsiung-nu) about the danger of the vastly superior Chinese population. He admonished him to avoid adopting a Chinese way of life. In a similar case, centuries later during the confrontation between the Turks (T'u-chüeh) and the T'ang dynasty, a famous Turkic minister, Tonyukhukh, again warned the Turkic leaders not to accept Chinese culture and to avoid sedentary ways. The advice of both men was to maintain a policy of cultural distance to prevent both the nomadic Hsiung-nu and the Turks from being assimilated into the Chinese.

The Chinese population during these early periods was not nearly so great as in modern times, but it was still large enough to pose a great threat to the nomadic leaders. Chinese sources give the population of Fomer Han (2 A.D.) as almost ninety-six million. Other records give the T'ang population as about forty-eight million (740). One may only speculate as to how much greater the problem had become by the period covered in this paper. In the middle of the nineteenth century, the Chinese population is given as 426,730,000 (1848). Certainly the pressure of the Chinese against the Mongols had become unimaginably strong.

Government documents confirm that the cultivation of Mongol lands occurred to a limited extent during the early years of the Manchu-Ch'ing dynasty (1626–1911). However, farming in Mongolia was not encouraged by the Manchu authorities who wanted to maintain the area as a military reserve. But as the Chinese population grew under Manchu domination, the importance of cultivating fertile grazing fields in Inner Mongolia could not be overlooked in resolving the problem of overpopulation in China. As the situation changed in China in the latter part of the eighteenth century, the Ch'ing court adopted a new policy of colonizing Mongol lands to alleviate the problem of famine in North China. Thus, the migration of Chinese refugees into southeastern Mongolia was allowed under the rationale of "borrowing Mongol land to nourish Chinese people" (借地養民 chieh-ti yang-min). Nevertheless, this was still intended as a temporary measure and the basic policy forbidding Chinese to farm in Mongolia continued.

The entire situation changed during the middle of last century following times of trouble in China, including the Opium War (1839–42), the Second Opium War or the Anglo-French War with China (1857–60), the T'ai-p'ing Rebellion (1850–64), and the continued penetration of Tsarist Russia into what was considered Ch'ing territory. With the military and economic incursions of Western imperialism and with internal rebellions, the agrarian economy of China declined greatly causing widespread poverty and distress among the peasantry. The concurrent penetration of Russia awakened great concern in the Ch'ing court for the power vacuum to the north, not only in Manchuria but also in Mongolia. As a reaction, and in order to resist the threat from the north as well as relieve internal population pressures, the Manchu rulers relaxed the policy forbidding migration into border areas and actually began to encourage it. As a result, millions of Chinese peasants flowed into Mongolia. This policy has continued unabated in Inner Mongolia and other non-Chinese border areas up to the present day.

During the mid-nineteenth century crises of war and rebellion, Inner Mongolian volunteer forces were recruited under the leadership of Prince Senggerinchin, and they fought valiantly for their Manchu overlords. But with the changing policies of the Manchu court, Mongolian attitudes also changed. Rather than Mongolian recruits fighting loyally for the Manchu court, nomadic people arose spontaneously as "Mongol Bandits," fighting for their own land and people.

In modern Mongolian history, two leadership groups, the lay nobility and the high lama ecclesiastics, are viewed as the twin pillars of Mongolian quasi-feudalism. Some leaders from both groups are regarded as traitors to their own people, selling public land for personal gain. Traditionally there was no private possession of land in nomadic society. Rather, the concern was grazing rights. The key socio-political relationship was between the lord *(noyan)* and his subordinates *(arad)* in a quasi-feudalistic system, while the key economic unit was the grazing field *(notugh,* Chs. *Yu-mu*游牧 *)*. Land was the common property of all the people — not the private property of the lord. He had no legal right to dispose of it, and thus there are many instances of "Mongol bandits" who revolted against their own lord, as well as against the Chinese settlers. Mongol leaders who stood against their princes, attacked the Chinese, or who led rebellions and nationalistic movements are the heroes of the Mongolian people in modern times.

Perhaps the problem of the *noyan* or princes should be explained. Under Manchu domination they were required to make regular official visits to Peking, where they imitated the luxurious life-style of the Manchu nobility or aristocrats in the capital, greatly increasing burdens on their own people. Under Manchu domination the Mongolian people were also plagued by the economic exploitation of Chinese merchants.

An additional problem was a decline in the overall productive power of Mongolia due to the increasing number of men who went into Buddhist temples as lamas or monks. As the economy of Mongolia was impoverished by the increase of taxes and corvée duties, the Mongolian nobility began to sell or to rent more and more land illegally to Chinese settlers. While this activity was unlawful, even court officials soon began to encourage secretly the leasing or sale of Mongolian lands for the monies to be gained. Eventually, the Ch'ing court was persuaded or pressured to adopt a new policy, and both Manchu and Chinese officials collaborated with greedy Mongolian officials and nobles to open Mongolian lands for Chinese settlers to cultivate.

As Chinese immigrants concentrated in particular areas, the Peking government established administrative offices of various types and levels such as *fu, hsien, chou,* and *ting* (府縣州廳). These Chinese organizations became an added problem as they encroached upon the administrative functions of the Mongolian banner units that had previously been autonomous or independent. Thus, the Mongolian people lost not only their life-line, i.e., their grazing fields, but they often lost the means to protect themselves through their own leaders and political organizations. In this situation of political encroachment and economic exploitation, betrayed by their own nobility and oppressed by both Manchu and Chinese officials, the people took up weapons in a struggle for their very survival. As Mongols struck in anger against the Chinese, Manchu officials, Chinese immigrants, and many of their own despised leaders, there emerged many movements composed of so called "Mongol Bandits" *(Meng-fei).*

The Chinese terms *tse* (賊), *k'uo* (寇), and *fei* (匪) are commonly applied to bandits and robbers, at times to rebellious or revolutionary groups, and even to foreign enemies. There are, for example, the *Huang-chin-tse* (黃巾賊) or Yellow Turban rebels of the Late Han in 184 A.D., the *Wo-k'uo* (倭寇) or Japanese raiders of the sixteenth century, and the *Nien-fei* (捻匪) or Nien rebels of the 1850s and 1860s. In our own day, the Chinese Communists are referred to by the Kuomintang as *Mao-fei* (毛匪 Mao Tse-tung bandits). Conversely, Peking brands its enemies as *pang* (幫 the gangs). Thus *Meng-fei* included both common bandits and political rebels. At times the term was used interchangeably with *ma-tse* (馬賊 "bandits on horseback"), *ma-ta-tzu* (馬韃子 "Tatars on horseback"), or *hu-fei* (鬍匪 "bearded bandits").

A list of so called "Mongol bandits" was published in Chinese newspapers at the beginning of the Republic (1912), but interestingly they were all Chinese. It should be made clear that while some of these roving bands were Chinese groups, others were armed, revolutionary Mongol groups taking direct action to protect their own people. A similar situation existed on the southwest and northwest borders of China where rebellious Moslem groups arose as *Hui-fei* (回匪 Moslem bandits).

After the Manchu pacification of the Chakhar uprisings in Inner Mongolia (1675), there were virtually no rebellious disturbances for some two centuries. But in the latter part of the nineteenth century, ethnic disturbances became increasingly more common due to the factors explained above. Attention was first focused on this phenomenon in the West by Owen Lattimore in his *Mongols of Manchuria*. It has been studied more recently by Walther Heissig in his article, *Some New Information on Peasant Revolts* and *Peoples Uprising in Eastern [Inner] Mongolia in the 19th Century* (1861–1901). Limited by time and space, it is impossible in this paper to discuss in detail each separate case of "Mongol Bandits." However, a simple outline will suffice. Documentation and sources are omitted due to space restrictions.

I. Bandit Types:
    A. The pure bandit type who robbed both Chinese and Mongols:
        1. Example: The Liu-Lama Band of the Tümed Right Flank Banner (Ch'aoyang District), Josotu League, 1851–52.
        2. "Bandits on horseback" *(ma-tse)*: The Jilanggha Taiji case of Keshigten Banner, Juu-Uda League, 1890, is typical of many groups on horseback.
    B. Heroic Robin Hood type bandits who only robbed Chinese:
        1. The Bilinggha-Milsengge Band of Josotu League, 1862–68. This group looted Chinese towns near Mukden, Ch'aoyang, Chiench'ang, Ch'inghomen, and along the Great Wall. They were protected by Mongols in Mongol territory until their capture by Manchu forces.
        2. The Baghadorji — Shobghor group of Kökekhota-Tümed and Ulanchab League, 1870. This group robbed the Chinese in the vicinity of Kökekhota and north of the Mongnai Mountains (Ta-ch'ing Shan). They had support from Mongol officials of the Muu-Mingghan banner, Ulanchab League.

II. Revolts against the Tyranny of Native Overlords:
   A. Examples of the assassination of princes:
      1. The case of Prince Sewangnorbusangbu, *Jasagh* of Tüshiyetü (Khorchin Right Middle) Banner and Chief of the Jerim League: This prince led a life of luxury while causing his people to suffer under heavy taxation and mistreatment. In 1901 banner officials and the people rebelled spontaneously, forcing him to hang himself. As a result the leaders, such as Khuwaliyasun, Toghtogh, Namkhainingbu, Khuwaliyan, and more than thirty people were executed by the Manchu-Ch'ing court.
      2. The case of Prince Lhonjalnortsan's assassination, The Aukhan Banner: This prince and *jasagh* of the Aukhan Banner was assassinated by his own bodyguard, Fujuri, in Peking in late 1904 (or early 1905). The court handled the case in the same manner as that of Prince Sewangnorbusangbu above.
   B. Popular uprisings of the common people:
      1. The Lao-t'ou-hui movement, Tüment Left Banner, Josotu League, 1860–67: The fertile grazing fields of this banner were increasingly cultivated by the Chinese settlers, and the Mongols' livelihood was steadily deteriorating. The elders (老頭 *lao-tou*) of this banner organized an association (會 *hui*) and led the people in armed resistance against the exploitative and corrupt banner administration. After an investigation, many leaders including Chojintai, Namsarai, Chaghanbator, and Enkebatur were executed.
      2. Rebellion of the Eight *Sumun*, Tümend Right Banner, Josotu League, 1861–70: This event was influenced by the *Lao-t'ou-hui* movement above. Popular leaders, i.e., Ch'angming, Danjur, Derchinjab, and others, stirred up the people in eight *sumun* (local units) of the banner to refuse military service and the payment of taxes. This was a mass movement against both Manchu and Mongolian authorities. The leaders were killed or exiled.
      3. The Revolt at Töküm in Jasaghtu Banner, Jerim League, 1899–1901: This armed revolt was a cooperative movement among the people of Jasaghtu and its neighboring banners whose livelihood was depressed because of poor administration and high taxes. Leaders of the uprising, Ghombosangbu and Wang-lo-hu, were outsiders who came in to help foment the popular uprising. Russian forces were also involved in this incident.
III. Movements Opposing Manchu and Chinese Colonization:
   1. The Bayanöljei incident, Urad Front Banner, Ulanchab League, 1856: Bayanöljei, a high official of Urad Front Banner, led a group in burning Chinese settlements and in killing the settlers.
   2. The *Dughuilang* movements of Jeünghar (Ordos Left Front) Banner, Yekejuu League (Ordos), 1906–8: In 1902 I-ku, Manchu Governor-General of Suiyuan, forced the banners of both Yekejuu and Ulanchab Leagues to open their land to Chinese settlers for cultivation. In 1906, a *dughuilang*-type, popular, secretly planned movement, broke out in the Jeünghar Banner and its leaders were killed by I-ku. Later, the Mongols under the leadership of Dampil *taiji* organized another *dughuilang* and the situation became more serious. Finally, Dampil and six other persons were executed by I-ku (1908) and the movement was crushed.

Still later, Governor-General I-ku was tried and imprisoned in part because of his actions in these cases.

3. The Choghdalai Rebellion in Jalaid Banner, Jerim League, 1907: After the Boxer Rebellion (1900), the Manchu-Ch'ing court carried out a policy of land development and Chinese settlement north of the Great Wall. A special focus was on eastern Inner Mongolia, and Jalaid was one of the main areas. As a backlash, in 1907, Choghadalai the *meiren* of the banner, led a group that killed Khafenggha, a Mongol collaborating with the Chinese. Then the group rose in armed rebellion and destroyed the Chinese administrative offices and settlements. This movement continued for almost one year.

4. The Bayandalai Uprising of Tümed Left Banner, Josotu League, 1908: This was purely an uprising of the common people without any leadership from the upper class. This armed rebellion, led by Bayandalai, a commoner, destroyed Chinese settlements in the districts of Changwu, T'aoan, Huaite, and T'uch'üian, all of which were Chinese districts (or counties) established within the Jerim League. This revolt was finally crushed by Chinese forces.

5. Togtogh *taiji's* anti-Chinese Revolt, Eastern Inner Mongolia, 1908–11: Toghtogh was a *taiji* (noble) of Ghorlos Front Banner, Jerim League, where Chinese colonization in Mongol lands was quite advanced. Toghtogh started his armed attacks on the Chinese settlements and government offices in 1908. Soon this revolt against the Manchus and Chinese was supported by the people of the four banners of Jailaid, Süke-Güng (Khorchin Right Rear), Tüshiyetü (Khorchin Right Middle), and Jasaghtu (Khorchin Right Front) in the Jerim League. Toghtogh, a talented leader of guerrilla warfare, led his partisans in attacks on Chinese settlements in the districts of Ch'angch'un, Talai, and T'aoan. He was able to dominate the northern half of the Jerim League for several years from a stronghold in the Great Hsingan Mountains. His men continued their heroic fight against the Ch'ing regime and the Chinese settlers until 1911, when Toghtogh and his group went to Outer Mongolia to join the Mongolian Independence Movement. This was the greatest *"Meng-fei"* incident of the late Ch'ing dynasty.

6. Ghombojab's Rebellion in Jarud Left Banner, Juu-uda League, 1913: Prince Dobjai, *Jasagh* of this banner, was a corrupt official who collaborated with Chinese officials to sell banner land to Chinese settlers. Ghombojab, *tusalghchi* (vice-head) of the same banner opposed the prince's policies. He gathered the people, killed the prince, raided the Chinese city of Kailu, and destroyed the Chinese settlements within the three banners of Left Jarud, Right Jarud, and Aru-Khorchin of the Juu-uda League. Finally, outnumbered by Chinese forces, they gradually escaped to Outer Mongolia.

7. The Ghadaa *meiren* Incident, Darkhan (Khorchin Left Middle) Banner, Jerim Leagues, 1929–30 (?): A few years before the Manchurian Incident (1931), the Chinese development of Mongolian lands in the Jerim League was forcibly carried out by General Ts'ou Tso-hua (鄒作華). The Manchu wife of Namjilsereng, Prince of the Darkhan Banner, a corrupt woman who collaborated with the Chinese for personal gain, was the main promoter of Chinese settlement and cultivation. An administrator *(meiren)* of the same banner,

Ghadaa, strongly opposed her policy. He struggled in vain to stop the Chinese colonization and finally gathered his followers in an armed rebellion against her, her husband (Prince Nemjilsereng), and the Chinese.

8. The "3-26 Incident" — revolt of 26 March 1943 — of Jasagh (Ordos Right Front Last) Banner, Yeke-juu League, 1943: During the Sino-Japanese War (1937–45), Jasagh Banner became one of the centers of Mongolian politics. Under General Fu Tso-yi's (傅作義) command, General Ch'en Ch'ang-chieh (陳長捷) and his troops garrisoned in Jasagh Banner promoted Chinese settlement on Mongol lands. Loroi, a young Mongolian garrison officer of Jasagh Banner, began an armed revolt on 26 March killing several Mongols (who collaborated with the Chinese) and attacking the Chinese forces. He had the full support of the people and the banner officials in exterminating the Chinese division. Ch'en Ch'ang-chieh escaped with only a few followers. The tense situation continued for almost a year. Because of the war against the Japanese and the nearby Communist forces in Yenan, the Chinese National Government in Chungking adopted a passive posture to placate the Mongols. Ch'en was punished as a scapegoat. However, the Chinese authorities Yao Tsung (姚琮) trapped Loroi by trickery and executed him.

IV. "Mongol Bandits" as Rebels against the Chinese:

1. The Rebellion of Utai and Rashiminjur, Jerim League, 1912: Utai as Prince of the Jasagh (Khorchin Right Front) Banner had the Mongolian farmers from Josotu League cultivate the banner lands instead of the Chinese. He was shrewd and ambitious and tried to play the Russians against Manchu-Chinese power. For doing so he was attacked by the Ch'ing court. In 1912, seeing the fall of the Manchu-Ch'ing dynasty, Utai cooperated with Rashiminjur, Prince of the Süke-Güng (Khorchin Right Rear) Banner, in a rebellion against Peking. At one point they even occupied the key cities of T'aonan and K'ailu, but were eventually defeated by the Chinese forces and fled to Outer Mongolia.

2. Babujab's Revolt in Eastern Inner Mongolia, 1913–16: The collapse of the Manchu-Ch'ing Dynasty and the establishment of the Republic of China (1912) did not improve the situation of Inner Mongolia. Babujab, an ambitious man from Sürüg (or Tümed Left Banner) with a deep hatred against the Chinese for their colonization of Mongol lands, soon became involved in a Japanese supported, Manchu restoration movement. After the failure of Prince Gungsangnorbu's Inner Mongolian independence movement, Babujab obtained Japanese arms and supplies and rebelled against the Chinese regime. He fought in the Jerim and Juu-uda Leagues, and attacked the Chinese centers of Mukden, Kirin, and Heilungkiang Provinces, and to the south and west in the Jehol and Chakhar areas. He also had some connection with the Urga Government of Outer Mongolia. He was killed in 1916 while attacking the city of Linhsi, northern Jehol, and his troops scattered. Some of them joined the Outer Mongolian forces and some returned to their homes.

3. The Mugdenbo Incident of Chakhar, 1917: Mugdenbo, a young, learned official of Ükerchin (later Mingghan Banner) of Chakhar, gathered several thousand young Mongols and in 1917 carried out a military rebellion against the Chinese Republic in a struggle for independence. Without support from any outside

powers, his group was soon crushed by Chinese forces before the rebellion was really in motion.

V. The Anti-Christian Movements:
By the time of the Boxer Rebellion in North China in 1900, Western Inner Mongolia was offended by missionary activity, especially in the Dalad Banner, Yeke-juu League, the Dorben-ke'üd Banner of Ulanchab League, and the Alashan Banner. However, Mongolian opposition to the Christian churches was quite different from the Chinese Boxers. The Mongols hated the church not only because it propagated a faith contrary to Buddhism, but because the church supported Chinese occupation of Mongol lands. In the settlement of the Boxer Rebellion, the churches received more land from the Mongolian banners, thus increasing the hatred. Therefore, until the end of the Ch'ing Dynasty there were always problems between the pastoral Mongols and the Chinese settlers under church protection.

VI. Factional Movements of Mongols Allied with One Chinese Group against Another:
These are a rare group of cases among the many on record. The Toghtokhu Incident in the Bingtu (Khorchin Left Front) Banner of Jerim League, 1861, will serve as a typical example. Toghtokhu, a *taiji* of the Bingtu Banner allied himself with a group of Chinese settlers and fought against another group of Chinese immigrants. His group killed twenty eight Chinese settlers before he was arrested and executed by the Manchu-Chinese authorities.

VII. Massacres of the Mongols by Chinese Settlers:
By the latter part of the Manchu-Ch'ing dynasty, the southern region of both Juu-uda League and Josotu League were heavily settled by the Chinese, many of whom were deeply influenced by the historically rebellious White Lotus Society (白蓮教 Pai-lien Chiao), a militant Buddhist Sect. In 1891, a group of Chinese in the Ch'aoyang and Aukhan Banner areas organized the Chin-tan-t'ao (金丹道) society (the way of golden pills), to fight for the restoration of the Chinese, the extermination of the Manchus and Mongols, and against the foreign Christians. They killed the prince of Aukhan, disrupted the three Kharachin banners of Josotu League, and killed men, women, and children in these areas. This revolt was crushed by the Manchu-Chinese forces and by Mongolian volunteers.

The cases mentioned above and the historical data available suggest that the so-called "Inner Mongolian Peasant Revolution," as interpreted by Chinese Communist writers, was mainly Mongolian ethnic-nationalistic movements against Chinese colonization, and not, as often construed, cooperative movements or class struggles against oppressive Mongolian princes and corrupt Chinese officials. Even in cases of revolts against tyrannical Mongolian overlords, they were still carried out solely by Mongols acting alone and without any Chinese involvement.

Chapter 15

The Sinicization of the Mongolian Ruling Class in the Late Manchu-Ch'ing Period

(Originally published in *Transactions of the International Conference of Orientalists in Japan*, Tōhō Gakkai [The Institute of Oriental Culture], 1984, 28–29:52–69)

A Brief Account of the Historical Background

From the early periods of Asian history there was a separation between the nomadic peoples of the arid plateaus of North Asia and the sedentary agricultural society of China in the monsoon region to the south. This division ran approximately along the line of the Great Wall and not only separated two different geographical areas, but also marked a great break between two very different cultures and societies. Historically, this gap was the basis of a long, painful confrontation between two radically different worlds. The cultural differences of the two areas perpetuated mutually antagonistic feelings. Thus, the nomadic peoples were motivated to differentiate themselves from their southern neighbors. Very early there appeared various farsighted leaders, such as Chung-hang Yüeh and Tonyukhukh, who realized the delicate situation which threatened the existence of the nomads as a separate nation. These leaders warned their people to be alert to the dire results of Sinicization. The nomadic peoples became conditioned by geography and culture to protect themselves against pressures from the vast Chinese population to amalgamate the two peoples.

During the reign of Khubilai Khan, some leaders suggested that the main cause of the downfall of Kitan and Jurchen powers was their adoption of Chinese Buddhism and Confucian teachings. This suggests that the Kitan and Jurchen were Sinicized. Regardless of the detail or one's view of the problem, a dominant concern for non-Chinese nomadic peoples was the historical trend toward Sinicization. Logically, then, there was a strong resistance to assimilation into the greater Chinese population. It is clear from the historical record that various Sinicizing influences did indeed create problems among non-Chinese peoples such as the Kitans and Jurchen, and eventually brought their downfall.

Historically, almost all North Asian nomadic or pastoral peoples who involved themselves deeply with the Chinese, especially those who came to rule China, were assimilated by the Chinese. An exception were the Mongols who still survive as a separate nation. Even so, from the middle of the nineteenth century the Sinicization of the Mongolian ruling class is an undeniable fact and requires study. The Mongols, though they maintained their identity, faced the same problems that the earlier Kitans and Jurchens had experienced.

A century and a half after the fall of the Yüan Dynasty (1386), a Ming Chinese writer, Hsiao Ta-heng (蕭達亨) wrote *Pei-lu feng-su* (北虜風俗 Customs of the North Barbarians). This book shows no sign of Sinicization among the Mongols. During the latter half of the sixteenth century, the Mongols were converted not to Chinese Buddhism but to Tibetan Buddhism. Buddhism changed the militaristic Mongolian horsemen into a more quiescent people who had little concern for this world, but focused on metaphysical concerns. This was also a primary cause for the decline of the Mongolian population. At the same time, this Tantric form of Tibetan Buddhism eventually became a unique national characteristic of the Mongolian people and a factor in their resistance to various cultural influences from outside, including Chinese assimilation. Moreover, Buddhist leaders became a key factor in the Outer Mongolian Independence Movement of 1911.

The process of Sinicization not only caused some Mongolian ruling nobles to lose their national identity, separating them from their fellow countrymen, but it also accelerated the assimilation of the Mongolian people on all levels of society into the Chinese population. Yet, the threat of rapid Sinicization also awakened Mongolian nationalistic feelings and a will to strive for both cultural and political survival. There were at least two main tendencies among the Mongols: first, there arose among the common people the will to struggle against their Sinicized nobles who betrayed them for their own selfish interests; and, second, there were movements among the intellectuals to introduce modern ideologies which stirred up Mongolian nationalist aspirations for survival and national development.

The Cause and the Fact of Sinicization

The Manchus, as a minority, seized power in the Middle Kingdom in 1644. In order to insure their rule over the Chinese majority, they worked hard to maintain the Mongols as their allies. For this purpose they tried to sever contact between the Mongols and the Chinese and to direct Mongol contacts toward the Manchus. It was in the interests of the Manchus to prevent Mongolian Sinicization. However, this process came, nevertheless, as a by-product of their own policies. From the middle of the last century, Manchu Sinicization accelerated Mongolian Sinicization. Following is an analysis of the reasons behind the process.

Manchu-Mongol intermarriage

A policy of intermarriage as a strategy for preserving peace was a long standing practice between the north Asian nomadic peoples and the sedentary agricultural Chinese. This practice was initiated at the time of the confrontation between the Hsiung-nu and the Han Dynasty some two hundred years before Christ. Although the attitude toward this practice differed through the years, it contributed to some extent to peace between these two hostile worlds. The Manchus also adopted intermarriage as a policy to win Mongol support for the Manchu confrontation with the Chinese, and this was carried on continuously during the Ch'ing Dynasty (1644–1911).

The pattern of the Mongolian-Manchu intermarriages can be divided into four categories: 1) the daughters of Mongolian nobles married Manchu emperors; 2) the daughters of Mongolian nobles married Manchu nobles; 3) Manchu princesses married Mongolian nobles; and 4) the daughters of the Manchu nobles married Mongolian nobles. Among these four categories of intermarriage the first and the second had minor influence on the matter discussed in this paper, but the third and the fourth categories were the main reasons accelerating the Sinicization trend among the Mongolian nobility. The most prominent system of intermarriage was *chih-pei efu* (指備額駙) or the registration for the imperial selection of sons-in-law. All the names of Mongol nobles between the ages of fifteen and twenty were recorded in the court files. The emperor would then make the final decision about which princess or daughter of the imperial household would go to which particular Mongolian noble family.[1]

From the middle part of the Manchu-Ch'ing dynasty this selection of *efu* was mainly directed to the noble families of the following thirteen banners of southeastern Inner Mongolia: the Khorchin Left Flank Central Banner, Khorchin Left Flank Front Banner, Khorchin Left Flank Rear Banner, Khorchin Right Flank Central Banner, Khorchin Right Flank Front Banner, Ba'arin Right Flank Banner, Aukhan Banner, Naiman Banner, Ongni'ud Right Flank Banner, Kharachin Right Flank Banner, Kharachin Left Flank Banner, Kharachin Central Banner, and the Tümed Right Flank Banner.[2] The reasons for this policy shift are not clear, though it was probably due to the close relationships which the Manchu court developed through continual intermarriage and the gradual change from a nomadic pastoral life to a more sedentary, agricultural style. These conditions made southeastern Inner Mongolia more attractive to the more Sinicized Manchu nobles.

Once the Manchu daughters were given in marriage to the Mongolian nobles, the Manchu court encouraged them to remain in Mongolia. It was their role to represent the imperial presence in the Mongolian banners and to influence the people. Because they were discouraged from returning to Peking, they brought their style of life to the places where they were to live. The consequence was the Sinicization of the Mongol ruling class as these princesses and noble daughters brought Chinese influence to Inner Mongolia. Thus, Sinicization of the Mongols was accelerated especially in southeastern Mongolia.[3]

The process of rotating imperial audiences

During Ch'ing times all of the Mongolian ruling princes, higher ranking nobles, and even influential lamas were required to travel to Peking for imperial audiences on a rotating basis. This institution, known in Chinese as *nien-pan* (年班 classified yearly rotation), was quite similar to the system in Tokugawa Japan, known as *sankin kotai*. The Manchu court divided Mongolian nobles into several groups and ordered them to proceed to the capital by rotation to attend the imperial audience at the beginning and end of each year. The frequency of their rotation was decided according to their distance from Peking. In other words, those who were located nearby had to attend more often. During their stay in Peking the emperor received them, gave them formal and semiformal banquets, and sometimes entertained them with the music of Chinese operas. Following is a condensed record of such an event that took place in the twenty-fifth and twenty-sixth year of Tao-kuang (1845–46).

On the *i-wei* day of the 12th month of the 25th year (4 January 1846), the Emperor Hsüang-tsung received a group of Mongolian princes and nobles inside the Shen-wu Gate,[4] and again on the *kuei-muo* day of the same month (13 January) he received another group outside the same gate.[5] On the *keng-hsü* day (20 January), the Emperor provided a banquet for the Mongol princes, *beile, beise*, dukes, *efus* (imperial sons-in-law), *taiji* and the Jangjiya Khutughtu at the Grand Yurt of the Fu-ch'en Palace, and bestowed gifts upon them according to their ranks.[6] On the *ping-ch'eng* day (26 January), at Pao-ho Hall, the Emperor gave a national banquet for the outside subordinates, such as: princes, *beiles*, *beises*, dukes, *efus*, *taijis*, and *tabnangs* (the sons-in-law of the Mongolian Borjigid clan) of Khorchin, Üjümüchin, Kharachin, Aukhan, Abagha, Jalaid, Ongni'ud, Khalkha, Sünid, Ba'arin, Ordos, Köke-naur, Yeke-mingghan, Chakhar,[7] Torghud, Tümed, Naiman, and the envoys of Korea and Vietnam. During the banquet the Emperor ordered the Mongol nobles of Right Flank and those of Left Flank to proceed to the front of the Throne and bestowed wine upon them.[8] On the *wu-wu* day of the first month of the 26th year of Tao-kuang (28 January 1846), the Emperor gave a banquet for some Mongolian nobles and the envoys of the foreign subordinates and bestowed gifts upon them according to their ranks.[9] On the *i-hai* day of the same month (14 February 1846), the Emperor provided food for the Mongolian nobles and the foreign envoys at *Shan-kao shui-ch'ang*.[10]

Evidently, these events were designated to show the Mongols the imperial goodwill. Besides these activities during their stay in the capital, the Mongol nobles and their followers naturally had close contact with Manchu nobles, Manchu-Chinese officials, and Chinese merchants who were active in Mongolia. At the same time, besides the regular rotation of annual imperial audiences, the Mongolian ruling class also had to proceed to the capital to attend various important ceremonies of the imperial household, such as enthronements, marriages, birthday celebrations, and funerals. All these occasions gave them an acquaintance with life in Peking, a culture which they desired to bring back to their homeland. When their wives were the daughters of the already Sinicized Manchu nobility, then the acceleration of the Sinicization process was much faster.

Mongolian service in the capital

In the early Ch'ing period, except for the Mongolian Eighter Banners stationed in the capital and organized into the Manchu political system, all Mongol nobles, after finishing their business in Peking, had to return to their own grazing lands, even though they were given residences in Peking. Later, because more complex relations developed between the Mongolian ruling class and the court, more Mongol nobles were assigned to official services in the capital and allowed to stay there longer.

Since they joined the officialdom or the state bureaucracy of the Ch'ing nation, they had to adapt to the customs of their Manchu and Chinese associates. Because these customs and cultural ways were regarded as having status and honor, they were admired by other Mongol nobles. In fact, those who were assigned to live and serve in the capital had to become quite Manchu-like (which meant Sinicized), otherwise it would have been impossible for them to accomplish their assigned tasks. For instance, Tsereng, a Prince of Khalkh who assisted the Manchus to fight the Jeünghar (Dzungar) Mongols, was given an imperial princess in marriage and also a residence in the capital. His descendants were continually assigned to services in the court. In the late Ch'ing period, Nayantu, who succeeded to the rank and position of the family, was continuously assigned different positions in the court. In 1896, he was made the *Ch'ung-wen-men cheng chien-t'u*, the Superintendent of the Customs Bureau at Ch'ung-wen Gate, which was one of the richest positions in the Ch'ing Empire. In 1901, when the Empress Dowager Tz'u-hsi and Emperor Kuang-hsu were returning to Peking from Sian through Honan Province after the Boxer Rebellion (1900), Nayantu was assigned to offer sacrifices at the Shrine of Chu

These events suggest that Prince Nayantu had to be fully Sinicized, otherwise there would have been no possibility of coping with the involvements and problems related to this high national position or of being qualified as an imperial envoy to offer complex sacrifices to Chinese historical figures.

The descendants of Senggerinchin, Prince of Khorchin, who led Mongolian "volunteers" to fight against the T'ai-ping, Nien rebels, and the invading Anglo-French forces in the middle of 1880s, also held positions similar to that of Tsereng. Besides these special cases, the Ch'ing court usually appointed some Mongol nobles to serve at court with the titles Ch'ien-ch'ing meng hsing-tsuo (乾清門行走) and yü-ch'ien hsing-tsuo (御前行走), which mean, "Minister to Serve at the Chien-ch'ing gate" and "Minister to Serve Before His Majesty." Although these officials had no real power they were positions of imperial favor. Occasionally, the Emperor summoned some capable Mongol nobles to the capital and assigned them positions of real service. Under these conditions, those assigned were inevitably Sinicized sooner or later.

Administrative necessity as a factor in assimilation

By the late Ch'ing Dynasty, not only the Manchu ruling class, but also most so-called Manchu Bannermen were thoroughly Sinicized. The use of the Manchu language was used in official functions and the demand for officials who knew Mongolian diminished. The Mongol officials who had learned Manchu found it impossible to carry out real administrative contacts with Sinicized Manchu bureaucrats who were not able to read and speak Manchu or Mongolian. After the Ch'ing court revised its policy and allowed more Chinese to settle in Mongolia, this situation became more serious than ever.

In 1828 (eighth year of Tao-kuang) the office of the Military Governor of Jehol faced the problem that no one could translate Mongolian documents into good Manchu.[12] Later in the same year, the Military Governor of Jehol reported to the Emperor that the Chinese magistrates under his jurisdiction usually took the side of Chinese settlers in disputes and were often not favorable to Mongols.[13] Eight years later (1836), a man by the name of Mujinggha (probably a Manchu) was assigned as an *amban* of Chakhar, but could not understand Mongolian, and consequently his appointment was turned down by the Emperor.[14] Facing difficulties in their official contacts, the Mongols had to learn Chinese in order to deal with their Chinese or Manchu counterparts.

The influence of book translations

Originally Manchu policy prohibited Mongols from learning Chinese, and conversely the Mongols had no desire to study the language. However, later the entire situation changed and circumstances encouraged the Mongols to transgress the Manchu prohibitions.

After the Mongolian conversion to Tibetan Buddhism and the translation of Buddhist scriptures, more Mongols learned to read. Manchu rulers, in order to "brain wash" the Mongols, and strengthen their loyalty and obedience to the imperial court, distributed the Confucian classics translated into Mongolian from Manchu editions. Early in the Yüan Dynasty, these classics were translated by the Mongol court, but after the downfall of the dynasty, all translations disappeared except for the Book of Filial-Piety *(Hsiao-ching 孝經)*. The reappearance of these Confucian books in Mongolian during the Manchu period provided the Mongols some philosophic teachings in addition to their own Buddhist traditions. This opened the eyes of some with scholarly inclinations to a whole new field of knowledge and helped change the original negative Mongolian attitudes toward Chinese culture. This was also the reason some Mongol nobles invited Chinese teachers to tutor their younger generations.

Earlier, before their Sinicization, the Manchus had translated for their enjoyment many Chinese novels, such as the *San-kuo yen-i* (三國演義 Romance of the Three Kingdoms), *Chin-ku ch'i-kuan* (今古奇觀 Grotesque Tales Past and Present), *Liao-chai chih-i* (聊齋誌異 Records for Mysterious Tales), and *Hung-lo meng* (紅樓夢 Dream of the Red Chamber). Later, Mongol intellectuals with good Manchu and Chinese language backgrounds put these literary works into Mongolian. The influences of these translated novels was no less than that of the Confucian scriptures, for they increased curiosity about Chinese culture among the literate Mongols, especially in southeastern Inner Mongolia.

In the middle of the nineteenth century, the well-known Mongolian writer, Injannashi,[15] wrote a historical novel, *Köke sudar*, in the style of *San-kuo yen-i*, and a romantic novel, *Nigen dabkhur asar*, following the pattern of the *Hung-lo meng*. These works again reflect the author's Sinicized feelings and his high esteem for Chinese culture.

Analyzing the above mentioned influences leading to the Sinicization of the Mongolian ruling class, one may conclude that while it was not the purpose of the Manchu court, nevertheless, the gradual Sinicization of the Mongolian nobility was undoubtedly a by-product of their own policy.

The Process of Sinicization

The Sinicization process of the Mongolian upper class is also clearly reflected in edicts of the Ch'ing court. It must be kept in mind that gradual Sinicization of the Mongols could damage their relationship with the Manchus and cause the Mongols to be drawn to the Chinese side. Also, Sinicization would definitely damage those Mongolian military characteristics which had sustained the Manchus in their conquest of China. Therefore, the Manchu court issued again and again edicts warning the Mongols against contamination by "bad Chinese customs." However, these efforts were never effective and failed to insulate the Mongols from the Chinese and the rest of the world.

Early in 1815 (twentieth year of Chia-ch'ing), the Emperor Jen-tsung issued a decree warning Mongols not to give up their old traditions or learn "bad" Chinese customs, such as building houses and watching dramas and plays.[16] In 1818 the Emperor again issued a decree prohibiting Mongol nobles from gathering young people and training them to perform operas.[17]

In the eighth year of Tao-kuang, Emperor Hsüan-tsung punished Keshingge, the *jasagh* of Kharachin (probably the Karachin Central Banner) for secretly performing Chinese operas at his residence. In an edict the Emperor emphasized that the Mongol tradition was to practice archery and horsemanship and to follow a simple way of life without luxuries. He noted that Chinese customs were wasteful nonsense. He advised the Mongols to keep their good traditions and refine their techniques in archery and horsemanship.[18]

In 1836 (the sixteenth year), the Emperor decreed that the Mongols should use only Manchu or Mongolian names, not Chinese.[19] In 1839 (the nineteenth year) the court prohibited Mongols from hiring Chinese scribes as clerks and tutors.[20] In 1853 (the third year of Hsien-feng), Emperor Wen-tsung decreed that the imperial council should stop the Mongols from using Chinese names, learning Chinese language and literature, and preparing documents in Chinese.[21] In 1876 (the second year of Kuang-hsü), a court edict forbade the Mongols to use Chinese language in documents and declared that Chinese who served in Mongolia as scribes should be arrested and extradited to their home towns as punishment.[22]

These various court ordinances show the Manchus' ostensible eagerness to exhort the Mongols to keep their good "old traditions" and not to adopt "bad Chinese customs." The real purpose was to force the Mongols to maintain their nomadic, martial traditions, to live in yurts, to maintain their archery and horsemanship, and to be militarily prepared when a military reserve was needed. Simply speaking, the Manchu design was to keep the Mongols loyal and unsophisticated. Thus, the Manchus felt it was important to keep the Mongols from any contact with things Chinese. None of these decrees were effective.

The very things the court wanted to stop, i.e., dwelling in houses, watching Chinese operas, enjoying the Peking life-style, were all the things that the Mongol nobles learned to appreciate from their Manchu wives and from their required stay in the capital during their yearly court audiences. Later in the mid-nineteenth century, when the Ch'ing Empire began to suffer foreign invasions and internal rebellions, one result was a great Chinese immigration into southern Mongolia. These new developments forced the Mongol leaders to attend to other matters. The reason the Mongols began to learn Chinese was mentioned earlier and need not be discussed again. Since the Manchus, including the Emperor, had used Chinese or semi-Chinese names for years, it was impossible totally to prohibit the Mongols from adopting them. On the other hand, the Mongolian nobles and officials who had to deal with the Manchu nobles and high official needed the honorary name, *tzu* (字), to facilitate their associations in official and social contacts.

From the middle of the Ch'ing Dynasty, the court's main solution to famine and poverty in the northern provinces was to settle the distressed Chinese in the southern territories of Inner Mongolia. With the increase of the Chinese population, both the Mongol officials and the common people had no choice but to associate with the new settlers, and they gradually learned some Chinese. When conflicts arose between the two peoples, it was more effective to prepare documents in Chinese, if possible. Otherwise, it was difficult for Manchu or Chinese officials to understand the situation and to settle the problem. This was another reason the Mongols hired Chinese scribes and tutors.

The Mongols did not petition the throne to remove the prohibitions, but neither did they obey the injunctions. Among the above mentioned trends, the matter of hiring Chinese tutors was probably the most significant development in the process of Mongolian Sinicization. The use of Chinese scribes and tutors was at first an administrative necessity, but gradually it became an important method of educating young Mongols. The existence of Chinese home tutors was not only overt, but in some areas it actually developed into sizeable schools. In 1902, Gungsangnorbu, the Prince of Kharachin,[23] started a modern school based upon the experience of home tutors in the banner, and also upon new insights that he had gained both from Peking and Japan. By this time, even the Ch'ing court had to recognize the new *status quo*. In 1906 (thirty-second year of Kuang-hsu), in the name of the Emperor, the court delivered a tablet to the school bearing the inscription *Yu-ti Meng-chiang* (牖迪蒙疆), meaning "Enlightenment for the Mongol Territory."[24] This school taught not only in Chinese, but some courses were in Mongolian and even Japanese. Consequently, besides creating a new generation of Mongolian intellectuals, this school also served to advance Sinicization.

Influences and Contributions

From the middle of the nineteenth century, there were great cultural changes in Mongolian society, especially in the southern territory of Inner Mongolia where the trend to Sinicization advanced rapidly. The "old customs" that the Manchu court desired to maintain were disappearing. In some places the Mongols were even outnumbered by Chinese settlers. In the late 1930s, it was rare to see a Tümed Mongol of the Köke-khota area under the age of fifty who could still speak fluent Mongolian. Although assimilation had occurred, it did not mean the extermination of the Mongol people. In actuality, it created militant feelings of nationalism and the desire for national survival.

As discussed earlier, the continual practice of intermarriage, yearly imperial audiences, and various official assignments influenced many southern Mongolian nobles to feel that their traditional nomadic way of life was not as magnificent or comfortable as the life they experienced in Peking. Thus, they were inclined to imitate the luxurious life of the Manchu nobles. They began to build large residences and to live according to the luxurious standards of Peking. This greatly added to the burden of the Mongol herdsmen who were obligated to support these frivolous expenditures of their overlords. As the needs of the nobles increased, they would collect more and more taxes from the people under their jurisdiction. The heavy financial burden caused the covetous princes and dukes to open grazing lands to cultivation by Chinese. They even sold the land illegally. In addition, they took out high interest loans from Chinese merchants. This further increased the peoples' burden and stirred their hatred. Consequently, in 1901, Sewangnorbusangbu, the notorious prince of Khorchin Right Flank Central Banner, was killed by his own people.[25]

Together with these events, the increase in Chinese settlers farming pastoral lands compelled a great number of Mongols to give up their traditional pastoral way of life and turn to agriculture. Those who refused to change took their cattle and retreated to lands with less water which were not good for agriculture or for animal raising. In addition, in times of conflict, the Chinese settlers were usually supported by the Chinese magistrates. Mongol officials who collaborated with the Chinese were also useless. Under these desperate circumstances, some angry herdsmen rose in armed revolt. As we have seen, this was the genesis of the so-called Mongol bandits. Judging from the history of these tragic events, all the "Mongol bandits" came from areas where their own overlords were Sinicized in the worst sense.

Nevertheless, the influences of the Sinicization on the Mongolian ruling class were not always negative. The introduction of Chinese books and literature broadened the knowledge of Mongolian literates and opened their eyes to their situation in a world context. Consequently, their desire for change was stirred. Gradually cultural and social changes shook the foundation of Mongolian feudalism.

The growing influence of Sinicization also threatened conservative and nationalistic Mongolian leaders, thereby stimulating a demand for a nationalistic movement. Finally, at the beginning of this century, these two opposite streams of ideology joined, lending strength to the struggle for national existence.

Internally, the hatred of the common people against their Sinicized ruling class became the root of anti-feudalistic movements aimed at democracy. At the same time, there appeared a spark of anti-religious activities, and this was initiated in part through the reading of Chinese books. The "Mongol bandits" also added their influence to the growing nationalistic movement.

Before the end of the Manchu rule there were a few enlightened Mongol nobles, educated in Chinese ways, who submitted demands for change to the Ch'ing court. In the thirty-fourth year of Kuang-hsü (1908), Gungsangnorbu, the Prince of Kharachin, petitioned the throne for eight items: 1) to establish banks as soon as possible; 2) to hasten the construction of railroads; 3) to develop mineral resources; 4) to develop farming, industry, and commercial enterprises; 5) to take special care of diplomatic matters; 6) to popularize and elevate education; 7) to modernize military forces; and 8) to establish a police administration.[26]

The next year Ghonchughsereng,[27] Prince of Khorchin, petitioned the court on the following items: 1) to control religion to stop superstition; 2) to develop education to increase the knowledge of the people; 3) to train Mongolian troops to fortify border defense; and 4) to select land for cultivation to protect the livelihood of the people.[28]

The Ch'ing court assigned these two petitions to appropriate officials for their discussion. However, no positive response was given. This suggests that even to the end of their rule the Manchus had no willingness to accept constructive results of Sinicization among the Mongol nobles.

Notes

1. *Ch'ing-tai pein-cheng t'ung-kao* (清代幼政通考), a reproduction of the *Li-fan yüan shih li* (理藩院事例) of the *Ta-Ch'ing hui-tien* (大清会典), printed by the Mongolian and Tibetan Commission, Taipei, 1981, 20.

2. Recorded by the author from the Kang-hsi edition *Li-fan yüan tse-li* (理藩院則例).

3. For more information on intermarriage, see Sechin Jagchid, "Mongolian-Manchu Intermarriage in the Ch'ing Period," *Zentralasiatische Studien*, Bonn: Universität Bonn, 1986, 19:68–87.

4. *Ch'ing shih-lu* (清実錄), Hsüan-tsung, vol. 424, the entry of the *i-wei* day of the twelfth month of the twenty-fifth year of Tao-kuang. The Shen-wu Gate is the north gate of the Imperial Forbidden City.

5. Ibid., the entry of *kuei-muo* day.

6. Ibid., the entry of *keng-hsu* day.

7. This was not a Chakhar noble but a Ö'elüd *güng* who was living among the Chakhars.

8. Hsüan-tsung, 424, the entry of *ping-ch'en* day.

9. Hsüan-tsung, 425, the entry of *wu-wu* day of the first month of the twenty-sixth year of Tao-kuang.

10. Ibid., the entry of *i-hai* day. *Shan-kao shui-ch'ang* (山高水長) means "lofty mountains and long rivers," and it was probably located in the imperial garden *Yüan-ming yüan* (圓明園) that was destroyed by the Anglo-French allied forces in 1860.

11. *Ch'ing shih-lu*, Te-tsung, vol. 393, the entry of *wu-wu* day of the ninth month of the twenty-seventh year of Kuang-hsü.

12. Hsüang-tsung, 141, the entry of *ping-chen* day of the eighth month of the eighth year of Tao-kuang.

13. Ibid., 145, entry of *chia-wu* day of the tenth month of the eighth year of Tao-kuang.

14. Ibid. 272, entry of the *keng-wu* day of the twelfth month of the sixteenth year of Tao-kuang.

15. For the life and works of Injannashi, see John G. Hangin, *Köke Sudar; A Study of First Mongolian Historical Novel by Injannashi*, Weisbaden, 1973. Some scholars suggest that *Hung-lo Meng* was translated directly into Mongolian from the Chinese and not from the Manchu edition.

16. *Ch'ing-tai pein-cheng t'ung-k'ao*, 303.

17. Ibid.

18. Hsüan-tsung, 143, entry of *chi-yu* day of the third month of the eighth year of Tao-kuang.

19. *Ch'ing-tai pein-cheng t'ung-k'ao*, 304. There was no mention about the Sanskrit-Tibetan names. Probably they were considered as Mongolian names.

20. Ibid.

21. *Ch'ing shih-lu*, Wen-tsung, vol. 103, entry of the *hain-muo* day of the eighth month of the third year of Hsien-feng.

22. *Ch'ing-tai pein-cheng t'ung-k'ao*, 304.

23. For Gungsangnorbu, see Jagchid, "Gungsangnorbu: Forerunner of Inner Mongolian Modernization," *Zentralasiatische Studien*, 1978, 12:147–58.

24. Te-tsung, 561, entry on the *kuei-yu* day of the sixth month of the thirty-second year of Kuang-hsü.

25. Ibid., 483, entry of *ping-tzu* day of the fifth month of the twenty-seventh year of Kuang-hsü.

26. Ibid., 586, entry of the *kuei-muo* day of the first month of the thirty-fourth year of Kuang-hsü.

27. Ghonchughsereng was the Prince of Khorchin Left Flank Front Banner. Around 1912, he went to Outer Mongolia and joined the Urga Government, but he was disappointed and returned.

28. Hsüan-t'ung, 21, entry of *keng-ying* day of the twelfth month of the first year of Hsüng-tung which is 20 January 1911.

Part IV
The Modern Period

Chapter 16

Prince Gungsangnorbu and Inner Mongolian Modernization

(Originally published in *Symposium of the History of the Republic of China*, Taipei, 23–28 August 1981, 2:466–500)

Background of Era

The beginning of the twentieth century was a critical period in Mongolian history. Confronting the people were problems of surviving under foreign aggression, of avoiding assimilation by large domineering neighbors, and of guiding their stagnant and isolated society from outmoded traditions toward modernization, self-sufficiency, and self-rule. Since that time many types of Mongolian leaders, i.e., revolutionaries, nationalists, and militant reformers, have appeared. Of them, Gungsangnorbu (1871–1931), the Prince of Kharachin,[1] was the most outstanding, for he was a proponent of Mongolian modernization. His career marked an epoch in the hardships and struggles of the Mongolian people.

From the seventeenth century, when the Mongols came under Manchu dominance, their power and morale began to decline. Through shrewd political manipulation, Manchu rulers separated the Mongols into numerous feudal-like units which over a century lapsed into tribalism and localism leaving them fragmented and weakened.

In addition, Manchu religious policy[2] turned the militant Mongols into a decadent people concerned only about the next life with little care for their daily existence. Traditional Buddhist scriptures dominated intellectual activity blocking the Mongols from the beginnings of modern knowledge and leaving them to a dismal fate.

Meanwhile, ties between feudalistic Mongolian leaders and the Manchu imperial household were being strengthened. The Manchu leaders allowed feudalistic self-rule for each administrative unit, the banner, and thus the Mongols felt they were ruled by their own lords and not by a foreign people. The Manchu rulers did not want Mongolian power weakened, for the Mongols had been their allies prior to their occupation of China. Yet, neither did they want to see the emergence of a too-powerful Mongolia. They wanted Mongolian forces available to the imperial household when needed.

Following their long rule in China, the Manchu ruling class became more and more Sinicized. Following their defeat by the Anglo-French allied forces (1856–60), and the expansion of Tsarist Russia toward the Far East, the lands of the Manchus and Mongols which originally had been the base of Manchu power, were now recognized as mere border regions. The occupied area of China had become the heartland of the Empire. Moreover, in order to address the famine in overpopulated North China and to prevent further infiltration of aggressive Russian power into the north, the Manchu-Ch'ing court sent Chinese peasants to settle in the Mongolian border lands. Consequently, previously forbidden land was opened to the Chinese. Through the support of the Manchu regime and

Chinese officials, multitudes of Chinese refugees and settlers rushed into Mongolia, and the best parts of the Mongolian grazing lands were turned into farm land. Through the collaboration of some self-seeking Mongolian nobles and the Manchu-Chinese officials, the Mongolian grazing lands were progressively occupied by the Chinese. As a result, the common Mongolian herdsmen became dissatisfied and began to hate their princes and the Manchu-Chinese officials. Thus came uprisings against the Chinese settlers and Mongolian and Manchu-Chinese officials.

Manchu-Ch'ing administrative policy and regulations gave each banner only limited power of jurisdiction over its Mongolian people, but no power over the Chinese. The growing number of Chinese settlers seriously threatened the self-rule of the Mongolian banners. The Manchu authorities established Chinese institutions such as *fu* (府), *hsien* (縣), *chou* (州), and *t'ing* (廳) as pretexts for controlling the Chinese, when actually they were penetrating and weakening the jurisdiction of Mongolian banners. Thus, two contradictory jurisdictions existed among the Mongols and Chinese.

Because their political privileges were curtailed, some enlightened Mongols began to question the goodwill of the Manchu court. As a result, the rehabilitation of Mongolian political integrity, the maintenance of their economic rights, and Mongolian survival became critical questions and necessitated new policies. In addition, Mongolia was being squeezed between China and Russia, and eastern Mongolia was greatly influenced by Japanese power. Finding solutions to these situations was a task of extreme importance for the Mongolian leaders. Until the time of Gungsangnorbu, there had been no real discussion of the problems in their entirety among the Mongols or with their counterparts, the Manchu-Chinese officials.

After the Opium War (1840–42), the Anglo-French campaign (1856–60), and the Russian intervention, the power of the Manchu-Ch'ing Empire declined greatly. After the Sino-Japanese War (1894–95), Japan began to compete with Russian influence in Korea, Manchuria, and eastern Inner Mongolia, creating a confrontation which eventually turned into the Russo-Japanese War (1904–5). Following the victory over Russia, Japan established its influence in East Asia and was even able to challenge Western powers.

With all these changes and under the slogan of "using barbarians against barbarians," a group of Chinese elite reluctantly decided to accept modern civilization to preserve the dynasty. This modernization movement eventually became one of the main factors that led to the Chinese revolution and to Mongolian social change.

The conflict between Britain and Tsarist Russia in Tibet and the expansion of Russia's influence in Mongolia, prompted many Mongolian and Tibetan leaders who were already dissatisfied with Manchu rule to work for new outlets for their people. The power struggle between Japan and Russia in Mongolia did not cease at the end of the Russo-Japanese war. Concurrently, the changing situation of China caused more Chinese settlers to rush into Inner Mongolia, bringing Mongols in this area under the threat of assimilation.

The above circumstances constitute the background of Gungsangnorbu's era. Kharachin, Gungsangnorbu's native domain, is located in the southernmost part of Inner Mongolia near the Great Wall. The distance from his residence to Peking was only about 250 miles. Consequently, Kharachin was on the forefront of Mongolian contact with Chinese culture and civilization. The leaders of Kharachin maintained special contact with Peking.

His Early Life

On 26 June 1871, Gungsangnorbu was born at the princely residence, Wanginkhoroon,[3] of the Kharachin Right Flank Banner, Josotu League. He was the eldest son of Prince Wangdudnamjil. A younger sister of Shih-to, Prince Li[4] of the Manchu imperial house, is generally recognized as Gungsangnorbu's "official" mother. She was known as a wise and gracious lady who had an especially strong influence on Prince Gung.[5] However, his natural mother, whose name is unknown, was actually a Mongolian wife of Prince Wangdudmanjil.

As a youth, Gungsangnorbu demonstrated considerable intelligence and studied diligently. His father invited scholars of the Banner to teach him Mongolian and Manchu history and literature. He also became conversant with traditional Mongolian Buddhist philosophy, which included the study of Tibetan and Sanskrit texts with their esoteric terminology. Prince Wangdudmanjil requested Ting Chin-t'ang (丁錦堂), a famous scholar of Shantung Province, to tutor his son (then in his early teens) providing a classical Chinese education. As a result, Gungsangnorbu became a respectable scholar in the classical Chinese model. In addition, he enjoyed writing Chinese calligraphy, composing poetry, and painting. Fearing that his son might become a weak, cultured literati, Prince Wangdudnamjil insisted that Gungsangnorbu also learn the Mongolian military arts, including horsemanship and archery, together with Chinese *kung-fu*. By the time he was twenty years of age, Gungsangnorbu was accomplished in both the literary and military arts.

Prince Wangdudnamjil in his later years was chronically ill and consequently Gungsangnorbu, as his father's official representative, had to deal with many political affairs of the Banner at an early age.[6] When he was only twenty-one, a bloody incident, known as the Chin-tan-tao (金丹道) Rebellion,[7] broke out in the neighboring Aukhan Banner of Juu-uda League and spilled over into Kharachin.

During the middle 1700s, the number of Chinese settlers in Inner Mongolia began to increase, especially in the banners of the Josotu, Juu-uda, and Jerim Leagues. For centuries uncultivated land had been plentiful and the Mongols were entirely unconcerned about the Chinese settlers. Moreover, because of the Chinese agriculture, the income of the Mongol banners and the people increased significantly. But, in later decades, the Chinese took the best pasture and farming land for cultivation while the price of various manufactured goods purchased by the Mongols increased limitlessly. As their standard of living fell, the Mongols of Gungsangnorbu's generation began to worry about their economic situation, and thus took measures to limit the increasing migration of Chinese settlers and to increase the rent on their lands worked by the Chinese.

As the population of Chinese settlers steadily increased, both Manchu and Chinese local officials became more sympathetic to them. As a result, the frequency and seriousness of land problems between the Mongols and the Chinese increased. Ambitious Chinese settlers went so far as to takeover completely Mongol lands.

With the accumulation of problems, the situation in Aukhan Banner, Juu-uda League, in 1891 was extremely critical following the suppression of the White Lotus Sect *(pai-lien chiao)* to the south and inside the Great Wall. The Chinese who had migrated into the Aukhan Banner organized the so-called Chin-tan-tao movement under the slogan *"Sao-pei mieh-hu (掃北滅胡),"* "Sweep clean the northern territory and exterminate the Mongols." This sect encouraged Chinese settlers to kill every Mongol they met. Having adopted red turbans as part of their dress or identification, these Chinese rebels became known as "Red Caps" ("Ulan Malghait" in Mongolian and "Hung-mao-tzu" (紅帽子) in Chinese).

Violent rebellion soon spread into the four southern banners of Juu-uda League, thus threatening the banners of the Josotu League, including that of Gungsangnorbu. The Mongols were inadequately prepared and consequently suffered defeat. The Manchu court dispatched troops to pacify the rebellion, but they did not arrive in time. Many Mongols, including women and children, were killed. Fortunately the Kharachin Right Flank Banner Mongols were able to organize militia forces and to prevent the rebels from penetrating deep into their territory. Even though the rebellion was put down by the end of January 1891, animosities between the Mongols and the Chinese were deepened.

Another event which strongly influenced Gungsangnorbu's views at least as much as the Chin-tan-tao rebellion was the First Sino-Japanese war (1894–95) which changed the balance of power in East Asia. After defeating China, Japan emerged as a new Asian power because of her reforms carried out during the Meiji Restoration. As a result of the war and the Sino-Japanese treaty signed at Shimonoseki, Japan obtained special privileges in Southern Manchuria. This gave Japan direct interest in Mongolian affairs. While the Manchurian fruits were robbed from Japan by the Triple Intervention of Russia, Germany, and France, her *"Man-Mo"* (Manchuria-Mongolia) policy was continued and strengthened.

A third event which further heightened Gungsangnorbu's apprehension was a growing movement to promote Chinese colonization of virgin Mongolian lands. Among the proposals, the petition of Hu P'in-chih,[8] the Governor of Shansi Province, to the court is the best-known. This petition soon led to the framing of a new policy toward Mongolia by the Ch'ing court.[9]

Assumption of Rule and Relations with the Manchu

When Prince Wangdudnamjil died in 1898, Gungsangnorbu succeeded him. His succession coincided with one of the most historically significant events of modern Chinese history, the Hundred Days Reform *(Wu-hsü cheng-pien* 戊戌政變*)*. Not far removed from the scene of this significant incident, Prince Gung was motivated to study the issues and the underlying differences between the policy of the reform faction and the wishes of conservatives.

As a new ruling *jasagh* of Kharachin, Prince Gung was required by tradition to go to Peking to present himself at court as a Mongol vassal and to be confirmed in his new position. He was honorably received by the Empress Dowager Tz'u-hsi and granted the special honor of riding a horse through the gate of the imperial palace — the Forbidden City.[10] This first contact with the court came just a few months after the suppression of the Hundred Days Reform.

Another contact came in January 1900 just as a new crisis was approaching. The Boxers *(I-ho-t'uan* 義和團 *)* were already active in Shan-tung and their threat appeared to be spreading toward Peking. In a meeting, the Empress Dowager proposed that Prince Gung raise Mongol troops to fight for the Manchus, but this never occurred due to changes in the situation. It is significant that the troubled court called on a

Mongolian leader. The tensions in Peking created by zealous reformers on the one hand and reactionary Boxers on the other undoubtedly posed problems for Gungsangnorbu as he became involved in the world of Chinese power politics. These problems rose in part because of resistance to progressive reform measures and the age-old policy against change in Mongolia.

The Boxer Rebellion in North China eventually brought the invasion of the allied forces including Britain, the United States, Germany, France, Austria, Italy, Russia, and Japan. Peking was occupied, forcing the Empress Dowager and the court to escape to Sian. During this crisis, governors in Southern China, including Chang Chih-tung[11] and Li Hung-chang,[12] ignored the Empress' order to attack the foreign powers. Instead they sought an end to hostilities. Meanwhile some of the leaders of the Mongolian Banners, such as the Alashan and Dalad Banners of the Yeke-juu League and Dörben-ke'üd Banner of Ulanchab League, seeing the anti-foreign movement, encouraged their people to attack foreign mission centers.[13]

The Kharachin Mongols under the leadership of Gungsangnorbu adopted a policy similar to that of Chang Chih-tung and Li Hung-chang and remained uninvolved in this ill-advised movement. Despite this, some Boxers moved north of the Great Wall and approached Kharachin. To deal with this new threat, Gungsangnorbu dispatched banner troops to block them, a move which saved Kharachin and neighboring regions from invasion. Several missionary stations were also saved from attack and the lives of Western missionaries spared.[14] Such important steps, taken early in the career of Prince Gung, demonstrated his potential for decisive leadership. There is no evidence of any direct contact between him and the reform faction. However, it is obvious that his enlightened views were inclined toward those of the progressive reformers. This is clear from his own proposals for change.

After succeeding his father, Gungsangnorbu undertook reform measures within his domain. He abolished certain notorious "feudalistic" practices, a type of progressive action that became typical of his reign. During the Ch'ing dynasty, Mongol princes enjoyed many privileges of nobility much like those of a feudal lord. They worried little about the livelihood of their people at whose expense they led a comparatively luxurious life. They spent great sums of money during their visits to the capital to attend court and pay tribute. One reform of Prince Gung was to regularize the finances of his banner. Recognizing the problems and disadvantages of certain traditional practices, Gungsangnorbu established a Bureau of Income and Expenditure. His objective was to support the administrative expenditures with money earned from the agricultural and forest properties of the Banner and to tax the people only if this was not sufficient. In addition, no extraordinary tax was to be levied on the people. This fiscal policy lightened significantly the burden of the common people.

In the summer of 1900, in connection with his development plans, Prince Gung petitioned the court for permission to develop a gold mine in his banner and to use the income to train the new army earlier proposed. The Empress Dowager authorized the petition and then referred it to court ministers for consultation.[15] It was vetoed by conservative advisors at court.

In order to plan for the future of Mongolia and to develop his banner's power, Gungsangnorbu realized he must strengthen Mongolian military capabilities and the Mongolian economy. Thus, seizing the propitious time of the foreign occupation of

Peking, he presented a plan to the court for training more troops. However, the Empress Dowager herself strongly opposed Prince Gung's request, no doubt out of concern for the implications of military power in the hands of a non-Manchu people on the border.

Thus, the Manchu rulers revealed their hostility toward any modernization in the wake of their defeat by the foreign powers. Their attitude also changed toward Gungsangnorbu, for they became extremely suspicious of the young, ambitious Mongol leader. Their role for him was that of an ideal court puppet, uninvolved in state affairs.

The attitudes expressed by the Empress Dowager did not mean, however, that the Manchu rulers placed no importance on Mongolian military support. Soon after their chastisement of Prince Gung, the court, in a decree to Prince Serengnamjilwangbo, Chief of Josotu League, again encouraged the Mongolian banners to strengthen their military power to protect the borderlands against the enemy.[16] It is evident, however, that the Manchus did not want an ambitious Mongolian leader such as Gungsangnorbu to emerge after the Boxer Rebellion.

The years following the Boxer Rebellion were even more critical to modern Inner Mongolian history. Every Mongolian banner was required to make contributions so the court could pay the Boxer indemnities required by the Allied powers. The Alashan Banner and those of the Ulanchab and Yeke-juu Leagues, which were involved in anti-Christian movements, were severely punished by the court and forced to hand over fertile tracts of land to foreign missions. These lands eventually became centers for Chinese settlements and for cultivation of Mongolian soil.

Because of the Boxer Rebellion, Russian forces occupied Manchuria and a part of eastern Inner Mongolia for two years (1900–1902). Later, in 1903, the Russians completed the Eastern China Railroad in Manchuria and enlarged the railroad's influence in eastern Inner Mongolia. This caused more problems for the Mongols. Prince Utai[17] of the Khorchin Right Flank Front Banner of Jerim League became one of the leading pro-Russian leaders in Inner Mongolia. Meanwhile, the Japanese stepped up their activities against Russia in the same area.

Near the end of 1901, after more than a year of exile, the Empress Dowager and Emperor Kuang-hsü returned to Peking. The court undertook certain reform measures forced upon it by the Chinese situation and world conditions. The court issued imperial decrees to implement the reforms. With the reforms in the capital, Gungsangnorbu, with his own reforms in mind, obtained an audience with Emperor Kuang-hsü in early 1902. The details and results of these discussions are not known.[18] However, encouraged by the changed attitude of the court, Prince Gung once again presented a petition in the spring of 1903 concerning a new military training plan. This time the court not only accepted the plan but encouraged Prince Gung to carry it out in earnest.[19] Thus, the general outlines of Gungsangnorbu's plan for reform and development within his own banner, previously blocked by the negative attitude of the Empress Dowager and her court, was fortuitously encouraged by developments in the aftermath of the Boxer Rebellion.

Especially important was the establishment in 1902 of the first modern school in Mongolia, the *Töb-ig erkilegchi surghaghuli*, known in Chinese as the *Ch'ung-cheng hsüeh-t'ang* (崇正學堂).[20] Before 1902, public education was nonexistent in Mongolia. What little education was carried out, apart from the informal transfer of information, was by private tutoring. This was along traditional Chinese lines among the elite or in Buddhist monasteries where many people sent their sons to become lamas.

Because of the general illiteracy among the common people, it was virtually impossible to involve them in public works and other projects which Prince Gung was planning. His educational reform was opposed by some conservative banner nobility who did not want the common people involved in banner politics. There was also opposition from the common people themselves who, because of their long tradition of illiteracy, felt it troublesome for their children to be taken from them and put in schools. Gungsangnorbu was prepared to meet these challenges, however. He established his new school on a system of free education and avoided increasing the people's taxes by setting aside a large tract of public land, as well as some of his own private property, to support the school. The school was launched with a Mongolian and Chinese faculty.

The school's curriculum was a mixture of traditional and modern subjects. Mongolian and Chinese were used as languages of instruction. The main subjects taught were mathematics, geography, and history, along with the traditional calligraphy, gymnastics, and music. The school would seem very small and primitive today, but it was the first modern school in all of Mongolia with the possible exception of the Buriyad area. What is more remarkable, it challenged the conservatives in Mongolian society who were dominant. Further, it ran counter to the basic interests of the Empress Dowager T'zu-hsi and powerful reactionaries at court who had been implacably opposed to such modernizing movements.

Visit to Japan — A Turning Point

For several years, Gungsangnorbu had desired to visit the United States to gain ideas useful to his modernization policies. He was particularly eager to attend the famous 1902 St. Louis Exposition, but the Manchu court objected. This, however, did not dampen his zeal to learn about the United States.[21]

A turning point in Gungsangnorbu's life occurred during a visit to Peking when he became acquainted with Japanese diplomats. It seems they encouraged Gungsangnorbu to visit Japan. The trip was another remarkable first for the Prince, especially since it was not easy for a Mongol prince to gain permission to travel abroad. Unfortunately, a detailed record of his visit to Japan with his objectives and actual itinerary, activities, contacts, and negotiations are not available. It is known, however, that he visited such cities as Osaka, Kyoto, and Tokyo, and that he attended an exposition in Osaka which gave him an opportunity to see new industrial developments. His visit came a quarter of a century after Japan's momentous Meiji Restoration in 1867. Hence, Japan's modernization was considerably advanced and demonstrated graphically what could be done in nation-building with a deliberate policy of modernization.

Gungsangnorbu was warmly welcomed by many leaders of Japan's commercial and industrial cities, and he met such important political figures as Okuma Shigenobu who discussed with him the situation in Mongolia, China, and the world. From such men, Prince Gung gained encouragement in his plans for the modernization of Mongolia.[22] Having already developed a deep interest in education, Prince Gung was especially impressed with coeducation in Japan and the positive influences of education on girls. At the same time, he was also impressed with Japan's military schools.[23]

Exactly how and why Gungsangnorbu decided to visit Japan is not clear. According to one Kharachin elder, it was related to an incident during the foreign occupation of

Peking at the time of the Boxer Rebellion. The Russians occupied Yung-ho-kung, the imperial Lamaist temple near the Russian Orthodox chapel, and severely abused the lamas. Later, the temple was put under jurisdiction of a Japanese force, which brought full protection to the lamas and their temple.[24] Because of this incident many Mongols in Peking came to admire Japan, and this made it easy for the Japanese to contact the Prince.

Banner Reforms and Educational Development

After returning to Mongolia, Prince Gung established two new schools in Kharachin in addition to the one already mentioned. The first was a military school named *Töb-ig sakigchi cherig-ün surghaguli (Shou-ch'eng wu-pei hsüeh-t'ang,* 宗正武備学堂). In this undertaking he was assisted by two Japanese officers, Captain Ryutaro Ito and Lieutenant Shiro Yoshiwara whom he invited to serve as teachers in the school. This new educational institution proved to be a heavy financial burden, and, because it was impossible to increase the tax burden on the people, Gungsangnorbu had to find new revenue sources. He finally leased a section of land to the Chinese for agricultural development to support the military school.

The second of Gungsangnorbu's educational establishments was a school for young women. Again he obtained the assistance of a Japanese educator, Miss Misako Kawahara.[25] This school, named *Yü-chen niu-tzu hsüeh-t'ang* (豫正女子学堂 Girls' School for the Development of Integrity), opened officially in November with an enrollment of thirty to forty students. The purpose of the institution was to prepare young women to be mothers of future Mongolian leaders. Thus, attention was given especially to subjects dealing with the development of healthy bodies, keen intellect, and pleasant personalities. Included in the curriculum were the Mongolian, Japanese, and Chinese languages, history, geography, mathematics, home economics, science, painting, sewing, and music. Instead of charging the students' parents for educational expenses, wealthy people of the banner were encouraged to support the school with donations. The Prince's younger sister was enrolled in the school,[26] and it is readily apparent that he believed that the education of both men and women was extremely important to Mongolia's future.

Another undertaking of major importance was Gungsangnorbu's action which countered the feudal class consciousness of his people. As he listened to explanations and observed for himself what had happened in Japan following the abolishment of feudalism during the Meiji restoration, he became conscious of how Mongolia's traditional class system was preventing unity among the people. Such disunity hindered preparation for future national unity and modernization. Upon his return from Japan, Gungsangnorbu exhibited a marked change in his views toward the traditional class system. The Prince undertook to abolish class customs, claiming that all people in Kharachin were of the same origin. Furthermore, he made it known that henceforth personal qualifications and competence would be considered in recruiting people for various banner offices. Class distinctions would no longer be the main consideration. Gungsangnorbu's reforms are undoubtedly an important reason why so many more modern Mongolian leaders came from Kharachin rather than from other banners. Apparently Gungsangnorbu's changes were a bit too progressive for the traditional Ch'ing court and generated serious concern among many Manchu and Chinese officials.

As noted earlier, the political situation in northeast Asia was complicated after the turn of the century by the intense competition between Japan and Russia. In Inner Mongolia, Gungsangnorbu tended to adopt a pro-Japanese stance. His reasons for this are not entirely clear since basic information is lacking. It is possible, however, that a Russian occupation of Manchuria might have been viewed as a threat by many Mongolian leaders, especially since it would bring Russian merchants into eastern Inner Mongolia.[27] Because of these trends, Gungsangnorbu was apprehensive about Russia. When the Russo-Japanese War broke out, Prince Gung served as an indirect supporter of the Japanese.

Misako Kawahara, who had become a teacher at Gungangnorbu's girls' school, returned to Japan during the Russo-Japanese War, and Ryuzo Torii and his wife Kimiko[28] assumed her duties. Torii later became a famous archaeologist while his wife was a specialist in folklore. During the war, Japanese officers teaching at Gungsangnorbu's military school also had to leave and the school was closed several years later. These difficulties did not reduce Prince Gung's interest in education, however. He selected seven young students to be educated in Japan, the first Inner Mongolian group to be sent abroad to study. Included in this group were four boys and three girls. It is true that prior to this, a group of Buriyad Mongol students living in the vicinity of Lake Baikal had been sent to Russia to study at the University of Kazan. However, the Kharachin Mongol group was the first to be sent to Japan. Although this educational venture did not fully accomplish Gungsangnorbu's purpose, the young Mongols were exposed to Western political thought and to modern ideologies. They became a progressive element, known as "radicals" by some, working to abolish "feudalistic traditional institutions." They, of course, influenced other Mongolian students in their struggles for democracy or socialism.

Proposal for Greater Reformation

Constrained to make reforms to maintain the influence of the Ch'ing court, the Empress Dowager dispatched to Europe, in connection with a plan to draw up a constitution, six ministers to gain insight into problems involved in modernization. This encouraged Gungsangnorbu to petition the court to authorize important reforms in economic, political, military, and educational fields in the four eastern leagues of Inner Mongolia.

Unfortunately Gungsangnorbu's plan is not among the Ch'ing documents thus far made available, possibly because it was considered a secret matter and buried. It is known, however, that his petition was carefully studied by the Manchu court and by the Army Training Bureau.[29] A point-by-point report by Yao Hsi-kuang,[30] an official of this bureau, provides some of the details. The most important points of Prince Gung's proposal may be summarized as follows.

1. Mongolian troops should be recruited and trained along modern military lines.

2. A comprehensive and uniform land tax should be adopted in Mongol territories cultivated by Chinese settlers.

3. The opium tax, presently being collected by the military-governor of Jehol, should be increased to 10 percent and be transferred to Mongolian banner offices to be used in developing education.

4. A unified tax should be established in Mongolian salt deposits, and this revenue should be divided between the central government and the Mongolian banners.

5. An official bank for eastern Inner Mongolia should be established to accelerate commercial and economic development.

6. Banner ownership of Mongolian lands should be recognized, and the revenue therefrom should be divided between the Mongolian Banners and the Chinese districts *(hsien)*.

7. A standard tax should be established on livestock exports from the Mongolian banners, and the revenue should be used by the banners for education and military training.[31]

Yao Hsi-kuang, who made a detailed study of the plan, was not favorably impressed. He believed that:

1. The training of Mongolian troops, along with other reforms in the banners, should be controlled by the court, not by the banners.

2. The land tax revenue should go to the central government, not to development of the Mongolian areas.

3. The 10 percent increase in the opium tax would be too great a burden for the farmers. Moreover, any such revenue should go to the Peking Military Training Bureau.

4. Mongolian salt revenue should go to the court, not to Mongolian banners. It could, however, be used to establish a national bank in Mongolia.

5. A Mongolian bank should be established as soon as possible to forestall Russian and Japanese influence.

6. The salt revenue could be utilized in part for the development of the Mongolian economy, but revenue from land development should not be used for this.

7. Further cultivation of Mongol land should be opened, without controls, to free and fair competition between the Mongols and Chinese.[32]

Yao Hsi-kuang, alarmed at Gungsangnorbu's initiative and long-range protection of Mongolian rights, submitted another report to the Military Training Bureau, and proposed three types of expansion into Mongolia: population migration, land development, and the expansion of administrative institutions.[33]

Yao Hsi-kuang's report was clearly a reaction to Gungsangnorbu's plans. Provoking a good deal of thought among high Manchu and Chinese officials at court, Prince Gung's proposal was viewed with great suspicion. From this time forth, Mongolian loyalty to the Manchu-Ch'ing court was questioned. In a related development, Manchu Prince Su, also known as Shan-ch'i,[34] was appointed in the winter of 1905 as head of the Ministry of Dependencies *(Li-fan yüan)* and subsequently sent on an official, high level inspection tour of the Mongolian banners.[35] This development was no doubt a response to the ambitious activities and proposals of Gungsangnorbu. Fortunately for Prince Gung the new head of the Ministry of Dependencies was his brother-in-law, a personal friend, and therefore, inclined to support rather than to oppose him.

On his tour of inspection, beginning in late spring of 1906, Prince Su was instructed to accomplish five major objectives: 1) to establish intimate relations with the Mongols and to persuade them to support the imperial court; 2) to encourage Mongol leaders to train troops; 3) to encourage the Mongols to establish schools; 4) to investigate the potential for mineral development in Mongolia; and 5) to properly survey and map Mongolian territory. These imperial instructions seem to be a compromise between Gungsangnorbu's original proposal which favored the Mongols and the plan suggested by Yao Hsi-kuang which favored the court.

Arriving in Kharachin in early May 1906, Prince Su was warmly welcomed by Gungsangnorbu and his wife, Shan-kun,[36] Prince Su's sister. During his stay in Kharachin, Prince Su visited the new schools where he gave a speech emphasizing that the development of Karachin would benefit all of Mongolia and also the Ch'ing Empire, because Kharachin was a valuable Mongolian center and an integral part of the empire. He stressed that the Mongols and the Manchus were one great family. Around the middle of May, Prince Su and his group, accompanied by Gungsangnorbu, proceeded on a five month circuit through Inner Mongolia, visiting most of the banners of the four eastern leagues, which in this case included Josotu, Juu-uda, Jerim, and Shilin-ghol.[37] According to Mongolian leaders the tour of inspection seemed to confirm, to the satisfaction of those concerned, that a threat of rebellion against the Manchu court did not exist.[38] Nevertheless, both the proposals of Gungsangnorbu and Shan-ch'i were finally refused by the court, and none of them materialized before the death of Tzu-hsi in 1908 and the end of the Manchu dynasty in 1911.

This failure did not stop Gungsangnorbu's efforts for reform in Mongolia, however. In the early spring of 1908, he presented another petition to the court. The purpose was twofold: to confirm Mongolian rights and to protect Inner Mongolia from incursions by Russia and Japan. The main points were: 1) to establish banks as soon as possible; 2) to hasten construction of railroads; 3) to develop mineral resources; 4) to develop farming, industrial, and commercial enterprises; 5) to give special attention to diplomatic matters; 6) to popularize and elevate education; 7) to modernize military forces; and 8) to establish a police administration.[39] In addition to these eight points, the Prince selected Ujümüchin as the best district for the future development of animal husbandry. He recommended that the court select capable young Mongols to study the modern care of livestock and to establish a large company to manage animal products.

Also in his petition the Prince pointed out that two thirds of the Mongolian land in Josotu, Juu-uda, and Jerim leagues were already under cultivation and that cultivation of land in Yeke-juu and Ulanchab leagues was beginning. He drew attention to the fact that following this cultivation, Chinese settlers rushed in and that Chinese administrative units were then established in the Mongolian banners of these two leagues. There was no separation in the political functions of the Mongolian *banner* and the Chinese *hsien*, and consequently conflict between the two sets of institutions was inevitable. Gungsangnorbu stressed to Peking that a separation of jurisdictions according to the nature of the problem was needed to avoid further conflicts.

The above cases reaffirm that Gungsangnorbu's knowledge of world affairs, as well as of domestic problems, was both broad and deep. Moreover, his proposals foreshadowed the later Mongol struggle for autonomy and independence caused by conflicts between the *banners* and the *hsien* districts and the problem of Chinese cultivation of Mongolian lands. Prince Gung's petition was accepted by the court and assigned for careful study to various ministries concerned. This proposal, however, like those preceding it, died in the hands of Manchu ministers and Chinese advisors.

Gungsangnorbu's two schools, during all of these changes, continued to be a personal financial burden. Eventually he sold many antiques and other valuable possessions to obtain needed funds. He petitioned the Emperor to advance him the equivalent of five year's salary as a loan for the support of the schools, and this request was authorized by the court.[40] As a result of Prince Gung's promotion of Mongolian education at great personal sacrifice, the neighboring Kharachin Left Banner began to establish schools, as did Prince Ghonchoghsurung's[41] Khorchin Left Flank Front Banner of the Jerim League.

In order to finance his work, Gungsangnorbu had to seek resources that would not only maintain themselves but would also provide revenue. In an effort to develop gold mining, he tried to get a contract with a Dutch company. But his effort was contrary to Manchu policy and therefore was stalled.[42] Still, Gungsangnorbu's attempt reveals his progressive attitude and his open-mindedness toward the modern technology of the West.

The Manchu court was now living on borrowed time. In 1908 the Empress Dowager Tz'u-hsi and Emperor Kuang-hsü died several hours apart. Three year old P'u-yi was then placed on the throne with his father Tsai-feng, Prince Ch'un, as Regent.[43] These deaths foreshadowed the demise of the dynasty itself. This was naturally a critical period for Mongolia, and adjusting to the new and changing circumstances was difficult. Other changes included a proclamation by the Ch'ing Court of a constitutional monarchy and a popular demand through the provinces for the immediate establishment of a national assembly or parliament.

In the same year 1909, under heavy pressures for more reforms, the court finally proclaimed the establishment of the *Tzu-cheng yüan* (資政院 The House of Political Consultation) as a preliminary base for a national parliament. In the summer of 1910, the court convened the first meeting of this new "parliament" and appointed as members approximately one hundred Manchu nobles and outstanding Chinese leaders, together with Gungsangnorbu and several other Mongolian princes.[44] This organization was merely nominal, however, and accomplished nothing substantial for Chinese democracy.

At this time, Gungsangnorbu submitted a petition to the Court concerning problems in Jerim League, eastern Inner Mongolia, in which he emphasized the need for several important measures: 1) there should be a clear-cut division of power between the Mongolian Banners and the Chinese *hsien;* 2) in the banners where Chinese *hsien* had already been established, the Chinese officials should collect the rents and the taxes from the Chinese settlers and divide the revenue among the banners; 3) such local affairs as education and police should be administered by each banner; and 4) Mongolian banners should take precedence in land problems and law cases involving both Mongols and Chinese.

Prince Gung's original petition is not available, but the points mentioned above are listed in a report of Hsi-liang, Governor-General of Manchuria, who studied the petition.[45] It appears that Gungsangnorbu made great concessions to the Chinese administration in his petition, but only by his policies could the rights of Mongolian banners be protected. His petition indicates the rapid changes that had taken place in eastern Inner Mongolia in the decade following the Boxer Rebellion. Along with Hsi-liang's report, Prince Gung's proposals were again studied by the court officials and judged unacceptable.

Finally, in the autumn of 1910, the *Li-fan pu*[46] (Ministry of Dependencies) petitioned the court to make a thorough change of policy toward Mongolia. It encouraged the Mongols to learn and use the Chinese language, to cultivate virgin Mongolian land, to settle Chinese immigrants in Mongolia, and to establish intermarriage between the Mongols and the Chinese. This petition was officially authorized by the court.[47]

A Move Toward Independence

As these changes were being implemented, a critical situation developed in Mongolia and Tibet. British troops which had occupied Tibet in 1904 were under the command of Colonel Francis Younghusband and withdrew from Lhasa in 1910. Chao Erh-feng then entered Tibet with Chinese troops and occupied Lhasa to reassert Chinese rule. This move forced the Thirteenth Dalai Lama to flee south to India. As a result, the Tibetans opposed Manchu-Ch'ing rule even more fiercely than before, and thus the situation in Tibet as well as Outer Mongolia became increasingly more tense because of the pressure the Manchu *ambans* (ministers) exerted on leaders in these areas. Just as the Mongols turned to Tsarist Russia for assistance in their struggle against the Manchus, the Tibetans sought British support. Of course, Gungsangnorbu was keenly aware of all these events, and they influenced his thinking to some degree.

In China, and particularly in the capital, rumors of revolution increased daily, and tension and distress prevailed in the imperial household. During 1911, as revolutionary activity multiplied in central and southern China, Yüan Shih-k'ai[48] was appointed Prime Minister. His personal ambition soon led to the abdication of the dynasty, and he became the all-powerful figure in Peking.

The fall of the Manchu dynasty and the Republican Revolution, which broke out 10 October 1911, were turning points in modern history for both the Chinese and the Mongols. Outer Mongolian leaders were quickly ordered to force the retreat of the Manchu officials from Mogolian territory and to proclaim their independence from the Manchu-Ch'ing dynasty. Revolutionary forces proclaimed the establishment of the Republic of China in January 1912 with Nanking as the capital and Sun Yat-sen as President. Meanwhile, the Manchus convened an imperial council presided over by Empress Lung-yü, widow of the Emperor Kuang-hsü, to discuss the fate of the dynasty. Prince *Ch'ing, I-k'uang*,[49] who conducted, persuaded the Empress to accept the advice of Yüan Shih-k'ai to abdicate. Interestingly, Prince Gungsangnorbu and several other Mongol princes opposed abdication. Prince Gung made it known that if the court did surrender, he would consider proclaiming the independence of the eastern Inner Mongolia from any new regime.[50] The reasons for Gungsangnorbu's position are not given. However, the overt anti-Manchu propaganda of the revolutionaries that logically included other non-Chinese like the Mongols, was no doubt the main factor.

With Outer Mongolia's declaration of independence and the tense situation within Inner Mongolia, representatives of the Ch'ing court, who were involved in arranging an abdication, and the leaders of the newly established Republic of China met to discuss the Mongolian problem and that of other minorities who had traditionally recognized the suzerainty of the dynasty. Because this was one of the most serious problems, a public policy statement was issued, stating that all nationalities in China would be treated equally. There would be no change or removal of the established rights and privileges of the different nationalities. The Mongolian problem also influenced the revolutionary leaders to establish the Republic as a commonwealth of five nationalities — Chinese (Han), Manchu, Mongol, Moslem, and Tibetan.[51]

Mongolian leaders clearly knew that the Mongols alone were not powerful enough to resist domination from Peking, and they tried to seek foreign aid. Among the world powers only two countries had much interest in Mongolian problems — Japan and Russia. Before seeking assistance from Japan, both Gungsangnorbu and Ghonchogsurung visited the Deputy Minister of Russia in Peking and discussed with him the possibility of Russian assistance. The Russian diplomat indicated that his country was sympathetic with the independence movement and would help the Outer Mongols but not the Inner Mongols because of geographical distance.[52] As a result these determined Mongolian leaders had no choice but to seek help from Japan.

By this time Japan was greatly worried about the growing instability in China. Some Japanese officials even attempted to persuade the Manchu leaders to retreat to Manchuria and establish a new regime under Japanese patronage. Following the abdication of the Manchu court, Prince Su escaped from Peking to Dairen, established a loyalist party, the *Tsung-she-tang* (宗社党), and planned to restore the Manchu dynasty. Meanwhile, Gungsangnorbu's plan for independence was supported by several leading Inner Mongolian nobles. The Japanese committed to assist Prince Su in his plan for a restoration, and apparently were also willing to help Gungsangnorbu in his plan for an independent Inner Mongolia. No doubt they expected to gain concessions from such activities. This was clearly in line with their *Manmo seisaku* (満蒙政策), i.e., the Japanese policy for expansion in Manchuria and eastern Inner Mongolia.

Immediately following the Manchu abdication in January 1912, Gungsangnorbu returned to Kharachin and convened a conference of princes and leaders of the Josotu and Juu-uda leagues. Delegates from Jerim League also attended. They assembled at Ulan-khada (Ch'ih-feng 赤峰) to discuss the Mongol course of action in the China crisis. Gungsangnorbu, key leader and spokesman at the conference, made it very clear that he favored establishing an independent Mongolia.[53] His Manchu wife, Shan-k'un, a strong-minded woman, differed with her husband and tried to influence the conference from the outside to adopt a policy for the rehabilitation and support of the Manchu dynasty.[54]

The Mongolian leaders realized that proclaiming independence from Peking was a very risky undertaking. The inclination of many of the princes was to establish close relationships with the Urga government in a move to organize a unified pan-Mongolia. In order to be better informed about the new developments in Outer Mongolia, Gungsangnorbu sent Lobsangchoijur[55] as his personal representative to Urga. Through this man the Boghda Khan, the Eighth Jebtsundamba, appointed Gungsangnorbu as leader of the six leagues of Inner Mongolia. Before Lobsangchoijur's return Prince Gung journeyed to Peking under the "persuasion" of Yüan Shih-k'ai. This journey did not betray his hope for independence, but rather was an effort to defuse Yüan's threats to use military force against Gungsangnorbu's area, located not far north of the Great Wall and Peking.

Another factor that hindered Gungsangnorbu's plan for independence was Japan's changing policy. At the beginning of the revolution the Japanese government was suspicious of Yüan Shih-k'ai, and anxiously tried to establish an independent *Manmo* state — Southern Manchuria and eastern Inner Mongolia. But following the consolidation of his power in Peking, Yüan manifested a favorable attitude toward Japan. Consequently, the Japanese cabinet decided not to run the risk of supporting Gungsangnorbu and Prince Su.[56]

Career in Peking and Chinese Politics

Apparently it was the failure to gain Japan's support that convinced Gungsangnorbu to go to Peking in accordance with the "invitation of President Yüan Shih-k'ai." Once in the capital, Prince Gung was not favorably impressed by Yüan Shih-k'ai. He was, however, impressed by the progressive and broadly liberal attitude of Sun Yat-sen. He felt that Sun Yat-sen was an open-minded progressive leader — a great statesman — and that he would sincerely try to establish a commonwealth of the five nationalities.[57]

In spite of his misgivings, Gungsangnorbu was brought into the new Republican government by Yüan Shih-k'ai, for Gung was an outstanding leader. The old Ministry of Dependencies *(Li-fan Yüan)* was abolished because of its negative history and poor image. In its place was established in July 1912 the Mongolia-Tibetan Affairs Bureau *(Meng-Tsang shih-wu-chü* 蒙藏事務局 *)*, directly under the supervision of the Prime Minister. Initially, Yao Hsi-kuang was appointed acting director of this office and served for about three months. However, in September Yüan Shih-k'ai appointed Gungsangnorbu as director, maintaining Yao on the staff as vice-director.[58] This change was most probably an attempt to block Gungsangnorbu from executing any future plans to develop a powerful Mongolia. The Mongolian problem could not be ignored, for both Outer Mongolia and Tibet had declared independence from the new Republic.

About this time, in August 1912, Sun Yat-sen was reorganizing his revolutionary party as a new *Kuomintang* and included Gungsangnorbu as one of its key leaders. Details on how this came about are not yet available, but the position was probably a nominal one. When the new political party was launched with a governing committee *(li-shih-hui* 理事會*)*, Sun was sustained as chairman of the core group, with Gungsangnorbu, Huang Hsing,[59] Sung Chiao-jen,[60] Wang Ch'ung-hui,[61] and others listed as members.[62] It seems that Gungsangnorbu's contact and support of Sun Yat-sen distressed Yüan Shih-k'ai, and he thus granted Prince Gung position and honor but no actual political power or self-government for the Mongolian people.

In one definite sense, Gungsangnorbu was the loser in all of this. His move to Peking and subsequent involvement in Chinese officialdom placed him, the single most outstanding Inner Mongol leader, in the web of Yüan Shih-k'ai. A prototype of the warlords, Yüan Shih-k'ai made certain compromises and extended certain rewards to placate the Mongols, while he misled them and neutralized any real power they might have had. Moreover, in the establishment of a parliamentary assembly within the new Republican government, Yüan did not allow the Mongols to occupy all of the seats reserved for them. He insisted instead that some of his personal supporters be seated in the assembly as substitute representatives for the Mongols. These included Tsao Ju-lin,[63] Wang Jung-pao,[64] and others.[65] This political game disillusioned the Mongols and caused them to distrust Yüan Shih-k'ai and the Chinese government even more.

Founding the Mongolian-Tibetan Academy

Gungsangnorbu was not to be daunted, however. As director of the Mongolian-Tibetan Office, he drew together the Mongolian and Tibetan representatives in Peking. In 1913 he submitted a proposal to the government for the establishment of a Mongolian-Tibetan Academy in Peking to educate young Mongols and Tibetans. Prince Gung's proposal was passed by the parliament and the academy was established. Many young students were brought in from the outlying leagues and banners of Inner Mongolia. The establishment of this academy was a very progressive step and received strong support among young Mongolian intellectuals. But the conservative princes and officials still looked askance at modern education and took a dim view of the work of Gungsangnorbu's academy.

His hard work as a pioneer in establishing the Mongolian-Tibetan Academy proved to be a mixed blessing for Gungsangnorbu. Because of it, he lost support among some senior banner leaders in Inner Mongolia and at times drew strong opposition from the conservative group of Mongolian leaders residing in Peking.

This school, established essentially through the personal efforts of Gungsangnorbu, had great significance for Mongolia because many future leaders gained their most significant educational training there. The Mongol leaders trained at the academy include Pai Yün-ti (Serengdungrub)[66] and Li Yung-hsin,[67] organizers of the Inner Mongolian Kuomintang Movement, who later served as officials in Nanking. Ulanfu (Yün Tse)[68] and others who later rose to prominence as Inner Mongolian Communist leaders were also students at the school. The academy trained many leaders who participated in the Inner Mongolian Autonomous Movement of 1933. However, there were difficulties, for Gungsangnorbu's students constantly pressed him for more progressive reforms while conservatives blamed him for liberal ideas the school introduced which led to unrest in Inner Mongolia. Regardless of problems created by students of the academy, Gungsangnorbu's enthusiasm for the school did not wane. Furthermore, he continued to be interested in the development of education in all of Mongolia.

A negative influence hanging over Prince Gung's plans and enthusiasm was Yao Hsi-kuang, the vice-director of the Mongolia-Tibetan Affairs Office. The conflict between these two men became so intense that Yüan Shih-k'ai was forced to remove Yao in order to placate the Mongols. Even though Yao was removed, the policy of the Peking Government toward the Mongols was no more liberal. When the government realized that the problem in Mongolia and Tibet could not be easily solved, they upgraded the Mongolian-Tibetan Affairs Office and on 18 May 1914 established the Mongolia-Tibetan Ministry *(Meng Tsang Yüan* 蒙藏院*).*[69] Gungsangnorbu was promoted to the post of General Director *(tsung-ts'ai,* 總裁*)* and his ministry became directly responsible to the president, not to the prime minister. His position, while remaining essentially a hollow office that gave him no real power in Mongolian affairs, did, however, afford him a degree of influence in some decisions.

Mongolia, North China, and Warlords

The period of the First World War included an event that held important implications for Japanese penetration into the Asian mainland, including Mongolia. In 1915, Japan, through pressure on the government of Yüan Shih-k'ai and the infamous "Twenty-one Demands," attempted to force certain concessions in Manchuria and eastern Inner Mongolia from the Chinese.[70] Nothing is yet known about Gungsangnorbu's impression of or response to this development, but no doubt he tried to avoid involvement in this delicate problem. In the meantime, during the war the Chinese, Russians, and Mongols met at Khiakta to decide the status of Outer Mongolia. The final treaty reduced Mongolia from independence to autonomy. It recognized Russian concessions gained in Mongolia, but also reconfirmed Mongolian subordination to Chinese suzerainty.

While Gungsangnorbu struggled in the capital with various problems, working within the system of the new Republic and attempting through established channels to protect Mongolian rights and improve the situation of his people, one of the largest rebellions in modern Mongolian history broke out in 1915 and ranged widely over Mongolia. Gungsangnorbu had no direct connection with this somewhat confused movement and maintained a rather sympathetic neutrality. The key figure in the rebellion was Babujab[71] from the Tümed Banner. Following the collapse of the Manchu-Ch'ing dynasty and the Chinese revolution, Babujab joined Prince Su's loyalist Party (Tsung-shê-tang). Through Prince Su, Babujab was able to gain the support of the Japanese army which not only equipped him but lent advisors to organize troops drawn mainly from the Josotu, Juu-uda, and Jerim Leagues.

Branded a "Mongol bandit" *(Meng-fei)*, Babujab, under the slogan of Manchu imperial restoration, rapidly attracted a large number of troops, estimated by some at over ten thousand. With these, he fought a guerrilla war ranging over the territory of eastern Chakhar, Jehol, Kirin, and Mukden. Some of his units reached as far north as Heilungkiang Province. During this time, he established some direct or indirect relationships with the Outer Mongolian government.

Gungsangnorbu, though a relative of Prince Su by marriage and somewhat sympathetic to a Manchu restoration, was not a member of the loyalist party that supported Babujab. At least he was not known to be an active member of the group. He maintained neutrality toward Babujab's movement, not merely because he was a ranking official in the Peking government, but because he saw that Babujab's goals were confused, his troops not well organized, and their actions in some areas which they occupied were deplorable. Finally, in 1916, during a campaign in Juu-uda League (northern Jehol), while attacking the administrative and military center of Lin-hsi District, Babujab was killed. Soon thereafter his troops scattered.

The dust had not settled on the Babujab incident when a new problem arose to challenge Gungsangnorbu's leadership abilities. Yüan Shih-k'ai attempted to establish a new dynasty with himself as emperor.[72] For the Mongolian leaders in Peking, this was a delicate situation, and most of them chose under political pressure to support Yüan's move. Gungsangnorbu did not openly oppose Yüan's bid to become emperor, but his decision not to become involved placed him in a difficult position among his Mongolian friends and further highlights his independence.

From before the turn of the century, pressure on Mongolia had increased each decade, regardless of whether there was a strong central government or not. This growing pressure was the primary concern of Gungsangnorbu and other Mongolian leaders. Nineteen sixteen, the year Yüan Shih-k'ai died, was the turning point, bringing not only new problems for Mongolia but also a worsening of old ones. The lapse of China into warlordism, partly a result of the death of Yüan, meant a weak government in Peking and created less security in the provinces and Inner Mongolia.

Various strong men, essentially warlords, ruled Peking after the passing of Yüan Shih-k'ai. Chang Hsüen,[73] a conservative, taking advantage of the turbulence in North China politics, attempted a restoration of the Manchu Imperial House.[74] Gungsangnorbu, once loyal to the Manchus, did not become involved in this movement, but avoided it as he had done Yüan Shih-k'ai's attempt to create his own dynasty. Gungsangnorbu's responses to both these situations during the early Republican period attest to his clear understanding of Chinese politics.

Warlord politics continued in Peking, and with the failure of the restoration movement, Tuan Ch'i-jui[75] took power as Prime Minister, supported by a warlord group known as Anfu Clique (安福系) which dominated North China. Sun Yat-sen, alienated from the warlord regimes in Peking, left for Canton to establish a new government. Gungsangnorbu, involved as he was in the Peking government, even at times against his better judgment, did not go south. Yet, he did not attempt to stop a group of Mongolian leaders who did follow Sun Yat-sen to set up a rival government.[76] This action may have been due to his earlier contacts with and admiration for Sun Yat-sen, as well as his personal disappointment with the warlord leadership in Peking.

Conservatives and Liberals in Confrontation

Meanwhile, many Outer Mongolian leaders, having been disillusioned with the Russians and the problems arising out of autonomy, were turning back to a pro-Chinese alignment. Shortly after the May Fourth Movement in 1919, Tuan Ch'i-jui, in order to relieve the internal political struggles in North China, dispatched an expedition of Chinese troops to Outer Mongolia under the command of Hsü Shu-cheng.[77] A tough, harsh, and high-handed man, Hsü pressured the Mongols to abolish their autonomy and "willingly" return to the fold of China. Next, in 1920, the Russian Civil War between the Bolsheviks and the White forces in Siberia spilled over into Outer Mongolia. Distressed in the extreme by Hsü Shu-cheng's oppression, Mongolian leaders in Urga sent two missions to Russia to ask for assistance. The mission to the White Russians soon brought Baron Ungern-Sternberg and his troops into Mongolia to force the Chinese to leave. In October 1920, the Chinese forces were driven out of Outer Mongolia by Mongolian-Russian allied forces. The Mongols proclaimed what was known as the Second Declaration of Independence for Outer Mongolia on 22 March 1921.

Another Mongolian mission was sent to the Bolshevik forces, including the revolutionary leader Süke-bator, who met Lenin and was able to obtain assistance. The Russian Red Army, together with forces of the Mongolian People's Revolutionary Party, occupied Urga in 1921 and established a communist government.

With the rise of the socialist revolution in northern Mongolia, excitement grew among young students and intellectuals in Inner Mongolia, bringing high hopes for self-determination and the unification of all Mongolian peoples. As young Mongols became more militant, conservative leaders became more defensive, and Gungsangnorbu was still caught in the middle and criticized by both sides.

While conservative warlord politics was working itself out on one level in China and the borderlands, progressive and radical groups were busy on another. The Chinese

Communist Party was organized in 1921. The Soviet Union dispatched Karakhan as its ambassador to Peking where he was warmly welcomed. The Mongolian problem continued to plague Sino-Soviet relations, however, and negotiations did not go smoothly. In the meantime, Adolph Joffe, a delegate of the Comintern, arrived in Canton to negotiate for a united front, and the Kuomintang-Communist cooperation was a result. At the same time, Outer Mongolian leaders sent their representatives to Canton to consult with Sun Yat-sen.[78] Both sides agreed to a joint political venture in Inner Mongolia and Pai Yün-t'i, Gungsangnorbu's former protégé, was chosen to assist in the venture. Pai had been working with Sun Yat-sen in Canton for some time and now had his opportunity to rise to prominence. He immediately proceeded to Peking to begin his work and was greatly encouraged by the arrival of Sun Yat-sen in December 1924. An even more fortuitous development for Pai's movement, however, was a victory in North China of Feng Yü-hsiang,[79] who had links with the Comintern. He could provide supplies and protection under which Pai Yün-t'i could operate.

The name of the new Inner Mongolian political party founded by Pai Yün-t'i and his followers was symbolic of the nature of the united front. To the Chinese it was known as the *Nei-meng-ku Kuomintang*, the Inner-Mongolian Kuomintang. To the Mongols it was known as the *Obör Mongghol-un arad-un khubisghaltu nam*, the Inner Mongolian People's Revolutionary Party. Both sides felt that this new party was an extension of its own party, and it gained support from the Chinese Kuomintang, from the Comintern, and from the Mongolian People's Revolutionary Party in Ulan Bator. In this context a group of students were sent to Ulan Bator and to Russia for training. Ulanfu (Yün Tse), one of those who studied in Russia, later became the leading Mongolian Communist figure in China.

Sometime during his organizing activities, Pai Yün-t'i consulted with Gungsangnorbu regarding the movement. Prince Gung, as an experienced leader of the Mongol nation, told Pai that if the Mongolian people fought among themselves they would endanger their survival. He stressed that class warfare would only weaken the Mongols and handicap their struggle against outside enemies.[80] However, Pai was not inclined to accept Gungsangnorbu's counsel.

When the Inner Mongolian People's Revolutionary Party or the *Nei-Meng-ku Kuomintang* was formally organized in Kalgan in 1925, Dambadorji,[81] as leader of the Mongolian People's Revolutionary Party from Ulan Bator, attempted to lend his support. Most significant was his advice to Pai Yün-t'i, essentially the same as that which Gungsangnorbu had given him. The first priority of the Mongolian people must be to maintain internal unity and to defend themselves against external enemies. Strife among the people themselves would be a serious and dangerous development.[82] The new party gained some popularity, but apparently it was not able to integrate the people into a solid organization. As a last attempt, Pai threw himself and his party into the struggles with the Chinese warlords, hoping to gain concessions for the Mongols in eastern Inner Mongolia. Pai's Mongol troops supported Feng Yü-hsiang against the warlord of Manchuria, Chang Tso-lin,[83] but the venture failed. Feng was forced to retreat toward northwest China, and Pai and his party had no recourse but to move west to take refuge in the Yeke-juu League and in some parts of Ninghsia region. Here they joined local radicals and caused considerable bloodshed in a struggle with conservatives of that area while attempting to establish tough reforms. As a result of this action, certain conservatives in western Inner Mongolia grew to hate the radical Mongols who came into their area, and they also blamed Gungsangnorbu. They felt that his schools had brought new ideas into Mongolia, had undermined tradition, and had thus encouraged radical actions among the younger generation.

Prince Gung: The Passing of an Era

After the establishment of the Republic of China and its lapse into warlordism, Inner Mongolia's virgin lands became a target for Chinese warlords and corrupt officials to appropriate and to sell to Chinese settlers for personal power and monetary gain. Several selfish Mongolian princes collaborated with the Chinese warlord Chang Tso-lin and others for further exploitation of Mongolian land. By 1925 Feng Yü-hsiang had been appointed the Director General of Military Cultivation in the Northwest (*Hsi-pei tun-k'en tu-pan* 西北屯墾督辦) and was planning to settle Chinese soldiers and their families in western Inner Mongolia. In this crisis Gungsangnorbu and his group in Peking mobilized both radical and conservative Mongols to petition against any further Chinese cultivation of Mongolian lands. They demanded that Tuan Ch'i-jui and his government stop the warlords from exploiting the Mongols.[84] In this situation the young ambitious Prince of Sünid, Demchugdungrub,[85] was a leading figure against the powerful warlord, Feng Yü-hsiang. This petition was accepted by the Peking Government, but no restrictions were placed on the warlords. Meanwhile, this incident made Gungsangnorbu even more unpopular among the officials of North China.

Meanwhile, a political situation was developing in China that would decide the fate of the nation. While Chang Tso-lin proclaimed himself Generalissimo of China in Peking (1927), the Kuomintang's Northern Expedition was launched to unify China. When it reached Nanking and established a new government, Pai Yün-t'i separated from his Communist attachments and gave his support to the new government.

This was a particularly difficult year in North China, and for a few months Gungsangnorbu did not go to his office in the Mongolian-Tibetan Ministry. His absence was reported to be due to illness, but it is debatable whether his illness was physical or "political." Following the victory of the Kuomintang forces with which Pai Yün-t'i had allied himself, Pai sent a group of his followers to Peking, ousted Gungsangnorbu's staff from the Mongolian-Tibetan Ministry, and assumed control in the name of the new Central Government in Nanking.

As for Pai and his group, although they won some status and reputation in the Kuomintang party, they did not gain any real political advantages for the Mongols which they claimed to represent. Moreover, the policy of the new government toward Mongolia, influenced by such old warlords as Feng Yü-hsiang and Yen Hsi-shan, was soon revealed to be inconsistent with Sun Yat-sen's doctrine: "The government should help the weaker and smaller nationalities inside the country to carry out their self-determination and self-rule." Contrary to Sun's liberal policy, clearly stated in his *Outline for Nation Building* (*Chien-kuo ta-kang*),[86] six new provinces were formed — Jehol, Chahar, Suiyüan, Ninghsia, Chinghai, and Hsikang — all of them former Mongol territories with the exception of Hsikang which was Tibetan. This new action by the government was a shock to the Mongols, and they became greatly disillusioned about the possibility of gaining self-rule.

A brilliant young intellectual, Wu Ho-ling,[87] a Kharachin graduate from Peking University and former administrative assistant to Gungsangnorbu, devised a means for organizing and uniting the Mongolian leagues and banners in an effort to protect themselves. In 1928 he proposed that a Mongolian Delegation, drawn from the representatives of all banners, go to Nanking to negotiate with the new government for Mongolian rights on the basis of Sun Yat-sen's pronouncements on self-determination and self-government for minority nationalities. Struggles between various Mongolian and Chinese factions over a Mongolian settlement continued, and the government was finally persuaded to convene a Mongolian Conference *(Meng-ku hui-i)* in Nanking in 1930. Out of this conference came a basic Law for the Organization of the Mongolian Leagues, aimaghs,[88] and Banners *(Meng-ku meng-pu-ch'i tsu-chih-fa* 蒙古盟部旗組織法 *)*.

A few months after the creation of this law which could lead to self-rule and democracy for Inner Mongolia, Gungsangnorbu died of poor health in Peiping on 14 January 1931. After the death of the Prince, the National Government in Nanking recognized his contribution to his people and his service to the Republic with a governmental decoration. After some delay, due to Japan's occupation of eastern Mongolia, Prince Gung was buried in 1934 in his ancestral tomb in Kharachin.

Gungsangnorbu was probably modern Mongolia's most progressive leader at the turn of the century. He was a skilled administrator and statesman. His understanding of the international and internal situations, it seems, was greater than that of any other contemporary Mongolian leader and of most Chinese leaders. Unfortunately, he lived in a period when reactionary forces were too strong to permit a natural and gradual evolution of the progressive ideas he espoused. When these forces were removed, long overdue social change took the form of revolution, rather than the peaceful reform favored by Prince Gungsangnorbu. Under different circumstances Gungsangnorbu might have become the recognized leader of his people. As it was, he was the scapegoat for both the Mongolian liberals and conservatives during most of his life. The problems that Prince Gung noted but failed to solve eventually became the point of irreconcilable contradiction between Mongolian and Chinese administrations and resulted in an Inner Mongolian movement for autonomy in the 1930s.

Notes

1. The tribal name of Kharachin originally was Uriyangkha and was located outside of the Great Wall. The nobles were the descendants of Jeleme, a general under Chinggis Khan. During the Manchu-Ch'ing period the Kharachin was divided into three banners, the Right Flank, the Left Flank, and the Central. After the Communist takeover, the Right Flank and the Central were combined into one banner.

2. Sechin Jagchid, "The Manchu-Ch'ing Religious Policy Towards Mongolia," *Tractata Altaica*, Wiesbaden, 1976 (chapter 10 in this work).

3. The name Wangin-khoroon means "the camp of the prince." The Chinese name of the residence was K'a-la-chin wang-fu, but it was commonly known as Wang-yeh-fu. At present it is known as Ta-ying-tzu.

4. Shih-to's (世鐸) rank was Prince Li (礼王). See "The List of the Sons of the Emperors" *(huang-tzu shih-hsi-piao)* II, *Ch'ing shih*, Taipei, 1971, 163:2031.

5. Hsing Chih-hsiang (邢致祥), *K'a-la-ch'in yu-ch'i cha-sa-k'o ch'in-wang Kung-sang-no-erh-bu chih shih-lüeh* (喀喇沁右旗札薩克親王貢桑諾爾布之事略 A Short Biography of Prince Gungsangnorbu, *jasagh* of the Kharachin Right Banner), Kharachin, 1938, 9. Hsing Chih-hsiang was originally a scribe of Prince Gung's banner. Later he was appointed the teacher at the banner's school and soon afterward promoted to school principal. Prior to Japanese occupation he was made one of the top officials of the banner. He was known as a man who was very knowledgeable about the history of Kharachin, and his work, though simple, is reliable.

6. Hsing Chih-hsiang, 9–10.

7. See *Ch'ing shih-lu* (清實錄), Te-tsung, 302–4, which covers the period of Kuang-hsü's seventeenth year (1891). See also Paul Hyer, "The Chin-tan-tao (金丹道) Movement — a Chinese Revolt in Mongolia," *Altaica*, Helsinki, 1977, 105–12.

8. Hu P'in-chih's (胡聘之) proposal may not be the first, but it was influential for the Chinese settlement on Mongolian soil.

9. Te-tsung, 406, entry of *kuei-yu* day, sixth month, twenty-third year of Kuang-hsü (1897), and 415, entry of *hsin-yu* day, twelfth month of the same year.

10. *Tung-hua-lu* (東華錄), entry for *ting-hai* day, twelfth month, twenty-fourth year of Kuang-hsü. Ibid., entry for *chia-wu* day, fifth month, twenty-sixth year of Kuang-hsü (1900).

11. For further information on Chang Chih-tung, see Arthur W. Hummel, ed., *Eminent Chinese of the Ch'ing Period* (Washington, 1944), 1:27–31. See also *Ch'ing shih*, *chüan* 438, *chüan* 224.

12. For further information on Li Hung-chang (李鴻章), see Hummel, 1:464–71. See also *Ch'ing shih* (清史), *chüan* 412, *chuan* 198.

13. Te-tsung, 481, entries of the days of *ting-ch'ou*, *wu-yin* and *hsin-ssu*, third month, twenty-seventh year of Kuang-hsü (1901); Te-tsung, 483, entry of *i-ch'ou* day, fifth month, same year; Te-tsung, 497, entry of *hsin-wei* day, second month, twenty-eighth year of Kuang-hsü (1902); Te-tsung, 507, entry of *hsin-wei* day, eleventh month, same year.

14. This information was personally related by the elders of Kharachin to the author. See also Hsing Chih-hsiang, 14–15.

15. *Tung-hua-lu*, see entry of *chia-wu* day, fifth month, twenty-sixth year of Kuang-hsü (1900).

16. Te-tsung, 477, entry of *ping-ch'en* day, twelfth month, twenty-sixth year of Kuang-hsü (1900).

17. For further information on Utai, see Tatsuo Nakami (中見立夫), "Khaisan and Udai: Two Southern Mongols under the Bogdo Khan Regime," *The Toyo Gakuho*, vol. 57, January 1976.

18. Te-tsung, 491, entry of *ken-tzu* day, twelfth month, twenty-seventh year of Kuang-hsü (1901).

19. Ibid., 497, entry of *i-ch'ou* day, third month, twenty-eighth year of Kuang-hsü (1902).

20. Misako Ichinomiya (一宮操子) (Kawahara 河原), *Moko miyage* (蒙古土産 Mongolian souvenir), (Tokyo, 1909), 126. Hsing Chih-hsiang, 14–15. Also see Jagchid, *Pein-chiang chiao-yü* (邊疆教育 The Education of the Border Areas of China), (Taipei, 1961), 43–44. The school continued as a normal school

to train school teachers for southeastern Inner Mongolia until the end of World War II, 1945.

21. Issac Taylor Headland, *Court Lift in China*, (New York, 1905), 218–21.
22. Hsing Chih-hsiang, 17–18.
23. Ibid., 15–17.
24. This information was personally related to the author by many Kharachin elders and many elderly lamas of Yüng-ho Kung. See Kokuryukai, ed., *Toa sengaku shishi kiten* (東亞先覺志士記傳), Tokyo, 1966, 2:266–69.
25. Misako Kawahara later married Mr. Ichinomiya, Director of the Bank of Japan, and served as a literary woman in the imperial palace of Japan. According to Kawashima she was sent to Kharachin as an agent for the Japanese intelligence organization. See Tsutomu Aida (会田勉), *Kawashima Naniwa ou* (川島浪速翁 The Elder Kawashima Naniwa), (Tokyo, 1940), 96–97.
26. Hsing Chih-hsiang, 18–20.
27. See *Tung-san-sheng cheng-lüeh* (東三省政畧), "Mongolian Affairs" (1), 2:3b–4a. On the problem of Utai, see note 18.
28. Ryuzo Torii was a famous Japanese archaeologist who worked a good deal on the Kitan Liao cities and the tombs in the Ba'arin Banner of Inner Mongolia. Kimiko, his wife, was a famous writer in folklore. For information on their activities in the Kharachin, see Kimiko Torii, *Dozukugaku yori mitaru Moko* (土俗学より見たる蒙古 Ethnographical Observations on Mongolia), (Tokyo, 1927), 26–29, 929, 970, and 984–85.
29. *Lien-ping ch'u* (練兵處), the Army Training Bureau, was established in the twenty-ninth year of Kuang-hsü (1903) for the purpose of military modernization.
30. Yao Hsi-kuang (姚錫光) was a native of Tan-tu (丹徒 present-day Chen-chiang), Chaing-su Province. By 1906 he was a high official serving in the *Lien-ping ch'u*. He was appointed to accompany Prince Su on his inspection trip to eastern Inner Mongolia. Later Yao published his opinions on Mongolian policy in his book *Ch'ou-meng ch'ü-i* (籌蒙芻議).
31. Yao Hsi-Kuang, *Ch'ou-meng chü-i* (a discussion of Mongolia Policy), (Peking 1908, republished in Taipei, 1965), 1a–22b.
32. Ibid., 23a–72a.
33. Ibid., 23–72a.
34. For further information on Shan-ch'i, (善耆) Prince Su (肅親王), see Hummel, 1:281, under *"Haoge, Prince Su."* See also Tsutomu Aida, 127–38.
35. Te-tsung, 550, entry of the *jen-tzu* day, tenth month, thirty-first year of Kuang-hsü (1905).
36. For further information on Shan-Kun (善坤), see Ichinomiya, 131–33. See also Kawahara (Ichinomiya) Misako, *Karachin ohi to watakushi* (喀喇沁王妃と私 The Princess of Kharachin and I), (Tokyo, 1969).
37. Yao Ksi-kuang, 2:1a and 60a–75b; Torii, 788–825 and 933–36.
38. This information was related to the author by his father, Lobsangchoijur, who was then a secretary to Prince Su during the latter's travel in Mongolia. Prince Su's official report has not yet been found.
39. Gungsangnorbu's petition was recorded in the *Tung-san-sheng Meng-wu kung-tu hui-pien* (東三省蒙務公牘彙編 A collection of the Documents of

the Mongolian Affairs in the Three Eastern Provinces), Chu ch'i-ch'ien (朱啓鈐), ed., 1909, reprinted in Taiwan, no date, 5:447–57. For the abstract of Prince Gung's second petition, see Te-tsung, 586, the entry of *kuei-mou* day, first month, thirty-fourth year of Kuang-hsü (1908).

40. Ibid., 523, entry of *chia-ch'en* day, eleventh month, twenty-ninth year of Kuang-hsü (1903).

41. Ghonchoghsurung was a progressive-minded leader who followed Prince Gung's policy and developed education in his banner. After the failure of the Inner Mongolian independence movement, he went to Outer Mongolia and joined the Urga Government. He returned one year later, however.

42. Te-tsung, 551, entry of *ting-muo* day, first month, twenty-ninth year of Kuang-hsü (1903), and 533, entry of *i-yu* day, seventh month, thirtieth year of Kuang-hsü (1904).

43. For further information on Tsai-feng (載灃), Prince Ch'un (醇親王), see Hummel, 1:385–86, under the biography of I-huan, the father of Tsai-feng.

44. *Ch'ing shih-lu* Hsüan-tung, 34, entry of *chia-hsü* day, fourth month, second year of Hsüan-tung (1910).

45. Ibid., 29, entry of *kuei-ch'ou* day, first month, second year of Hsüan-tung (1910). For Hsi-liang (錫良), see a biography in *Ch'ing shih, chüan* 450, *chuan* 236.

46. Originally the name was *Li fan Yüan,* but the *yüan* was changed to *pu* in the year 1906 as a sign of modernization. At this time other changes also took place in the governmental institutions.

47. Hsüan-tung, 41, entry of *ting-hai* day, eighth month, second year of Hsüan-t'ung (1910).

48. Yüan Shih-k'ai was the first President of the Republic of China. See H. L. Boorman, ed., *Biographical Dictionary of Republic of China* (New York: Columbia University Press, 1967), 4:78–79.

49. I-K'uang (奕劻), Prince Ch'ing (慶親王), was appointed the Prime Minister in 1911 when the Ch'ing Court reorganized its government to satisfy the demand for modernization. He resigned just prior to the abdication and supported Yüan Shih-k'ai as his successor.

50. See *Chung-hua-min-kuo shih-shih chi-yao pein-chi wei-yuan hui* (The Editing Committee of the Important Historical Events of the Republic of China), ed., *Chung-hua-min-kuo shih-shih chi-yao* (中華民國史事記要), 1912 (The Important Historical Events of the Republic of China, 1912), (Taipei 1971), 98–101. See also Aida, 121–24.

51. *Chung-hua-min-kuo shih-shih chi-yao,* 103–4, 111–12, 175, 180–81, and 193–94.

52. Aida, 147–48, Kawashima's telegram No. 65 to Japanese general-staff's office.

53. Jagchid, *Meng-ku chih chin-hsi* (蒙古之今昔 Mongolia Present and Past), (Taipei, 1954), 214.

54. This information was related to the author by several of the Kharachin elders who attended the Ulan-khada conference.

55. Lobsangchoijur (1866–1945) is the father of the author. During the official travel of Prince Su in Inner Mongolia, Lobsangchoijur was recommended by

Gungsangnorbu to Prince Su as his secretary. When the Thirteenth Dalai Lama left Tibet and visited Peking, Lobsangchoijur was a secretary to the high lama. After his return from Urga, he first was elected as a Mongolian Member of the Chinese Parliament in 1912 and then was appointed as a representative of Tibet by the Thirteenth Dalai Lama to the Chinese Parliament. He retired from political activities after the Japanese occupation of Kharachin in 1933. The record here is taken mainly from a conversation of the author with his father.

56. Aida, 164–67; *Toa sengaku shishi kiten,* 346–48. See also Ken Kurihaya (栗原健), *Tai manmo seisakushi no ichimen* (对满蒙政策史の一面 One Side of the History of the Policy Towards Manchuria and Mongolia), (Tokyo, 1966), 96–98 and 139–44.

57. From a conversation of the author with Mr. Todob (Tu-tuo-po (鸾多博), d. 1968, the eldest son of Gungsangnorbu.

58. See Liu Shou-lin, ed., *Hsin-hai i-hou shih-chi-nien chih-kuan-piao* (辛亥以後十七年職官表 The Name List of the Officials from 1912–28), (republished in Hong Kong, 1974).

59. For information on Huang Hsing, see Howard L. Boorman, ed., *Biographical Dictionary of Republic of China* (New York, 1968), 2:192–97. See also, Hsi-ch'iu (惜秋), *Min-ch'u feng-yün jen-wu* (民初風雲人物), (Taipei, 1966), 1:1–105.

60. For information on Sung Chiao-jen, see Boorman, 3:192–95. See also Huang Chi-lu ed., *Ko-ming jen-wu chih* (革命人物志), (Taipei, 1969), 2:332–46.

61. For information on Wang Ch'ung-hui, see Boorman, 3:376–78. See also Huang, 1:179–80.

62. Chang ch'i-yün (張其昀), *Tang-shih kai-yao* (党史概要), (Taipei, 1950s), 144. See Li Shou-k'ung (李守孔), *Min-ch'u chih kuo-hui* (民初之國会), (Taipei, 1964), 60–61.

63. For information on Tsao Ju-lin (曹汝霖), a pro-Japanese politician, see Boorman, 3:299–302.

64. Wang Jung-pao (汪榮寶) was later appointed Chinese Minister to Japan for a long period.

65. The legal number of Mongolian members of the two houses in the Chinese Parliament was fifty-three. Among these, more than fifteen seats were occupied illegally by Chinese. See Li Shuo-kung, 154 and 159.

66. For information on Pai yün-ti (白雲梯) see Boorman, 1:6–9, ref. Buyantai.

67. Li Yung-hsin (李永新), a Kharachin Left Banner man, died in 1975. He was one of the leading Mongolian members in the Koumintang. After the National Government moved to Taiwan, he was appointed the Minister of the Mongolian-Tibetan Affairs Commission during the Tibetan revolt against the Chinese Communists in the late 1950s.

68. Ulanfu, see Paul Hyer, "Ulanfu and Inner Mongolia Autonomy Under the Chinese People's Republic," *Mongolia Society Bulletin,* 1969, 8:24–62. See also Boorman, 3:349–53.

69. *Meng-tsang wei-yüan-hui* (The Mongolian-Tibetan Commission), ed., *Meng-tsang wei-yüan-hui chien-shih* (蒙藏委員會簡史 A Simple History of the Mongolian Tibetan Commission), (Taipei, 1971), 9–10.

70. "The Twenty-one Demands" were imposed on Yüan Shih-k'ai while he was attempting to make himself monarch of China. These demands were composed of five documents. The second one was a draft of a treaty concerning southern Manchuria and eastern Inner Mongolia. In this proposal Japan demanded prerogatives on economy, transportation, and land and mining developments. These demands were imposed on the Chinese side on 18 January 1915 as an ultimatum, and except for a few articles, they were agreed upon by Yüan shih-k'ai's government on 25 May 1915. This agreement was not accepted by the people or the new government after the collapse of Yüan, however, and it was finally abolished following the conference on the Limitation of Armaments, Washington, D.C., 12 November 1921–6 February 1922.

71. Jagchid, unpublished manuscript, "The Political Problems of Inner Mongolia of Recent Three Centuries." See also Aida, 214–92, and *Tao sengaku shishi kiten*, 625–61.

72. Yüan declared his monarchical system 12 December 1914, and announced the title of his reign as Hung-hsien (黃史). He was forced to abdicate on 22 March but remained as the president. He died 6 June 1915.

73. For information on Chang Hsüen, see Boorman, 1:68–72.

74. The restoration, beginning 1 July 1917, ending 12 July 1917, lasted for only twelve days.

75. For information on Tuan Chi-jui, (段祺瑞) see Boorman, 3:330–35.

76. From the Mongolian members in the Parliament, there were Pai Jui (白瑞), Chidaltu, Altanochir, and Uribatu.

77. For information on Hsü Shu-cheng (徐樹錚), see Boorman, 2:143–46.

78. See Sun Yat-sen's speech on 20 January 1924, *Meng-tsang wei-yüan hui* (Mongolian-Tibetan Commissions), ed., *Meng-tsang-ch'eng-t'se chi fa-ling hsüan-chi* (蒙藏政策及法令選集 A Selection of Policy and Regulations Towards Mongolia and Tibet), (Taipei, 1966), 4–5; See also Robert A. Rupen, *Mongols of the Twentieth Century* (Indiana University, 1964), 1:185–86.

79. For Feng Yü-hsiang, see James Sheridan, *Chinese Warlord, The Career of Feng Yü-hsiang* (Palo Alto: Stanford University Press, 1966).

80. This information was related to the author by Mr. Pai Yün-ti.

81. Dambadorji, (1899–1934) the first secretary of the Mongolian People's Revolutionary Party, was a nationalistic leader and strongly advocated unification of both Inner and Outer Mongolia. Because of this he was removed from his important position by Moscow communist authorities (1928). See also William A. Brown and Urgunge Onon, translation, *History of the Mongolian People's Republic* (Harvard, 1976), 770, n.101. See also Rupen, 1:193–94.

82. This was related to the author by Prince Demchugdungrub and Mr. Pai Yün-ti.

83. For information on Chang Tso-lin, see Gaven McCormack, *Chang Tso-lin in Northeast China*, 1911–28, (Palo Alto, 1977).

84. The date was 27 April 1925. See Pan-su (半粟) (pen name), *Chung-shan ch'u-shih-huo Chung-kuo liu-shih-nien ta-shih-chi* (中山出世後中國六十年大事記 The Important Events of China, Sixty Years after the Birth of Sun Yat-sen, 1866–1928), (Shanghai, no date; reprinted in Taipei, no date).

85. For information on Prince Demchugdungrub (De Wang, 1920–66), see unpublished biography by Jagchid.

86. *Chien-kuo ta-kang* (建國大綱 Outline of National Building) was one of the most important documents written by Sun Yat-sen himself. It was as important as his famous work, *San-min chu-i* (三民主義 The Three Principles of the People). Both were known as the guidelines of the Kuomintang and the government.

87. For information on Wu Ho-ling, see Boorman, 4:353–56, under his Mongolian name Unenbayin.

88. *Aimagh* is an old term in Mongolian social institutions which means a clan alliance. The modern Mongolian term *aimagh* means "province." In Inner Mongolia, historically, it meant a group of people and its land. In Chinese it is translated into *pu* (部), but its strict meaning is not exactly what the English *tribe* means.

Chapter 17

The Rise and Fall of Buddhism in Inner Mongolia (Part II)

(A continuation of chapter 9)

Changing Conditions and the Decline of Lamaist Buddhism

At the turn of the twentieth century, rapid changes in the Asian situation posed serious problems to the existence of the Mongols as a nation. By this time, Tibetan Buddhism had already mingled with traditional Mongolian culture and had become an integral part of the Mongolian national character. It also had become one of the main reasons for the decline of the Mongols as a nation. When Outer Mongolia declared its independence from China in 1911, many were concerned about protecting its religious faith,[1] while other enlightened Mongolian intellectuals carried out campaigns against Buddhism, advocating strict controls over religion for the sake of the survival and development of the Mongolian nation.

Prince Ghonchoghsurung of the Khorchin Left Front Banner of Jerim League was the first to openly advocate strict controls on Buddhism and its activities. In 1910, one year before the Independence Movement in Outer Mongolia, he presented a memorial to the Manchu-Ch'ing Court in which he proposed that "in order to abolish superstitious religion, [Buddhism] must be put under strict control."[2] In 1903 Prince Gungsangnorbu established his modern schools. Students who attended these schools began to doubt the teachings of the lamas and to recognize Buddhism as a factor in the decline of the Mongols. Soon afterwards, Prince Gungsangnorbu sent several students to study in Japan. Following their return to Kharachin, modern thought and an anti-Lamaist Buddhist movement began to spread rapidly.

As mentioned, in addition to its political and economic goals, the 1911 Independence Movement sought the protection of the Yellow Faith. The leader of the movement was the Eighth Jebtsundamba Khutughtu.[3] Because of his incomparable personal influence in religious matters, the movement won enthusiastic support from the Khalkha people. However, soon after independence various conflicts broke out, eventually creating the conditions for the Communist Revolution of 1921 and its subsequent socialist reforms.

The independence of Outer Mongolia was a great temptation to the Inner Mongols. But because the prestige of the Jebstundamba Khutughtu south of the Gobi was not as great as it was among the Khalkha Mongols, the goals of the revolution in Inner Mongolia, as planned by the Outer Mongolian leaders, could not be achieved. By this time, the Peking Government of the Republic of China (successors of the Manchu-Ch'ing Dynasty), in order to halt further expansion of the Jebtsundamba Khutughtu's influence in Inner Mongolia, followed the footsteps of the abdicated Manchu Court and proclaimed its policy of protection and patronage of the Yellow Religion.

During this crisis, the high lamas who had the greatest influence over the Inner Mongolian people were the Jangjia Khutughtu and the Kanjurwa Nom-un Khan of the Dolonor Monastery. A power struggle over ecclesiastical administration had long existed between these two lamas and their disciples. The Sixth Kunjurwa Nom-un Khan was sympathetic to the Outer Mongolian Independence Movement and because of this was killed in 1913 by so-called "bandits," i.e., disguised Chinese soldiers stationed at Dolonor.[4] Consequently, the Sixth Jangjia Khutughtu, still a young man, was urged by his politically ambitious disciples to intervene in Mongolian politics. He openly showed his support for the newly established Republic of China which supported his interests. He was subsequently rewarded with the title of *Hung-chi kuang-ming ta-kuo-shih* (宏济光明大國師 Great National Master of Spacious Relief and Enlightenment). Henceforth, until his death (1950s) the Sixth Jangjia Khutughtu was frequently entangled in Inner Mongolian politics. During the period of the Peking Government (1912–28) he was a political opponent of Prince Gungsangnorbu who was then the Director of the Mongolian-Tibetan Ministry and the main promoter of an Inner Mongolian modernization movement. The Mongolian-Tibetan Academy founded by Gungsangnorbu in Peking early became an active center of anti-feudalistic and anti-Buddhist activity. In 1924, with the death of the Eighth Jebtsundamba, traditional religious influence greatly diminished, and the Mongolian Peoples' Republic was established. These new events on the north of the Gobi greatly attracted the attention of the students at the Mongolian Tibetan Academy and encouraged more anti-religious activities in Inner Mongolia.

In the early 1920s, a political conflict broke out between the two great Masters of Tibetan Buddhism, the Thirteenth Dalai Lama and the Ninth Panchen Erdeni. Finally, the latter was forced from power and sought refuge in China and Mongolia. During his stay in the "lower land," he created the last "high tide of Buddhism" in Inner Mongolia. The princes, nobles, and common people gave their support to this great Master, Prince Demchügdüngrüb[5] of the Sünid Right Banner, Shilinghol League, and even proposed building a temple for him. The proposal was warmly received, and in 1932(?) the last great monastery in western Inner Mongolia was dedicated to him in Sünid Banner.

In 1931 Japan invaded Manchuria, and eastern Inner Mongolia soon fell into the hands of the invaders. The Japanese militarists, in order to strengthen Mongolian local governmental organizations and thus win the support of Mongolian intellectuals, abolished the old quasi-feudalistic system and began the extensive construction of schools. In order to please the conservatives, the Japanese also carried out a policy of patronizing Buddhist monasteries, but did not exempt lamas from conscription for military services. The Japanese ostensibly favored Lamaist Buddhism, but subtly withdrew the traditional privileges of the Mongolian ecclesiastical class. This greatly reduced the interest of parents in sending their sons to the monasteries. According to the statistics of 1938, there were in the Mongolian districts of "Manchuria" or *Manchukuo* 662 lamaseries. Among a Mongolian population of approximately 930,000 there were about 29,000 lamas, comprising about 3 percent of the entire population and 6 percent of the males.[6] This represents a sharp decline in eastern Inner Mongolia in the number of lamas from the beginning of the century. The trend was especially pronounced in the 1930s.

Political developments in western Inner Mongolia reached a crisis in 1933 with the Autonomous Movement. This was a cooperative political undertaking of nobles and conservative leaders under the leadership of Prince Demchügdüngrüb and supported by liberal intellectuals. However, confronted with heavy pressures from the Chinese warlords of nearby Shansi and Suiyan Provinces and conforming to the influences of long-standing feudalistic regionalism, some princes and nobles began to turn away from the movement. At this time, the Ninth Panchen Erdeni was residing at the monastery of Batu-kha'alagh-yin Süme (Chs. Pai-ling-miao) in Darhan Banner, Ulanchab League, which was also a center of the Autonomous Movement. Conservative nobles gathered there continually to visit the Tibetan masters for prayers and counsel. Because the Ninth Panchen Erdeni was himself very sympathetic to Prince Demchügdüngrüb and his Autonomous Movement, the Panchen Lama's answers to doubts regarding the movement were encouraging, leading most of the nobles who lacked confidence to support the movement.[7]

The Sixth Jangjia Khutughtu was then at the Buddhist center of Wu-tai-shan in Shansi Province, where he was persuaded by Yen Hsi-shan, leading warlord of the Shansi-suiyuan faction, to express openly his opposition to Mongolian autonomy. Just prior to this, the Jangjia Khutughtu had been appointed *Meng Chi-hsüan-hua-shih* (蒙旗宣化使) "Propagation Emissary to the Mongolian Banners," by the National Government in Nanking, with the hope that through his "propagation" the problem of the Mongolian Autonomous Movement would be resolved. The Sixth Jangjia arrived in Peiping (Peking) from which he planned to travel to Inner Mongolia and carry out his mission of subverting the Autonomous Movement. On his arrival in Peiping, however, the Mongolian students studying there unexpectedly published in the local newspapers a declaration opposing religious interference in Mongolian politics by a Tibetan ecclesiastical politician, i.e., the Jangjia Khutughtu. The students threatened bodily harm to the lama and demanded that he return to Wu-tai-shan immediately.[8] Under this threat of death, the Sixth Jangjia quietly returned to Wu-tai-shan.

This was the first overtly anti-Buddhist Movement in Inner Mongolian history. Needless to say, it was criticized by the conservatives. Nevertheless, it saved the Autonomous Movement from possible destruction through religious interference. The Ninth Panchen Lama's support of Mongolian autonomy was secret, but the Sixth Jangjia's opposition to Mongolian self-rule was an open failure. As a result, most young intellectuals became even more determined to stand against the traditional religion in order to maintain the existence of the nation. In this crisis, many conservative leaders understood the very real problem facing the Mongol nation, but their personal faith prevented them from participating in the movement against Lamaist Buddhism.

In 1937, the Second Sino-Japanese War (1937–45) broke out and western Inner Mongolia came under Japanese occupation. However, because of the struggle for autonomy, Mongolian national consciousness was much stronger in the west than in the Mongolian areas of "Manchukuo." Therefore, in order to prevent opposition from the Mongols, the Japanese army interfered less in the internal affairs and administration in western Mongolia than they had in eastern Inner Mongolia. Nevertheless, the Japanese military prepared various "lama policies." One objective was to "Japanize" the Tibetan Buddhism of Inner Mongolia in order to gain further psychological control over the Mongols.[9] The Koyasan Monastery (高野山) near Osaka, headquarters of the Shingon Sect (真言宗) of esoteric Japanese Buddhism, became the reeducation center for Mongol lamas, the hope being that this Japanese center would become the "holy land," replacing the Tibetan monasteries. This kind of religious infiltration or manipulation caused Mongolian devotees great concern, for it faced them with what they saw as a sort of religious imperialism.

This period was a major turning point in modern Inner Mongolian history. The Mongols had to struggle for their national existence against threats from the outside, and internally they had to quicken the modernization process and improve their livelihood. Among the many critical political demands, they saw that high priority had to be given to the task of breaking the deadlock posed by the traditional religion. Though conservative leaders recognized the necessity of changing their religious institutions, they dared not advocate changes for fear of jeopardizing their religious faith or future life.[10] Younger radical leaders felt, however, that the salvation of the Mongolian nation lay in the eradication or extreme modification of Lamaist Buddhism. Differences over political policy between the two schools of thought created considerable difficulties.

According to statistical data gathered by the author during his term as an official in the Shilin-ghol League office in 1943, there were 10,930 lamas in a total population of 52,706 (21 percent of the total population).[11] These statistics need no further comment as to their harmful effects upon population growth, the economy, and the existence of the nation itself. This internal crisis and the infiltration of Japanese Buddhism from the outside eventually forced leaders of the two western Inner Mongolian camps to forge a mutually-acceptable policy. Much of this policy was a reformation. However, the term "purification" was generally preferred because of the sensitivities of believers who composed the vast majority of the population. The main points of the new policy were:

1. The Buddhist doctrine of the Yellow Religion is correct, holy, and should be respected. But it must be purified to redevelop the pure truth of its original holy teachings. Impure elements from outside should not be allowed. This was meant to hinder the introduction of Japanese influences.

2. The monastery and temple system, because of defects present, should be regulated according to the *bainin yosun*, or rule of discipline.

3. Lamas should be experts in Buddhist scripture and their competence be demonstrated by examination. All lamas from eighteen to fifty years of age must take the examination. Those who fail will return to secular life. This examination should be given each year to all lamas who turn eighteen. The examination should be regulated by banner and league officials in cooperation with the ecclesiastical officials of the monastery.

4. Lamas who are the only male family member or the only son must return to lay life in order to maintain the family line.

5. Henceforth, if there are three sons, one may become a monk. If there are more sons, not more than half may become monks.

6. The competence of the lamas must be heightened, i.e., they must learn both Mongolian and Tibetan. Mongolian literature is an important item on the examination.[12]

7. Lamas should participate in productive activities and in each monastery a training quarter and a small factory should be set up. Lamas under eighteen years must be involved in the training.[13]

In Shilin-ghol League from 1942 to 1944 more than fifteen hundred lamas, 14 percent of the total, were returned to secular life. This moderate reformation policy, though not as effective in reducing the number of lamas as the general conscription law carried out in the Mongolian district of *Manchukuo*, was the only Buddhist reformation in Inner Mongolian history that was internally motivated and formulated without outside interference. It is clear that the dominant position of Buddhism within the Mongol society had already weakened it, for otherwise the reforms would not have been possible.

Staff officers of the Japanese occupying forces felt that this religious reformation would anger the Mongolian people and somehow weaken Japanese control. Therefore, the Japanese contacted religious leaders individually and attempted to implement a "Lama Policy" of their own. In opposition to this scheme, conservative Mongolian leaders under Demchügdüngrüb decided to establish, in accordance with the old Manchu-Ch'ing regulations, a *Lama Tamagha* (Lamaist Affairs Office) to bring together Lamaist leaders, including pro-Japanese lamas, and organize them into a single unit under the supervision of Prince Demchügdüngrüb himself. This resulted in a behind-the-scenes struggle against Japanese measures, which was carried out under the pretext of restoring traditional Tibetan Buddhist doctrines and discipline on the precedent of the old regulations of the Manchu-Ch'ing Dynasty. Though the Japanese military authorities in Inner Mongolia were displeased, they could find no pretext to stop the Mongols from reforming their own religion, since it was in the name of restoration and purification.

Postscript

With the end of the Second World War in 1945, the Soviet Red Army and the Mongolian Revolutionary Army entered Inner Mongolia. This occupation ended the long era of Tibetan Buddhism in Mongolia. Soon the whole of Inner Mongolia came under the control of the Chinese Cummunists and all religious activities were abolished or fundamentally altered. At first, the Chinese Communists organized a religious unit to manipulate all lamas and believers. But after the Cultural Revolution in the 1960s, all lamas disappeared and the monasteries were either closed or used for other purposes. Religious music, activities, prayers and ceremonies, that had long been a part of the people's lives became no more than a matter of history.

On the other side of the Gobi in the Mongolian People's Republic, after undergoing drastic changes for several decades, religious activities began again on a very small scale in the 1940s. The famous monastery of old Urga (Ulan Bator), Gandan Keid, the old center of Buddhist faith in Mongolia, was opened to the people for worship and a few lamas were allowed to perform religious ceremonies. Even an institute of Buddhism has now been opened in Ulan Bator. Buddhism there today, unlike Buddhism in Inner Mongolia, enjoys relative freedom from harassment.

Notes

1. Chen Ch'ung-tsu (陳崇祖). *Wai-Meng chin-shih shih* (外蒙近世史) The History of Modern Outer Mongolia), Peking 1921, reprinted in Taipei, 1965, 10.

2. The entry for the *keng-yin* day of the twelfth month of the first year of Hsüan-t'ung (1909), "Hsüan-t'ung chen-chi (宣統政紀)" of the *chüng-shih-lu* (清實錄).

3. The Eighth Jebtsundamba Khutughtu was reincarnated in Tibet in 1874. He was brought to Urga, Mongolia, and was installed there the same year. At the time of Outer Mongolian independence in 1911, he was enthroned and was given the title of *Boghda*

Khan (the Holy Emperor). In 1915 Outer Mongolia changed its position from independence to autonomy and the president of the Republic of China gave him the title of *Khutughtu Khan*. In 1920, the Urga Government abolished its autonomy under pressure from the Chinese warlord Hsü Shu-cheng. In 1921, the Outer Mongols declared their independence again, and the Eighth Jebtsundamba recovered the old title of *Boghda Khan*. In the same year, the Mongolian People's Revolutionary Party took power. Because the influence of Buddhism was still great, the Eighth Jebtsundamba — although he lost his political power — was still recognized as the nominal head of the state. In 1924 he died, and the Party announced the formal name of Outer Mongolia to be the Mongolian People's Republic. At the same time, it announced that no incarnation of the Jebtsundamba would ever be reinstalled.

4. The author was personally informed about this matter by the late Fifth Kanjurwa Khutughtu and some old lamas at Dolonor.

5. Prince Demchügdüngrüb (1902–66) was also known in Chinese as Te Wang (Prince De).

6. Zenrin kyokai (善隣協会), *Moko taikan* (蒙古大観), Tokyo, 1938, 264.

7. Information is from the author's personal contact with Prince Demchügdüngrüb.

8. At this time the author was studying at Peking University, was one of the members of the Mongolian Students' Association in Peiping, and attended the anti-Jangjia movement.

9. For instance, the learned Japanese monk, Hashimoto Koho, who studied in many Mongolian monasteries was also an active spy of the Japanese army. Major Yukei, the head of Japanese military intelligence office *(tokumu kikan* 特務机関*)* at Jabsar (Te-hua) was a monk, who especially focused on religious matters in Mongolia. As for earlier Japanese concerns with Mongolian religion, see Kokuryukai (黒龍会), *Toa Senkaku shishi kiden* (東亜先覚志士記伝), Tokyo, 1966, 2:266–67.

10. All Mongolian nobles took at least several high lamas as teachers to whom they gave their oath of obedience, and they would never do anything contradictory to their oath. Consequently, they refused to criticize the religion, religious affairs, and especially their personal teachers, such as, the Sixth Jangjia Khutughtu.

11. According to the 1942 statistics of the Shilinghol League Office.

12. The lamas mostly recited only the Tibetan scriptures and neglected the Mongolian edition. Therefore, the young lamas were forced to learn Mongolian.

13. The author as an official of the Shilin-ghol League Government was personally involved with religious reform work for three years.

Chapter 18

Mongolian Nationalism in Response to Great Power Rivalry (1900–1950)

(Originally published in *Studies on Mongolia, Proceedings of the First North American Conference on Mongolian Studies,* Henry G. Schwarz, ed., Center for East Asian Studies, Western Washington University, 1978. Reprinted with permission.)

Nationalism versus Imperialism in Asia

The nineteenth century was a century of imperialism, as well as one of nationalism. The stimulant to nationalism in Asia was largely the intrusion of imperialism, and in the twentieth century the main historical events in Asia stemmed from earlier trends. Mongolia, however, located in inner Asia and rather insulated, was less influenced by the outside. Yet, it was impossible even for Mongolia to resist the great influences of imperialism and nationalism.

Before the Western powers arrived, a consistent theme in East Asian history was the struggle for existence involving competition or cooperation between the nomadic peoples north of the Great Wall and the sedentary, agricultural Chinese to the south. Throughout their long history there were struggles between these two because of the differences in ethnic origins and culture. Therefore, in Chinese history there was always a dichotomy defined as "the civilized Chinese versus the Barbarians." In order to resolve this distinction between the two great peoples, more learned and farsighted Chinese stated that "those barbarians who willingly accept Chinese civilization should be acknowledged as Chinese." However, this phenomenon was due to differences in cultures and not to nationalistic feelings or problems of the nineteenth and twentieth centuries. With the European colonization of Asia, the actors and the plot of the drama began to change. Great pressures from the outside awakened nationalistic feelings among the Asian people. Thus stimulated, Asian people arose and fought foreign intrusions and oppressions. However, peoples inside Asian countries were also set against one another. This phenomenon is a principal factor in Asian politics even today.

Early Manchu-Mongol Relationships

In the seventeenth century the Manchus began to establish the Ch'ing empire. Because of geographical and cultural factors, they were successful in establishing an alliance with the Mongols to fight the agricultural Ming dynasty. Later, at the time of the Manchu-Jeünghar War (1688–1750), the Khalkha and most other Mongol tribes generally supported the Manchu emperor and fought their Jeünghar Mongol brothers. Under pressure from the Jeünghars, the Khalkha princes assembled to discuss a surrender to either the Manchus or to the Russians. This suggests that there was still nothing like the nationalism of today. However, during the above war, when Emperor Chien-lung executed a Mongol prince (1775) contrary to an old tradition which forbade the execution of descendants of Chinggis Khan, the Khalkha Mongols were infuriated and a rebellion broke out. Common blood and traditions could unify the Mongols against common enemies. Such factors were the roots of nationalism, but modern Mongol nationalistic movements go beyond these.

A cardinal dictum in Manchu policy toward the Mongols was to avoid the feeling that the Mongols were dominated by others. The Manchus allowed a quasi-feudalistic autonomy at the local level in Mongolia and gave the Mongols limited privileges of self-rule. Psychologically this satisfied the Mongol demand that Mongolia be ruled by Mongols.

Russian expansion toward the east caused worry in the Manchu court and among the Chinese ministers. In the early stages of Manchu rule, Manchu generals or officials stationed in Mongolia were merely symbols of the suzerainty and power of the emperor. Their duty was to supervise but not to interfere in the internal administration of the Mongol leagues and banners. Later, because of an increasing Russian presence, they began to inject themselves into internal Mongolian administrative affairs, and this was highly offensive to the Mongolian ruling class. Also, because of expanding Russian influence in Mongolia, the Manchus tightened their control over the Mongols. These actions caused some Mongol nobles to suspect that they were no longer the "beloved ones" of the court in Peking, i.e., they were no longer trusted by the emperor. They began to sense discrimination based on ethnic origins. Thus, ethnicity eventually became a foundation stone of nationalism, although it was some time before it reached the ordinary people.

While ruling China for two and a half centuries, the Manchus became more and more Sinicized. To them the Mongols were no longer important allies, but merely a defensive buffer zone for China. The Manchus then began to carry out a policy of settling Han Chinese in Mongol territory. The cultivation of Mongol soil by Chinese settlers angered the cattle raising Mongol people. Hence, they fought against Manchu officials who favored the settlers over themselves. In addition, some selfish Mongol nobles aligned themselves with the Manchus for personal gain. This further provoked the people and deepened their hatred of both the Manchu authorities and their own ruling class. These events created the fertile ground for nationalism in the minds of the Mongol common people.

The Russian and Japanese Expansion and the Mongolian Response

The arrival of European powers by sea stimulated a greater reaction among the Chinese than the intrusions of the Russians by land. For instance, the Opium War (1840–42) ushered Chinese history into an entirely new era. Fear of and hatred toward the West and dissatisfaction with the Manchu court found expression in nationalistic feelings and revolutionary thought among the Chinese people. Ideologies such as democracy and republicanism which came from the West along with the gunboats were condemned as false teachings. Even so, they became more and more popular. These developments took place south of the Great Wall and were not particularly influential in frontier areas such as Mongolia. Yet, it is difficult to say that they had no effect at all.

During the period of Western imperialism, Japan was the only country in Asia able to protect itself, to avoid domination, to modernize, and to become powerful. However, she soon adopted the same imperialistic pattern with which the West had threatened her. The violence and terror practiced by Japan against her Asian neighbors was worse than that of the Western powers. This was a great stimulant to Chinese nationalism. After Japan dominated Korea, she decided her next move would be the domination of "Man-Mo" (満蒙 Japan's standard term for southern Manchuria and eastern Mongolia). This, of course, impacted significantly the Inner Mongolian ruling class. Japan's actions caused the Mongols apprehension but also generated thoughts about their future. The spectacular achievements of Japan's Meiji reformation impressed Prince Gungsangnorbu. In spite of the opposition of conservative Mongols and Manchu officials, he went to Japan to learn about the larger world. His observations made him even more inclined to Japanese contacts and modern thought. He established modern civilian and military schools and dispatched students to study in Japan. He invited teachers from south of the Yangtze river, as well as Japan. New thoughts came with them and unexpectedly served to popularize nationalistic and democratic ideologies in Eastern Inner Mongolia.

One result of Tsarist Russia's eastern expansion was the subjugation of the Buriyad Mongols in the Lake Baikal area. However, in order to win the friendship of the Khalkha Mongols then under Manchu domination, the Russian government reduced their interference among the Buriyad. Later, Buriyad Mongol intellectuals went to the Russian center of Kazan to study. When they returned they brought new thoughts on the nationalism and modernization then developing in Russia. In the year 1901 the Tsar abolished his lenient policies and adopted instead an aggressive policy of Russianization which aroused the resentment of the Buriyad people. This situation provided an incentive for Mongol intellectuals returning from Kazan to spread the seeds of nationalism. Very early it was these Buriyads who introduced a knowledge of Russia and the modern world to the Khalkhas of Outer Mongolia.

When Russia's expansion was checked by the British in the Near East, they concentrated their energies in the Far East, and, therefore, Chinese-Turkistan (Sinkiang) and Mongolia became the first stages in their march. No sooner had Russian expansion toward the East begun than it was confronted with Japan's westward expansion. Conflict between these two powers eventually led to the outbreak of the Russo-Japanese War (1904). Finally, the Russians were compelled to retreat from Port Arthur and the Southern part of Eastern Mongolia and Manchuria. Consequently, the only alternative left to the Russians was expansion into North China via Mongolia.

The three great powers of Northern Asia — the Ch'ing empire of China, Japan, and Tsarist Russia — all met as opponents in Mongolia. In order to strengthen their administration over Mongolia, the Ch'ing settled more Chinese in the country, and the result was increased antagonism from the Mongol people. At the same time, both the Japanese and the Russians were seeking to win the Mongols, and in doing so exploited Mongol nationalism by trying to persuade the Mongols to separate from China and join them. Consequently, both the aggressors (Japan and Russia) and the defenders (the Manchus and Chinese) stimulated the growth of Mongol nationalism. However, nationalism cannot be transplanted from one people to another. It must have its roots among its own people. In the case of Mongolia, nationalism was manipulated by foreign powers in the beginning, but after its growth, it became the distillate of the Mongol spirit. No foreign power could control its growth. No foreign power could cut its Mongol roots.

The Chinese Revolution and Outer Mongolian Independence

The Boxer Rebellion and occupation of Peking by the allied forces in 1900 revealed the weakness and ineptitude of the Ch'ing dynasty. The Chinese revolution against the Manchus in 1911 gave the Mongols an opportunity for self-rule or for independence. However, because Manchu power still existed in Mongolia, the Mongols had no alternative but to seek Russian assistance. Of course, the Russians did not permit such an opportunity to slip through their fingers, and they gave oral promises of assistance. In the winter of 1911, a conference of lay and religious nobility, as well as representatives of the people, was assembled in the name of their religious leader, the Eighth Jebtsundamba, Living Buddha of Urga (now Ulanbator). The conference decided to declare independence from Manchu rule. This was the first great event in Mongolian history arising from nationalism. One reason the Mongols declared independence at this time was because they realized that the end of the Manchu dynasty was near, and they hoped that by proclaiming independence they could prevent a new Chinese government from claiming sovereignty over Mongolia in the future.

The new independent regime of Urga tried to include in its territory all lands occupied by Mongol peoples. However, the Tsarist government had its own plans which were contradictory to Mongolian hopes. Fearing the interference of Japan and other European powers and looking forward to a close future relationship with China, the Russians dared not fully support the Mongol adventure. Thus, Russia asked the Mongols to limit their objectives to the territory of Outer Mongolia. However, the independence movement soon spread to all corners of Mongolia. Inner Mongols supported the movement and became important officials in the new independent Mongol government.

After the establishment of the Chinese Republic (1912), Sun Yat-sen and other leaders realized that with the end of Manchu rule it was no longer necessary to emphasize a national revolution. Rather, unity of the Chinese nation was needed to prevent other nationalities from separating further from China. Therefore, they declared the new republic to be a commonwealth of five nationalities, i.e., the Hans, the Manchus, the Mongols, the Uighurs, and the Tibetans. This no doubt appealed to some Mongols. A more important factor, however, was that Inner Mongolia was close geographically to Peking, and its military power was too weak to resist the new Chinese government. There was no choice but to follow Peking. Also, in order to win the confidence of the Mongols, the Peking government issued a statement protecting the privileges of the old Mongol conservative ruling class. While this superficially settled the Inner Mongolian problem, disappointed leaders of the common people soon set out on a new road toward nationalism.

After the establishment of the republic, the Peking government gave top priority to the Mongolian problem in negotiations with the Russians. At the same time the Russians, in order to maintain the status quo on the frontier, signed a treaty with the Mongols in which the latter paid a high price for Russian protection of their independence from China. Also, in order to protect the privileges that they gained from the Mongols, the Russians, in their negotiations with the Chinese, agreed to recognize Chinese suzerainty over Mongolia as a compromise with Peking. In exchange, the Chinese were to recognize all privileges the Mongols had conceded to the Russians. The Mongols have never forgotten the Russian betrayal, for in reality they were not ruling themselves and their national existence was jeopardized. Naturally this furthered ideas of Mongol nationalism.

The final compromise between the Chinese and the Russians on the Mongol problem was created in a Sino-Russo-Mongol tripartite conference which took place at Khiakta, a border town between Russia and Mongolia (1914–15). The Russians sought to protect their privileges in Mongolia. In effect they joined with the Chinese to force the Mongols to give up their independence and to accept a lower level of "autonomy." This conference cooled the Russian-Mongol relationship. Consequently, the Mongols looked to the Japanese, already an influence in Eastern Mongolia. Thus, the tide of Mongol nationalism began to work against Russian influence in eastern and western Mongolia.

The Pan-Mongolian Movement

Russian defeats in Europe and a lax Chinese policy toward Mongolia warmed the relationship between Peking and Urga during World War I. Also, because of the difficulties in internal politics, a depressed economy, and threats from outside (the Bolsheviks and the Japanese in Siberia), a portion of the old conservative princes began to suggest the abolition of their autonomy and a return to the earlier quasi-feudalistic arrangement of the Manchu period. Of course, this was unacceptable to Mongol nationalists, and Mongol unity began to disintegrate.

Meanwhile, the power of the Peking government was held by an unpopular clique of pro-Japanese warlords. In order to offset criticism among the people, this group tried to use military power to recover Outer Mongolia and reestablish their reputation. This plan was executed by General Hsü Shu-cheng (徐樹錚), commander-in-chief of forces dispatched to Mongolia. Because of his heavy hand on the Mongol leaders and people and his personal insult to the Living Buddha, the Mongols were again provoked. The result was a new opportunity for radical nationalists to influence the government. When a new civil war erupted inside China, the Mongols proclaimed independence from China for a second time.

The Bolshevik Revolution and the collapse of the Tsarist regime provided an opportunity for the Buriyad Mongols of Siberia to seek independence. The intrusion of the Allied expeditionary forces into Siberia gave the Mongols a chance to contact foreign powers other than the Russians. Of these, Japan was the most important. Taking advantage of this opportunity, Buriyad Mongol intellectuals began to espouse a pan-Mongolian movement. They hoped that all Mongols could be united into one organization to fight for national independence. Self-determination, as set forth in the Fourteen Points of Woodrow Wilson, became a main objective. The Buriyad intellectuals' pan-Mongol call was echoed by nationalists in Inner Mongolia, many of whom went to Siberia to attend a conference in 1918. However, this particular nationalistic movement did not last long. The reasons are as follows.

1. The Buriyad Mongols tried to include Outer Mongolia in their organization as one of its several units. However, Outer Mongol leaders saw themselves as the leaders of all Mongolia and rejected the proposals of the Buriyads.

2. The movement was supported by Japanese agents and this caused suspicion among the Outer Mongols. They wanted no involvement with the Japanese.
3. A delegation of the pan-Mongolian organization failed to attend the Paris Peace Conference to work with world leaders for the self-rule of the Mongolian people.

Contacts with other countries of the world were in vain, but the ideology of pan-Mongolianism was not extinguished. It is still a slogan that attracts the attention of all the Mongol people, because cultural Mongolia is larger than political Mongolia. Those people who speak the Mongolian language belong to the Mongol nation, and those areas in which Mongol people live are Mongol lands. It is an emotional, not a legal matter.

The Emergence of the Mongolian People's Republic

While a Chinese Army was still stationed in Urga, a group of young Mongol patriots headed by Sükebator, who hated foreign domination and the old ruling nobles for selfishly betraying the people, secretly established in 1919 an organization to work for independence and democracy. Naturally these young people were influenced both by radical Russians and by their Buriyad compatriots. Sükebator and one of his comrades were secretly appointed emissaries by Jebtsundamba to contact Lenin and seek help. They did not accomplish their mission, but while in Russia they were indoctrinated as revolutionaries in the Communist tradition. Later, however, their group was transformed into the Mongolian People's Revolutionary Party. Lenin agreed to dispatch the Red Army to assist in the "liberation" of the Mongol people from the oppression of the White Russians and Mongol "feudal lords." Consequently, a Buddhist realm was turned into a Communist satellite. Following two interim steps in 1921 and 1924, Outer Mongolia formally adopted the name of the Mongolian People's Republic and became the first satellite of the Soviet Union. Lenin resolved the Russian minority problem in Europe and Central Asia through the clever policy of keeping a communistic core but sugarcoating it with nationalism. He further allowed minority peoples to practice self-rule within the limitations of communism. With the establishment of the Mongolian People's Republic, Russian policy became quite attractive to nationalists in Inner Mongolia. Thus, it became easier for Russian influence to penetrate the southern portion of Mongolia.

The constitution of the Soviet Union allowed member states the freedom to either join or withdraw from the Union. However, control from Moscow soon became more strict than during the Tsarist period, and, consequently, the Buriyad people failed to achieve the independence they hoped would come after the communist revolution. Although the Russian government changed, the expansionist policy of the Tsarist period remained. First, the Russians demanded that Outer Mongolia allow Tannu-Uriyankhai (now Tannu Tuva) "self-determination" and separation from Mongolia. Soon they demanded that these same Mongols, who were to be given "self-determination," be annexed as part of Russian territory. This heightened anti-Russian feeling among the Mongols, and as a result of their objections, many Mongol nationalists were liquidated for being "counter revolutionaries" and "spies" of such foreign countries as China and Japan. During Stalin's era especially, many intellectuals were put to death. Such oppression caused an opposite effect to that desired as Mongol nationalism became even stronger. During the third decade of this century the spirit of Mongolian nationalism was deeply nurtured by the blood of thousands of martyred patriots. It was a period of strong nationalistic feelings against Soviet oppression. Living testimonies to this were the many Mongols who escaped from the Russian sphere to Inner Mongolia while the writer was living there.

The Chinese Kuomintang and the Inner Mongols

When the 1911 Chinese Revolution fell short, Sun Yat-sen advocated another revolutionary stage against the warlords of North China in order to unify the nation. Cooperation between the Kuomintang and Communists was the strategy chosen to accomplish the goal. This new situation provided the radical nationalists of Inner Mongolia an opportunity to make open contact with their Outer Mongolian compatriots. Some of them, with the cooperation and help of Canton, Urga, and Moscow started a revolutionary party (1924) which was known in Chinese as the Inner Mongolian Kuomintang. However, its real name in Mongolian was The Inner Mongolian People's Revolutionary Party. The existence of this party was made possible only by the united-front of the Kuomintang and the Comintern. Because the leaders of the party were quite radical, they overemphasized the need for internal social revolution instead of uniting against foreign domination. This eventually resulted in a struggle between the leftist and conservative wings of the nationalist movement. Therefore, it became impossible for nationalists to carry on activities in Inner Mongolia. On the other hand, because of the split in China between the Kuomintang and the Communists (1927) and the purge of Mongolian nationalists, such as Dambadorji in Urga, it became impossible for an Inner Mongolian nationalist movement to survive to the north or the south of the Gobi. Finally, the Inner Mongolian party disbanded, but their ideologies, including nationalism, democracy, communism, and the Three People's Principles of Sun Yat-sen, were by no means exterminated in Inner Mongolia.

During the Northern Expedition (1926–28), the leaders of the Kuomintang made attractive propaganda from Sun Yat-sen's doctrines which sought to help the weak and small minorities in China to practice self-determination and self-government. This attracted the officials and intellectuals of Inner Mongolia who had been oppressed by warlords for years. They hoped that under the new government it might be possible for them to enjoy a high level of autonomy. Consequently, Mongol leaders sent a delegation to Nanking (1928) to petition that Sun Yat-sen's doctrines be put into practice. However, while the Northern Expedition was successful, many of the old local warlords remained in power and only outwardly cooperated with the new revolutionary regime in Nanking. Consequently, new reform policies were blocked by them, especially in the remote provinces and border areas. The demands for a greater degree of self-government among the Mongol people were neglected by the Central Government. As the warlords of northeast and northwest China became even more powerful, their old policies of exploiting the Mongol people continued. Politically the warlords damaged the integrity of the Mongolian league and banner units, and they turned the Mongolian pasture lands into Chinese farms by force of arms. By the early 1930s, Mongolian intellectuals had more education, experience, and opportunities to speak out. Their voices became more influential in Mongol society. Distressed by poor conditions under the warlords, they were attracted to a new conservative leader, Prince Demchüghdöngrüb. They supported him as their leader and raised the Mongol nationalist movement to its most important level in modern Mongolia.

Japanese Aggression and the Inner Mongolian Autonomous Movement

After the Manchurian Incident (1931), the Japanese army, in order to win the sympathy of the Mongol people and facilitate control of the land which they occupied, allowed the Mongols under a puppet regime to practice a certain degree of self-government. They were also allowed to organize a special district under the central administration of "Manchukuo." This "autonomy" or "self-government" did not mean that the Mongols were exempted from the domination of the Japanese. Rather, the new arrangement made a clear distinction between the Mongol territories and those of the Chinese. It halted the old struggles between the peoples, and released the Mongols from the exploitation of warlord days. Of course, in the long run, it was hoped that a liberal policy toward eastern Inner Mongolia might help the Japanese carry forth their campaign against China, enable them to occupy other parts of Mongolia, and counter the propaganda of the Soviet Union. With Japan's expansion, the situation in western Inner Mongolia became more strained. It was evidently impossible for the Chinese government to protect the Mongols from the aggression of the Japanese army. On the other hand, Japanese agents began to deal directly and separately with the old ruling princes of Inner Mongolia, trying to draw them to the Japanese side.

In the autumn of 1933, Prince Demchügdüngrüb and his conservative followers joined with the more radical nationalists and promoted a conference for Mongol autonomy at Bat-khaalagh *süme* (Pai-ling-miao). This movement, supported by all the leaders of Inner Mongolia, decided to petition the National Government in Nanking demanding a high level of autonomy for the Mongols. Of course, the problem was too complex and controversial for the Mongols and the Chinese government to settle easily. Discovering that Chinese opinion as expressed in the newspapers was inclined to be sympathetic to the autonomous movement, Japanese papers began to show great sympathy and concern for the Mongols. Consequently, Chinese opinion cooled and began to move away from supporting the movement. Thus, the Japanese posed as supporters of Mongolian nationalism, thereby turning the Mongolian request for autonomy into a beachhead for the Japanese invasion of China. The reasons why the Japanese adopted this course of action may be analyzed as follows.

1. Japan wanted to become a sponsor of the Mongolian nationalist movement which they felt could be molded to their goals and used by them.

2. They hoped to break the relationship between the National Government and the Mongols.

3. The autonomous movement attracted the intellectuals of eastern Mongolia, already under Japanese domination. Unless the Japanese could bolster the hopes of these Mongols, they would loose their support. Thus, a Japanese failure in western Mongolia could lead to serious problems in Manchuria.

4. Japanese activity in Mongolia was quite important to Japan's psychological warfare against the Soviet Union.

5. It was a good policy for winning the friendship of the Outer Mongolian people, thus making possible future expansion, as well as diminishing the Russian sphere of influence.

The Mongol nationalist movement finally bore fruit in the spring of 1934 when the Nanking Government agreed to allow the Mongols to establish an Autonomous Political Council under the sovereignty and supervision of the central government. However, by this time it was becoming difficult for the Chinese army to resist Japanese expansion to the west along the north side of the Great Wall. Therefore, the local warlords persuaded the central government to divide the unified and autonomous Mongolian organization, thereby weakening it. Thus, they helped push Mongol nationalistic groups which were not originally pro-Japanese into Japan's fold. Simultaneously, a climax in the anti-Russian movement was reached in Outer Mongolia. Due to the success of Japan's policy in Inner Mongolia, some Outer Mongolian leaders tried to establish an alliance with the Japanese to counter-balance the Russians. However, the whole effort ended in purges and tragedy.

Mongolian Nationalism against Japan

Immediately following the outbreak of the Sino-Japanese War on 7 July 1937, North China was easily overrun by the Japanese. Seizing this opportunity, the Mongols, who had been allied with the Japanese, tried to establish an independent government or an autonomous regime of their own. However, in the new order, to balance the Chinese and the Mongols, the Japanese military forced the Mongols to accept the merger of two purely Chinese regimes into their regime. Thus was established the so-called "Meng-chiang" (Mongolian Territory) regime. Their aims were: 1) to continue to sponsor a Mongolian government in order to show their goodwill toward the Outer Mongols; and 2) to dissolve the nationalistic idealism of the Mongols in western Inner Mongolia by providing a Chinese counterbalance, thus facilitating Japanese control over the Mongols. However, this policy met with failure, because the Japanese lost the confidence of the Mongols when the latter became disillusioned by the broken promises and treachery of the Japanese military.

The earlier pro-Japanese stance of the Mongols stemmed from their nationalism, and paradoxically the development of an anti-Japanese spirit came from the same source. Open Mongol defiance under the pressures of the Japanese was yet another manifestation of nationalism. The Japanese treated Mongols in the area of "Manchukou" quite heavy-handedly, and there were a number of executions. In contrast, the Japanese had to compromise with the Mongols in the so-called Mengchiang area, because this region was intended to be a showcase to impress Mongols under both Soviet and Chinese domination.

During the Sino-Japanese war, sovereignty over Mongol areas was very complicated. The National Government in Chungking, "the false regime" of Wang Ching-wei in Nanking, and the Japanese puppet regime occupying Manchuria, all claimed rights to Mongolia. The "Mengchiang" regime was the center of much attention. The Chinese government at Chungking could not control this area at all. The claims of the "puppet government" in Nanking were supported by a powerful faction in the Japanese army.

However, all these claims, whether Chinese or Japanese, were rejected by the Mongols because of the strength of their nationalism.

The Western section of Inner Mongolia was not occupied by the Japanese, but remained under the domination of the old Chinese warlords. The Mongols here were not greatly influenced by Japanese expansion, but they were influenced by a newly established force to the south, i.e., the Yenan Soviet of the Chinese Communists. Concurrently, in this area of the Ordos, a conflict occurred over Chinese cultivation of Mongolian soil, a conflict which finally resulted in combat between the Mongols and the Chinese Nationalist army. This provided opportunity for the Chinese Communists to exploit Mongolian nationalistic feelings in an effort to win them to their side.

When the Chinese Communists were still in Kiangsi, they stated that the minority nationalities of China, such as Mongols and Tibetans, would have the freedom either to unite with the Chinese or to separate from them. After the Chinese Communist Party established a base in the northern part of Shensi province, they began to recruit and train Mongol cadres. The Communists pressed their movement among all the different nationalities but especially among the Mongols. The Mongol nationalists had decided that if it seemed beneficial to the founding of a Mongol nation, they would not be too critical of the competing ideologies. Instead, they would be pragmatic rather than dogmatic. Thus, they were easily swayed by competing political forces, and by the propaganda of the Russian, Chinese, and Outer Mongolian Communists.

In 1939 a minor war broke out between the Japanese and the Russians along the border of Outer Mongolia and Eastern Inner Mongolia. Both sides mobilized their Mongol troops for battle. But, because of the success of Outer Mongolia's propaganda campaign utilizing common nationalistic feelings, the Mongol troops of "Manchukuo" rejected the expansionist fight against their brothers on the enemy side. As a consequence, the Japanese faced large losses militarily, as well as in prestige. Interestingly, the Japanese later transported these same Mongol troops to the vicinity of the Great Wall to fight against Chinese Communist forces, and there they won victories. This case and others indicate the strength of Mongolian nationalist sentiment during the war period. It is not difficult to imagine why both the Russian and Chinese Communists tried to win these people for themselves.

The Yalta Agreement and Its Impact on Mongolia

At the end of the Second World War the unification of Inner and Outer Mongolia became an idealistic dream of the Inner Mongolian people. The Yalta Agreement (1945) provided for the recognition of the independence of Outer Mongolia through a plebiscite. However, the fate of the people in Inner Mongolia was not nearly so fortunate. Their dreams were dashed. When the war ended (1945) much of Inner Mongolia was occupied by combined Russian and Outer Mongolian forces. Some Inner Mongolian leaders, encouraged by the Russians and Outer Mongols, established two temporary political regimes in a transitory attempt at self-government. However, because of the Soviet policy toward the Chinese Communists these regimes finally came under the domination of the Chinese Communists. Civil war in China soon broke out and the power of the Kuomintang government reached Inner Mongolia. However, they did not solve the Mongol problem. The nationalistic feeling of the Mongols were ignored, and Inner

Mongolia again fell into the hands of the same old warlords, who now bore new position titles given them by the Chinese central government. The Chinese Communist propaganda proclaimed that the rights which were refused the Mongols by the Kuomintang would be allowed by the Chinese Communists. Thus, they won the more radical Mongol nationalists to their side. In order to increase the effectiveness of their propaganda against the Kuomintang, the Communists condemned chauvinistic "Great Han nationalism." Also, the Communists and their supporters stated that all minority nationalities in China should enjoy the right of regional autonomy. With this slogan, it was quite easy for the Communists to draw many non-Chinese nationalities, including the Mongols, from the side of Kuomintang to their own.

The Last Inner Mongolian Autonomous Movement

During the long civil war between the Kuomintang and the Communists, there was a group of Mongol nationalists who discovered that the slogans of the Chinese Communists were false, and that the Communists would never allow true nationalism. They hoped that the Kuomintang government would grant them real self-determination and self-rule. Encouraged by the nationalistic feeling and dedication of those around him, Prince Demchügdüngrüb personally petitioned Chiang Kai-shek in Chungking (1945) for an acknowledgment of Mongol rights. He hoped that Mongolia could become a member of a Greater Chinese Confederation or a member of a Chinese Commonwealth. Chinese leaders, however, evaded the issue or failed to give a positive answer, and consequently many Mongol nationalists were attracted to the Communists. Even so, there were still large numbers who continued their struggle against communism. Finally, a remnant of Mongol nationalists held a conference at Alashan in Western Inner Mongolia (1949). They established an autonomous government, but no sooner had they accomplished this than the whole of the Chinese mainland was occupied by the Communists, and this autonomous Mongol regime fell with the rest. This was the last attempt of prominent Inner Mongolian nationalists to establish self-determination in their homeland.

Inner Mongolia Under the Chinese Communists

After the new Communist regime was established in Peking, their constitution proclaimed that China was a great family, that all nationalities were members of this family, and that a family can never be allowed to separate. They conveniently forgot their earlier liberal promises in Kiangsi to the minority nationalities. However, in order to appease the Mongols, to deal with the force of nationalism, and to follow the doctrine of Leninism, they established an Inner Mongolian Autonomous Region under the leadership of a Sinicized Mongol, Ulanfu. On one hand, they condemned chauvinistic "Great-Han nationalism," and on the other they condemned "local nationalism." The latter they used as a pretext to liquidate Mongol nationalists. However, blood is thicker than water. Although Ulanfu was carefully controlled by the Chinese Communist Party and in spite of the fact that he was very Sinicized, he still tried to protect the special position of Inner Mongolia. He sought to maintain the existence of the Inner Mongolian people and their cultural traditions, and he also tried to establish a closer relationship between them and the Outer Mongols.

After the death of Stalin, Russian pressure on Outer Mongolia was markedly relaxed. Yet, even though Stalin was condemned by the Russians, the Mongols still insisted that his statue remain in the plaza of Ulanbator. It was a reminder of the past and demonstrated that Mongolia was an independent country outside Russian rule. Also, in order to arouse their people, some intellectuals recently planned a great celebration for the eight hundredth birthday of Chinggis Khan, intending to reestablish him as a symbol for the Mongol people. This was not allowed by Kremlin leaders, of course, but it was a most striking testimony to the continuing strength of Mongol nationalism. After the split between the Soviet Union and the Chinese Communists, all relations between Inner and Outer Mongolia were cut off. The Chinese still tried to win the Outer Mongols to their side, but because Mao Tse-tung claimed Outer Mongolia as Chinese territory, the leaders in Ulanbator dared not draw too near to Peking.

At the time of the Great Proletarian Cultural Revolution and the concurrent power struggle, Ulanfu and his comrades were all purged. During this period Ulanfu and other Mongol nationalists tried to utilize Mongolian nationalism as a weapon to fight Mao Tse-tung. They even advocated "Mongolia for the Mongols," but were suppressed by the Chinese People's Liberation Army and lost their political power. This movement caused heavy damage in the Inner Mongolian Autonomous Region and the names of the leaders of the region all became Chinese. Mongol names no longer appeared. Mongol territories were cut to pieces, since areas in the eastern and the western part of Mongolia were severed from the main body of the so-called Inner Mongolian Autonomous Region. A great number of Chinese were forced to settle in Mongolia and the Mongols, even in their homeland, have become a minority. (This paper was prepared in 1978 and today the Inner Mongolian Autonomous Region has been restored to its original size).

Chinese Communists still outwardly condemn the "Great Han nationalism" but are actually assimilating the Mongols. This is the greatest threat that the Mongol people have ever faced. Yet, their nationalistic feelings are certain to resist this great oppression. The Soviet Union, in order to limit the Chinese Communists and win minority nationalities to their side, unceasingly broadcast propaganda that Mao and his colleagues were "chauvinistic oppressors of the minorities." They often pointed to events occurring in Inner Mongolia, in Sinkiang, and even in Tibet which were embarrassing to the Chinese. On the other hand, the Chinese Communists condemned the Russians for "colonizing Outer Mongolia." Thus, both sides were and are trying to win these non-Russian and non-Chinese minority peoples to their respective sides. Of course, in the midst of this struggle Mongol nationalism is one of the most important facts in deciding the Mongol future. As previously mentioned, nationalism was stirred by outside influences, and once established it became the living spirit of the nation. Now, unless the people die out, it will never be extinguished by a foreign power. The existence of these nationalistic feelings will prolong the life of the Mongol nation and is raising it to great heights in Outer Mongolia. From now on, no matter what may happen in Asia, the nationalistic movement of the Mongol people will still be an important issue to be resolved among the northern Asian peoples.

Chapter 19

Discrimination Against Minorities in China

(Originally published in *Case Studies on Human Rights and Fundamental Freedoms, A World Survey*, for the Foundation for the Study of Plural Societies, by Martinus Nijhoff, The Hague, 1976, 391–403)

Whether China is a country of different, equal, and freely allied peoples or a state of a powerful nationality dominant over the others is a question with different answers depending on the interpreter.

The critical role of minority peoples in China may be seen in the fact that Peking has recognized publicly that minority peoples occupy about three-fifths of the present territory of the People's Republic of China, even though minorities number only about 6 percent of the total population. Historical China is quite different from the China of the present day, and its historic traditions are changing. Nevertheless, China is still China, and its traditions are unceasingly influencing present circumstances. Historically, China or the "Middle Kingdom" was a state where "All under heaven is the realm of our king, and all inhabitants are his subjects."[1] In other words, the "Middle Kingdom" was the center of the world, the domain of the "Son of Heaven," and all the peoples on earth were vassals of the Son of Heaven. Accordingly, the world order, as viewed by the Chinese, centered in the Middle Kingdom. All peoples were not equal in status but subordinate to their superior, the Middle Kingdom, according to Chinese ideology. Various peoples under the direct rule of the Son of Heaven, after a long process of intermingling or amalgamation, gradually became one nationality. They adopted the name *Hsia* (夏), meaning "great or magnificent." They also called their state *Hua* (華), meaning "glorious" or "beautiful." Finally a combination of these two words, *Hua-hsia*, gave rise to another name for the "Middle Kingdom." The term *Hua-hsia* has the implication that peoples outside the Middle Kingdom are "*Yi-ti* (夷狄)," uncivilized, animal-like barbarians, or foreigners. Consequently, the strict differences between *Hua-hsia* (Chinese) and *Yi-ti* (non-Chinese) became one of the most important political/cultural slogans used by Confucius (551–479 B.C.), his contemporaries, and his followers. Later, after the great and powerful Han dynasty (206 B.C.–220 A.D.) was established, the word *Han* (漢) together with the old term *Hua-hsia* became formal names of the Chinese as a people and of the Middle Kingdom as a country.

Chinese and "Barbarians"

The Chinese generally spoke of the alien peoples on its four borders as Eastern *Yi* (夷), Southern *Man* (蠻), Western *Ch'iang* (羌), and Northern *Ti* (狄). The character *man* is a basic character showing a group of worms, and the character *ti* is a dog beside the fire. These characters themselves are proof of Chinese condescension toward and discrimination against other peoples. According to the official history of the Han dynasty:

The barbarians were covetous for gain — human faced but animal hearted. . . . As for clothing, food, and language, the barbarians are entirely different from the people of the Middle Kingdom. They live in the cold wilderness of the far north. They wander to find grazing fields for their flocks and hunt game to sustain their lives. Mountains, valleys, and the great desert separate them from us. This barrier, which lies between the "interior" is created by Heaven and Earth. Therefore, the sage rulers, considering the alien ones beasts, neither established contact with them nor subjugated them. It would cost a huge sum and we would be deceived if any agreement were established with them. It would involve our troops in vain actions and cause the enemy to fight back, if an invasion were carried out against them. Their land is impossible to cultivate and it is impossible to rule them as subjects. Therefore, they are always to be considered as outsiders, never as citizens. Our administration and teachings have never reached their people. Our Imperial Calendar has never been bestowed upon them. Punish them when they come in and guard against them when they retreat. Receive them when they offer tribute as a sign of admiration for our righteousness. Restrain them continually and make it appear that all blame is on their side. This is the proper policy of the sage rulers toward the barbarians.[2]

This was the policy of the Han court toward the northern non-Chinese nomadic peoples, but it may be said generally that this was the foundation of Chinese policy toward all non-Chinese peoples from before the Christian Era to the beginning of the twentieth century. Since this contemptuous attitude could not support the ideology that "All the people on earth are the subjects of our king," and in order to reach the political goal of unification of the *tien-hsia* (天下) or the realm under heaven, a new monistic theory of the origin of non-Chinese people was developed. According to this notion, the ancestors of both the Hsiung-nu (the nomadic peoples) on the north and the ancestors of the Pai-yüeh (百越 the "hundred yüeh" or tribe peoples of Southeast Asia) on the south were the descendants of Yü (禹), founder of the legendary Hsia dynasty (2205–1767 B.C.). This baseless theory provided a rationalization for the rulers of ancient China to carry out a unilateral unification of and domination over neighboring peoples. Moreover, it also became the ideological base for the establishment of the new Republic of China (1912) as a Commonwealth of the "five peoples": Chinese (Han), Manchus, Mongols, Moslems, and Tibetans. Sun Yat-sen (1866–1925) formulated a theory advocating a "Chung-hua (Chinese) Nationality" (Chung-hua min-tsu 中華民族) and this became the official terminology of the Kuomintang Party. Presently the term is also used by the Chinese Communist regime. Historically, whether willing or not, the "Han" Chinese people, centered in the Middle Kingdom, were forced to have relations with the non-Chinese people around them and inevitably obliged to interact with them through both peace and war.

Conquest and Cultural Assimilation

Throughout the history of China there have been five dynasties of conquest[3] and seventeen dynasties of infiltration.[4] Among the five dynasties, the Mongolian Yüan dynasty (1260–1368)[5] and the Manchu-Ch'ing dynasty (1644–1911) not only unified the whole of China but also were two of the last five great dynasties[6] of Chinese history.

The terms "dynasties of conquest" and "dynasties of infiltration" are used only by Western and Japanese scholars, and not by Chinese historians. The traditional Chinese view was that "barbarians" who adapted Chinese ways were recognized as Chinese. Thus, when non-Chinese people occupied a part or all of the territory of the Middle Kingdom and established a Chinese like court, their khans would be recognized as "Sons of Heaven" with the "Mandate of Heaven" bestowed upon them as a natural consequence. The differentiation between Chinese and "barbarians" was not determined by race or origin but rather by cultural distinctions. A non-Chinese people who willingly accepted Chinese culture were considered Chinese and were no longer treated as "barbarians." However, there was another strong tradition running counter to this broad-minded ideology which may be outlined as follows. First, all non-Chinese people who did not establish a Chinese style rule over Chinese people were without exception called *yi-ti* or "barbarians." Secondly, if a non-Chinese people who had established a Chinese-type dynasty were later overthrown, returned to their native land, and resumed their native way of life, they lost their qualification to be associated with the Middle Kingdom and returned to their original status as "barbarians" or "people beyond culture" *(hua-wai-jen 化外人)*. A case in point is the Chin (金) dynasty (1115-1234). After its collapse the people immediately were called *Nüeh-chen*, or Jurchen, again. Later, two groups emerged from among the Jurchen and one, which had assimilated some Chinese ways, was known as "Ripe" *(shu)* Jurchen, while the group which was more remote and resistant to Chinese power was known as the "Raw" *(sheng)* Jurchen.[7] After the collapse of the Yüan dynasty, the Mongols were included in the "Book of Foreign Countries" *(Wai-kuo chuan)* in the *Ming shih*, the official history of the Ming Dynasty. Later they were listed in Ch'ing dynastic records in the "Accounts of the Subordinates" *(Fan-pu 藩部)* together with the Tibetans and Uighurs. Therefore, whether peoples who had established dynasties in China were regarded as Chinese and associated with the Middle Kingdom depended on their role in Chinese history and the stage of development being considered. This naturally involved problems of cooperation, amalgamation or assimilation, prejudice, discrimination, suppression, or liquidation regarding the peoples involved in Chinese history. These factors are continually developing, even at the present time.

Historically and geo-politically the Chinese exhibit patterns in the development of power which moves from the north to the south. The famous Great Wall did not actually achieve its purpose of stopping waves of military incursions by nomadic peoples into China. At the same time the expansion of Chinese power moved from north China into central China and forced unassimilated non-Chinese people in the Yangtze River valley and beyond to retreat or move into the mountainous areas of southwest China and southeast Asia. As long as they did not accept Chinese culture, they were regarded as barbarians or savages by the rulers of the Middle Kingdom and could never obtain an equal position with Chinese citizens. The people of northern China were much stronger than the peoples of south China, so the southerners were usually assimilated by the Chinese and disappeared in the great "human sea" of the Chinese population. Over a period of time they have helped the growth of the Chinese population and richly enhanced the content of Chinese culture. What began as conquest, however, ended in self-annihilation by the northern peoples. In response to this threat and in order to ensure the continued existence of themselves and their culture, the non-Chinese people adopted various sorts of dual systems. All these were usually neglected in the official Chinese histories. Chinese historians have recognized the Sinicized part of cultural mutations as part of the orthodox civilization of the Middle Kingdom, but the non-Chinese elements were overlooked. Consequently before their Sinicization, conquered people all over China were recorded by Chinese historians as *Yi-ti* or uncivilized, uncultured people. Western scholars of Asian studies have been greatly influenced by Chinese materials, and have often simply translated the term *Yi-ti* as "barbarians." The term *Yi-ti* was, in fact, not applied merely to neighboring non-Chinese peoples, but was also broadly applied to all nationalities in the world, with the exception of Chinese.

Reciprocal Prejudice and Discrimination

Historically the prejudice of Chinese against non-Chinese was not one-sided, for actually all non-Chinese dynasties reciprocated with prejudiced and unequal treatment against the Chinese people. All founders of dynasties of conquest titled themselves *kuo-tsu* (國族), the "national race," and their language *kuo-yü* (國語), the "national language," to show that their status was superior to the subordinate Chinese. Consequently, discriminatory treatment was unavoidable. For instance, at the time of the Yüan dynasty, the Mongols divided the people under the Great Khan into four categories according to the cultural differences and the phase in which they were subjugated, i.e., first, *Kuo-tsu*, the Mongols; second, *Se-mu* (色目), central and western Asians and peoples of non-Chinese origin; third, *Han-jen* (漢人), the northern Chinese; and fourth, *Nan-jen* (南人), the southern Chinese. These political positions were hierarchical and entailed certain rights, obligations and differing degrees of privileges. Some Chinese records actually indicated that the Mongols divided their underlings into ten categories: 1) officials, 2) clerks, 3) Buddhist monks, 4) Taoist monks, 5) physicians, 6) artisans, 7) hunters, 8) ordinary people, 9) Confucian scholars, and 10) beggars. An alternative arrangement seems to have been: 1) officials and 2) clerks, with 7) artisans, 8) prostitutes, 9) Confucian scholars, and 10) beggars being placed last. The records on this subject are unreliable.[8] The Mongols raised the position of artisans because economic necessities required their services. This was different from the Chinese who traditionally divided the social strata into four, i.e., 1) officials and literati, 2) farmers, 3) workers, and 4) merchants. Of course, there was great disagreement between the Mongols and their conquered Chinese subjects on the whole matter of social status.

In the courts of pure Chinese dynasties there were also many non-Chinese officials, some of whom reached the highest official circles. This was especially evident during the Former Han (206 B.C.–8 A.D.) and the T'ang (618–907) dynasties, but these were merely individual cases and did not involve cooperation of different nationalities. Later, at the time of the Ming dynasty (1368–1644), many Mongolian officials served at the Chinese court, in spite of the fact that war between the Ming and the Mongols never ceased.

Historically, the dynasties which united present-day China — including Manchuria, Mongolia, Turkistan, and Tibet — under one political administration were the Mongolian Yüan and the Manchu-Ch'ing dynasties, never Chinese dynasties themselves. The question whether the founders of these two dynasties, the Mongols and the Manchus, were Chinese citizens or foreigners brings different answers from the Mongols and Manchus on one side and the Chinese on the other. At the time of the Ch'ing dynasty there were some scholars who demanded an enforced distinction between the *Hua-hsia* (Chinese) and the *Yi-ti* (non-Chinese) based on the old Confucian tradition. Wang Fu-chih's[9] view is one of the best-known examples. He said:

> There are two great distinctions under Heaven — the distinction between *Hua-hsia* and *Yi-ti*, and the distinction between good-hearted men and the wicked. Originally the difference between the two, the root and the branch, the beginning and the end was not clear, but the distinction was emphasized by the early sage-kings in order to separate the two. As for the *Yi-ti*, they live in a different type of land from the *Hua-hsia*, and because of their different environment, their temperament is different. Consequently, differentiations in custom and teachings arise. Since their customs and teachings are different, their entire behavior is different from ours.
>
> As for the *Yi-ti*, if you exterminate them it is not unmerciful. If you plunder them it is not unjust. If you cheat them it is not unrighteous. Why? Because justice and righteousness or a mode of intercourse between men do not apply to a different species.
>
> As for the uncultivated land [of the *Yi-ti*], it should be occupied by civilized peoples, in order to make manifest the virtue of Heaven and to establish imperial rule. However, this is the will of Heaven, and must not be forced by men. Since Heaven wished the cultivation of this land, then the sage leaders will accomplish it. If sage leaders do not undertake the task themselves, then it will be carried out by the rulers with wise and strong men.[10]

Here Wang states quite precisely what is only implicit in the thoughts of other Chinese leaders and people, but which was obvious in both policy and action. These ideas, and many like them, are evidence of Chinese prejudice toward non-Chinese people who were looked upon as uncivilized barbarians or even savages, not to be treated as human beings. Such ideas rationalized Chinese aggression against neighboring, smaller, and less sophisticated nationalities. These ideas are the forerunners of the present day Chinese Chauvinism or "Great Han Chauvinism," of which Chinese leaders are aware and to which they at times refer. These ideas about minority peoples were current during the Manchu-Ch'ing dynasty. The Manchu rulers would ordinarily be regarded as "barbarians," but being seated on the throne of the Son of Heaven in the Middle Kingdom, they were regarded as *Kuo-tsu*, the National race, and no longer as *Yi-ti* (barbarians). Therefore, these derogatory statements about barbarians did not arouse the anger of the Manchu rulers. The Manchus were the last imperial dynasty, and also the last dynasty of conquest in Chinese history. But the Manchus established a Chinese-style court and consciously assimilated Chinese culture. In so doing they also copied traditional Chinese discriminatory patterns toward the people under their rule and looked down upon them as *Yi-ti* (especially to the southwestern nationalities) from their own seemingly superior position as a Sinicized people.

Manchu Policy on Nationality

The cardinal Manchu principle toward subordinate peoples was a kind of national segregation policy, i.e., both Manchus and Mongols were forbidden to intermarry with Chinese, although intermarriage between the Manchus and the Mongols was encouraged. Since the Mongols and Tibetans had the same religion, Lamaistic Buddhism, and since the Manchus themselves favored this religion, intercourse between Mongols and Tibetans was not prohibited. Nevertheless, the Mongols were strictly forbidden to learn Chinese or adopt Chinese customs. This was a political policy designed to separate and facilitate the control of the two peoples. Like the Mongols, the Turkic-Uighur peoples in Chinese Turkistan were also segregated from the Chinese. Their Moslem religious antagonisms were cleverly manipulated by the Manchu court to segregate Mongols and Tibetans from these Turkic peoples with whom they otherwise had many cultural elements in common.

Since the Mongols were allies of the Manchus before the latter occupied China, they did not immediately lose their favored position after the dynasty was established. However, the Manchus did carry out a brutal policy of suppression against disobedient Mongol groups. They exterminated the entire Jeünghar (Dzungar) tribe (1755) and massacred the majority of the Khoshod tribe (1724).

In the early days of the dynasty, as noted above, the Manchus generally forbade the Mongols to have contacts with the Chinese. They did, however, permit Chinese merchants to go to Mongolia to trade. This was a significant change in Chinese policy toward the northern peoples.[11] By the middle of the nineteenth century, as a defence against an increasing Russian threat from the north, the Manchu court decided to allow Chinese immigration and settlement on Mongolian lands. Following the peasant settlers came Manchus and Chinese magistrates to establish a Chinese-style administration in Inner Mongolia. The net result was that power was removed from the hands of the Mongolian officials and good grazing lands were taken from the Mongolian herdsmen. This policy eventually caused the Mongolian people to rise against Manchu rule in the independence movement of Outer Mongolia in 1911.

Manchu policy toward the Moslems in Sinkiang (Chinese Turkistan) and other areas was even more high-handed. Their religious customs were not regarded with favor, and from the time of the Manchu occupation of Chinese Turkistan (1758–60) until after the establishment of the Republic of China (1912), rebellions, uprisings, and bloodshed between the Moslems and the Manchus and the Chinese peoples occurred repeatedly.

The Manchu policy toward the Tibetans was more mild at the beginning of the dynasty, but eventually the power of the Tibetan theocratic government was assumed by the Manchus. Manchu rulers then began to separate the land of Kham from Tibet and made it a part of Szechuan province, known as "Chuanpien." Under the new Chinese Republic, this area was reorganized as the Chinese province of Hsikang. This was the reason the Thirteenth Dalai Lama sought help from the British and declared independence from the Ch'ing (1911).

The Manchus continued the rather repressive measures of early Chinese dynasties toward the southwestern non-Chinese peoples. The policy was one of assimilation by force through "Changing the aboriginal rule into a standard (Chinese) administration" (*Kai-t'u kuei-liu* 改土歸流). There was much bloodshed in this conflict and the policy finally pushed these non-Chinese peoples deeper into the mountain valleys and cut them off from modern civilization.

The Manchus adopted the Confucian doctrine emphasizing filial piety and loyalty toward the Chinese, the most important of their subject peoples. Thus, they carried on the traditional examination system, recruiting Chinese intellectuals into the imperial bureaucracy under non-Chinese rulers. All this they did quite successfully. The Manchus were quite adept in the art of politics. But they did not escape the established historical course, for they were eventually assimilated into the Chinese mass, losing their own system of writing and language, essential elements in maintaining identity as a distinct people. Paradoxically, this Manchu dynasty was supported by its Chinese vassals and by the Chinese masses, and their rule continued until the second decade of this century.

Modern Chinese Nationalism and Minorities

In modern times a Chinese sense of nationalism, like that of other Asian peoples, was stimulated by Western imperialism. As the Chinese people awakened, they came to feel that one reason for their inability to change and meet the threat of the Western powers was the fact that they were ruled by reactionary *Yi-ti*, the Manchu barbarians. Therefore, in a desire for self-salvation, they moved to overthrow Manchu domination. This was a basic factor in the revolution led by Sun Yat-sen and his followers. Their slogan was "expel the Tatar barbarians and recover China."[12] This seemingly revolutionary slogan, however new in appearance, was actually very old. Consequently, this revolution, because of historical and cultural circumstances, was a quite unprogressive, narrow-minded nationalism. After the abdication of the Manchu imperial court whose non-Chinese origins were already being obscured, Chinese revolutionary leaders began to realize that a narrowly conceived nationalist revolution might become a pretext for separatist movements among non-Chinese nationalities long associated with China. Consequently, they revised their slogans and began to issue propaganda for the "establishment of a commonwealth of the five peoples: the Han (Chinese), Manchus, Mongols, Moslems, and Tibetans." The new Government of the Republic formally proclaimed the equality of all nationalities, and especially recognized both Mongolia and Tibet as integral parts of China, no longer subordinate but having rights of self-rule.[13] However, these idealistic declarations did not bear fruit for most non-Chinese peoples. On the contrary, their land was occupied by an increasing stream of Chinese settlers, and political power was usurped by Chinese warlords in the border areas. There was established a special administrative agency for the Mongols and Tibetans known as the Mongolian Tibetan Ministry,[14] but it was only a nominal office without power. Apart from this office there was virtually no way to redress grievances. All important posts were occupied by Chinese officials and there were no offices for minority peoples except a handful of Sinicized Manchus.

Sun Yat-sen and his Kuomintang Party had their own views regarding the nationality and the minority problem in China. In his *San-min-chu-i* (Three People's Principles), Sun Yat-sen pointed out that "the virtue of the people of China (Middle Kingdom) was much superior to that of foreign peoples. Therefore, although the Sung dynasty (960–1276) was ended by Mongols intruding from outside, the latter were eventually assimilated by the Chinese. Following this the Ming dynasty (1368–1644) also was extinguished by aliens. The Manchus at their end were also assimilated by the Chinese."

Consequently, the position of these non-Chinese peoples and their "Chinese citizenship" becomes uncertain. In another instance, in his *Chien-kuo-ta-kang* 建國大綱 Outline of Nation Building), Sun Yat-sen clearly suggested that "the Government must sustain these weak and small nationalities, making it possible for them to achieve self-determination and self-rule." Sun Yat-sen like most great leaders was not entirely consistent. Of these two contradictory statements, the first was evidently traditional while the second was influenced by modern Western political thought. The former view predominated and the oneness of a monolithic Chinese Nation *(Chung-hua min-tsu)* was stressed. Within this, non-Chinese peoples were recognized merely as *tsung-tsu* (宗族) or minor branches of the *Chung-hua min-tsu*. Consequently, the self-determination concept was forgotten as conservative voices dominated in the decades following the revolution. The political position and economic rights of non-Chinese peoples were largely ignored to their detriment, especially by the local warlords and magistrates. In order to maintain their national integrity and very existence, they were forced to contend against direct rule and exploitation by the Chinese or "Han" people's rule. The best known example of a minority nationalist struggle was the Inner Mongolian Autonomous Movement which broke out in 1933. This is concrete evidence of a reaction to discrimination against minorities in China. During the Second Sino-Japanese War (1937–45), a struggle for self-determination took place among the non-Chinese nationalities in Sinkiang (Chinese Turkistan).[15] This was a continuation of struggles against the Chinese rule extending far back in history. It was influenced by the Soviet Union, was a response to the notorious oppression of the Chinese leftist warlord Sheng Shih-tsai, and another case of a minority struggle against "Chinese chauvinism."

In 1947, a new constitution was established by the Republic of China and included several articles resulting from compromises on such things as equality for nationalities, local autonomous rights, and economic claims by minorities.[16] However, this constitution was not ratified because of the military situation in China created by the Chinese Communist movement.

After their occupation of the Chinese Mainland, the Communists established their own constitution (1954) in which they emphasized the unity of all nationalities, or in plain words, the unification of the "great family of nationalities" and the privilege of being a member of the "family."[17] What was conspicuous by its absence was any stress on the right of self-determination, which had been prominent before the Communist regime was established. Peking did, however, establish many autonomous regions, both large and small, for the Mongols, Uighur, Tibetans, Moslems, Chuang, and many other different non-Chinese nationalities. At the same time they proclaimed that "all national autonomous areas are inseparable parts of the People's Republic of China." During the "Great Proletarian Cultural Revolution" (1966–68), most of the leadership of these autonomous regions was assumed by the Chinese. Among all these regions the Inner Mongolian Autonomous Region was the most politically sensitive, and, therefore, many nationalistic leaders were liquidated under the pretext of being narrow nationalists, national separatists, or local nationalists. Finally, two-thirds of the Inner Mongolian territory was divided and absorbed by neighboring Chinese provinces.[18] In addition, the Chinese Communists dispatched great numbers of Chinese immigrants to non-Chinese areas, settling them under duress and making the non-Chinese peoples minorities even in their own homelands. These were all calculated steps for the final assimilation of minorities into the Chinese mass. The Tibetan uprising against the Chinese in 1959 was important evidence of the intense pressure the Chinese Communists brought on the Tibetan people. The Tibetans, like other non-Chinese minorities, felt that they were struggling against Chinese chauvinistic despotism. As for the political strategy of the Chinese Communists toward non-Chinese minorities, in order to reduce their hatred against the Chinese, they emphasize class struggles among the people themselves, and point out that the common enemy of both minorities and Chinese is nothing but exploitation by the old capitalistic ruling class. They stress that if "class" is exterminated, then there will be no more oppression of either Chinese or non-Chinese peoples. However, blood is much thicker than ink, and if Mao Tse-tung and his successors use nationalism as a weapon to fight against his former "big brother," the Soviet Union, then inevitably non-Chinese people will also use nationalism to struggle for their own existence against outside rule by the Chinese. In this process, if the non-Chinese minorities are not assimilated by the Chinese, then it seems quite unlikely that Chinese prejudice or discrimination against them will cease.

Notes

1. Verse Pei-shan (北山) of the Hsiao-ya Section of the *Book of Songs* (詩經), compiled in the later years of Confucius (551–479 B.C.).

2. Han-shu 94 B, "Account of the Hsiung-nu" B, 32ab. The work of the famous historian Pan Ku (A.D. 33–92).

3. The five dynasties of conquest were: 1. Tabghach-Wei (386–557) 2. Kitan-Liao (907–1125) 3. Jurchen-Chin (1115–1234) 4. Mongolian-Yüan (1260–1368) and 5. Manchu-Ch'ing (1644–1911).

4. The era of Chinese history from 304 to 439 A.D. was known as the "Five Barbarians and Sixteen Kingdoms Period." The so-called Five Barbarians were the Hsiung-nu, Hsien-pi, Ti (氐), Ch'iang (羌), and Chieh (羯). Thirteen of the Sixteen Kingdoms were established by these five non-Chinese peoples. These brief non-Chinese dynasties or kingdoms were the Han, Former Chao, Later Chao, Former Yen, Later Yen, Southern Yen, Former Ch'in, Later Ch'in, Western Ch'in, Later Liang, Southern Liang, Northern Liang, and Hsia. In addition there were the Northern Chou (557–81) founded by the Yü-wen Clan of the Hsin-pei people; the Later T'ang (907–36) founded by the Sha-t'ou Turks, the Chin (936–46) and Han (946–51), both of which were also founded by the Sha-t'ou Turks.

5. The Mongolian empire was established by Chinggis Khan in 1206. The Mongols occupied Peking in 1215 and all of North China in 1234. Khubilai Khan ascended the throne in 1260 and unified all of China in 1267. The title "Yüan" was adopted in 1271.

6. T'ang (618–907), Sung (960–1276), Yüan (1260–1368), Ming (1368–1644), and Ch'ing (1644–1911).

7. The terms "ripe" and "raw," "white" and "black" have roughly the same meaning. The latter were usually applied to such southwestern minorities as the White Yi and the Black Yi.

8. See *Ta-yi-lüeh-hsü* (大義略敘) by Cheng Ssu-hsiao (鄭思肖), reprinted in Taipei, under the title of *Tieh-han hsin-shih* (鉄函心史). Khubilai

and other Mongol Khans usually honored learned men and exempted them from corvée duty. Therefore, these records are not reliable.

9. Wang Fu-chih (王夫之) was in his days a famous scholar of the latter seventeenth and early eighteenth centuries (he was also known as Wang Chuan-shan 王船山). His works are frequently quoted even today in the field of political thought.

10. See Wang's work, vols. 3 and 4, *Tu t'ung-ch'ien lun* (讀通鑑論).

11. Chinese traditional policy toward the northern non-Chinese peoples was to embargo exports and was designed to cut off economic supplies. Because of this the nomadic peoples were forced, by their great need for agricultural products, to plunder across the Chinese border.

12. This was the slogan of the Hsing-chung-hui (興中會) established by Sun Yat-sen in 1894. Later his party was reorganized into the T'ung-meng-hui (同盟會), in 1905, and the slogan also changed to: "Repel the Tatar barbarians and establish a republic."

13. *Meng-ku tai-yü tiao-li* (蒙古待遇條例 Regulations for the Treatment of Mongolia) promulgated by the Republican Peking Government, 1912 and 1919.

14. During the Ch'ing dynasty this office was known as the *Li-fan yuan*, or Ministry of Outer Dependencies. After the National Government was established in Nanking, it was reorganized as the Mongolia-Tibetan Affairs Commission. Under Communist rule it is now the Nationalities Affairs Commission *(Min-tsu shih-wu wei-yuan-hui* 民族事務委員會).

15. Fourteen nationalities are counted in Chinese Turkistan: Chinese, Tung-kan (東干 Sinicized Moslems, but different from ordinary Chinese Moslems), Mongols, Manchus, Sibe (a branch of the Manchus), Solon (A Tungusic-Manchu people), Uighur, Kazak, Tatar, Uzbek, Kirgiz (Burut), Tajik (Persian), and Taranchi (meaning agriculturalists).

16. Articles 5, 119, 120, 168 and 169, in the Constitution of the Republic of China, 1947.

17. See Articles 3, 67, 68, 69, 70, 71, 72 in the Constitution of the People's Republic of China. See article 3 particularly.

18. This paper was published in 1975. Now the territory of the Inner Mongolian Autonomous Region has been reestablished as it was.

Chapter 20

The Inner Mongolian Kuomintang of the 1920s[1]

(Originally published in *Proceedings of Conference on Dr. Sun Yat-sen and Modern China*, Taipei, 1986, 3:178–208)

Background of the Era

In 1912 an unprecedented historical change took place in China caused by the impact of Western and democratic thought. The revolutionaries, under the leadership of Dr. Sun Yat-sen, ended a several-thousand-year tradition of monarchism and founded the first republic in Asia. This influenced not only the Middle Kingdom but all Asia. Although the situation in Outer Mongolia will be excluded from discussion in this paper, it should be stressed that the situation of Inner Mongolia became quite unstable toward the latter part of the nineteenth century. It became a crucible of conflicting interests between China, Japan, and Russia. Consequently, the Bolshevik Revolution influenced even the Mongolian herdsmen's steppe lands.

Enlightened Mongol leaders realized that with the changing situation it would be better not to cling to the past but to move forward toward modernization. Conservatives, however, insisted that the only way to maintain social order was to preserve the integrity of traditional institutions. Moreover, there were some who wanted to draw support from foreign powers to counterbalance the internal struggle. Even though the opinions of these groups were different, they were still able to unite to achieve a common goal. When they lacked such a goal, splits reoccurred. These, in brief, were the major forces in Mongolian society during the late Ch'ing and the Republican periods.

The premier leader of the Inner Mongolian reformists was Gungsangnorbu,[2] the Prince of Kharachin. As noted in chapter 16, he was influenced by the success of Japan's Meiji Restoration, as well as by the failure of China's Hundred Days' Reform of 1898, the Boxer Rebellion, China's defeat in 1900, and the humiliation of the Treaty of 1901 which China was forced to sign with Western colonial powers. He believed that the way to rehabilitate Mongolia was modernization and the development of education. He overruled objections, abolished the traditional class discrimination between the nobles and the commoners in his own domain, and established modern schools. He personally visited Japan and invited several teachers to Mongolia. He also sent several students to study in Japan to bring back new knowledge and thereby accelerate Mongolian modernization. On their return these students brought back new knowledge and techniques as Gungsangnorbu had expected, but they also returned with anti-feudalistic and democratic ideas. In short, the policy of Prince Gung enlightened the Inner Mongols to a degree, and a tendency toward change developed which the conservatives could not contain.

The founding of the Republic based on the five races — Han (Chinese), Manchus, Mongols, Moslems, and Tibetans — should have been cause for great celebration among its peoples. However, because of poor communication many Mongols were wrongly informed, believing that this newly-established nation was for the benefit of the Han-Chinese only. Even the Mongolian translation of the formal title of the Republic was misleading.[3] At the beginning of the Republic, the Mongolian problem was discussed by the delegates of both the south (the revolutionaries) and the north (the government in Peking), but they were not able to formulate a complete and satisfactory policy. Thus, Peking not only failed to be responsive to Outer Mongolia, but also created instability in Inner Mongolia.

Pressured by the tense situation of the Outer Mongolian Independence Movement, the Peking government promulgated the Regulations for the Treatment of Mongolia and confirmed that "the original ruling power of the Mongolian princes and nobles should be preserved as is. . . . The succession of hereditary title and ranks will be allowed to continue as usual, and the prerogatives that they enjoy in their banners will be maintained unchanged."[4] This proclamation had no effect on the Outer Mongolian situation. Nevertheless, it eased the anxiety of some Inner Mongolian conservatives, and at the same time blocked the movement of the Inner Mongols toward the democracy promised by the Republic to all its people. Concurrently, Yüan Shih-k'ai[5] reinforced Chinese authority in the three special territories of Jehol, Chakhar, and Suiyüan and encroached upon the Mongolian leagues and banners.

In 1913, in order to win goodwill, Yüan Shih-k'ai appointed Gungsangnorbu to be the General Director of the Mongolian-Tibetan Ministry. In this position, Prince Gung continued his concern for education and devoted his efforts to the founding of the Mongolian-Tibetan Academy in Peking to further the modernization of Mongolia and Tibet. Although this academy had little effect on the Tibetans, it has a great influence on Mongolia, especially in the political sense. In order to realize his plans, Prince Gung assigned several of his former students recently returned from Japan, such as Enkebürin, Altanochir (also known by his Chinese name Chin Yung-ch'ang 金永昌), and others to be teachers in the newly established Mongolian educational center. These young intellectuals used this opportunity to preach democracy. Soon young Mongols studying in other colleges and schools gathered and made the academy their headquarters for Mongolian reformation.

One result was that Gungsangnorbu became a target of conservative Mongol leaders. However, from the point of view of the young liberal Mongols, Prince Gung was still a feudal lord and lacked courage to bring real reforms to Mongolia. In actuality, in the early Republican period he was one of the most enlightened persons in the entirety of Peking officialdom. In the autumn of 1912, when Sun made his first official visit to Peking, Prince Gung was one of his admirers.[6] He joined Sun's Kuomintang and was elected as one of the seven members of the governing committee, together with Huang Hsing, Wang Ch'ung-hui,[7] and others.[8] These events inclined some liberal-minded Inner Mongols toward the Kuomintang.

Later, following the downfall of Yüan Shih-k'ai, civil war broke out, especially in north China, and Inner Mongolia was severely compromised both economically and politically by local warlords. Moreover, some selfish Mongolian regional princes, neglecting the rights and benefits of the common herdsmen, collaborated with shrewd Chinese merchants, greedy officials, and covetous warlords, and betrayed their own people by unlawfully selling public grazing lands for personal gain. This led to the emergence of the so-called Mongolian Bandits (Chs. *Meng-fei*).[9] In addition, the Japanese "concern" for eastern Inner Mongolia, as revealed in the "Twenty-one Demands,"[10] was seen as a threat by Mongolian intellectuals who feared that Mongolia would be the next Korea. These circumstances plus the situation of a students' movement (1919) deeply influenced Mongolian intellectuals in Peking and created a hotbed of anti-feudalism, as well as opposition to warlordism and foreign intervention.

Earlier, in 1917, Sun, alienated from the warlord regime in Peking, founded a rival government in Canton. At this time, a group of Mongolian delegates to the Chinese Parliament, e.g., Altanochir, Pai Jui, and others, because of their sympathy for Sun's policies, joined his party. Soon after, the Kuomintang, under the leadership of Sun and reinforced by the party organization, put forward slogans like "down with imperialism," "eradicate the warlords," "limit capital," and "land for the tillers." Soon the *Three Principles of the People,* the *Outline of Nation Building,* and the "Declaration of the First National Congress" were all publicized. All these attracted the hearts and minds of numerous young Mongolian activists. Of them, Serengdüngrüb, better known by his Chinese name Pai Yün-t'i (白雲梯),[11] and his friends were the most active.

Outer Mongolia, after its independence in 1911 and a period of autonomy (1915–19), abrogation of autonomy (1920–21), and its second independence (1921–24), was transformed into the Mongolian People's Republic. Its foreign support also changed from Tsarist Russia to the Soviet Union. Although its activities were all under the direction of the Third International or the Comintern, its existence as an independent nation was still a great stimulant for its fellow Mongols south of the Gobi. Of course, the princes, nobles, high lamas, and the members of the feudalistic privileged class were shaken by its drastic socialistic changes. However, for the young intellectual activists it seemed to be a way that Inner Mongolia should follow.

At the same time, in a so-called United Front Policy, the Chinese Kuomintang was allied with the Russians and accommodated the communists within the party. This caused some Mongols to feel that the two parties, at least on some issues, had similar views because of the guidance of the Third International. The People's Revolutionary Party of Outer Mongolia also took advantage of this opportunity to accelerate its activities. On one hand, they sent a governmental delegate, B. Dantzen, to Canton to visit with Sun. He was well received by the latter. The welcoming speech of Sun[12] impressed many Mongolian intellectuals who were already inclined toward the Kuomintang party. On the other hand, Outer Mongolia sent Buyannemekü,[13] a well-known writer, as a party representative to Peking to influence the students of the Mongolian-Tibetan Academy. At the same time, Li Ta-Chao,[14] one of the founders of the Chinese Communist Party, personally took the responsibility to develop party work among the Mongol youth. Thus, the Inner Mongolian Kuomintang, the first political party in modern Inner Mongolian history, was organized against this complicated historical background and amidst this environment of conflict.

The Formation of the Inner Mongolian Kuomintang

Before discussing the formation of the party, perhaps it is necessary to provide some background on its important founder, Serengdüngrüb (Pai Yün-t'i). A native of the Kharachin Central Banner, his home was not too far from the banner of Prince Gungsangnorbu. Pai was greatly influenced by the new educational developments and eagerly received modern knowledge. He entered the Mongolian-Tibetan Academy soon after it was established. He became well acquainted with two of his fellow Mongolian students: Merse (also known by his Chinese name Kuo Tao-fu 郭道甫) and Fu Ming-tai (富明泰), both from the Dakhur region of northeastern Inner Mongolia. Also, because of his liberal inclinations, he was encouraged by his revolutionary tutors Enkebürin and Altanochir, became involved in political activities, and finally entered the Chinese Kuomintang in 1919.

At the time of the split between north and south China, Pai was continually traveling between Peking, Shanghai, and Canton to make contacts, and he was early recognized by Sun Yat-sen. In 1920, Sun appointed him a Special Commissioner for Party Affairs in Mongolia and the three Special Regions of Jehol, Chakhar, and Suiyüan. Pai himself firmly believed that the only way to save the Mongol people from greater problems was to espouse Sun's doctrine. In 1924, after attending the First National Congress of the Kuomintang, Pai earnestly preached the ideas of the *Outline of Nation Building*. "The Government should assist the weak and small nationalities in China to be able to carry out self-determination and self-rule." He received an enthusiastic response and won over many young intellectuals to the party. However, at about the same time, his two good friends Merse and Fu Ming-tai went to Ulan-bator and joined the Mongolian People's Revolutionary Party. In 1923 and 1924 they established a Mongolian Youth Party in the Hulun-buir area.

Meanwhile, following mutual recognition between the Republic of China and the Soviet Union and the arrival in Peking of the first Soviet Ambassador, Lev M. Karakhan, there existed a naive and idealized spirit toward the new Russian regime. In addition, the founding of the Mongolian People's Republic on the north of the Gobi had created a psychological change among many young Mongols. Grasping this opportunity, the Chinese Communists began their activities in the Mongolian-Tibetan Academy.

Notwithstanding the Mongol liberals in Peking, Gungsangnorbu was still the leading figure. However, the conservatives, headed by Tawangburjal (Prince of Alashan Banner) and the Jangjia Khutughtu (a leading high lama), blamed Prince Gung for the new ideas he had introduced which had led to so much trouble and unrest in Mongolian society. At the same time, the radical intellectuals constantly pressed him for more progressive reforms. Regardless of problems among the radicals and students of the Mongolian-Tibetan Academy, his educational enthusiasm did not wane. Among the Mongol teachers in the academy, Altanochir was openly active because of his position in the Chinese Parliament. Enkebürin outwardly went about his work as an educator quietly, but in reality encouraged his pupils to organize politically. Merse and Fu Ming-tai frequently came to Peking and actively worked among the Mongol students both inside and outside the academy. Sayinbayar, a radical from Jerim League of eastern Inner Mongolia, opened his house to the Mongolian intellectuals, and gradually it became the center for discussions about the future of Mongolia. Also, Bayantai (Yü Lan-chia, a former student of the Army Academy at the end of the Ch'ing Dynasty), Mandaltu (Li Tan-shan, a former clerk at a Mongolian newspaper in Harbin founded by the Russians in the first decade of the 1900s), and I-Dechin (a graduate from the Japan Military Academy) — all from Gungsangnorbu's banner — and Yao Ching-T'ao (son of Yao Shan, an influential nationalistic leader of Keshighten area of Juu-uda League) became close friends of Pai. About this time, in the early 1920s, Wangdannima and Shini-lama, two leaders of the *dügüileng* movement (a nonviolent peoples' rebellion) from the Yeke-juu League of southwestern Inner Mongolia, took refuge at Yung-ho kung, the great lamasery in Peking. Thus, these various individuals gathered together as comrades who cherished the same ideas of anti-warlordism, anti-feudalism, and a struggle for the rights of the common people.

A group of Mongol members of the Chinese Parliament in Peking went to Canton to join Sun's government, as mentioned earlier. At the same time there were at least two young Mongols, Dügürengsang (Pai Hai-feng) and Wu Yün-chu from Gungsangnorbu's banner, in the Whampoa Military Academy where they probably joined both the Chinese Kuomintang and possibly the Communist Party. This is a brief account of the more politically active members of the Mongolian Society in Peking. They tried to make contacts with the local Mongols, but failed to convince many to accept their new ideas which differed so radically from old Mongolian traditions. This unsuccessful attempt probably prevented the party later established from winning the support of the great majority of their countrymen.

Since Pai Yün-t'i was the most important liaison person and was recognized by Sun, he gradually became the center of the group and the leader in founding the party. The political situation in Peking suddenly changed because of the Kuomintang's alliance with the Soviets and the mutiny of Feng Yü-hsiang[15] against Wu P'ei-fu.[16] Tuan Chi-jui,[17] the leader of Peking officialdom, invited Sun to Peking for consultation on the reunification of China. At this point Pai presented his plan for the formation of an Inner Mongolian party to support the Kuomintang revolution. His proposal was accepted by Sun and the Kuomintang authorities.

The news of the Pai group's activities greatly disturbed Mongolian society in Peking. However, Gungsangnorbu did not try to impede them. In order to win some support from this enlightened feudal prince, Pai went to visit him and asked for assistance. Prince Gung replied that he had done his best to protect the rights of the Mongols but from that time on the matter should be the responsibility of younger generations.[18] Upon hearing these comments from the Prince, Pai was greatly encouraged and realized that there would be no hindrance from this most influential Mongol leader. On the other hand, Sun's health was rapidly deteriorating. In order to grasp the trend of the time, on 1 March 1925 Pai and his group established their party in Kalgan, a city along the Great Wall between Inner Mongolia and China proper, under the aegis of the pro-Russian warlord, Feng Yü-hsiang, and the Comintern.

Those attending the First Congress numbered 125. Sun sent Li Lieh-ch'un and Hsü Ch'ien[19] as representatives of the Chinese Kuomintang. Feng Yü-hsiang was one of the guests of honor. The delegates from the Mongolian People's Republic were Dambadorji,[20] Chairman of the Central Committee of Mongolian People's Revolutionary Party, Gendun,[21] Amur,[22] Nasunbatu, and Buyannemekü. An impressive ceremony was held and the congress elected Pai, Merse, Bayantai, I-Dechin, Sayinbayar, Yao Ching-t'ao, Fu Min-tai, Mandaltu (Li Tan-shan), Altanochir, Wangdannima, Shini-lama, Jiyaatai, Li Yü-chih, and twenty-one other persons as members of the Central Committee. Pai, Merse, Altanochir, Fu Ming-tai, Sayinbayar, Yao Ching-t'ao, and Mandaltu were confirmed as members of the Executive Committee. Pai was Chairman, with Merse as Secretary General, and Altanochir as Director of the Organizational Department.

The above record is based upon conversations between the author and Pai. However, according to some other sources, the conference held in the spring of 1925 was only a preliminary one. According to this interpretation, the first congress was held 27 October 1925 at Kalgan. This source also states that representatives of the Chinese Communist Party, the Comintern, and Feng Yü-hsiang attended the ceremony and delivered congratulatory speeches.[23]

The congress adopted (in Chinese) the party name *Nei Meng-ku Kuomintang* (內蒙古國民黨 the Inner Mongolian Kuomintang). However, its Mongolian name was *Totughadu Mongghol-un arad-un khubisghaltu nam*, meaning the Inner Mongolian People's Revolutionary Party.[24] The difference between the Mongolian and Chinese titles clearly suggests the complicated political background of the new party. It was designed to appeal to both the Chinese and the Mongols and to imply that this new party was an extension of neighboring fraternal organizations. Consequently, it gained support from the Chinese Kuomintang, the Mongolian People's Revolutionary Party, the Comintern, and the Chinese Communist Party. This naturally brought with it some influence or control from the institutions concerned.

Among the leaders of the party, Pai, Yao Ching-t'ao, Altanochir, and others were the members of the Chinese Kuomintang. Merse and Fu Ming-t'ai were from the Mongolian People's Revolutionary Party, and Li Yü-chih (李裕智), a Chinese, was from the Chinese Communist Party. Ochirov, a Buriyad Mongol, was appointed by the Comintern as its representative to serve the party as an advisor. As this list of leaders indicates, pro-Chinese moderates were able to control early party affairs. Even so, the Comintern immediately showed a special concern for the party's activities.

Besides settling the matter of leadership, the Congress resolved to establish an officer training school and an armed force. In addition, it issued a declaration which stressed: 1) We, the Mongols, have been oppressed by imperialists for years, and now the light of national liberation is dawning; 2) We will put down reactionary dark rule; 3) The sufferings of the Mongolian people were caused by the heavy extortion of the feudal princes and the special prerogatives of their class, i.e., they sell public lands for selfish personal gain; and 4) We should do our best to struggle for the equality of Mongolia and the well-being of our people.

The party program established the following points. 1) The goal in founding the Republic of China was to establish a commonwealth for the five peoples — Han-Chinese, Manchus, Mongols, Moslems, and Tibetans. However, only suffering and distress has occurred among the Inner Mongolian people. Therefore, we must eradicate tyrannical warlords. 2) The imperialists — Japan, Great Britain, the United States, and France — have exploited the civil wars between the warlords for personal gain. Japan is building railroads in northeastern Mongolia in order to colonize the territory. We must ally ourselves with the weak and small nationalities to stop it. 3) Since the 1911 Revolution, the aims of the Chinese Kuomintang have consistently been in line with that of our party. We must join in a common effort to overthrow the imperialists, to eradicate the warlords, and to establish a republican commonwealth for the well-being of the five peoples. 4) Feudalistic aristocratic institutions that extort wealth from the people of Inner Mongolia should be overthrown and replaced by self-rule. 5) We must protect the traditional public lands of the Inner Mongolian people and stop princes or feudal lords from selling it at will. 6) Princes, feudal lords, shrewd merchants, and corrupt officials are bitterly detested by the Inner Mongolian people. We must concentrate our strength and seek to benefit our fellow Inner Mongols as we struggle together for the fulfillment of the people's revolution[25] of China. 7) All the nationalities in China should enjoy the right of self-determination in order to overthrow the imperialists and to eradicate the warlords. All our Inner Mongolian people should enjoy the rights of democracy and political freedom and should be treated equally without discrimination based on sex or origin.

In a preliminary policy statement the new party announced certain objectives. They were as follows:

1. Politics: The feudal system should be abolished and power should be handed over to the people. A congress of Inner Mongolian People's Representatives should be established through a system of elections.

2. Economy: All lands controlled by the feudal lords should be handed over to public offices established through elections by the people. Problems over lands in areas settle by both Mongols and Chinese should be solved through negotiations under principles profitable to both sides. Offices established through general elections should assume the responsibility of dealing with land profits and of abolishing exorbitant taxes and levies. The people should have no obligation to pay the debts of the feudal lords who owe merchants either in or out of the country. Domestic industrial and consumption cooperatives should be established to promote the well being of the people.

3. Culture and education: Public primary schools, middle schools, and colleges should be established to carry out compulsory education. The tuition and fees of the children of poor families should be waived. People should enjoy the freedom of religious belief. However, to defraud others of their wealth in the name of religion should be prohibited.[26]

Judging from these proposals, policies of this party were quite moderate and contained virtually no contradictions with the doctrines of the Chinese Kuomintang. The key demand for the abolition of feudalistic institutions did not conflict with the common principle of democracy. However, the new terminology used in these documents was familiar only in the political vocabulary of Outer Mongolia. This demonstrates that these documents were set down by some Outer Mongolian writers or someone quite sophisticated in the socialistic terminology common in Outer Mongolia. They also suggest that from its inception the party was heavily influenced by the Mongolian People's Revolutionary Party of Outer Mongolia. Even so, its party platform was still close to that of the Chinese Kuomintang. Since this was the peak of Sino-Soviet friendship and cooperation, it may be safely assumed that the Third International approved of what was set forth.

The Activities

It has already been mentioned that the founding of this Inner Mongolian political party was guided and supported by both the Chinese Kuomintang and the Comintern with its branches being the Mongolian People's Revolutionary Party and the Chinese Communists. At first, most of its leaders were moderates who tended to lean toward the ideology of the Chinese Kuomintang. However, due to geographical location and political changes in north China, the involvement of the Comintern gradually increased. Consequently, the problem of the party's basic aims became a priority issue — that is, whether to first unify the people, struggle against outside pressures, and strive for Mongolian national survival and equality, or whether to give priority to an internal struggle for social change. In other words, from the beginning, within the party there were conflicting views between nationalistic and socialistic leftist factions.

Pai Yün-t'i indicated that while he was visiting with Gungsangnorbu and seeking support for the founding of the party, the prince warned him that if the Mongols fought among themselves, they would be weakened and handicapped in their struggle against enemies from the outside. Pai also confirmed that when Dambadorji, the nationalist leader of the Mongolian People's Revolutionary Party, was in Kalgan, he too advised that the first priority of the Mongol people must be to maintain internal unity and defend themselves against external enemies. Struggles among the Mongols would be a serious and dangerous development.[27] However, this advice from elder statesmen was not effective enough to help Pai's party decide its basic policy, and it continued to have a foot in two camps. The main obstacles were created by the Comintern, as well as the limitations of the political situation. The most obstinate enemies of Mongol survival were warlords and the covetous officials under them. However, the party was organized under the shadow of the pro-Russian warlord Feng Yü-hsiang who had greatly troubled the Mongolian banners, forcing them to give up their grazing lands to cultivation because of the presence of surplus troops. His actions were as notorious as those of Chang Tso-lin[28] in Manchuria. Nevertheless, the Mongolian party was not only unable to condemn Feng as a warlord and demand his withdrawal, but had to side with him in the unpopular civil war against Chang. Finally, the Mongol troops were defeated together with Feng's forces. Unable to gain any success in the external struggle, they turned their attention inward and tried to make a breakthrough by carrying out a socialistic revolution against feudalism and the old traditions of Mongolia. Here they met stern resistance and a counterattack from the conservatives. Thus, they failed to achieve the unification of the Mongol people or to strengthen their influence over Inner Mongolia.

According to the resolutions of its first congress, the party began to organize military forces, i.e., the Inner Mongolian People's Revolutionary Army (Chs. *Nei-Meng-ku kuo-min Ke-ming-chün* 内蒙古国民革命军), with Pai as Commander-in-Chief and I-Dechin as Chief-of-Staff. Yao Ching-t'ao, assigned to recruit the troops, returned to his birthplace in the Keshingten Banner of Juu-uda League in eastern Inner Mongolia. With the influence of his father, Yao Shan, and the support of Bükejiyaa, the *jasagh*[29] of the banner, he not only recruited many young militants but also brought the Peace Preservation Troops of the Keshingten Banner into the cavalry of the Revolutionary Army. By the end of 1925, Yao and his troops, after joining Feng Yü-hsiang, fought against Chang Tso-lin, defeated his forces, and took over several districts including Linhsi, Chingpeng, and Kailu. They executed the Chinese magistrates and the heads of the Cultivation Bureau, all of whom were bitterly hated by the Mongol people. This act of revenge was cheered not only by the common herders but also by several conservative ruling princes. But not long afterwards the whole army of Feng was compelled to retreat to the northwest. With this setback, the Inner Mongolian Kuomingtang (or the Inner Mongolian People's Revolutionary Party) had to move its general headquarters from

Kalgan to Paotou and then to Ninghsia. Meanwhile, the party's academy for officers located at Keshigten, was forced to move to Paotou and Ninghsia where it trained several hundred cadets. The troops that Yao recruited from his home banner were never able to return. Because of this tragic situation, Yao himself never returned to Keshigten.

While the recruiting of troops was taking place, the Third International sent a Kharachin Mongol, Wu Tzu-ch'eng, disguised as a merchant from Tientsin, to eastern Inner Mongolia with a great sum of money. However, on the way Wu met with bandits, was killed, and the money disappeared. With the loss of this financial support the party was not able to fulfill its plans for this area.[30]

For propaganda purposes, the party published *Mongghol-un arad-un sedgül* (Mongolian People's News). Also, several groups of students were sent to Ulan-bator and to Moscow for further political training. Yün Tse (雲澤 later known as Ulanfu), Yün Jun (Ulanfu's older brother), Dügürengsang (also known as Pai Hai-feng), Öljeiodsor, Jung Chao, and Pai Yün-lung were among them.

When the party's general headquarters moved to Paotou, Wangdannima and Shini-lama returned to their old base in Yeke-juu League, organized their old comrades of the earlier *dügüileng* movement, recruited some radical horsemen, and established an armed force under the name of the Inner Mongolian People's Revolutionary Army. Wangdannima was made the Commander and Li Yü-chih, a Chinese Communist, the deputy. Through the endeavors of the party's general headquarters, they obtained some armaments and supplies from the Third International via Ulan-bator. They also founded an officer's training center with Wang Ping-chang, another Chinese Communist Party member, as its director.

This evidence suggests that of the entire party organization only this group was inclined to the extreme left. This was not due only to the inclinations of their leaders, Wangdannima and Shini-lama. Rather, it was also caused by earlier historical conditions in the Uushin Banner. From the end of the Ch'ing Dynasty, an anti-Han-Chinese, anti-cultivation movement had already occurred in this area. The action was known as *dügüileng*, as will be explained. When the people started the movement, they sat in the form of a circle to indicate that all present should take equal responsibility. The movement was non-violent but stubbornly resisted paying taxes and levies and boycotted all duties until their demands were accepted by the ruling regime.

After the founding of the Republic, Mongolian ruling princes, usually under the pressure of border officials, agreed to open public grazing lands to Chinese cultivation. Consequently, *dügüileng* movements increased. Soon after, due to the heavy oppression from the Ma Fu-hsiang[31] and Ching Yüeh-chiu, the commander of the Chinese army in the areas of Ninghsia and northern Shensi, members of the *dügüileng* movement took violent measures in opposition to the violence of the warlords. They had to struggle both against their own feudal prince, as well as having to fight against armed interference from the outside. When their power could not match that of the enemy's, they usually went underground. Both Wangdannima and Shini-lama were leaders who earlier barely escaped execution by Ma Fu-hsiang. Consequently, after joining the new party, it was easy for them to accept the more militant approach of the leftists. However, their radical tendencies were not welcomed by Pai Yün-t'i and his moderate group. In addition, their drastic actions created resistance from the conservative leaders and dissatisfaction among the great majority of Mongolian people. The blame for these actions was one more problem that plagued Pai and his party.

In Yeke-juu League, under the leadership of Wangdannima and Shini-lama, the party recruited many members and organized them into several party cells. They also retaliated against Tegüsamughulang, the ruling prince of Uushin banner, and forced him to flee to Yülin to join warlord Ching Yüeh-shiu. The revolutionaries took over the banner office and put it under party control. They declared the establishment of democratic rule and undertook some projects to meet the needs of the common herdsmen. However, their approach was too drastic and not only undermined the support of the majority of the people but also caused serious splits in their ranks.

Early in the winter of 1926, Wangdannima died at Paotou amidst rumors that he was poisoned by his opponents. After his death Pai Yün-t'i dispatched Sayinbayar with a contingent of cavalry to the Yeke-juu area to re-establish order, to mediate peace between Shini-lama and the League government, and to check any interference by the troops of Ching Yüeh-hsiu from northern Shensi. However, Sayinbayar's mission was rejected by all sides and resulted in still more violence and bloodshed. This additional failure in Yeke-juu again resulted in strong feelings of aversion toward the Inner Mongolian Kuomintang. By the end of the same year, Li Yü-chih, the deputy commander of Wangdannima's forces, was killed by bandits while he was transporting guns from Paotou to his troops. Again, it was rumored that this was an assassination by the moderate group in the party, and this caused Wang Ping-chang, another Chinese Communist member, to flee Ninghsia where the party general headquarters were then located. Following these events the Inner Mongolian party's connections with the Chinese Communists became somewhat strained.[32]

Meanwhile, the party's relations with the Chinese Kuomintang continued without serious problems. Moreover, through the arrangement made by the Soviet Advisor, Michael Borodin, and Feng Yü-hsiang, their contact became ever more active and concrete. In the middle of March 1929, Pai sent Sayinbayar to Hankow to represent him at the Third Conference of the Central Committee of the Chinese Kuomintang's Second Congress. The committee passed two resolutions regarding Outer and Inner Mongolia.[33] The one on Outer Mongolia states:

1) A mutual exchange of representatives should be made to assist the cooperation of the two parties in China and Mongolia. 2) The national self-determination of Outer Mongolia should be recognized. 3) A branch office of the Chinese Kuomintang should be established in Outer Mongolia to recruit party members there. 4) The terms of mutual assistance between Outer Mongolia and the Northwest (Feng Yü-hsiang) should be settled.

The resolution on Inner Mongolia says:

1) Our party should establish party offices in Inner Mongolia and in the area of the Three Special Districts of Jehol, Chakhar, and Suiyüan. Party affairs of the Inner Mongolian people should be managed by the Inner Mongolian Party Branch and be recognized by the Party Central Committee. 2) The Central Committee should dispatch staff members to guide Inner Mongolian party affairs and political discipline. 3) The Central Committee should issue a statement confirming its intention to assist the Inner Mongolian national liberation

movement. 4) Realizing Inner Mongolia's necessity to establish cavalry forces and propaganda units, funds in the amount of one hundred thousand *yüan* should be delivered by the Central Committee and be allocated in stages over six months.

The resolution on Outer Mongolia was no doubt passed through persuasion by Borodin, and yet the pro-Chinese attitude of some Outer Mongolian leaders should not be overlooked. It is evident that the Chinese Kuomintang handled the Mongolian Party as an extension of its own party in these resolutions on Inner Mongolian affairs. However, the Inner Mongolian Kuomintang had its own unique character, and its affairs should not be confused with Chinese party matters in the Three Special Districts. It was resolved, as noted above, that staff members should be sent from the Kuomintang party headquarters in China to its branch in Inner Mongolia in order to maintain close relationships. Meanwhile, an anti-Communist movement emerged inside the Chinese Kuomintang and a split between the right and left wings was inevitable. Though the resolutions on the Inner Mongolian Kuomintang were passed, they never materialized under the adverse conditions existing in both China and Mongolia.

In early April a Chinese anti-communist movement was set in motion. At a meeting of the Central Supervisory Committee of the Kuomintang held in Shanghai, the Mongolian members in the Executive Committee, Pai-Yün-t'i and Enkebatu, were identified as suspects. Tsuo Lu,[34] under his pen name Hai-pin, in a published article on the matter stated: "The conference held in Hankow under the domination of the Communists agreed 'to preserve the name of Inner Mongolian Kuomingtang' and promised to ally it with our party. The Inner Mongolian Kuomintang in Inner Mongolia is exactly the same as the Outer Mongolian Kuomintang [People's Revolutionary Party] in Outer Mongolia. It is evident that Inner Mongolia would eventually follow the same footsteps of Outer Mongolia and become ostensibly independent, but being in reality an underling of Soviet Russia. The conspiracy is the same."[35]

The Alashan Banner, located west of the Alashan Mountains (Chs. Ho-lan shan) with its capital at Ting-yüan-yin (presently Bayan-nor) occupies an important strategic position in western Inner Mongolia with links to Kokonor, Tibet, and Outer Mongolia. Its ruling prince, Tawangburjal, was one of the key conservative leaders in Mongolian society in Peking. On the other hand, because of its geographical proximity to Outer Mongolia, Alashan was also susceptible to trends and events there. In the winter of 1926, while the headquarters of the party was in Ninghsia, Merse, the Party Secretary General, and Ochirov, a Representative of the Third International, along with others, entered Alashan secretly to propagate the radical doctrines of the Inner Mongolian party. There was then in Alashan a group of discontents headed by a blood relative of Twangburjal, named Dechinyishinorbu. He was in league with T'ien Hsieh-an and Meng Hsiung. They accepted Merse's advice to form a secret organization. In early April 1927, with arms from Feng Yü-hsiang's troops in Ninghsia, they attacked the banner office, occupied it, and killed the top official representing the ruling *jasagh*. They declared the formation of a new revolutionary political office, and established Headquarters for the Second Route unit of the Inner Mongolian People's Revolutionary Army. Dechinyishinorbu made himself head of the office and commander of the army with T'ien Hsieh-an as Chief-of-Staff. They then confiscated the properties of Prince Tawangburjal, promised to establish democratic rule, and abolished the heavy tax system. After several months this revolutionary regime was overthrown by the conservatives of the banner. Later Dechinyishinorbu and Meng Hsiung were killed while T'ien Hsieh-an escaped. In 1931, Ochirov was again sent to Alashan by the Comintern, but this time was caught and killed by Alashan soldiers.[36] This armed revolt and the events in southwest Yeke-juu League shook all Inner Mongolia for a period of time.

On 6 April 1927, Chang Tso-lin sent armed men and police to seize the Soviet Embassy in Peking. They found many secret documents and arrested the well known Chinese Communist Li Ta-chao and others. Meanwhile, anti-communist purges continued in the territories occupied by Chinese Kuomintang forces. With the unfavorable situation, the Third International ordered the Inner Mongolian Kuomintang to move its party headquarters from Ninghsia to Ulan-bator. In the late fall of that year a special conference was conducted by Matvei Innekenevich Amgaev, a new representative of the Third International assigned to the party. The stated purpose of the conference was to discuss past successes and failures. In reality it was to remove all moderate leaders from the Central Committee who had connections with the Chinese Kuomintang and to elevate the leftist members in their stead. Attending were Pai Yün-t'i, Merse, Altanochir, Yao Ching-t'ao, Mandaltu, Fu Ming-t'ai, and Bayantai. Among other members of the Central Committee, Möngke-oljei attended, along with forty or more representatives from Yeke-juu and other areas of Inner Mongolia. A group of students whom the party had earlier sent to Moscow and Ulan-bator attended. These included Dügürengsang (Pai Hai-feng), Yün Jun (older brother of Ulanfu), and Pai Yün-lung. Dambadorji, with several leaders of the Outer Mongolian People's Revolutionary Party, also joined the conference. The meetings continued for almost a month and the trend was not favorable to Pai Yün-t'i and his group. Even though Dambadorji showed support for Pai, there was no way to match the pressure from Amgaev. The final decisions of the conference were: 1) to relieve Pai Yün-t'i, Merse, and Altanochir of their duties, but to allow Pai and Merse to continue as members of the Central Committee; 2) to expel Altanochir, Yao ch'ing-tao, Mandaltu, and Bayantai from the Central Committee; and 3) to elect Möngke-öljei, Yün Jun, Dügürengsang, Pai Yün-lung, Fu Ming-tai, and others to the Central Committee, with Möngkle-öljei as Chairman and Pai Yün-lung as Secretary-General. Hearing that Amgaev was planning to detain Pai Yün-t'i and his supporters in Ulan-bator, Dambadorji warned Pai and prepared an automobile to spirit him out of Ulan-bator by night, allowing him to escape to Inner Mongolia. Following Pai's escape, his friends also returned one after the other.[37]

After returning to his headquarters at Ninghsia, Pai convened an urgent conference of his party and supported by his old comrades, issued an anti-Soviet, anti-communist declaration stating: 1) The Inner Mongolian Kuomintang will faithfully follow the decision of the First Party Congress and continue the struggle against feudalism and its related institutions; 2) It will not allow communism to be implemented in Inner Mongolia; 3) It will strive for a victory of the people's revolution under the leadership of the Chinese Kuomintang. In November 1927 Pai went to Nanking, personally representing the Inner Mongolian Kuomintang, and petitioned for unification with the Chinese Kuomintang. His request was accepted. Since then the vicissitudes of the Inner Mongolian Kuomintang have been relegated to historical discussions.

Epilogue

The visit of Pai Yün-t'i to Nanking ended the Inner Mongolian Kuomintang, but its influence did not cease. As mentioned earlier, from the beginning of the party there was a conflict between the right and the left. Later, when the party disintegrated, the right-wing moderates, accepting Pai's leadership, joined the Chinese Kuomintang, but the left-wing radicals continued to follow the old line of the "Inner Mongolian People's Revolutionary Party." For example, Shini-lama continued as a leading figure of the left wing. No matter what Pai advocated, Shini-lama and others still carried out social revolution as before, not even hesitating to clash with the troops of Sayinbayar that were dispatched by Pai. Nevertheless, their extremist activities angered the majority of the Mongolian people as well as their own supporters. Finally, in early spring of 1929 Shini-lama was killed by his own people. Thus, the unrest in the southern Yeke-juu area that arose with the founding of the Inner Mongolian Kuomintang was resolved, but the legacy later made both Uushin and Otogh banners a springboard for the Chinese Communists to enter Inner Mongolia after their occupation of north Shensi.

After Pai arrived in Nanking, he was well received by both the Kuomintang Party and the National Government. He also maintained quite a good personal relationship with Feng Yü-hsiang based on their old friendship. However, Feng did not allow Pai's armed forces to be stationed in the vicinity of his power base in Ninghsia. During the Chinese New Year holidays of 1928, Feng secretly ordered his troops to disarm Pai's Mongolian forces. Under false pretenses, they invited Pai's two cavalry regiments to the city of Ninghsia for a banquet, opera, and bathing. Catching them off guard, the Mongolian troops were captured and disarmed. Li Yung-hsin, who was then a regimental chief, demanded to know why such action was taken and was told by Feng's man: "It was demanded by Pai Yün-t'i himself."[38] From then on this misinformation caused a strain between Li and Pai that existed until their last days.

After losing their military power, any remaining influence of the Inner Mongolian Kuomintang was virtually eliminated from Inner Mongolia by the conservatives except in Uushin Banner and its vicinity. Nevertheless, Pai and his clique continued to influence Mongolian affairs in the Kuomintang and in the National Government in Nanking. Following a proposal by Pai, the government agreed to establish the Mongolian-Tibetan Affairs Commission to assume the responsibilities previously handled by the Mongolian-Tibetan Ministry in Peking.

In June 1928, Kuomintang forces occupied Peking, changing its name to Peiping. The Mongols faced the new situation with conflicting feelings. Sun Yat-sen's words concerning the Mongolian future in *Outline of Nation Building* and other important documents provided them with great hopes, but they were worried because no Mongols had contact with the new government except for the Inner Mongolian Kuomintang group. There was the fear that this group's advocacy of social revolution might become the guiding principle of the government's new policy toward Inner Mongolia. In the meantime, on Pai's recommendation, Mandaltu (Li Tan-shan) and Bayantai were sent to Peiping to take over the offices of the Mongolian-Tibetan Ministry, but their arrogant behavior was deeply resented by the Mongolian society.

In order to establish direct contact with and to present their opinions to the new government, the conservatives decided to send a Mongolian delegation to Nanking. The leader of this group was Wu Ho-ling (吳鶴齡 Ünenbayan),[39] a Kharachin Mongol intellectual who earlier was a teacher in the Mongolian-Tibetan Academy and an official in the Mongolian-Tibetan Ministry. When Pai was forming his party, Wu was invited to join. However, because of differences in their political views, they were never able to get together. This was one reason why Wu wanted to lead the conservative group to confront the Inner Mongolian Kuomintang clique. His proposals eventually gained a favorable response from the local banner and league leaders, and a Mongolian Delegation was organized in Peiping without hindrance.

Though much of what they advocated was different, both Pai and Wu's groups had a common goal, i.e., the implementation of the principles and promises of Sun Yat-sen for the Mongols and other minorities. Both proposed a unification of all Mongols under one autonomous organization separated from the non-Mongolian administration of the Three Special Districts of Jehol, Chahar, and Suiyuan. While the Mongols were awaiting a positive response to their proposals, the Chinese Kuomintang Central Political Committee passed a resolution on 29 August 1928, to elevate the six special districts of Jehol, Chahar, Suiyuan, Ninghsia, Ch'inghai (Kokonor), and Hsik'ang (Kham) to the status of provinces. This was a great disappointment for the Mongols. Pai, then a member of the Central Political Committee, not only remained silent but also refused to accept any blame in the matter or to resign from his post.[40] This situation created a very unfavorable image of Pai and his group. Their reaction only accelerated the internal struggle among the Mongols, for it seemed Pai had no courage to resist outside pressures. The criticism from Wu Ho-ling was extremely severe.

The Mongolian Delegation, with Wu as its spokesman, arrived in Nanking in the middle of October 1928 to oppose the establishment of the new provinces in Inner Mongolian territory. It appealed for the preservation of the original Mongolian league and banner institutions and proposed the formation of a unified Mongolian autonomous administration. The appearance of Wu's Mongolian Delegation in the new capital was a serious challenge to Pai and his group. They were no longer the only body representing the Mongols to the government. Wu's sharp criticism damaged their position and upset the status quo. Thus, in order to defend their position of supremacy, Pai and his group retaliated by labeling Wu and his delegation as "feudalistic remnants." This brought an open split and a clash between the two factions. Meanwhile Rinchinrakhba, a delegate from Yeke-juu League, accused Pai and his followers of certain murders in Yeke-juu and petitioned the government to put them on trial. This confrontation resulted in a defeat for both sides, and a political loss for the entire Mongolian people. Even later when the Mongolian-Tibetan Affairs Commission was set up, the post of Minister fell into the hands of a shrewd Shansi warlord-politician, Yen Hsi-shan.[41]

Following these struggles, Pai, a personal acquaintance of Wang Ching-wei,[42] joined Wang's clique, became a member of the anti-central government group, and thereby destroyed his prestige within the party. Although he was usually elected a Standing Member of the Central Executive Committee of Kuomintang and was even Minister of the Mongolian-Tibetan Affairs Commission in 1948 and 1949, nevertheless, all the positions he later held were merely nominal and without any real function.

Some of the old Inner Monoglian Kuomintang group remained in Nanking, while some left. For instance Mandaltu (Li Tan-shan) was appointed a Member of the Mongolian-Tibetan Affairs Commission. I-Dechin was appointed an instructor of

Mongolian language and literature at the Army University in Nanking with the rank of Lieutenant General. Yao Ching-t'ao was appointed a Member of the Control Yüan and later a Member of the National Government, but was never really involved in politics. Only Li Yung-hsin and his group of middle-ranking cadres worked faithfully in the Border Area Party Affairs Section of the Central Committee of the Chinese Kuomintang until the retreat to Taiwan. Altanochir and Bayantai, disappointed in their hopes, returned to their native district of Kharachin. Only Sayinbayar continued to be concerned with the Mongolian students in Peiping, and his house again became a gathering spot for young Mongol intellectuals. Later, when Prince Demchügdüngrüb (Te Wang) initiated his famous Autonomous Movement, Sayinbayar and the active young intellectuals zealously joined the movement.

After Pai left Ulan-bator, Merse and Fu Ming-t'ai were sent back to their homes in Hulan-buir. In the winter of 1929, taking advantage of a Soviet invasion of northern Manchuria, they initiated a Hulun-buir independence movement in Hailar. The next spring as the Soviet troops withdrew, Fu returned to Outer Mongolia, while Merse, accepting an offer from Chang Hsüeh-liang,[43] proceeded to Shenyang (Mukden) and established the Normal Academy of the Northeast Mongol Banners.

At this school Merse educated many outstanding young Mongol intellectuals, and at the same time sowed the seeds of nationalism and socialism in the young minds. Later the students of this school contributed tremendously to Inner Mongolian politics, economy, and education. The outbreak of the Manchurian Incident in 1931 stopped the functioning of this school. Merse disappeared on his way to Outer Mongolia.

The Japanese invasion, the unsettled problems of Mongolia, and increasing political and economic encroachment by the border provinces, such as Suiyuan, etc., upon the lands of the Mongolian leagues and banners created conditions appropriate for Prince Demchügdüngrüb to attempt another breakthrough. In the fall of 1933, he initiated an Inner Mongolian Autonomous Movement for the unification of all Mongols to resist the Japanese invasion and oppression from the border provinces. With the hope of fulfilling a common purpose, the ruling princes of the leagues and banners, the Mongolian officials in both Nanking and Peiping, and virtually all intellectuals joined the movement wholeheartedly. Sayinbayar, for instance, was one of the most active of the group. Even the students educated in Russia and Outer Mongolia, like Dügürengsang (Pai Hai-feng) and other leftists, joined the movement until Japanese suppression in Inner Mongolia became really serious.

Those leftists in Ulan-bator — such as Dügürengsang, Yün Tse (Ulanfu), Temürbaghan, and others — who, following the direction of the Third International, struggled against Pai Yün-t'i's leadership, were sent back to Inner Mongolia to carry out an underground movement. Later, most of them joined the Chinese Communist Party. Most of those who remained in Outer Mongolia were unmercifully purged and killed during the Stalin period.[44]

During the civil war of the late 1940s and the establishment of the Inner Mongolian Autonomous Region, the Chinese Communist Party put Ulanfu (Yün Tse), Kuei Pi, and many former members of the Inner Mongolian Kuomintang (also known as the Inner Mongolian People's Revolutionary Party) in important positions. However, with the Cultural Revolution (1966–76), a conflict grew between Ulanfu and his opponents who were in power. Finally, because of the nationalistic sentiment of the Mongols, Ulanfu and his group were removed from their positions. Some hundred thousand people were involved in this radical movement and most of them were accused of crimes linked with a so-called *Nei-min-tang* (内民党), an abbreviation of the *Nei-meng-ku jen-min knming-tang* (内蒙古人民革命党) a Chinese translation meaning the Inner Mongolian People's Revolutionary Party. In reality it had not existed for years, but radical Red Guards fabricated charges based on old stories.

Now the "Gang of Four" period is over, and not only has Ulanfu reemerged on the political stage but even the Inner Mongolian People's Revolutionary Party's history has been recognized. However, the records concerning the party which have been published are usually deliberately misquoted concerning the political aims of the party. They not only vilify Pai Yün-t'i and most other founders of the Inner Mongolian People's Revolutionary Party (the Inner Mongolian Kuomintang) but also try to weaken its relationship with the Chinese Kuomintang and the Outer Mongolian People's Revolutionary Party. Undue stress and importance are given to the guidance and support of the Chinese Communist Party and the Comintern within the Mongolian Party.

In brief, the era of the Inner Mongolian Kuomintang is over. Most of its founders have died. Yet, considering the depressed situation of Inner Mongolia in the 1920s, one cannot but admire the strong will and courageous activities of those involved in so distinguished an event in the history of modern Mongolia. They were influenced by the doctrines of Sun Yat-sen, and most of them believed that the best way to save the Mongolian people was to follow his guiding principles. Later, however, they became confused, but this was a general trend due to the circumstances of the time. Their plans for Inner Mongolian survival and reformation were never implemented, in part because of the confusion of their policies. Yet, their failure to implement Sun's teachings is not the only reason for the continuing problems of Inner Mongolia. The roots of the problems lie in the past, but they have also had an impact on the current situation.

Notes

1. There are only limited materials on the rather rare subject treated in this paper. In my memory, only Paul Hyer presented a paper entitled "The Kuomintang on China's Frontier: The Case of Inner Mongolia," in 1967, at the Western Conference of the Association of Asian Studies, Albuquerque, New Mexico. Recently one or two articles have been published in Inner Mongolia. However, they are written with a certain political bias, and therefore, distortion is inevitable. The Soviet Mongolian specialist S. D. Dylykov has written a pioneering article on the subject, but it is marred by the same problem. One purpose of this paper is to preserve the historical facts about this period of Inner Mongolia and to correct some mistaken interpretations. The author is persuaded that his personal contact and conversations with most of the leading persons involved should shed some light on the problem.

2. For Gungsangnorbu, see Sechin Jagchid, "Prince Gungsangnorbu and Inner Mongolian Modernization: *Symposium on the History of the Republic of China*, (Taipei, 1981) 2:466–500 (chapter 16 in this work).

3. The first Mongolian translation of the Republic of China was *Domdadu Bügüde Nairamdaghu Irgen Ulus*. Although the meaning of the word *irgen* means people during the Ch'ing period, it was used as the term for the non-Manchu-bannerman which meant

the ordinary Han-Chinese. Consequently, the *Irgen Ulus* was explained as the Han-Chinese nation.

4. *Chung-hua Min-kuo shih-shih chi-yao* (中華民國史事記要), A Record of the Historical Events of the Republic of China. edited by the National Historical Bureau, July–December 1912, (Taipei, 1972), 147–48.

5. Yüan Shih-K'ai was the first president of the Republic of China. See H. L. Boorman, ed., *Biographical Dictionary of the Republic of China* (New York: Columbia University Press, 1967), 6:78–79.

6. From a conversation of the author with Mr. Todob, the eldest son of Gungsangnorbu.

7. For information on Huang Hsing (黃興) and Wang Ch'ung-hui (王寵惠) see Boorman, 2:192–97 and 3:376–78.

8. Chang Ch'i-yün (張其昀), *Tang-shih chi-yan* (党史記要), An Outline of the History of Kuomintang. (Taipei, 1964), 60–61.

9. See Jagchid, "An Interpretation of 'Mongol Bandits' (*Meng-fei*)," *Altaica* (Helsinki, 1977), 113–21 (chapter 14 in this work).

10. "The Twenty-one Demands" was imposed on Yüan Shih-k'ai while he was attempting to make himself the monarch of China. These demands were composed of five documents, the second one of which was a draft of a treaty concerning southern Manchuria and eastern Inner Mongolia. In this proposal Japan demanded prerogatives on economy, on transportation, and on land and mining developments. These demands were imposed as an ultimatum on the Chinese on 18 January 1915, and except for a few articles were agreed upon by Yüan Shih-k'ai's government on 25 May 1915. This agreement was not accepted by the people or the new government following the collapse of Yüan, however, and was finally abolished after the Conference on the Limitation of Armaments, Washington, D. C., 12 November 1921–6 February 1922.

11. Pai Yün-ti also had another name, Buyantai. See Boorman, 1:6–9; and Wu Hsiang-hsian (吳相湘), *Min-kuo Pai-jen-chuan* (民國百人傳) Biographies of One Hundred Persons of the Republic of China.) (Taipei, 1971), 6:169–73.

12. See *Meng-tsang Cheng-tse chi fa-ling hsüan-chi* (蒙藏政策及法令選集), A Selection of Policy, Law, and Regulations toward Mongolia and Tibet 1, edited by Mongolian-Tibetan Affairs Commission (Taipei, 1966), 4–5.

13. Buyannemekü, a famous writer and a member of the Mongolian Revolutionary Youth League Central Committee, was executed in 1937 and posthumously "rehabilitated" in 1967. See William A. Brown and Urgunge Onon, translation, *History of the Mongolian People's Republic* (Harvard, 1976), 806, n1, and 825, n20.

14. For Li Ta-chau (李大釗), see Boorman, 2:329–33.

15. For Feng Yü-hsiang (馮玉祥), see James Sheridan, *Chinese Warlord, The Career of Feng Hühsiang* (Stanford University Press, 1966).

16. For Wu P'ei-fu (吳佩孚), see Boorman, 3:444–50.

17. For Tuan Chi-jui (段祺瑞), see ibid.,3:330–35.

18. From a conversation of the author with Pai Yü-t'i. See also Wu Hsiang-hsiang, 170.

19. For Hsü Ch'ien (徐謙) and Li Lieh-chün (李烈鈞), see Boorman, 2:118–22 and 312–16.

20. Dambadorji, (1899–1934) the first secretary of the Mongolian People's Revolutionary Party, was a nationalistic leader and strongly advocated unification of both Inner and Outer Mongolia. Because of this, he was removed from his important position by Moscow Communist authorities (1928). See also Brown and Onon, 770, n.101. See also Robert A. Rupen, *Mongols of the Twentieth Century* (Indiana University, 1964), 1:193–94.

21. Gendun was Chairman of the National Little *Khural* (Committee) and later the prime minister (1932–36). He was liquidated in 1939. See Brown and Onon, 813, n.94.

22. Amur (or Amar) was the prime minister of the Mongolian People's Republic (1928–30) and was purged in 1939. See ibid., 808, n.52 and 809, n.55.

23. Odkhonbilig, "*Ulus-un totughadu-yin nigedüger khoyadughar khubisghaltu dain-u üye-yin totughadu Mogghol-un arad-un khubisghaltu nam* (The Inner Mongolian People's Revolutionary Party during the Period of the First and Second Revolutionary Wars inside the Country)," *Mongghol teüke-yin tokai ügülel-üd* (Essays on Mongolian History), Höhhot, 1981, 325. See also Rupen, 1:188.

24. The Mongolian word *arad* can be translated into Chinese *kuo-min* (國民) or *jen-min* (人民). The former is used by the Chinese Kuomintang (KMT) and the latter is used by the leftist parties.

25. The phrase "people's revolution" here is *kuo-min ke-ming* (國民革命). It was one of the slogans of the KMT of that period and the official purpose of their Northern Campaign.

26. For the record of these documents see Odkhonbilig, 334–37.

27. This was related to the author by Prince Demchugdungrub and Pai Yün-t'i.

28. For information on Chang Tso-lin (張作霖), see Gaven McCormack, *Chang Tso-lin in Northeast China, 1911–28*, (Palo Alto, 1977).

29. The Mongol word *jasagh* means a ruler of a banner. Usually a *jasagh* was a *taiji*, a member of an aristocratic family of the Chinggisid.

30. The author learned this information from many Kharachin elders. It was also confirmed by Pai Yün-t'i.

31. For Ma Fu-hsiang (馮玉祥), see Boorman, 2:464–65.

32. Cf., Odkhonbilig, 362 and 369–70.

33. *Chung-hua min-kuo shih-shih chi-yao*, January–June (Taipei, 1977), 301–2.

34. For Tsuo Lu (鄒魯), see Boorman, 3:317–18.

35. The article's title is "*Su-o yü Meng-ku*" (蘇俄與蒙古 Soviet Russia and Mongolia) and is recorded in *Ch'ing-tang shih-lu* (清党實錄 The Records of Party Cleaning). The pages are not complete. Both publisher and date are not clear. The book is preserved in the Harold B. Lee Library at Brigham Young University.

36. Odkhonbilig, 356–58 and 400. Jorigh, "*Alashan khushighun-u Shiou san-ye-yin kereg-ün tokhai*. (On the Shiou-san-ye incident of Alashan Banner)," and Lo Yung-hu, "*Shiou san-ye-yin kereg-ün eki adagh* (The Beginning and the End of the Shiou-san-ye Incident)." Both are in *Obör Mongghol-un teüke-yin materiyal* (The Inner Mongolian Historical Materials), Hohhot, 1981, 4:1–69.

37. Based on the author's conversation with Pai Yün-t'i. However, according to Odkhonbilig, the event took place between August and September 1927.

38. From the author's conversation Li Yung-hsin (李永新), a Kharachin Mongol, who died in 1975 in Taiwan. He was one of the leading Mongolian members in

the KMT. After the government moved to Taiwan, he was appointed the Minister of the Mongolia-Tibetan Affairs Commission in the late 1950s.

39. For Wu Ho-ling, see Boorman, 4:353–56, under his Mongolian name Unenbayan.

40. The author discussed this event with Pai Yün-t'i. According to his explanation, on the day of the meeting he was sick and phoned Feng Yü-hsiang, who was to chair the meeting, and asked whether he should attend. Feng replied, "There would be no important matters taken up. Better stay home and rest." However, Feng himself raised the proposal and had it passed. Nevertheless, the minutes of that meeting need to be checked to find what the record reveals.

41. For Yen Hsi-shan (閻錫山), see Boorman, 4:47–50.

42. For Wang Ching-wei (汪精衛), see ibid., 3:369–78.

43. For Chang Hsüeh-liang (張學良), see ibid., 1:61–68.

44. From a conversation of the author with K'ang Hsi-ch'en (康壐臣), a Kharachin intellectual who was sent by the Inner Mongolian Kuomintang to Ulan-bator to study in the 1920s. Later he was purged and exiled to the countryside. He deserted to Peiping in 1945.

Chapter 21

The Inner Mongolian Autonomous Movement of the 1930s

(Originally presented at the *Conference on Chiang Kai-shek and Modern China*, Taipei, 26–30 October 1986)

The twentieth century has been an era of great change in the world. Even landlocked Mongolia in continental Asia has found it impossible to avoid the currents and tides creating historical changes. At the turn of this century, the critical situation in East Asia and the influence of Chinese modernization movements led Prince Gungsangnorbu[1] to light the torch of reform. He advocated new ideas for modernization, established modern schools, and sent students abroad to study. His actions accelerated the Mongols' inclinations toward modernization. At the same time, his work created a conflict between a newly emerging intellectual group and traditional conservative leaders. Moreover, this conflict led to demands for social reform which ran counter to traditional Mongolian ways.

In Asia, the early twentieth century saw the height of imperialistic aggression as both Russia and Japan expanded their influence in Mongolia and Manchuria. The results in northern Mongolia included the independence of Outer Mongolia (1911), the American-Japanese expedition in Siberia (1918), a Pan-Mongolian movement (1919), the founding of the Mongolian People's Revolutionary Party (1921), the communistic revolution in Outer Mongolia (1921), and the establishment of the Mongolian People's Republic (1924). All these were linked and had a tremendous impact on Inner Mongolia.

In the 1920s, the Chinese Kuomintang Party was reorganized and promulgated *The Three Principles of the People* and the *Outline of Nation Building*. Dr. Sun Yat-sen declared in the latter: "The government should help the weaker and smaller nationalities inside the country to carry out self-determination and self-rule." A group of young Mongolian intellectuals enthusiastically responded to this new line. With Serendöngrüb (Pai Yün-t'i)[2] as a key leader, and with support from both the Chinese Kuomintang and the Comintern, a group known as the Inner Mongolian Kuomintang (also called the Inner Mongolian People's Revolutionary Party) was founded in 1925.[3] This new political party, which originally had as its goal the establishment of Mongolian self-rule, eventually lost the support of the majority of the people because it promoted radical social revolution against traditional institutions, thereby coming into conflict with powerful conservative groups. Although these initial endeavors ended in failure, their impact did not entirely disappear.

The above events, combined with a growing dissatisfaction among the Mongolian people and a desire for change, eventually culminated during the 1930s in the rise of the Inner Mongolian Autonomous Movement. In due time, the various factions came under the new leadership of Prince Demchügdüngrüb (commonly known as Te Wang). At this historic moment, the real leader of the National Government, Chiang Kai-shek, realizing the problems and the demands of the minority peoples, adopted a conciliatory policy toward the Mongols. Thus, he was able to win the trust of Demchügdüngrüb and other leaders. The net result was that while the Mongols were increasingly critical of the authorities in the border provinces, they continued to have confidence and hope in the leadership of the central government. This mentality had great impact on Inner Mongolian leaders during the Japanese occupation and the postwar period.

The Inner Mongolian Autonomous Movement and the Mongol problems during the 1930s have been so overshadowed and distorted by the propaganda of Fu Tso-yi[4] and his associates that it is still difficult for most researchers to interpret the facts properly. This is one reason the author has selected this topic for discussion.

Reasons Behind the Rise of the Inner Mongolian Autonomous Movement

The reasons for the rise of the Inner Mongolian Autonomous Movement can be divided into three main categories: 1) conflicts among the Mongols; 2) external pressures; and 3) an economic crisis.

In 1928, Chiang Kai-shek's Northern Campaign succeeded in restraining the remnants of warlordism and temporarily unifying the nation. Only then was official contact between the National Government in Nanking and the Mongolian leagues and banners established. The guidelines of the Kuomintang, as delineated in the *Outline of Nation Building* and other important documents, provided the Mongols with great hope. Yet, the government established no concrete programs to implement the guidelines. In addition, the establishment of the Jehol, Chahar,[5] Suiyüan, Ninghsia, and Ch'inghai provinces in Mongolian regions disappointed league and banner leaders.[6] These leaders were also worried that only Mongols with whom the Nanking government would have any contact would be former members of the Inner Mongolian Kuomintang, a group of people whose inclinations for social revolution might influence governmental policy toward Inner Mongolia. In order to establish direct contact with the National Government and to present their opinions, these leaders and other conservative Mongols decided to send a Mongolian delegation to Nanking. Even though the only goal of this delegation was to secure protection for traditional Mongolian political and economic rights, its arrival in the new capital was construed as a challenge to the former Inner Mongolian Kuomintang clique which could no longer claim to be the only group representing the Mongols to the government. This confrontation resulted in defeat on both sides and afforded an opportunity for two old warlords, Yen Hsi-shan[7] and Feng Yü-hsiang,[8] to continue their former exploitations of the Mongols.

Because of the ardent interests and the common goals of Mongol conservatives and moderate reformers, the formation of the Mongolian Delegation created, at its outset, a temporary alliance between the two groups. However, as time wore on and the delegation failed to produce any concrete results, the conservatives and moderates began to go their separate ways. Pai Yün-t'i's loss of influence and prestige among the Mongols gave Yen Hsi-shan the chance to become the first Minister of the National Government's Mongolian-Tibetan Affairs Commission. The Mongolian Delegation was reorganized as the Nanking Office of the Mongolian League and Banner Delegates, with Wu Ho-ling[9] as its head. At this juncture Chimedsampil, the Jerim League Chief, and Demchügdüngrüb,

Deputy-Chief of Shilinghol League, openly withdrew their support from the body. As a result, Mongolian political life was split into three factions: the radicals, the moderate reformers, and the conservatives. The conservatives persisted in their insistence that the old feudalistic institutions could not be reconciled with *The Three Principles of People*, the basis of the Kuomintang's party line. Pai Yün-t'i's group, although located in the Kuomintang Central Headquarters and still enjoying some support from Mongolian intellectuals and students, lost its political base in the local Mongolian leagues and banners. Wu Ho-ling and his group were wedged between the two above factions. However, as a result of Wu's strategies and political acumen, his group was supported by most of the league and banner leaders and was able to work as a liaison between the central government and local Mongolian authorities.

In order to solve the problems of the local Mongolian administrations and their involvement with the provincial organizations, the government finally convened the Mongolian Conference in the summer of 1930 (at Nanking) and passed the "Draft of the Organizational Law of the Mongolian Leagues, Tribes, and Banners." Later the next year, the National Government promulgated this draft as law. At the time of the conference, Yen Hsi-shan and Feng Yü-hsiang started a civil war. They allied themselves with Wang Ching-wei,[10] convened the "Enlarged Conference" *(k'uo-ta hui-yi* 擴大會議*)* in Peiping (Peking) and rebelled against the central government. Consequently, all transportation lines under the control of Yen and Feng were inaccessible to western Inner Mongolian delegates and officials, and they were unable to travel to the Mongolian Conference in Nanking.

The Organizational Law guaranteed the existence, status, and functions of the leagues, tribes, and banners, and it regulated relations between them and the concerned provinces. Nevertheless, it did not protect the feudalistic privileges of the old ruling class. It did quite the opposite, for it emphasized the powers and rights of a council elected by the people. Wu Ho-ling and his group praised the law as protection for local Mongolian political institutions and as enhanced support for democracy in Mongolia. However, in the opinion of Demchügdüngrüb and other conservatives, not only did the law not contain any new and meaningful provisions, but even worse, it abrogated the old guarantee confirmed by the Peking government in *The Regulations for the Treatment of Mongolia* (issued in 1912 and 1919). It failed to uphold the concept that "the original ruling power of the Mongolian Princes and nobles should be preserved as is." For these reasons, Demchügdüngrüb opened an attack on the law and on Wu Ho-ling, its promoter. The law was also utterly ignored by the provincial governments. It is, therefore, evident that the promulgation of this law did not bring about any resolution to the real problem. Instead, it produced a great split among Mongolian leaders. This turn of events disappointed both the liberals and the conservatives. The setbacks gradually led the Mongols to be suspicious of the authority and prestige of the central government, and made them realize that a resolution of this deadlock would have to be effected through their own efforts.

According to Ch'ing law, Chinese (Han) criminals in Mongolian regions were to be judged by the Manchu-Chinese authorities in accordance with Chinese law, as long as there was no interference with Mongolian matters. Even the military governors (*chiang-chün* 將軍 or *tu-t'ung* 都統） stationed at strategic positions in Mongolia did not directly administer Mongolian affairs. Later, in the wake of the influx of Chinese migrants into Mongolia, the Ch'ing court began to establish geographical divisions of *chou* (州) and *hsien* (縣) as a means of dealing with complicated Chinese affairs.[11] By the end of the Ch'ing Dynasty, officers of these *chou* and *hsien* began interfering in the Mongol banners. Warlordism emerged soon after the establishment of the Republic, and the posts of the above-mentioned military governors and *hsien* and *chou* magistrates were soon occupied by minor warlords and their henchmen. These areas were mismanaged, exploiting Chinese and Mongols alike. However, because they were Chinese, strong nationalistic feelings of antagonism arose among the Mongols. In 1938, even after the old administrative districts had been changed into provinces, those appointed as governors and magistrates of the provinces were still persons formerly associated with the previous warlordism. T'ang Yü-lin (湯 玉 麟), Governor of Jehol Province, was one of the most notorious of these appointees. Not only were these newly appointed provincial governors as harsh to the Mongols as they had been before the Northern Campaign, but they also dared openly to ignore the law as well as orders issued by the central government regarding Mongolian interests. In addition, the ruling Mongol nobles were seeking ways to preserve their own feudalistic privileges by protecting the integrity of the league and banner system. Even with the total absence of these shortcomings, it would still have been impossible to set up parallel systems of administration in the same area and avoid conflict.

After the Manchurian Incident of 1931, and especially after the fall of the Jehol area in early 1933 (when the eastern half of Inner Mongolia was occupied by the Kwantung Army), the remaining western portion of Inner Mongolia became a target for the next Japanese offensive. Neither the provincial governments along the border nor authorities of North China could stop Japanese aggression. This constant threat produced deep feelings of insecurity among the Mongol leaders. In order to keep their territories from being annexed, these leaders wanted to form a united front for dealing with the Japanese and Fu Tso-yi, a person widely regarded as the symbolic leader of the border provinces.

To solve the problems of famine and overpopulation in northern China in the middle of the nineteenth century, the Ch'ing court began encouraging refugees to settle in southern Inner Mongolia. This was done under the rationale of "borrowing land from the Mongols to nourish the Chinese (借 地 養 民)." The lands put under cultivation were the best grazing areas of the Mongol herders. Of course, every increase in cultivated land was accompanied by a commensurate decrease in the amount of land available for domestic animals, the very life blood of the Mongol people. In nomadic societies, pasture lands were traditionally regarded as part of the public domain and could not be sold by anybody. Yet, the covetous Manchu-Chinese officials collaborated with unscrupulous merchants and bribed or forced greedy Mongolian lords to sell or lease more and more land illegally to the settlers. Thus, the herders lost not only their pastures but their livelihood. Being pressed into such dire straits fanned the flames of resentment among many herders, and some took direct, forceful action in an attempt to protect the public pastures as part of the struggle for their very survival. The Manchu-Chinese officials, being concerned only with their own interests and relations with the Ch'ing court, deliberately ignored the political and nationalistic reasons behind such actions and labeled these Mongols as "bandits." The ensuing indiscriminate massacres of these herders led to the rise of the so-called "Mongol Bandits" (*Meng-fei* 蒙 匪)[12] of the late Ch'ing and early Republican era. Factors leading to the establishment of an independent

Outer Mongolia were many, and the "Mongol bandits" was more than likely one of the most important factors.

During the period of warlordism (1917–28), both Chang Tso-lin[13] and Feng Yü-hsiang forced the Mongolian leagues and banners to put land under cultivation in order to supply food for the warlords' armies. After the establishment of the National Government, the old Shansi warlord Yen Hsi-shan appointed Wang Ching-kuo (王靜國) as Commander for Military Cultivation *(t'un-k'en ssu-ling* 屯墾司令 *)*, stationed him at Pao-t'ou, and charged him with the responsibility of forcing the Yeke-juu and Ulan-chab banners to relinquish their pasture lands and open them to cultivation for Yen's former soldiers. This action led directly to the Inner Mongolian Autonomous Movement of 1933.

All of the circumstances and factors mentioned above made it abundantly clear to almost all Mongols, whether the feudalistic ruling class or the conservatives, the radicals or the reformers, that the Mongolian problem was deadlocked. Mongols saw that there was no way to resist simultaneously the Japanese aggression and the political and economic exploitation from the Chinese border provinces. To many, the only way out of such a desperate situation was the initiation of a movement for autonomy.

The Autonomous Movement

At the zenith of the struggle between Demchügdüngrüb and Wu Ho-ling, a group of activist anti-Wu intellectuals joined Demchügdüngrüb in order to exert heavier pressures upon Wu. Soon they realized that Demchügdüngrüb was not a young and powerful prince struggling for the selfish interests of the feudal class, but that he was dedicated to the destiny of his own people, the Mongols. These intellectuals decided, therefore, to place themselves completely under his leadership. The cooperation of these young intellectuals had great impact on Demchügdüngrüb. Not only did it increase his personal confidence, but it also gradually guided him in a more progressive direction.

In the early summer of 1933, Demchügdüngrüb went to Üjümüchin to visit Prince Sodnamrabtan (commonly known as Prince So), Chief of the Shilinghol League. Prince So was the most prestigious member of the nobility in Inner Mongolia at that time. He was conservative and just, but he had no political ambitions. Knowing that Prince So was antagonistic toward Japanese aggression, Demchügdüngrüb persuaded him to unite all the leagues and banners together to form a united front with which to confront the Japanese. Although Prince So had no vested interest in the organization of such a body, he was greatly distressed by the Kuantung Army's demand for the establishment of a special service (intelligence) office *(tokumu kikan* 特務機関*)* in his banner, and therefore he agreed to support Demchügdüngrüb's efforts. He immediately convened the leaders of the ten banners of the Shilinghol League at his residence to discuss measures for coping with the new situation. At the meeting it was decided that Demchügdüngrüb would contact the leaders of the other leagues and carry out plans for autonomy.

Having received support from Prince So and the leaders of the Shilinghol League, Demchügdüngrüb went to Beyile-yin Süme (Pai-ling-miao 百靈廟 in Chinese) to meet with Prince Yondonwangchugh (commonly known as Prince Yon), Chief of the Ulanchab League, to discuss the proposal. Prince Yon was then under pressure from Wang Ching-kuo to put the land of Ulanchab under military cultivation, and consequently he too agreed to support the proposal. Only the Yeke-juu League, located south of the Yellow River and the Peiping-Suiyuan Railroad, and thus closely watched by Fu Tso-yi, was not visited by Demchügdüngrüb personally. Even so, the Deputy-Chief of the league, Prince Altanochir, was reached through secret contacts and agreed to give his support. The Chakhar banners in the vicinity of Shilinghol were contacted separately. For the sake of political harmony, Prince So wished to have Prince Yon lead the movement and convene a conference of all Mongolian leaders by the end of September in Beyile-yin Süme. They planned to discuss at this conference the future of the Mongol people and to issue a declaration of Inner Mongolian Autonomy.

This call for autonomy was enthusiastically supported by all Mongols and unified the different factions in a struggle for a common goal. Of all the group, the Mongolian intellectuals and students in Nanking and Peiping were especially zealous in their support of this movement.

Fu Tso-yi and his clique not only tried to keep the delegates of the Yeke-juu League from attending the conference, but they also took advantage of the nationwide anti-Japanese sentiment to prevent Mongolian autonomy by misrepresenting the movement as a plot to cooperate with Japanese aggression. In a similar attempt to crush the fledgling movement, Yen Hsi-shan induced the central government to dispatch the Jangjia lama as a special government emissary to Beyile-yin Süme. It was Yen's hope that the lama, to whom the Mongolian nobles and conservatives were devoted, would be able to persuade the delegates to stop the conference. When this politically oriented lama arrived at the Peiping railroad station, he was immediately met by Mongolian students demonstrating against him. That same day the Peiping newspapers published the news of Mongolian opposition to religious interference in politics. Seeing this drastic change in Mongolian society, the Jangjia lama decided to remain in the old capital and cease going to Inner Mongolia for political purposes.

In order to formulate a government response to this conference, Wang Ching-wei, Chief of the Executive *Yüan*, gathered the Mongol leaders in Nanking for consultation and dispatched the Interior Minister, Huang Shao-hung,[14] and the Vice-Minister of the Mongolian and Tibetan Affairs Commission, Chao Pi-lien, as government emissaries to Mongolia. After their arrival in Peiping, the two emissaries met with Ho Ying-ch'in[15] and Huang Fu (the two top leaders of military and political affairs in North China), Sung Che-yüan, governor of Chahar Province, the Jangjia lama, and several Mongolian princes and members of the nobility. They deliberately did not meet with delegates of the Peiping Mongolian Association or with the delegates of the Mongolian student body in Peiping, thereby showing their unwillingness to hear the opinions of Mongol intellectuals.

After their visit to Peiping, the two emissaries went to Kuisui (Hohhot) and stayed there for ten more days to discuss measures with Fu Tso-yi and his colleagues. They arrived at Beyile-yin Süme on 10 November to talk with Yodonwangchugh and Demchügdüngrüb. After several days of argument and negotiation, they finally reached an agreement containing eleven articles. The Mongol leaders were grateful, because the emissaries from the central government accepted, albeit conditionally, their earnest requests for the conclusion of an agreement. In order to show their faith in the government and the commitment of the emissaries, the Mongolian side did not ask Huang and Chao to affix their signatures to the document.

Huang and Chao left Beyile-yin Süme in a magnificent send-off ceremony and arrived again at Kuisui to consult with Fu Tso-yi. The two emissaries then took the route through T'aiyüan, the capital city of Shansi, to talk with Yen Hsi-shan for several days before returning to Nanking to report on their negotiations with the Mongols and to present to the government the agreement they had reached. At the very moment Mongol delegates charged with the responsibility of offering thanks arrived in the capital from Beyile-yin Süme, the newspapers published the eleven articles for Mongolian autonomy as passed by the Kuomintang Central Political Committee. Because these eleven articles did not constitute an accurate version of the agreement reached with the Mongol leaders in Beyile-yin Süme, a public outcry arose from the Mongol community in Nanking. It turned out that the Central Political Committee's articles were not the articles agreed to at Beyile-yin Süme at all, but were eleven completely modified articles worked out in negotiations with Fu Tso-yi and Yen Hsi-shan at Kuisui and T'aiyüan. Only the numbers of the articles had remained unchanged. Indignant Mongols petitioned the government and angrily demonstrated in the streets.

The government was indeed embarrassed by the perfidious deeds of Huang Shao-hung and Chao P'i-lien. Wu Ho-ling, head of Nanking's Office of Mongolian League and Banner Delegates, bypassed the Ministry of Interior Affairs and Mongolian-Tibetan Affairs Commission and contacted Wang Ching-wei, Chief of the Executive *Yüan* directly in order to work out an acceptable draft. Policy dictated that such an important matter have the approval of Generalissimo Chiang Kai-shek, so this draft was submitted to him for his decision.[16] Approval was immediate, and the draft was passed without delay by the Party's Central Political Committee under the title *Principles for Implementation of Mongolian Autonomy*. This draft, which satisfied the demands of the Mongols, is reproduced below.

1. A Mongolian Local Autonomous Political Affairs Committee shall be established at an appropriate locality in Mongolia. The said Committee and its administration of the political affairs of the leagues and banners shall be under the direct jurisdiction of the Executive *Yüan* and the guidance of concerned offices in the central government. Persons appointed as chairman and members of the said Committee are to be Mongols. The budget of the Committee shall be issued by the central government. The central government shall station a high-ranking official at the locality of the Committee to provide guidance and to mediate in disputes between the [Mongol] leagues and banners and the [Chinese] provinces and *hsiens*.

2. All league offices shall be converted into league governments, and banner offices into banner governments. Internal organization of these offices-turned-governments are to remain unchanged. Expenditures of the league governments shall be subsidized by the central government.

3. The Chakhar tribe shall be established as a league in order to put it on an equal footing with other leagues. The administration and organization of the Chakhar tribe shall remain unchanged.

4. The jurisdictions and ruling powers of the leagues and banners are to remain unchanged.

5. The current cultivation of pasture lands shall cease. Henceforth, local [Mongolian] economic development shall be based upon improvements in animal husbandry and growth in related industries. (In instances where leagues and banners give their consent, cultivation shall be allowed.)

6. The integrity of all taxes and rents of the leagues and banners, as well as of private rents of the Mongol people, shall be ensured.

7. A percentage of all local taxes collected in league and banner territories by the provinces and *hsien* shall be returned to the leagues and banners for allocation as construction funds. Decisions concerning the allocation of tax revenues shall be made separately.

8. There shall be no additional *hsien* or *she-chih-chiu* (設 治 局 sub-*hsien*) established in league and banner territories. (When exigencies dictate otherwise, the establishment of additional *hsien* or *she-chih-chu* must still be approved by the concerned leagues and banners.)

Following the political solutions approved by the Central Political Committee, as contained in the *Outline of the Temporary Organization of the Mongolian Local Autonomous Political Affairs Committee,* Yondonwanchugh and twenty-four others were appointed as committee members, with Yodonwangchugh as Chairman, Sodnamrabtan and Shaghdurjab as Deputy-Chairmen, Demchügdüngrüb as Secretary-General, and Wo Ho-ling as Head of the Counselors. In addition, Ho Yin-ch'in, Acting Chairman of the Peiping Branch of the Military Committee, was appointed as the Mongolian Local Autonomy Director-Chief and Chao Tai-wen, Head Counselor of the T'aiyüan Pacification Headquarters, was appointed as the Deputy-Director-Chief. On 23 April the Mongolian Local Autonomous Political Affairs Committee (or the Mongolian Political Committee for short) was officially established at Beyile-yin Süme.

Thus, the final decision solved the problems of Inner Mongolian Autonomy. Because the decision helped the Mongols achieve more and lose less, it was warmly welcomed and enhanced the Mongols' confidence in the central government. It convinced the Mongol leaders that the Kuomintang and the National Government did have an enlightened policy toward them and other minorities. However, this progressive policy was never realized due to the hindrances by high-ranking frontier officials. All decisions made by the central government concerning Mongol interests were completely ignored by these frontier officials. Consequently, the Mongols had to bypass these provincial authorities and deal with the central government directly. This caused the provincial officials to be even more antagonistic toward the Mongols. This unfortunate state of affairs continued unabated until the withdrawal of the National Government to Taiwan in 1949.

The Mongolian Political Committee that emerged soon ran into conflicts with Fu Tso-yi and his Suiyüan Provincial Government. According to the seventh article of the *Principles of Mongolian Autonomy,* a percentage of all tax revenues collected by the provincial governments in Mongolian territory was to be returned to the leagues and banners. This article also specifies that the Committee had the right to negotiate with the provincial governments. Because the issues of land revenues were very complex, the committee decided that the first matter to be negotiated with the Suiyüan Provincial Government should be the tax on opium. At Khashaatu of the Urad Central Banner, the

Siuyüan Provincial Government had established a tax bureau to collect the so-called "special tax" on opium being transported from the Kansu and Ninghsia areas through Mongolian grasslands on its way to markets in Peiping and Tientsin. Talks on the opium tax continued for some time, but all of the petitions and requests of the Mongolians were rejected. This deadlock in negotiations resulted in both sides sending troops to the tax bureau in Khashaatu for a military confrontation. Pressure from the central government prevented any bloodshed, but the problem of the opium tax remained unresolved.

In the political arena, Fu Tso-yi prevented the Yeke-juu leaders from joining the work of the Mongolian Political Committee. He also attempted to disrupt the administration of the Mongolian leagues and banners. Prior to the formation of the Mongolian Political Committee there had already occurred in the Urad Front Banner a struggle for succession to *jasagh* (feudal leader). Prince Yon, Chief of the Ulanchab League, had recommended that Shalabdorji become the *jasagh*. The National Government, through the instrumentality of the Mongolian-Tibetan Affairs Commission, recognized Shalabdorji as the legitimate successor to this position. In the late summer of 1935, Shalbdorji had his soldiers unlawfully confiscate the property of his opponents. These opponents escaped injury and lodged a complaint with Prince Yon, the League Chief and also Chairman of the Mongolian Political Committee. In adjudicating this matter, Prince Yon summoned Shalabdorji to Beyile-yin Süme for a discussion with the persons who had lodged the complaint against him. Knowing that he would be unable to defend his illegal actions in such a discussion, Shalabdorji defected to Kuisui and sought the backing of Fu Tso-yi. Seeing an opportunity to disrupt the league and banner system and hinder the jurisdiction of the Mongolian Political Committee, Fu had Wang Ching-kuo send his troops from Paot'ou to the Urad Front Banner for "pacification." As a response, the Mongolian Political Committee sent its troops to the same spot. An armed clash was avoided only after the National Government punished Shalabdorji in November by suspending him for eight months from his position as *jasagh*.

Early in 1675, the Chakhar Mongols rebelled against Manchu rule. After the rebellion was quelled, the Ch'ing court abolished the Chakhar Mongols' feudalistic system of self-rule and split them into eight banners and four pastures. On top of this, the court placed the Chakhar Mongols under the jurisdiction of the Manchu Military Governor of Chahar[17] to serve as a warning to other Mongols who might also have considered rebelling. Under the Peking government of the Republican period, this system of administration remained the same, except that the governors were no longer Manchus. After the National Government was founded, the four Left Flank banners and the four pastures were put under the jurisdiction of the newly established Chahar Province, and the four Right Flank banners were put under the jurisdiction of Suiyüan Province. Consequently, the Chakhar leaders struggled for years to have their status changed to that of a league. Their request was granted by the Central Political Committee, but actual implementation was again blocked by the provincial governments of Chahar and Suiyüan.

In summary, then, the high point in cordial relations between the Mongols and the National Government was reached with the resolution for Mongolian autonomy and the establishment of the Mongolian Political Committee. These two concessions were widely appreciated by the Mongol people and were the main reasons that Demchügdüngrüb and the other Inner Mongolian leaders always maintained their goodwill toward the Chinese central government. However, these good relations were unable to continue due to Fu

Tso-yi's interference and the Japanese invasion, which eventually brought about the collapse of the Inner Mongolian autonomous regime under the National Government.

The Japanese Invasion and the Disintegration of the Mongolian Political Committee

Following the Manchurian Incident, the Japanese established Pu-yi, who had abdicated from the Manchu-Ch'ing imperial throne, as their puppet and used his name to seduce conservative Mongolian princes and nobles. Under the pretence of replacing the leagues with a system of Mongol "self-rule," the Japanese established the Kingghan ("Hsing-an" in Chinese) provinces and abolished all *hsiens* in banner territories. In order to win the hearts of the Mongol intellectuals, the Japanese completely abolished the feudal institutions in the territories they occupied. However, this simply made it easier for the Japanese to penetrate the banner organizations.

The Japanese occupation of eastern Inner Mongolia further stimulated the rise of Mongolian patriotism and nationalism. It also led some intellectuals to join the anti-Japanese camp of the Chinese. Some Mongol intellectuals turned their hopes toward Outer Mongolia. Later, a larger group of disillusioned Mongols left "Manchukuo" and joined the regime under the leadership of Demchügdüngrüb in western Inner Mongolia.

In the spring of 1933, the Japanese annexed the Jehol area into "Manchukuo," and Li Shuo-hsin[18] surrendered. Because Li was a Mongol, the Japanese reorganized his group into a "strategic column" which would assume the risks associated with Japanese "work" in western Inner Mongolia. Li was then directed to take Dolonor (To-lun), a strategic area between the Chakhar and Shilinghol leagues. The fall of Dolonor provided Feng Yü-hsiang a chance to emerge at Kalgan as the Commander-in-Chief of the Allied Anti-Japanese Army. He recovered Dolonor for a period of time and then lost it again. The fall of Dolonor aroused the fears of the Mongols, as did also the appearance of Feng Yü-hsiang, because memories of forced military cultivation of pasture lands were still fresh.

Soon after the fall of Dolonor, the Japanese Kwangtung Army convened the Chakhar banners for a meeting and dispatched envoys to demand that the banners of Shilinghol League send delegates to celebrate Pu-yi's enthronement as the "Emperor of Manchukuo." Politically, these demands could have been rejected without hesitation. However, because of Mongol dependence on food supplies from areas under Japanese control, formulation of a response to these demands was a delicate matter. Also, at this time, the Kwantung Army asked Prince So to permit the establishment of a special service (i.e., intelligence) office in his Üjümüchin Banner. This unreasonable request, was, of course, rejected, and it led Prince So to respond favorably to Demchügdüngrüb's overtures for a united front for a collective defence and self-rule. Prince So's resolute attitude was praised by the central government, but neither he nor the united front was able to halt the Japanese advance. During the high tide of the Beyile-yin Süme autonomous movement, the Kwantung Army again sent its agents to set up a special service office in Üjümüchin. Prince So informed the agents that since the central government had not given its approval for the office, he could not provide any supplies or protection. He also forbade his people to make any private contacts with the Japanese. Prince So's adamant position, combined with the severity of the ensuing winter, forced the Japanese to withdraw. However, their withdrawal was only temporary.

The situation in North China during the summer of 1935 changed dramatically as a result of the "Ho Ying-ch'in-Umezu Agreement." Worried by deteriorating circumstances, Demchügdüngrüb proceeded to Peiping for talks and consultations with General Ho Ying-ch'in about the situation in Inner Mongolia. The General's advice to Demchügdüngrüb was to "deal with the Japanese in a dignified but inoffensive manner." Under the circumstances, this may well have been the only advice the General could possible have given. Soon afterwards, the organizations and troops of the central government were forced to withdraw from the Peiping and Tientsin area. The Japanese, while agreeing to allow Sung Che-yüan's forces to fill the resultant power vacuum, orchestrated the so-called "Changpei Incident." As a result, Sung's troops were forced to withdraw from the north to the south of the Great Wall. This effectively put all the Chakhar and Shilinghol banners out of the political reach of the National Government.

It was almost exactly at this same time that Itagaki Seishiro, the Kwantung Army's Deputy Director of Staff Officers, came to Üjümüchin along with his staff officer Tanaka Ryukichi to visit Prince So. Itagaki confided to Prince So that if the Mongols would strive for independence, Japanese assistance would be made available. Prince So replied that such an important matter would have to be decided upon by all the Mongol leaders, and that he personally could not make any decision. Moreover, Prince So continued, Mongolia was still part of the Chinese territory. Such matters should be taken up and negotiated between the two governments of China and Japan. After having been rebuffed in this manner, the Japanese concentrated their Mongolian efforts on Demchügdüngrüb.

During the winter of the same year, the Chinese National Athletic Meet took place in Shanghai. Because the wrestlers were mostly from Üjümüchin, Prince So was able to send one of his officials to accompany them. Prince So's personal delegates (one of whom was the author) met secretly in Nanking with General Ho Ying-Ch'in to report on Itagaki's visit and to ask for instructions. In view of the situation in North China, the only advice the General was able to offer was that the matter should be "handled with care."

After the Japanese began concentrating their efforts on Demchügdüngrüb, agents began pouring into his banner, the Sünid Right Flank, under cover of the Zenrinkyokai (Good Neighborliness Association). These agents openly set up clinics, schools, and intelligence operations. News of Demchügdüngrüb's collaboration with the Japanese filtered through Fu Tso-yi's propaganda agency to the Chinese newspapers. Here it should be pointed out that by this time the Japanese "special service offices" had already been established in both Peiping and Tientsin, and that even in Fu Tso-yi's own city of Kuisui, there was a "residence" of Major Haneyama which was engaged in the same "special service."

In the winter of 1935 the Hopei and Chahar Political Affairs Committee *(Chi-Cha cheng-wu wei-yüan-hui* 冀察政務委員会 *)* was established under Japanese pressure in Peiping with Sung Che-yüan as Chairman. During this same time the Japanese Kwantung army directed Li Shuo-hsin's troops to occupy all Chinese *hsien* north of the Great Wall near Kalgan. This cut the Mongol areas of Chakhar and Shilinghol off from the other side of the Great Wall. Seeing this change, Wu Ho-ling, as Head of the Nanking Office of Mongolian League and Banner Delegates, asked for permission to return to Mongolia. His request was granted by the Generalissimo Chiang

Kai-shek, who reminded Wu that he should do his best to impede or delay Japanese actions but to do so secretly.

The first moves the Japanese made in their newly occupied Mongolian territory were the conversion of the Chakhar tribe into a league and the establishment of a league office for the management of administrative affairs. These changes were effected in January 1936. Through these measures the Japanese were able to dominate the Chakhar banners. Shilinghol, however, was a different story. Because of its solid feudalistic institutions and the prestige of both Prince So and Demchügdüngrüb, the Japanese were unable to penetrate the administration of its leagues and banners.

In order to curb the pro-Chinese activity in Mongolia, the Japanese assassinated Nimaodsor, a Mongol who had a close relationship with Nanking, on the day after the formation of the Chakhar League Office. A Japanese plot to kill Wu Ho-ling was discovered and foiled by Demchügdüngrüb. This miasma of terror infiltrated Mongolian political life and permitted Demchügdüngrüb to see the viciousness of the Japanese "friends."

By the end of 1935, Inner Mongolia was covered with heavy snows, and most of the Mongols' animals had died in the severe cold. This precipitated a shortage in the food supply. Grain from Suiyüan was normally imported by the Mongols, but this source was cut off due to Fu tso-yi's embargo on grain sales to the Japanese enemy. The Japanese were finally able to supply some food for the Mongols, but along with this relief came demands that all Chinese troops under Li Shuo-hsin be reorganized into the "First Mongolian Army." In response, Demchügdüngrüb himself assumed the position of commander-in-chief and recruited young Mongols into his "Second Mongolian Army," which he stationed in pastoral areas. Disillusioned Mongol youth in "Manchukuo" came to join this armed force.

As mentioned earlier, one of the reasons for establishing the autonomous movement was to form a united front with which to resist Japanese advances. However, after the Japanese occupation of Mongolia became a *fait accompli*, the situation changed and resistance became less feasible. It was under these circumstances that a group of Mongol intellectuals, together with the majority of the Peace Preservation Troops of the Mongolian Political Committee, left Beyile-yin Süme and defected to Kuisui. As they were leaving, they issued an open telegram making it clear that their actions were motived solely by patriotic indignation at the Japanese invasion of their homeland. They did not, however, lay the blame for this invasion upon Demchügdüngrüb personally. These anti-Japanese acts by the Mongols had great propaganda value for Fu Tso-yi, and he immediately saw to it that newspapers all over the country sensationalized the matter. However, after the propaganda value of these Mongols had been exhausted, Fu gave them a very cold reception and disarmed them as a group.

Before this unfortunate incident, Prince Yon, concerned about Fu Tso-yi's malfeasance and the growing Japanese influence, had resigned from his official positions as Chief of the Ulanchab League and Chairman of the Mongolian Political Committee. In order to placate the Mongols, the Nanking authorities made him a member of the National Government and appointed Prince So to replace him as Chairman of the Mongolian Political Committee. This action did not, however, help the deteriorating conditions that had so worried Prince Yon. On 25 January 1936 the National Government, acting on the advice of Fu Tso-yi and Yen Hsi-shan, announced the establishment of the Suiyüan Mongolian Local Autonomous Political Committee. Shaghdurjab, Chief of the Yeke-juu League, was appointed as Chairman of this committee, and Yen Hsi-shan was selected as its Director-Chief. Jurisdiction over Ulanchab, Yeke-juu, and Tümed banners, which had been administered by the original Mongolian Political Committee, was turned over to the new committee. On 23 February this Suiyüan Mongolian Political Committee was formally organized at Kuisui. Guests appearing at the ceremonies marking the committee's organization included Fu Tso-yi, Yen Hsi-shan's delegate, and the Japanese Major Haneyama. A committee declaration stressed that the guiding policies of the Committee were "good neighborliness and vigilance against communism *(mu-lin fang-kung* 睦鄰防共 *).*" In these days the word *"lin"* (neighbor) in this type of context meant Japan. Mongols were therefore greatly puzzled at the apparent inconsistency in Fu Tso-yi's attitudes toward the Japanese. Mongols and Tibetans had experienced similar feelings during the last years of the Ch'ing when Manchu authorities had forbidden the Mongols and Tibetans to compromise with Russia and Britain. Later the Ch'ing court itself concluded the very compromises it had earlier prohibited.

It was during this period of unstable political life that Prince So died. On 21 July the National Government ordered the Mongolian Political Committee at Beyile-yin Süme to disband. In its stead the government established the Chahar Mongolian Local Autonomous Political Committee and appointed Demchügdüngrüb as its Chairman. It seemed that the government wanted to maintain the Chahar Mongolian Political Committee as a symbol of Chinese ties with the Mongolian territory already lost to the Japanese. Demchügdüngrüb and other Mongol leaders also preferred to maintain this nominal relationship, rather than to sever all contacts with the National Government. Nevertheless, Demchügdüngrüb did not withdraw his staff members from Beyile-yin Süme as ordered.

Following the acceleration of the "Concentration on Northern China" campaign, the "help" given to Mongols from the Kwantung Army became unbearable. With the formation of the Mongolian Military Government, "assistance" by Japanese "advisors" became mandatory.

During the course of these developments the Kwantung Army executed Ling Sheng, Governor of Kingghan North Province (the Hulan-buir area), along with some of his followers, after having convicted him on trumped-up charges of spying for Outer Mongolia. Ling Sheng, a stern conservative, was strongly anti-Japanese and wielded considerable influence among the Hulun-buir Mongols. Because of Ling Sheng's intractably conservative attitudes and policies, his Japanese "advisors" were actually treated as such, and were thus unable to dominate the administration of Kingghan North Province. The Japanese regarded Ling Sheng and his followers as hostile figures and had them executed to serve as a warning to others who refused to "cooperate."

Confrontations with Fu Tso-yi and certain moves by the Japanese caused Demchügdüngrüb's course to be altered. Nevertheless, he still hoped that the situation might change and that the central government, under the leadership of Chiang Kai-shek, would provide some future solution to the Mongolian problem. For this reason, he refused to sever completely his ties with the Nanking government. The Japanese, of course, would not tolerate such a refusal. Demchügdüngrüb stressed constantly that his newly recruited Mongol troops lacked training, and he refused to send them to be sacrificed needlessly on the battlefront. Seeing in this situation an opportunity to advance his own career, Tanaka Ryukichi worked through the Special Service Office at Tientsin and got Wang Tao-yi to recruit some local Chinese bandits for an attack on the eastern border of Suiyüan. This attack, which was carried out in the name of the Mongolian regime, was warded off by Fu Tso-yi's forces, and Wang's group of bandit-soldiers was annihilated. Then, Tanaka brought from Tientsin Wang Ying, son of the local Suiyüan tyrant Wang T'ung-ch'un, to gather bandits and gangs of hoodlums into a so-called "Righteous Army of the Great-Han (Ta-han Yi-chün 大漢義軍)." Tanaka combined this "Righteous Army" with Li Shao-hsin's Chinese forces (the so-called "Mongolian First Army") and launched a larger attack on Fu Tso-yi's troops. This led to the outbreak of the "War of Eastern Suiyüan." Imbued with a strong anti-Japanese sentiment, the entire nation of China supported Fu's resistance against the enemy. Fu was eventually able to repel the invasion and also to take Beyile-yin Süme, thus achieving for himself a victory of both military and political dimensions. Although Tanaka Ryukichi suffered a military defeat, he had achieved his goal of severely straining the ties between Demchügdüngrüb and the Chinese central government.

Before the guns began to blaze, Demchügdüngrüb, in his capacity as Chairman of the Chahar Mongolian Political Committee, had issued an open telegram to Fu Tso-yi which enumerated past conflicts between Fu and the Mongols as the reason for the attack. The telegram made it clear that this attack was not intended as a hostile act against the central government. Soon after the Sian Incident, Demchügdüngrüb, again in his official capacity, issued a telegram announcing that the rescue of the leader (Chiang) was a matter of top priority, and that the Mongolian-Suiyüan conflict should be put on hold until the central government could settle the matter. Thus, Demchügdüngrüb was able to halt further developments in the incident created and orchestrated by Tanaka Ryukichi.

Following the outbreak of the Marco Polo Bridge Incident in 1937, Kalgan, Tat'ung, and Kuisui fell one after the other to the Japanese. Under the personal command of Tojo Hideki, the Kwantung Army advanced through the southern territory of western Inner Mongolia and eliminated any remaining vestiges of Mongol self-rule. Even so, western Inner Mongolia's background of politically autonomous movements, tenuous but still viable relations with the Chinese government, and political importance in relation to Outer Mongolia, induced the Japanese to be much more lenient toward western Inner Mongolia than they were toward the "Manchukuo" portion of eastern Inner Mongolia.

Nonetheless, high-handed Japanese policy prompted widespread Mongolian nationalism and anti-Japanese sentiment. In Japanese-controlled areas of Inner Mongolia, none but a handful of lackeys were supportive of the Japanese invasion and occupation. Among the Mongols opposed to Japanese rule, the radicals leaned toward Outer Mongolia and the Soviet Union. Most of the moderates (including Demchügdüngrüb) hoped that an eventual victory by Chiang Kai-shek and his allies would bring a new and progressive solution to Mongolia's problem. These hopes were especially high immediately following the Japanese-Soviet Khalkha River Battle, the outbreak of the Pacific war, and the collapse of Japan's militarism. The conflicting political ideologies between the radicals and the moderates did lead to some contentions, but all Mongols were equally apprehensive about the prospect of Fu Tso-yi's return to power in Suiyüan.

In short, the Inner Mongolian autonomous movement won general support because it helped in the struggle for national survival and was a means by which Mongols could resist collectively Japanese aggression as well as encroachment from border provinces. The establishment of the Mongolian Political Committee brought about a period of nominal Mongol autonomy, but Japanese interference brought this period to an end.

Notes

1. For Gungsangnorbu, see Sechin Jagchid, "Prince Gungsangnorbu and Inner Mongolia Modernization," *Symposium on the History of the Republic of China* (Taipei, 1981) 2: 466–500 (chapter 16 of this work).

2. For Serendöngrub (Pai Yün-t'i) see Jagchid, "The Inner Mongolian Kuomintang of the 1920s," *Proceedings of the Conference on Dr. Sun Yat-sen and Modern China* (Taipei, 1986) 3:178–230 (chapter 20 of this work).

3. Ibid.

4. For Fu Tso-yi see *Fu Tso-yi p'ing-sheng* (傅作義的平生 *The Life of Fu Tso-yi)*, (Peking, 1985). See also Howard L. Boorman, ed., *Biographical Dictionary of the Republic of China* (New York, 1967) 2:47–51.

5. The word "Chahar" is used for the name of the province Cha-ha-erh (察哈尔) to differentiate it from the Mongolian tribe "Chakhar."

6. The banner is a basic unit of local administration and is comparable to a district or county (Chinese *hsien*). The league is an administrative unit composed of several banners.

7. For Yen Hsi-shan (阎锡山), see Boorman, 4:47–52.

8. For Feng Yü-hsiang (馮玉祥), see James Sheridan, *Chinese Warlord: The Career of Feng Yü-hsiang* (Stanford University Press, 1966). See also Boorman, 2: 37–43.

9. For Wu Ho-ling (吳鶴齡), see ibid., 3:350–53.

10. For Wang Ching-wei (汪精衛), see ibid., 3:369–76.

11. The *hsien* is a Chinese district or county, the basic local administrative unit. The *chou* (州) was a sub-hsien; this administrative unit was abolished in the late 1920s.

12. See Jagchid, "An Interpretation of 'Mongolian Bandits' (Meng-fei)," *Altaica* (Helsinki, 1977), 113–21 (chapter 14 of this work).

13. For Chang Tso-lin (張作霖), see Gavan McCormack,*Chang Tso-lin in Northeast China*, 1911–27, (Palo Alto, 1977).

14. For Huang Shao-hung (黃紹竑), see Boorman, 2:205–8.

15. For Ho Ying-ch'in, see ibid., 2:79–84.

16. For Chiang Kai-shek's views and policies toward Inner Mongolian Autonomy, see his speech *Chung-kuo chih pien-chiang wen-ti* (中國之边疆問題 On China's Frontier Problem), 7 March 1934, *Tsung-t'ung Chian-kung ssu-hsiang yen-lun tsung-chi — yen-chiang* (總統蔣公思想言論總集—演講 The Collection of President Chiang's Thoughts and Speeches — Lectures) (1981, Taipei), 105–10.

17. See note 5.

18. Li Shuo-hsin (李守信) was a Mongol from the Tümed Banner of the Josotu League. He left Mongolian society quite young and therefore was entirely Sinicized. He could not even speak the Mongolian language. His original troops were all Chinese; no Mongols were involved.

Part V
Folklore and Shamanism

Chapter 22

Chinggis Khan in Mongolian Folklore

(Originally published in *Proceedings of the International Conference on Sinology*, October 1981, Taipei, 287–310)

Prior to the emergence of Chinggis Khan, the Mongols were merely one small, unknown tribe among many in Inner Asia. Through Chinggis Khan came the political unification of fragmented peoples having a common origin, language, and culture, but who were scattered over what is present-day Mongolia. Chinggis Khan not only founded an empire that occupied some two-thirds of the known world of his time (r. 1206–27), but he also began a rule over Mongolia which continued through his descendants — the Chinggissid princes — until 1949.[1] It is not an exaggeration to state that without Chinggis Khan there never would have been a unified Mongolian nation. The name of Chinggis Khan is inseparably linked with the fate of the Mongolian people.

Chinggis Khan was responsible for establishing a system of laws and public institutions, as well as promoting the development of a writing system for the Mongols. Through phenomenal military victories, he improved the standard of living and gave stability to his people. The *Secret History of the Mongols*, the earliest Mongolian record, probably written in the 1240s, records Chinggis Khan's hope, i.e., "To enjoy happiness, their [the people's] feet should be set firmly on grass-covered lands and their hands should grasp the [rightful] places."[2] This may be interpreted to mean placing a herder's staff in the people's hand and providing them good grazing lands.

It was probably Chinggis Khan, the supreme strategist, who first exercised extensively the "human sea warfare tactic"[3] in his invasions of western Asia. But, those whom he drove before him into the valley of death were enemies, alien inhabitants of newly occupied territories, not his own people. He always carefully minimized sacrificing his own people's lives. He was harsh and severe toward the enemy, but considerate to his underlings. He did not liquidate his own supporters, meritorious generals, or important vassals after his rise to power as did many founders of Chinese dynasties.[4] Notwithstanding the fact that his reputation was clouded among his enemies, he was honored and even worshipped as *örüshiyeltü boghda khaghan*, merciful divine emperor, in the traditions of his own people. Not only was he glorified as a great historical and national hero, the model of a perfect man, but he was also deified as a god, the divine protector of the Mongolian nation. A great ruler of the past, he is still alive in the hearts of the Mongols. Chinggis Khan's significance as a nationalistic symbol has been manifested on numerous occasions in recent decades. Only a few examples will be noted here.

In Outer Mongolia, after the socialist revolution in the 1920s, Chinggis Khan became an anti-hero, a symbol opposed to Marxism-Leninism, a hindrance to the international communist scheme. The *History of the Mongolian People's Republic*, published by the Institute of History of the Academy of Sciences of the Mongolian People's Republic, states:

> Intellectuals not understanding the difference between patriotism and manifestations of national pride on the one hand and bourgeoisie nationalism on the other, boasted about the conquests of Chinggis Khan and Mongolian feudalism and characterized the period of the development of Mongolian feudalism as if it were a "Golden Age."[5]

In 1962, on the occasion of the 800-year anniversary of the birth of Chinggis Khan, the nationalistic leaders of the Mongolian People's Republic government and party (Temür-ochir, Tsende, and others) planned a great national celebration, expressive of Mongolian patriotism. Of course, the result of such an action might have been to instigate a political crisis in the Soviet Union by inciting nationalistic insurrections among non-Russian national minorities in Central Asia and Siberia. Consequently, under pressure from Moscow, Temür-ochir and Tsende were banished from their leadership positions and Ilichev, the top Kremlin theoretician, was sent to Ulan-bator with a delegation to take care of the problem.[6]

In Inner Mongolia Chinggis Khan was regarded as the symbol of national freedom during the autonomy movement of the 1930s. During the Sino-Japanese War (1937–45), the National Government of China, in order to circumvent a Japanese plot in Mongolia, ordered the removal of Chinggis Khan's relics from Ejen-khoroo in Ordos, western Inner Mongolia, to Hsing-lung Mountain near Lanchou, Kansu Province. While the Japanese occupied eastern Inner Mongolia, they established a shrine to Chinggis Khan at Wang-yin süme (presently Ulan-khota) to cultivate good will among the Mongols. After the Communist takeover, the relics removed to Kansu were officially brought back to the original site in Ordos and an enormous mausoleum to Chinggis Khan was established as an expression of the concern by the new regime for the vitality of the strategic Mongolian minority.

In Taiwan, a significant group of Mongolian leaders residing on the island, sponsored by the government of the Republic of China, continue to celebrate a day of commemoration and veneration for Chinggis Khan with a traditional memorial service on the twenty-first day of the third lunar month each year. All these events suggest that Chinggis Khan is still a symbol of unity to the Mongols, a symbol of their unique national heritage.

Historically, accounts of supernatural parentage for Chinggis Khan were recorded quite early, but the deification of this founder of the nation arose only with the passage of time. The *Secret History of the Mongols* emphasizes that a mandate of Heaven *(Tenggeri)* was granted him through the supernatural birth of his ancestors.[7] According to the *Secret History*, Chinggis Khan always expressed earnest devotion to *Möngke Tenggeri*, the supreme god of early Mongolian Shamanism. With his great success and victories, Chinggis Khan gradually came to believe that Heaven was on his side, that he was the lord of the universe, trusted by Heaven.[8] According to the same record Heaven revealed to a high shaman that the nation would be given to Temüjin, later entitled Chinggis Khan, and not to Jamukha, his opponent.[9]

The Persian historian, Ata-Malik Juvaini (1226–83), also recorded in his famous work, *The History of the World Conqueror*, that God spoke to Kököchü *Teb-tenggeri*, a leading shaman declaring that: "The earth was given to Temüjin and he should be named as Chinggis Khan."[10] In the same period the Armenian historian, Girgor of Akanc' recorded in his *History of the Nation of Archers,* that God sent an angel in the form of a golden eagle to deliver his will and commandments to Chinggis Khan.[11] This Armenian legend is obviously a Christianized version of a Mongolian mythical tale emphasizing the supernatural character of Chinggis Khan. In a similar vein the seventeenth century Mongolian historian, Sagang Sechen, in his *Erdeni-yin tobchi* (the Chinese translation is known as *Meng-ku yüan-liu*), records:

> On three consecutive mornings before the day that [Temüjin] ascended the khan's throne there appeared a five colored sparrow sitting on a perfectly square white rock singing, *"chinggis chinggis . . ."* Thereafter the fame of the Blessed Divine Chinggis Khaghan spread abroad throughout [the universe]. The rock spontaneously split in two and a precious jade seal appeared.[12]

A similar tale is recorded in the *Altan tobchi,* edited and compiled by Lobsangdanjin, a learned lama of the latter part of the seventeenth century.[13] However, it is not recorded in the *Secret History*. This indicates that the mythical bird tale was fabricated after the death of Chinggis Khan and increasingly took on the qualities of a myth as time passed. With the expansion of Mongolian power, legends of Chinggis Khan were promulgated differently in different areas. They all served to enhance the "supernatural nature" of the world conqueror.

The actual worship of Chinggis Khan was not limited to his *Altan uragh* (golden-descendants), but was a general practice of the common Mongols. After the fall of the empire, internal turmoil and external oppression occurred and reoccurred in Mongolia. The need for protection, the hope for tranquility, and a recollection of the glories of the past regime all combined to elevate Chinggis Khan to the realm of a supernatural demigod. Tales of the omnipotent power of the Khan were also fabricated to satisfy a void in the hearts of the people. Chinggis Khan in the minds of the people took on magical powers and was able to transform himself into different forms when necessary. These tales appear constantly in the Mongolian materials concerning Chinggis Khan which were written several centuries after the collapse of the empire. For instance, Sagang Sechen recorded in his *Erdeni-yin tobchi:*

> [The two meritorious younger brothers of Chinggis Khan] Khasar[14] and Belgütei[15] talked to each other. "This Lord [Chinggis] is ruling unreasonably and compelling [us] incomprehensibly. It [his power] is nothing [alone] but is dependent upon [us] — i.e,. the marksmanship of Khasar and the strength of Belgütei." . . . Soon after, the Lord, knowing this, in order to correct the youngsters' arrogance, transformed himself into a poor old man and strolled among the yurts to sell a long, deeply arched bow. Khasar and Belgütei met [him] and said, "Old man, this bow of yours is good for nothing except to [shoot] small arrows at birds." The old man smiled and said, "You two youngsters, why underrate it before trying? Test it, then [you] will know." Belgütei's strength was not able to string [the bow] so the old man strung it. [Even so] Khasar was unable to draw it. Then, in their presence, the [common] old man changed into a grey-haired elderly [gentle] man on a white-faced gray mule,[16] took back the long, deeply arched bow, drew a whistling golden arrow,

shot at the cliff and chopped off half of it. . . . Then the two [brothers] said, "He is not an old man. He is the Lord transformed." From that time they repented and behaved properly.[17]

In the section about Chinggis Khan's eradication of the Tangut Hsia (Tangghud in Mongolian) dynasty, Sagang Sechin relates Chinggis' magical confrontation with the enemy chief.

Shidurghu Khaghan[18] [of the Tangghud] transformed himself into a snake, and then the Lord transformed himself into a *Karaudi*,[19] the king of all birds. [Shidurghu Khaghan] then transformed himself into a tiger, but the Lord was transformed into a lion, the king of all beasts. [Shidurghu Khaghan] transformed himself into a boy, whereupon the Lord was transformed into Khormusta[20] [the king of heaven]. Finally, Shidurghu Khaghan was exhausted and captured.[21]

When discussing the internal struggle and subsequent emergence of the Oirad power against the Chinggisid leaders, Sagang Sechen wrote:

Toghon *Taishi*[22] [of the Oirad] mounted a fine palomino horse . . . circled the Lord's *ordo* [the eight white yurts for worship] three times, and as [his] horse pawed the ground with its hooves he said, "You are a blessed one whose yurt is white. I Toghon, am also of blessed seed. . . ." [The guards] . . . said, ". . . Your word . . . is a grave blasphemy. You should bow to the Divine Lord and beg a pardon for your life." [Toghon] refused and said, "Why should I ask [forgiveness] for my life from others? Now the entire Mongol nation is mine. I should have the khan's title as the other Mongol khans before me." He then placed offerings before the Lord and turned back. [Suddenly,] a striking sound come from the Lord's golden quiver. His guards rushed back and discovered that a long-range arrow in the middle hole [of the quiver] was still waggling. Just then blood began pouring from Toghon *Taishi's* nose and mouth and suffering came upon him. When [they] undressed him and tried to comfort [him], a wound was seen between his two shoulder bones as if it had been pierced by an arrow. Going back to check the Lord's quiver, blood was found on both the point and shaft of a long-range arrow that inserted in the middle hole [of the quiver]. It was then realized that [Toghon's action] was not pleasing to the Lord.[23]

This mystical story was not only recorded in Sagang Sechen's work but also in other materials of his period and later, such as the *Altan tobchi, Chinggis Khaghan-u chidagh,* and others.

According to the venerable record of the *Secret History,* the early Mongols traditionally worshipped their ancestors *(yekes)* with sacrificial burnt offerings *(tüleslhi)*.[24] After the empire was established, the ceremonies of imperial ancestor worship became even more sophisticated and institutionalized under Khubilai Khan (r. 1260–94). A Chinese dynastic history, the *Yüan shih,* notes:

On the *ting-ch'ou* day of the . . . tenth winter month . . . of the third year [of Chih-yüan, 1266] the Imperial Ancestral Temple was completed. The prime-ministers, An-tung and Bayan,[25] declared: "There shall be a regulation of the ancestral genealogies, honorable posthumous temple titles, offerings, and temples for the four emperors [Chinggis Khan, Ogödei Khan, Güyüg Khan, and Möngke Khan], their spirit tablets, the meritorious ministers with whom [they] share sacrifices, ceremonial clothing, and instruments." [The Emperor] commanded the Deputy Prime Minister, Chao Pi[26] to assemble the court officials for discussions and it was decided [to establish] eight [memorial] halls.[27]

The following is recorded in the "Monograph on Worship and Offering" in the same history in the section on Ancestral Temples.

The ritual of worship and offerings to their ancestors included the sacrifice of animals, the offering of *kumis,* and the words of prayer which should be offered by a Mongolian shaman. This was their customary national tradition.[28]

These excerpts from the *Yüan shih* suggest that after the Mongolian Yüan Dynasty was established in China their rituals of ancestor worship were somewhat Sinicized. Nevertheless, they still maintained the Shamanistic tradition in the ceremonies.

The aforementioned "eight halls," which the Chinese *Yüan shih* records as *pa shih,* the Mongolian materials refer to as *naiman chaghan ger,* "the eight white yurts" (tents of worship). The *Meng-ku yüan-liu* (the Chinese version of the *Erdeni-yin tobchi*), calls them *pa pai shih.*[29] The *Chaghan teüke,*[30] said to be a primary source of records from the time of Khubilai Khan (r. 1260-94), confirms that "Khubilai Khan worshipped the *altan gege'en* [the Ancestral Golden Spirit], and established a complete set of rules [for the ceremonies].[31]

With the collapse of Mongolian imperial power (1368), the ancestral temple in China was, of course, discontinued. However, the institution of the *naiman chaghan ger* continued in Mongolia and became the center of a Chinggis Khan cult. Here the later khans came to pay their respects and to declare their sovereignty.[32] The Ordos tribe took care of the *naiman chaghan ger* located on the south of the loop of the Yellow River. The word *Ordos* is the plural form of *ordo* meaning the yurt or *ger* of an honorable one. At present, the center of the cult of Chinggis Khan is at Ejen Khoroo,[33] the Lord's camp or the Lord's Headquarters in the Ordos region. No doubt this cult originated from the early institution of the *naiman chaghan ger.*

Ejen Khoroo is located at Altan-shire'en in the southern part of Jiün-wang Banner (Ordos Left Flank Center Banner) near the northern boundary of the Jasagh Banner (Ordos Right Flank Front End Banner). Later, the Communists combined these two banners under the new name of Ejen Khoroo Banner, and a new shrine or mausoleum was established on the original site to commemorate Chinggis Khan. According to the *Meng-ku yu-mu chi* (Record of Mongolian Grazing Lands), the well-known work of the Ch'ing specialist Chang Mu states: "The burial place of Yüan T'ai-tsu [Chinggis Khan] is located at the far northwest corner of the fortress of Yü-lin [northern Shensi]; the name of the place is Chaghan-ger [the white yurt]." But this specialist mistakenly locates this historically important place in the Otogh Banner (Ordos Right Flank Middle Banner) area.[34]

The traditional offering days were the twenty-first day of the third lunar month of spring, the fifteenth day of the fifth month of summer, the twelfth day of the ninth month of autumn, and the third day of the tenth month in the winter. In addition to this, ceremonial offerings were made on the Khan's birthday, the sixteenth day of the fourth month; the Khan's memorial day, the twelfth day of the seventh month; and the day of the Khan's enthronement, the sixteenth day of the twelfth month. Also, there were offerings on the first day and the last day of each lunar year. In addition to these, regular offerings were made on the first day of each month and special or private offerings were made for various other reasons at undetermined times.

The *Chaghan teüke* records that Khubilai Khan announced the following national festival days: 1) the twenty-first day of the last month of spring (the third lunar month) to commemorate a historic occasion when Chinggis Khan tied up ninety-nine mares of his White Herd to milk them; 2) the fifteenth day of the middle month of summer (the fifth lunar month) as the summer festival day; 3) the twelfth day of the last month of autumn (the ninth lunar month) as the autumn festival day; and 4) the third day of the first month of winter (the tenth lunar month) as the day for *milaghad* ceremony of the Khan (a ritual of anointing newborn babies or other new important items).[35]

The birthday of Chinggis Khan is commonly celebrated on the sixteenth day of the fourth lunar month. However, the accuracy of this date is doubtful. The *Secret History* does not indicate the Khan's birthday. On the contrary, it indicates the sixteenth of the first month of summer, the *khulan tergel odür*, as an important Mongolian festival day.[36] Probably people later mistook the *khulan tergel ödür* as the birthday of the Khan. As for the holiday on the third day of the tenth lunar month, it is impossible to tell precisely whether Chinggis Khan was anointed on that day or if he anointed others.

The spring offering, the twenty-first day of the third lunar month, was the most important of the four ceremonial occasions. Its origin is also not clear. Perhaps it was to celebrate Chinggis Khan's victory over his chief enemy, Ong Khan of the Kereyid, a turning point in his career. From this victory Chinggis Khan never again met a setback, but achieved his goals.[37] On this day of celebration, all the banners of Mongolia sent envoys to Ejen-khoroo to pay respects and present offerings. Traditionally the *ongghon*, or imperial casket, was placed on a special large cart pulled by a white camel,[38] moved to the vicinity of the yurts, and placed in a temporary large tent pavilion covered with yellow satin in which the audience venerated the national hero.

The traditional administrative institutions of the cult at Ejen-khoroo were quite unique. The highest official was the *jinong*[39] who governed a group of five hundred families independent from any other Mongolian administration. The origin of the *jinong* can be traced back through Mongolian history. According to the *Chaghan teüke*, Khubilai Khan determined that both the Khan and the *jinong* should personally supervise the affairs of the cult of the "Ancestral Golden Spirits."[40]

After the fall of the empire there were long periods of division among the Mongols. In the latter part of the fifteenth century they were reunified under the reign of Dayan Khan (r. 1479–ca. 1516) who personally supervised the Left Flank Mongols. The administration of the Right Flank forces were assigned to his third son, Bars-bolod, as deputy *khan* (jinong). At the same time, he was recognized as the lord *(noyan)* or Ordos, one *tümen* of the Right Flank Mongols. The descendants of Bars-bolod hereditarily received the title of *jinong*, deputy khan.

In the Manchu-Ch'ing period Ordos was divided into seven banners and reorganized as Yeke-juu League. Among these seven banners the prince of the Jiün-wang Banner (Ordos Left Flank Central Banner), of the lineage of the eldest son of Bars-bolod, inherited the noble title of *jinong*. In the latter part of the Ch'ing period, the Manchu court ceased to recognize and honor this special lineage and transferred the title in rotation to the prince appointed as the governor of the league. In the Mongolian tradition a *jinong* was not only a person of very high noble rank, but also one assigned to administer the cult of Chinggis Khan.

The five hundred families under the jurisdiction of the *jinong* were called *darkhad* (a plural form of *darkhan* which originally meant a specially meritorious person freed from obligations of services and taxes). Here it means a group of people exempted from customary duties and assigned the honor of serving Chinggis Khan at his camp Ejen-khoroo. The ranks and functions of the *darkhad* had eight division: 1) *khonjin*,[41] the top official who administered the cult at Ejen-khoroo; 2) *Taishi* (a transliterated Chinese word *t'ai-shih*), the most honorable title for court officials of the Mongol empire and the Yüan dynasty;[42] 3) *Daibu* (another transliterated Chinese official term, *t'ai-fu*),[43] second to the *taishi* in handling the offering ceremonies and services; 4) *Tsaisang* (another borrowed Chinese word *tsai-hsiang*, meaning prime-minister), charged with the preparations of the ceremonies; 5) *Jisghal*, the director of ceremonies; 6) *Tüleger*, cared for the burnt offerings and the distribution of the sacrificial food to the attendants; 7) *Keshigten*,[44] probably descendants of the imperial bodyguards *(keshigten)* originally assigned to protect the *chaghan ger* of the Khan; and 8) *Khorchin*,[45] originally imperial guards equipped with bows and arrows who took care of the imperial yurt *(ordo)* and the keys. These positions were hereditary and show the strong historical tradition of the *ordo* and *keshighten* of the Mongolian empire. The secular administration of the *darkhad* was managed by a *darugha*,[46] known earlier in the empire period as *darughachi*.[47]

The organization of the cult is a little different from what one might expect as seen in the record in the *Chaghan teüke*.

> The head of the vassals who perform the offerings and manage the rituals of this general worship service is the *khonjin*, next are the *ilghaghchi taishi, jaisang [tsaisang]*, forty *ger-ün noyan* [officials of the yurts], and four *darkhad*. It was decided that the twelve *otogh* [groups] of the Ordos tümen [a main body of troops] should manage the affairs and articles for offerings ... with great care.[48]

The focal point of the cult at Ejen-khoroo is the *ongghon* of Chinggis Khan. This term *ongghon* generally means the tomb of an honorable person, a guardian spirit, or an object of worship. Here it means the imperial casket. However, what is contained in the *ongghon* has long been a closely kept secret and is not known to the world at large. Commonly it is said that this *ongghon* is the casket of Chinggis Khan and his first empress *(khatun)*, Börte. Yet, according to most Mongolian sources, the Khan's body was buried in Yeke-öteg Mountain of the Kentei Range.[49] Again, according to Chinese official documents and records, all deceased khans of the Yüan Dynasty were brought back and buried at Ch'i-nien-ku,[50] a very sacred and secret place in Mongolia.

In a conversation in 1949, a *darkhad* official told the author that traditionally each year on an auspicious day prior to the spring offering of the twenty-first day of the third month, the *Jinong*, the *khonjin*, and a few *darkhad* officials were obliged to change the yellow satin that wrapped the relics inside the casket. Before doing so, they had to make a very solemn oath that they would never speak to anybody about what they had seen or experienced. This is a very solemn taboo, and, therefore, this historical secret has never been made known to the world. Nevertheless, whether this *ongghon* is the real casket of the Khan or merely a symbol does not diminish the reverence the Mongols show toward this holy relic.

Another sacred item related to the Ejen-khoroo cult is Chinggis Khan's imperial standard,i.e., *khara-sülde*. It is symbolic of the protective spirit of the Mongol nation. It consists of a shaft wrapped with white leather topped by a gray-colored, fine steel spearhead. Under the spear-head is a ring with tassels made from the manes of one thousand dark-brown stallions. The *sülde,* or standard, is preserved in the middle of a wooden enclosure eighty *bere*[51] southeast of the main shrine *(khoroo)*. Four similar sacred spots exist where four "emissary standards" *(elchin sülde)* related to the main *khara sülde* are preserved. These *süldes* are similar to the main one but a little smaller. Traditionally, these four "emissary standards" are taken once every twelve years on a solemn procession through all seven banners of the Ordos.[52] The purpose of this ritual was to preserve the peace and welfare of the area. The *khara sülde* was said to be so powerful, sacred, noble, and untouchable that no one dared move it from its position. Nevertheless, it was believed that the power of the *khara sülde* could be felt in distant places. Consequently, in the 1930s when the Khan's *ongghon* was ordered moved from Ejen-khoroo to Lanchou by the National Government, it was only accompanied by one of the four *elchin süldes,* because no person dared touch the *khara sülde*. The author was told by a *darkhad* official that changes in the *sülde's* color were related to the tranquility or turmoil in a particular area. An elder *darkhad* attendant is inspired to discern the state of affairs.

To the Mongols the *sülde* embodied or was symbolic of the great guardian spirit of the ancient Shamanistic tradition. Before the unification of the fragmented nomadic tribes of Chinggis Khan, each clan or tribe apparently had its own *sülde*. However, after unification the *sülde* of Chinggis Khan became symbolic of the protecting spirit of the entire Mongol nation. Before the Communist revolution almost all Mongolian banners had a sacred and secret place to worship a *sülde*. Accompanying these symbolic *süldes* were relics of Chinggis Khan such as his sword, spear, arrow, bow, quiver, saddle, clothing, and boots. Traditionally, persons involved with this sacred place were forbidden to discuss the duties of their service. The location of the sacred place was isolated from the public and especially from strangers. Offerings to the *sülde* usually took place secretly though regularly. The formal, official offerings to Chinggis Khan were the only ones performed openly at government centers.

Following the introduction of Buddhism to Mongolia the native tradition of ancestor worship was influenced by the new religion. To link the Mongolian imperial lineage directly to Buddhism, Tibetan Buddhologists and historians drew upon the theories of reincarnation. They claimed that Khorichar-mergen, Chinggis Khan's ancestor who preceded him by twenty-one generations, was the reincarnation of Padmasambbava, a great master of Tantriyana and founder of the Buddhist faith in Tibet.[53] Beginning in the 1570s Buddhism again flourished in Mongolia, and as its influence expanded Mongolian Buddhist historians built upon Tibetan mythology. They not only deified Chinggis Khan, but also linked the Khan's genealogy to Tibetan and Indian legendary kings and to the Buddha himself.[54] With the rise of Manchu power in the early half of the 1600s other religious-political myths were created and spread among the Mongols. These held that the Tibetan pontiff, the Dalai Lama, is the transformed body of the great Boddhisattva,

Avalokitesvara, that the Manchu emperor was the Boddhisattva Manjushiri, and that Chinggis Khan was the incarnation of the Boddhisattva Vajrabani.[55]

Many records of performances of Buddhist prayers in the Mongolian ancestral temple are found in the *Yüan shih,* but still, the main service was carried out by the Mongolian shamans, the *bo'e*. Perhaps a detailed presentation of the rites and prayers will best serve as an example of the extent to which Buddhism and Chinese court traditions influenced the original Shamanistic rituals of Mongolian ancestor worship.[56]

At Ejen-khoroo the ordinary ceremonial rituals consisted of the following: 1) *khadagh*[57] (ceremonial silk scarf) offerings; 2) *jula*[58] (lamp) offerings; 3) incense offerings; 4) meat offerings; 5) wine[59] offerings; 6) recital of an *ochig* (also known as *sang,* an official prayer); 7) burnt sacrifices; 8) offerings to the relics; and 9) distribution of the sacrificial food.

Because the cult originally had no direct relationship with Buddhism, the rituals were not necessarily administered by a lama but were commonly carried out by laymen.[60] Nevertheless, since Buddhism became the common faith of the Mongols, these rituals were clearly influenced by such Buddhist religious objects as *khadaghs,* lamps, and incense. Of course, these could be remnants of Chinese ceremonies performed in the Yüan times in the imperial ancestral temple *(tai-miao* 太廟*).*

A firsthand account of one of the ritual ceremonies is appropriate here. In July 1949, while the *ongghon* of Chinggis Khan was still at Hsing-lung Mountain, Lanchou, Kansu Province, the author and the governor of Ulanchab League, Prince Rinchinsengge, a descendant of Khasar, the younger brother of Chinggis Khan, went to pay formal respects to the *ongghon*. I noted that the casket was about seven to eight feet long by four feet high, rectangular in shape and constructed of some dark brown metal overlaid with designs in silver. The chief *darkhad* explained that it contained the remains of both Chinggis Khan and his Empress *(khatun),* Börte. A similar but smaller casket, said to contain the remains of Khulan *Khatun,*[61] was placed on the far right side of the hall. On this occasion, distilled spirits and a whole boiled sheep were offered. If this ceremony had taken place at Ejen-khoroo or other centers in Mongolia, the distilled spirits would have been *araki* or *araja,* a strong liquor prepared from cow's milk, or *airagh,* fermented mare's milk commonly known as kumiss. The sacrifice of sheep would have included nine whole boiled animals. In Ejen-khoroo a horse was sometimes sacrificed.[62] Since nine is a lucky number according to Mongolian beliefs, the total offering should contain nine sacrificial categories with nine items in each category. At the ceremony in Lanchou, the attendants all knelt as the chief of the *darkhad* called out our names and titles in a loud voice as though in the presence of His Majesty, the Khan. We then knelt three times and executed nine bows toward the *ongghon.* At the beginning of the ceremony the head of our group, Prince Rinchinsengge, made an offering of a long *khadagh.* After the *jula,* incense, and meat were offered, the head *darkhad* chanted the *öchig* in a liturgical voice. He then offered the wine in a large vase-shaped bronze vessel about one and a half feet tall. While other *darkad* were still chanting, he took the wine and told us that it was a gift bestowed upon those present by the Khan. He took a drink first, performed nine kowtows (kneeling bows), and then passed it to those present for them to partake from the same vessel in an order according to rank. The ceremony seemed reminiscent of the ancient *ho-chan*[63] or royal wine party of the Yüan dynasty.

Nineteen forty-nine was a critical year for Inner Mongolia. Those attending the above ceremony, as they compared the situation then to the past glory of the Mongol nation, were unable to restrain their emotions and wept silently. All the *de'eji*, the choicest parts of the sheep offering, were put into a vessel containing fire and consumed as a burnt offering. Finally, after another set of three kneelings and nine bowings, we were ushered to a reception room where the boiled sheep was brought to us as *keshigh* — i.e., blessed food from the Khan — of which we partook with the *darkhad* officials attending the ceremony.

Soon after World War II anthropologist Frank Bessac visited Ejen-khoroo. In a ceremony he witnessed a *darkhad* leader, after chanting and offering *airagh* (mare's milk) to the four directions under heaven, required those present to bow to some of the effects of Chinggis Khan that were still present. He then had them touch his bowstring while kneeling on one knee and tied a *khadagh* around the neck of those present symbolizing that each had pledged himself to the cause of Chinggis Khan.[64]

In the ceremonies discussed above, the recital of an *öchig* or *sang* was an important part of the ritual. There are different editions of the prayers, but they are all quite similar. Below are the author's translations of some of the prayers.

Psalm/Prayer to the Divine Chinggis Khan[65]

Born with the mandate of Supreme Heaven,
Bearing majestic fame and divine title,
Governing all nations of the universe,
Chinggis Khaghan, you were born of Heaven!

With Heaven as the origin of His grace,
With imposing superior intelligence,
With matchless wisdom and virtuous rule,
Chinggis Khaghan, you were born with genius!

With the reputation of Temüjin, the hero,
With four beloved empresses,[66]
With four energetic brothers,[67]
With four powerful sons,[68]
Chinggis Khaghan, you were born universal Lord of all nations!

Beginning in the grace of the starry Heavens,
Born at Deli'ün-boltagh on the River Onon,
Assuming rule of the nation of Ong Khaghan,
And ruling the Kereyid multitudes,
Yet governing properly your own — the Ordos masses,
Chinggis Khaghan, you are the Lord of all nations!

With a most enlightened Empress Börtegeljin[69]
Who was with you before creation,
With the honorific title, Lord of the Sacred,
With the Golden descendants from the Borjigin [clan],[70]

With your companions Bu'urchi[71] and Mukhali,[72]
Chinggis Khaghan, you are the Lord of the entire universe!

With Empress Khulan who you met miraculously,
And accompanied by melodious songs,
With the nine heroic companions[73] who followed as one,
Chinggis Khaghan, you are the Lord of everything and all!

Ascending the Imperial throne at Ködege-aral[74] on the River Kerülün,
Bearing the great fame and flawless title,
Bearing in mind all things that have been spoken,
Chinggis Khaghan, you were born brilliant and wise!

Born in the image of sun and moon,
Absorbing the realm of Dayan Khaghan[75] of Naiman,
Taking possession of the realm of the great nation,
Chinggis Khaghan, your birth was auspicious in every reincarnation!

Leading thousands and thousands of your warriors,
At Ghurban-ulkhui of the River Tu'ula,
Brandishing standards and trumpets,
Under the luxuriant tree of the dancing festival,[76]
Chinggis Khaghan appointed the standard-bearer, Mukhali of the Jalair [clan].

Marching across the yellow hills,
Crushing your enemies, the three groups of Taichi'ud,
Eliminating all the insults against your Golden offspring,
Chinggis Khaghan, you bear the greatest fame!

Marching beyond the Khangghai Mountains,
Leading with your jade seal in your sleeve,
Training the rocklike troops,
Annihilating your alien foes,
Chinggis Khaghan, you bear widely known title and fame!

Marching beyond the Altai Mountains,
Leading your people and legions,
Destroying your envious enemies,
Chinggis Khaghan, you bear widely known title and fame!

Marching beyond the Jelemen Mountains,
Roasting your musk-deer and wild horse,
Subduing your obnoxious enemies,
Spreading widely your laws and ordinances,
Chinggis Khaghan, you were born destined to reign!

Marching beyond the Tobkhan Mountains,
Riding your horse, Dobuchagh-targhu,
Releasing your famous falcon,
Subduing the enemy Toghmagh[77] under your feet,
Chinggis Khaghan, you were born with standard, trumpets, and troops!

Leading expeditions in Sa'ari and Tabaghtai,[78]
Occupying Sultan Jalal-ad-Din's[79] state of Sarta'ul,[80]
Releasing your sharp-clawed gerfalcon
To catch and divide desired game,
Chinggis Khaghan, you have placed your descendants to rule over them!

Marching beyond the Shingkhula Mountains,
Subduing the people wearing *shirbegel*,[81]
Riding a fine horse,
Chinggis Khaghan, you imposed taxes and obligations upon Samarkand[82] and abroad!

Leading incursions into the land of Ölge,
Subduing the enemy Öchiyed[83] under your rule
In a century of greatness,
Chinggis Khaghan, your birth was auspicious!

Marching beyond the Munan Mountains,
Leading your own Mongol nation
To subdue the Tangghud state under your hand,
Causing Shidurghu Khan[84] to tremble,
[Oh] Lord you took the beauty, lady Gürbeljin![85]

Ruling all nations from where the sun rises to where it sets,
Enjoying the fine drink of port wine,[86]
Ruling nations and peoples,
[Oh] Lord, you bear the boundless honorific title and fame!

This day we offer effusive prayer to you.
Preparing various offerings we entreat you:
Grant Mercy and provide for the well-being of your descendants, offspring of Your Majestic Borjigin line,
Oh Chinggis Khaghan of divine birth!

Increase, we pray, your own — the Mongol masses.
Extend their lives and longevity.
Enlarge the size of their herds and animals.
Cause to flourish your own descendants and offspring.

On bended knee we pray with offerings to you.
Cause, please, your own religion to develop.
Multiply, we beg, your own treasury and herds.
From this day and forever, manifest, we beseech you, your will for comprehensive ordinances and expansive brilliant teachings.

The *sülde* of Chinggis Khan, according to ancient Shamanistic tradition, was believed to have the power to bless worshippers and curse enemies both spiritually and physically. Following are two examples of prayers or liturgies performed as offerings to the *sülde*.

I. *Offerings for the Golden sülde*[87] *of Chinggis Khaghan, and A Prayer to His Serene Holiness, the Ingenious Divine Chinggis Khaghan.*[88]

Recite *om a hum*[89] three times.

    O Lama, Protector of Law and the Supreme [Buddha] of the three epochs [past, present and future]; and the Divine Chinggis Khaghan, with limitless companions, the designated ministers and companions of the *ordo*,[90] palace of happiness; and all *tenggeri* [the heavens],[91] *luus* [the dragon kings],[92] guardians of riches, lords of land and waters located here about, and all wrathful deities, [we] invite [you] to condescend now to fulfill [our] needs and desires.

    A platform is prepared with jewels beyond compare and [we invite] the Great Chaghan Ubashi[93] and all his companions, intimate ministers, heavens, and dragon kings, to please be seated, happily and comfortably, on the cushion of eight beautiful lotus flowers.

In accordance with the holy offering, [we] present the choicest part of many tasty foods, the essence of *rashiyan*,[94] and the best tasting milk, to the Divine, Ingenious Chinggis Khaghan and his companions.

[We] offer *jula*[95] [the holy lamp], which is the full-blown, prosperous flame of a blazing fire.

[We] offer a great aroma of burning incense of sandalwood, balsam, and juniper. Oh, Chinggis Khaghan and [his] companions, please partake of the holy offerings and bestow *shidi*[96] [a divine use of power] to pacify all the evil obstacles.

Use, please, your divine power to resolve erroneous controversies.

Use, please, your divine power to enhance [our] wisdom and knowledge.

Bestow, please, the divine power to increase [our] courage and strength.

Through your command as Heavenly Khaghan, [exercising] your spontaneous, miraculous power as protector of wealth, and as the perfect heroic creator, crumble, please, into dust the defenses of the kings whose teachings are heretical; rule over the countries of the [people of] five colors in the four directions.

Use, please, thy great power, as great as the supreme eighty four thousand kings of the Khaghan that rotates the Wheel of the Law [of Buddha], to conquer violent malice.

[We] praise and worship you, Perfect Divine Guardian.

According to the merit of our offerings, praises, and prayers to thee our own Lord,

Multiply, please, our companions and herds.

Strengthen, please, the peace, bliss, and enjoyment of long life.

Reveal, please, those deeds [necessary] for the fulfillment of [our] special goals.

Oh, subdue please, the ill-will of men and nature.

Repel, please, military attacks.

Destroy, please, yea, behead, with [your] decisive thunderbolt and sword, hostile enemies that harm the league.[97] Dissect their main aorta.

Propagate, please, the religion of *vachir tarani*[98] in ten directions.
Bind, please, yea, incarcerate those who violate their oaths.
Send down, please, lightning upon those stubborn violent demons.
Repulse, please, the wild black wind, the hail, and the hoarfrost.
Regulate, please, the untamed land and water into a state of harmony.

With the benefaction of the three marvelous superiors, the Great Chaghan Ubashi, your ministers, and all your companions, please fulfill our wish.
Lama, Protector of the Law and the supreme [Buddha] of the three epochs [past, present and future], [you are] special divine protectors and lords of oaths.[99]
Fulfill, please, proper requests to our greatest satisfaction.
[We wish] everyday to enjoy the auspicious bliss of happiness.
[We seek] peace during the day and a sense of well-being at night.
Both day and night there will be tranquility and the auspicious bliss of the Supreme Three Jewels [Buddha, Dharma, and Sangha], forever and ever.
Let the fruit of good deeds be increased.
Let the auspicious bliss be fulfilled.

II. *The Prayer to the Golden sülde of Chinggis Khaghan Among the Early Mongols.*[100]

Bow to the Lama,[101]
Bow to the Buddha,
Bow to the Law,
Bow to the Buddhist Priests.

Upholding the fame of the Golden *sülde*,
Achieving great merit against difficult demons,
Defeating all enemies,
[We] bow and present offerings to you, oh wrathful Black *sülde*.[102]
Calling in a voice of urgency,
[We] bow and present offerings to you, oh Golden *sülde*.

Having a youthful countenance,
Holding your crescent thunderbolt spear fearsomely,
With knitted [angry] hair standing on end,
[We] bow and present offerings to you, oh young Divine *sülde!*

With your youthful countenance,
Being never deceived by any mysterious creature,
And with many ornaments around your face,
[We] bow and present offerings to you, oh Divine *sülde!*

Possessing the Immense power of *sulder*,[103]
On the summit of Mount Sumir,[104]
Causing Khomusta,[105] the Lord Khan of thirty three heavens[106] to kneel before you.
[We] bow and present offerings to you, oh Divine *sülde!*

Possessing tireless willpower,
And protecting all the creatures of this world,

Out of the suffering or terrible chaos,
[We] bow and present offerings to you, oh Divine *sülde!*

[Liberating] everyone from his demon foes,
Manifesting the supreme miraculous power of transformation,
And exterminating all demonic enemy forces,
[We] bow and present offerings to you, oh Divine *sülde!*

Possessing a fearless will,
Staring angrily downward with your thousand black eyes,
And treading a multitude of demons under your feet,
[We] bow and present offerings to you, oh Divine *sülde!*

Having a spirit of wrath,
Holding your [sharply] bladed lance,
And making a rosary out of the heads of numerous enemy troops,
[We] bow and present offerings to you, oh Divine *sülde!*

Providing merciful protection for multitudes of suffering people,
Manifesting a supreme, miraculous power of transformation,
And bestowing benevolent care,
[We] bow and present offerings to you, oh Divine *sülde!*

Marching with an Imperial Decree,
Defeating, oppressing, and destroying the shrewd, wrong, and arrogant
    malefactors,
[We] bow and present offerings to you, oh Divine *sülde!*

Suppressing disloyal ones who counter the Divine Command,
Punishing disobedient ones who counter the Laws of Buddha,
And arrogant ones who do wrong,
[We] bow and present offerings to you, oh Divine *sülde!*

Because there is misdirection in both the religion and nation,
Because evil ones increase and upright ones decrease,
[We beseech you to] bring peace and stability to the nation,
[We] bow and present offerings to you, oh Divine *sülde!*

Conquering the entire army,
Turning [them] into a pile of ash,
And manifesting the fullness of wrath,
[We] bow and present offerings to you, oh Divine *sülde!*

[We] bow and present offerings to you, oh Divine *sülde,*
That [you] might overpower the ambitions of the hated, evilhearted ones;
[We] bow and present offerings to you, oh Divine *sülde,*
That [you] might proclaim a celebration of the beneficial, good-hearted ones.

If an offering is presented once a day it will make possible all the enjoyments of
    good health, peace, and happiness, and the enjoyment of good times without
    natural disaster in summer and autumn. If an offering is presented once a day

it will make possible the defeat and repulsion of any kind of evil, anger, or violent enemies, thieves and bandits for a distance of a thousand *bere*.[107]

Liberating all the creatures from the world of darkness,
Bringing reincarnation through the power of the Law [of Buddha],
We bow and make offerings to you,
Oh Divine *sülde*, oh miraculous one!

Delivering tranquility in the midst of conflict and struggle,
Wiping out suffering and grief caused by the enemy,
We bow and present offering to you,
Oh Divine *sülde*, oh sharp annihilator of the enemy!

We pray [to you] because of your great fame.
[We] praise and bow to heaven in the direction of the bountiful, auspicious, and virtuous lords of earth.
Multiply, please, blessings and glories.
Fulfill, please, all desires.
Eliminate, please, obstacles and disasters.
Repulse, please, hateful enemies.
Cause, especially please, all our acts to be accomplished swiftly, without hindrance!

Recite the personal name [of the worshipper], then say:

According to the merit of virtue that I have fulfilled, may the Lord of the entire earth and the trusted Protector of the whole nation, the Divine Lord Chinggis Khanghan's Golden *khara sülde* with immense jurisdiction, absorb his [offering] into your light and bestow grace upon the offspring of the Khan, commoners, underlings, and all the masses of the nation. In order to deter any kind of enemy, prepare three categories of offerings that contain a pyramid [shaped] black *baling*[108] [together with] the finest, strong liquor, black tea, sugar, brown sugar, blood of a killed person, fragments of gold and silver, fragments of a steel [sword] that has been used to kill a person, and the finest part of flour and oil. [These] have to be divided and mixed evenly, and offered to the divine protector Vachirbani,[109] the Lord of Mystery.[110] Execute this prayer and offering to the Divine Lord Chinggis Khaghan according to the previously described manner on the top of an eminent mountain. If this prayer and offering are carried out in that location, it will repulse and exorcise all aggravating enemies, thieves, bandits, litigation, altercations, and scandals. For cases of dissension, altercation, and litigation, offer first the finest of strong liquor, black tea, and milk. This prayer offering to the Golden *khara sülde,* performed from the period of the Divine Chinggis Khaghan by large and small groups of the *Köke* Mongols,[111] should be presented on the top of a prominent mountain on such days as: the third day, the eighth day, and the fifteenth day of each month, or, on the fifteenth day of the first month of spring; the twelfth day of the first month of winter, and the twenty third day of the middle month of the same season.[112]

Reading from these prayers one perceives a Buddhist influence upon this once purely Shamanistic cult. Still, these prayers clearly indicate that the cult remained removed doctrinally from the teachings of Buddhism. The cult does not exceed the level of folk religion, but study of it does show how a Shamanistic ritual can survive confrontation with another religion (in this case Buddhism) by assuming the trappings or the coloration of that religion. On the other hand, this study also confirms that the Chinggis Khan cult was so firmly rooted in Mongolia that the Buddhists, although they endeavored to eradicate Mongolian Shamanism, had to make compromises in this special case.[113] In the later part of the eighteenth century the Panchen Eredeni, second great leader of the Lamaist-Buddhist world, came to Peking and Jehol. Accepting the request of the Ordos Mongols, this great lama authored a special sutra for the cult of Chinggis Khan. In this manner the Shamanistic cult of Chinggis Khan was once more drawn into the realm of Buddhism.[114]

From the above mentioned examples, it is evident that the Mongols strongly believed that a deified Chinggis Khan and his guardian spirit, the *sülde,* were omnipotent and could bring great blessings and protections to his people. At present these religious expressions have declined. However, the image of Chinggis Khan as a national hero still remains as a symbol of life and freedom in the hearts of his people. His name is still evoked in political disputes concerning Mongolian issues.

Notes

1. Chinggissid rule in Outer Mongolia ended in 1921 and in Inner Mongolia in 1949. Both happened through outside influence, i.e., the Bolshevik Revolution in Russia and the Communist takeover in China.

2. *Secret History of the Mongols,* sect. 279.

3. "Human sea warfare tactic" is a direct translation from the Chinese term *jen-hai chan-shu* (人海戰術) that was broadly used by the Chinese Communists during the civil war of the late 1940s.

4. One exception to this is the execution of the shaman Kököchü who ambitiously challenged the authority of Chinggis Khan. Nevertheless, the destruction was limited to the shaman himself and none of his household was punished. His father and brothers continued to maintain their ranks and positions without any demotion. See *Secret History,* 245, 256.

5. *History of the Mongolian People's Republic,* translated and annotated by William A. Brown and Urguange Onon (Harvard, 1976), 498.

6. *History of the Mongolian People's Republic,* 498, 630; Robert Rupen, *Mongols of the Twentieth Century* (Indiana University Press, 1964),1:320–22; and C. R. Bawden, *The Modern History of Mongolia* (London, 1968), 417–19.

7. *Secret History,* 1, 21.

8. Ibid., 80, 103, 117, 125, 246.

9. Ibid., 121.

10. Ata-Malik Juvaini, *The History of the World Conqueror,* English translation by John Andrew Boyle (University of Manchester, 1958), 1:39.

11. Grigor of Akanc, *History of the Nation of Archers,* English translation and annotation by R. P. Blake and R. N. Frye, *Harvard Journal of Asiatic Studies,* vol. XII, nos. 3, 4, (1949).
12. Sagang Sechen, *Erdeni-yin tobchi* (Ulan-bator, 1961), 86.
13. Lobsangdanjin, *Altan tobchi,* (Harvard University Press, 1952), 1:26–27.
14. Khasar, see biography in Tu Chi's (屠寄) *Meng-wu-erh shih-chi* (蒙兀兒史記), *chüan,* 22, *chüan* 4 (Reprinted in Taipei, 1962).
15. Belgutei, younger brother of Chinggis Khan from a different mother. See biography in *Yüan shih* 117, *chüan* 4.
16. Mules were not used in Mongolian pastoral-nomadic areas and were considered animals easily possessed by evil spirits. The most popular mule in folklore is the one ridden by Lhamu, the Tantric-Buddhist protector of the Law, and the word mule itself conveys to the Mongols a feeling of legendary mystery.
17. Sagang Sechen, 89–91. See also, *Chinggis Khaghan-u chidagh,* Peking edition, 1927, 12r–13v.
18. Sidurghu Khaghan was the last king of the Tangut or Hsi Hsia. His personal name is recorded in Chinese as Li Hsien (李晛).
19. *Karudi,* skr. *garuda,* commonly translated as phoenix, is a symbol of power, unlike the Chinese *feng-huang* (鳳凰), which is a symbol of beauty.
20. Khormusta (or Khormusda) was originally the Persian god Ormuzd (or Ahuramazda). In Mongolian folklore the role of Khomusta is similar to the Hindu god Indra and the Chinese god Yü-huang-ta-ti (玉皇大帝).
21. Sagang Sechen, 120.
22. Toghon *taishi* was a powerful leader of the Oirad Mongols. Later his son Esen *taishi* usurped the throne of the khan.
23. Sagang Sechen, 169–71.
24. *Secret History,* 70.
25. For An-tung's biography see *Yüan shih,* 126, *chuan* 13; for Bayan's biography see ibid., 127, *chuan* 14.
26. For Chao Pi's (趙璧) biography see ibid., 159, *chuan* 46.
27. "The Annals of Shih-tsu," 3, 8b, in ibid., 6, *chih* 6.
28. "Monograph on Worship and Offering," 3, the article on Ancestral Temple. Ibid., 74, *chih* 25, 1a.
29. See Sagang Sechen, 169, 211–212, 219. See also *Meng-ku yüan-liu ch'ien-cheng* (蒙古源流箋證), annotated by Chang Erh-tien (張爾田) (reprinted in Taipei, 1965), 6:6b, 8a, 12a.
30. The *Chaghan teüke* was first rediscovered by the Mongolian scholar, C. A. Zamcarno in Ejen-khoroo, Ordos, 1910, and was reprinted with the introduction by Walther Heissig in his *Die Familien und Kirchengeschichtsschreibung der Mongolen,* I (Wiesbaden, 1959). In the early 1970s, it was translated into English by a young Korean scholar, Ki Joong Song as a master's thesis at the University of California, Berkeley. According to Zamcarno, "the book might have been first compiled during Khubilai's reign." See Zamcarno, *The Mongol Chronicle of the 17th Century,* translated by R. Leowenthal (Wiesbaden, 1955), 50–55.
31. Ibid., Heissig edition, 1r–v.
32. Sangang Sechen, 212–19. *Meng-ku yüan-liu,* 6:8a, 12a.

33. The written form of Ejen-khoroo is Ejen-Khorogha.
34. Chang Mu (張穆), *Meng-ku yu-mu chi* (蒙古游牧記), 6:9b. First printed in 1867.
35. *Chaghan teüke*, 12r–v. Zamcarno, 53.
36. *Secret History*, 81.
37. Sechin Jagchid, *"Ch'eng-chi-ssu-han ta-chi-jih ti li-shih yi-yi"* (成吉思汗大祭日的歷史義意 The historical significance of the great offering day of Chinggis Khan), *Chung-yang hih-pao* (Central Daily News) (Taipei, 5 May 1961).
38. A white camel is considered by the Mongols to be an animal of high honor and good luck. In the Manchu-Ch'ing period the most honorable present from the Mongol khans to the Manchu emperors was the symbolic white camel.
39. *Jinong* is commonly defined as a deputy-khan. There are several explanations for the origin of the word. However, the author and his colleague, Gombojab Hangin, agree that it is a combination of the *Yüan* princely title *Chin-wang* (晉王) in Chinese and *jin-ong* in Mongolian. The meaning is the Prince of Chin (advance). The Chinggisids who bore this title were usually assigned to service in the *ordo* of Chinggis Khan. See "The Biography of Hsien-tsung (顯宗 Ghamala)" 11a, *Yüan shih*, 115, *chuan* 2.
40. *Chaghan teüke* 2r.
41. The title *Khonjin* does not appear in materials of the Mongolian empire and the Yüan dynasty, but appears quite often in records dating from the middle of the sixteenth century as a title of a noble of less importance. It did not continue in usage after the Mongols came under the domination of the Manchus.
42. *Taishi* or *tayishi* is a Mongolian loan word from the Chinese title *tai-shih* (太師). See Henry Serruys, "The Office of Tayisi in Mongolia in the 15th Century," *Harvard Journal of Asiatic Studies*, vol. 37, no. 1, 1977.
43. *Daibu* is another word borrowed from Chinese, but it is difficult to determine whether it is *t'ai-fu* (太傅 grand imperial tutor) or *tai-fu* (大夫 an honorable title for court officials).
44. On *keshigten*, the imperial guards, see *Secret History*, 224–34. See also "Monograph on Military Affairs," 2, entry for *ch'üeh-hsüeh* (怯薛) (*keshigten*), 1b–3b, in the *Yüan shih* 99, *chih* 47.
45. On *khorchin*, see Jagchid, *"Yüan shih huo-erh-ch'ih kao"* (A study on the Khorchi of the *Yüan shih*), *Pien-cheng hui-k'an* (Taipei, October 1966).
46. On *darugha* or *darughachi*, see Jagchid, *"Shuo yüan shih chung ti ta-lu-hua-ch'ih"* (On the *darughachi* of the *Yüan shih*), *Bulletin of the College of Art, Taiwan University*, no. 13, December 1964.
47. These are also recorded in *Sui-Meng chi-yao* (綏蒙紀要 An Important Record of the Mongols in Suiyuan Province), edited by Suiyuan Provincial Government, 1937, 140–62.
48. *Chaghan teüke*, 1v. The same book also gives a long list of the officials assigned to this cult (9r–v).
49. *Altan tobchi* 1:104–5.
50. See the ending paragraphs of all the annals of the emperors in the *Yüan shih*. For Chinggis Khan see ibid., 1, *chi*, 1, "Annals of T'ai-tsu," 23b.
51. *Bere*, an approximate measure of distance about one and a half miles.

52. The *elchin süldes* are divided into four groups: one for the Otogh (Right Flank Center) Banner, one for the U'ushin (Right Flank Front) Banner and Jasagh (Right Flank Front) Banner, one for the Jiün-wang (Left Flank Central) Banner, and one for the Jeünghar (Left Flank Front) Banner and Dalad (Left Flank Rear) Banner.

53. Kun dgah rdo rje, *Hu-lan deb ther*, Japanese translation by Shoju Inaba and Hisashi Sato (Kyoto, 1964), 78, 84. See also Hjigs-med nam-mkhah, *Chen-po hor-gyi-yul-du dam-paihi-chos ji-tar-ebyun-bahi-tshul-bsad-pa rgal-bahi bstan-pa-rin-po-che gsal-bar-byed pahi-sgon-me*, Japanese translation by Koho Hashimoto (Tokyo, 1940), 14.

54. See Sagang Sechen, *Chinggis Khaghan-u chidagh;* Lobsangdanjin, *Altan tobchi;* and Shiregetü Guushi Dharma, *Altan kürdun migghan kegestü bichig* (reprinted in Copenhagen, 1958).

55. *Hjigs-med nam-mkhah*, 15. *Chaghan teüke*, 5v.

56. "Annals of Shih-tsu," 6, 13a, *Yüan shih*, 9. *chi* 9. See also ibid., "Monograph of Worship and Offering," 3, 2b, 74, *chih* 25.

57. A *khadagh* is a white or light blue silk scarf about three to six feet long with Buddhist designs on it. The presentation of a *khadagh* symbolized a wish that the receiver gain blessings and flourish further. It is also a symbol of honor.

58. *Jula* is a lamp used in religious ceremonies. It was originally used by the shamans but was gradually taken into Buddhist practices.

59. According to *Chaghan teüke* it contains *airagh* (kumiss), *ariki* (ordinary liquor), and *araja* (strong liquor), 2r.

60. In the autumn of 1944 when the new Chinggis Khan shrine at Wang-yin sume (present Ulan-khota) was formally dedicated, shamans *(bo'es)* were especially brought in to perform the ceremonies instead of the lamas.

61. On Khulan Khatun, see brief biographies in K'o Shao-wen (柯紹忞) *Hsin Yüan shih* (新元史) 104, *chuan* 1, and *Tu Chi* 19, *chuan* 1.

62. Depending upon the size of the ceremony, a horse would sometimes be sacrificed as an offering. This is a continuation of an old tradition before the Mongol nation was thoroughly converted to Buddhism in the 1570s.

63. *Ho-chan* (喝盞), the original Mongolian term is *ötög*, see Yü Chi (虞集), *Tao-yüan hsüeh-ku-lu*, *chüan* 16. "The inscription of the Meritorious Deeds of the House of Su-tu-ssu (Süldüs)" (*Ssu-pu pei-yao* edition reprinted in Taipei, 1966), *chüan* 16, 7b.

64. See Jagchid and Paul Hyer, *Mongolia's Culture and Society* (Boulder, Colorado, 1971), 108. Frank Bessac, professor of anthropology at the University of Montana, a colleague of the author, traveled broadly in Mongolia after World War II.

65. B. Rintchen, *Les Materiaux Pour L'étude du Chamanisme Mongol. Band 3*, (Weisbadan, 1959), 67–69. See also Ch. Damdinsürung, *Mongghol uran jokiyal-un degeji jaghun bilig orusibai* (One Hundred Selections from Mongolian Literature) (Ulan Bator, 1959), 73–86.

66. The four empresses of Chinggis Khan were Börte, Khulan, Yesüi, and Yesügen. See *Yüan shih* 106, *piao* 1, "The Table of the Empresses" 1b–3b.

67. The four younger brothers of Chinggis Khan were Khasar, Khachi'un, Odchigin, and Belgütei.

68. The four sons of Chinggis Khan were Jochi, Chaghadai, Ögödei, and Tolui.

69. Börtegeljin, also known as Börte, was the first or senior wife of Chinggis Khan. See her brief biography in *Yüan shih* 114, *chuan* 1. See also biographies in K'o Shao-wen, *Hsien Yüan shih* 104, *chuan* 1, and T'u Chi, *Meng-wu-erh shih* 19, *chuan* 1.

70. Borjigin (or Borjigid in plural form) is the clan name of Chinggis Khan and the Chinggisid lineage.

71. For Bu'urchi or Bo'urchu's biography seen *Yüan shih* 119, *chuan* 6.

72. Mukhali, see biography, ibid.

73. The nine heroic companions of Chinggis Khan, according to the record of the *Altan tobchi*, were Mukhali, Cho-mergen, Bo'urchu, Surkhan-shira, Jeleme, Jebe, Kharakiru, Bo'urol, and Shigi-khutughu, 2:106).

74. Ködege-aral (or Kode'e-aral) was not recorded as the place for the enthronement of Chinggis Khan in either the *Secret History* or the *Yüan shih*. However, it was recorded as the place that Ögödei Khan ascended the throne. See *Secret History*, 202, 269, *Yüan shih* 1, *chi* "Annals of T'ai-tsu" 14b and ibid., 2, *chi* 2, "Annals of T'ai-tsung" 1a.

75. For Dayan (or Dayang) Khan's biography see Tu Chi 21, *chuan* 3.

76. See *Secret History*, 57.

77. The Toghmogh were a Turkic people in Central Asia also known as the Kipchak.

78. Sa'ari (or Saghari) was the Khan's headquarters in western Mongolia. Tarbaghtai is also known by its Chinese name, Ta-ch'eng, in Northern Sinkiang.

79. Jalal ad-Din, in the original text it is Jalijin. He was the son of Muhammad and was the last sultan of Khorezm. See Juvaini, 2:396–426.

80. Sarta'ul was the Mongolian term for Khorezm. Chinese versions of the *Secret History (Yüan-ch'ao pi-shih)* translate Sarta'ul as Hui-hui, Moslems.

81. *Shirbegel*, A conical metal case worn on the end of the braids on both sides of a married woman's breasts.

82. Samarkand, in the original text is Shimiskel. This Mongolian name of Samarkand was transliterated into Chinese as Hsueh-mi-ssu-kan in the *Yüan shih* (*chi* 1, 20b). The *Secret History* gives it as Shimiskhab (257).

83. Öchiyed (or Üchiyed) does not appear in the *Secret History*. Although it was recorded by Sagang Sechen and Lobsangdanjin in their works, sections concerning much later events, it is still difficult to identify them and why they were called enemies.

84. Shidurghu Khan, see note 18.

85. The name Gürbeljin does not appear in the *Secret History* nor the *Yüan shih*, but Sagang Sechen records her as the wife of the Tangut Khan Shidurghu.

86. Port wine, *boro darasu* in Mongolian, imported from Central Asia, was a favorite drink of the Mongolian imperial household and nobles. However, there is no record to prove that it was enjoyed by Chinggis Khan himself. The *Secret History* does record that his successor, Ögodei Khan, regretted distractions due to port wine (281).

87. The Golden *sülde, Altan sülde* in Mongolian, is a general term for the protecting spirit of Chinggis Khan. The word *altan* or golden was used in an honorific way for any item that belonged to Chinggis Khan — for instance *altan amin,* the Golden Life, *Altan uragh,* the Golden Descendants, and *altan jilo'a,* the Golden Reign. See Henry Serruys, "Mongol *Alton* 'Gold' — Imperial," *Monumenta* Serica 21 (1962): 357–78.

88. Rintchen, 59–60.

89. *Om a hum,* are Sanskrit-Tibetan Buddhist liturgical words commonly placed at the beginning of most prayers to express the wish that the words will become eternal.

90. The *Ordo,* imperial yurts, were maintained even after the death of the Khan. See Yanai Wataru (箭内瓦), "*Gencho ordo ko* (元朝斡兒朶考)," *Toyo gakuho* (東方學報) vol. 10, nos. 1–3, 1920.

91. According to Mongolian Shamanism there are thirty-three heavens or *tenggeri,* some merciful and some fearful. Among these various *tenggeri,* the *odghan tenggeri* is the supreme god, also known as *möngke tenggeri,* the Everlasting Heaven. See note 106.

92. *Luus* or dragon kings are deities of different localities. They are also known as *nibdagh* and *shabdagh* and the *oboos* are their shrines.

93. *Ubashi,* Srk. *upasaka,* a layman who has taken Buddhist vows. The Chaghan-ubashi is also known as Chaghan-ebügen, the White Old Man who is considered to be a deity of long life. The legend is probably influenced by the Chinese tale of Lao-shuo-hsing (老壽星), Cf., Heissig, *The Religion of Mongolia* (translated from the German edition by Geoffery Samuel) (London, 1980), 76.

94. *Rashiyan* or *arashiyan,* skr. *rasayana* the holy water.

95. *Jula,* see note 58.

96. *Shidi,* skr. *siddhi,* saintly or magical power.

97. League, *chighulghan* in Mongolian and *meng* (盟) in Chinese, was a local administrative unit that governed several banners. Thus, the seven banners of the Ordos tribe were organized into the Yeke-juu League.

98. *Vachir tarani,* skr. *Vadjra dharani,* magic Buddhist thunderbolt spells.

99. According to Mongolian Buddhist belief, the deities who make a decision to protect the Buddhist law should give their oath to confirm their obligations as protectors.

100. Rintchen, 60–63.

101. The word *lama* here means a master or *guru* who gives the authority or power to one qualified to recite a sacred formula or scripture. Also involved is the custom that the *baghshi* and *shabi,* the master and disciple, relationship should be established through an oath with the status of the *baghshi* being very sacred, authoritative, and absolute.

102. The Black *sülde* or the *khara sülde* is the main *sülde* of Chinggis Khan. In order to express honor to the protecting spirit of the Khan it is also sometimes addressed as the Golden *(altan)* sülde.

103. *Sülder* is a cognate of the word *sülde.* See *Secret History,* 63.

104. Skr. Semeru, Mong. Somber, is the holy Buddhist mountain in the center of the universe. Around this mountain there are four great continents. On the south is *Zambu tib* where our world is located.

105. For Khormusta, see note 20.

106. This concept of thirty-three *(sudarasun)* heavens is of Buddhist origin but has also been adopted by Mongolian Shamanism. See note 91.

107. *Bere,* see note 51.

108. *Baling* is an offering to deities usually made of rye flour and butter kneaded into various shapes — often a round pole shape or pyramid. Some are coated with red-colored butter.

109. Vachirbani also known as Ochirbani in Mongolian and Vadjarpani in Sanskrit.

110. Mystery means Tantriyana Buddhism.

111. The Mongols call themselves *köke Mongghol,* "the blue Mongols," and the color blue is held as a symbol of the Eternal Heaven *(Möngke tenggeri).*

112. These are the fifteenth day of the first lunar month, the twelfth day of the tenth month, and the twenty-third day of the eleventh month.

113. Another compromise made by Buddhism toward Mongolian tradition was the allowance of the worship of local deities — i.e., the *nibdagh* or the *luus* (the Dragon King) in their shrine the *oboo* — thus ranking these deities as lower, protecting spirits of the Proper Law of the Buddha.

114. Facsimiles of this sutra are attached to an article by the well-known Japanese Tibetan Buddhologist, Tada Tokan, in "Chinggis Khan kyo ni tsuite" (On the Sutra of Chinggis Khan), *Gogaku ronshu,* Series I (Keio University: Tokyo, 1948).

Chapter 23

Shamanism Among the Dakhur Mongols

(Originally published in *Proceedings of the 6th East Asian Altaistic Conference*, December 1981, Taipei)

Foreword

Of the Mongols, the Dakhur Mongols[1] who live in the northeastern corner of Mongolia are the only people who were not converted to Buddhism but maintained their older Shamanistic practices. The Dakhur differ linguistically from other Mongols in their dialect, which is a mixture of the Mongolian and Tungusic languages. If we consider the religious practices of the Dakhur Mongols relative to their geographical locations, we find that those who inhabit the valleys of the Nomor and Noni Rivers have retained perhaps 90 percent of their traditional practices, and that those who inhabit the Hulun-buir area, although having adopted Buddhism, still retain many of their original beliefs.

Sources of information concerning the religious traditions of the Dakhur Mongols are limited, and the few sources available are either very simple or highly subjective. For many years it was my intention to write something of the Dakhur's religious traditions to fill this gap in Mongolian cultural history. However, I put it off, not feeling adequately qualified in the fields of anthropology or folklore nor having completed any field study in those areas. In my younger days, I had many Dakhur friends with firsthand knowledge of this area, and I often talked at length with them about their religious customs. But, to my regret, I made no record of the conversations.

Therefore, I felt most fortunate when, in the summer of 1978, Mr. Jirgalang stayed in my home in Provo, Utah, for several days during a visit to the United States from Taiwan. Capitalizing on this opportunity, I made a list of questions which I asked him at intervals during his stay. His answers, which I carefully recorded and then submitted to him for review, will be the foundation for this paper.

Jirgalung is of the Dedül family and his Chinese name is Te Ku-lai (德古來). He is over seventy years of age and the oldest living Dakhur Mongol in the non-Communist world. Hence, he is probably the best available source for information on the ways and customs of his kinsmen. As a young man he studied at the Normal University of Peiping (Peking). He then went to Japan for further study at Nagasaki, after which he threw himself into politics, working for the development of Mongolia. He is now a member of the National Legislature in the Republic of China. He is a careful man and is not given to flowery or rambling speech. Therefore, the information he imparted, which comprises some 90 percent of what follows, may be regarded as highly reliable. The other 10 percent is the analysis and synthesis of the author.

The Shaman — Costume and Ritual

Shamanism is originally a primitive pantheistic religion. While a general sketch of its common features is possible, it differs significantly among the various regions and peoples where it is found. Hence, the Shamanism of the Dakhur Mongols differs from that found in other areas of Mongolia. Furthermore, Shamanism in other regions was largely suppressed with the arrival of Buddhism in the 1570s. Thus, Shamanism became an "underground religion" throughout Mongolia except among the Dakhur and two other small groups, i.e., the Buriyad of the Lake Baikal area and the Bö'echül of the Sünid Left Banner of the Shilinghol League in Inner Mongolia.

The word *shaman* is a Tungusic-Manchu term. The Mongol terms for a shaman are *bo'e* for a male and *idughan* for a female. In Dahkur, the shaman, regardless of sex, is called *yadghan*, and was a title which followed rather than preceded the bearer's name; e.g., Sayintob *yadghan*, Saran *yadghan*, and so forth. If he or she is a well known shaman, a local or clan name rather than a given name precedes the title; e.g., Dedül *yadghan* would designate a shaman from the village inhabited chiefly by the Dedül.

A shaman was usually an adult — almost none were under eighteen years of age. The older shamans were generally recognized as being most powerful, and hence the most honored and trusted. There were more male than female shamans, but this had no bearing on their position or treatment. Not all female shamans married, though the position did not hinder marriage, except when pride in their position and authority was a source of irritation to their husbands. One of Jirgalang's distant uncles was married to a *yadghan*.

In Dakhur society the position of the shamans was generally the same as that of other individuals. Thus, shamans formed no exclusive class nor organization, but were self-supporting individuals. This was in contrast to the lamas or Buddhist monks of Mongolia who gathered in monasteries with an organization, discipline, and a doctrinal philosophy. These formed an honored class in society exempt from taxes and other civil obligations. The shamans of the Dakhurs were ordinary members of the community who labored to maintain a living by herding, farming, or other common occupations. Shamanism was traditionally a part-time job. There have been very few shamans who worked at that vocation exclusively.

In return for a shaman's services, such as the offering of a prayer, a family would usually give no more than a piece of meat. If the shaman came from afar, the family would also pay for the transportation, but not if the shaman were from the vicinity. The shaman's obligations were to please the gods, to exorcize evil spirits, to pray for the family, and to cleanse them. The shaman's role was to be of service to the spirits of the gods and not primarily to gain a livelihood. The highest material reward given to a shaman was the ceremonial presentation of a coat — known as *jagh-barin* — as a gift. Such coats were usually used ones.

Shamans originated mainly from the ordinary people and rarely from the elite of a village or clan. Shaman candidates were usually selected by the elder shamans of an area. Many were mentally abnormal (though not necessarily insane), and abnormality seems to have been an asset in performing the role and duties of a shaman.

In Dakhur Mongol dialect the costume of a shaman is called *samachiki*. It is a gown worn tight around the wrists, waist, and especially at the thighs. There is no specific color for this gown, but all were embroidered with flowers and other designs around the waist. There were strips of embroidered material, very colorful and attractive and attached at the waist, which hung down. Around the upper body were hung nine round bronze or copper mirrors called *toli*. These mirrors, three or four inches in diameter, were hung four in the front and five in the back. A central mirror on the back was somewhat larger than the others. When a shaman danced, the mirrors would strike each other with a jangling noise. Shamans also wore a very tight cap made of leather or cloth, on the top of which was fastened a bronze bird. In the birds beak was a ring which dangled as the shaman danced. Around the fringe of the cap were fastened short strips which hung to about eye level. In the left hand, during the dance or chant, the shaman held a round, drum-like instrument of about one and a half to two feet in diameter called an *ontor* which he would beat with a small "whip-like" leather instrument held in the right hand. The drum was similar to that used by shamans in other regions of Mongolia. The whip symbolized the whipping of a horse to hasten it on a journey to the spirit world.

The main reasons for inviting a shaman to pray were to heal diseases, to exorcize evil spirits, and to please the gods. Of course, a shaman's services might also be sought to bring peace and good fortune or to cleanse the family. A shaman was almost never invited for the purpose of cursing. Curses between shaman and shaman have been known, but were quite rare. It was also very rare that the shaman's advice would be sought in matters of birth, marriage, or death. However, if a person, an animal, or even a tree were struck by lightning, a shaman would be invited to come and pray to the god of thunder, *Daril barkhan*, to please and pacify the god. Unlike customary Buddhist practices, a shaman was not asked to come and pray on specific days.

Besides regular shamans *(yadghan)*, there were also *baghchi* who were considered shamans of a lesser degree. These were invited only when no *yadghan* was available. The difference between the *yadghan* and the *baghchi* was that the former were able to point out which god was involved and perform an appropriate ceremony to mollify it, while a *baghchi* could only pray to the gods or spirits in general.

In some Dakhur districts, which had become agricultural and thus led a sedentary village life — districts that were subsequently more Sinicized, especially in centers of communication or where a postal station was established by the Manchu-Ch'ing — there was usually a shaman called a *ghiamun*, or in Chinese *chan-bang-tzu* (站棒子). These were known as the soldiers of Wu San-kuei (吳三桂),[2] a Chinese general who surrendered to the Manchus. *Chan-bang-tzu* were usually Chinese and were considered as third class shamans by the Dakhurs.

Objects of Belief in Dakhur Society

Shamanistic objects of belief may be divided into three categories: 1) the Heavens *(tenggeri)*; 2) the Gods *(barkhan)*; and 3) the Evil Spirits *(shürkül)*.

Tenggeri or the heavens are the highest objects of worship in the Dakhur pantheon. This is true in Mongolian Shamanism in general. However, the Dakhur shamans treated all heavens equally. There was no differentiation as in other types of Mongolian Shamanism which referred to Odghan Tenggeri (Highest Heaven) or Möngke Tenggeri (Everlasting Heaven) as the greatest among all heavens, gods, and spirits. In Dakhur belief the heavens were not numbered nor was there any distinction between the heavens of the west and east or of mercy and wrath. At the time of the Mongolian Empire, the highest ranking *bö'e* (male shamans), because they were able to communicate with heaven, were entitled *teb-tenggeri*, or, in Chinese, *kao-tien-jen* (告天人).[3] Their duty was to communicate with heaven and bring *jigharin* (instructions of heaven) to earth. Of course, this is the primary goal of all shamans, who should be in communion with *tenggeri* as well as gods and spirits.

Barkhan (gods) in common Mongolian is *Burkhan*, a transliteration from the Sanskrit word Buddha. In the Dakhur dialect, the word *barkhan* includes all the gods and even some spirits. The word for spirit or guardian spirit in the common Mongolian language is *sakighulsun* in written form and *saikhus* in colloquial speech. After the Mongols were converted to Buddhism, the word *sakighulsun* took the Buddhist meaning of "Protector of the True Law." However, these words were not part of the common vocabulary of Dakhur Shamanism. The word *barkhan* in Dakhur dialect includes all spirits above the earth. The following are some of the well known *barkhans* in the Dakhur pantheon.

Khojor is the most important god of a clan. This word is *ijaghur* in modern, written Mongolian and *khuja'ur* in the *Secret History of the Mongols*. The word itself means "origin." Therefore, *khojor* in Dakhur Shamanism also connotes the ancestor and the origin of a clan, and is thus a clan diety.

Khotan barkhan is the most popular god among the Dakhur people. The word *khotan* or *khota* means city or village, and may be compared to the Chinese city deity *ch'eng-huang* (城隍). This has led to the misconception that these two gods have similar functions in folk-religion. However, the Khotan-barkhan of the Dakhurs is not identifiable with the Chinese city-god, but rather is similar to the Chinese local deity *tu-ti* (土地).

There were no images of *Khotan barkhan* that are kept or venerated, but only painted portraits which depict a man and wife and sometimes children. These portraits were placed in a shrine in the northwest corner of the yard in back of the main house. The shrine was a small wooden structure supported by four wooden pillars. This shrine was called *barkhan ger* which means "house of the *barkhan*." Sometimes it was flanked by two smaller shrines or wooden frames. The significance of these secondary structures is lost, for even members of the older generation like Jirgalang do not remember their significance.

Niyang-niyang barkhan. *Niyang-niyang* is a word borrowed from the Chinese word *niang-niang* (娘娘) which means queen or goddess, such as the Chinese Tzu-sun niang-niang (子孙娘娘) — the goddess of offspring — among others. *Niyang-niyang barkhan* is also displayed in portraits placed beside a south window on the west side of one's house or placed atop a cabinet to show honor. This goddess may have been introduced by the Manchus to the Dakhurs from Chinese folk-religion.

Auliin barkhan in common Mongolian is *Aughala-yin burkhan* in the written language and *Uuliin burkhan* in colloquial speech. The terms refer to the god or gods of the mountains. In other parts of Mongolia these deities are called *nibdagh shibdagh*. Among the Dakhur Mongols, *Auliin barkhan* are divided into two categories — *Yeke-shira* and *Bagha-shira*, which may be translated "greater yellow deity" and "lesser yellow deity" respectively. The *Yeke-shira* is a supernatural being or fox-spirit and the *Bagha-shira* is a weasel spirit. Both types of deities are represented in portraits, always of a husband and wife. The husband is called *aimdan* and the wife *emden*. If the portrayal is of *Yeke-shira*, there will be a fox at the couple's feet, and if it is of *Bagha-shira*, there will be a weasel in the same position. These portraits are placed in a small wooden shrine on the roof of a barn or storehouse. The *Auliin barkhan* are similar to the *Hu hsien* (狐仙), fox spirits, and *Huang hisen* (黃仙), weasel spirits, of North Chinese folk religion. It is difficult to determine whether this similarity is coincidental or, if not, which is the derivative and which the original. Although the *Yeke-shira* and *Bagh-shira* were deities, hunting of animals was essential to the existence of the Dakhurs and the fox was not spared. In winter, the well-off Dakhur usually wore a fox-fur hat and gown. The Dakhurs rationalized that if a particular fox were a supernatural spirit it surely could not be caught by mortal hunters. As for the weasel, it was commonly killed by dogs in the yard. The people were not concerned with the death of this animal, although they were troubled when weasels harmed their chickens or stole eggs. These animal deities were believed to have dual personalities and could do either good or bad, depending on how the people treated them.

Daril barkhan is the Dakhur god of thunder. The word *daril* is probably identical to the standard Mongolian word *dayiral* which means "that which causes sudden or accidental death." Sudden death was seen as the snatching away of life by a god or evil spirit. However, in the vocabulary of the Dakhur, *daril* means the striking of lightening and *Daril barkhan* was the deity who controlled the phenomenon. This deity had no portrait but was symbolized by a piece of yellow cloth, sometimes painted with a dragon or a sun, or, like the Chinese symbol, with two dragons, one on either side of a fiery pearl.[4] Sometimes a shape like an eyebrow was cut out of silver paper and pasted to the cloth above the design. Often, however, there was no design at all. This cloth representation for a god was known as *kideng*. At the time of worship, the people might stack wood in a teepee-shaped frame and place a cloth *kideng* on the top and worship it. After the ceremony the *kideng* would be placed in storage. If a person were struck by lightning, this was thought to mean that he or she had been adopted by the *Daril barkhan*, and was qualified to become a *daril barkhan* and the spiritual messenger of a *yadghan*. Those who died of strange diseases were believed to become Shamanistic messengers.

Ghal barkhan and *Toghon barkhan*: *Ghal barkhan* is the traditional god of fire while *Toghon barkhan* is the god of pots and of the stove. Sometimes these two gods were viewed as one. They were worshipped on the twenty-third day of the twelfth lunar month, the same day the Chinese worshipped *Tsao-wang* (灶王), their god of the stove. Fire worship was an ancient tradition in Mongolia and the date of the ceremonies associated with it varied from place to place — from the eighth lunar month to the twelfth lunar month. However, the worship of the stove was practiced only in agricultural, and hence usually in Sinicized areas — where it became mixed with fire worship — and was never practiced among the nomadic groups who worshipped only fire. Fire, which possesses the power of cleansing, has been considered holy in Mongolian society from the earliest times. This could possible be linked to the ancient Persian religion of Zoroastrianism. In more recent Dakhur society, the holy function of fire faded, and the fire god's position was taken over by the god of the stove.

Jiyaachi (*jiyaghachi* in written Mongolian) is the god of destiny. However, in Dakhur society, *Jiyaachi* is both the god of travel and the god of hunting. This is because in early Dakhur society the main reason to travel was to hunt. This god was represented in portraits which were placed on the roof under the main house's west chimney. One purpose of Dakhur hunting was to collect sable furs and tender deer horns for trade and gifts. This was usually done during fall and winter, and it might take two or three months. The day before departure, Dakhur hunters would thoroughly stock a wagon with food and supplies and then drive it about one mile into the wilderness. There they would worship and supplicate *Jiyaachi* for a safe journey and abundant success in the hunt. The ceremony they performed was called *mör orkhan*, a travel prayer. This prayer ceremony, called *mör gharkhu* in common Mongolian, was only carried out at the commencement of a long journey. The word *mör* means footprints or tracks, and the Mongols desired *chaghan mör* — white or blessed tracks. A man with *chaghan mör* meant a man of good luck. In records from the Yüan period, this is called *pai-tao-tzu* (白道子).[5] The god of hunting in common Mongolian is known as *Manakhan tenggeri*. When the Dakhurs worshipped *Jiyaachi barkhan*, they would burn incense and sprinkle liquor offerings, the burning of incense being a common practice in Eastern religions. The sprinkling of wine in Dakhur vocabulary is *airki chichin*, *airki* being the common Mongolian term for liquor. The sprinkling ceremony in common Mongolian speech is *sachuli*. A *sachuli* offering was either *airagh* (kumis), fermented mare's milk, cow's milk, or liquor. The liquid was carried in a cup held high in the left hand. The method of sprinkling was to dip the middle finger of the right hand into the cup and then flick the liquid off the finger into the air, repeating the action three times. Among the Dakhurs the ceremony was the same as among the Mongols, except that liquor was used.

Doloon od is the Mongolian term for the Big Dipper constellation. This term meaning "seven stars" is written as *Dologhan odu*. It is pronounced *Doloon od* in both common Mongolian and the Dakhur dialect. However, in common Mongolian conversation the term *Doloon öbgön* is used when referring to the constellation as a deity. This term, written as *Dologhan ebügen* means "the seven old men." It should be noted that these "seven old men" were not kindly, pleasant old fellows, but rather fierce and angry old men, especially among the Buriyad Mongols. However, among the Dakhur the *Doloon od* were the supreme symbol of all heavenly deities, more important than the sun, moon, or other stars.

Manghai were very rough images about two to three feet high carved from tree trunks. Their faces were painted black. It is now unclear whether they were male or female. They were placed at one side of a yard entrance where they were exposed to the elements and would eventually rot and disintegrate. No veneration was given to these images, and they were never placed inside the yard. They may have some relation to the *Dai-chang-kun* (大将軍)[6] of Korea. However, the Korean *Dai-chang-kun* might be unpainted or painted very colorfully and always appeared in pairs, a male and a female. They looked rather fierce with threatening open mouths, and were erected in front of the house or at the entrance to the village. They were believed to possess the power to frighten away evil spirits. Both the *Manghai* of the Dakhurs and the Korean *Dai-chang-kun* may have evolved from early Tungusic traditions. Whether the word *manghai* in Dakhur and the Mongolian word *mangghas* are related or not is a matter for further linguistic study. The word *mangghas* in common Mongolian vocabulary means "monster."

Oboo refers to the shrine of the local deity of mountains or water. The word *oboo* has the same meaning in Dakhur and colloquial Mongolian and is written *obogha*.[7] In other parts of Mongolia, the terms *nibdagh* and *shibdagh* are used to refer to local deities in general, as is the word *luus* which means "dragon king." An *oboo*, a center for the worship of such local deities, was a pile of stones on top of which were tree branches. In other areas of Mongolia an *oboo* consisted of thirteen such piles but among the Dakhurs only one. The *oboo* was originally an ancient Shamanistic tradition, but after the Mongols were converted to Buddhism *oboo* worship was absorbed into the Buddhist ceremonies. Sacred Buddhist words were printed on the stones and on small flags of various colors which were tied to the erected branches. The Dakhurs, as has been mentioned, did not become Buddhist, and no such sacred words or flags appear on their *oboos*.

Offerings to an *oboo* were very formal and ceremonial in other parts of Mongolia, but were performed quite simply among the Dakhurs. At the time of worship among the Dakhurs, an animal was sacrificed, boiled, and placed before the *oboo*. After the sacrifice, those who attended divided and ate the offered meat. If the ceremony were a prayer for rain, they would conclude by bathing in a river, a practice not observed among other Mongolian tribes. A prayer for rain and subsequent bathing suggest that the spirit of the *oboo* was *luus* the "dragon king," the deity who held power over water.

Ilmün khan was the king of the underworld. He was also an important and honored god, although no ceremony was conducted for him.

Shirkül was a general term for all ghosts and spirits which roamed the earth making mischief. It was these spirits that the *yadghan* was to exorcize.

Shamanistic Ceremonies

Among the Dakhur Mongols, ceremonial worship centered around chanting and dancing. The term for such dancing is *yadghaljibei*. As has been mentioned, the primary motive in inviting a shaman was to heal the sick. Although their methods were certainly outside the realm of modern scientific medicine, their efficacy, at least in the eyes of the Dakhurs, may be illustrated by two firsthand accounts. Jirgalang relates how his father, though a believer in Shamanism, had no faith in the powers of his distant aunt (mentioned earlier). One day his father became ill, and there was no doctor nor any *yadghan* available other than his distant aunt. He therefore consented to invite her, and his condition improved considerably after her ceremony. However, she said that she was unable to completely heal him, and suggested that a more powerful shaman be invited. After performing his ceremony, the second shaman instructed the old man to take a bath in cold water. Upon doing as he was told, he was completely healed without having taken any medicine. In earlier days I had a friend, Mr. Jui-yung (瑞永), whose younger brother was a shaman. Jui-yung told me that his brother was able to "suck" a wound, sore, or tumor from a person's body with his mouth. Upon doing so he might spit it onto a tree upon which a scar would later appear. This seems similar to the practice of Chinese witches or shamans or to the *Chu-yu-k'o* (祝由科) of Hunan province. Jui-yung, who related this to the writer as a fact, was a graduate of Waseda University in Japan and not at all a superstitious man.

The Shamanistic prayers and ceremonies of the Dakhurs are a branch of Northern Asian practices in general, all of which follow the same basic procedures, i.e., prayer by chanting, beating of drums, dancing, and a fainting trance which is viewed as the means of communication with the spirits for the purpose of receiving their instructions.

The performances of the Dakhur *yadghan* may be divided into two stages, one inside the house and one outside in the yard. (The Dakhurs of the Noni River valley were mostly sedentary and lived in houses.) In preparing to perform, a *yadghan,* after dressing in the costume of a shaman, would sit on the *khangji* in Mongolian, and *kang* (炕) in Chinese[8] — a raised brick or mud porch — and, taking a drum in hand, would close his eyes and begin to chant. This chanting is known in Dakhur as *onghor jarbai* and in common Mongolian as *bö'e-yin daghudalgha.*[9] It is usually a very long song composed in rhyme and sometimes includes meaningless sounds. While chanting, a *yadghan* would beat his drum with a short whip-like instrument (described above). The *yadghan* was sometimes accompanied by another drummer called *ontar daghachi* who was not necessarily a shaman. The drum of the accompanist was always smaller. This part of the ceremony was called the "invocation of the gods," *ongghor jaran.* The word *onghor* in common Mongolian is *ongghon* and refers to objects of worship.

Continuing to beat the drum and chant, the shaman, when moved, would stand and begin to dance. The basic pattern of the dance was to first move forward and then back, then to hop, and then to turn faster and faster while beating and chanting at an increasingly rapid tempo, thereby showing that he was drawing nearer and nearer to a state of communication with the gods or spirits. A climax was finally reached when, after a state of apparent madness, the shaman suddenly fell to the ground unconscious.

The length of time that a shaman remained in this trancelike state varied. An older, more experienced shaman was generally able to pass into a trance and speak as an oracle in a short period of time and regained consciousness quickly. Before he came back to his senses, the shaman revealed, in the voice of a spirit, what demon was afflicting the sufferer or by which god he or she was being punished, and hence to which god prayer and sacrifice should be made in order to be healed. Sometimes during the ceremony the shaman would fan the victim with his drum, holding it in both hands, to exorcize the evil spirit. At other times he would take the large mirror from the center of his back and throw it into the yard, discerning by how it landed the procedures for healing or some other desired information.

When the ceremony was performed in the yard, the *yadghan's* dance would circle a fire where the sacrificial meat was boiling, and at the end of the ceremony he would use his drum to fan the flames. The ceremony performed in the yard followed the same basic steps as that inside a house, although an indoor ceremony was generally preferred for the healing ritual, unless the house were too small for the dance.

During a *yadghan's* communication with a spirit or deity, the instructions he transmitted were usually in the form of a long narrative and always in rhyme. Sometimes the shaman's vocabulary during this narrative was incoherent to all but a few elderly people, who, by experience, were able to interpret it at least in part.

In performing a ritual to cure illness, a shaman would usually reveal that the ill person had been cursed by a particular god or possessed by a particular spirit. Hence, he would instruct the sufferer or sufferer's family to make an offering or prayer to a certain god, usually *Auliin barkhan* (the fox or weasel god) to bless the sufferer or to cast out the evil spirit. The most common offering designated was a chicken, although a pig, sheep, or wild antelope might also be designated by the shaman. The ritual of sprinkling liquor *(airki chichin)* described above was also mandatory.

The offering or sacrifice was placed on an altar known as *delkin* which means "universe" in common Mongolian. This altar was constructed of four poles bound together near the top to form a stand on which a board large enough to hold the sacrifices was placed. On the top of the highest pole of the altar was hung a straw image of a dragon or bird. At the time of the offering a *yadghan* would dance, chant, and beat the drum, although not repeating the trance phase since all necessary instructions had previously been received during the initial ceremony.

If lightning had struck a man, animal, or even a tree or the ground, a shaman always seemed to find out about it and encourage the family to rectify the inauspicious state of affairs through his services. Death which came in any sudden or unexpected way, such as a strange disease or suicide, also necessitated a special Shamanistic ceremony and offering. Of various deaths, a person killed by lightning was believed to have become a *barkhan*, and hence offerings had to be made to the spirit of the deceased. Such a spirit was also believed to become the medium of the *yadghan* whose services had been used to rectify the state of affairs resulting from the unique death.

In cases of long illness, or of recovery from such an illness, a shaman would also be invited to perform. Such a performance was called *dorbor ichin*, the essential part of which was the fanning of the patient or of the fire with a drum. The *dorbor ichin* also had to be carried out in the dark of night.

Another important function of the *yadghan* was divination. This usually took the form of interpreting omens, whether good or bad, and often included finding lost animals. These practices were common to Shamanism throughout Asia. Divination was usually performed by reading the cracks which appeared in the shoulder bones of sheep or other domestic animals after the bones had been placed in a fire. The message in this crack "writing" could give instructions for finding a lost animal or healing the disease of a sufferer. The most able and powerful shamans could discern such messages without needing to first burn the bones.

Sometimes, if a family were able to invite a well-known shaman to their dwelling, the people of the vicinity would come and invite him to heal or help them. Hence there would often be a series of Shamanistic performances in the area.

Customs Related to Shamanistic Belief

The most important day of the year among the Dakhurs was, not surprisingly, the day of the lunar new year. Many of this day's customs were also linked with the last day of the previous year. The main deities worshipped at this time were *Tenggeri* (Heavens), *Doloon od* (the Big Dipper), and *Khotan barkhan* (the household deity). The worship of these deities was carried out in the yard at midnight of the old year's last day and again at dawn of the new year's day. The worship of heaven was performed by bowing *(kou-tou)* at least three times to the southwest. Then one would turn to the northeast and bow again to the Big Dipper. This custom differs from that of other Mongolian subgroups who bowed only at dawn, one toward the east — the direction of sunrise — and then in turn to the south, west, and north. The bowing of the Dakhurs, as described above, to the two directions southwest and northeast, sufficed for the Khotan barkhan who received no separate bows.

The *Doloon od* was especially important to the Dakhurs at this time of year. When offerings were made to this deity, they were in the form of chalice shaped lamps made of flour dough with butter placed in the bowl for fuel and with a cotton wick. These lamps were called *jula,* and were seven in number for the seven stars. This practice was similar to the Chinese Taoist tradition of *Chi hsing teng* (七星燈). Before bowing to *Doloon od,* these lamps were lit and presented. The whole ceremony was called a *jula bairin.*

In those homes where members of the older generation had died during the past year, extra bedding was prepared for them, or rather for their spirits, at new year's time. By the bed, the deceased person's favorite pipe and tobacco was also set out. This custom was called *or joghan,* or *oru jokyan* in written Mongolian. Before exchanging new year's congratulations, all family members were required to bow before the specially prepared beds. Guests who came to call also bowed and offered liquor to the beds before offering new year's salutations to the family. The *or joghan* ritual was repeated during the new year season (the first to fifteenth day) for three years after the death of the family members.

The day to worship *Toghon barkhan* (the god of the stove and pot) was the twenty-third day of the twelfth lunar month, as well as new year's day. The last day of the year was also an important one. On that day incense was burned and offerings made before all the *barkhans,* although all religious ceremonies (as described above) were performed on the following day. In Dakhur society, other then these two days, there were no notable religious holidays.

Birth and death are the most important events in any society, and Dakhur society was no exception. When a baby was born, whether boy or girl, the parents would hang a small bundle of grass on their door. Unfortunately, the symbolic meaning of the grass bundle and the purpose of this custom are yet to be discovered. All we now know is that it was a sign to visitors not to enter for a given period of time.

After death, the body was buried underground with a mound of raised earth over the grave. On this occasion there were no Shamanistic rites of any kind performed among the Dakhurs. Even where they lived among the Chinese, the Dakhurs would not call on a geomancer (風水先生) to determine the time or place of burial, for all such matters were decided privately by the family. If the deceased was a child, the family would dress the body in new, clean clothing and take it from the home into the wilderness. There they would erect a *delkin* (as described above for making sacrifices) and place the body on it. For three years after the child's death, the family, especially the mother, would visit the *delkin,* often bringing food for the deceased. For adults no *delkin* was constructed unless the circumstances of death were extraordinary. Burial customs among the Dakhurs did not differ due to social position or status.

Among the Dakhurs there was no reciting of scriptures at the time of death, or at any other time, except among those inhabiting the Hulun-buir area who had been converted to Buddhist practices. Among the Noni Dakhurs a lama might be called to recite scriptures for the blessing of the family, but only very rarely. Traditionally most doctors were lama doctors who specialized in smallpox immunization. The dire need for such immunization among the Dakhurs was the original reason for inviting lamas.[10]

Notes

1. After the occupation of the area by the Chinese Communists, the Dakhur Mongols were classified separately from the Mongolian nationality, and an autonomous district was established for them inside the Inner Mongolian Autonomous Region. The policy of the Chinese Communists has been to classify the Dakhurs as a separate and independent minority from the rest of the Mongolian people — a policy to which the Dakhur leaders outside the People's Republic of China are opposed.

2. Wu San-kuei: see biography in *Ch'ing shih*, 235.

3. Kao-tien jen: This title was given to religious leaders during the time of the Mongol Empire. When Chinggis Khan was conquering North China, he gave the title to the famous Chinese monk Yin chien (印箭), also known as Hai-yun *fa shih* (海雲法師). As for Teb-tenggeri, see F. W. Cleves, "Teb-Tenggeri," *Ural-altaishe Jahrbucher*, 39 (1967), 248–60.

4. Two dragons and jewel: These symbols are undoubtedly influenced by the Chinese tradition. However, the meaning of the eyebrow-like form of silver paper is lost.

5. Pai-tao-tzu, see T'ao Tsung-yi (陶宗儀), *Ch'u ching lu* (輟耕錄), chuan I, Shih-chieh shu-chü reprinted edition (Taipei, 1963), 32.

6. *Dai-chang-kun:* This name means "Great General" and refers to the posts which appear at the front of the house or village in Korea. The male is called *Chun-ha dai-chang-kun* (天下大將軍) or "Great General Under Heaven," and the female is called *Chi-ha yun-chang-kun* (地下大將軍) or "Female General Under Earth."

7. *Oboo:* Not always a shrine. The *oboo* might also be a "road sign," as it were, which told the directions of a marked border or boundary. Even so, it would have religious significance as a symbol of the deity of the location.

8. *Khanji* (*kang* in Chinese): a raised portion of the floor with smoke channeled beneath it for warmth.

9. With reference to the chanting of the Mongolian shaman, see Rintchen, *Folklore Mongol, Asiatisch Forschungen*, Band 7, 11, (Weisbaden, 1960, 1963).

10. In early days, both Mongolian and Tibetan lamas gave smallpox vaccinations in the form of a snuff placed in the nostril which was sometimes so powerful as to cause scars on the face. The original vaccination given by the lamas was supposed to be effective for sixty years. The old Chinese equivalent was good for thirty years and the present day version of the vaccination is said to be efficacious for three years.

Index

Index

A

Abadai Taiji, 125, 132, 133
Abagha, 134, 197
Afghanistan, 97, 98
agricultural: activity, 180-81, 179; areas, 186; Chinese, 173, 195, 240; civilization, 91; development, 214; economy, 187; kingdom, 34; people, 3, 6, 8, 136, 173, 176; production, 180; products, 5, 13, 14, 16, 174; society, 3, 6, 194; state, 12, 174; territories, 3
airagh (mare's milk), 307, 308
Alashan, 158–59, 167, 211, 212, 250, 272, 273
Altai mountains, 175, 309
Altaic, 34; nomads, 131, 174; people, 90, 121, 142
Altan Khan, 10, 15, 121, 125, 131–33, 135, 155, 156, 177, 180
Altan tobchi, 51, 54, 56, 58, 59, 61, 64, 301
Altan uragh (see Golden descendants)
amban (minister), 146, 163, 198, 219; of Tibet, 147
Amdo, 134
American-Japanese expedition in Siberia, 281
Amurtsana, 175
ancestors (yekes), 52, 300, 302
Anfu Clique, 224
Anglo-French forces, 198, 207
animal products, 174, 217
anti-religious activity, 202
arad (people), 145, 162, 163, 166, 188
archery, 199, 200, 209
Arigh-bukha, 71, 74
assimilation, 186-87, 198, 201, 207, 259
Ata-Malik Juvaini, 300
Aukhan, 182, 196, 197, 209
autonomous, 178, 224, 244, 246, 247, 264; Mongol regime, 250; movement, 235–36, 276, 292; power, 176
Avalokitésvara, 107, 306
Ayur-shiridara, 91, 142
ba'atur ("brave man" or "hero"), 53

B

Babujab, 192, 223

Bal-mo khri-btsun, 90
bandi (gelun), 150, 159, 160
banner, 146, 150, 151, 162, 163, 165, 176, 182, 183, 188, 193, 196, 207–9, 212, 227; offices, 216
Baron Ungern-Sternberg, 224
Batu-kha'alagh-yin Süme, 236, 247
Belgütei, 68, 301
bestowals, 3, 7, 9
Beyile-yin Süme (Pai-ling-miao), 285–94
bö'e (male shamans), 83, 307, 323, 325
bökö ("wrestlers"), 53
Bolshevik, 224, 244; Revolution, 262
Bon ("Black Faith"), 90
bon-po (Bon priest), 90, 91
Bo'orchu, 52, 59, 60, 63
booty, 13, 22, 27
border: encroachments, 3; lands, 43, 187-88, 207, 224; provinces, 276, 284, 285
Borjigid, 56, 308, 310
Borodin, Michael (Soviet advisor), 271
Börte, 53, 305, 307
Börtegeljin, 308
Boshoghtu Khan, 133
Bsod-nam rgya-mtsho, 132
Boxer Rebellion, 150, 191, 193, 197, 210–12, 214, 218, 243, 262
Buddha, 90, 101, 104, 109, 111, 122, 135, 142, 146, 149, 311, 312, 325
Buddhism, 62, 63, 64, 71, 75, 77, 84, 85, 88, 102–3, 106, 108–9, 112, 114–15, 121–26, 131–32, 135–36, 143, 150–51, 156–57, 163, 177, 188, 193, 207, 236, 238, 245, 314; administration, 114; affairs, 89, 113; anti-Buddhist movement, 234, 236; ceremonies, 328; conflict with Taoists, 105, 112–13; elders, 103; monks, 24, 86, 101, 105, 123, 125; negative influences of, 149; scripture, 237
Bureau of Mongol Affairs (Meng-shih-chu), 183
Buriyad, 178, 213, 215, 242, 244, 245, 267, 323
Bu'urchi, 308

C

Canton, 224, 225, 246, 264–66

Central Asia, 16, 17, 46, 47, 56, 87, 173, 174, 177, 245, 300; steppes, 67
Central Capital, 25, 31
Chaghadai, 52, 58, 59, 60, 84
Chahar (Province), 282, 286
Chakhar (tribe), 125, 134, 149, 158, 163, 182, 189, 192, 197, 198, 223, 226, 263, 265, 271, 275, 286, 289, 290, 292
Ch'ang-ch'un Chen-jen, 84–87, 89
Changpei Incident, 291
Chang-tsung (Chin Emperor Ma-ta-ke, r. 1190–1208), 44
Chang Hsüeh-liang, 184, 276
Chang Tso-lin, 184, 225, 226, 269, 273, 285
Chao Hung, 68
Chao P'i-lien, 286, 287
Cheng-yi Sect, 96, 113
Ch'i Dynasty (550–77), 14
Chiang-chün (general), 162
Chiang Kai-shek, 250, 281, 282, 287, 291, 293, 294
chibghancha (nun), 150
Ch'ien-lung (r. 1736–95), 136–37, 143, 145, 147–48, 150–51, 155, 157, 161, 240
Chimhai, 180
Chin, 18, 35, 36, 44, 45, 96, 104; Dynasty (1115–1234), 254
Ch'in, 179; Dynasty, 6, 101, 179
Ch'in Shih-huang-ti (r. 246–210 B.C.), 96
Chinese: administration style, 257; administrative units, 217; agriculture, 180, 183, 186; army, 245; bandits, 294; Buddhism, 85, 87, 91, 94–96, 101, 194; captives, 23; chauvinism, 178, 185, 259; cities, 23, 28; colonization, 178-79, 181, 190-93, 210; commonwealth, 221, 250, 253, 267; Communists, 178, 185, 189, 193, 238, 249, 250, 253, 259, 260, 264, 267, 268, 271, 276; court, 6, 11; cultivation, 182-84, 249, 270; culture, 84, 90, 199, 208, 254; discrimination, 260; education, 209; emperors, 7; farmers, 178-79; farms, 246; forces, 193; frontier, 6; fugitives, 179; government, 243, 247; hsien, 217–18, 287; immigrants, 183, 188, 219, 257;
institutions, 208; intellectuals, 98, 101; magistrates, 183, 184, 201, 257; manpower, 21, 23, 27; masses, 141; merchants, 197, 201, 257, 263; migrants, 185, 283; Minister of Colonization, 183; monks, 90, 91; Nation (Chung-hua min-tsu), 259; nationalism, 242; officials, 193, 215; Parliament, 264, 266; peasants, 183; People's Liberation Army, 251; population, 178, 186, 187, 194, 195, 200, 254; power, 31, 185; princess, 7, 11; refugees, 22, 24, 187, 208; Republic, 184, 243; revolution, 246; revolutionary leaders, 258; rule, 219; scholars, 86, 89, 90, 104–5; scribes, 200; settlement, 182-84, 191, 212; settlers, 179-84, 188, 193, 198, 201, 208–10, 215, 217, 226, 241; suzerainty, 173; teachers, 199; tutors, 200; urbanization, 31; warlords, 225–26
Ch'ing, 18, 293; court, 6, 148, 150–51, 156, 159, 161, 176, 192, 198-99, 210, 215, 289; documents, 160; Dynasty (1644-1911), 136, 149, 155, 157, 169, 176, 182, 184, 195, 200, 211, 217, 240, 243, 270, 284; law, 158, 168, 283; rulers, 176
Chinggis Khan (r. 1206–27), 4, 13, 16, 17, 35, 43–46, 51–64, 68, 83–85, 87, 89, 94–107, 113, 133, 145, 155, 241, 251, 279; Golden sülde, 312, 314; khara-sülde, 306; as symbol of national freedom, 300
Chinggisid: leaders, 302; princes, 17, 46, 299
Chinghai (Kökönor), 226, 275, 282
Ch'i-nien-ku, 305
Chin-tan-t'ao: Rebellion, 209–10; society, 193
Ch'iu Ch'u-chi, 96–98, 100, 102, 106–7, 113
choijung (Protector of the Law of Buddha) 146, 161
Chou Dynasty (559–81), 14, 15
Christian, 71, 75, 77, 84, 87, 121, 126, 131, 193; anti-Christian movement, 236; priests, 88, 105
Ch'üan-chen Sect, 84–86, 96, 98, 100, 102, 104, 106, 113

Index

Chung-hua (Chinese) Nationality, 253
Chungking, 250
Chung-tu (Central Capital — Peking, also see Jungdu), 41, 45, 108
clan system, 52
Comintern, 225, 246, 264, 266–73
common: herdsmen, 183, 271; Mongols, 301; people, 134, 183, 202, 213, 241, 262, 266
Communist, 90, 178, 185, 192, 222, 226, 245, 246, 264, 299, 303; anti-Communist movement, 272–73; Party, 225, 266; Revolution, 234
Confucian, 41, 52, 84, 85, 103; filial-piety, 98; scholars, 86, 100–1, 104, 108, 110, 197; teachings, 194; temple, 107; tradition, 256
Confucius (551–479 B.C.), 24, 101, 103, 109, 252; teachings, 87
conservative, 213, 222, 246, 262–63, 270, 281, 283, 285; leaders, 224; ruling class, 243
cooperatives, 268
corvée duties, 106, 135, 188
counter revolutionaries, 245
cultivation, 187, 209, 212, 216, 241, 269; anti-cultivation movement, 270
cultural: change, 64, 201; differences, 5, 194; distance, 3, 5, 6, 90, 187; similarities, 47
Cultural Revolution, 238, 251, 259, 276, 277

D

Dairen, 220
Dakhur, 265, 326, 328–31; dialect, 325; hunters, 327; Mongols, 322, 323
Dalai Lama, 132, 136, 143–48, 158, 161–62, 306; Fifth Dalai Lama, 133, 148, 159; Fourth Dalai Lama, 156; Sixth Dalai Lama, 148; Third Dalai Lama (Bsod-nams rgya-mtso), 121, 133, 156; Thirteenth Dalai Lama, 219, 235, 257
Dambadorji, 225, 246, 266, 269, 273
darkhad, 306, 308
darkhan (title), 305
Dayan Khan (r. 1479–ca. 1516), 126, 175, 304, 309
Deli'ün–boltagh, 308

Demchügdüngrüb, 226, 235–36, 238, 246, 250, 276, 281–83, 285–86, 288–94
democracy, 215, 218, 242, 245, 246, 262, 268, 271, 283
Dge-lug-pa (Yellow Religion or Sect), 88, 126, 132–33, 136, 143, 145, 148, 156, 158, 177, 234, 237
Director General of Military Cultivation, 184, 226, 285
Doloön-nor, 134, 137, 144, 147, 148, 158, 164, 166, 235, 290
Dörben-ke'üd, 134
Dowager Tz'u-hsi, 197, 210–13, 215, 218
dügüileng movement, 266, 270
Dutch, 218
dynasties of conquest (dynasties of infiltration), 16, 34, 253–55

E

Earth (Etügen), 51, 83, 114, 253
East Asia, 58, 83, 87, 208, 210
Eastern Capital (Tung-ching), 31, 39
Eastern China Railroad, 212
Eastern Tümed, 134
ecclesiastical nobels, 134
economic: aim, 176; base, 186; dependence, 7; development, 27, 186; exploitation, 188, 285; factors, 177; gain, 14; lifeline, 6; necessity, 6; need, 3, 10, 186; power, 8; rights, 208; satisfaction, 9, 14; unit, 188
education, 216–18, 222, 268; free, 213; reform, 213
Ejen-Khoroo, 300, 303–8
elders (ötögüs), 52
emissary standards (elchin sülde), 306
Erdeni-yin Juu, 184
Esen, 15, 121, 124–25
Eurasian steppes, 55
Europe, 133, 245; colonization of Asia, 240; powers, 241, 243
Evil Spirits, 324

F

farming, 5, 180, 187, 217; lands, 14, 179
Feng Yü-hsiang, 225, 226, 266, 267, 269, 271, 272, 274, 282, 283, 285, 290

feudal: anti-feudal movement, 202, 264, 266; class, 285; lord, 136, 155–56, 162, 165, 176, 211, 245, 267; Mongolian leaders, 207; practices, 211; princes, 267; privileges, 134, 163, 283–84; regionalism, 236; ruling class, 285; society, 155; system, 268; traditional institutions, 215, 290; units, 136
fief (yu-mu), 165
filial: love, 52; piety, 258
foreign: aggression, 207; intervention, 264; occupation, 211; power, 251, 262
Former Han Dynasty (206 B.C.–8 A.D.), 255
fragmentation and rule, 137
France, 210, 211, 267
frontier market, 8
Fu Ming-tai, 266, 267, 273, 276
Fu Tso-yi, 184, 282, 284, 286–94

G

Galdan Khan, 133, 143, 148, 175
Gandan Keid, 238
gege'en, 157, 159, 161, 164, 166
gelüng, (see bandi)
General Director of Colonization, 184
geographical: distance, 6, 220
Germany, 210, 211
Ghadaa meiren Incident, 191
Ghonchoghsurung, 220, 234
Ghorlos, 134
Gobi, 21, 131–32, 136, 141, 145, 156, 174, 178, 180, 234, 235, 238, 246, 246, 264; steppes, 12
Golden Bomba Bottle, 146–47, 161–62
Golden descendants (Altan uragh), 132–33, 156, 301, 308, 309
Governor General of Sheng-Ching (Mukden), 183
grazing field (notugh), 165, 179, 182, 187, 188, 201, 263, 269, 284
Great Britain, 208, 211, 219, 257, 267
Great Han: chauvinism, 256; nationalism, 250–51
Great Khan of Mongolia, 8, 52, 57, 60, 95, 255
Great Wall, 6, 9, 12, 14–16, 21, 27, 28, 31, 35, 42, 44, 54, 90, 122, 126, 131, 173, 177, 179, 180, 182, 183, 186,

189, 191, 194, 208, 211, 220, 240, 241, 248, 249, 254, 291
guerrilla warfare, 191
Gungsangnorbu (1871–1931), 192, 200, 202, chapter 16, 234, 242, 262–66, 269, 281; modernization policies of, 213
Güüshi Khan, 133
Güyüg Khan, 68, 73, 88, 89, 105, 126, 303

H

Hailar, 276
Hai-ling (Wan-yen Ti-ku-nai, r. 1148–61), 36, 38–40, 42
Hai-yün (Buddhist monk), 95, 97, 100, 102–7
Han, 6, 8, 220; court, 11, 253; Dynasty (206 B.C.–220 A.D.), 4, 7, 174, 176, 179, 187, 195, 252
Han Chinese, 179, 258, 263; anti-Han Chinese, 270; revolution (1911), 141
Han Hsüan-ti (r. 73–49 B.C.), 10
Han Kao-ti (r. 140–88 B.C.), 11, 14
Han Wu-ti (r. 140–88 B.C.), 96
heads of the clans, 27
Heaven (Tenggeri), 51, 52, 83, 95, 98–100, 106, 114, 135, 253, 256, 300, 308, 311, 324, 325, 327, 330
Heilungkiang, 192, 223
herdsmen, 176, 201, 263
high lama, 133, 14, 155, 188, 264
Ho Ying-ch'in, 286, 288, 291
Hohhot (see Köke-Khota)
Ho-hsi (Tangut), 71
Hopei and Chahar Political Affairs Committee, 291
horsemanship, 199-200, 209
Ho-ti (Han emperor, r. 89–105), 174
Hsi, 34, 36, 39, 40, 45
Hsi-ching (Western Capital), 27
Hsia (Tangut), 24, 36, 47
Hsiao Ta-heng, 194
hsien (prefecture), 290, 291, 288
Hsien-pei, 6, 13, 179
Hsiung-nu, 4, 7, 8, 10, 11, 13, 16, 18, 136, 179, 187, 195, 253
Hsü Shu-cheng, 224, 244
Hsü T'ing, 69

Index

Huang Shao-hung, 286, 287
Hulun-buir, 185, 265, 276, 322, 331
Hundred Days Reform, 210
hunting, 5, 34, 173, 176
idughan (female shaman), 323

I

I-ku, 183, 190
illiteracy, 213
immortal, 106, 113
Imperial: Ancestral Temple (tai-miao), 302, 307
Imperial audiences, 197, 201
Imperial Instructor (ti-shih), 98–99, 106, 115, 121, 133, 144
Imperial son-in-law, 163, 196, 197
imperialism, 240, 258, 267, 281
independence, 146, 157, 184, 234, 243, 245
India, 90
Indian: masters, 91
Injannashi, 199
Inner Asia, 14, 31, 34, 35, 89, 176; nomadic people, 16
Inner Jasagh, 158, 166
Inner Mongolia, 8, 31, 42, 43, 61, 90, 131, 134, 136, 137, 148, 151, 162–65, 178, 180, 182, 184, 187, 188, 191, 192, 193, 196, 199, 201, 208, 209, 215, 217, 219, 222–27, 234, 235, 238, 243, 246–50, 263–68, 272–73, 281, 285, 290, 307; autonomous movement, 184, 222, 227, 259, 276, 281, 282, 286, 290, 294; Autonomous region, 250, 251, 276; economy, 276; education, 276; history, 237; Japanese occupation of, 300; Kuomintang (People's Revolutionary Army and Party), 222, 225, 246, 267, 269, 270, 272, 274, 277, 281, 282; leaders, 282, 289; people, 267, 268; problem, 243; reformation, 277; ruling class, 242
intellectuals, 224, 234, 244, 246, 251, 263, 281, 285
Islam, 84, 121, 131; activities, 126
Itagaki Seishiro, 291

J

Jamukha, 59, 62, 63, 300
Jangjia Khutughtu, 134, 137, 142, 147, 158, 164, 166, 196, 235, 265, 286; First Jangjia Khutughtu, 148; Sixth Jangjia Khutughtu, 148, 236
Japan, 196, 200, 210, 211, 213, 215, 217, 220, 234, 242, 243, 245, 262, 263, 267, 281, 322
Japanese, 90, 192, 201, 208, 212, 214, 222, 238, 244, 245, 247, 249, 263, 290–93, 300; advisors, 293; aggression, 284–86; anti-Japanese, 248, 290, 293–94; army, 247; Buddhism, 236–37; domination, 247; expansion, 248–49; influence, 216; invasion, 276, 290; Kwangtung Army, 290–94; militarists, 235; military, 236, 248; occupation, 236, 282, 292; officials, 184, 214, 215; scholars, 254; Soviet Khalkha River Battle, 294; Special Service Office (tokuma kikan), 285, 290, 291, 294
jasagh (law code), 57
jasagh (ruling prince), 134, 145, 147, 150, 156, 162, 164, 166, 181–83, 190-91, 199, 210, 269, 289
jasagh lama, 134, 147, 159, 164–65
Jasaghtu Khan Aimagh, 165
Jebon (Hbas-spuñs), 137
Jebtsundamba Khutughtu, 145, 147, 148, 155, 157, 158, 161, 164–69, 245; Eighth Jebtsundamba Khutughtu, 146, 148, 157, 169, 234, 243; Fifth Jebtsundamba Khutughtu, 132, 136; First Jebtsundamba Khutughtu, 137, 143, 144, 160, 163; Second Jebtsundamba Khutughtu, 137, 143, 160, 162
Jehol, 144, 147, 148, 192, 226, 263, 265, 271, 275, 282, 284, 290, 315
Jerim League, 183, 190–93, 209, 212, 217, 218, 220, 223, 234, 265, 282
Jesuit missionaries, 176
Jeünghar (Dzungar) Mongols, 133, 157, 164, 175–77, 197, 240, 257
Jigmed-namkha, 110, 156
jinong (title), 304
Jochi, 59, 84
Joffe, Adolph, 225

Josotu League, 164, 182, 189–93, 209, 210, 212, 217, 220, 223
Jou-jan (Juan-juan), 12, 179
Jungdu (Peking, see also Chung-tu), 16, 17, 64
Jurchen-Chin, 7, 8, 18, 23, 29, 30, 34, 38, 40, 42, 43–47, 57, 64, 71, 100, 194, 254; court, 41; Dynasty (1115–1234), 16, 35, 37, 38, 180; military forces, 42; rulers, 37, 46
jurisdiction, 208, 217
Juu-Modo, 175
Juu-Uda League, 182, 189, 191–93, 209, 210, 217, 220, 223, 265, 269

K

Kalgan, 225, 267, 269, 270, 291, 294
K'ang-hsi (r. 1662–1722), 137, 148, 175
Kanjur, 133, 135
Karakhan, Lev M. (Soviet ambassador), 225, 265
Karma-pa, 121, 126
Kara Kitai, 42, 46, 47
Kashmir, 88, 90, 113
Kereyid, 52, 62, 63, 87, 126, 304, 308
Kerityeds, 88
Kerülün River, 309
keshig (bodyguard), 68
khadagh, 122, 144, 307
Khaidu, 71, 73
Khalkha, 125, 133, 136, 143, 145, 148, 156, 159, 160, 164–67, 175, 184, 197, 234, 240, 242; Mongols, 132, 175; nobles, 133
Khanbaligh (Peking, see also Jungdu), 90, 121, 123, 125, 126
khara (lay element), 162
Kharachin, 180–82, 193, 196–97, 199–200, 202, 207–10, 214, 217, 220, 227, 262, 264, 275, 276; elder, 213; Mongols, 68, 211
Khara-khorum, 78, 89, 105, 121, 122, 180
khariyatu (underlings), 163
Khasar, 52, 55, 301
Khashaatu, 288, 289
Khiakta, 223, 244
Khorchin, 159, 183, 196–98, 212, 218, 234

Khorezm (Central Asia), 17, 99
Khoshod Mongols, 133
Khri-ssron lde-btsan, 90
Khubilai Khan (r. 1260–94), 17, 58, 60, 73–74, 84–87, 89–90, 97, 104–5, 107–8, 110, 125, 131, 137, 142, 144, 194, 303, 304
khubilghan (reincarnation), 144–47, 157–62
khural, 178
khutughtu, 134, 144, 147, 157–58, 162
kingdom on horseback, 21, 22
Kingghan provinces, 290, 293
Kirgiz, 21, 180
Kirin, 192, 223
Kitan, 7, 16, 21–23, 25–28, 30, 34, 36–37, 39, 42, 45–47, 71, 194; Kitan-Liao Dynasty (907–1125), 13, 27, 29, 31, 35, 38, 40, 43, 180; leaders, 31, 38; military support, 27; Mongolian alliance, 43; nobles, 27; rebels, 41; rulers, 34; scholar, 86
Kö'elün, 52, 53, 55, 56, 60
Köke Mongols, 314
Köke-Khota Tümed (Hohhot), 132, 134, 137, 158, 164, 166, 180, 189, 201
Kököchü, 300
Kökönor, 90, 133, 137, 162, 165, 166, 175, 197, 272
Korchin, 134
Korea, 23, 25, 29, 71, 90, 197, 242, 264, 327; monks, 91
Kötön, 84, 89, 99, 107, 126
Koyasan Monastery, 236
Kuang-hsü, 197, 212, 218, 219
Kuantung Army, 284, 285
Kubilai, 99
Kuei-hua City (Köke Khota), 166
Kueisui (Hohhot), 286, 287, 291–94
Kumbum, 137
kumis, 303, 307
K'ung Yuan-t'suo, 103–4
Kuomintang, 189, 221, 225, 246, 249, 250, 253, 258, 263–68, 271–76, 281–83, 287–88; Communist cooperation, 225; Northern Expedition, 226, 246, 284
Küriyen (Urga), 167

Index

L

Lake Baikai, 242
Lake of Kökönor (Chinghai) 132
lama, 122, 134, 137, 145, 146, 149–51, 159, 161, 163, 166, 212, 234–36, 311, 312, 323, 331; feudal lord, 169; policies, 236; tamagha (Lamaist Affairs Office), 134, 137, 147, 238
Lamaist, 142; administration, 147; Buddhism, 141, 143, 148, 315; institutions, 144; leaders, 238; nobles, 134, 159, 162, 169; temples, 143; world, 147
Lanchou, 300, 306, 307
Land of Pine and Desert, 35, 40, 47
land tax, 215
Lao Tzu, 101, 107–8, 111
Later Chin Dynasty (936–46), 16
Later T'ang Dynasty (923–35), 16, 26
Law for the Organization of the Mongolian Leagues and Banners, 227
Law of Buddha, 85–87, 89, 101–2, 107, 110, 134–25, 132, 156–60, 311, 313
lay: feudal lord, 169; lords, 145; nobles, 144, 146, 155, 157, 162, 169, 188; noyans, 161, 166; power, 145
league, 150, 165, 227; chighulghan, 147
league and banner system, 183–84, 241, 246, 263, 275, 276, 282, 283, 285, 287, 288, 289
leftist, 246, 276
Lenin, Nikolai, 224, 245, 299
Lhasa, 143, 146, 147, 162, 219
Li Shuo-hsin, 290, 291, 292, 294
Li-fan Yüan, 146–47, 149–50, 158–62, 165, 216, 219, 221
Liao (see also Kitan), 29, 35, 36, 37, 45; Dynasty (907–1125), 16
Liao-tung (Southern Manchuria), 44
liberals, 283
Lighdan Khan (r. 1604–33), 125, 132, 135
Lin-huang, 23, 31, 41
Ling Sheng, 293
Liu Ping-chung, 85, 104–5, 108
living Buddha, 134, 161, 244
localism, 207
loyalist party, 223
Luus, 135, 311, 327

M

Manchu-Ch'ing, 68 133, 136, 142, 143, 146, 157, 172, 181, 195, 217, 220, 240, 253, 255, 257, 262, 267, 324; authorities, 293; Chinese, 192; court, 134, 136, 144-48, 150, 159, 161, 168, 181, 182, 188, 191, 201, 207, 210, 213, 234, 257, 304; domination of Mongolia, 133, 148, 188, 207; Dynasty (1644–1911), 141, 174, 187, 192, 193, 196, 219, 223, 238, 243, 253, 255, 258; imperial throne, 290; emperors, 137, 142, 144–45, 156, 161, 164, 166, 169, 175, 195, 240; Imperial House, 207, 224; Jeüngharian War (1688–1750), 133, 184, 240; lamas, 143; language, 198; law, 134; leaders, 220; magistrates, 183, 184; Military Governor of Chahar, 289; Mongol intermarriage, 195, 201; nobles, 195, 197, 201, 218; officials, 181–83, 208, 215, 284; overlords, 188; period, 155, 168, 304; policy toward Mongolia, 136, 149, 241; power, 243, 306; princesses, 195; religious policy, 149, 207; restoration, 223; rule, 289; rulers, 56, 136, 141, 151, 155, 176, 187, 198, 207, 212
Manchukuo, 235–37, 247–49, 290, 292, 294
Manchuria, 25, 34, 42, 43, 132, 141, 184, 187, 212, 220, 223, 225, 235, 242, 247, 255, 269, 276, 281
Manchurian Incident, 191, 247, 276, 284, 290
Mandate of Heaven, 254
Manichean religion, 179
Man-mo, 242; Manmo seisaku, 220
Mantzu (South China), 108
manufactured goods, 174
Mao Tse-tung, 189, 251, 260
Mao-tun (r. 209–174 B.C.), 11, 14
Marco Polo Bridge Incident, 294
markets, 3
May Fourth Movement, 224
Meiji Restoration, 210, 213, 214, 242, 262
Mencius, 101, 103

Meng-chiang (Mongolian Territory), 248
merchants, 268
mergen ("experts in archery"), 53
Mergid, 53, 56, 57, 67
Merse (Kuo Tao-fu), 265–67, 272, 276
Middle Kingdom, 4, 9, 12, 13, 22, 141, 146, 149, 173, 195, 252–54, 256, 258, 262
military: actions, 14, 311; aid, 16; arts, 209; capabilities, 211; civilian system, 150; conscription, 235; exploitation, 67; forces, 217, 269; Governor of Jehol, 198, 216; governors, 283; influence, 7; objective, 16; power, 174, 212; purpose, 3; reserve, 187, 200; resources, 36; school, 214; strength, 11, 38, 43; support, 212; tactics, 41; threat, 7, 13; value, 67
Ming, 8, 10, 180; court, 12, 122; Dynasty (1368–1644), 121–22, 124–25, 131, 174, 175, 240, 255, 258; forces, 121; frontier, 6
minority nationalities, 227, 250, 252, 282
Misako Kawahara, 214, 215
moderates, 283, 294
modern: civilization, 176, 258; ideologies, 215; school, 212
modernization, 207, 237, 262, 281
Mohammedan teachers, 71, 75, 77
monasteries, 212, 235, 238
Monastery of Badghar (Wu-tan-chao), 137
Möngke Khan (r. 1251–59), 46, 71, 73, 86–89, 101, 104–11, 303
Möngke Tenggeri, 51, 83
Mongol-Ming relationship, 7
Mongolia, 6, 21, 25, 27, 30, 56–58, 78, 87, 90, 95, 234
Mongolian, 6, 10, 13, 16, 18, 30, 44–47, 52, 56, 62–64, 68, 70, 72, 78, 83, 85, 87, 88, 90, 91, 243, 249, 262; 1930 Conference in Nanking, 227, 283; administration, 182, 283; agriculture, 181; areas, 182; armies, 74, 79, 292; art, 135; authorities, 114, 283; autonomy, 223, 236, 275, 286, 295; Bandits (Meng-Fei), 184, chapter 14, 201–2, 223, 263, 284; banners, 216–18; Communist, 225; conquest, 100; conservatives, 265; court, 17, 87, 105–7, 111, 113, 121, 198; culture, 51; custom, 98; Delegation, 227, 275, 282; economy, 136, 211, 324; education, 218; empire, 16, 54, 56, 83, 84, 86, 126, 137, 180, 305; emperors, 71, 156; enlightened, 208; evolution to an agricultural state, 178; farmers, 180; feudal lords, 168; feudalism, 176, 201, 300; First Army, 294; forces, 45, 149; frontier, 178; government, 248; grazing lands, 208; herdsmen, 184, 201, 208, 257; horsemen, 195; independence, 223, 264; intellectuals, 199, 201, 222, 235, 242, 264, 265, 276, 290, 283, 286; interests, 288; invasion, 44; khans, 83, 84, 115, 125, 135; khans' choice of religion, 131; Lamaism, 143; land, 183, 188, 217, 219, 226, 257; landowners, 182; leaders, 97, 188, 202, 207, 214, 215, 217, 220, 223, 224, 244, 283, 284, 286, 287; liberals, 263, 265; males, 149-50; masses, 310; ministers, 89; monarch, 99; monks, 137; moral value, 52; nation, 245, 299, 307; nationalism, 242, 245, 247, 248, 251, 294; nationalists, 249–51; nobles, 13, 89, 132–33, 151, 157, 163, 165, 169, 182–83, 188, 195–202, 286, 290; officials, 188, 255; overlords, 193; pastoralists, 181, 193; pastures, 173, 178, 183, 185, 246; people, 61, 155, 157, 188, 207, 224, 225, 271, 281, 286; pilgrims, 137; poor, 182; population, 136, 151, 178, 195; power, 31, 37, 46; princes, 176, 196, 219, 270; problem, 220, 221, 225, 282, 285; quasi-feudalism, 144, 188; reformation, 263; regions, 282; religious policies, 113; reunification, 157; royal family, 87; royal house, 89, 121, 156; rule, 115; rulers, 17, 84, 90, 107, 131; ruling class, 90, 122, 151, 194, 201, 241; shaman, 303; Shamanism, 300; social structure, 155; society, 56–59, 60, 62, 88, 133, 135, 143-44, 149, 155, 162, 201, 238, 213, 246, 262, 266, 286; soldiers, 70; students, 276, 283, 286; territories, 215, 247; theocratic monarch, 155; traditionalist, 88; traditions, 58, 266; tribes, 43, 133, 176, 240, 328; troops, 210, 215, 216,

Index

293; volunteers, 149, 193; Youth Party, 265
Mongolian Eight Banners, 149, 197
Mongolian Local Autonomous Political Committee, 248, 287–89, 292–95
Mongolian Military Government, 293
Mongolian People's News, 270
Mongolian People's Republic, 175, 184, 185, 235, 238, 245, 264–66, 281, 300
Mongolian People's Revolutionary Party, 224, 225, 238, 245, 165–68, 281
Mongolian-Russian allied forces, 224
Mongolian-Suiyüan conflict, 294
Mongolian-Tibetan Academy, 83, 222, 235, 263–65, 275
Mongolian-Tibetan Affairs Bureau (Meng-Tsang shih-wu-chü), 221, 274–75, 282, 286, 287, 289
Mongolian-Tibetan Ministry (Meng-Tsang Yüan), 222, 226, 235, 258, 263, 274–75
Mongolian-Yüan Dynasty (1260–1368), 142, 253, 255; khans, 134
Moscow, 245, 246, 270
Moslem, 220, 253, 258, 259, 262, 267; bandits, 189
Mukden (Shenyang), 144, 165, 189, 192, 223, 276
Mukhali, 52, 60, 85, 95, 97, 308, 309

N

Naiman, 54, 62, 67, 88, 126, 309
naiman chaghan ger (the eight white yurts), 303
nai-po, 25
Na-mo (Namu), 88, 89, 106–10
Nan-ching, (Southern Capital), 26
Nanking, 122, 219, 226, 227, 246, 248, 273, 274, 282, 286, 287, 291, 292
National Government, 192, 227, 247, 274, 276, 281–83, 285, 289–93, 300, 306; in Chungking, 248; in Nanking, 226, 236, 246
nationalism, 56, 64, 195, 201–2, 240–41, 244, 248, 249, 258, 260, 276, 290; local, 250; movements, 188; narrow minded, 258
nationalistic leaders, 300
nationalities, 220, 221, 226

Nei-min-tang, 277
Nein-fei rebellion, 149
Nestorian, 87, 88, 126
Ninghsia, 225, 226, 270, 272–75, 282
noble lama, 144, 156, 160
nobles, 236, 245, 262–64
nomadic: areas, 186; chief, 176; culture, 44, 89, 91, 115; group, 6, 12, 326; invasion, 186; khan, 7; Kitans, 37; lands, 31; life style, 51, 186; livelihood, 165; martial traditions, 200; Mongolian society, 136; pastoralism, 90; people, 3, 5, 6, 8, 9, 10, 12, 14, 34, 67, 173, 176–77, 186, 194–95, 253; population, 31; power, 3, 175–77, 180; quasi-feudal system, 143, 162; rulers, 7, 11; society, 6, 52, 55, 58, 60, 70, 186, 284; state, 11, 173, 175; tribe, 30, 131
non-Mongol, 178, 184
non-Russian national minorities, 300
Noni River, 322, 329
Normal Academy of the Northeast Mongol Banners, 276
North Asia, 126, 174, 194, 242, 251, 328
North China, 16, 17, 45, 77, 84, 89, 100, 104, 112, 178, 187, 193, 211, 224–26, 246, 248, 269, 291
Northern Yüan State, 174
notugh (fief), 155, 162–63, 165
noyan (nobles), 102–3, 155–56, 159, 162, 188, 304, 305
Nurhachi (r. 1616-27), 142

O

oboo, 327, 328
öchig (sang), 308
Office of Mongolian League and Banner Delegates, 282, 287, 291
Oghul Ghaimish, 68, 73
Ögödei Khan (r. 1229–41), 17, 46, 60, 68, 71–72, 84–86, 88–89, 101–7, 302
Oirad, 12, 56, 124, 156, 159, 175, 302; leaders, 126; Mongols, 132; rulers, 123
Ong Khan, 52, 62, 63, 68, 304, 308
ongghon, 304, 305, 307, 329
Önggüd, 88, 126
Ongni'ud, 182
Onon River, 308

opium tax, 216, 288, 289
Opium War (1839–42), 187, 208, 241
ordo, 31, 104, 303, 305, 311
Ordos, 132, 134, 159, 179, 183, 197, 249, 300, 303, 304, 306
Organizational Law of the Mongolian Leagues, Tribes, and Banners, 283
Orkhon River, 180, 184
Otogh, 274
Outer Jasagh, 168-69
Outer Mongolia, 90, 132, 148, 162-63, 175, 180, 184, 191, 192, 219, 223, 262, 271, 276, 281, 290, 294; forces, 249; leaders, 219, 224, 225, 242, 244; independence, 219, 249; Independence Movement, 149, 169, 178, 195, 220, 234–35, 257, 263; People's Revolutionary Party, 264, 273, 277
Outline for Nation Building (Chien-kuo-ta-kang), 226, 259, 264–65, 274, 281, 282

P

Pacific war, 294
Padmasambhava, 88, 90
Pai Yün-t'i (Serengdüngrüb), 222, 225, 264, 266–76, 281, 282
pan-Mongolianism, 245, 281; organization, 245
Panchen Erdeni, 132, 136, 143, 145-48, 158, 162, 315; Ninth Panchen Erdeni, 235, 236
Pandita Gaene'en Keid, 151
Pao-t'ou, 270, 271, 285, 289
Parhae, 23, 26, 27, 28, 29, 30, 34, 36
pastures (ch'ün-mu), 37, 284
peace, 7, 8, 14
Peiping Mongolian Association, 286
Peiping-Suiyuan Railroad, 286
Peking (Peiping), 15, 16, 17, 22, 24, 42, 45, 64, 137, 143, 144, 146, 147, 148, 162, 188, 189, 192, 196, 200–1, 208, 211, 212, 214, 220, 221, 222, 224, 225, 236, 243, 244, 250–52, 259, 263, 264, 265, 266, 273, 274, 275, 276, 283, 286, 289, 291, 315, 322
People's Republic of China, 252, 259
Persian religion, 179

Phags-pa Lama, 88–90, 98–99, 104, 107–11, 125, 131
political: freedom, 268; gain, 3; organization, 188; party, 225; prestige, 9; privileges, 208; rebels, 189
Prince Su (Shan-ch'i), 216, 217, 220, 223
private property, 165
pro-Chinese, 90, 272, 292; moderates, 267
pro-Japanese, 215, 248; lamas, 238; warlords, 244
pro-Russian warlord, 266
proto-Mongol peoples, 179
psychological: coup, 100; warfare, 63, 247
public land, 213
P'u-yi, 218, 290

Q

quasi-feudal, 144, 155, 244; institutions, 62; nomadic system, 133; society, 157, 168; system, 64, 141, 235; units, 163
radical groups, 224, 225, 237, 246, 265, 283, 285, 294
rebellion, 35, 39–41, 43–47, 71, 78, 141, 143, 148, 176, 187–88, 192–93, 210, 217, 223, 289

R

Rebellion of Eight Sumun, 190
Red Guards, 277
Red Sect (Snying-ma-pa), 88, 122, 132–33
reforms, 262, 265, 285
Regulations for the Treatment of Mongolia, 263, 283
reincarnation (khubilghan), 134, 145, 146, 157-62
religious: faith, 234; reformation, 238
Republic of China, 148, 192, 219, 226, 234, 235, 253, 257, 265, 300, 322
revolution, 40, 219, 223, 224, 243, 267, 268
Righteous Army of the Great Han (Ta-han Yi-chün), 294
Roman Catholic Church, 126
royal marriage, 3, 7, 11, 14, 91

Index

Russia (also Soviet Union), 177, 192, 208, 210–11, 214–15, 217, 220, 223–25, 240, 243–45, 247–48, 251, 259–60, 262, 264–66, 272, 276, 281, 294, 300; anti-Soviet, 273; Communists, 249; expansion in Central Asia, 175; forces, 212, 249; influence, 216, 241; invasion (1929), 276; Kremlin, 251, 300; Mongol relationship, 244; power, 207; power toward China, 183; Red Army, 224, 238, 245; Soviet domination, 248; Soviet oppression, 246; Soviet embassy, 273; Soviet policy, 249; Tsarist, 173–75, 187, 207–8, 242–45, 264
Russianization, 242
Russo-Japanese War (1904–5), 208, 215, 242

S

Sagang Sechen, 10, 125, 301, 302
sakighulsun (godly spirit), 100
Samarkand, 310
San-min-chu-i (Three People's Principles), 246 258, 264, 281, 283
Sanskrit texts, 209
Sarta'ul, 309
Sa-skya Pandita, 84, 90, 99, 125, 144
Sa-skya-pa, 83, 84, 88–90, 106, 121, 126, 131
Sayinbayer, 265, 266, 271, 274, 276
Sayin Noyan Aimagh, 156, 165
schools, 217–18, 234–35, 242, 281, 291
Sechen Khan, 168–69
Secret History of the Mongols, 16, 51–53, 58–60, 62, 64, 67–68, 72, 123, 165, 299, 300, 304, 325
secular power, 144
self-determination, 207–8, 221, 226–27, 243, 245–47, 250, 258–59, 265, 267, 268, 281, 290
semi-nomadic, 90
Sengerinchin, 149, 188–89
Serendöngrüb (see Pai Yün-t'i)
shabinar (lay disciples), 134, 145, 156, 158, 159, 163–66
Shaghdurjab, 288, 293
Shalabdorji, 289
shaman, 59, 324, 329

Shaminism 51, 87, 90, 95, 121, 125–26, 131, 142, 323, 328; background, 90; beliefs, 100, 135; ceremony, 328, 330; faith, 126; gods, 83; ritual, 307, 314; tradition, 88
Shang-ching, (Supreme Capital), 23, 31
shangsadba (lama official), 163, 164
Shangtu, 108
Shansi, 285; Province, 236; warlord, 275
Shigi-khutughu, 52, 64, 84, 102, 104
Shih-tsung (Chin emperor, r. 1161–89), 40, 42, 43, 99
Shilin-ghol League, 137, 151, 178, 185, 217, 235, 237, 283, 285, 286, 290, 323
Shini-lama, 265, 266, 270, 271, 274
shira (yellow—theocratic element), 162
Shira-mören, 22
Shun-chih (Ch'ing emperor, r. 1644–61), 149, 159
Sian Incident, 294
Siberia, 173, 176, 224, 244, 281, 300
Silk Road, 16, 179
Sinicization, 17, 35, 42, 151, 179, 183, 255; areas, 326; Buddhism, 90; Kitans, 35, 37, 44, 47; Manchu, 258; nomads, 21; of the Mongolian ruling class, chapter 15; people, 256; regime, 16
Sinkiang (Chinese Turkistan), 242, 251, 257, 259
Sino-Anglo-French War (Second Opium War, 1857–60), 149, 187, 208
Sino-Japanese War (1894–95), 210
Sino-Japanese War (1937–45), 192, 236, 248, 259, 300
Sino-nomadic relationship, 22, 31
Sino-Russo-Mongol tripartite conference, 244
Sino-Soviet relations, 225, 268
slaves, 27
social: changes, 201, 264, 281; revolution, 224, 269, 274, 281
socialism, 215, 269, 276
Sodnamrabtan (commonly known as Prince So), 285, 290–93; death of, 293
Son of Heaven, 7, 9, 10, 60, 88, 90, 100, 103, 131, 141, 146, 252, 254
Sorkhaghtani Beki Khatun, 86, 87, 104
Southern Manchuria, 210, 221
Southern Sung Dynasty (1127–76), 17, 36, 70, 98, 112

spiritual boy, 157
Sron-btsan sagam-po, 90
Ssu-ma Ch'ien, 8, 11, 13, 27, 178
Sui period (589–618), 11
sui-pi ("yearly payment"), 13, 25
Suiyüan Province, 226, 236, 263, 265, 271, 275, 276, 282, 292, 294
Suiyüan Mongolian Local Autonomous Political Committee, 293
Suiyüan Mongolian Political Committee, 293
Suiyüan Provincial Government, 288
Süke-bator, 224, 245
sula noyan (noble at leisure), 163
sülde, 306, 310, 312, 314, 315; sulder, 312
sumu (household unit), 150
sumun janggis (official), 164
Sun Yat-sen (1866–1925), 219, 221, 224–27, 243, 246, 253, 258, 259, 262, 264–66, 274–75, 277, 281
Sung, 25, 37, 38, 39, 41, 43, 100; Dynasty (960–1276), 7, 13, 197, 258; tombs, 112
Sung Che-yüan, 286, 291
Sung-Mo, 35
Sünid, 134, 159, 197, 226, 235, 291, 323
Supreme Three Jewels (Buddha, Dharma, and Sangha), 312
suzerainty, 219, 223, 241

T

Tabghach Wei Dynasty (386–556), 12, 21, 26, 16, 179
tabunang (see Imperial son-in-law)
Taichi'ud, 53, 54, 62, 309
taiji (title), 150, 163-64, 193, 197
T'ai-ning Garrison, 125
Tai-p'ing Rebellion (1850–64), 149, 187
taishi (title), 305
Tai-tsung (Ch'ing emperor, r. 1627-43), 142, 181
Taiwan, 276, 288
Tanaka Ryukichi, 291, 294
T'ang Dynasty (618–907), 7, 9, 16, 21, 27, 101, 179, 187, 255
Tang-hsiang (Tangut), 7, 23, 302, 310
Tannu-Uriyankhai (now Tannu Tuva), 245

Tantric, 195; Buddhism, 115; teachings, 90
Tantryana Tibetan Buddhism, 115
Taoist, 4, 71, 75, 77, 85, 86,94, 96, 101, 103, 106, 108–15; influence, 87; monks, 24; priests, 106; temples, 101
Tashilumpo, 147
Ta-tan (Eastern Mongols), 123, 125, 175
Tatar, 56, 69, 258
Ta-tu (Peking), 76, 78
Ta-t'ung, 26, 27, 104, 294
taxes, 135, 216, 268, 288
Tayang Khan, 54
Temüjin (see also Chinggis Khan), 51, 53–55, 60, 63, 67–68, 300, 301, 308
theocratic: leaders, 162; lords, 145; nobles, 146, 161, 165, 166, 168; power, 144, 145, 147, 148; quasi-feudalist system, 163-65
Third International (see Comintern)
Three Garrisons (Uriyangkha), 122
Tibet, 88–91, 113, 131, 137, 141, 142, 145, 147, 148, 157, 158, 175, 208, 219, 226, 237, 249, 251, 255, 272, 306
Tibetan, 7, 16, 90, 91, 131, 141, 148, 220, 222, 243, 253, 257–59, 262, 267; area, 166; art, 135; Buddhism, 83–84, 88–91, 107, 121, 126, 131–32, 136, 142-43, 155-56, 177, 195, 198, 234, 238; Buddhologists, 306; empire, 90; lamas, 90, 122, 155, 157; lamaseries, 156; language, 135; monks, 136, 143; mythology, 306; religious leaders, 133; society, 90; texts, 209; uprising, 260
t'ien-shih (Toaist priest), 113
Ting-yüan-yin (Bayan-nor), 272
ti-shih (see Imperial instructor)
Toghontemür Khan (r. 1333–68), 91, 121
Togtogh taiji, 191
Tojo Hideki, 294
Tolui, 84
Törölbaikhu, 133
trade, 5, 6, 7, 136, 177, 181
Transoxianian, 17
tribalism, 35, 56, 207
tributaries, 9
tribute, 3, 5, 6, 7, 9, 12, 169; of nine white, 169
Tsereng, 197
Tsongkha-pa, 126, 132

Index

Tsung-she-tang (party), 220
Tuan Ch'i-jui, 224, 226, 266
T'ü-chüeh, 15
Tu-fan, 7, 16
Tümed, 121, 131, 156, 163, 181, 182, 196, 223, 293; Mongol, 201
Tümen Khan (r. 1558–92), 132
Tung-ching (Eastern Capital), 25
Tungusic, 26; languages, 322; Manchus, 90, 323; Parhaes, 22
Turkistan, 141, 255
Turks, 9, 12, 14, 15, 18, 21, 27, 177, 187; empire, 179
Tüshiyetü Khan Aimagh, 143, 145, 157, 165, 168, 169
tu-tieh (official diploma), 149-51
tu-t'ung (military governor), 163
Tu'ula River, 309
T'u-yü-hun, 23
Twenty-one Demands, 223, 264

U

Uighur, 7, 15, 16, 18, 21, 22, 34, 53, 58, 71, 87, 88, 90, 136, 179, 243, 257, 259; traders, 24
Uiryangkha Mongols, 180
Üjümüchin, 134, 178, 197, 217, 285, 290
Ulan Bator (see Urga)
Ulanchab, 183, 185, 217, 293; banners, 285; League, 137, 189–90, 212, 236, 285, 292, 307
Ulanfu (Yün Tse), 222, 225, 250, 251, 270, 276, 277
Ulan-khada, 220
ulus, 22
underlings, 27
Union of Soviet Socialist Republics (see Russia)
United States, 211, 213, 267
Urad, 134, 159, 289
Urga (Ulan Bator), 144, 147, 149, 163-64, 184, 220, 224–25, 238, 243–46, 251, 265, 270, 273, 276, 300
Urga Government of Outer Mongolia, 192
Uriyangkha, 125
Utai, 212
Uushin, 274; Banner, 270, 271

V

Vajrabani, 306
Vietnam, 90, 197

W

Wan-yen Wu-lu, 40
Wang Ching-wei, 248, 275, 283, 286, 287
Wang Mang (r. 9–23), 10, 11
Wangdannima, 265, 266, 270, 271
Wang-yin süme (Ulan-khota), 300
war, 7, 12, 14, 39, 53, 177, 188; civil, 121; cost of, 4; objective in, 4
War of Eastern Suiyüan, 294
warlordism, 224, 246–50, 267, 269, 284, 285; anti-warlordism, 266
Wei Dynasty (see Tabghach Wei Dynasty)
Wen-ch'eng Kung-chu, 90
West Capital (Ta-t'ung), 38, 42
Western Asia, 87
Western: imperialism, 187, 242; missionaries, 193, 211; powers, 240, 258, 262
Western Region, 84, 90
White Lotus Society (Pai-lien Chiao), 193, 209
White Russians, 224
World War I, 222, 244
World War II, 238, 249
Wu Ho-ling, 227, 275, 282, 283, 285, 287, 288, 291, 292
Wu-huan, 179
Wu-tai mountain, 105, 137
Wu-tai-shan, 147, 236
Wu-ti (r. 140–87 B.C.), 174

Y

Yalavaj, 17
Yalta Agreement, 249
Yang-lien-chen-chia, 112
Yangtze River, 41, 96, 112, 113, 114, 242, 254
Yao Hsi-kuang, 215–17, 221
Yao Shu, 87, 89, 108
yearly payment, 3, 7
Yeh-li-k'o-wen (Nestorian Christians), 87
Yeh-lü A-pao-chi, 22, 23, 24, 26, 28

Yeh-lü Ch'u-ts'ai, 17, 35, 84, 86, 96, 102, 104, 107
Yeh-lü family, 39, 46
Yeh-lü Liu-ko, 44, 45, 46
Yeh-lü Ta-shih, 46
Yeh-lü Wo-wo, 37
Yeh-lü Yen-hsi (r. 1101–25), 38
Yeke-juu League, 190, 192, 193, 211–12, 217, 225, 266, 270, 271, 273, 275, 285, 286, 289, 293, 304
Yeke-öteg Mountain, 305
Yellow Religion or Sect, (see Dge-lug-pa)
Yellow River, 26, 72, 103, 166, 179, 184, 286, 293
Yen (Peking), 35, 95, 104
Yen Hsi-shan, 184, 226, 236, 275, 282, 283, 285, 286, 287, 293
Yenan, 192, 249
Ying-tsung (Ming emperor, r. 1436–49, 1457–64), 15
Yesügei, 53, 56
Yi-la Wo-wo, 42, 43
Yin Chien (Hai-yün Fa-shih), 85, 86, 88, 94
Yi-ti (non-Chinese), 252, 256, 258; dynasties, 255; minorities, 260, nationalities, 258; officials, 255; peoples, 146, 256–59
Yondonwanchugh (Prince Yon), 285, 286, 288, 289, 292
Yüan, 58, 87, 94, 102, 156; court, 17, 133; Dynasty (1260–1368), 12, 53, 70, 78, 84, 90–91 100, 113, 121–26, 131, 134–36, 143-44, 174, 180, 194, 198, 254, 255, 303, 305, 307; emperors, 68, 73, 113; imperial household, 125; state, 104
Yüan Shih-k'ai, 149, 219–24, 263
yu-mu (see fief)
Yung-cheng (Ch'ing emperor, r. 1723–35), 137, 143-44, 148, 163
Yung-ho-kung, 137, 146-47, 214, 266
Yung-lo (Ming emperor, r. 1402–24), 15, 174
Yü-wen Mao-chao, 36

Z

Zenrinkyokai (Good Neighborliness Association), 291